Understanding
Sports Law

Understanding the First Amendment,
Seventh Edition
Russell L. Weaver

Understanding Immigration Law,
Third Edition
Kevin R. Johnson, Raquel Aldana,
Bill Ong Hing, Leticia M. Saucedo,
and Enid Trucios-Haynes

Understanding Insurance Law, Sixth Edition
Robert H. Jerry, II and Douglas Richmond

Understanding Intellectual Property Law,
Fourth Edition
Tyler T. Ochoa, Shubha Ghosh,
and Mary LaFrance

Understanding International Business
and Financial Transactions,
Fourth Edition
Jerold A. Friedland

Understanding International Criminal Law,
Fourth Edition
Ellen S. Podgor, Roger S. Clark,
and Lucian Dervan

Understanding International Law,
Third Edition
Stephen C. McCaffrey

Understanding Jewish Law, Second Edition
Steven H. Resnicoff

Understanding Juvenile Law, Fifth Edition
Martin Gardner

Understanding Labor Law,
Fifth Edition
Douglas E. Ray, Calvin William Sharpe,
and Robert N. Strassfeld

Understanding the Law of Terrorism,
Second Edition
Erik Luna and Wayne McCormack

Understanding the Law of Zoning
and Land Use Controls, Third Edition
Barlow Burke

Understanding Lawyers' Ethics, Fifth Edition
Monroe H. Freedman and Abbe Smith

Understanding Local Government,
Second Edition
Sandra Stevenson

Understanding Modern Real Estate
Transactions, Fourth Edition
Alex M. Johnson, Jr.

Understanding Negotiable Instruments
and Payment Systems, Second Edition
William H. Lawrence

Understanding Nonprofit and Tax Exempt
Organizations, Third Edition
Nicholas P. Cafardi and Jaclyn Fabean Cherry

Understanding Partnership
and LLC Taxation, Fifth Edition
Jerold A. Friedland

Understanding Patent Law, Third Edition
Amy L. Landers

Understanding Products Liability Law,
Second Edition
Bruce L. Ottley, Rogelio A. Lasso,
and Terrence F. Kiely

Understanding Property Law,
Fifth Edition
John G. Sprankling

Understanding Remedies, Fourth Edition
James M. Fischer

Understanding Sales and Leases of Goods,
Third Edition
William H. Henning, William H. Lawrence,
and Henry Deeb Gabriel

Understanding Secured Transactions,
Fifth Edition
William H. Lawrence, William H. Henning,
and R. Wilson Freyermuth

Understanding Securities Law,
Seventh Edition
Marc I. Steinberg

Understanding Sports Law
Timothy Davis, N. Jeremi Duru

Understanding Taxation of
Business Entities, Second Edition
Walter D. Schwidetzky and Fred B. Brown

Understanding Torts, Sixth Edition
John L. Diamond, Lawrence C. Levine,
and Anita Bernstein

Understanding Trade Secret Law
John G. Sprankling and Thomas G. Sprankling

Understanding Trademark Law, Fourth Edition
Mary LaFrance

Understanding Trusts and Estates,
Seventh Edition
Roger W. Andersen and Susan Gary

Understanding White Collar Crime,
Fifth Edition
J. Kelly Strader and Todd Haugh

Understanding
Sports Law

Timothy Davis
JOHN W. AND RUTH H. TURNAGE PROFESSOR OF LAW
WAKE FOREST UNIVERSITY SCHOOL OF LAW

N. Jeremi Duru
PROFESSOR OF LAW
AMERICAN UNIVERSITY WASHINGTON COLLEGE OF LAW

CAROLINA ACADEMIC PRESS
Durham, North Carolina

Copyright © 2023
Carolina Academic Press
All Rights Reserved

Library of Congress Cataloging-in-Publication Data

Names: Davis, Timothy, 1954-author. | Duru, N. Jeremi, author.
Title: Understanding sports law / Timothy Davis, N. Jeremi Duru.
Description: Durham, North Carolina : Carolina Academic Press, LLC, 2022. |
   Series: Understanding series
Identifiers: LCCN 2022016679 (print) | LCCN 2022016680 (ebook) | ISBN
   9781531019846 (paperback) | ISBN 9781531019853 (ebook)
Subjects: LCSH: Sports—Law and legislation—United States. | School
   sports--Law and legislation—United States. | College sports—Law and
   legislation—United States. | Sex discrimination in sports—Law and
   legislation—United States. | Discrimination in sports—Law and
   legislation—United States. | Sports for people with disabilities—Law
   and legislation—United States. | Athletes with disabilities—Legal
   status, laws, etc.—United States. | Sports injuries—United States.
Classification: LCC KF3989 .D38 2022 (print) | LCC KF3989 (ebook) | DDC
   344.73/099—dc23/eng/20220526
LC record available at https://lccn.loc.gov/2022016679
LC ebook record available at https://lccn.loc.gov/2022016680

Carolina Academic Press
700 Kent Street
Durham, North Carolina 27701
Telephone (919) 489-7486
Fax (919) 493-5668
www.cap-press.com

Printed in the United States of America

Contents

Preface

This book is about the legal issues and concepts that emerge from relationships existing within American sport. It captures the legal doctrine and rules arising from judicial decisions, state and federal legislation, and the private law created by associations and other sport entities.

Collectively, the principles of law discussed in this book comprise what is commonly referred to as sports law, which covers an array of substantive legal doctrine. Certain of these substantive concepts are introduced to law students during their first or second years of law school (*e.g.*, contracts, constitutional law, and torts). Other principles encompass doctrine to which most law students will have had limited exposure (*e.g.*, antitrust and labor law) before enrolling in a survey sports law course. The challenge in drafting this book has been striking a balance between articulating these concepts so that they are accessible to multiple audiences while exploring the complexity of the legal issues that frequently arise in sports. We hope this book strikes a satisfactory balance as it strives to provide an in-depth yet accessible overview of the law of sports.

The primary audiences for this treatise are law students, law professors, and practitioners. As alluded to above, law students taking sports law are confronted with learning and applying several familiar and unfamiliar bodies of law in a single course. This treatise will assist students in synthesizing these discrete bodies of law. It should also prove beneficial to students seeking a deeper understanding of unfamiliar and often complex doctrine and how it is uniquely situated in sports.

This book will also serve as a helpful resource to law professors who teach sports law and to practitioners. Sports law is also often taught by adjuncts who frequently specialize in either amateur or professional sports law matters, but not both. Thus, some sports law professors may lack a comprehensive and in-depth knowledge of legal issues traversing both amateur and professional sports. This treatise will facilitate these professors acquiring knowledge of areas of law outside their respective fields of expertise. We anticipate this book will also provide a quick reference to practitioners who will find that the referenced cases, statutes, and other materials provide a point of departure for engaging in a more detailed examination of topics within sports law.

Because sports law encompasses a vast array of different substantive areas, we elected to adopt an organizational structure that attempts to coherently present the material. To facilitate this, the treatise uses a similar structure to that employed in the leading sports law casebooks. In most instances, the material is organized according to the level of sports participation — high school, college or professional. Thus, Chapter

1 focuses primarily on the legal issues resulting from conflicts (*e.g.*, eligibility disputes) frequently arising in the relationships between high school athletes and their schools. Much of the discussion revolves around the constitutional law dimensions of this relationship.

While constitutional law issues are explored in Chapter 2 — which examines the legal issues emerging from college athletes' relationships with their universities — the chapter also offers an overview of the legal principles that govern the contractual aspects of the relationship. These relationships are examined against the backdrop of the NCAA's significant, yet shifting, governance role in college athletics. Similarly, Chapter 7 illustrates legal issues (*e.g.*, league governance and commissioner authority) unique to professional sports.

Where substantive issues and the rules governing their resolution transcend the level of sports participation, this book addresses the relevant principles typically without regard to the level of the sport. This approach is illustrated by Chapter 11, which addresses tort liability, where many of the salient concepts apply irrespective of the level of participation. Similarly, Chapter 5 explores legal principles involving gender equity issues, which at times are unique to a particular level of sport and at other times arise regardless of the level of sport.

While this book's primary focus is on articulating the current legal principles governing relationships in sport, it often discusses the historical evolution of such rules in order to contextualize and foster an understanding of today's controlling principles. Therefore, the treatise presents the doctrine adopted by the majority of courts. Where there is a significant divergence in judicial approaches regarding what is the predominant view, however, we state both majority and minority rules and the rationales supporting each.

This book can serve as a helpful companion to a casebook or as a stand-alone resource. It summarizes the rules of law emerging from the principal cases found in the leading casebooks. The materials are not restricted, however, to an articulation of those rules and cases. It attempts to frame the factual and legal contexts in which such cases arise and such rules are developed to demonstrate the relationships between the array of concepts extant in sports law.

It is not unusual for legal casebooks to pose provocative and challenging questions without providing answers or guidance on how to discover the answers. This book raises such questions, but also provides answers. In addition to providing an up-to-date articulation of law as described in the text, the book contains extensive footnotes that support the propositions in the text and provide resource materials, which may prove particularly helpful to practitioners and researchers. To increase its value to readers, the treatise provides a detailed table of contents that will serve as a quick roadmap of the book's content.

Part I

Legal Issues in
Amateur Athletics

Chapter 1

Legal Issues in Interscholastic (High School) Athletics

§ 1.01 Introduction

This chapter examines legal issues impacting the opportunity of high-school-aged athletes to participate in organized sports activities. The chapter's primary focus are the constitutional law principles that determine the outcome of lawsuits filed by athletes when age, transfer, good conduct, and other rules limit their eligibility to participate in organized high school athletics. The predicates to such claims, state action status and the existence of a property interest in athletic participation, are also examined. The chapter begins, however, with a brief overview of the different organizations which provide outlets for young athletes to pursue their athletic interests. Thereafter, the chapter returns to its primary focus—legal issues that arise in organized high school athletics.

§ 1.02 Youth Sports Organizations

[A] Organized High School Athletics

Organized high school (interscholastic) athletics provides the most convenient setting within which high-school-aged children can participate in competitive athletics. High schools usually offer an array of sports such as football, track and field, basketball, softball, baseball, and soccer.[1] Less popular and lesser known offerings include canoeing, rodeo, synchronized swimming, bass fishing, and quidditch.[2] High schools also operate sports on seasonal schedules, enabling athletes to play multiple sports within the same year.[3] High schools typically offer two levels of participation oppor-

---

1. *High School Sports*, NCSA, https://www.ncsasports.org/articles-1/high-school-sports (last visited June 13, 2021).
2. *Top 5 of the Most Unusual Sports Played in High School*, ITG NEXT (Nov. 5, 2020), https://itgnext.com/top-5-of-the-most-unusual-sports-played-in-high-school/.
3. *See* NCHSAA, https://www.nchsaa.org/sports (last visited June 14, 2021).

tunities — varsity and junior varsity.[4] Varsity teams represent their high schools at the highest level and are usually comprised of older and more experienced athletes, while junior varsity is typically made up of younger and less experienced athletes.[5] As discussed, *infra*, organized high school athletics are regulated at the school, school district, and state levels, the latter is most commonly regulated through interscholastic athletic associations.

[B] Club/Travel Sports

Clubs/travel sports teams allow students to participate on teams that are independent of an athlete's school even though some high schools have affiliations with club teams. Club sports can offer an elevated level of play and schedules that conform well with college coaches' recruiting schedules.[6] The year-round nature of club sports gives athletes more time to focus on honing their skills, while at the same time providing college coaches more time to evaluate athletic participants.[7] Thus, club sports often play an important role in a high school student-athlete's odds of securing a college athletic scholarship.[8] A 2021 survey found: 88% of female and 77% of male college soccer players, respectively, participated in club soccer in high school; 94% of female college softball players and 85% of male college baseball players, respectively, participated in club softball or baseball in high school; and 79% of female and male college athletes in swimming participated in club swimming in high school.[9] The survey also revealed, however, lower participation rates for other sports. Only 24% of college football players participated on a high school club football team, and approximately 30% of female and male college track and field athletes participated on a club track and field team.[10]

The Amateur Athletic Union ("AAU"), which was established in 1888 to promulgate standards and uniformity in amateur sports, exemplifies club/travel sports.[11] AAU offers sport participation to youth athletes, including those who are high-school-aged.[12] Within AAU, groups of athletes form independent teams that compete against each other in AAU tournaments.[13] AAU teams are not restricted by school zones, so teams can be comprised of players even if they attend high schools in different dis-

---

4. Tanya Mozias Slavin, *What is the Difference Between Varsity & Junior Varsity*, THE CLASSROOM, https://www.theclassroom.com/difference-between-varsity-junior-varsity-6936387.html (last updated June 27, 2018).

5. *Id.*

6. *High School vs. Club Sports: Understanding the Benefits*, NCSA, https://www.ncsasports.org/recruiting/how-to-get-recruited/club-sports (last visited June 13, 2021).

7. *Id.*

8. *Id.*

9. *Id.*

10. *Id.*

11. *Id.*

12. *About the Amateur Athletic Union*, AAU, https://aausports.org/page.php?page_id=99844 (last visited June 13, 2021).

13. *What is AAU Basketball (Including Pros and Cons)*, BASKETBALL FOR COACHES, https://www.basketballforcoaches.com/what-is-aau-basketball/ (last visited June 13, 2021).

tricts.[14] This allows for the best players to compete against high-level competitors, which, in turn, affords players an effective means of gaining substantial exposure. AAU sponsors tournaments involving matches between AAU teams.[15]

Basketball is the sport in which AAU has gained the most significant foothold among high-school-aged children. The prominence of AAU basketball is demonstrated by the number of NBA players entering the league over the past ten years who participated to varying degrees in AAU basketball.[16] The organization offers, however, opportunities in 41 different sports,[17] including track and field, golf, hockey, diving, football, table tennis, baseball, and martial arts.[18] Apart from basketball, AAU-run sports overall have not received the level of recognition that accompanies interscholastic sports participation.[19]

Notwithstanding the benefits of club sports, concerns have been raised that club teams encourage or force athletes to specialize in one sport, which can result in higher rates of physical injuries.[20] Other concerns relating to athletes' participation on club teams include: schedule conflicts that impede an athletes' ability to play for their school teams;[21] athletes' considerable time commitment to their sports;[22] and, the cost associated with participating on club teams.[23]

[C] Olympic Development Programs

Olympic development programs ("ODP") provide high school athletes the opportunity to receive high-level training in an Olympic sport. ODPs are great options for athletes dedicated to a particular sport and offer experience that can catapult an athlete onto an Olympic team. Benefits of participating in ODPs include athletic development, quality instruction from nationally licensed head coaches, exposure, and quality competition.[24]

U.S. Soccer's ODP can provide a direct pathway to the professional ranks for male and female high school players.[25] In most states, players are selected through open

---

14. *Id.*

15. *Id.*

16. Logan Furey, *What Is AAU Basketball? And Whether You Should Find a Team*, GMTM (Jan. 10, 2021), https://gmtm.com/articles/what-is-the-deal-with-aau.

17. *Id.*

18. AAU, https://find.aausports.org/ (last visited June 13, 2021).

19. *Id.*

20. 9ine Point, *Youth Club Sports: Pros and Cons*, 9INE POINT MAGAZINE, https://www.9inepointmag.com/athlete/youth-club-sports-pros-and-cons/ (last visited June 13, 2021).

21. *Id.*

22. *Id.*

23. *Id.*

24. *Id.*

25. Examples of other ODP sports are cycling, water polo, and sailing. USA CYCLING, https://usacycling.org/team-usa/olympic-development-academy (last visited June 13, 2021); USA WATER POLO, https://usawaterpolo.org/sports/2018/12/19/odp-national-team-pipeline.aspx (last visited June 13, 2021); *Frequently Asked Questions About US Sailing's Olympic Development Program (ODP)*, US

tryouts,[26] which are conducted by coaches affiliated with the ODP program in their particular state[27] Players are evaluated based on their: (1) technique; (2) tactics; (3) fitness and athletic ability; and (4) psychological make-up (attitude).[28] The selected athletes are placed on ODP teams.[29] The program is divided into four geographic regions, each of which offers a regional camp for ODP teams in each eligible age group.[30] These camps are designed to expose players to high-level competition; athletes who play at a high level and perform well during camps are identified as potential players for the national team pool or national team camp.[31]

[D] Playing Professionally/Joining a Professional Club's Academy

High school athletes may also opt to play professionally or join a professional team's sports academy, but few athletes in the United States follow this course because opportunities are either limited or nonexistent in many sports. This is a more common path in Europe. For example, European soccer leagues emphasize youth sports development through their leagues' football academies.[32] (In the United States, promising athletes are afforded the opportunity to develop their skills through participation in NCAA athletics.) European athletes under the age of majority often sign with a club's sports academy before they reach high school.[33] If the club deems a player sufficiently talented, the player will eventually be offered a contract to play for the club's senior team. For example, UEFA Champions League star Christian Pulisic excelled in the Dortmund academy and debuted in the Bundesliga, Germany's highest soccer league, at the age of 17.[34]

Signing with a professional team's academy is also available in the U.S. United States Men's Soccer National Team ("USMNT") star Tyler Adams took this path.[35] At the age of ten, Adams signed with the academy of the New York Red Bulls, a Major League Soccer ("MLS") team.[36] When he was 16, Adams debuted with the Red

---

SAILING, https://www.ussailing.org/olympics/olympic-development-program/olympic-development -program-faqs/ (last visited June 13, 2021).

26. *About ODP*, US YOUTH SOCCER, https://www.usyouthsoccer.org/about-odp/ (last visited Jan. 1, 2022).

27. *Id.*

28. *Id.*

29. *Id.*

30. *Id.*

31. *Id.*

32. *See, e.g.*, Multiple Contributors, *Barcelona, Lionel Messi, and the Napkin: Oral History of his Transfer, Arranged 20 Years Ago*, ESPN (Dec. 14, 2020), https://www.espn.com/soccer/barcelona/story/ 4263107/barcelonalionel-messi-and-the-napkin-oral-history-of-his-transferarranged-20-years-ago.

33. *Academy Player Wages 2020*, PLAYERSCOUT, https://playerscout.co.uk/football-academies/do- academy-players-get-paid/ (last visited June 14, 2021).

34. *Id.*

35. *Tyler Adams*, NEW YORK RED BULLS, https://www.newyorkredbulls.com/players/tyler-adams/ (last visited June 13, 2021).

36. *Id.*

Bulls' USL affiliate team (U.S. second division for soccer) and then joined the senior MLS New York Red Bulls at the conclusion of that season.[37]

Soccer is not the only sport in which an American high school athlete can pursue professional opportunities. It is relatively uncommon, however, given the presence of intercollegiate athletics in the U.S. and NCAA rules prohibiting student-athletes from playing professionally if they want to retain their eligibility to compete in intercollegiate athletics.[38] Recently, however, high school basketball players electing to forgo college by playing professionally has become somewhat less rare given the emergence of entities such as the NBA G League[39] and Overtime Elite.[40] These organizations provide an opportunity for high school basketball players, who are ineligible to enter the NBA draft because they are not one year removed from high school, to play professionally and forgo playing college basketball. Other high-school-aged athletes have elected to play professionally overseas. Charlotte Hornets superstar LaMelo Ball took this route when he signed with Lithuanian club Prienu Vytautas at the age of 16 to play basketball.[41] The move was met with much criticism at the time, but ultimately worked out well for Ball, who performed exceptionally well in his debut NBA season,[42] winning NBA rookie of the year honors.[43] Other Olympic sports have also had high schoolers reach the pinnacle of their sports during their high school years. This was the case for American snowboarder Chloe Kim, who won a gold medal in South Korea at the Olympics in 2018 at the age of 17, which led to her securing several lucrative sponsorship contracts.[44]

§ 1.03 Legal Issues in Interscholastic Athletics

Most high-school-aged athletes participate in sports that are offered by their schools. In 2018–19, just under eight million (7,937,491) athletes participated in high school athletics.[45] At the high school level, state interscholastic athletic associations, school districts, and high schools regulate athletic participation by students. Legal

---

37. *Id.*

38. Matthew Stross, *The NCAA's "No-Agent" Rule: Blurring Amateurism,* 2 Miss. Sports L. Rev. 167, 172 (2013).

39. NBA G League, *NBA G League 101,* https://gleague.nba.com/ (last visited Jan. 13, 2022).

40. Bruce Schoenfeld, *The Teenagers Getting Six Figures to Leave Their High Schools for Basketball,* N.Y. Times (Nov. 30, 2021).

41. *Id.*

42. *Lamelo Ball,* NBA, https://www.nba.com/player/1630163/lamelo_ball (last visited June 14, 2021).

43. *Id.*

44. Matthew J. Belvedere, *Snowboarding Gold Medalist Chloe Kim: I Won't Work with Sponsors Whose Messages I Don't Agree With,* CNBC, https://www.cnbc.com/2018/02/13/snowboarding-gold-medalist-chloe-kim-needs-to-agree-with-sponsors-messages.html (last updated Feb. 13, 2018) (last visited Jan. 15, 2022).

45. *2018–19 High School Athletics Participation Survey* (2019), https://www.nfhs.org/media/102 0412/2018-19_participation_survey.pdf. (last visited Jan. 14, 2022).

issues arise most frequently when a governing body rules that an athlete is ineligible to participate because of the violation of a rule and the athlete challenges the ineligibility determination. Athlete challenges often involve allegations of violations of their procedural and substantive due process rights arising from the Fourteenth Amendment of the U.S. Constitution and state constitutions. Athletes have also asserted that eligibility criteria infringe upon other constitutional rights such as their First Amendment rights to associate and speak freely, and Fourth Amendment protections against unreasonable searches and seizures.

Courts have afforded high school athletes limited constitutional protections. This judicial reluctance is derived from the general rule that, except in limited circumstances, high school athletes possess neither a property nor a liberty interest in athletic participation. Policy considerations also result in courts limiting their willingness to extend to athletes the protection of the First and Fourth Amendments. Following a discussion of high school eligibility rules and the predicates to a constitutionally protectable property interest, we examine the general rule that athletes do not have a constitutionally protectable right to participate in high school athletics.

[A] Eligibility Rules and Judicial Deference

[1] Eligibility Rules Overview

Athletes have asserted constitutional challenges to a range of eligibility regulations, including transfer, age eligibility, outside competition, good conduct, and personal appearance rules. Athletes have also challenged policies requiring that they submit to drug tests as a prerequisite to their participation in interscholastic sports.[46] Transfer rules generally require an interscholastic athlete to lose a year of athletic eligibility when they transfer to a school without a corresponding change in their residence. Transfer rules seek to "discourage school switching by athletes and recruiting of athletes by member schools."[47] Age eligibility rules generally prohibit students over a certain age (usually 19 or older) from participating in interscholastic athletics. A

---

46. Hageman v. Goshen County Sch. Dist. No. 1, 256 P.3d 487, 503–05 (Wy. 2011) (holding school drug testing policy violated neither the Wyoming nor United States Constitutions).

47. See Simkins ex rel. Simkins v. S. Dakota High Sch. Activities Ass'n, 434 N.W.2d 367, 369 (S.D. 1989) (upholding a transfer rule against an equal protection challenge, stating "[t]he purpose of the transfer rule is to discourage school switching by athletes and recruiting of athletes by member schools."). See also Ind. High Sch. Athletic Ass'n. v. Watson, 938 N.E.2d 672, 676 (Ind. 2010) (stating purpose of transfer rule is "[t]o preserve the integrity of interscholastic athletics and to prevent or minimize recruiting, proselytizing and school 'jumping' for athletic reasons...."); Morgan v. Oklahoma Secondary Sch. Activities Ass'n, 207 P.3d 362, 376 (Okla. 2009) ("The [transfer] rule serves two purposes: 1) to prevent recruitment of athletes; and 2) to preclude transfer students from displacing existing team plyers."); Ind. High Sch. Athletic Ass'n v. Carlberg, 694 N.E.2d 222, 240 (Ind. 1997) ("[T]he IHSAA views the [transfer] rule as 'a deterrent to students who would transfer schools for athletic reasons and to individuals who would *seek to recruit* student-athletes to attend a particular school for the purpose of building athletic strength.").

principal reason underlying age eligibility rules is the belief that "the use of older athletes constitute[s] a danger to the health and safety of the younger ones."[48] Athletes have also been ruled ineligible because of their failure to comply with a fifth-year rule, the principal purpose of which is to prevent students from competing in a "fifth year in high school, when [a student] is more mature, physically developed and presumably more proficient" while at the same time "competing with younger, less developed students, a situation which could lead to injuries."[49]

Outside competition rules generally prohibit high school athletes from competing on another team or participating in a "non-school activity or event in [the same] sport during that sports season."[50] Violations of this rule can result in athletes losing their athletic eligibility.[51] A Colorado appellate court summarized the rationales underlying outside competition rules as including:

> 1) assuring fairness to other students who may wish to participate on the school team, 2) providing balance between school teams, 3) providing balance with respect to the individual student's participation in athletics, 4) promoting team loyalty, and 5) ensuring that student athletes do not endanger their well-being by over-extensive athletic competition and stress.[52]

Athletes have been rendered ineligible for athletic participation because they failed to comply with academic eligibility rules.[53] In *Board of Education v. New Jersey State*

---

48. Trofimuk v. Penn. Interscholastic Athletic Ass'n, 1978 Pa. D. & C.3d 712, 713, 716 (Pa. D. & C. 1978); *see also* Baisden v. West Virginia Secondary Schs. Activities Comm'n, 568 S.E.2d 32 (W. Va. 2002).

49. Pratt v. New York Pub. High Sch. Athletic Ass'n, 133 Misc. 2d 679, 682 (N.Y. Sup. Ct. 1986); *see also* Bingham v. Oregon Sch. Activities Ass'n, 24 F. Supp. 2d 1110, 1113 (D. Or. 1998) (stating "OSAA's purpose in enforcing the Eight Semester Rule is threefold: 1) to ensure safety; 2) to promote competitive fairness; and 3) to encourage students to graduate in four years."); Lyon v. Illinois High Sch. Ass'n, 2013 WL 140926, at *5 (N.D. Ill. Jan. 11, 2013) (granting an injunction precluding the application of an "eight-semester" rule to render athlete ineligible).

50. Zuments v. Colo. High Sch. Activities Ass'n, 737 P.2d 1113, 1114 (Colo. App. 1987).

51. *See id.* (upholding constitutionality of an outside competition rule that stated "members of any high school sport may not compete on any other team, nor in any non-school activity or event in that sport during that sports season"); *see also* Cikraji v. Snowberger, 2014 Colo. Dist. LEXIS 2510, at *2, *19 (D. Colo. 2014) (dismissing a plaintiff's complaint challenging outside competition rule); E. N.Y. Youth Soccer Ass'n v. N.Y. State Pub. High Sch. Athletic Ass'n, 108 A.D.2d 39, 40–41 (N.Y. Ct. App. 1985) (upholding the constitutionality of an outside competition rule).

52. *Zuments*, 737 P.2d at 1115.

53. Brewer v. Purvis, 816 F. Supp. 1560, 1564 (M.D. Ga. 1993) (discussing an academic eligibility rule requiring students to be "on track" to graduate in order to participate in athletics); Spring Branch I.S.D. v. Stamos, 695 S.W.2d 556, 558, 562 (Tex. 1985) (reversing a temporary injunction issued by the district court enjoining enforcement of a no-pass, no-play academic eligibility rule); Bailey v. Bd. of Educ. of Kanawha, 321 S.E.2d 302, 305, 319 (W. Va. 1984) (rejecting constitutional challenges to academic eligibility rules); J.M. v. Montana High Sch. Athletic Ass'n, 875 P.2d 1026, 1031 (Mont. 1984) (upholding academic eligibility rule); David J. Shannon, *No Pass, No Play: Equal Protection Analysis Under the Federal and State Constitutions*, 63 IND. L.J. 161, 161–162 (1987) (discussing the arguments for and against academic eligibility rules and judicial challenges to them).

Interscholastic Athletic Association,[54] the court stated academic eligibility rules seek to prevent "red-shirting"[55] and "athletically gifted pupils who are not meeting academic standards from replacing other students who are maintaining academic standards but who might not have the same athletic prowess."[56] It further stated such rules attempt to "maintain[] a uniform progression among all member schools within a four-year cycle and equaliz[e] competition within these schools."[57]

Good conduct rules, which seek to "instill in students a respect for good citizenship in the form of positive peer pressure,"[58] generally prohibit students from engaging in conduct that renders them "unworthy to represent the ideals, principles and standards of [their] school."[59] Finally, personal appearance standards prohibit high school athletes from wearing clothing or having grooming styles, such as "hair styles which create problems of health and sanitation, obstruct vision, or call undue attention to the athlete."[60] Schools also maintain that appearance standards "promote discipline, maintain order, secure the safety of students, and provide a healthy environment conducive to academic purposes."[61]

---

54. 2012 WL 5199617 (N.J. Super. Ct. Oct. 23, 2012).

55. Although the NCAA disavows redshirting as an official NCAA term, it provides the following definition: "What a 'redshirt' season refers to is a year in which a student-athlete does not compete at all against outside competition. During a year in which the student-athlete does not compete, a student can practice with his or her team and receive financial aid." NCAA, *As a Division II Student-Athlete ... Do You Know,* NCAA.org, https://www.ncaa.org/sports/2014/3/27/as-a-division-ii-student-athlete-do-you-know.aspx (last visited Jan. 14, 2022).

56. Bd. of Educ. v. New Jersey State Interscholastic Athletic Ass'n, 2012 WL 5199617 at *1 (N.J. Super. Ct. App. Div. Oct. 23, 2021).

57. *Id.*

58. T.W. v. S. Columbia Area Sch. Dist., 2020 WL 7027636, at *1 (M.D. Penn. 2020).

59. Bunger v. Iowa High Sch. Athletic Ass'n, 197 N.W.2d 555, 557 (Iowa 1972) (invalidating conduct rule regulating alcohol); *see also* Smith v. Chippewa Falls Area Unified Sch. Dist., 302 F. Supp. 2d 953, 955–56 (W.D. Wis. 2002) (holding that a student, who violated alcohol policy, possessed no property interest and was also afforded due process if such an interest arose); Butler v. Oak Creek-Franklin Sch. Dist., 172 F. Supp. 2d 1102, 1107–08 (E.D. Wis. 2001) (invalidating athlete's 12-month suspension from sports for violating alcohol-related good conduct rule); Bush v. Dassel-Cokato Bd. of Educ., 745 F. Supp. 562, 564 (D. Minn. 1990) (upholding constitutionality of rule prohibiting athletes from attending parties where alcohol was served); Brands v. Sheldon Cmty. Sch., 671 F. Supp. 627, 628 (N.D. Iowa 1987) (stating a student violated a discipline policy since his conduct was "detrimental to the best interests" of the school district).

60. Hayden v. Greensburg Cmty. Sch. Corp., 743 F.3d 569, 572 (7th Cir. 2014) (finding grooming rule regulating length of haircuts violated the Equal Protection Clause and Title IX): *see also* Davenport v. Randolph Cty. Bd. of Educ., 730 F.2d 1395, 1396 (11th Cir. 1984) (upholding a "grooming policy [that] prohibited team members from having beards, wearing mustaches extending beyond the corners of their mouths, or growing sideburns below the ear lobes."); Karr v. Schmidt, 460 F.2d 609, 610 (5th Cir. 1972) (validating rule limiting the length of male students' hair); Dunham v. Pulsifer, 312 F. Supp. 411, 413 (D. Vt. 1970) (deeming as unconstitutional grooming policy regulating length of male athletes' hair); Humphries v. Lincoln Parish Sch. Bd., 467 So. 2d. 870, 871 (La. App. 2d Cir. 1985) (upholding validity of policy requiring that football players be clean shaven).

61. *Hayden,* 743 F.3d at 571.

[2] Judicial Deference

As the following discussion demonstrates, courts generally reject high school athletes' constitutional challenges to athletic eligibility rules. In so doing, courts rely on well-established constitutional doctrine, such as the failure of athletes to establish a constitutionally protectible property interest. Judicial reluctance to rule in favor of high school athletes is also a reflection of a policy determination to afford considerable deference to the eligibility determinations of interscholastic athletic associations, school districts, and schools.

The importance of deference was revealed in *Isabella v. Arrowhead Union High School District*.[62] In that case, a high school athlete violated her school's code of conduct. The athlete invited classmates to her home, some of whom brought and consumed alcohol. After becoming aware of the incident, the athlete's school suspended her for four soccer games.[63] The athlete asserted multiple constitutional challenges, including one alleging violation of her substantive due process rights. Rejecting the athlete's claim, the court reasoned "courts defer to a school's classification or construction of its own rules, even if erroneous, so long as they were not so irrational or arbitrary as to shock the conscience."[64]

The court in *Art Gaines Baseball Camp, Inc. v. Houston*[65] took the same approach in ruling on a challenge to an eligibility rule brought not by an athlete, but by the owner of a sports camp. The plaintiff challenged the legality of a rule providing that high school students attending a camp that specialized in a specific sport for more than two weeks during the summer would lose their eligibility to represent their schools in the same sport the immediately following school year.[66] The plaintiff alleged the rule harmed his economic interests.[67] Relying on the notion of deference, the court stated that "[a]long with entrusting the education of our children to teachers and administrators, we also entrust the control and supervision of the extracurricular activities incident to that education."[68] The court further explained that member schools voluntarily joined the athletic association and that chaos would result without

---

62. 323 F. Supp. 3d 1052 (E.D. Wis. 2018).

63. *Id.* at 1056–57.

64. *Id.* at 1062–63; *see also* Starego v. N.J. State Interscholastic Athletic Ass'n, 970 F. Supp. 303, 306, 310 (D. N.J. 2013) (affording deference to athletic association in regard to an age-eligibility rule dispute); Morgan v. Oklahoma Secondary Sch. Activities, 207 P.3d 362, 366 (Okla. 2009) (discussing a long-standing policy of deference to athletic associations partially due to their status as voluntary associations); Lilly v. Vermont Headmasters Ass'n, Inc., 648 A.2d 810 (Vt. 1993) (stating, "the VHA, as an educational association entrusted with the regulation of extracurricular activities, is entitled to deference in interpreting its rules."); Foskett v. Massachusetts Interscholastic Athletic Ass'n, 2021 WL 837091, at *5 (Mass. Super. Ct. Jan. 26, 2021) (stating courts must "accord the MIAA deference given its experience and competence" in regulating interscholastic athletics).

65. 500 S.W.2d 735 (Mo. Ct. App. 1973).

66. *Id.* at 736.

67. *Id.* at 741.

68. *Id.* at 740.

those rules. Finally, the court noted that it was "obvious that the members are in the most advantageous position to appreciate the regulations under which they must act to achieve desired goals. A court should not interfere with the enactment of those regulations as long as they are reasonable and do not infringe on public policy or law."[69]

[B] Athlete Due Process Claims

[1] Procedural Due Process

The Fourteenth Amendment of the U.S. Constitution precludes state actors (*i.e.*, public entities) from depriving any citizen of property without due process of the law.[70] Procedural due process concerns the type of notice and hearing to which a person is entitled before being deprived of a property or liberty interest.[71] Assuming that an athlete has a constitutionally protectible interest, procedural due process generally only requires a high school athletic association, a school, or some other governing body to provide a student with notice and an opportunity to be heard.[72] As alluded to above, however, the existence of a property or liberty interest is a prerequisite to a cognizable procedural due process claim.[73] This in turn requires that a plaintiff have a "legitimate claim of entitlement to a benefit — not simply a unilateral expectation or an abstract need."[74]

[2] Predicates to Cognizable Procedural Due Process Claim

[a] Property or Liberty Interest

Section 1983 is the procedural vehicle by which athletes pursue actions alleging that a state actor engaged in conduct that impermissibly deprived the athlete of their property and/or a liberty interest.[75] Therefore, a plaintiff seeking redress for due process violations must establish a protectible property interest of which she or he was deprived without sufficient procedural due process.[76] The property interest itself is not created by the Constitution. Rather, it is created and defined by "rules or understandings that stem from an independent source of law such as state law."[77] A

---

69. *Id.* at 741.

70. U.S. CONST. amend. XIV.

71. *See* ERWIN CHEMERINSKY, CONSTITUTIONAL LAW: PRINCIPLES AND POLICIES 591 (6th ed., Wolters Kluwer 2019).

72. *See* St. Patrick High Sch. v. New Jersey Interscholastic Athletic Ass'ns, 2010 WL 715826, at *3 (D. N.J. 2010) (citing Goss v. Lopez, 419 U.S. 565, 575 (1975)).

73. *See, e.g.,* Ryan v. California Interscholastic Fed'n, 94 Cal. App. 4th 1048, 1064 (Cal. Dist. Ct. App. 2001).

74. *Id.*

75. 42 U.S.C. § 1983 (2018).

76. Bd. of Regents of State Colleges v. Roth, 408 U.S. 564, 569–70 (1972); *see also* Walsh v. Louisiana High School Athletic As'n., 616 F.2d 152, 159–60 (5th Cir. 1980); Albach v. Odle, 531 F.2d 983 (10th Cir. 1976).

77. *Roth*, 408 U.S. at 577.

right arising out of contract provides such an independent source. Moreover, "[t]o have a property interest in a benefit, a person clearly must have more than an abstract need or desire for it. He must have more than a unilateral expectation of it. He must, instead, have a legitimate claim of entitlement to it."[78]

[b] State Actor Status

In addition to establishing a constitutionally recognized property interest,[79] a plaintiff must also establish that the body making an adverse eligibility determination was a state actor. Because private schools and their athletic governing organizations are not state actors, student-athletes at private schools do not possess federal constitutionally-based claims.[80] On the other hand, athletes may be able to pursue such claims against public high schools and school boards, because they are state actors.[81] Until 2001,[82] it was less than clear whether interscholastic associations were, similarly, state actors. The Supreme Court's decision in *Brentwood Academy v. Tennessee Secondary School Athletic Association*[83] brought clarity.[84] In *Brentwood,* a lower court found that Brentwood Academy, a member of the Tennessee Secondary School Athletic Association, violated the Association's rule against undue influence in recruiting.[85] The school sued the Association, claiming the TSSAA's enforcement of the rule constituted

78. *Id.* at 577.

79. CHEMERINSKY, *supra* note 71, at 591 (stating "[p]rocedural due process, as the phrase implies, refers to the procedures that the government must follow before it deprives a person of life, liberty, or property. Classic procedural due process issues concern what kind of notice and what form of hearing the government must provide when it takes a particular action.").

80. *See* Commonwealth v. Considine, 860 N.E.2d 673, 677–78 (Mass. 2007) (rejecting plaintiff's challenge to an alleged unreasonable search because it was conducted by a private school); Wajnowski v. Connecticut Ass'n of Schs., 1999 Conn. Super. LEXIS 3448, at *5, *13–14 (Conn. Super. Ct. Dec. 17, 1999) (finding no state action because of a lack of evidence that the subject organization received funds from the state).

81. *See* NCAA v. Tarkanian, 488 U.S. 179, 191 (1988); Anderson v. Ind. High Sch. Athletic Ass'n, 699 F. Supp. 719, 727–28 (S.D. Ind. 1988) (holding an athletic association did not engage in state action because "[t]here is simply no evidence whatsoever that a state supported institution ... caused, directed, or controlled the implementation of [a] transfer rule.").

82. *See* Mitchell v. Louisiana High Sch. Athletic Ass'n, 430 F.2d 1155, 1157 (5th Cir. 1970) (stating "[w]hile it is clear that LHSAA's disqualification of the students is state action for constitutional purposes, neither of appellee's allegations raises a substantial federal question."); B.C. v. Bd. of Educ., 531 A.2d 1059, 1068 (N.J. Super. Ct. App. Div. 1987) (concluding that state action arose from "activities of the Athletic Association in sponsoring, administering, regulating, and supervising interscholastic athletics....").

83. 531 U.S. 288 (2001).

84. Christian Heritage Acad. v. Okla. Secondary Sch. Activities, Ass'n, 483 F.3d 1025, 1030 (10th Cir. 2007) (citing *Brentwood* in finding the state athletic association's conduct constituted state action); Cmtys. for Equity v. Mich. High Sch. Athletic Ass'n, 459 F.3d 676, 692 (6th Cir. 2006) (affirming district court's finding that the Michigan High School Athletic Association is a state actor); A.H. v. Ill. High Sch. Athletic Ass'n, 263 F. Supp. 3d 705, 720 (N.D. Ill. 2017) (finding that Illinois High School Athletic Association is a state actor).

85. Brentwood Acad. v. Tenn. Secondary Sch. Athletic Ass'n, 13 F. Supp. 2d 670, 673–76 (M.D. Tenn. 1998).

state action and violated plaintiff's First and Fourteenth Amendment rights.[86] The Court held TSSAA was a state actor because of "the pervasive entwinement of public institutions and public officials in [TSSAA's] composition and workings."[87] The Court identified the following facts in support of its finding of top down and bottom up entwinement: 84% of TSSAA's membership was comprised of public schools and their personnel (*e.g.*, principals) who acted within TSSAA in their official capacities; TSSAA's administrative staff were treated as state employees; and state board of education members served in an *ex officio* capacity on important TSSAA committees (*i.e.*, the board of control and legislative council).[88]

[c] Exhaustion of Administrative Remedies

Under common law, a voluntary association may require its members "to exhaust all internal remedies within the association before resorting to any court or tribunal outside of the association," something known as the "exhaustion doctrine."[89] Thus, when a private organization has adopted rules and procedures for reviewing internal decisions, these procedures and rules "must be exhausted before a plaintiff can seek redress in a court."[90] Only under exceptional circumstances will courts intervene in a voluntary association's affairs without a plaintiff, against whom an adverse decision was made, having exhausted all of the association's remedies.[91]

The exhaustion doctrine also applies to administrative rulings taken pursuant to administrative rules or regulations. Accordingly, the exhaustion doctrine creates a potential impediment to high school athletes seeking redress against adverse eligibility determinations made by interscholastic athletic associations, public schools,[92] and school boards.[93] *Kanongata'a v. Washington Interscholastic Activities Association* illustrates the application of the exhaustion doctrine.[94] There, the Washington Interscholastic Athletic Association ruled an athlete ineligible to play football because he violated a "four-year season limitation rule" and committed an academic cheating violation.[95] The athlete sued, alleging the association's determination violated his federal constitutional rights and his rights under the Individuals with Disabilities

---

86. Brentwood Acad. v. Tenn. Secondary Sch. Athletic Ass'n, 531 U.S. 288, 293 (2001).

87. *Id.* at 298.

88. *Id.* at 299–302, 305.

89. Fla. High Sch. Athletic Ass'n v. Melbourne Cent. Cath. High Sch., 867 So. 2d 1281, 1284, 1287–88 (Fla. Dist. Ct. App. 2004).

90. *Id.* (citing 6 Am. Jur. 2d *Associations and Clubs* § 30 (1999)).

91. *Melbourne Cent. Cath. High Sch.*, 867 So. 2d at 1288.

92. *See* McIntyre v. El Paso Indep. Sch. Dist., 499 S.W.3d 820, 825 (Tex. 2015) (stating the Texas Education Code requires a person "to exhaust administrative remedies when they are aggrieved by the school laws and no exceptions to exhaustion applies.").

93. *See* Sutterby v. Zimar, 156 Misc. 2d 762, 763–66 (Sup. Ct. N.Y. 1993) (deeming premature challenge to school's denial of student's transfer waiver request); *but see* Lar v. Billings Sch. Dist., 2018 U.S. Dist. LEXIS 151251, at *2–4, *14–21 (D. Mont. 2018) (distinguishing cases in which athletes were required to exhaust administrative remedies).

94. 2006 WL 1727891, at *20 (W.D. Wash. June 20, 2006).

95. *Id.* at *4–5.

Education Act ("IDEA").[96] It was undisputed that the student had not exhausted the administrative remedies required under the IDEA. Thus, the court held that the athlete could not pursue his IDEA-based claim because he had not exhausted IDEA administrative remedies.[97] The court also rejected the athlete's argument that the futility exception to the exhaustion doctrine warranted not dismissing his lawsuit.[98] The court held that the applicability of the futility exception was fact intensive and, therefore, summary judgement was premature.[99]

[3] Majority Rule: Procedural Due Process Not Required Because of Absence of Property or Liberty Interest

In *Goss v. Lopez*,[100] the U.S. Supreme Court held that the right to a public grade-school education is protected by the Due Process clause.[101] Even though subsequent courts have recognized the importance of participation in extracurricular activities, including athletics, as an important component of the educational process, courts have rejected efforts by athletes to extend *Goss* to encompass athletic participation.[102] An illustrative case is *Albach v. Odle*,[103] where an athlete challenged a transfer rule that imposed a one-year ban on participation in interscholastic high school athletics to any student who transferred from the plaintiff's home district to a boarding school or a boarding school to a home district.[104] The athlete invoked *Goss*, but the court held that the educational process referred to in *Goss* consists of multiple inseparable components but a property interest subject to constitutional protection does not exist in each of these separate components, including athletics.[105]

---

96. *Id.* at *1, *4–5.

97. *Id.* at *20.

98. *Id.*

99. *Id* at *21; *see also* Univ. Interscholastic League v. Buchanan, 848 S.W.2d 298, 300–01, 303 (Tex. Ct. App. 1993) (finding that exhaustion under IDEA did not apply in this dispute regarding age eligibility rule); Caso v. New York Pub. High Sch. Athletic Ass'n, 78 A.D.2d 41, 43–46 (N.Y. App. Div. 1980) (discussing exhaustion of available administrative remedies regarding violation of outside competition rule).

100. 419 U.S. 565 (1975).

101. *See id.* at 573.

102. *See* Haverkamp v. Unified Sch. Dist. 689 F. Supp. 1055, 1056, 1058 (D. Kan. 1986) (finding athlete removed from varsity cheerleading squad possessed no constitutionally protected property interest notwithstanding the possibility of future education or career opportunities); *Ryan*, 94 Cal. App. 4th at 1059 (upholding an eligibility rule because athlete possessed no property interest in athletic participation despite the athlete's superior athletic abilities).

103. 531 F.2d 983 (10th Cir. 1976).

104. *Id.* at 984.

105. *Id.* at 985.

The position expressed in *Albach* has been adopted by the majority of federal and state courts.[106] For example, the Third Circuit[107] has ruled that athletes possess no constitutionally protected property interest in extra-curricular activities, including athletics.[108] In *Angstadt*, a student was not permitted to play basketball at a public high school because she failed to meet all eligibility requirements.[109] The student and her parents filed suit asserting a lack of due process, even though they conceded that "no property interest exists in participation in extracurricular activities, including sports, as a general principle, under the United States Constitution."[110] The Third Circuit held that the athlete possessed a property interest under neither the U.S. Constitution nor a Pennsylvania state statute. Regarding the latter, the court noted the relevant state statute required students to satisfy all requirements to participate in extra-curricular sports, but the athlete had failed to do so.[111] It is also notable that assuming an athlete possesses a property interest, in most cases, no claims lie because the athlete receives all the due process to which the athlete was entitled.[112]

Federal district courts have followed circuit courts in holding that student-athletes do not possess constitutionally protectible interests in athletic participation.[113] In *Maki v. Minn. State High Sch. League*,[114] an athlete sought a preliminary injunction against a one-year varsity athletics participation ban stemming from a transfer rule, in which the school district found that an "Intolerable Conditions at the Sending

---

106. Courts have refused to find a constitutionally protectible property interest in a range of disputes including: DeLaTorre v. Minn. High Sch. League, 202 F. Supp. 3d 1046, 1048, 1058 (D. Minn. 2016) (transfer rule); Immaculate Heart Cent. Sch. v. N.Y. State Pub. High Sch. Athletic Ass'n, 797 F. Supp. 2d 204, 207–08, 218 (N.D.N.Y. 2011) (classification policy dispute); Perry v. Ohio High Sch. Athletic Ass'n, 2006 WL 2927260, at *1, *3 (S.D. Ohio 2006) (transfer rule); Dominic J. v. Wyo. Valley W. High Sch., 362 F. Supp. 2d 560, 563, 572 (M.D. Penn. 2005) (drug policy); White-Ciluffo v. Iowa Dep't of Educ., 2017 WL 2469216, at *1, *6 (Iowa Ct. App. 2017) (rule prohibiting competition between high school and college athletes).

107. *Accord* Brindinsi v. Regano, 20 Fed. Appx. 508, 510 (6th Cir. 2001) (finding no property or liberty interest in interscholastic athletics conferring due process to student not permitted to join cheerleading squad); Davenport v. Randolph County Bd. of Educ., 730 F.2d 1395, 1397–98 (11th Cir. 1984) (in a grooming policy dispute, court holds student had no property interest in participation).

108. Angstadt v. Midd-West Sch. Dist., 377 F.3d 338, 344 (3d Cir. 2004).

109. *Id.* at 340.

110. *Id.* at 344 citing Appellants Brief at p. 29.

111. *Id.*

112. DeLaTorre v. Minnesota State High Sch. League, 202 F. Supp. 3d 1046, 1049, 1060 (D. Minn. 2016) (rejecting due process challenge to a transfer-eligibility rule because athlete received sufficient due process). *See also* T.W. v. S. Columbia Area Sch. Dist., 2020 WL 5751219, at *6 (M.D. Pa. Sept. 25, 2020) (finding a school district established a property interest in extra-curricular participation, the court concludes athlete failed to establish he had not been afforded due process); St. Patrick High Sch. v. New Jersey Interscholastic Athletic Ass'n, 2010 WL 715826, at *3, *4 (D. N.J. Mar. 1, 2010) (assuming plaintiff had a property interest in playing in a tournament, court finds athletic association procedures afforded sufficient due process to athlete).

113. *Accord Isabella*, 323 F. Supp. 3d at 1057–63 (adopting majority rule that there is neither a property right in athletic participation nor a violation of substantive due process).

114. 2016 U.S. Dist. LEXIS 181778 (D. Minn. Dec. 27, 2016).

School" exception did not apply.[115] The athlete asserted that she had a protected property interest in interscholastic varsity athletic participation entitling her to due process. Adhering to Minnesota precedent, the court concluded "that the right to a public education under Minnesota law does not include eligibility for interscholastic varsity athletic competition."[116] Thus, the court held that the student was unlikely to prevail on her procedural due process claim. The court also concluded that even if the athlete possessed a right to due process, she had been afforded sufficient due process.[117]

As illustrated by *Ryan v. California Interscholastic Federation-San Diego Section*,[118] state courts[119] have also generally refused to confer upon high school athletes a constitutionally protectible property or liberty interest in athletic participation. *Ryan* involved a challenge by an Australian exchange student to a transfer rule that precluded his participation in athletics because he had already exhausted eight semesters of high school in Australia.[120] Rejecting the athlete's claim, the court held, "[o]ur conclusion is consistent with the overwhelming majority of other states whose appellate courts have held that students do not possess a constitutionally protected interest in their participation in extracurricular activities and, specifically, in interscholastic sports."[121]

A federal district court examined whether an athlete had a liberty interest in his reputation in *J.K. v. Minneapolis Public Schools*.[122] In that case, a school district administratively transferred a baseball player to a different high school after he allegedly participated in the sexual assault of a teammate.[123] The athlete asserted that the transfer damaged his reputation.[124] In assessing the student's liberty interest challenge, the court stated that in order for the student to successfully invoke due process protection based on a liberty interest in his reputation, he was required to establish: "(1) damage to his reputation and (2) a tangible burden of some kind."[125] The test adopted by the court has been referred to as the "stigma-plus" test. The court found that plaintiff failed to satisfy his burden given that the facts showed his school record would not

---

115. *Id.* at *10.
116. *Id.* at *17.
117. *Id.* at *18.
118. 94 Cal. App. 4th 1048 (Cal. Ct. App. 2001).
119. Other state courts adopting this general rule include: Menard v. La. High Sch. Athletic Ass'n, 30 So. 3d 790, 792, 795 (La. Ct. App. 2009) (holding in a transfer-rule dispute athlete had no protected interest in interscholastic athletics); Taylor v. Enumclaw Sch. Dist., 133 P.3d 492, 494, 496–97 (Wash. Ct. App. 2006) (stating, "participation in interscholastic sports is not a constitutionally protected property interest" in case involving violation of alcohol policy); Edwards v. O'Fallon Twp. High Sch. Dist. No. 203 Bd. of Educ., 706 N.E.2d 137, 138, 140 (Ill. Ct. App. 1999) (holding, in a challenge to drug use prohibition, that "participation in interscholastic athletics does not rise to the level of a protected interest.").
120. *Ryan,* 94 Cal. App. at 1054–55.
121. *Id.* at 1061.
122. 849 F. Supp. 2d 865 (D. Minn. 2011).
123. *Id.* at 867–69.
124. *Id.* at 878–79.
125. *Id.* (citing Gundersson v. Hvass, 339 F.3d 639, 644 (8th Cir. 2003)).

reflect the reason for the transfer.[126] The court also noted other Minnesota authority holding "no property or liberty interest exists in a student's participation in extracurricular activities."[127]

[4] Exceptions to the Majority Rule

Courts adopting the majority rule that student-athletes have no constitutionally protected interest in athletic participation have invoked exceptions to afford athletes relief.[128] One such exception arises where a school or school district has a policy that requires process, such as a hearing, before an athlete is rendered ineligible to participate in athletics. For example in *Tiffany v. Arizona Interscholastic Association*,[129] a student-athlete was rendered ineligible to participate in interscholastic athletics because of a "nineteen-year-old" eligibility rule, when he turned nineteen before his senior year began.[130] The court initially held that Tiffany failed to "raise his interest in interscholastic athletics to a level warranting the safeguards of the due process clause."[131] The court ruled, however, that even though the association's bylaws specifically provided that its executive board must exercise discretion in considering hardship waivers to its eligibility rules, the board had failed to follow the bylaws. Rather, the board "adopted a policy of not making any exceptions to the nineteen-year-old eligibility requirement."[132] Thus, the court held that the administrative board's actions invoked administrative law principles and its actions were unreasonable, arbitrary, and capricious in failing to consider the student-athlete's waiver request.[133]

Another case illustrating an exception to the majority rule comes from the Supreme Court of Appeals of West Virginia in *Baisden v. West Virginia Secondary Schools Activities Commission*.[134] There, a West Virginia interscholastic athletic association's rule prohibited 19-year-old athletes from participating in interscholastic athletics. Pursuant to this rule, an athlete was declared ineligible to play football be-

---

126. *Id.* at 878–79.

127. *Id.* at 876 (citing Peterson v. Indep. Sch. Dist. No. 811, 999 F. Supp. 665, 674 (D. Minn. 1978)). For discussion on liberty interests in high school athletics, *see also White-Ciluffo*, 902 N.W.2d at *1–2, *6 (finding no liberty or property interest in interscholastic competition where athlete challenged rule prohibiting high school athletes from competing in games against college athletes representing their universities); *Ryan*, 94 Cal. App. 4th at 1054–56, 1066 (finding neither due process nor liberty interest entitling athlete to due process).

128. *See* Miss. High Sch. Activities Ass'n, v. R.T., 163 So. 3d 274, 275, 279–80 (Miss. 2015) (adopting general rule that an athlete has no legally protectible right to athletic participation, but holding that if a school creates a sports program and establishes eligibility rules, the school or athletic association must follow those rules); Paige v. Ohio High Sch. Athletic Ass'n, 999 N.E.2d 1211, 1213, 1216 (Ohio Ct. App. 2013) (in student-athlete transfer eligibility dispute, holding that the appeal of preliminary injunction in favor of student was moot because athlete had graduated from high school).

129. 726 P.2d 231 (Ariz. Ct. App. 1986).

130. *Id.* at 232.

131. *Id.* at 236.

132. *Id.*

133. *Id.*

134. 568 S.E.2d 32 (W. Va. 2002).

cause he turned 19 before the cut-off date.[135] The lower court granted a permanent injunction against enforcement of the rule.[136] The appellate court analyzed the applicability of the rule, noting that the student's learning disability caused him to remain in high school when he was 19. The court stated that the age rule may be waived "where a reasonable accommodation of disabilities" is justified.[137] After stressing the need to make individualized determinations of whether the age eligibility rule should be waived, the court ultimately concluded that the facts did not warrant waiver as a reasonable accommodation.[138]

[5] The Minority Rule: Athletes Possess a Property Interest in Athletic Participation

A minority of courts recognize that a high school athlete has a property or liberty interest in participating in interscholastic athletics.[139] In *Duffley v. New Hampshire Interscholastic Athletic Ass'n*,[140] the plaintiff-athlete alleged an interscholastic athletic association's "Semester Rule," which prohibited student-athletes from competing in interscholastic athletics for more than eight consecutive semesters, improperly denied him eligibility to participate in interscholastic athletics during what would have been his ninth semester.[141] Like the jurisdictions mentioned above, the court considered whether student-athletes had a constitutionally protected interest in interscholastic athletics. In departing from the majority rule,[142] the court reasoned that the state's Department of Education had promulgated rules stating that extracurricular activities, "including athletics, should be considered part of the curriculum."[143] According to the court, this supported the idea that "interscholastic athletics are considered an integral and important element of the educational process in New Hampshire."[144] The court further reasoned that a student's ability to attend college could hinge on the right to participate in interscholastic athletics, which entitles students to procedural due process and a property interest in interscholastic athletics.[145] For these reasons, the court found participation in interscholastic athletics must be viewed as a right entitled to protection, not merely a privilege.[146] The court's ruling conflicts with the majority rule which provides that a high school athlete's athletic participation could

---

135. *Id.* at 36.

136. *Id.*

137. *Id.* at 44.

138. *Id.*

139. *See* Stone v. Kansas State High School Activities Ass'n, 761 P.2d 1255, 1257 (Kan. Ct. App. 1988) (disagreeing with courts that hold student's interest in participating in extracurricular activities is "'not of constitutional magnitude.'").

140. 446 A.2d 462 (N.H. 1982).

141. *Id.* at 467.

142. *Id.*

143. *Id.*

144. *Id.*

145. *Id.*

146. *Id.*

position the athlete to receive a college scholarship is insufficient to give rise to a property interest.[147]

[C] Athlete Substantive Due Process Challenges

The Fourteenth Amendment restricts the ability of state actors to deprive citizens of their life, liberty, or property without procedural and substantive due process of the law.[148] As discussed, *supra*, procedural due process concerns the type of notice and hearing that a person is entitled to before being deprived of a property or liberty interest.[149] In contrast, substantive due process examines whether a state actor had a sufficient justification for taking action that deprives a person of a property or liberty interest.[150]

> Whether there is such a justification depends very much on the level of scrutiny used. For example, if the law is in an area where only rational basis review is applied, substantive due process is met so long as the law is rationally related to a legitimate government purpose. But if it is in an area where strict scrutiny is used, such as for fundamental rights, then the government will meet substantive due process only if it can prove that the law is necessary to achieve a compelling government purpose.[151]

Thus, notwithstanding any procedural protections provided, substantive due process prohibits a state actor from taking actions that are "unreasonable, arbitrary, or capricious" and thereby infringe upon a person's fundamental rights or liberty interests.[152]

Courts have not been receptive to student-athletes' substantive due process claims.[153] In *White-Ciluffo v. Iowa Department of Education*,[154] a track and field high school athlete was declared ineligible for two seasons after she competed against college athletes representing their colleges.[155] The court dismissed the athlete's substantive due process claim because she failed to establish a property or liberty interest in athletic participation.[156] In reaching this result, the court adhered to precedent establishing that athletes possess no constitutionally protected right to athletic participation and

---

147. Fla. High Sch. Athletic Ass'n v. Melbourne Cent. Catholic High Sch., 867 So. 2d 1281, 1284, 1288 (Fla. Ct. App. 2004) (stating, in a case involving anti-recruiting rule violation, that the possibility of a scholarship is not a protectable property interest).

148. U.S. CONST. amend. XIV.

149. *See* CHEMERINSKY, *supra* note 71, at 591.

150. *Id.* at 592.

151. *Id.*

152. 16C C.J.S., 16C C.J.S. *Constitutional Law* § 1821 (2020) ("A claim of violation of Fourteenth Amendment substantive due process requires proof that a defendant's conduct shocks the conscience or interferes with rights implicit in the concept of ordered liberty, or offends judicial notions of fairness, or is offensive to human dignity, or is taken with deliberate indifference to protected rights.").

153. *See, e.g.*, Isabella A. v. Arrowhead Union High Sch. Dist., 323 F. Supp. 3d 1052, 1063 (E.D. Wis. 2018) (ruling plaintiff's substantive due process claim was without merit).

154. 902 N.W.2d 590 (Iowa Ct. App. 2017).

155. *Id.* at *1.

156. *Id.* at *6.

that "a plaintiff [must] first demonstrate a due process right is at stake before [the court] will examine whether a governmental action has infringed upon that right."[157]

McGhee v. Talladega City Bd. of Education[158] produced a similar outcome. In that case, plaintiffs took issue with the defendant's hiring of a coach and the coach's alleged retaliatory conduct that refused to permit one of the players to join a high school's basketball team.[159] Dismissing the plaintiffs' claims, the court reasoned "[b]ecause no constitutional right arises to play interscholastic sports, receive a college scholarship, or participate in a gifted program, being denied the opportunity to play interscholastic sports, receive a college scholarship, or participate in a gifted program does not implicate substantive due process."[160]

Assuming that a court were to find that a high school athlete's athletic participation gives rise to a property or liberty interest, courts are nevertheless unlikely to find an athlete's substantive due process rights are violated. Consider *Hayden v. Greensburg Community College School Corp.*[161] In that case, parents on behalf of their minor son challenged a policy, which "require[d] boys playing interscholastic basketball at the public high school in Greensburg, Indiana, to keep their hair cut short."[162] Plaintiffs argued, *inter alia,* that "the hair-length policy arbitrarily intrude[d] upon their son's liberty interest in choosing his own hair length, and thus violates his right to substantive due process."[163] Plaintiffs contended that their son's right to determine the length of his hair amounted to a fundamental liberty interest. In rejecting this argument, the court stated, "the government need only demonstrate that the intrusion upon [a non-fundamental] liberty is rationally related to a legitimate government interest."[164] Given plaintiffs' inability to "demonstrate [that] the hair-length policy lacks a rational relationship with a legitimate government interest," the court concluded that the policy survived rational basis review.[165]

An alleged violation of an athlete's substantive due process rights was also at issue in *T.W. v. S. Columbia Area Sch. Dist.*[166] There, a student-athlete violated a school district's good conduct rule forbidding students who participated in extracurricular

---

157. *Id.* at *6.

158. 2020 WL 6384428 (N.D. Ala. Oct. 30, 2020).

159. *Id.* at *2–3.

160. *Id.*

161. 743 F.3d 569 (7th Cir. 2014); *see also* Johansen v. Louisiana High Sch. Athletic Ass'n, 916 So. 2d 1081, 1088 (1st Cir. 2005) (concluding plaintiffs' substantive due process claim must fail because they possessed no liberty or property interest in interscholastic athletics).

162. *Hayden,* 743 F.3d at 571.

163. *Id.*

164. *Id.* at 576.

165. *Id.*

166. 2020 WL 5751219 (M.D. Pa. Sept. 25, 2020); *see also* Scott v. Minnesota State High Sch. League, 2016 WL 7735565, at *4–5, *9 (D. Minn. Dec. 27, 2016) (rejecting, in a transfer-rule case, the substantive due process argument because plaintiffs "d[id] not identify a legitimate substantive due process right"); Brands v. Sheldon Cmty. Sch., 671 F. Supp. 627, 633–34 (N.D. Iowa 1987) (finding a plaintiff's substantive due process rights were not violated because the student was not treated arbitrarily and capriciously and their right to sexual privacy was not violated); Mancuso v. Massachusetts Interscholastic Athletic Ass'n, Inc., 900 N.E.2d 518, 522, 532–33 (Mass. 2009) (concluding athlete

activities from "attending any event in which underage drinking, smoking, or drug use is occurring."[167] The athlete asserted that the discipline (*i.e.,* suspension from athletic participation) imposed for his breaking the rule violated his right to substantive due process.[168] The athlete's parents also asserted a violation of their "substantive right ... as parents to direct and control their children's upbringing and education."[169] Applying a rational basis standard, the court found "even if [the] parents could establish such a right, they have not satisfied their burden of showing that the District's policy is irrational or shocks the conscience."[170] Thus, "they have failed to establish a likelihood of success on the merits of their substantive due process claim."[171]

§ 1.04 Athlete Equal Protection Challenges

[A] The Standards of Review

The Equal Protection Clause of the Fourteenth Amendment protects persons against "intentional, arbitrary discrimination by governmental officials."[172] In examining a plaintiff's equal protection claim, a court adopts one of three standards of review. A strict scrutiny standard is applied where a plaintiff's equal protection claim implicates a fundamental right such as freedoms protected by the Bill of Rights (*e.g.,* freedom of speech and religion) and other rights (*e.g.,* the right to marry and the right of parents to "direct the education and upbringing of [their] children").[173] Courts also apply a strict scrutiny standard of review where the plaintiff is a member of a suspect class (*e.g.,* race, color, national origin, or religion).[174] "Where strict scrutiny is used, ... then the government will meet substantive due process only if it can prove that the law is necessary to achieve a compelling government purpose."[175]

In instances in which the challenged governmental action does not implicate a fundamental right or suspect criteria, the action's constitutionality is examined under a rational basis standard, which "requires only that the classification rationally or reasonably further a legitimate governmental purpose."[176] The third standard of review — intermediate — imposes "a heightened scrutiny ... but not a scrutiny as intense

---

challenging fifth-year rule had "no property interest in her participation in interscholastic athletics and therefore suffered no violation of due process); Lilly v. Vermont Headmasters Ass'n, Inc., 648 A.2d 810, 811–12 (Vt. 1993) (applying the arbitrary and capricious standard in a challenge over an eight-semester rule).

167. *T.W.,* 2020 WL at *1–3.

168. *Id.* at *4.

169. *Id.* at *5.

170. *Id.*

171. *Id.*

172. Hayden v. Greenburg Cmty. Sch. Corp., 743 F.3d 569, 577 (7th Cir. 2014).

173. *Id.* at 575.

174. 16C C.J.S. *Constitutional Law* § 1277 (2020).

175. CHEMERINSKY, *supra* note 71, at 546.

176. 16C C.J.S. *Constitutional Law* § 1279 (2020).

as that applied in cases involving suspect classifications or fundamental rights. Under this analysis, the statutory classification must be substantially related to a governmental objective."[177] Quasi-suspect classifications giving rise to an intermediate standard of review include sex and legitimacy status.[178]

[B] Equal Protection: Rational Basis Standard of Review

As is true of their due process challenges, high school athletes have met with little success in lawsuits asserting adverse eligibility determinations violated their equal protection rights. *Niles v. University Interscholastic League* is illustrative.[179] In that case, a high school athlete, who resided in Texas, moved to California with his mother for the spring semester before returning to Texas to resume playing football the following fall.[180] The athlete was subsequently declared ineligible for athletic participation pursuant to an athletic association rule requiring that a student have been a resident of the school district for at least one year prior to participating in athletic events. The athlete appealed the ruling, arguing that it violated his equal protection rights by "creating an invidious classification between students residing with their parents and those residing apart from their parents."[181] The court rejected this argument, stating "'[w]here ... the classification created by the regulatory scheme neither trammels fundamental rights or interests nor burdens an inherently suspect class, equal protection analysis requires that the classification be rationally related to a legitimate state interest.'"[182] The court added that the athletic association's rules promoted "the state's legitimate interest in equalizing competition," and thus, there was no equal protection violation.[183]

---

177. *Id.* at §1278.

178. *Hayden*, 743 F.3d at 577 (stating that "gender is a quasi-suspect class that triggers intermediate scrutiny in the equal protection context; the justification for a gender-based classification thus must be exceedingly persuasive.").

179. 715 F.2d 1027 (5th Cir. 1983).

180. *Id.* at 1028–29.

181. *Id.* at 1029.

182. *Id.* at 1031 (quoting Walsh v. Louisiana High School Athletic Ass'n, 616 F.2d 152, 160 (5th Cir. 1980)).

183. *Id.; accord* B.A. v. Miss. High Sch. Activities Ass'n, 983 F. Supp. 2d 857, 861, 864 (N.D. Miss. 2013) (applying rational basis standard in athlete-eligibility dispute); Jones v. W. Va. State Bd. of Educ., 622 S.E.2d 289, 295–96 (W. Va. 2005) ("treating public and nonpublic school children differently with respect to participation in interscholastic sports does not violate equal protection" in constitutional challenge asserted by a home-schooled athlete); Reid v. Kenowa Hills Pub. Sch., 261 Mich. App. 17, 21, 30–31 (Mich. Ct. App. 2004) (concluding that "'participation in high school interscholastic athletics does not constitute exercise of a fundamental right'" in action brought by home-schooled students); Letendere v. Mo. State High Sch. Activities Ass'n, 86 S.W.3d 63, 69 (Mo. Ct. App. 2002) (finding rule precluding athletes from competing in two sports concurrently did not infringe upon athlete's equal protection rights because it was rationally related to the association's legitimate interest of serving the best interests of students).

Bailey v. Truby is also illustrative.[184] The West Virginia State Board of Education instituted a new policy requiring students participating in extracurricular activities to: (1) "maintain a 2.0 grade point average" and (2) "meet state and local attendance requirements."[185] The rule, which was challenged in a consolidated proceeding, was upheld by the West Virginia Supreme Court.[186] The court concluded the requirements were "a legitimate exercise of [the West Virginia State Board of Education's] power of 'control, supervision, and regulation' of extracurricular activities."[187]

[C] Equal Protection: Heightened Standard of Review

An intermediate standard of review was applied by the court in *Leffel v. Wisconsin Interscholastic Athletic Association*.[188] In that case, high school girls were denied permission to compete for roster spots on boys' baseball, tennis, and swim teams. Of the three sports, swim was the only sport offered to girls.[189] Plaintiffs challenged an interscholastic athletic association's constitutional provision prohibiting "all types of interscholastic activity involving boys and girls competing with or against each other."[190] In regard to equal protection, the court framed the pertinent inquiry as whether "the defendants violated the equal protection clause by denying female high school students the opportunity to qualify for a position on a boys varsity interscholastic team engaging in a contact sport where no separate team is provided for girls, or where the separate team provided does not have a comparable program."

In addressing this issue, the court applied an intermediate level of scrutiny. Quoting *Craig v. Boren*,[191] the court stated "to withstand constitutional challenge, previous cases establish that classifications by gender must serve important governmental objectives and must be substantially related to achievement of those objectives."[192] The court rejected the defendant's justifications for the policy — "differences in athletic abilities" and the enhanced risk of injury to girls if they competed against boys.[193] It concluded that excluding girls "from all contact sports in order to protect female high

---

184. 321 S.E.2d 302 (W. Va. 1984).

185. *Id.*

186. *Id.* at 305, 319.

187. *Id.* at 319.

188. 444 F. Supp. 1117 (E.D. Wis. 1978).

189. *Id.* at 1119. The court rejected plaintiffs' claim that where a school offers a girls' team in a particular sport, girls should be permitted to try out for that team where the boys' team competes at a higher level. *Id.* at 1121.

190. *Id.* at 1120. This provision was later amended to prohibit all types of interscholastic activity involving boys and girls competing with or against each other "except ... as prescribed by state and federal law [*i.e.*, Title IX]...." *Id.*

191. 429 U.S. 190 (1976).

192. *Leffel*, 444. F. Supp. at 1122.

193. *Id.*

school athletes from an unreasonable risk of injury is not fairly or substantially related to a justifiable governmental objective in the context of the fourteenth amendment."[194]

A heightened level of scrutiny does not guarantee a favorable ruling for a plaintiff,[195] as illustrated by *B.C. ex rel. C.C. v. Bd. of Educ.*[196] A male student-athlete challenged a ruling that he could not play on a high school girl's hockey team.[197] The court adopted a heightened level of review in stating that its determination of whether to afford plaintiff relief would hinge on whether the sex-based classification served an important governmental objective that was "substantially related to the achievement of the objective of promoting overall athletic equality for both sexes."[198] The court nevertheless found that the school's application of the rule survived an equal protection challenge because it "operates to achieve equality of athletic opportunity for both sexes."[199]

§ 1.05 The Constitutionality of Mandatory Drug Testing Policies

[A] Introduction

Many school districts have implemented mandatory drug testing policies that apply exclusively to students who participate in extra-curricular activities, including

---

194. *Id.; see also Hayden*, 743 F.3d at 576–82 (finding that a policy requiring boy athletes to have a certain hair length but not girls qualified for intermediate scrutiny and violated equal protection rights); Brenden v. Indep. Sch. Dist., 477 F.2d 1292, 1294 1300 (8th Cir. 1973) (finding high school league "failed to demonstrate that the sex-based classification fairly and substantially promotes the purposes of the League's rule."); Hecox v. Little, 479 F. Supp. 3d 930, 973–74 (D. Idaho 2020) (granting a preliminary injunction after affording transgender athletes heightened scrutiny as a quasi-suspect class in regard to the constitutionality of a law excluding "transgender women from participation on women's teams"); Beattie v. Line Mountain Sch. Dist., 992 F. Supp. 2d 384, 387, 395 (M.D. Pa. 2014) (ruling athlete likely to prevail on the merits of her equal protection claim against a gender restriction rule on the school's wrestling team); Packel v. Pa. Interscholastic Athletic Ass'n, 334 A.2d 839, 840, 843 (Pa. Commw. Ct. 1975) (finding that a rule banning girls from competing or practicing against boys in any contest violated equal protection).

195. *See* Clemons v. Shelby Cnty. Bd. of Educ., 818 Fed. App'x 453, 466–67 (6th Cir. 2020) (stating, in a challenge to a "girls-only tryout policy," that "[a]ssuming that holding tryouts for MLCHS girls and not boys constituted disparate treatment, that disparity survives heightened scrutiny."); Bukowski v. Wisconsin Interscholastic Athletic Ass'n, 726 N.W.2d 356, at *1, *4, *6 (Wisc. Ct. App. 2006) (ruling against a prospective student-athlete's gender-based equal protection claim because he failed to adequately develop his constitutional arguments).

196. 531 A.2d 1059 (N.J. Super. Ct. App. Div. 1987).

197. *Id.* at 1060.

198. *Id.* at 1065.

199. *Id.; see also* Bucha v. Illinois High Sch. Ass'n, 351 F. Supp. 69, 73 (N.D. Ill. 1972) (applying rational basis review to a challenge to a sex-based participation exclusion rule and finding that athletes' equal protection rights were not violated); Kleczek v. R.I. Interscholastic League, 612 A.2d 734,735, 738, 740 (R.I. 1992) (holding that the intermediate scrutiny test applies to gender-based challenges, instead of strict scrutiny).

athletics.[200] Students, including student-athletes, have asserted constitutional challenges primarily based on the alleged infringement of their Fourth and Fourteenth Amendment rights under the U.S. Constitution. The Fourth Amendment protects persons against unreasonable searches and seizures.[201] The Fourteenth Amendment extends this protection to prohibit unreasonable searches and seizures by state officers, including public school officials.[202] High school athletes' constitutional challenges to drug testing policies have met with limited success, as the majority of courts have upheld the constitutionality of mandatory, random, and suspicionless drug testing of high school student-athletes.

[B] Majority Rule: Drug Testing Policies Are Constitutional

The U.S. Supreme Court addressed the constitutionality of a school district's mandatory, random, and suspicionless drug testing policy in *Vernonia School District 47J v. Acton*.[203] In that case, high levels of drug use in the district's schools[204] resulted in the district implementing a drug testing program. The policy required that "[s]tudents wishing to play sports must sign a form consenting to the testing and must obtain the written consent of their parents."[205] An athlete was ruled ineligible for athletic participation after his parents refused to sign the consent forms. The athlete's parents, on his behalf, filed suit alleging the policy violated the Fourth and Fourteenth Amendments.[206]

Commenting first on why drug tests could be administered without a warrant, the court stated, "the warrant requirement 'would unduly interfere with the maintenance of the swift and informal disciplinary procedures [that are] needed,' and 'strict adherence to the requirement that searches be based upon probable cause' would undercut 'the substantial need of teachers and administrators for freedom to maintain order in the schools.'"[207] Discussing the drug policy's intrusion of privacy, the Court noted that historically minors possessed only a limited expectation of privacy.[208] It added that minors' reduced privacy expectation is further circumscribed for athletes for two primary reasons: 1) the communal undress in locker rooms that is an inherent aspect of athletic participation; and 2) athletes by voluntarily participating in athletics subject themselves to a higher degree of regulation with a concomitant expectation of intrusion

---

200. *See* Schaill v. Tippecanoe County School Corp., 679 F. Supp. 833, 836 (N.D. Ind. 1988).
201. US CONST. amend. IV.
202. New Jersey v. T.L.O., 469 U.S. 325, 336–37 (1985); Elkins v. U.S., 364 U.S. 206, 213 (1960).
203. 515 U.S. 646 (1995).
204. *Id.* at 649.
205. *Id.* at 649–50.
206. *Id.* at 651–52.
207. *Id.* at 653 (citing *New Jersey v. T.L.O.*, 469 U.S. 325, 340 (1985)).
208. *Id.* at 654.

upon "normal rights and privileges."[209] The Court found that the actual drug testing conducted under the policy resulted in a negligible intrusion on privacy.[210] The Court also held that the government's interest in deterring drug use was important and "perhaps compelling."[211]

The Court further shaped the contours of its *Vernonia* ruling in *Board of Education v. Earls*,[212] in which a school district adopted a drug testing policy requiring all middle and high school students to consent to testing in order to participate in extracurricular activities, including athletics.[213] The Court identified the students' limited privacy interests, the voluntary nature of extracurriculars, the confidentiality of the results, and the importance of curtailing student drug use as reasons to uphold the policy against the Fourth Amendment challenge.[214] "[T]esting students who participate in extracurricular activities is a reasonably effective means of addressing the School District's legitimate concerns in preventing, deterring, and detecting drug use."[215] The four dissenting justices differentiated sports from other activities stating that "[i]nterscholastic athletics ... require close safety and health regulation; a school's choir, band, and academic team do not."[216]

Courts have also upheld the constitutionality of mandatory drug testing policies under state constitutions. In *Hageman v. Goshen Cnty. Sch. Dist. No. 1*,[217] after a survey revealed a high level of drug activity among a county's students, a school district implemented a mandatory drug testing program for interscholastic athletes.[218] Analyzing the policy's constitutionality under Article 1, § 4 of the Wyoming Constitution, which protects against unreasonable searches and seizures, the court concluded that the new policy was constitutional.[219] It found that the policy was a reasonable intrusion on athletes' right to privacy because they possessed a reduced expectation of privacy and the school district had a compelling interest in protecting students' safety.[220] The court held that the policy was rationally related to the district's interest in deterring student drug and alcohol use.[221]

---

209. *Id.* at 657.

210. *Id.* at 658.

211. *Id.* at 661.

212. 536 U.S. 822 (2002).

213. *Id.* at 826.

214. *Id.* at 831–35, 838.

215. *Id.* at 837.

216. *Id.* at 846; *accord*, Todd v. Rush County Schools, 133 F.3d 984, 986 (7th Cir. 1998) (stating the "linchpin of this drug testing program is to protect the health of the students involved"); Schaill v. Tippecanoe County School Corporation, 864 F.2d 1309, 1312 (7th Cir. 1988) (upholding the school district's drug testing policy, in part, because of athletes' diminished expectation of privacy).

217. 256 P.3d 487 (Wyo. 2011).

218. *Id.* at 490–91.

219. *Id.* at 503.

220. *Id.*

221. *Id.*; *accord*, Weber v. Oakridge School District, 56 P.3d 504, 506 (Or. Ct. App. 2002) (upholding drug testing as condition to participating in athletics).

[C] Minority Rule:
Drug Testing Policies Are Unconstitutional

In contrast to *Hageman,* athletes have in some cases successfully invalidated drug testing policies under state constitutions. For instance, in *York v. Wahkiakum Sch. Dist. No. 200,*[222] a random suspicionless drug testing policy for athletes was ruled unconstitutional under the Washington state constitution. In that case, two students and their parents sought to invalidate the drug policy under a state constitutional provision analogous to the Fourth Amendment.[223] The court reached this result for the following reasons: (1) athletes' diminished expectation of privacy in a locker room did support a reduced expectation of privacy in regard to random drug testing; (2) the school district possessed no authority of law to conduct random drug tests since the drug testing was viewed as a "warrantless search"; (3) the policy did not invoke the federal or state special needs exception; and (4) there existed Washington state law precedent striking down suspicionless searches.[224]

§ 1.06 Athlete First Amendment Claims

[A] Free Speech

Under the First Amendment, "Congress can make no law ... abridging the freedom of speech, or of the press."[225] As the Supreme Court noted, however, in *Virginia v. Black,*[226] "the protections afforded by the First Amendment ... are not absolute."[227] This holds true in the context of public high schools.[228] The seminal case regarding student freedom of speech rights generally is *Tinker v. Des Moines Indep. Comm. Sch. Dist.*[229] In that case, a public high school punished three students who wore black armbands in protest of the Vietnam War.[230] The Court refused to uphold the school's disciplinary actions against the students, stating:

---

222. 178 P.3d 995 (Wash. 2008).
223. *Id.* at 998–99.
224. *Id.* at 1001–05; *see also* Theodore v. Delaware Valley School District, 836 A.2d 76, 90–91 (Pa. 2003) (noting the district's failure to suggest any specialized need to drug test).
225. U.S. Const. amend. I.
226. 538 U.S. 343 (2003).
227. *Id.* at 358.
228. *See* Tinker v. Des Moines Indep. Comm. Sch. Dist., 393 U.S. 503, 506 (1969) (stating "it can hardly be argued that either students or teachers shed their constitutional rights to freedom of speech or expression at the schoolhouse gate.").
229. *See* Morse v. Frederick, 551 U.S. 393, 410 (2007) (concluding schools can regulate speech advocating illegal drug use); Hazelwood School Dist. v. Kuhlmeier, 484 U.S. 260, 273 (1988) (holding "educators do not offend the First Amendment by exercising editorial control over the style and content of student speech in school-sponsored expressive activities so long as their actions are reasonably related to legitimate pedagogical concerns"); Bethel Sch. Dist. No. 403 v. Fraser, 478 U.S. 675, 683 (1986) (holding schools can regulate students' vulgar and offensive language).
230. Diane Heckman, *Does Being a Student-Athlete Mean You Have to Say You're Sorry?: First Amendment Freedom of Speech, Apologies and Interscholastic Athletic Programs,* 293 Ed. Law Rep. 549, 555 (2013).

A student's rights, therefore, do not embrace merely the classroom hours. When he is in the cafeteria, or on the playing field ... he may express his opinions, even on controversial subjects ... if he does so without "materially and substantially interfering with the requirements of appropriate discipline in the operation of the school" and without colliding with the rights of others.[231]

Pursuant to the *Tinker* standard, whether a limitation on student speech will survive constitutional scrutiny generally turns on: (1) whether the speech would "materially and substantially interfere with the school's ability to educate" and (2) whether the speech substantially interferes with the rights of others.[232] Although the *Tinker* standard is not universally applied by courts addressing the regulation of student speech,[233] courts often rely on it, particularly in cases involving interscholastic athletes. It is also important to note that student-athletes are subject to more restrictions, including free speech, than the student body at large.[234] Thus, the few cases that have addressed interscholastic athletes' right of free speech hold that interscholastic student-athletes are subject to regulation on their freedom of speech rights when the speech "materially disrupts" or "substantially interferes" with the team.

In the athletic context, courts generally focus on whether athlete speech "materially disrupts"[235] or "substantially interferes" with the athletic team. *Lowery v. Euverard*[236] illustrates a court applying the *Tinker* standard in the interscholastic context.[237] Several high school football players became dissatisfied with their coach's methods and circulated a petition critical of the coach.[238] The defendant, Euverard, learned of the petition and demanded that the players discontinue its circulation.[239] When the athletes refused to comply, they were dismissed from the team.[240] The Sixth Circuit relied on *Tinker* in determining whether the athletes' First Amendment free speech rights were

---

231. *Tinker*, 393 U.S. at 512–13.

232. Heckman, *supra* note 230, at 557.

233. Morse v. Frederick, 551 U.S. 393, 406 (2007) ("*Tinker* is not the only basis for restricting student speech."); Bell v. Itawamba Cnty. Sch. Bd., 799 F.3d 379, 390–91 (5th Cir. 2015) (noting that there are exceptions to the *Tinker* standard, where *Tinker* does not apply to student speech, such as offensive/lewd speech and school sponsored communications).

234. *See* Lowery v. Euverard, 497 F.3d 584, 589 (6th Cir. 2007) (*citing* Veronia Sch. Dist. 47J v. Acton, 515 U.S. 646, 657 (1995)).

235. *See* Pinard v. Clatskanie Sch. Dist. 6J, 467 F.3d 755 (9th Cir. 2006) (finding interscholastic athletes' petition did not violate the First Amendment because there was no substantial disruption, but that athletes' boycott was not protected because it resulted in substantial disruption); T.V. v. Smith-Green Community Sch. Corp., 807 F. Supp. 2d 767, 771, 782, 784 (N.D. Ind. 2011) (finding plaintiff student-athletes' First Amendment rights were violated because their online post of "raunchy" photos did not constitute substantial disruption, even though actual disruption is not required under *Tinker*); Killion v. Franklin Reg. Sch. Dist., 136 F. Supp. 2d 446, 455 (W.D. Penn. 2001) (holding student-athlete's suspension violated the First Amendment because the defendants could not satisfy the substantial disruption test under *Tinker*).

236. 497 F.3d 584 (6th Cir. 2007).

237. *Id.*

238. *Id.* at 585.

239. *Id.* at 586.

240. *Id.*

violated.[241] The court stated that the athletes had a right to express their opinion about Euverard. It differentiated the athletes' right, however, to express an opinion and their right to continue voluntarily playing football for a coach they were trying to undermine.[242] The court concluded the coach's dismissal of the athletes did not infringe upon their free speech rights given that the petition would undermine the coach and foster disunity on the team.[243] It added "*Tinker* does not require teachers to surrender control of the classroom to students, and it does not require coaches to surrender control of the team to players."[244]

A Tenth Circuit case, *Seamons v. Snow*,[245] also examined an interscholastic student-athlete's free speech rights. Brian Seamons, a high school football player, was assaulted in the locker room by a group of teammates.[246] Seamons reported the incident to the police and school authorities, and after doing so was allegedly asked by the coach and a team captain to apologize to the team for making the report.[247] Seamons refused, and his coach dismissed him from the team.[248]

Seamons and his parents filed a lawsuit asserting, *inter alia*, a violation of Seamons's free speech rights.[249] The Tenth Circuit overturned the district court's summary judgment in favor of defendants.[250] The court reasoned that there were significant factual disputes, such as whether the coach actually asked Seamons to apologize, the scope and intent of the coach's request for an apology, and whether Seamon's failure to apologize was a significant factor in his dismissal from the team.[251] The court protected the interscholastic athlete's free speech rights (at least at the summary judgment stage), even where there was "disruption" or "interference" within the team.

The Eight Circuit implicitly adopted the *Tinker* standard in *Wildman v. Marshalltown School District*.[252] There, Rebecca Wildman, a high school sophomore basketball player, circulated a letter containing explicit language that called for team members to speak out against the varsity basketball coach's selection of players for the varsity and junior varsity teams.[253] After the basketball coaches became aware of the letter, they demanded Wildman apologize as a condition to her return to the team the following school year.[254] Wildman refused and was not allowed to return to the team,

---

241. *Id.* at 587.
242. *Id.* at 599–600.
243. *Id.*
244. *Id.* at 601.
245. Seamons v. Snow, 206 F.3d 1021 (10th Cir. 2000).
246. *Id.* at 1023.
247. *Id.* at 1023–24.
248. *Id.* at 1024.
249. *Id.*
250. *Id.* at 1027.
251. *Id.* at 1027–29.
252. Wildman v. Marshalltown Sch. Dist., 249 F.3d 768 (8th Cir. 2001).
253. *Id.* at 770.
254. *Id.*

prompting her to file suit alleging the First Amendment prohibited the school from disciplining her for distributing the letter.[255] The Eight Circuit held that the athlete's speech was unprotected because the coaches' response was reasonable.[256] The court emphasized that Wildman's inability to return to the team would not disrupt her education. In granting summary judgment for defendant, the court distinguished *Seamons*[257] because Wildman's letter called for insubordination. This implicitly satisfied the *Tinker* disruption standard.[258]

In 2021, the U.S. Supreme Court issued an important ruling involving students' free speech rights. In *Mahanoy Area Sch. Dist. v. B.L.*,[259] a public high school student tried out for her school's varsity cheerleading team.[260] The student was not selected but was instead offered a position on the junior varsity team.[261] In reaction, the student posted a vulgar message on her "Snapchat story," which was seen by many of her peers.[262] The student's speech (the post), which "took place outside of school hours and away from the school's campus,"[263] was reported to the school. She was suspended from the junior varsity cheerleading squad for the year, prompting the student and her parents to sue the school district.[264]

The Court began its analysis by quoting *Tinker*'s admonition that students do not "shed their constitutional rights to freedom of speech or expression," even "at the school house gate."[265] It added, however, that "courts must apply the First Amendment 'in light of the special characteristics of the school environment.'"[266] The Court then identified the three categories of speech that a school has an interest in regulating under appropriate circumstances, which are:

> (1) "indecent," "lewd," or "vulgar" speech uttered during a school assembly on school grounds …; (2) speech, uttered during a class trip, that promotes "illegal drug use"; and (3) speech that others may reasonably perceive as "bear[ing] the imprimatur of the school," such as that appearing in a school-sponsored newspaper....[267]

Quoting *Tinker* again, the court stated that schools have a "special interest in regulating speech that 'materially disrupts classwork or involves substantial disorder or invasion of the rights of others.'"[268] The Court also recognized this special interest, which vests

---

255. *Id.* at 770–71.
256. *Id.* at 772.
257. Seamons v. Snow, 206 F.3d 1021 (10th Cir. 2000).
258. *Id.*
259. 141 S. Ct. 2038 (2021).
260. *Id.* at 2043.
261. *Id.*
262. *Id.*
263. *Id.*
264. *Id.*
265. *Id.* at 2044 (quoting *Tinker*, 393 U.S. at 506).
266. *Id.* (quoting Hazelwood Sch. Dist. v. Kuhlmeier, 484 U.S. 260, 266 (1988)).
267. *Id.* at 2044 (internal citations omitted).
268. *Id.* at 2045 (quoting *Tinker*, 393 U.S. at 513).

schools with "additional license to regulate" student on-campus speech, extends, under certain circumstances (*i.e.*, severe peer-to-peer bullying and threats made against teachers), to off-campus speech.[269]

Finally, the Court identified three features of speech that diminish schools' regulatory authority over student speech. First, because schools rarely stand *in loco parentis*, off-campus speech normally falls "within the zone of parental rather than school-related responsibility."[270] Second, "from the student speaker's perspective, regulations of off-campus speech, when coupled with regulations of on-campus speech, include all the speech a student utters during the full 24-hour day."[271] The Court stated because of this, courts should be skeptical of a school's regulation of off-campus speech because "doing so may mean the student cannot engage in that kind of speech at all."[272] Third, the Court identified the societal interest in protecting unpopular expression that fosters the "marketplace of ideas" and is an important democratic value.[273]

Having established the analytical framework for its ruling, the Court affirmed the district and circuit courts' decisions in favor of the plaintiff. It stated that the three above-described features that diminish a school's authority to regulate off-campus speech applied to the case before it. The Court reasoned that notwithstanding the vulgarity of the student's language, she was engaged in criticism of her community, which not only failed to place her language outside of First Amendment protection but did not amount to fighting words.[274] Noting that the student's speech occurred outside of school hours and away from school, the Court also emphasized that plaintiff's words neither identified the school nor any member of the school community and was communicated to her "private circle of Snapchat friends."[275] Taken together the Court concluded these features of plaintiff's speech diminished the school's interest in "punishing B.L.'s utterance."[276] The Court also found that the nature of plaintiff's speech diminished any interest the school possessed in prohibiting vulgar speech critical of a school's team or coaches.[277] The Court pointed to facts establishing that: (1) the speech occurred outside of school time; (2) the speech did not occur under circumstances where the school stood *in loco parentis* and plaintiff's parents had not delegated to the school their responsibility to control the student's behavior and there were no general efforts by the school to reduce the use of vulgar language by students when they are away from school;[278] and (3) there was no evidence that plaintiff's speech resulted in "the sort of 'substantial disruption' of a school activity or a threat-

---

269. *Id.*
270. *Id.* at 2046.
271. *Id.*
272. *Id.*
273. *Id.*
274. *Id.* at 2046.
275. *Id.* at 2047.
276. *Id.*
277. *Id.*
278. *Id.*

ened harm to the rights of others that might justify the school's action."[279] Finally, the Court found that there was no evidence that the plaintiff's speech led to any loss of team morale.[280]

[B] Freedom of Religion

Under the First Amendment of the U.S. Constitution, "Congress shall make no law respecting an establishment of religion or prohibiting the free exercise thereof."[281] The constitutional right of freedom of religion has two components: the Free Exercise Clause, which allows persons to freely exercise their religious beliefs without government interference, and the Establishment Clause, which is commonly referred to as separation of church and state.[282]

Free exercise of religion claims have primarily arisen in the following interscholastic athletic contexts: (1) a coach permitting student athletes to pray or the requirement that athletes participate in religious activities, such as prayer, during athletic events;[283] (2) the eligibility of athletes, who were homeschooled for religious reasons, to compete interscholastically;[284] (3) athletes' rights to wear religious attire in sports when competing;[285] and (4) the interscholastic eligibility of athletes transferring to different schools for religious reasons.[286] As the following discussion reveals, some courts analyze the constitutionality of alleged infringement of an athlete's free expression of religion by examining the "burden" imposed on a student-athlete who is denied the right to engage in or is forced to participate in a religious practice.[287] Other courts engage in an analysis that balances the respective burdens imposed on the athlete and the burdens imposed on a school or school district if it is judicially required to grant a religious-based accommodation or if it is precluded from requiring an athlete to engage in a religious practice.[288]

Robbins v. Indiana High Sch. Athletic Ass'n[289] illustrates a court's adoption of the undue burden standard.[290] In that case, a volleyball player at a public high school

---

279. *Id.* (quoting *Tinker*, 393 U.S. at 514).

280. *Id.* at 2048.

281. U.S. CONST. amend. I.

282. Diane Heckman, *One Nation Under God: Freedom of Religion in Schools and Extracurricular Athletic Events in the Opening Years of the New Millennium*, 28 WHITTIER L. REV. 537, 540–41 (2006).

283. *See* Keller v. Gardner Community Consol. Grade Sch. Dist., 552 F. Supp. 512, 513 (N.D. Ill. 1982).

284. *See* Reid v. Kenowa Hills Public Sch., 680 N.W.2d 62, 65 (Mich. Ct. App. 2004).

285. *See* Menora v. Illinois High Sch. Athletic Ass'n, 683 F.2d 1030, 1031 (7th Cir. 1982).

286. *See* Walsh v. Louisiana High Sch. Athletic Ass'n, 616 F.2d 152, 158–59 (5th Cir. 1980) (finding transfer rule did not violate the First Amendment).

287. *See* Wisconsin v. Yoder, 406 U.S. 205, 220 (1972) (stating "a regulation neutral on its face may, in its application, nonetheless offend the constitutional requirement for government neutrality if it unduly burdens the free exercise of religion.").

288. *See* Sherbert v. Verner, 374 U.S. 398, 403 (1963) (adopting a test that balances a student's hardship against the government's interest), *abrogated by* Holt v. Hobbs, 574 U.S. 352 (2015).

289. Robbins v. Indiana High Sch. Athletic Ass'n, 941 F. Supp. 786 (S.D. Ind. 1996).

290. *Id.* at 788. *See also* Doe v. Duncanville Independent Sch. Dist., 70 F.3d 402, 406 (5th Cir. 1995) (appearing to apply neither a burden imposed on the plaintiff nor a balancing of the burdens

transferred to a private high school after converting to Catholicism.[291] The relevant transfer rules would have prevented her from participating in interscholastic athletics for a year following the transfer.[292] The player sought to enjoin the enforcement of the transfer rules, asserting that it burdened the "parents and students' First Amendment right to the free exercise of their religion."[293] Although the federal district court noted that the transfer rules did not create a religious classification, it was appropriate to determine whether the rules "unduly burden[ed] [plaintiffs'] free exercise of religion."[294] The court ultimately decided against plaintiffs because of the absence of evidence that either Robbins or her parents' rights to practice religion had been unduly burdened in this case. The court stated that "[t]he transfer rules on their face do not classify in terms of religion" and "there is no evidence in the record that the new Transfer Rule unduly trammels upon the religious beliefs of Robbins or her parents…."[295] Accordingly, the court adopted a rational basis, rather than strict scrutiny, standard of review in ultimately upholding the constitutionality of the transfer rules.[296] The court found that "Robbins fail[ed] to meet her burden that she will be irreparably harmed if not allowed to participate on [her school's] varsity volleyball team. The IHSAA's ruling will not keep Robbins from fully practicing her religion…."[297]

In *Reid v. Kenowa Hills Public Schools*,[298] the Michigan High School Athletic Association refused to permit children who were homeschooled for religious reasons to participate in interscholastic athletics in the school districts in which the children resided.[299] The Association applied a rule requiring students seeking to participate in interscholastic athletics to be enrolled at a school for at least twenty hours per week.[300] In ruling against the children and their parents, the Michigan Court of Appeals found the rule did not burden the plaintiffs' exercise of their religious beliefs because the students and their parents had a choice between home schooling and participating in interscholastic athletics.[301]

A balancing of the burdens standard was applied in *Hadley v. Rush Henrietta Central School District*.[302] An athlete was prevented from playing high school lacrosse because of his refusal, on religious grounds, to take a tetanus vaccination.[303] Assessing

---

approach in finding that coach-led prayer sessions during practice and before games of a public school's basketball team violated the Establishment Clause).

291. *Robbins*, 941 F. Supp. at 786, 789.
292. *Id.* at 786.
293. *Id.* at 786, 792.
294. *Id.* at 792 (citing Wisconsin v. Yoder, 406 U.S. 205 (1972)).
295. *Id.*
296. *Id.*
297. *Id.* at 793.
298. 680 N.W.2d 62 (Mich. Ct. App. 2004).
299. *Id.* at 65.
300. *Id.*
301. *Id.* at 69–70.
302. 409 F. Supp. 2d 164, 166 (W.D. N.Y. 2006).
303. *Id.*

the parties' respective interests, the court concluded a balancing of hardships (or burdens) favored granting an injunction.[304]

> Allowing Hadley a fair opportunity to participate, however, will not impose a significant burden on the School District or the school community. Plaintiffs have offered to provide the defendant with a full waiver of liability for any and all injuries resulting from his failure to receive a tetanus vaccination, and such a waiver shall be given by plaintiffs to the defendant as a condition of his participation in lacrosse or any other extra-curricular activity. Accordingly, the School District may not be held liable should Hadley contract any disease or suffer any injury as a result of his refusal to be vaccinated. Moreover, because tetanus is a bacterial infection, and not a disease that is spread by human contact, there is no danger that it could be spread to other players, students, coaches, or teachers should Hadley contract tetanus.[305]

A balancing of the burdens test was also employed in *Keller v. Gardner Community Consolidated Grade School District 72C*.[306] The student attended a catechism class at a Catholic Church once a week that conflicted with basketball practice.[307] He and his father asserted that a rule not authorizing this as an excused absence based on religious observance infringed on his freedom of religion.[308] The court balanced the "burden on the individual who is denied the benefit because of religious practice, with the burden that would be imposed on the government if it extended the benefit to someone who because of their religious practice failed to meet a generally imposed requirement for eligibility for the benefit."[309] In upholding the coach's rule, the court found that Keller could have taken the class at another church within the district that would not have posed a schedule conflict and that the school had an important interest in maintaining the basketball practices while not giving unfair exemptions.[310]

---

304. *Id.* at 167–70. In *Menora v. Illinois High Sch. Athletic Association*, 683 F.2d 1030, 1032 (7th Cir. 1982), student-athletes wanted to wear yarmulkes fastened by bobby pins, despite a ban against unsecure headwear. The court applied both the *Yoder* and *Sherbert* tests and remanded the case to allow the students to propose a more secure head covering. *Id.* at 1032; Scott C. Idleman, *Religious Freedom and the Interscholastic* Athlete, 12 MARQ. SPORTS L. REV. 295, 332, 335 (2001) (suggesting a different outcome if the case were decided today).

305. *Hadley*, 409 F. Supp. 2d at 169.

306. 552 F. Supp. 512, 514 (N.D. Ill. 1982).

307. *Id.*

308. *Id.*

309. *Id.* at 514.

310. *Id.* at 515–16. Where conflicts exist between athletic activities and religious obligations, schools and athletic associations are permitted to attempt to accommodate religious beliefs in developing a schedule for the season. If the religious observance is not mandatory, accommodations are not required. *See* Idleman, *supra* note 304, at 332.

Chapter 2

Legal Issues in College Athletics

§ 2.01 Introduction

Given that intercollegiate athletics is a multi-billion-dollar industry, it is not surprising that disputes arise implicating diverse legal principles. With issues such as gender discrimination and liability for injuries in college sports reserved for discussion elsewhere in this treatise, this chapter examines legal disputes implicated by the contractual relationship between college athletes and their colleges and universities. Notably, contract law serves only as the point of departure for framing this relationship. A thorough understanding of the legal status of the college athlete/university relationship requires resort to other substantive areas of law, including antitrust, workers' compensation, labor law, and constitutional law, all of which have been instrumental in shaping the contours of the relationship. Although this chapter provides a detailed review of these principles, it initially discusses the historically prominent role the National Collegiate Athletic Association ("NCAA") has exercised in regulating intercollegiate athletics, including the relationships between college athletes and their institutions.

§ 2.02 College Athletics and the National Collegiate Athletic Association

[A] Introduction: Institutional Control and Governance

The NCAA, which was formed in 1905 and currently consists of approximately 1,100 colleges and universities, is the organization that regulates major college sports programs in the United States.[1] Through its promulgation of rules and regulations,

---

1. *See* Matthew J. Mitten, Timothy Davis, N. Jeremi Duru & Barbara Osborne, Sports Law & Regulation: Cases, Materials, and Problems 103–07 (5th ed. 2020) (providing an overview of the history of the NCAA and also noting other bodies that govern college athletics including the National Association of Intercollegiate Athletic Association (consisting of approximately 250 colleges and universities), the National Christian College Athletic Association (consisting of approximately 90 colleges), and National Junior College Athletic Association (consisting of more than 500 junior and community colleges)).

the NCAA sets national standards for the governance of intercollegiate athletics. Critical components of the NCAA's governance model are premised on principles articulated in the NCAA constitution and bylaws. One such principle is that of institutional control, which places accountability for the governance of intercollegiate athletics programs within the auspices of each member institution.[2] Thus, notwithstanding the significant role the NCAA has played historically in promulgating policies and regulations, each of its member institutions is responsible for ensuring that their athletics programs adhere to those policies and rules. In short, each institution has the responsibility to "control its intercollegiate athletics program in compliance" with NCAA rules and regulations.[3] "The institution's responsibility for the conduct of its intercollegiate athletics program includes responsibility for the actions of its staff members and for the actions of any other individual or organization engaged in activities promoting the athletics interests of the institution."[4]

Integral to the notion of institutional control is the principle of shared governance.[5] The NCAA Manual states that an institution's president or chancellor has ultimate responsibility for the conduct of an institution's intercollegiate athletics program.[6] As the institution's chief executive officer, the president must establish a tone that clearly identifies the role of athletics within the overall university culture. College presidents cannot, however, realistically be involved in the day-to-day operation of their institutions' athletics programs.[7] This responsibility is delegated to the director of athletics, who manages the details of the athletics programs and implements the institutionally developed policy.[8]

The NCAA Manual provides that "[i]ntercollegiate athletics programs shall be maintained as a vital component of the educational program, and student-athletes shall be an integral part of the student body."[9] Thus, the institutional governance model also envisions that other stakeholders within a college or university, including faculty, trustees, administrators, and students, share governance responsibility.[10] In this regard, the NCAA Manual states that "[a]dministrative control or faculty control, or a combination of the two, shall constitute institutional control."[11] Nevertheless, each university president is responsible for knowing the manner in which each university department, including athletics, conducts its operations.[12] The principle of

2. NCAA, 2021–22 Division I NCAA Manual § 2.1.1 (hereinafter NCAA Manual).

3. *Id.* at § 2.8.1.

4. *Id.*

5. *Id.* at § 19.2.1.

6. *Id.* at § 6.1.1.

7. David F. Salter, Blueprint for Success: An In-Depth Analysis of NCAA Division III Athletics, and Why It Should be the Model for Intercollegiate Reform 62 & 86 (1993).

8. *Id.* at 65–66.

9. NCAA Manual, *supra* note 2, at § 2.5. *See also* NCAA Manual, *supra* note 2, at § 20.9.1.7.

10. *See id.* at § 6.1.

11. *Id.* at § 6.01.1.

12. Salter, *supra* note 7, at 62–63.

educational primacy is best served by each university president receiving input from all relevant perspectives.[13]

The principle of institutional control and governance is also reflected in the respective relationship that institutions and the NCAA have with college athletes. The NCAA governance model imposes upon each institution the responsibility for attending to the educational, health, and athletic interests of its student-athletes.[14] It is the college or university that recruits student-athletes, contracts with them, and determines the quality of their overall college experiences. It is also the institution that takes direct action against an athlete by making them ineligible for athletic participation if an athlete violates an NCAA rule. Thus, the NCAA can take no direct action against a student-athlete. It is also true that the NCAA cannot take any direct action against an institution's employees.[15]

[B] Autonomy Schools and the NCAA's Amended Constitution

In 2011, the NCAA's governance structure was modified to create what is referred to as the autonomy conferences, which consist of the Atlantic Coast Conference, the Big-Ten Conference, the Big 12 Conference, the Pac-12 Conference and the Southeastern Conference.[16] These conferences are commonly referred to as the Power 5 conferences. The NCAA Constitution grants the autonomy conferences the authority to "adopt or amend" legislation in the autonomy areas.[17] The autonomy conferences and "their member institutions are granted autonomy ... to permit the use of resources to advance the legitimate educational or athletics-related needs of student-athletes and for legislative changes that will otherwise enhance student-athlete well-being...."[18] Areas of autonomy include legislation relating to: (a) student-athlete financial aid; (b) student-athlete health and wellness; (c) balancing the athletic and educational demands on student-athletes time; (d) "pre-enrollment [e]xpenses and [s]upport"; and (e) student-athlete academic support.[19]

In January 2022, NCAA member institutions modified the organization's constitution.[20] The adoption of the amendment is the first step in what represents an effort toward decentralization of NCAA governance. Articulated reasons for the new constitution include allowing the NCAA to "better meet the needs of ... stu-

13. Tanyon B. Lynch, *Quid Pro Quo: Restoring Educational Primacy to College Basketball*, 12 MARQ. SPORTS L. REV. 595, 609–15 (2002).

14. NCAA MANUAL, *supra* note 2, at §2.2.

15. Nat'l Coll. Athletic Ass'n v. Tarkanian, 488 U.S. 179, 184 (1998).

16. NCAA MANUAL, *supra* note 2, at §5.02.1.1.

17. *Id.* at §5.3.2.1.1.

18. *Id.* at §5.3.2.1.2.

19. *Id.*

20. Corbin McGuire, *NCAA Members approve new constitution*, NCAA.ORG (Jan. 20, 2022), available at https://www.ncaa.org/news/2022/1/20/media-center-ncaa-members-approve-new-constitution.aspx.

dent-athletes" and establish a governance model that will set the organization on "a sustainable course for college sports for decades to come."[21] The new constitution adheres to the principles of institutional control.[22] It also continues to prohibit member institutions from compensating student-athletes for their athletic services.[23] The constitution authorizes, however, each division to establish: (a) its organizational structure, including creating new divisions or subdivisions;[24] (b) academic eligibility rules;[25] (c) guidelines for student-athletes to receive compensation for their names, images and likenesses from third parties;[26] and (d) "policies and procedures for enforcement of Association rules and regulations."[27] The new constitution also grants student-athletes "voting representation on the NCAA Board of Governors, Division I Board of Directors, and Divisions II and III's Presidents Councils."[28] As the forgoing overview suggests, the next step of the process will involve the divisions and conferences promulgating legislation pursuant to the authority they have been granted by the amended constitution.

[C] The NCAA Enforcement Structure

The NCAA has a well-established enforcement structure consisting of bylaws, a description of conduct that violates bylaws or constitutional provisions, and the penalties that may result from violations committed by institutional stakeholders including coaches, staff, athletes, and supporters of an institution's athletic program (commonly referred to as boosters). In 2013, the NCAA enacted major changes to address deficiencies in its enforcement structure.[29] Although the following discussion focuses primarily on the current enforcement regime, where it is necessary to provide context, it also examines aspects of the pre-2013 enforcement regime.

[1] Classification of Violations

[a] Pre-2013: Major and Secondary Violations

Prior to the 2013 amendments, violations of NCAA rules were classified as major or secondary. The NCAA Manual defined a secondary violation as one that was "iso-

---

21. *Id.*

22. NCAA, NCAA CONSTITUTION § 1(E) (adopted Jan. 20, 2022), https://ncaaorg.s3.amazonaws.com/governance/ncaa/constitution/NCAAGov_Constitution121421.pdf (last visited Jan. 23, 2022).

23. *Id.* at § 1(B).

24. *Id.* at §§ 2(B)(1) & (3).

25. *Id.* at § 2(B)(2).

26. *Id.* at § 2(B)(4).

27. *Id.* at § 2(B)(5).

28. *Id.* at § 2(E)(1).

29. Timothy Davis & Christopher T. Hairston, *Majoring in Infractions: The Evolution of the National Collegiate Athletic Association's Enforcement Structure*, 92 OREGON L. REV. 979 (2014) (discussing the 2013 amendments to the NCAA enforcement structure and the rationale underlying the changes).

lated or inadvertent in nature, provides or is intended to provide only a minimal recruiting, competitive or other advantage and does not include any significant impermissible benefit (including, but not limited to, an extra benefit, recruiting inducement,
preferential treatment or financial aid)."[30] Under the forgoing definition, a violation
was major rather than secondary if it could not be characterized as either isolated or
inadvertent.[31] Consequently, the pre-2013 enforcement structure defined a major violation as consisting of any violation that was not classified as a secondary violation
because in such an instance it was not isolated, not inadvertent, or it resulted in more
than a minimal recruiting or competitive advantage.[32]

An example of a major infraction relating to impermissible benefits involved Reggie
Bush, who was a member of the University of Southern California ("USC") football
team.[33] The NCAA's Committee on Infractions ("COI") report stated that sports
agents bestowed upon Bush and his family gifts including: (1) airline tickets; (2) lim-
ousine services, which were often requested by Bush or his parents; (3) cash that facilitated Bush's purchase of a car; (4) the purchase of a home for use by Bush's parents
(with the understanding that Bush's parents would pay the agents only $1400 of the
approximately $4500 monthly cost); (5) $10,000 in cash to enable Bush's family to
purchase furniture for the house; and (6) substantial cash payments to Bush.[34] The
rules violations were discovered after Bush left USC.

The COI concluded that Reggie Bush violated NCAA rules prohibiting college
athletes, or their friends or relatives, from accepting transportation and other benefits
from agents where the benefits were not available to the student body generally.[35]
Additionally, Bush violated an NCAA bylaw prohibiting representation agreements
between student-athletes and agents.[36] Bush's violation of NCAA amateurism bylaws
resulted in him retroactively losing his eligibility to participate in intercollegiate athletics.[37] Applying its rule of restitution, the COI vacated all of the USC football team's
victories in which Reggie Bush played when he was ineligible for intercollegiate
athletic competition.[38] As a result of these infractions, the NCAA vacated the football
team's last two victories of the 2004 football season, which included the team's January
2005 Orange Bowl win and all of its wins during the 2005 season.[39] The January 2005

---

30. NCAA, 2012–13 NCAA Division I Manual § 19.02.2.1.

31. *Id.*

32. *Id.* at §§ 19.02.2.1, 19.02.2.2.

33. NCAA Public Infractions Decision, University of Southern California Public Infractions Report (2010) [hereinafter USC Infractions Decision], available at https://web3.ncaa.org/lsdbi/search/miCaseView/report?id=102369 (identifying Reggie Bush as "student-athlete I").

34. *See generally id.*

35. *Id.*

36. 2012–13 NCAA Division I Manual, *supra* note 30, at § 12.1.2(g).

37. *Id.* at 12.01.0.

38. USC Infractions Decision, *supra* note 33, at 57.

39. *Id.* at 57–58.

victory was notable because USC was designated as the Bowl Championship Series (BCS) winner, and the violation required USC to vacate its National Championship.[40]

[b] Post-August 2013 Classification: Levels I-III Violations

The NCAA's enforcement structure now classifies infractions as Level I, Level II or Level III.[41] Level I infractions, which are labeled "Severe Breach of Conduct," are intended to encompass the most serious rules violations that "seriously undermine or threaten the integrity of the NCAA Collegiate Model ... including any violation that provides or is intended to provide a substantial or extensive recruiting, competitive or other advantage, or a substantial or extensive ... impermissible benefit."[42] Illustrations of severe breaches that would constitute Level I violations include: (1) a lack of institutional control; (2) academic fraud; (3) the failure of the institution or an involved person to cooperate with the NCAA in a violation investigation; (4) individual unethical or dishonest conduct; (5) a head coach's failure to promote compliance in an athletic program and monitor the activities of assistant coaches that result from a Level I violation; (6) making cash inducements to prospective student-athletes; (7) intentional or reckless violations of NCAA rules; and (8) collective Level II and III violations.[43]

Level II violations, labeled "Significant Breach of Conduct," encompass infractions that result in "more than a minimal but less than a substantial or extensive recruiting, competitive, or other advantage."[44] Conduct giving rise to Level II violations includes: (1) the provision of impermissible benefits that are less than minimal but more than substantial; (2) violations involving conduct that compromises the integrity of the NCAA's collegiate model of intercollegiate athletics; (3) an institution's failure to monitor unless such failure is substantial or egregious; (4) "systemic violations that do not amount to a lack of institutional control"; (5) "multiple recruiting, financial aid, or eligibility violations that do not amount to a lack of institutional control"; (6) a failure by a head coach to promote compliance in a program and to monitor the activities of assistant coaches that result from a Level II violation; and (7) "[c]ollective Level III violations."[45]

---

40. *Id.*; *see also* Lynn Zinser, *U.S.C. Loses Its 2004 B.C.S. National Championship*, N.Y. Times (June 6, 2011), available at https://www.nytimes.com/2011/06/07/sports/ncaafootball/usc-stripped-of-2004-bcs-national-championship.html.

41. The modifications initially provided a Level IV violation for incidental matters. On April 14, 2017, the NCAA eliminated the Level IV violation classification. Moving forward, what would have been a Level IV violation will be processed as a Level III violation. NCAA, NCAA LSDBi, Division I Proposal, *Infractions Process — Violation Structure — Incidental Infraction (Level IV Violations — Elimination of Level IV Classification Division)* (Apr. 14, 2017), https://web3.ncaa.org/lsdbi/search/proposalView?id=100647 (last visited Jan. 23, 2022).

42. NCAA Manual, *supra* note 2, at § 19.1.1.

43. *Id.*

44. *Id.* at § 19.1.2

45. *Id.*

Level III infractions involve violations that are isolated or limited and provide only a "minimal recruiting, competitive, or other advantage" and a "minimal impermissible benefit."[46] Conduct amounting to Level III violations includes: "[i]nadvertent violations that are isolated or limited in nature; or (b) [e]xtra benefit, financial aid, academic eligibility and recruiting violations, provided they do not create more than minimal advantages."[47]

The 2013 amended bylaws and enforcement structure place greater responsibility on head coaches. The bylaws create a presumption that a head coach is:

> responsible for the actions of all institutional staff members who report, directly or indirectly, to the head coach. An institution's head coach shall promote an atmosphere of compliance within his or her program and shall monitor the activities of all institutional staff members involved with the program who report, directly or indirectly, to the coach.[48]

Therefore, it is now more difficult for a head coach to succeed with an argument that he or she was unaware of bylaw violations committed by those who report to the head coach. The NCAA takes actions indirectly against a coach or another institutional employee for Level I and Level II violations through its use of a show cause order submitted to a coach's institution.[49] Such an order issued by the COI instructs the institution to take further disciplinary action against a coach or other employee where the COI concludes the actions taken by the institution are inadequate.[50]

[2] The Infractions Process

[a] Enforcement Staff Investigation

The NCAA infractions process begins when the NCAA's enforcement staff receives information regarding a potential violation of the NCAA constitution and bylaws.[51] The enforcement staff determines whether the information warrants initiating an investigation or whether the matter can be resolved without an investigation.[52] If, based on the information provided, the enforcement staff concludes initiating an investigation is necessary, the enforcement staff will conduct a full investigation.[53] Before it launches an inquiry involving an enrolled athlete or a current institutional staff member, however, the enforcement staff will send a Notice of Inquiry to the institution's president or chancellor. The Notice formally notifies the institution of the nature of the enforcement staff's inquiry. It also advises the institution that if the enforcement staff uncovers information of possible Level I or Level II violations, the

---

46. *Id.* at § 19.1.3.
47. *Id.*
48. *Id.* at § 11.1.1.1.
49. *Id.* at § 19.9.5.4.
50. *Id.* at §§ 19.9.5.4 & 19.9.9.
51. *Id.* at § 19.5.1.
52. *Id.*
53. *Id.*

institution will be duly notified and the matter will be processed accordingly. The Notice will also advise the institution if only Level III violations are involved.

After an investigation, if the enforcement staff determines "there is sufficient information to conclude that a hearing panel of the Committee on Infractions could conclude that a violation occurred,"[54] the enforcement staff will issue a Notice of Allegations to the institution and/or involved individuals.[55] The Notice of Allegations sets forth the alleged bylaws breached, the possible level of each alleged violation, and possible hearing procedures. The Notice of Allegations will also invite the institution and involved individuals to answer the allegations.[56] In addition, the Notice will identify the information on which the allegations are based and any mitigating and/or aggravating factors.[57]

[b] Committee on Infractions

The NCAA Manual describes the COI's role: "The hearing panel assigned to a case shall hold a hearing to make factual findings and to conclude whether violations of the NCAA constitution and bylaws occurred and, if so, to prescribe appropriate penalties."[58] After the hearing, the COI will issue a written report that contains a "statement of the findings of facts, conclusions of violations, penalties, corrective actions, requirements and (for institutions) any other conditions and obligations of membership."[59]

[c] Infractions Appeals Committee

The institution has the right to appeal the COI's findings and determinations to the Infractions Appeals Committee ("IAC").[60] An institution that seeks to appeal a finding of an infraction and/or the penalty imposed must submit a notice of appeal within fifteen days of the COI panel's decision.[61] The IAC is not involved in processing appeals of Level III violations.[62] Instead, appeals of Level III violations will be submitted to a COI panel.[63] With respect to Level I and II violations, appeals can be processed via written submission or videoconference in addition to traditional in-person oral presentations before the IAC.[64]

Substantively, a COI determination can be set aside only if the appealing party demonstrates to the IAC that new information is available, or that the initial decision

---

54. *Id.* at § 19.7.1.
55. *Id.*
56. *Id.* at § 19.7.1.1.
57. *Id.*
58. *Id.* at § 19.7.7.
59. *Id.* at § 19.8.1.
60. *Id.* at § 19.10.2.
61. *Id.*
62. *Id.* at § 19.12.4.
63. *Id.*
64. *Id.* at § 19.10.2.1.

was rooted in prejudicial error.[65] Moreover, a COI panel's factual findings and conclusions that violations occurred cannot be set aside unless the appealing party establishes:

(a) A factual finding is clearly contrary to the evidence presented to the panel;

(b) The facts found by the panel do not constitute a violation of the NCAA constitution and bylaws; or

(c) There was a procedural error and but for the error, the panel would not have made the finding or conclusion.[66]

[3] Alternative Dispute Resolution Processes

[a] Negotiated Resolution

The NCAA enforcement process provides for three infractions resolution mechanisms that serve as alternatives to the aforementioned process. The first is a negotiated resolution. At any time after an investigation has begun and before a summary disposition (described below) or before a COI infractions hearing, the institution and the enforcement staff may enter into a negotiated resolution. A written negotiated resolution must, among other things, briefly describe the case, state the agreed-upon violations and penalties, and contain a "[w]aiver of appellate opportunities."[67] The negotiation resolution is subject to review and approval by a panel of three COI members.[68] A negotiated resolution will be rejected by the hearing panel only if "it is not in the best interest of the Association or the agreed-upon penalties are manifestly unreasonable...."[69]

[b] Summary Disposition

In a case before the COI that involves Levels I and II violations, the enforcement staff, institution, and involved individuals can jointly agree and elect to use another alternative: summary disposition.[70] The relevant parties are required to submit a written report that contains: (a) "proposed findings of fact" and a summary of the information on which the findings are based, (b) "a statement identifying the violation(s)"; (c) "the parties' agreement on the overall level of the case"; (d) a list of mitigating and aggravating circumstances; and (e) a stipulation that a thorough investigation was conducted.[71]

The summary disposition process is efficacious where the enforcement staff and institution agree to the violations, the findings of fact, and the penalties to be imposed. A COI panel will conduct a review of the thoroughness of the investigation and the

65. *Id.* at §19.8.2.1.
66. *Id.* at §19.10.1.2.
67. *Id.* at §19.5.12.1.3.
68. *Id.* at §19.5.12.
69. *Id.* at §19.5.12.2.
70. *Id.* at §19.6.
71. *Id.* at §19.6.

written report.[72] The panel will then either accept or reject the proposed findings of fact, violations, and penalties.[73] If the former, the COI will prepare a report of its decision.[74] If the latter, the case will proceed to a hearing before a panel of the COI.[75]

[c] Independent Accountability Resolution Process

In 2018 — with an effective date of 2019 — the NCAA established the Independent Accountability Resolution Process ("IARP"), which now resolves "select infractions cases involving allegations of Level I or Level II violations."[76] The IARP was created in the aftermath of recommendations made by the Commission on College Basketball.[77] The IARP is designed to serve as the dispute resolution mechanism to handle complex cases and to "minimize perceived conflicts of interest" through use of an "independent structure...."[78] The factors that may give rise to a complex case include: violations of the NCAA's core values; failing to prioritize academics or athlete well-being; the potential for the imposition of severe penalties; or "conduct that is contrary to the cooperative principles of the existing infractions process."[79]

Under this process, cases will be heard by a panel consisting of individuals external to the NCAA. The components of the IARP structure are: the Independent Accountability Oversight Committee, which will administer the process; (b) Infractions Referral Committee, which will decide whether to refer cases for consideration by the IARP; (c) Independent Resolution Panel, which will hear cases referred to the IRAP; and (4) Complex Case Unit, which is the investigatory arm of the IRAP.[80] The IARP will receive a case if the IRC finds that: "the Association's interests are best served by resolving the case under the independent accountability resolution structure, including when a case involves unique policy issues or factors that, when weighed in totality, could impede accurate and effective resolution of the case under the internal infractions structure."[81]

As of November 2021, six cases had been referred to the IRAP.[82] Each of the cases involved institutions that were implicated in a basketball scandal involving alleged payments made to coaches and assistant coaches to direct players to particular colleges

---

72. *Id.* at § 19.6.4.1.

73. *Id*, at § 19.6.4.

74. *Id.* at § 19.6.4.3.

75. *Id.* at § 19.6.4.5.

76. *Id.* at § 19.11.1.

77. Independent Accountability Resolution Process, https://iarpcc.org/ (last visited Dec. 29, 2021).

78. *Id.*

79. *Id.*

80. NCAA MANUAL, *supra* note 2, at § 19.11.2.

81. *Id.* at § 19.11.3.1. The specific factors for referral include alleged infractions implicating NCAA core values; a lack of acceptance of core principles of self-governance; the "scope, scale and duration of the case, and other factual complications"; and "increased stakes, including potential penalties, or other pressures driving institutional decision-making." *Id.* at § 19.11.3.1.1.

82. IARP: Referred Cases, https://iarpcc.org/referred-cases/ (last visited Dec. 29, 2021).

and universities.[83] During the convention at which the NCAA members approved a new constitution, the membership also suspended the IRAP.

[4] Enforcement Penalty Structure

The NCAA enforcement regime includes a penalty structure that sets forth core penalties that may be decreased or increased depending on the level of violation and the presence of mitigating and aggravating circumstances. Aggravating factors include: (a) the presence of multiple Level I violations; (b) the institution's history of Level I, Level II or major violations; (c) lack of institutional control; (d) obstructing an investigation; (e) unethical conduct; (f) the intentional or blatant disregard of the NCAA constitution and bylaws; and (g) the premeditation with which violations were committed.[84] Mitigating factors include: (a) an institution's prompt self-detection and disclosure of violations; (b) acknowledgement of violations; (c) exemplary cooperation; and (d) the unintentionality of the violations.[85] For example, a standard penalty range for a Level I violation is 1 to 2 years of competition restrictions, including postseason competition bans.[86] The presence of aggravating circumstances could increase the range of a postseason ban to 1 to 5 years.[87] On the other hand, mitigating factors could reduce the range of a postseason ban to 0 to 1 year.[88]

The impact of aggravating circumstances on the penalty imposed is illustrated by an infractions case involving Oklahoma State University.[89] The case involved allegations of improper inducements, extra benefits, unethical conduct, and a failure to cooperate. The associate head coach took cash bribes of $18,150 and $22,000 from two financial advisors who sought access to college basketball players with NBA potential.[90] The COI found that Oklahoma State had committed violations. The COI issued a show cause order requiring any member institution that employed the associate head coach from June 5, 2020, through June 4, 2030, to show cause why restrictions on athletically related activities imposed on the associate head coach should not apply.[91] The COI explained that the length of the show cause order was justified by aggravating circumstances, including multiple Level I violations committed by the associate head coach, the associate head coach's unethical conduct, and his intentional and blatant disregard for the NCAA constitution and bylaws.[92]

---

83. Mitch Sherman, *Everything You Need to Know about the College Basketball Scandal*, ESPN (Feb. 23, 2018), available at https://www.espn.com/mens-college-basketball/story/_/id/22555512/explaining-ncaa-college-basketball-scandal-players-coaches-agents.

84. NCAA Manual, *supra* note 2, at § 19.9.3.

85. *Id.* at § 19.9.4.

86. *Id.* at Figure 19-1.

87. *Id.*

88. *Id.*

89. NCAA, Public Infractions Decision, Oklahoma State University (Jun. 5, 2020), available at https://web3.ncaa.org/lsdbi/search/miCaseView/report?id=102864.

90. *Id.* at 1.

91. *Id.* at 20.

92. *Id.* at 18.

§ 2.03 The College Athlete and University Relationship

[A] Amateurism and the Collegiate Model

This chapter examines the contours of the college athlete and university relationship and legal disputes that emerge from the relationship. Understanding the relationship, however, requires understanding the NCAA's model of intercollegiate athletics and the athlete's role therein. Accordingly, we begin with a discussion of the NCAA's collegiate model of intercollegiate athletics.[93]

> Student-athlete success is paramount, both academically and athletically. The collegiate model should embed the values of higher education, including shared responsibility and accountability; this model must be protected and sustained. In the collegiate model of athletics, amateurism is the student-participation model that guides the relationship between students and institutions. In the collegiate model of athletics, the guiding principles should be based on fair opportunities to compete among institutions with similar commitments to intercollegiate athletics.[94]

Whether described as the collegiate model or alternatively as the amateur/education model of intercollegiate athletics,[95] the NCAA defines college athletes as amateurs.

> Student-athletes shall be amateurs in an intercollegiate sport, and their participation should be motivated primarily by education and by the physical, mental and social benefits to be derived. Student participation in intercollegiate athletics is an avocation, and student-athletes should be protected from exploitation by professional and commercial enterprises.[96]

In attempting to foster the NCAA's amateurism principle, NCAA bylaws define what constitutes an athletic scholarship and otherwise impose limits on the consideration that universities can provide in exchange for the services of their athletes.[97]

> Moreover, college athletics is considered an integral part of the educational purpose of colleges and universities. In this regard, NCAA Bylaw 1.3.1 articulates the basic purpose of intercollegiate athletics.

> The competitive athletics programs of member institutions are designed to be a vital part of the educational system. A basic purpose of this Association is to maintain intercollegiate athletics as an integral part of the educational program and the athlete as an integral part of the student body and, by doing

---

93. NCAA Manual, *supra* note 2, at xii.

94. NCAA Working Group on Collegiate Model — Enforcement, Final Report 2 (2012), https://dokumen.tips/documents/final-report-ncaa-working-group-on-collegiate-model-enforcement-august-2012.html.

95. Timothy Davis, *Intercollegiate Athletics: Competing Models and Conflicting Realities*, 25 Rutgers L.J. 269 (1994).

96. NCAA Manual, *supra* note 2, at § 2.9.

97. *Id.* at § 15.01.

so, retain a clear line of demarcation between intercollegiate athletics and professional sports.[98]

The promotion of the educational component of the collegiate model has resulted in a host of bylaws that seek to ensure that only educationally-prepared high school athletes will be permitted to participate in intercollegiate athletics and that college athletes will benefit educationally following their matriculation. Examples of such rules include initial eligibility requirements,[99] progress toward degree requirements,[100] and rules regarding academic progress rates.[101]

As discussed, *infra*, the values residing in the collegiate model and its accompanying rules have a direct impact on the athlete and university relationship. Moreover, the willingness of courts to adopt the NCAA's articulated vision of intercollegiate athletes has had a profound impact on the judicial resolution of disputes between college athletes and their institutions.

[B] Contractual Principles

[1] Introduction

Courts have defined the legal relationship between scholarship athletes and their institutions as a contractual agreement.[102] The contours of the parties' respective

---

98. *Id.* at § 1.3.1.

99. Initial eligibility rules establish minimum academic standards that high school graduates must meet in order to participate in intercollegiate athletics and receive a scholarship. Historically, these standards are comprised of high school grade point averages, core courses taken in high school, and performance on standardized college entrance exams (*i.e.*, ACT and SAT scores). *Id.* at § 14.1.

100. NCAA MANUAL *supra* note 2, at § 14.4.1 and § 14.4.3.2. Promulgated in 2002, NCAA "satisfactory progress rules" require that student-athletes enroll in a curriculum that will facilitate their ability to obtain a college degree. *See Academic Progress Rate Timeline*, NCAA (last visited Apr. 24, 2020), http://www.ncaa.org/about/resources/research/academic-progress-rate-timeline.

101. In May 2004, the NCAA developed a metric known as the Academic Progress Rate (APR), which is calculated by examining each intercollegiate athletic team of member institutions. NCAA MANUAL, *supra* note 2, at § 14.02.2. The measure focuses on whether scholarship players on each team have remained academically eligible to participate in intercollegiate athletics and whether the players have chosen to remain enrolled at the school. *NCAA News Archive — 2003*, NCAA NEWS (Sept. 1, 2003), https://ncaanewsarchive.s3.amazonaws.com/2003/Division-I/athlete-graduation-rates-continue-climb-9-1-03.html. Teams are awarded one point for meeting each of these standards during a given semester, resulting in each athlete potentially earning the school a maximum of two points per semester and four points per year. *Id.* A failure of a team to reach a 930 benchmark exposes a college to penalties including scholarship and recruiting restrictions and a team's loss of postseason competition eligibility.

102. Ross v. Creighton Univ., 957 F.2d 410, 417 (7th Cir. 1992) (stating to prevail, a college athlete must point to an identifiable contractual promise); Milo v. Univ. of Vermont, 2013 WL 4647782, at *5 (D. Vt. Aug. 29, 2013) (recognizing the relationship between scholarship athletes and their colleges as contractual); Jackson v. Drake Univ., 778 F. Supp. 1490, 1493 (S.D. Iowa 1991) (analyzing an athlete's breach of contract claim solely based on the explicit obligations set forth in the financial aid agreement); Begley v. Corp. of Mercer Univ., 367 F. Supp. 908, 909–10 (E.D. Tenn. 1973) (discussing obligations arising from a contract entitled "Student Aid Contract For Athletes"); McAdoo v. Univ. of N.C. at Chapel Hill, 736 S.E.2d 811, 821 (N.C. Ct. App. 2013) (stating that in financial aid agreement,

rights and obligations are shaped by the terms set forth in the principal contract documents, the National Letter of Intent ("NLI") and an athletics financial aid agreement, as well as by NCAA, athletic conference, and institutional rules and policies.

An analysis of reported decisions reveals that in resolving issues relating to the athlete and university contractual relationship, courts give primacy to the contract documents by refusing to imply terms into the parties' contract,[103] which would expand the obligations that institutions owe to their athletes. Similarly, courts are reluctant to recognize the enforceability of oral promises made by institutional representatives to college athletes[104] or to permit athletes to recover on promissory estoppel claims.[105]

[2] The Express Contract Terms and Conditions

[a] The National Letter of Intent

Pursuant to an NLI, a student-athlete promises to attend the institution named in the NLI and to compete in intercollegiate athletics for that college or university.[106] The validity of the NLI is conditioned on the occurrence of events including the signature of the student-athlete and the athlete's parents or legal guardian, and the

---

the university promised to pay for tuition and board in exchange for the athlete conducting himself "in accordance with all UNC, ACC, and NCAA regulations"); Taylor v. Wake Forest Univ., 191 S.E.2d 379, 381 (N.C. Ct. App. 1972), *cert. denied*, 192 S.E.2d 197 (N.C. 1972) (finding that the student aid application created a contract); Barile v. Univ. of Va., 441 N.E.2d 608, 615 (Va. 1981) (stating a contractual relationship arises when college athletes execute a financial aid or scholarship agreement); Sams v. Bd. of Trs., 65 Ill. Ct. Cl. 127, 131 (2013) (describing the relationship as contractual). *But see* Rensing v. Indiana St. Univ. Bd. of Trustees, 444 N.E.2d 1170, 1174–75 (Ind. 1983) (holding no contractual relationship exists between an athlete and the university for purposes of Workmen's Compensation Act).

103. *See Ross*, 957 F.2d at 417 (stating an identifiable contractual promise must be pointed to in a breach of contract claim); *Jackson*, 778 F. Supp. at 1493 (holding there was no right to play when the financial aid agreement did not explicitly say so); *Taylor*, 191 S.E.2d at 381 (relying on contractual terms to define the relationship).

104. For cases in which courts refuse to give effect to oral promises and statements, see Eppley v. Univ. of Delaware, 2015 WL 156754, at *3, *4 (D. Del., Jan. 12, 2015) (stating coach's oral promises regarding scholarships are unenforceable); Searles v. Trustees of St. Joseph's College, 695 A.2d 1206, 1211–12 (Me. 1997) (holding that an oral promise by a university to pay costs of an athlete's medical injuries suffered playing basketball is unenforceable); Giuliani v. Duke Univ., 2010 WL 1292321, at *6 (M.D.N.C., March 30, 2010) (finding that a previous coach's oral promises to an athlete were unenforceable); Hairston v. Southern Methodist Univ., 441 S.W.3d 327, 337 (Tex. Ct. App. 2013) (holding that the statute of frauds renders unenforceable a university's oral scholarship promise to a prospective athlete).

105. *See* Hall v. NCAA, 985 F. Supp. 782, 796 (N.D. Ill. 1997) (stating that a student-athlete's promissory estoppel claim against the NCAA has "no greater than a negligible chance of success"); Williams v. Univ. of Cincinnati, 752 N.E.2d 367, 377 (Ohio Misc. 2001) (finding that an athlete failed to provide enough evidence for a promissory estoppel claim). *But see* Fortay v. Univ of Miami, Civ. A. No. 93-3443, 1994 WL 6231, *1 (D. N.J. Feb. 17, 1994).

106. *About the National Letter of Intent*, NAT'L LETTER OF INTENT, nationalletter.org/aboutThe Nli/index.html (last visited Jan. 24, 2022).

athlete having received, at the time the NLI is executed, the institution's written offer of an athletic scholarship for at least one academic year.[107] Moreover, the NLI will be considered null and void if: (1) the named institution notifies the athlete, who has completed an application for admission, that the athlete has been denied admission; (2) prior to the beginning of fall classes, the athlete fails to meet NCAA initial eligibility requirements; (3) the athlete attends no college or university for one full academic year; or (4) the named institution discontinues the athlete's sport.[108] The NLI is void-able by the athlete if personnel at the named institution commit NCAA rules violations that require the athlete to seek eligibility reinstatement by the NCAA's reinstatement staff.[109]

The validity of the NLI is not affected by a coach leaving the named institution after the athlete signs the NLI or after or before an athlete matriculates at the named institution.[110] Given that an important purpose of the NLI is to foreclose the recruitment of an athlete by other institutions, any such recruitment efforts must discontinue once the student-athlete and the named institution enter into an NLI.[111] An athlete who signs an NLI but does not attend the named institution for one full academic year will be penalized by being unable to compete at another institution for a full academic year and suffering the loss of one season of intercollegiate athletics competition in all sports.[112]

[b] Athletic Scholarships/Financial Aid Agreements

In exchange for an athlete's commitment, a college or university promises in a financial aid agreement to provide an athletic scholarship to the athlete for at least one academic year.[113] NCAA bylaws require that the scholarship agreement "shall give the recipient a written statement of the amount, duration, conditions, and terms of the award."[114] Before 2015, NCAA bylaws limited the duration of an athletic scholarship to one year, renewable annually. Legislation adopted in 2013 with an effective date of August 2015 authorized NCAA member institutions to award multiyear scholarships, ranging from a minimum of one year to a maximum of five years.[115]

---

107. *Financial Aid Requirement*, NAT'L LETTER OF INTENT, nationalletter.org/nliProvisions/index.html (last visited Jan. 24, 2022).
108. *Letter Becomes Null and Void*, NAT'L LETTER OF INTENT, nationalletter.org/nliProvisions/index.html (last visited Jan. 24, 2022).
109. *Id.*
110. *Coaching Changes*, NAT'L LETTER OF INTENT, nationalletter.org/nliProvisions/index.html (last visited Jan. 24, 2022).
111. *Recruiting Ban After Signing*, NAT'L LETTER OF INTENT, nationalletter.org/nliProvisions/index.html (last visited Jan. 24, 2022).
112. *Basic Penalty*, NAT'L LETTER OF INTENT, nationalletter.org/nliProvisions/index.html (last visited Jan. 24, 2022).
113. NCAA MANUAL, *supra* note 2, at § 15.3.3.1.
114. *Id.* at § 15.3.2.2.
115. *Id.* at § 15.3.3.1.

[i] Permissible Athletics Financial Aid

NCAA bylaws govern the items for which a college or university can provide athletics financial aid. Prior to August 1, 2015, an athletic scholarship was defined as follows: "[A] student-athlete could receive athletically related financial aid limited to tuition and fees, room and board, and required course-related books."[116] In January 2015, the NCAA autonomy schools passed true-cost-of-attendance legislation, effective August 1, 2015, that redefines permissible financial aid.[117] The legislation provides in part: "A student-athlete may receive institutional financial aid based on athletics ability ... and educational expenses awarded ... up to the value of a full grant-in-aid, plus any other financial ... aid up to the cost of attendance."[118] Cost of attendance is defined as "an amount calculated by an institutional financial aid office, using federal regulations, that includes the total cost of tuition and fees, room and board, books and supplies, transportation, and other expenses related to attendance at the institution."[119] Although the "cost of attendance legislation is mandatory for autonomy schools but permissive for non-autonomy schools,"[120] competitive pressures have prompted many non-autonomy schools to offer true-cost financial aid.[121]

[ii] Reduction or Cancellation of Athletic Scholarships

NCAA bylaws regulate the circumstances under which an institution may reduce or cancel an athletic scholarship during the term of the contract.[122] These NCAA bylaw provisions are typically incorporated into the financial aid agreement and become express terms of the student-athlete/university contract. Circumstances that justify reduction or cancellation include: (1) a failure by the athlete to remain academically eligible for intercollegiate athletic competition; (2) a student-athlete's voluntary withdrawal from their sport; (3) an athlete's fraudulent misrepresentation of information in the application; (4) an athlete engaging in misconduct resulting in the institution imposing a substantial disciplinary penalty; and (5) an athlete violating institutional rules and policies delineated in the financial aid agreement.[123]

Athletics financial aid agreements require athletes to comply with the rules and regulations of the particular institution, athletic conference, and the NCAA.[124] Examples of institutional rules that vest colleges with the discretion to cancel or reduce a schol-

---

116. Timothy Davis, *Expanding Student-Athlete Benefits: Are There Costs?*, 5 Miss. Sports L. Rev. 43, 44 (2015–16).

117. Timothy Davis, *A Thirty-Year Retrospective of Legal Developments Impacting College Athletics*, 30 Marq. Sports L. Rev. 309, 329 (2019).

118. NCAA Manual, *supra* note 2, § 15.1.

119. *Id.* at § 15.02.2.

120. Davis, *supra* note 116, at 45.

121. NCAA Manual, *supra* note 2, at 44.

122. *Id.* at §§ 15.3.4 & 15.3.5.

123. *Id.* at §§ 15.3.4.2 & 15.3.5.1.

124. *Id.* at § 15.01.5.

arship, include an athlete's: (1) poor class attendance; (2) hazing; (3) failure to notify a coach within 24 hours of being arrested or receiving a criminal citation; (4) excessively violating university parking regulations; (5) failing to report the dangerous conduct of teammates (*e.g.*, abusive relationship, drug abuse, and driving while under the influence); and (6) failing to adhere to a college's honor and judicial codes.[125] Athletic scholarship agreements also provide that financial aid must be reduced or cancelled if an athlete with remaining eligibility signs a contract with a professional team, accepts money for playing in a contest, or signs a contract with an agent for certain types of representation.[126] Student-athletes must also abide by rules of athletics conferences which may impose penalties for an athlete's failure to exhibit good sportsmanship, excessive celebration, and not adhering to social media policies.[127]

NCAA provisions specifically enumerate circumstances that will not justify an institution's reduction or cancellation of an athletic scholarship during the term of the agreement.[128] During the term of the agreement, reduction or cancellation is not permitted based on the athlete's athletic performance or contribution to the team or based on injury, illness or an athlete's mental condition.[129] For autonomy schools, an institution, after the term of an award, cannot refuse to renew a scholarship for any of these reasons.[130]

[3] *Rights and Obligations Arising from the Express Contract*

The NLI and financial aid agreement establish the core obligations of the parties consisting of the athlete remaining academically eligible for intercollegiate competition and participating in the institution's athletics program, and the institution's promise to provide financial aid. These core rights and obligations were discussed in the seminal case *Taylor v. Wake Forest University*.[131] In that case, Taylor attended Wake Forest on a football scholarship. As a result of his poor academic performance in his first semester, however, Taylor became ineligible to play.[132] Although Taylor's improved academic performance restored his athletic eligibility, he refused to return to the team.[133] Taylor argued that he had the discretion to discontinue playing football if, in his and his parent's judgment, athletic participation would impede his academic

---

125. *Id.* at §§ 15.3.4 & 15.3.5.
126. *Id.* at §§ 12.1.2 & § 12.3.
127. *See* James Hefferan, *Picking Up the Flag? The University of Missouri Football Team and Whether Intercollegiate Student-Athletes May Be Penalized for Exercising Their First Amendment Rights*, 12 DePaul J. Sports L. & Contemp. Probs. 44, 51 (2016); *McAdoo*, 736 S.E.2d at 821 (stating that in the financial aid agreement, the university promised to pay for tuition and board in exchange for the athlete conducting himself "in accordance with all UNC, ACC, and NCAA regulations").
128. NCAA Manual, *supra* note 2, at §§ 15.3.4.3 & 15.3.5.2.
129. *Id.*
130. *Id.* at § 15.3.5.3.
131. 191 S.E.2d 379.
132. *Id.* at 381.
133. *Id.*

achievement.[134] After Taylor refused to play football, the university terminated his athletic scholarship.[135] Taylor sued seeking to recover expenses incurred to finish his degree requirements.[136] Without discussion, the court assumed the existence of a contract between Taylor and the university.[137] It held that Taylor's refusal to participate in athletics, when he was both academically and physically able to do so, constituted a breach of "his contractual obligation," discharging the university's obligation to provide financial assistance.[138] Thus, the financial aid agreement imposes an affirmative and express contractual obligation on student-athletes to participate in sports. An athlete's failure to fulfill this obligation in good faith will discharge the university's obligation to provide financial aid.

[4] Contractually Implied Rights and Obligations

[a] Introduction

While the express contract documents detail the scholarship athlete's contractual obligations to the named institution, the only specifically enumerated obligation the documents impose on the university is to provide financial aid to a scholarship athlete. The absence of language in the NLI and athletic financial aid agreements expressly imposing other obligations on universities has led athletes to petition courts to recognize rights allegedly implicit in the parties' contract. These petitions have arisen in multiple contexts including whether colleges possess an obligation to provide an educational opportunity to student-athletes, and whether an athletic scholarship grants an athlete a property interest in athletic participation and a scholarship beyond the term set forth in the contract documents. As discussed below, courts generally are unwilling to imply these and other obligations into the athlete/university express contractual arrangement.

[b] Judicial Rejection of an Implied Duty of Educational Opportunity

In signing an NLI, an athlete acknowledges an intent to attend an institution as a regular student with the presumed intention to obtain an education.[139] The financial aid agreement conditions an athlete's right to an athletic scholarship on the athlete maintaining academic eligibility to compete in intercollegiate athletics. These documents and NCAA fundamental principles emphasize the student-athlete as an in-

---

134. *Id.* at 382.
135. *Id.* at 381.
136. *Id.* at 381–82.
137. *Id.* at 382.
138. *Id.*
139. *About the National Letter of Intent*, NAT'L LETTER OF INTENT, nationalletter.org/aboutThe Nli/index.html (last visited Jan 24, 2022).

tegral part of the student body and athletes' education being central to student-athletes well-being.[140] Therefore, it is not surprising that student-athletes have brought lawsuits claiming that colleges possess an implied duty to provide athletes with opportunities to develop academically. While creating narrow exceptions, courts have rejected such claims. *Ross v. Creighton University*[141] exemplifies the prevailing view.

Kevin Ross, who was a scholarship student-athlete recruited by Creighton to play intercollegiate basketball, sued Creighton alleging, *inter alia*, educational malpractice and breach of contract.[142] The court followed nearly unanimous precedent in lawsuits brought by non-athlete students[143] in dismissing Ross's educational malpractice claim and refusing to imply a duty that would allow student-athletes to attack the quality of the educational instruction.[144] The court articulated policy reasons for its decision, including: (1) the difficulty of determining a standard of care; (2) the difficulty in ascertaining causation (*i.e.*, whether the failure of the athlete to achieve academically was a consequence of the university's failure or some other factors); (3) the potential flood of litigation that would likely ensue; and (4) academic abstention.[145]

In recognizing a limited specific-promise exception to its rule precluding tort and contract claims alleging educational malpractice, the *Ross* court held that student-athletes present cognizable contract claims relating to educational services provided by their institutions only when athletes can "point to an identifiable contractual promise that the school failed to honor."[146] Similarly, a federal district court in *Jackson v. Drake University*,[147] rejected a scholarship athlete's claim that his university had engaged in conduct that undermined his ability to succeed academically. Recognizing the express contractual relationship between student-athletes and universities, the district court refused to find that Drake possessed an implied duty "to provide an atmosphere conducive to academic achievement."[148] The court reasoned that "where the language of a contract is clear and unambiguous, the language controls."[149]

The *Jackson* court also refused to imply a term into the parties' contract granting a student-athlete a right to athletic participation. The court stated: "the financial aid agreements do not implicitly contain a right to play basketball."[150] In addition to refusing to recognize an implied contract right to athletic participation, courts have also ruled that the student-athlete/university relationship gives rise to neither a fi-

---

140. NCAA MANUAL, *supra* note 2, at §§ 1.3.1. & 2.2.1.
141. 957 F.2d 410 (7th Cir. 1992).
142. *Id.* at 412.
143. *Id.* at 412 n.2.
144. *Id.* at 416.
145. *Id.* at 414–15.
146. *Id.* at 417.
147. 778 F. Supp. 1490 (S.D. Iowa 1991).
148. *Id.* at 1493.
149. *Id.*
150. *Id.*

duciary relationship[151] nor for liability of colleges for acts of student-athletes under a theory of respondeat superior.[152]

§ 2.04 Are College Athletes Employees?

[A] Workers' Compensation

State workers' compensation statutes allow workers to receive compensation for injuries and medical expenses "arising out of and in the course of employment."[153] In exchange for a simplified no-fault mechanism for compensation, injured workers relinquish the right to pursue tort or other statutory remedies against their employers for covered injuries.[154] Workers' compensation statutes are premised on the idea that costs associated with compensating workers for work-related injuries are a production-related cost of doing business.[155]

A threshold issue in determining a person's entitlement to workers' compensation benefits is whether a claimant can establish an employment relationship. The prevailing view is that the contractual arrangement between student-athletes and their colleges is not an employment relationship.[156] In reaching this result, a leading case focused

---

151. Hendricks v. Clemson Univ., 578 S.E.2d 711, 716 (S.C. 2003) (stating that no fiduciary relationship exists between an academic advisor and a college athlete); *see* McCants v. NCAA, 201 F. Supp. 3d 732, 749 (D.N.C. 2016) (finding no fiduciary relationship between athletes and the NCAA); Flood v. NCAA, 2015 WL 5785801, *1, *11 (M.D. Pa. Aug. 26, 2015) (stating courts recognize that no fiduciary relationship exists between athletes and their colleges and the NCAA) ("In short, while the NCAA oversees some aspects of intercollegiate athletics it is not a fiduciary for the thousands of student athletes who participate in those sports, and may not be held to the legal standards of a fiduciary relationship."); *Eppley*, 2015 WL 156754, at *4 (finding no fiduciary relationship is present between a coach and college athlete); Knelman v. Middlebury Coll., 898 F. Supp. 2d 697, 718 (D. Vt. 2012) (finding no fiduciary relationship between an athlete and a college regarding the student's status as a member of the hockey team); McFadyen v. Duke Univ., 786 F. Supp. 2d 887, 987 (M.D. N.C. 2011) (finding no fiduciary relationship between an athlete and a university); Sterman v. Brown Univ., 513 F. Supp. 3d 243, 255–56 (D. R.I. 2021) (no breach of fiduciary relationship occurred between a university and athletes after their sport was transitioned from varsity to club status).

152. *See* Townsend v. State of California, 191 Cal. App. 3d 1530, 1537 (Cal. Ct. App. 1987) (holding college athletes are not employees and universities are not liable under the doctrine of respondeat superior); Kavanagh v. Trustees of Boston Univ., 795 N.E.2d 1170, 1173–74 (Mass. 2003) (holding that the university is not responsible for an athlete's tortious conduct under the doctrine of respondeat superior); Hansen v. Kynast, 494 N.E.2d 1091, 1092 (Ohio 1986) (holding the university was not responsible for a non-scholarship athlete's in-game conduct under the doctrine of respondeat superior).

153. 5 LARSON'S WORKERS' COMPENSATION LAW Chapter 1 Synopsis (2019).

154. *Id.*

155. *Id.* at § 3.01.

156. *See* Graczyk v. Workers Compensation Appeals Bd., 184 Cal. App. 3d 997, 1007 (Cal. Ct. App. 1986) (finding that a football player did not have "a vested right in employment status at the time of his injury"); State Compensation Ins. Fund v. Ind. Comm'n, 314 P.2d 288, 289–90 (Colo. 1957) (holding the athlete and university did not enter into a contract for hire to play football and thus no employer-employee relationship arose); Rensing v. Indiana State Univ. Bd. of Trustees, 444 N.E.2d 1170, 1175 (Ind. 1983) (holding athlete was enrolled at university for educational opportunity and was not an employee).

on two factors critical in determining employee status:[157] the existence of a contract for hire and a university's right to control the details of the athletes' services.[158]

In *Waldrep v. Texas Employer's Insurance Ass'n,*[159] the plaintiff was a former scholarship football player at Texas Christian University who suffered an injury during a football game that left him paralyzed below the neck.[160] Waldrep filed a workers' compensation claim, and the state commission ruled that he was entitled to benefits.[161] The defendant appealed and a jury found that Waldrep was not an employee for workers' compensation purposes.[162] Because the jury did not specify the basis for its verdict, the issues before the Texas Court of Appeals were whether there was sufficient evidence to support the jury's finding that either there was no contract for hire between Waldrep and TCU or that the university did not have the right to direct or control Waldrep's work.[163] Under either alternative, the court held that sufficient evidence supported the jury's verdict.[164] Therefore, Waldrep was denied employee status for workers' compensation.[165]

The court examined the record and concluded that evidence that could have supported the jury's finding of no contract for hire included: NCAA rules and policies distinguishing amateur and professional athletics and which forbid the payment to student-athletes for athletic services; Waldrep and TCU's mutual understanding that he was a student and not an employee; and neither Waldrep's nor TCU's treatment of the athlete's athletic scholarship as compensation.[166] On the issue of the right to control, the court acknowledged that TCU exercised considerable control over its athletes but that there was also evidence on which the jury could have found that "TCU did not have the right to direct or control all of Waldrep's activities during his tenure at the school."[167]

---

157. The Restatement of Employment Law offers the following test for determining if an individual is an employee:

    (a) Except as provided in §§ 1.02 and 1.03, an individual renders services as an employee of an employer if:

    (1) the individual acts, at least in part, to serve the interests of the employer;

    (2) the employer consents to receive the individual's services; and

    (3) the employer controls the manner and means by which the individual renders services, or the employer otherwise effectively prevents the individual from rendering those services as an independent businessperson.

RESTATEMENT OF EMPLOYMENT LAW § 1.01 (Am. L. Inst. 2021).

158. Waldrep v. Texas Emp. Ins. Ass'n, 21 S.W.3d 692, 696 (Tex. Ct. App. 2000).

159. *Id.*

160. *Id.*

161. *Id.*

162. *Id.* at 697.

163. *Id.* at 698–702.

164. *Id.*

165. *Id.* at 702.

166. *Id.* at 700.

167. *Id.* at 702.

Similarly, in *Rensing v. Indiana State Univ. Bd.*,[168] the court acknowledged the contractual nature of a student-athlete/university relationship but reasoned that the absence of an express or implied intent to enter into an employment agreement negated the existence of an employer-employee relationship and that an athletics scholarship is a grant-in-aid rather than payment for services rendered.[169] This was also true in *Coleman v. Western Michigan University*,[170] where the court ruled no employment relationship arose after applying an economic reality test, which focuses on (1) the extent of the university's right to control and discipline the activities of the student-athlete; and (2) the extent to which plaintiff's sports participation was an integral part of the university's business.[171] The court stated: "[p]laintiff's scholarship did not subject him to any extraordinary degree of control over his academic activities. The degree of defendant's control over this aspect of plaintiff's activities was no greater than that over any other student."[172] Addressing whether the athlete's participation in sports constituted an integral part of the university's business, the court concluded that the university could effectively conduct its business without an intercollegiate football program.[173]

Two earlier decisions resulted in incongruent outcomes. In *University of Denver v. Nemeth*,[174] a student-athlete sought worker's compensation benefits for a back injury sustained during football practice.[175] The Colorado Supreme Court ruled that the plaintiff was an employee who was injured in the course of his employment.[176] Although it attempted to distinguish *Nemeth*, in *State Compensation Ins. Fund v. Industrial Commission*,[177] the court effectively overruled its earlier decision in holding that a scholarship student-athlete was not an employee of his university and therefore not entitled to workers' compensation benefits. In the other case, a California court determined that the essence of the student-athlete/university relationship is a contract for hire in which a scholarship is awarded in exchange for athletic services.[178] Finding that the athlete received an athletic scholarship in exchange for rendering athletic services, the *Van Horn v. Industrial Accident Commission*[179] court reasoned that one who participates for compensation as a member of an athletic team may be an employee for worker's compensation purposes in spite of the fact that academic credit is also awarded for such participation.[180] It is worth noting that Van Horn also worked

---

168. 444 N.E.2d 1170, 1175 (Ind. 1983).
169. *Id.*
170. 336 N.W.2d 224, 228 (Mich. Ct. App. 1983).
171. *Id.* at 225.
172. *Id.* at 226.
173. *Id.* at 227.
174. 257 P.2d 423 (Colo. 1953)
175. *Id.* at 424.
176. *Id.* at 430.
177. 314 P.2d 288 (Colo. 1957).
178. Van Horn v. Indus. Accident Comm'n, 219 Cal. App. 2d 457, 464 (Cal. Ct. App. 1963).
179. *Id.*
180. *Id.* at 465.

directly for the athletic department by lining the football field, for which he was paid by the hour.[181]

After *Van Horn*, the California legislature passed a statute excluding student-athletes from the scope of the state workers' compensation statute.[182] Other state statutes that exclude student-athletes from workers' compensation coverage include Oregon,[183] Hawaii,[184] New York,[185] and Vermont.[186]

[B] Fair Labor Standards Act and Unionization

[1] Fair Labor Standards Act

Scholarship student-athletes have also sought employee status for purposes of the Fair Labor Standards Act ("FLSA"). The FLSA was passed by Congress in 1938 and regulates overtime pay, recordkeeping, child labor, and minimum pay standards to ensure fair treatment for employees.[187] The benefits of the FLSA are only available to an individual defined as an employee.[188]

Courts have reached mixed results in considering whether to define student-athletes as employees for purposes of the FLSA. In *Dawson v. NCAA*,[189] a former college football player sued the NCAA and the Pac-12 Conference asserting they violated FLSA by failing to implement policies providing for the payment of a minimum wage to student-athletes.[190] On the threshold issue of whether student-athletes were employees, the court applied an economic reality test, focusing on the following facts on which the Supreme Court had previously relied in determining employee status:

---

181. *Id.* at 462.

182. Frank P. Tiscione, *College Athletics and Workers' Compensation: Why the Courts Get It Wrong in Denying Student-Athletes' Workers' Compensation Benefits When They Get Injured*, 14 Sports Law. J. 137, 146 (2007); *see also* Cal. Lab. Code § 3352(a)(7) (Deering Supp. 2013).

183. Or. Rev. Stat § 656.027 (2008) (stating that nonworkers who are not entitled to workers' compensation include "a person who has been declared an amateur athlete ... and who receives no renumeration for performance of services other than board, room, rent, housing, lodging, or other reasonable subsistence allowance").

184. Haw. Rev. Stat. Ann. § 386-1 (defining "employment" as not including "service for a school, college, university, college club, fraternity, or sorority if performed by a student who is enrolled and regularly attending classes and in return for board, lodging, or tuition furnished, in whole or in part").

185. N.Y. Workers' Comp. § 2(4) ("the term 'employee' shall not include persons who are members of a supervised amateur athletic activity operated on a non-profit basis, provided that said members are not also otherwise engaged or employed by any person, firm, or corporation participating in said athletic activity.").

186. 21 Vt. Stat. Ann. § 601(14(b)) (2018) (stating the term "worker" or "employee" does not include "an individual engaged in amateur sports even if an employer contributes to the support of such sports"). *But see* Neb. Rev. Stat. § 85-106.05 (2019) (holding an insurance program should cover college athletes).

187. Christine Colwell, *Playing for Pay or Playing to Play: Student-Athletes as Employees Under the Fair Labor Standards Act*, 79 La. L. Rev. 899, 905 (2019).

188. *Id.*

189. 932 F.3d 905 (9th Cir. 2019).

190. *Id.* at 907.

(1) the expectation of compensation, (2) the power to hire and fire, and (3) evidence that an arrangement was thought up and executed to evade the law.[191] After considering these factors, the court concluded the athlete had no expectation of receiving compensation from either the NCAA or Pac-12 because neither entity offered him a scholarship. It also noted that neither organization had the power to hire or fire him.[192] The court added that the substantial revenues that defendants derived from college football did not alter its analysis.[193] In dictum, the court added that "under California law, student-athletes are generally deemed not to be employees of their schools."[194] The court cited to California case and statutory authority to support this conclusion.[195]

A different result (including a different interpretation of FLSA's regulations) was reached in *Johnson v. NCAA*.[196] The *Johnson* court relied, in part, on an economic realities test in refusing to find as a matter of law that college athletes are not employees as defined by the FLSA.[197] The court first rejected defendants' characterization of U.S. Supreme Court precedent as standing for the proposition that athletes "are not employees of the schools they attend, and for which they compete in interscholastic athletics,"[198] because they are amateurs, and the Supreme Court has recognized that "[c]ollege athletics in the United States is defined by its century-old 'revered tradition of amateurism.'"[199] The court also rejected the defendants' argument that college athletes are amateurs based on language in FLSA's regulations. Interpreting the regulatory language and applying a seven-factor economic realities test, the court concluded:

> "[C]onstru[ing] the complaint in the light most favorable to the plaintiff," ... we find that the Complaint plausibly alleges that NCAA D1 interscholastic athletics are not conducted primarily for the benefit of the student athletes who participate in them, but for the monetary benefit of the NCAA and the colleges and universities that those student athletes attend. We further find that the Complaint plausibly alleges that the NCAA D1 interscholastic athletics are not part of the educational opportunities provided to the student athletes by the colleges and universities that they attend but, rather, interfere with the student athletes' abilities to participate in and get the maximum

---

191. *Id.* at 909.

192. *Id.*

193. *Id.* at 910.

194. *Id.* at 913.

195. *Id.* at 912–13 (citing Graczyk v. Workers' Comp. Appeals Bd., 229 Cal. Rptr. 494 (Cal. Ct. App. 1986)); Cal. Labor Code § 3352(k)). The court cited to *Shephard v. Loyola Marymount Univ.*, 102 Cal. App. 4th 837, 845 (Cal. Ct. App. 2 Dist. 2002), and held that a student-athlete was not an employee for purposes of the California Fair Employment and Housing Act. It also cited to *Townsend v. State of California*, 191 Cal. App. 3d 1530, 1537 (Cal. Ct. App. 1987), in which the court refused to characterize a student-athlete as an employee of his college for purposes of respondeat superior.

196. 556 F. Supp. 3d 491 (E.D. Pa. 2021).

197. *Id.* at 500, 508.

198. *Id.* at 500.

199. *Id.*

benefit from the academic opportunities offered by their colleges and universities. Accordingly, we conclude that the Complaint plausibly alleges that NCAA D1 interscholastic athletics are not the types of activities listed in FOH § 10b03(e) that 'do not result in an employer-employee relationship between the student and the school or institution.' FOH § 10b03(e). We further conclude, accordingly, that FOH § 10b03(e) does not require us to find, as a matter of law, that Plaintiffs cannot be employees of the ASD. Consequently, we deny the Motion to Dismiss as to this argument.[200]

The court refused to adopt defendants' argument that college athletes are not employees of colleges because the economic reality of the relationship is that athletes participate in intercollegiate sports without any expectation of payment.[201]

Applying an economic reality test, another court also refused to grant a defendant's motion to dismiss. In *Livers v. NCAA*,[202] a former student-athlete alleged that Villanova University's refusal to compensate him for his playing on the school's football team violated the FLSA.[203] The court ruled that allegations in plaintiff's amended complaint relating to the economic realities of the plaintiff's relationship warranted not dismissing plaintiff's action at that stage of the proceedings.[204]

[2] Unionization and the National Labor Relations Act

In regards to the NLRA, in 2015, Northwestern University scholarship football players sought to be recognized as employees as a step toward unionizing pursuant to the NLRA.[205] Focusing on the players' substantial time commitment to football, the extensive control that Northwestern exercised over all aspects of the players' lives, and the revenue generated by football, an NLRB regional administrator determined that the Northwestern football players fell within the NLRA's definition of employee.[206] Northwestern appealed the decision.[207]

In reversing the administrator's determination, the five-member board declined to exercise jurisdiction for policy reasons.[208] Stating that the underlying goal of the NLRA is to foster stability in labor relations, the board stated that exercising jurisdiction would undermine that goal.[209] Its reasoning was informed by: (1) the NCAA's significant control over member institutions through its regulatory regime; (2) the view that the NLRB's exercise of jurisdiction would disrupt the uniformity of the

---

200. *Id.* at 506.
201. *Id.*
202. No. 17-4271, 2018 WL 3609839, *1 (E.D. Penn. 2018).
203. *Id.* at *1.
204. *Id.* at *5–6.
205. Northwestern Univ., 362 NLRB 1350, 1350 (2015).
206. *Id.* at 1353, 1359, 1360.
207. *Id.* at 1350.
208. *Id.* at 1353–55.
209. *Id.* at 1355.

rules regulating college athletics given that the Board would only have jurisdiction over private schools in the NCAA (*i.e.*, the NLRB could only assert jurisdiction over 17 of the 125 football teams in the Football Bowl Subdivision);[210] and (3) the NCAA's initiation of reforms seeking to enhance student-athlete well-being.[211] The Board expressed concern about infringing on the NCAA's regulatory authority and potentially contributing to a collapse of the NCAA's regulatory and enforcement regimes.[212] Based on these policy considerations, the five-member NLRB declined to address the merits of whether student-athletes are employees.[213]

Based on the considerable control that colleges and universities exercise over their student-athletes, in September 2021, the NLRB's general counsel wrote an opinion sent to regional offices stating that athletes who attend private colleges and universities fall within the NLRA's definition of an employee.[214]

§ 2.05 College Athletes and Constitutional Rights

[A] Introduction

Student-athletes assert that entities, including their colleges and the NCAA, engage in conduct that violates the athletes' constitutional rights. They alleged infringement ranging from depravation of a property interest without procedural due process to denial of their First and Fourth Amendment rights. Our discussion first examines an issue that represents the intersection of contractual and constitutional principles — athlete allegations that their scholarship agreements create an implied right to athletic participation, which in turn creates a property interest of which the athlete cannot be deprived without due process.

[B] Do Student-Athletes Have Protectible Property or Liberty Interests in Athletic Participation?

The Fourteenth Amendment precludes state actors (*i.e.*, public entities) from depriving any citizen of property without due process of the law.[215] Section 1983[216] is

---

210. *Id.* at 1353–54.

211. Zachary Bock, *Student-Athletes as Employees: Unmasking Athletic Scholarships*, 36 N. Ill. U. L. Rev. 131, 139 (2016).

212. *Id.* at 139.

213. *Northwestern Univ., supra* note 205, at 1355–56.

214. NLRB, *NLRB General Counsel Jennifer Abruzzon Issues Memo on Employee Status of Players at Academic Institutions*, News & Publications (Sept. 29, 2021), https://www.nlrb.gov/news-outreach/news-story/nlrb-general-counsel-jennifer-abruzzo-issues-memo-on-employee-status-of.

215. U.S. Const. amend. XIV.

216. 42 U.S.C. § 1983 (2018).

the procedural vehicle by which athletes pursue actions alleging that a state actor engaged in conduct that deprived the athlete of their property and/or a liberty interest in contravention of their Fourteenth Amendment guarantees of procedural and substantive due process. Therefore, a plaintiff seeking redress for due process violations must establish a protectible property interest of which the plaintiff was deprived without sufficient procedural protection, including adequate notice and a fair hearing.[217] The property interest itself is not created by the Constitution. Rather it is created and defined by "rules or understandings that stem from an independent source such as state law."[218] A right arising out of contract provides such an independent source. Moreover, "'[t]o have a property interest in a benefit, a person clearly must have more than an abstract need or desire for it. He must have more than a unilateral expectation of it. He must, instead, have a legitimate claim of entitlement to it.'"[219]

Thus, a predicate to a student-athlete's procedural due process claims is establishing the existence of a property interest.[220] In addition, because private colleges and universities are not state actors, athletes would only have cognizable claims against public colleges and universities.[221] Therefore, the following discussion is offered against the backdrop of the state actor requirement and the difficulty student-athletes encounter in seeking redress for alleged constitutional violations by private entities such as the NCAA.[222]

The overwhelming majority of courts have held that the student-athlete/ university financial aid agreement does not create a property interest in athletic participation and competition.[223] An illustrative case is *Hysaw v. Washburn University*

---

217. Bd. of Regents of State Colleges v. Roth, 408 U.S. 564, 569–70 (1972); *see also* Jacobeit v. Rich Twp. High Sch. Dist. 227, 673 F. Supp. 2d 653, 665 (N.D. Ill. 2009); Kish v. Iowa Cent. Cmty. Coll., 142 F. Supp.2d 1084, 1096 (N.D. Iowa 2001); Austin v. Univ. of Or., 925 F.3d 1133, 1139 (9th Cir. 2019) (holding that even though athletes were not entitled to due process, they "received 'the hallmarks of procedural due process': notice and a meaningful opportunity to be heard") (internal citation omitted).

218. *Roth*, 408 U.S. at 577.

219. *Id.* at 577.

220. Erwin Chemerinsky, Constitutional Law: Principles and Policies 591 (6th ed., Wolters Kluwer 2019) ("Procedural due process, as the phrase implies, refers to the procedures that the government must follow before it deprives a person of life, liberty, or property. Classic procedural due process issues concern what kind of notice and what form of hearing the government must provide when it takes a particular action.").

221. *See Tarkanian*, 488 U.S. at 191.

222. *Id.* at 196 (holding that the NCAA is not a state actor).

223. *Accord Does v. United States Dep't of Homeland Sec.*, 843 Fed. App'x 849, 852 (9th Cir. 2021) (rejecting international students' claims alleging Department of Homeland Security Covid-19 related restrictions violated their property and liberty interest, and concluding "access to educational and athletic programs" as well as in the students' visas, does not give rise to a property or liberty interest); Awrey v. Gilbertson, 833 F. Supp. 2d 738, 741 (E.D. Mich. 2011) (finding that athletic scholarship agreement did not vest an athlete with a property interest in athletic participation); Gonyo v. Drake University, 837 F. Supp. 989, 994 (S.D. Iowa 1993) (stating athletes have no constitutional right to participate in intercollegiate athletics); Lesser v. Neosho Cty. Community Coll., 741 F. Supp.

of Topeka[224] where several scholarship African-American student-athletes' complaints of discriminatory treatment ultimately resulted in their decision to boycott team practices and meetings.[225] After the university refused to allow certain players to return to the team,[226] the players sued the university asserting that the university's dismissal of them from the team infringed upon their implied contractual right to play football which gave rise to a property interest of which they could not be deprived without the university affording them due process.[227] In refusing to imply a right to athletic participation in the parties' contract, the court stated "the only interests created by those agreements are interests in receiving scholarship funds. Any other terms plaintiffs attempt to read into those agreements are, without supporting evidence, no more than 'unilateral expectations.'"[228] Thus, *Hysaw* and other courts state that the essence of the athlete/university relationship does not support finding an implied right to athletic participation or a property interest in athletic participation.

An overwhelming number of courts have not been swayed by a theory advanced by scholarship athletes that the tangible economic benefits derived from athletic participation creates a property interest in athletic participation.[229] Courts generally hold that potential economic value of athletic participation is too speculative to create a constitutional right. For example, the court in *Colorado Seminary (University of Denver) v. NCAA*,[230] denied a student-athlete's claim of a property interest in athletic participation that allegedly arose because intercollegiate athletics provides a training ground for some athletes to play at the professional level.[231] The court held that:

854, 862, 864–65 (D. Kan. 1990) (finding there is no right to a position on a baseball team emerging from a Letter of Intent creating contract between athlete and college where contract was silent on issue); *see* Equity in Athletics, Inc. v. Dep't of Educ., 639 F.3d 91, 109 (4th Cir. 2011) (holding college athletes have no constitutionally protectible property interest in athletic participation); Hart v. NCAA, 550 S.E.2d 79, 85 (W. Va. 2001) ("participation in interscholastic athletics ... does not rise to the level of a constitutionally protected 'property' or 'liberty' interest."). *But see* Hall v. Univ. of Minnesota, 530 F. Supp. 104, 107–08 (D. Minn. 1982); Hunt v. NCAA, No. G76-370 C.A., slip op. at 7–8 (W.D. Mich. Sept. 10, 1976) (finding scholarship agreement entitles athletes to certain benefits including right to participate in intercollegiate athletics); Behagen v. Intercollegiate Conference of Faculty Representatives, 346 F. Supp. 602, 604 (D. Minn. 1972) (finding that potential for substantial economic benefits of athletic participation give rise to a property interest therein).

224. 690 F. Supp. 940 (D. Kan. 1987).

225. *Id.* at 942–43.

226. *Id.* at 943.

227. *Id.* at 944.

228. *Id.*

229. Brian L. Porto, Note, *Balancing Due Process and Academic Integrity in Intercollegiate Athletics: The Scholarship Athlete's Limited Property Interest in Eligibility*, 62 IND. L.J. 1151, 1159–60 (1987) (citing a number of theories brought forward to assert a property interest in athlete eligibility: economic, educational, scholarship per se, and contractual); Timothy Davis, *Student-Athlete Prospective Economic Interests: Contractual Dimensions*, 19 T. MARSHALL L. REV. 585, 605, 607–10 (1994) (analyzing the economic potential of collegiate athletics as a basis for a property interest, which has been primarily denied as being too speculative).

230. Colorado Seminary (University of Denver) v. NCAA, 417 F. Supp. 885 (D. Colo. 1976).

231. *Id.* at 895–96.

"while plaintiffs' characterization of the distinctive importance of collegiate athletics as a forum may be a sadly accurate reflection of the true significance of today's amateur athletic competition, the interest in future professional careers must nevertheless be considered speculative and not of constitutional dimensions."[232]

Likewise in *NCAA v. Yeo*,[233] the court was not persuaded by an intercollegiate and Olympic swimmer's argument that the damage to her international reputation if she were not permitted to compete in athletics distinguished her situation from that of athletes in cases in which courts refused to find a property interest in athletic participation.[234] The court stated: "Yeo's claimed interest in future financial opportunities is too speculative for due process protection. There must be an actual legal entitlement. While student-athletes remain amateurs, their future financial opportunities remain expectations."[235]

Hall v. Univ. of Minnesota[236] is a notable exception to the majority rule that there is no property interest in athletic participation. In that case, the court sided with the athlete in finding that the potential harm to his prospects of playing professional basketball required that the university afford him due process before determining his eligibility to play intercollegiate sports.[237]

[C] Does a Student-Athlete Have a Property Interest in a Scholarship?

The financial aid agreement between student-athletes and their universities creates a protectible property interest in the scholarship of which athletes cannot be deprived without due process. Lawsuits in which athletes assert constitutional challenges based on the existence of a property interest in their scholarships, however, have not been successful. In these cases, athletes typically allege that their property interest in athletics financial aid provides a premise for an alleged deprivation of their claimed interest in athletic participation. Yet, courts differentiate a property interest in a scholarship from a property interest in athletic participation. Thus, where a student-athlete is denied the ability to participate in intercollegiate sports, there is no constitutional violation when the university honors the terms of the athletic scholarship.[238]

Courts distinguish a college's revocation of an athletic scholarship from its failure to renew a scholarship.[239] Prior to the amended NCAA bylaws permitting multi-year

---

232. *Id.* at 895.

233. 171 S.W.3d 863 (Tex. 2005).

234. *Id.* at 870.

235. *Id.*

236. Hall v. Univ. of Minnesota, 530 F. Supp. 104, 107–08 (D. Minn. 1982).

237. *Id.*; *see also* Behagen v. Intercollegiate Conference of Faculty Representatives, 346 F. Supp. 602, 604 (D. Minn. 1972) (finding that potential for substantial economic benefits of athletic participation give rise to a property interest therein).

238. *See* Holden v. Perkins, 398 F. Supp. 3d 16, 21, 23 (E.D. La. 2019); *Hysaw*, 690 F. Supp. at 944; *Awrey*, 833 F. Supp. 2d at 741; Conard v. Univ. of Wash., 834 P.2d 17, 22 (Wash. 1992).

239. *Holden*, 398 F. Supp. 3d at 21, 23.

athletic scholarships, courts held that a college's refusal to renew a one-year athletic scholarship was not constitutionally protected given the absence of a property interest in the renewal of the scholarship. As discussed, *supra*, however, NCAA bylaws limit the right of colleges to revoke, reduce or cancel an athlete's scholarship during the term of the scholarship, whether the term is for a single year or is multi-year.

This leads to the related issue of the level of due process that a college must afford an athlete when a scholarship has been revoked or is not renewed. In *Austin v. Univ. of Oregon*,[240] two University of Oregon men's basketball players were accused of sexual assault.[241] Although they were not subjected to criminal prosecution, the athletes were found guilty of sexual misconduct under the university's disciplinary policies which resulted in the university suspending them.[242] The university decided not to renew the athletes' athletic scholarships.[243] The court assumed, without deciding the existence of a property interest, that plaintiffs were entitled to procedural due process.[244] In addressing the minimum due process required, the court held that the university disciplinary proceeding satisfied due process requirements in that the athletes received notice and a choice of a hearing with counsel.[245] A similar result was reached in *Mattison v. East Stroudsburg Univ.*, where an athlete was suspended for one year for smoking marijuana.[246] Ruling that the athlete possessed no property interest in athletic participation,[247] the court nevertheless examined whether the university's punishment of the athlete adhered to due process requirements.[248] It ruled that the university had met the requirements because the plaintiff was given notice and a hearing.[249]

[D] Student-Athletes' Liberty Interest

Student-athletes have asserted the existence of a liberty interest in their attempt to lay the foundation for asserting a violation of their Fourteenth Amendment procedural and substantive due process rights. As is true for athlete claims that they possess a property interest in athletic participation, the majority of courts reject athlete claims that actions depriving them of the ability to play intercollegiate sports infringe on their liberty interests.[250] Thus, in *Hysaw*, plaintiffs alleged they possessed a liberty

---

240. *Austin*, 925 F.3d at 1139.

241. *Id.* at 1135.

242. *Id.* at 1135–36.

243. *Id.* at 1136.

244. *Id.* at 1139.

245. *Id.*; *see also* Marcum v. Dahl, 658 F.2d 731, 735 (10th Cir. 1981) (ruling that college's decision not to renew scholarship did not violate due process after notice and an opportunity to have a hearing occurred).

246. Mattison v. East Stroudsburg Univ., 2013 WL 1563656, *1, *4 (M.D. Penn. 2013).

247. *Id.* at *4 (citing Angstadt v. Midd-West Sch. Dist., 377 F.3d 338 (3d Cir. 2004)).

248. *Mattison*, 2013 WL 1563656, at *4.

249. *Id.* at *4.

250. *See* Caldwell v. Univ. of N.M. Bd. of Regents, 510 F. Supp. 3d 982 (D. N.M. 2020) (holding a student-athlete did not have a liberty interest in a future professional basketball career because any such interest would be too speculative, but athlete possessed a liberty interest in his continued en-

interest that was infringed upon when their coach made derogatory statements that thwarted the athletes' ability to be recruited by another institution. In rejecting the plaintiffs' liberty interest claim, the court stated:

> A due process claim is made out only if the liberty interest allegedly violated is protectable under the Constitution.... The plaintiffs concede that no right to pursue a college football career exists.... Something more must be shown; a tangible interest must be established.... The court finds no tangible interest here.... While no constitutional right to a government job exists, the Supreme Court has noted that qualification for a government job is a "privileg[e] of first-class citizenship...." Plaintiffs have offered no reason why a right to pursue a collegiate athletic career should be afforded the same status....[251]

Likewise, in *Yeo*, the court ruled that the application of a transfer rule rendering a highly-regarded college swimmer ineligible for intercollegiate participation did not infringe upon her constitutionally protected liberty interest given that neither athletic participation nor her reputation as a swimmer created a liberty interest.[252] The court's refusal to recognize the athlete's reputation as giving rise to a liberty interest is consistent with U.S. Supreme Court precedent.[253] In rejecting plaintiffs' claims, courts have refused to equate athletic participation with interests that give rise to a liberty interest, including the right to be free of bodily restraint, the free exercise of religion, the right to marry, and the rights of parents to rear their children.[254]

[E] Student-Athletes and Substantive Due Process

The Fourteenth Amendment restricts the ability of state actors to deprive citizens of their life, liberty, or property without procedural and substantive due process of the law.[255] Procedural due process concerns the type of notice and hearing to which a person is entitled before being deprived of a property or liberty interest.[256] In contrast, substantive due process focuses on whether a state actor has a sufficient justification for taking action that deprives a person of a property or liberty interest.[257]

---

rollment at the university); *Holden*, 398 F. Supp. 3d at 23 (stating college athletes possess no liberty interest in athletic participation); Carrington v. Duke Univ., 2011 WL 13324486, 1, *52 (M.D. N.C. Mar. 31, 2011) (holding there is no property or liberty interest in athletic participation); *Equity in Athletics*, 639 F.3d at 94 (stating that participation in intercollegiate athletics does not give rise to a liberty interest); Brennan v. Bd. of Trustees for Univ. of Louisiana Sys., 691 So. 2d 324, 330 (La. Ct. App. 1997) (holding that athlete has no liberty interest in athletic participation in rejecting constitutional challenge by an athlete suspended after testing positive for anabolic steroids).

251. *Hysaw*, 690 F. Supp. at 945.

252. *Yeo*, 171 S.W.3d at 869–70.

253. *See* Paul v. Davis, 424 U.S. 693, 712 (1976) (stating that harm to reputation is neither a liberty nor a property interest).

254. *See generally* CHEMERINSKY, *supra* note 220, at 612–26 (explaining deprivations of liberty and property recognized by the Supreme Court as protected by procedural due process).

255. U.S. CONST. amend. XIV.

256. *See* CHEMERINSKY, *supra* note 220, at 591.

257. *Id.* at 592.

Whether there is such a justification depends very much on the level of scrutiny used. For example, if the law is in an area where only rational basis review is applied, substantive due process is met so long as the law is rationally related to a legitimate government purpose. But if it is in an area where strict scrutiny is used, such as for fundamental rights, then the government will meet substantive due process only if it can prove that the law is necessary to achieve a compelling government purpose.[258]

Thus, notwithstanding any procedural protections provided, substantive due process prohibits a state actor from taking actions that are "unreasonable, arbitrary, or capricious" and thereby infringe upon a person's fundamental rights or liberty interests.[259]

As is true of student-athletes' procedural due process claims, courts have not been receptive to student-athletes' substantive due process claims. The majority of courts hold that athletic participation does not create a property interest, a prerequisite to a cognizable substantive due process claim. The courts in both *Holden v. Perkins*[260] and *Equity in Athletics, Inc. v. Dep't of Educ.*[261] concluded that the athletes' failure to establish a protectible property or liberty interest in athletic participation warranted dismissal of their substantive due process claims.

Assuming that a court were to find that athletic participation gives rise to a property or liberty interest, a court will not necessarily find that an athlete's substantive due process rights were violated. In *Richard v. Perkins*,[262] the court assumed that the athlete had a property interest in athletic participation. The court then proceeded to articulate the standard for determining a violation of substantive due process:

> The standard for a substantive due process claim is whether the challenged government action would "shock the conscience of federal judges." ... To satisfy this standard, plaintiff must do more than show that the government actor intentionally or recklessly caused injury to the plaintiff by abusing or misusing government power.... Plaintiff must demonstrate "a degree of outrageousness and a magnitude of potential or actual harm that is truly conscience shocking." ... Conscience shocking behavior generally falls on the far side of the culpability spectrum, requiring plaintiff to show that the government actor performed with an intent to harm.[263]

---

258. *Id.*

259. 16C C.J.S. *Constitutional Law* § 1821 (2020) ("A claim of violation of Fourteenth Amendment substantive due process requires proof that a defendant's conduct shocks the conscience or interferes with rights implicit in the concept of ordered liberty, or offends judicial notions of fairness, or is offensive to human dignity, or is taken with deliberate indifference to protected rights.").

260. 398 F. Supp. 3d 16, 21, 23 (E.D. La. 2019).

261. *Equity in Athletics*, 639 F.3d at 109; *see also Carrington*, 2011 WL 13324486, at *52 (holding the absence of a property or liberty interest in athletic participation precluded plaintiff's substantive due process claim); *Colorado Seminary*, 477 F. Supp. at 896 (finding that because plaintiff athlete possessed no constitutionally protectible interest, athlete had no entitlement to due process).

262. 373 F. Supp. 2d 1211, 1220 (D. Kan. 2005).

263. *Id.* at 1220.

Applying this standard, the court ruled that defendants' removal of the athlete from the team did not shock the conscience.[264]

[F] Student-Athlete Fourteenth Amendment Claims against the NCAA

Student-athletes encounter two impediments in pursuing Fourteenth Amendment claims against the NCAA. First, the court in *NCAA v. Tarkanian*[265] ruled the NCAA is not a state actor, an essential requirement of a due process claim.[266] Moreover, athletes largely have been unable to convince courts that they possess a constitutionally protected property or liberty interest. For example, in *Yeo*, the court did not address whether the NCAA is a state actor.[267] The court nevertheless rejected the athlete's claim that the NCAA had infringed upon her due process rights. It held that the athlete possessed no constitutionally protected interest requiring that she be afforded due process.[268] Similar results were reached in cases decided before *Tarkanian*, in which courts rejected student-athlete due process claims either on grounds that the NCAA was not a state actor and/or the athletes possessed no constitutionally protectible interest.[269]

[G] Student-Athlete Freedom of Expression and Privacy Rights

[1] Freedom of Expression

The First Amendment limits federal and state governments' power to regulate citizens' expressions.[270] For a thorough discussion of this issue, we refer you to Chapter

---

264. *Id.; see also Holden*, 338 F. Supp. 3d at 22 (defining substantive due process as barring "arbitrary, wrongful government action regardless of the fairness of the procedures used to implement them.").

265. 488 U.S. 179 (1998).

266. Matthews v. NCAA, 79 F. Supp. 2d 1199, 1208 (E.D. Wash. 1999) (finding that the NCAA is not a state actor); Hawkins v. NCAA, 652 F. Supp. 602, 604 (C.D. Ill. 1987) (ruling the NCAA was not a state actor and that possible postseason participation by an athlete was not a constitutionally protected interest requiring due process); McDonald v. NCAA, 370 F. Supp. 625, 632 (C.D. Cal. 1974) (dismissing athletes' due process claims against the NCAA because it is not a state actor).

267. NCAA v. Yeo, 171 S.W.3d 863 (Tex. 2005).

268. *Id.* at 870. *Accord* Justice v. NCAA, 577 F. Supp. 356, 365 (D. Ariz. 1983) (NCAA deemed a state actor but court concludes athletes possessed no constitutionally protected interest); *see also Colorado Seminary*, 417 F. Supp. at 893, 896 (finding a student-athlete's future interest in playing at the professional level did not give rise to a protectible property interest); NCAA v. Gillard, 352 So. 2d 1072, 1080 (Miss. 1977) (concluding athletes have no constitutionally protectible property interest in playing football). *But see* Brian L. Porto, Note, *Balancing Due Process and Academic Integrity in Intercollegiate Athletics: The Scholarship Athlete's Limited Property Interest in Eligibility*, 62 IND. L.J. 1151, 1160 (1987) (citing *Hunt v. NCAA*, in which the court found a college athlete had a property interest against the NCAA).

269. *See* MITTEN, ET AL., *supra* note 1, at 162.

270. U.S. CONST. amend. I.

1 of this treatise, which addresses freedom of expression at the high school level. The paucity of reported decisions regarding the regulation of college-athlete speech warrants caution in reaching broad generalizations about the constitutionality of colleges' restrictions on athletes' free speech rights. With this in mind, however, the considerable regulation by colleges of their student-athletes and a school's interest in team unity provide the foundation for institutions to impose limited restrictions on college-athlete speech.[271] The few relevant cases to date suggest a judicial willingness to protect college-athletes' speech when the value of the speech extends beyond the interests of a particular athlete.[272]

In *Hysaw v. Washington Univ. of Topeka*,[273] the *Tinker* standard (see discussion in Chapter 1, *supra*) was applied in a case in which scholarship football players were dismissed from a team following their boycott of practices in protest of racial injustice.[274] Recall that in *Tinker v. Des Moines Indep. Cnty. Sch. Dist.*[275] the Court invalidated a school policy that resulted in the suspension of high school students who wore black arm bands in protest of the Vietnam War.[276] Recognizing the need to balance a student's freedom of expression with an institution's need to control conduct and exercise authority, the court articulated the following standard:

> When [a student] is in the cafeteria, or on the playing field, or on the campus during the authorized hours, he may express his opinions, even on controversial subjects..., if he does so without "materially and substantially interfering with the requirements of appropriate discipline in the operation of the school" and without colliding with the rights of others. But conduct by the student, in class or out of it, which for any reason—whether it stems from time, place, or type of behavior—materially disrupts classwork or involves substantial disorder or invasion of the rights of others is, of course, not immunized by the constitutional guarantee of freedom of speech.[277]

Returning to *Hysaw*, the plaintiff football players asserted that their dismissal from the team violated their First Amendment rights.[278] The defendant sought summary judgment arguing that because the "boycott severely disrupted the football

---

271. Diane Heckman, *Educational Athletes and Freedom of Speech*, 177 EDUC. L. REP. 15, 48 (2003) (stating, "[t]he overriding message from the case law is that the student-athlete who speaks out about his or her problem may not be protected by the First Amendment and therefore must be willing to suffer the consequences, which can include the loss or curtailment of athletic participation or loss of an athlete [*sic*] scholarship."); Hefferan, *supra* note 127, at 50 (concluding, "[a]ny analysis of the First Amendment rights of intercollegiate student-athletes must begin with an acknowledgment that student-athletes are 'special and different' from ordinary college students, and, therefore, are subjected to different regulations of their speech than the student body at large.").

272. *See* Hefferan, *supra* note 127, at 60; Meg Penrose, *Outspoken: Social Media and the Modern College Athlete*, 12 J. MARSHALL REV. INTELL. PROP. L. 509, 512 (2013).

273. 690 F. Supp. 940 (D. Kan. 1987).

274. *Id.* at 943.

275. 393 U.S. 503 (1969).

276. *Id.* at 513.

277. *Id.* at 512–13 (internal citations omitted).

278. *Hysaw*, 690 F. Supp at 942.

team and infringed upon the rights of others participating in the football program," the athletes' dismissal was reasonable in regard to time, place and manner.[279] Construing the "infringing upon the rights of others" language of *Tinker* narrowly, the court held that infringement occurs "only to activity which could result in tort liability for the school."[280] Acknowledging that the athletes' boycott undoubtedly hurt team morale and made practice more difficult, the court nevertheless ruled that there was an infringement of the athletes' rights.[281] The court concluded it would not "place the interests of participants in a university extracurricular activity above the rights of any citizen to speak out against alleged racial injustice without fear of government retribution."[282]

In contrast to *Hysaw*, an athlete complaint about a coach's management of a team resulted in a different result. In *Green v. Sandy*,[283] the court determined that "a student-athlete's expression of dissatisfaction with her team or coach causes great harm to team unity and therefore constitutes a disruption and disturbance which school officials have a right to prevent."[284] Similarly, courts will likely uphold restrictions on expressions resulting in adverse institutional action, such as the nonrenewal of scholarships, where the speech does not pertain to matters of public concern.[285] A university's restrictions on free speech have also been deemed reasonable when they conflict with a policy that seeks to avoid a college or university violating the Establishment Clause.[286]

[2] Religious Expression and the Establishment Clause

We also refer you to Chapter 1, *supra*, for a discussion of high school athletes and religious expression because much of that discussion is equally applicable to college student-athletes. As is true in the high school setting, whether a college athlete's rights have been wrongfully abridged under the Free Exercise Clause requires courts to balance a student-athlete's and an institution's respective interests.[287] This in turn requires a student-athlete to demonstrate that a state actor (*e.g.*, a public college or university), placed "a constitutionally significant burden on a practice that is sufficiently related

---

279. *Id.* at 943.

280. *Id.* at 946.

281. *Id.*

282. *Id.*

283. 2011 WL 4688639, *1 (E.D. Ky. Oct. 3, 2011).

284. *Id.*

285. *Marcum*, 658 F.2d at 735 (finding that the college's decision not to renew athletes' scholarships after the athletes told the press about their opposition to the coach was not a matter of public concern that invoked First Amendment protection); *Richard*, 373 F. Supp. 2d at 1217 (rejecting athlete's argument that appeal of university's decision not to renew his scholarship was a matter of public concern entitling him to First Amendment protections).

286. Williams v. Eaton, 468 F.2d 1079, 1082–84 (10th Cir. 1972) (affirming lower court's decision that allowed a coach to prohibit team members to wear an armband during a game protesting racial injustice because it would not violate the Establishment Clause).

287. Scott C. Idleman, *Religious Freedom and the Interscholastic Athlete*, 12 MARQ. SPORTS L. REV. 295, 301 (2001).

to the claimant's sincerely held religious beliefs."[288] Courts' mediation of conflicts between a student-athlete's religious expression and violations of the Establishment Clause is likely to follow the approaches adopted by courts adjudicating cases involving high school athletes. Student-initiated prayer and other religious activities will not likely conflict with the Establishment Clause at a public college or university unless a coach or administrator directs the prayer.[289]

[3] College Athletes and Privacy

[a] Drug Testing and Privacy

College athletes have argued that drug testing programs violate the Fourth Amendment's prohibition against unreasonable search and seizure[290] and similar protections provided in state constitutions. Courts have upheld the constitutionality of the NCAA's random and suspicionless drug testing program administered through colleges and universities.[291] In finding that the competing interests of colleges and the NCAA outweigh the privacy interests of athletes, courts emphasize athletes' diminished right to privacy given the control colleges exercise over multiple aspects of their athletes' lives.[292] Courts also focus on institutions' legitimate interests in protecting the health and safety of sports participants.[293] Stated one court:

> By its nature, participation in intercollegiate athletics, particularly in highly competitive postseason championship events, involves close regulation and scrutiny of the physical fitness and bodily condition of student athletes.... As a result of its unique set of demands, athletic participation carries with it social norms that effectively diminish the athlete's reasonable expectation of personal privacy in his or her bodily condition, both internal and external. In recognition of this practical reality, drug testing programs involving athletic competition have routinely survived Fourth Amendment "privacy" challenges.[294]

In validating the NCAA's drug testing program, the court in *Hill v. NCAA*[295] offered additional justifications, including: (a) the reasonableness of the drug testing given the advance notice and athlete's consent; (b) the view that athletic participation is not a right and athletes forgo certain individual rights as a cost of athletic participation; (c) the deterrence effect of drug testing; and (d) and the interest in fostering fair com-

---

288. *Id.*

289. *See* Doe v. Duncanville Indep. Sch. Dist., 70 F.3d 402, 406 (5th Cir. 1995).

290. *See* U.S. CONST. amend. IV.

291. Hill v. NCAA, 865 P.2d 633, 658 (Cal. 1994); Brennan v. Bd. Trus. Univ. La. System., 691 So. 2d 324 (La. App. 1997).

292. See *Hill*, 865 P.2d at 658; *Brennan*, 691 So. 2d at 329.

293. *See* Bally v. Northeastern Univ., 532 N.E.2d 49, 53 (Mass. 1989) (holding that a university drug testing program that conditioned participation in athletics on participating in the drug testing to be "indiscriminate" and "impartial[]" and thus was valid); *Hill*, 865 P.2d at 658; *Brennan*, 691 So. 2d at 329.

294. *Hill*, 865 P.2d at 658.

295. *Id.*

petition.[296] Similar justifications were stated by the court in *Brennan v. Bd. of Trustees for Univ. of Louisiana Sys.*, which also upheld the constitutionality of the NCAA's drug testing program.[297]

The Colorado Supreme Court struck down a non-NCAA drug testing program in *University of Colorado v. Derdeyn*.[298] The court ruled the University of Colorado's drug testing program violated the Fourth Amendment and Colorado's state constitution.[299] The case is distinguishable from *Hill* and *Brennan* in that Colorado's drug testing program lacked the level of safeguards present in the NCAA's drug testing regime (*i.e.*, it failed to provide for the confidentiality of test results).[300]

[b] The Right to Privacy and the Media

Because NCAA sports generate public interest, student-athletes' right to privacy is more attenuated than the privacy rights of other students. For example, in *Bilney v. Evening Star Newspaper Co.*, six members of the University of Maryland's men's basketball team experienced academic difficulties.[301] A newspaper published an article detailing their struggles, prompting the athletes to file suit asserting, *inter alia*, a tortious invasion of privacy claim.[302] The athletes asserted their academic standing was a private matter unaffected by any public interest.[303] The court disagreed, holding that the athletes were voluntary public figures by virtue of their positions on the basketball team and that their academic eligibility was a matter of "legitimate public interest."[304]

§ 2.06 College Athletics and Antitrust Law

[A] Introduction

As explored more thoroughly in Chapter 7, *infra*, antitrust law seeks primarily to protect consumer welfare and preserve competition. The antitrust law most applicable to college sports is the Sherman Act, which was enacted in 1890.[305] Section I of the

---

296. *Id.* at 659, 661.

297. *Brennan*, 691 So. 2d at 329–30.

298. Univ. of Colorado, Boulder v. Derdeyn, 863 P.2d 929, 930–33 (Colo. 1993); *see also* Stephen F. Brock et al., *Drug Testing College Athletes: NCAA Does Thy Cup Runneth Over*, 97 W. VA. L. REV. 53, 88 (1994).

299. Brock et al., *supra* note 298, at 85.

300. *Id.* at 81 (stating the program was also more intrusive because, in the third version of the testing, athletes were "selected using objective criteria that were supposed to detect drug use"); *Derdeyn*, 863 P.2d at 932 (stating all team members, such as managers and cheerleaders, were included in the drug test).

301. Bilney v. Evening Star Newspaper Co., 406 A.2d 652, 655 (Md. Ct. Spec. App. 1979).

302. *Id.*

303. *Id.* at 659.

304. *Id.*

305. 15 U.S.C. §§ 1–7.

Sherman Act prohibits any "contract, combination ... or conspiracy in restraint of trade or commerce"; Section 2 prohibits any "monopoliz[ation] or attempt to monopolize ... trade or commerce."[306] Pursuant to these provisions, the Sherman Act seeks to prevent anticompetitive behavior that unreasonably restrains competition. In college sports, athletes, coaches, colleges and other plaintiffs have challenged NCAA bylaw provisions as unreasonably restraining trade in violation of Section I of the Sherman Act.[307] As a jurisdictional matter, the Sherman Act, a federal statute, applies only to alleged anticompetitive conduct arising in interstate commerce. "Courts have consistently held that the NCAA ... is engaged in interstate commerce" and thus the organization's activities are subject to the Sherman Act.[308]

[B] Antitrust Law in College Sports: Before *O'Bannon v. NCAA*

Historically, judicial resolution of antitrust challenges to NCAA bylaws followed a pattern resulting in two lines of judicial precedent and reasoning. In cases that did not implicate NCAA eligibility rules and impacted what could clearly be viewed as commercial relationships, courts were more willing to use antitrust law to invalidate the challenged bylaw.[309] In cases involving athlete-eligibility rules, however, athletes were unsuccessful in antitrust challenges. In the latter cases, judicial precedent was influenced significantly by courts' unquestionable reliance on the principles and values undergirding the NCAA's definition of amateurism and conceptualization of college sports.[310] We begin, however, with two cases in which antitrust law provided the basis for invalidating NCAA bylaws unreasonably restraining what could be characterized as commercial relationships.

[1] NCAA v. Board of Regents

In the seminal case *NCAA v. Board of Regents*,[311] universities challenged an NCAA plan that limited the total number of games which could be televised and the number of games which any single member institution could appear on television.[312] The Court characterized the NCAA's television plan as constituting a horizontal price fixing and output limitation.[313] It noted that, in most instances, such restraints would be deemed per se unreasonable and thereby would violate the Sherman Act.[314] In the context of sports, however, the Court stated that a Rule of Reason analysis, which allows a defendant an affirmative defense asserting procompetitive justifications for

---

306. *Id.* at §2.

307. *Id.*

308. MATTHEW J. MITTEN, ET AL., *supra* note 1, at 216.

309. *Id.* at 310.

310. Davis, *supra* note 95, at 310.

311. 468 U.S. 85 (1984).

312. *Id.* at 99–101.

313. *Id.* at 99–100, 107–09.

314. *Id.* at 100.

the alleged restraint, is the appropriate analytical framework.[315] The Court reasoned that in sports "horizontal restraints on competition are essential if the product is to be available at all."[316] It added: "'[S]ome activities can only be carried out jointly. Perhaps the leading example is league sports. When a league of professional lacrosse teams is formed, it would be pointless to declare their cooperation illegal on the ground that there are no other professional lacrosse teams.'"[317]

Applying the Rule of Reason analysis it had adopted, the Supreme Court agreed with the plaintiffs in holding that the NCAA's television plan violated the Sherman Act. The NCAA argued that the television plan had no anticompetitive effect because it did not possess market power. In rejecting this argument, the Court stated:

> [A]s a matter of law, the absence of proof of market power does not justify a naked restriction on price or output. To the contrary, when there is an agreement not to compete in terms of price or output, "no elaborate industry analysis is required to demonstrate the anticompetitive character of such an agreement."[318]

The Court then added that a "naked restraint on price and output requires some competitive justification even in the absence of a detailed market analysis" for the defendant to avoid antitrust liability.[319] The Court found that the NCAA possessed market power and that the plan had an anticompetitive effect.[320] It then considered and rejected the NCAA's proffered procompetitive justifications — that the plan assisted the NCAA in marketing its broadcast rights,[321] was necessary to protect attendance at live games,[322] and maintained competitive balance among NCAA football programs.[323]

In dictum, the Court distinguished cases challenging NCAA amateurism rules from those regulating NCAA television contracts on the ground that the former regulates noncommercial matters while the latter regulates commercial activity. Thus, the Court suggested that NCAA eligibility and other rules most likely would survive antitrust scrutiny under the Sherman Act.

> A myriad of rules affecting such matters as the size of the field, the number of players on a team, and the extent to which physical violence is to be encouraged or proscribed, all must be agreed upon, and all restrain the manner in which institutions compete. Moreover, the NCAA seeks to market a particular brand of football — college football. The identification of this "product" with an academic tradition differentiates college football from and makes it

---

315. *Id.* at 113.
316. *Id.* at 101.
317. *Id.* (quoting R. Bork, The Antitrust Paradox 278 (1978)).
318. *Id.* at 109 (quoting Natl. Soc. of Prof. Engineers v. U.S., 435 U.S. 679, 692 (1978)).
319. *Id.* at 110.
320. *Id.* at 111.
321. *Id.* at 113–14.
322. *Id.* at 116–17.
323. *Id.* at 117–19.

more popular than professional sports to which it might otherwise be comparable, such as, for example, minor league baseball. In order to preserve the character and quality of the "product," athletes must not be paid, must be required to attend class, and the like. And the integrity of the "product" cannot be preserved except by mutual agreement....[324]

The Court also recognized the NCAA's vital role in college football retaining its character.[325]

[2] Law v. NCAA

In *Law v. NCAA,*[326] a restraint on commercial activity, salaries, was successfully challenged as violating Section I of the Sherman Act.[327] As a part of its efforts to control costs within college sports, the NCAA sought to restrict the salaries of part-time assistant coaches.[328] It developed a class of Division I entry-level basketball coaches known as a restricted-earnings coaches ("REC"). The annual athletic-related income of these coaches could not exceed $16,000.[329] The RECs sued, alleging the cap on salaries was an unreasonable restraint that violated Section 1 of the Sherman Act.[330] The district court found that the REC salary limitation violated Section 1 and enjoined the NCAA from enforcing it.[331]

In upholding the district court's finding, the Tenth Circuit characterized the REC salary limitation as a horizontal price-fix that would typically have been condemned as per se illegal.[332] The court stated: "By agreeing to limit the price which NCAA members may pay for the services of restricted-earnings coaches, the REC Rule fixes the cost of one of the component items used by NCAA members to produce the product of Division I basketball."[333] Consistent with *Board of Regents*, however, the court applied a Rule of Reason analysis in affirming the lower court judgment. In so doing, it established a framework for determining whether the price limitation violated Section 1 of the Sherman Act. It stated that plaintiffs bear the initial burden of "showing that an agreement had a substantially adverse effect on competition."[334] The burden then shifts to the defendant to proffer evidence of procompetitive effects of the restraint.[335] Assuming the defendant carries its burden, the plaintiff must show that the "challenged conduct is not reasonably necessary to achieve the legitimate

---

324. *Id.* at 101–02.
325. *Id.* at 102.
326. 134 F.3d 1010 (10th Cir. 1998).
327. *Id.*
328. *Id.* at 1013.
329. *Id.* at 1012.
330. *Id.* at 1015.
331. *Id.* at 1016.
332. *Id.* at 1017.
333. *Id.*
334. *Id.* at 1019.
335. *Id.*

objectives or that those objectives can be achieved in a substantially less restrictive manner."[336]

Finding that plaintiffs met their initial burden by "showing the naked and effective price-fixing character of the agreement,"[337] the court then assessed and rejected each of the NCAA's following asserted procompetitive rationales that: (1) the salary limitation retained entry level positions for younger coaches (the court ruled that altruistic values without an impact on competition do not sustain a defendant's burden);[338] (2) the limitation fostered competitive balance by "barring some teams from hiring four experienced coaches instead of three" (the court found that the REC position could be filled by experienced coaches);[339] (3) the limitation reduced costs (the court found the NCAA failed to present evidence that any cost savings would not be redirected within schools' athletic programs, and that in any event, a defendant's efforts to reduce cost without showing more, such as efficiencies that result in cost savings, are invalid as a procompetitive justification);[340] and (4) the limitation enhanced "competitive equity by preventing wealthier schools from placing a more experienced, higher-priced coach in the position of restricted-earnings coach" (the court found the NCAA presented no credible evidence to support this justification).[341]

[3] NCAA Student-Athlete Eligibility Rules

While *Board of Regents* and *Law* involved restraints on what were clearly commercial activities, a markedly different approach was adopted by courts in cases in which college athletes mounted antitrust challenges to the validity of NCAA eligibility rules. Prior to *O'Bannon v. NCAA*,[342] "courts uniformly rejected student-athletes' claims that the 'no-draft,' 'no agent,' and 'limited compensation' rules violated Section I of the Sherman Act."[343] Some courts reasoned that the noncommercial nature of NCAA amateurism-based eligibility rules removed them from the purview of antitrust regulation.[344] Other courts applied a Rule of Reason analysis in concluding that eligibility bylaws either had no anticompetitive effect[345] or were reasonable because they advanced and maintained the amateurism value (as articulated by the NCAA).[346]

---

336. *Id.*

337. *Id.* at 1021.

338. *Id.*

339. *Id.*

340. *Id.* at 1021–24.

341. *Id.* at 1024.

342. 802 F.3d 1049 (9th Cir. 2015).

343. Davis, *supra* note 95, at 306.

344. *Id.*; *see, e.g.,* Smith v. NCAA, 139 F.3d 180, 185–86 (3d Cir. 1998); Jones v. NCAA, 392 F. Supp. 295, 303 (D. Mass. 1975); *see also* Bassett v. NCAA, 528 F.3d 426, 430 (6th Cir. 2008) (stating that NCAA recruiting and extra benefits the violation of which resulted in sanctioning of coach were not subject to antitrust purview).

345. McCormick v. NCAA, 845 F.2d 1338, 1343 (5th Cir. 1988).

346. Davis, *supra* note 95, at 306; *see also* Deppe v. NCAA, 893 F.3d 498 (7th Cir. 2018); Agnew v. NCAA, 683 F.3d 328, 339 (7th Cir. 2012) (stating "[m]ost — if not all — eligibility rules ... fall comfortably within the presumption of procompetitiveness afforded to certain NCAA regulations," but

In *Banks v. NCAA*,[347] a student-athlete playing football for Notre Dame registered for the National Football League draft and consulted with an agent. The NCAA declared Banks ineligible to play football in his remaining year at Notre Dame.[348] Banks sought to permanently enjoin the NCAA and Notre Dame from enforcing the no-draft and no-agent rules, asserting that both rules violated Section 1 of the Sherman Act.[349] The Seventh Circuit affirmed the district court's holding that Banks had failed to establish that the no-draft and no-agent rules had an anti-competitive effect on trade.[350] The language of the court's opinion, and its allusion to the NCAA's stated purpose in particular, revealed the court's perception of college sports as resting on the amateur ideal:

> Because the no-draft rule represents a desirable and legitimate attempt "to keep university athletics from becoming professionalized to the extent that profit making objectives would overshadow educational objectives," the no-draft rule and other like NCAA regulations preserve the bright line of demarcation between college and "play for pay" football.... We consider college football players as student-athletes simultaneously pursuing academic degrees that will prepare them to enter the employment market in non-athletic occupations, and hold that the regulations of the NCAA are designed to preserve the honesty and integrity of intercollegiate athletics and foster fair competition among the participating amateur college students.[351]

A similar result was reached in *Gaines v. NCAA*,[352] where a student-athlete challenged the validity of the no-draft and no-agent regulations. The *Gaines* court's decision was premised on upholding rules that the court perceived as preserving amateurism and maintaining college athletics as an integral part of the collegiate educational process.

[C] *O'Bannon* and Its Progeny

[1] O'Bannon v. NCAA

O'Bannon represents a significant shift in judicial precedent regarding the application of the Sherman Act to NCAA eligibility- and athlete compensation-related rules.[353] In *O'Bannon*, a class of then current and former NCAA Division I men's basketball and football players filed a lawsuit in which they asserted that they were entitled to receive a share of the compensation that their institutions had earned from using the athletes' names, images and likenesses ("NILs") in videos, broadcasts and other footage.[354] The district court found that NCAA rules prohibiting athletes

---

also finding that "one-year limit scholarships and a limit on scholarships per term are not inherently or obviously necessary for the preservation of amateurism, the student-athletes, or the general product of college football").

347. 977 F.2d 1081 (7th Cir. 1992).
348. *Id.* at 1084.
349. *Id.*
350. *Id.* at 1084, 1086.
351. *Id.* at 1090.
352. 746 F. Supp. 738 (M.D. Tenn. 1990).
353. 802 F.3d 1049 (9th Cir. 2015).
354. *Id.* at 1055–56.

from receiving compensation for their NILs constituted an unlawful restraint of trade in violation of the Sherman Act in that the rules were more restrictive than required to maintain the NCAA's legitimate goal of maintaining amateurism.[355] The district court issued an injunction enjoining the NCAA from "prohibiting its member schools from giving student-athletes scholarships up to the full cost of attendance at their respective schools and [requiring Division I institutions to give] up to $5,000 per year in deferred compensation, to be held in trust for student-athletes until after they leave college."[356]

On appeal, the Ninth Circuit held that NCAA amateurism rules are not exempt from antitrust scrutiny and must be analyzed under the Rule of Reason.[357] Although the Ninth Circuit accepted the proposition that certain NCAA amateurism rules preserve the distinction between college and professional sports and, in so doing, preserve college sports as a distinctive product,[358] it rejected the NCAA's argument that its amateurism rules are valid under the Sherman Act as a matter of law. In this regard, the court stated that whether NCAA amateurism rules survive antitrust review "must be proved, not presumed."[359]

Similar to *Law*, *O'Bannon* recognizes that restraints on inputs are subject to antitrust purview.[360] It also holds that the NCAA's compensation rules regulate commercial activity and fixed an aspect of the "price" that recruits pay to attend college.[361] The appellate court also agreed with the district court that a proper alternative to the NCAA's compensation rule was to permit student-athletes to receive up to the full cost of attendance.[362] It disagreed, however, with the district court's deferred compensation award.[363]

> [T]he district court clearly erred in finding it a viable alternative to allow students to receive NIL cash payments untethered to their education expenses.... We cannot agree that a rule permitting schools to pay students pure cash compensation and a rule forbidding them from paying NIL compensation are both *equally* effective in promoting amateurism and preserving consumer demand. Both we and the district court agree that the NCAA's amateurism rule has procompetitive benefits. But in finding that paying students cash compensation would promote amateurism as effectively as not paying them, the district court ignored that not paying student-athletes is *precisely what makes them amateurs*.[364]

---

355. *Id.* at 1052–53.
356. *Id.* at 1053.
357. *Id.* at 1057.
358. *Id.* at 1076.
359. *Id.* at 1064.
360. *Id.* at 1053, 1063–64.
361. *Id.* at 1073.
362. *Id.* at 1075–76.
363. *Id.* at 1079.
364. *Id.* at 1079 (emphasis in original).

Notwithstanding the adverse finding, *O'Bannon* was a partial victory for the NCAA in that both the district and appellate courts agreed with the NCAA's argument that its compensation rules served two procompetitive purposes: "'integrating academics with athletics'" and "preserving the popularity of the NCAA's product by promoting its current understanding of amateurism."[365] The Ninth Circuit stated:

> [The] district court found, and the record supports that there is a concrete procompetitive effect in the NCAA's commitment to amateurism: namely, that the amateur nature of collegiate sports increases their appeal to consumers. We therefore conclude that the NCAA's compensation rules serve the two procompetitive purposes identified by the district court....[366]

The Ninth Circuit rejected, however, the NCAA's procompetitive justifications that its compensation rules promote competitive balance and that they increase output in the college education market.[367]

[2] Alston v. NCAA

Judicial adherence to the NCAA's articulated values and its definition of amateurism were further eroded in *In re NCAA Athletic Grant-in-Aid Cap Antitrust Litigation*,[368] the class action in which Shawne Alston was the lead plaintiff.[369] Judge Wilken, who adjudicated *O'Bannon*, held that student-athlete eligibility rules that limit: "(1) the grant-in-aid at not less than the cost of attendance; (2) compensation and benefits unrelated to education paid on top of a grant-in-aid; [and] (3) compensation and benefits related to education provided on top of a grant-in-aid[,]"[370] "constitute horizontal price-fixing agreements enacted and enforced with monopsony power."[371] Judge Wilken concluded:

> While Defendants have shown that limiting student-athlete compensation has some effect in preserving consumer demand for Division I basketball and FBS football as compared with no limit, Plaintiffs have shown that not all of the challenged rules are necessary to achieve this effect and that a less restrictive alternative set of rules would be virtually as effective as the set of challenged rules, without requiring significant costs to implement. The less restrictive alternative would remove limitations on most education-related benefits provided on top of a grant-in-aid, while allowing the NCAA to limit cash or cash-equivalent awards or incentives for academic achievement or graduation to the same extent it limits athletics awards. Limits on compen-

---

365. *Id.* at 1073.

366. *Id.*

367. *Id.* at 1072 ("We therefore accept the district court's factual findings that the compensation rules do not promote competitive [balance and] that they do not increase output in the college education market....").

368. 375 F. Supp. 3d 1058 (N.D. Cal. 2019).

369. *Id.*

370. *Id.* at 1101.

371. *Id.* at 1109.

sation and benefits not related to education and a limit on the grant-in-aid
at not less than the cost of attendance would remain.[372]

The court enjoined the NCAA from prohibiting universities from providing tangible
items related to the pursuit of academic studies (*e.g.*, computers, musical instruments,
and study abroad expenses).[373] It permitted the NCAA "to limit academic and graduation awards and incentives that are provided in cash or a cash-equivalent to a level
that the record shows is not demand-reducing or inconsistent with NCAA amateurism...."[374]

The Ninth Circuit affirmed, holding that the district court had not erred in finding
that the plaintiffs carried their burden of establishing that the pertinent NCAA rules
had "significant anticompetitive effects" in the market for student-athletes football
services.[375] It also upheld the district court's finding that certain NCAA rules — limits
on compensation unrelated to educational expenses and some "restrictions on cash
academic and graduation awards and incentives"[376] — served the procompetitive justification of preserving "amateurism," which "widens consumer choice" by distinguishing college and professional sports.[377] Finally, the Ninth Circuit affirmed the
district court's conclusion regarding the least restrictive alternatives. It stated, "[t]he
district court reasonably concluded that uncapping certain education-related benefits
would preserve consumer demand for college athletics."[378] The court stated the same
is true of permitting student-athletes to receive up to $5,600 for "athletic participation
awards."[379]

The decision provides another basis on which institutions can compete for college
athletes in that it expanded the breadth of permissible educational benefits institutions
can give to their athletes.[380] It is noteworthy that the court refused to invalidate all
NCAA limitations on the compensation that colleges and universities can give athletes
in exchange for their services. Both sides appealed.

The Supreme Court resolved the issues squarely before it in *NCAA v. Alston*.[381]
In that case, the NCAA argued that its rules should be exempt from "the normal operation of antitrust laws."[382] In contrast, the athletes challenged the "current, inter-
connected set of NCAA rules that limit the compensation they may receive in
exchange for their athletic services."[383] In an extensive analysis, the Supreme Court
disagreed with the NCAA's proposition that its rules are outside of the Sherman

---

372. *Id.*
373. *Id.*
374. *Id.* at 1106.
375. In re NCAA Grant-in-Aid Cap Antitrust Litigation, 958 F.3d 1239, 1256 (9th Cir. 2020).
376. *Id.* at 1258.
377. *Id.*
378. *Id.* at 1260.
379. *Id.* at 1262.
380. *Id.* at 1110.
381. 141 S. Ct. 2141 (2021).
382. *Id.* at 2147.
383. *Id.* at 2151.

Act's purview. It also rejected the NCAA's challenges to the district court's application of the Rule of Reason. The Court found that NCAA compensation limits "produce significant anticompetitive effects in the relevant market." Refusing to accept the NCAA's definition of amateurism, the Court stated that "the NCAA's conception of amateurism has changed steadily over the years."[384] The Court also concluded that the NCAA's evidence failed "to establish that the challenged compensation rules, in and of themselves, have any direct connection to consumer demand."[385] In short, the Court affirmed the lowers courts' decisions enjoining the "NCAA ... from limiting education-related compensation or benefits that conferences and schools may provide to student-athletes playing Division I football and basketball."[386]

It is important to note the issues that were not addressed in *Alston*. The Supreme Court refused to address the validity of the NCAA's limits on non-education compensation that colleges and university can provide to their athletes.[387] The Court noted that the lower courts specifically upheld those rules and the issue of whether NCAA limits on non-education compensation survives scrutiny under the Sherman Act was not before it.[388]

In a stinging concurrence, Justice Kavanaugh questioned, however, whether the remaining constraints will withstand antitrust scrutiny.

> [T]here are serious questions whether the NCAA's remaining compensation rules can pass muster under ordinary rule of reason scrutiny.... The bottom line is that the NCAA and its member colleges are suppressing the pay of student athletes who collectively generate *billions* of dollars in revenues for colleges every year. Those enormous sums of money flow to seemingly everyone except the student athletes.... [I]t is highly questionable whether the NCAA and its member colleges can justify not paying student athletes a fair share of the revenues on the circular theory that the defining characteristic of college sports is that the colleges do not pay student athletes. And if that asserted justification is unavailing, it is not clear how the NCAA can legally defend its remaining compensation rules.[389]

In the aftermath of the Court's *Alston* ruling, on June 30, 2021, the NCAA reversed its longstanding position and suspended its rules that "prohibit[ed] athletes from receiving compensation for the use of their names, images and likenesses."[390] This policy change followed the enactment of legislation and gubernatorial executive orders granting student-athletes the right to receive compensation for their NILs

---

384. *Id.* at 2152.
385. *Id.*
386. *Id.* at 2151–53, 2166.
387. *Id.* at 2147.
388. *Id.* at 2154.
389. *Id.* at 2167–68.
390. Dan Murphy, *NCAA Clears Student-Athletes to Pursue Name, Image and Likeness Deals*, ESPN (June 30, 2021), https://www.espn.com/college-sports/story/_/id/31737039/ncaa-clears-student-athletes-pursue-name-image-likeness-deals.

from parties other than their institutions.[391] Additional states will likely enact similar NIL legislation in 2022 and 2023.[392] Federal legislation has been proposed with the hope that it will achieve uniform NIL guidelines.[393]

[3] House v. NCAA

In another potentially important antitrust action, *House v. NCAA*,[394] college athletes seek to invalidate NCAA bylaws "prohibiting student-athletes from receiving anything of value in exchange for the commercial use" of their names, images, and likenesses.[395] The ramifications of the case are potentially significant in that the ultimate outcome of the issues raised in *House* could determine whether athletes can receive a share of the lucrative revenues that colleges and universities earn from their television and endorsement deals. The challenged rules allegedly prohibit student-athletes from using their NILs to: (1) receive NIL-related income from outside employment; (2) "promote their own business"; and (3) derive income from "their social media posts, personal brands, viral videos depicting their athletic performances, apparel sponsorships, and other opportunities related to the use of their NIL."[396] Plaintiffs also challenge NCAA rules that allegedly prevent its member institutions and conferences from sharing with student-athletes revenue derived from broadcasting contracts with television networks, marketing contracts, and media sponsorships.[397]

Plaintiffs allege that the relevant rules constitute an illegal price fix in that they set at zero the amount athletes can be paid for the use of their NILs.[398] This allegation is connected to the proposition that lies at the heart of plaintiffs' claim — colleges compete for the services of college athletes by offering a unique bundle of goods and services including full cost-of-attendance scholarships, tutors, academic support services, and state of the art athletic facilities.[399] The plaintiffs assert that permitting colleges and conferences to share in the revenue produced, in part, by athletes' NILs will add to the bundles of goods and services that form the basis of what colleges use to compete for the services of athletes.[400]

---

391. Steve Berkowitz, *NCAA Adopts Temporary Policy on Name, Image, and Likeness in Seismic Shift for College Sports*, USA TODAY (June 30, 2021, 9:00 AM), https://www.usatoday.com/story/sports/college/2021/06/30/ncaa-adopts-name-image-likeness-policy/7813970002/; Rudy Hill & Jonathan D. Wohlwend, *College Athletes Now Allowed to Earn Money from Use of Their Name, Image, and Likeness*, NAT'L L. REV. (July 1, 2021), https://www.natlawreview.com/article/college-athletes-now-allowed-to-earn-money-use-their-name-image-and-likeness.

392. Hill & Wohlwend, *supra* note 391.

393. Dan Murphy, *Everything you need to know about the NCAA's NIL debate*, ESPN.COM (Sept. 1, 2021), https://www.espn.com/college-sports/story/_/id/31086019/everything-need-know-ncaa-nil-debate (last visited Jan. 23, 2022).

394. 545 F. Supp. 3d 804 (N.D. Cal. 2021).

395. *Id.* at 808.

396. *Id.*

397. *Id.*

398. *Id.* at 810.

399. *Id.* at 809.

400. *Id.*

Absent these nationwide restraints, Division I conferences and schools would compete amongst each other by allowing their athletes to take advantage of opportunities to utilize, license, and profit from their NILs in commercial business ventures and promotional activities and to share in the conferences' and schools' commercial benefits received from exploiting student-athletes' names, images, and likenesses. Conferences and schools would also compete for recruits by redirecting money that they currently spend on extravagant facilities and coaching salaries to marketing programs and educational resources designed to help their student-athletes develop and grow their personal brand value.[401]

Thus, plaintiffs contend that by virtue of the challenged bylaws, the NCAA, Power 5 athletic conferences, and their member institutions have conspired to unreasonably restrain trade in violation of Section 1 of the Sherman Act.[402]

The court denied the NCAA's motion to dismiss the complaint. In denying the motion, Judge Wilkins reasoned: "There is a reasonable inference that competition among schools and conferences would increase and this increased competition would incentivize schools and conferences to share their broadcasting and other commercial revenue with student-athletes even if the students-athletes lacked publicity rights in broadcasts."[403]

---

401. *Id.* at 809.
402. *Id.* at 810.
403. *Id.* at 816.

Chapter 3

Legal Issues Arising in International and Olympic Sports

§ 3.01 Introduction

Sport is a global phenomenon. Virtually all societies feature some sort of organized sports competition. In some cases, sports are played exclusively in one city or nation.[1] Most sports, however, such as soccer, baseball, swimming, skiing, and track and field, have cross-border reach, touching people from different nations and bringing them together in competitions. These sports are featured at the Olympic Games and other high-level global competitions, such as the FIFA World Cup and the World Baseball Classic. Certain of these sports also inspire athletes to travel internationally in search of opportunities to play in different nations' domestic leagues.[2] This results in teams comprised of players from different countries. In the United States, it is common for teams in the National Hockey League, National Basketball Association, Major League Baseball and Major League Soccer to include players born outside of the U.S. In other instances, the leagues themselves include teams located across national borders. The National Hockey League, for instance, which is headquartered in New York City in the United States, has teams based in both the United States and Canada.[3]

Organized sports competitions that transcend national borders require a robust regulatory and adjudicatory system fashioned to address the transnational character of sporting competition and legal issues emanating therefrom. This chapter will familiarize you with the role played in regulating international sports by several organizations and institutions, including the International Olympic Committee, the Court of Arbitration for Sport, and the World Anti-Doping Agency. The chapter

---

1. *Home Game Limited Series* (Netflix, 2020). Calcio Storico, a frenzied combination of boxing, wrestling, and rugby dating to the 16th Century, is played in Florence, Italy with only native Florentines permitted to participate. In Bali, jockeys riding abreast on wooden ploughs suspended between pairs of water buffalo race against each other in a sport called Makepung Lampit. Other cities, provinces, and countries, have their own particularized sports of great local import, but largely unknown and unplayed elsewhere. *Id.*

2. *See, e.g., NBA Rosters Feature 107 International Players from 41 Countries*, NBA (Dec. 22, 2020), https://www.nba.com/news/nba-rosters-feature-107-international-players-from-41-countries.

3. *See Teams*, NHL, https://www.nhl.com/info/teams (identifying 32 NHL teams, seven based in Canada, and 25 based in the United States).

then turns its focus to exploring the governance of Olympic sports in the United States. It also addresses regulations impacting international athletes' participation in American sports leagues.

§ 3.02 The Regulatory and Governance Framework in International Sport

[A] The Olympic Games — Structure and Governance

The Olympic and Paralympic Games make up the world's most celebrated international sports competition. The International Olympic Committee ("IOC"), based in Lausanne, Switzerland, operates the Olympic Games and Paralympic Games ("the Games"). The IOC sits atop a complex web of organizations critical to the operation of the Games.[4] Most importantly, each country that participates in the Olympics has its own National Olympic Committee ("NOC"), which generally organizes that nation's Olympic and Paralympic efforts and manages its national contingent of athletes.[5] In the United States, this organization is called the United States Olympic and Paralympic Committee ("USOPC").[6] The Amateur Sports Act of 1978 charges the USOPC with supervising the nation's participation in the Olympics and Paralympics.[7]

Each country has a National Governing Body ("NGB") (also known as a "National Federation") that governs each Olympic sport. For instance, in the United States, the NGB for track and field sports is USA Track & Field ("USATF") and the NGB for gymnastics is USA Gymnastics ("USAG").[8] Each NGB reports to the NOC.[9] The NGB in a particular sport serves as that sport's "coordinating body for amateur athletic activity."[10] This includes holding competitions and determining, through periodic qualifying events and trials, which athletes will represent a country at the Olympic Games and other international competitions.[11]

---

4. Int'l Olympic Comm., Olympic Charter, R2, R15 (2020); *see also Overview*, INT'L OLYMPIC COMM., https://olympics.com/ioc/overview (describing the IOC's collaboration with several different stakeholders); *Who Organizes the Paralympic Games*, INT'L OLYMPIC COMM., https://olympics.com/ioc/faq/roles-and-responsibilities-of-the-ioc-and-its-partners/who-organises-the-paralympic-games (explaining that the Paralympic Games are supervised by the International Paralympic Committee, which is recognized by the IOC).

5. Olympic Charter, *supra* note 4, at R27.

6. 36 U.S.C. § 220501(b)(7).

7. *Id.* at § 220503(3).

8. *See About USA Gymnastics*, USA GYMNASTICS, https://usagym.org/pages/aboutus/pages/about_usag.html; *About*, USA TRACK & FIELD, https://www.usatf.org/about.

9. Olympic Charter, *supra* note 4, at R29.

10. 36 U.S.C. § 220523(a)(3).

11. *Id.* at § 220523(a)(5)–(7).

Each sport has an international sports federation ("IF"), which functions as the umbrella organization[12] over various nations' NGBs and is responsible for organizing international competitions for that sport.[13] As worldwide governing bodies, IFs also establish competition rules and eligibility thresholds for participants in those competitions.[14] Returning to track and field and gymnastics as examples, the track and field IF is World Athletics (formerly, the International Amateur Athletics Federation ("IAAF") and the gymnastics IF is the Fédération Internationale de Gymnastique ("FIG").[15]

All IFs are independent from each other, as are NGBs. Moreover, the relationship between NGBs and the sporting structures in their respective nations differ substantially. In some nations, each NGB operates the professional league for its sport, giving the NGBs extraordinary power. In other nations, NGBs have no direct connection to professional leagues, rendering them less powerful actors on their nations' sporting landscape.

As international athletic exchange and involvement increased and became more complex through the twentieth century, the IOC created other organizations to assist in regulating international sport. Chief among these are the Court of Arbitration for Sport ("CAS") and the World Anti-Doping Agency ("WADA").[16]

[B] The Court of Arbitration for Sport

CAS was founded in 1983 as an arbitral body to resolve disputes that develop in international sport.[17] CAS hears disputes that generally fall into two categories: commercial and disciplinary disputes.[18] The commercial disputes CAS hears include disputes involving the execution of contracts, player transfers, and fee/salary disagreements among sports clubs, athletes, and athlete agents.[19] The disciplinary disputes it hears are mostly drug-related, but it hears other disciplinary matters as well, including those involving in-game violence and referee abuse.[20] CAS also addresses athlete ineligibility determinations made on various grounds by various sports governing bodies.[21] Importantly, CAS does not automatically have jurisdiction over

---

12. *International Sports Federations*, INT'L OLYMPIC COMM., https://olympics.com/ioc/international-federations.

13. Olympic Charter, *supra* note 4, at R25.

14. *Id.* at R26.

15. *See id.* (listing officially recognized international federations).

16. *History of the CAS*, COURT OF ARBITRATION FOR SPORT, https://www.tas-cas.org/en/general-information/history-of-the-cas.html [hereinafter *History of the CAS*]; *Who We Are*, WORLD ANTI-DOPING AGENCY, https://www.wada-ama.org/en/who-we-are.

17. *History of the CAS, supra* note 16.

18. *Id.*

19. *Id.*

20. *Id.*

21. *See* Matthew J. Mitten & Timothy Davis, *Athlete Eligibility Requirements and Legal Protection of Sports Participation Opportunities*, 8 VA. SPORTS & ENT. L.J. 71, 78–81 (2009).

parties to a dispute. Parties must agree to submit to CAS jurisdiction.[22] That said, all IFs have submitted to CAS jurisdiction and many, in turn, pressure NGBs, event organizers, athletes, and other stakeholders with whom they work to sign contracts agreeing that any potential dispute with the IFs will be resolved by CAS.[23] Consequently, CAS is the principal tribunal for hearing disputes (including doping disputes, see, *infra*) in the international sport realm.[24]

The International Council of Arbitration for Sport ("ICAS"), which is a twenty member group of luminary lawyers and judges with expertise is sports, has developed and updates the Code of Sports-Related Arbitration ("CAS Code"), which governs CAS and its operations.[25] CAS operates principally in two languages, English and French, and all of its roughly 400 arbitrators, appointed by ICAS, must speak one or the other language.[26] Despite use of the word "Court," CAS is not a court, but an arbitral tribunal.[27] For any particular matter, the assigned arbitral panel consists of between one and three arbitrators.[28] The CAS Code's procedural rules and Swiss law combine to establish the procedural rules governing all CAS arbitrations.[29] These procedural rules facilitate a modicum of uniformity across CAS arbitrations handled by different arbitrators in different places at different times. Because CAS arbitrators selected to hear a matter have the authority to determine the relevance of proffered information,[30] CAS does not have formal rules with respect to the submission of evidence during arbitrations.[31] Unlike a court, CAS arbitral proceedings are closed to the public.[32]

[1] CAS Dispute Resolution

CAS panels hear disputes of all kinds in various contexts. CAS ordinary arbitration involves first instance contract and commercial disputes, including disputes: between athletes and their managers; regarding international broadcasting rights; and between

---

22. Court of Arbitration for Sport, Code of Sports-Related Arbitration, R27 (2020) [hereinafter CAS Code].

23. Matthew J. Mitten, *The Court of Arbitration for Sport and Its Global Jurisprudence: International Legal Pluralism in a World without National Boundaries,* 30 Ohio St. J. on Disp. Resol. 1, 9 (2014).

24. *Id.*

25. Mitten, *supra* note 23, at 10; CAS Code, *supra* note 22, at art. S4, S6, S14.

26. *See* CAS Code, *supra* note 22, at art. S6, S14, R29; *List of Arbitrators,* CAS, https://www.tas-cas.org/en/arbitration/liste-des-arbitres-liste-generale.html.

27. CAS Code, *supra* note 22, at art. S12 (stating that CAS panels have the responsibility of resolving disputes through arbitration and/or mediation).

28. *Id.* at art. S3.

29. *Id.* at art. R45.

30. *Id.* at art. R44.2.

31. *Id.* at art. R44.1. As such, legal disputes regarding procedure during CAS arbitrations sometimes arise. *Compare* Federal Tribunal Decision 4A_318/2020 of December 22, 2020 (overturning CAS's decision to ban Chinese swimmer, Sun Yang, for a doping violation because an arbitrator in the decision did not disclose the existence of his impartiality towards Yang and a Chinese tradition, which he had explicitly shared on social media), *with* Federal Tribunal Decision 4A_362/2013 and 4A_448/2013 (denying that the admission of an illegally obtained video recording in a CAS hearing violated a fundamental Swiss rule of procedure).

32. *See* CAS Code, *supra* note 22, at art. R43, R44.2.

NGBs and IFs.[33] Notably, there is no uniform body of substantive law that necessarily applies to all disputes. The parties can select the law that will govern resolution of a dispute.[34] If the parties cannot agree, Swiss law will govern.[35] When a dispute requires expedited attention in the days before and during the Olympic Games and other major international sporting events, the CAS Ad Hoc Division hears the matter.[36] CAS sends arbitrators to the events to perform this function. Matters referred to the Ad Hoc Division include eligibility determinations, doping disqualifications, and allegations that judges were biased in awarding points for performance — matters in which substantial prejudice would potentially come to bear if resolution were delayed.[37] The Olympic Charter (or the particular charter documents for the event at issue), together with private rules established by the National Olympic Committees or other organizations involved in the dispute, generally serve as the "law" the Ad Hoc Division draws upon in reaching its conclusions.[38] Generally, Ad Hoc Division determinations, which must be delivered in writing, are made within 24 hours.[39]

In addition to hearing first instance disputes, CAS hears appeals from determinations made by sports governing bodies, such as NGBs and IFs.[40] This occurs through the Ad Hoc Division if the international competition at issue is about to begin or is in progress and expedition is required. Otherwise, the CAS Appeals Division will hear the matter. In either case, the CAS panel's review is *de novo*.[41] Under the CAS Code, a CAS arbitration panel has "full power to review the facts and the law," and having done so, it "may issue a new decision which replaces the decision challenged or annuls the decision and refers the case back to the previous instance."[42]

D'Arcy v. Australian Olympic Committee[43] is illustrative. In that case, Nick D'Arcy, a member of the Australian National Swim Team, became intoxicated and engaged in a bar fight shortly after qualifying for the team.[44] When attempting to qualify for the team, D'Arcy had agreed to abide by the Australian Olympic Committee ("AOC") "Ethical Behaviour Bylaws," which required he not "engage or participate in conduct which, if publicly known, would be likely to bring him into disrepute or censure."[45] Finding that D'Arcy's violent conduct violated the "Ethical Behaviour Bylaws," the AOC Executive Body dismissed D'Arcy from the team.[46] D'Arcy appealed the decision

33. *History of the CAS, supra* note 16.
34. *Id.*
35. *Id.*
36. Arbitration Rules for the Olympic Games, art. 2, 5.
37. *Id.* at art. 1.
38. *Id.* at art. 17.
39. *Id.* at art. 18.
40. CAS Code, *supra* note 22, at art. R47.
41. *See* CAS Code, *supra* note 22, at art. R57
42. *Id.*
43. Australian Olympic Committee, Inc. v. D'Arcy, CAS 2008/A/1539, Arbitral Award, 119 (2008).
44. *Id.* at 139.
45. *Id.* at 122.
46. *Id.* at 119.

to CAS, where the AOC argued that CAS should employ a deferential standard of review that would require the CAS panel to "limit its review to whether the decision appealed against was obviously or self-evidently so unreasonable or perverse that it could be said to be irrational."[47] The CAS panel refused, noting that its duty is to make an "independent determination of whether the appellant's contentions are correct, not to limit itself to assessing the correctness of the 'award or decision' from which the appeal was brought."[48] Applying *de novo* review, the CAS panel upheld D'Arcy's dismissal from the team.[49]

Although CAS panels exercise *de novo* review, they do not generally question international sports governing body rules with respect to athlete eligibility,[50] as long as the sports governing body does not apply the rules in bad faith.[51] This is the case even if the rules grant the sports governing body substantial discretion. Consider *Bauer v. Austrian Olympic Committee and Austrian Ski Federation.*[52] In that case, Daniela Bauer, an Austrian freestyle skier, challenged her exclusion from the Austrian team that competed in the 2014 Winter Olympics in Sochi, Russia.[53] Although Bauer met the International Ski Federation qualification requirements, the Austrian Ski Federation ("ASF") recommended to the Austrian Olympic Committee ("AOC") that she not be placed on the team because her skill level was "not sufficient" for her to achieve a "positive result at the Olympics."[54] The AOC accepted the recommendation and did not select Bauer for the team. The CAS panel found for the AOC and the ASF.[55] The panel determined that the ASF's regulations granted the ASF significant subjective discretion in making recommendations for the Olympic team, and the panel refused to second guess that grant of discretion.[56] The panel did encourage the ASF to establish and publish clear, objective criteria with which to assess Olympic hopefuls going forward.[57] In the absence of such objective criteria, however, the panel concluded the ASF did not exercise its discretion in an arbitrary, unfair, or unrea-

---

47. *Id.* at 126.

48. *Id.* at 134.

49. *Id.* at 120.

50. *See, e.g.,* Arbitration CAS 2009/A/1768, Hansen v. FEI, 1, 49 (upholding a Fédération Equestre Internationale (FEI) decision on appeal stating, "[i]t is not for CAS to write the Rules of FEI."); Arbitration CAS ad hoc Division (O.G. Sydney 2000) 003, Miranda v. IOC, award of 13 Sept. 2000 in Court of Arbitration for Sport, CAS Awards — Sydney 2000, 29 (2000) (upholding decision by the Cuban Olympic Committee to use its discretion to disallow former national team athlete from competing for the nation to which the athlete immigrated).

51. Matthew J. Mitten & Timothy Davis, *Athlete Eligibility Requirements and Legal Issues 2.0, in* HANDBOOK ON INTERNATIONAL SPORTS LAW (James A. R. Nafziger & Ryan Gauthier, eds., Edward Elgar Publishing, 2d. ed. 2021); *See, e.g.,* Arbitration CAS 95/142, L. v. FINA, award of 14 Feb. 1996, in Vol. 1 DIGEST OF CAS AWARDS 1986–1998 225, 243–44 (Matthieu Reeb 2004) (stating that in exercising its authority, a sports governing body must not act in "bad faith").

52. Daniela Bauer v. Austrian Olympic Committee & Austrian Ski Federation, CAS OG 14/01, Arbitral Award, 1 (2014).

53. *Id.*

54. *Id.* at 6.

55. *Id.*

56. *Id.* at 5.

57. *Id.* at 10.

sonable manner and presented a legitimate sports performance justification for recommending Bauer's exclusion.[58] Had the criteria been ambiguous, rather than simply subjective, the CAS panel would likely have reached a different outcome in *Bauer*. CAS jurisprudence indicates ambiguous rules should be construed in the complaining athlete's favor.[59]

The illicit use of performance-enhancing drugs ("PEDs") is a major concern in international sports competition, and CAS has established the CAS Anti-Doping Division ("CAS ADD") to focus specifically on resolving disputes related to athletes' use of PEDs. The CAS ADD exists to hear first-instance anti-doping cases pursuant to a delegation of power from the IOC, the IFs for Olympic sports, and other sport entities that are signatories to the World Anti-Doping Code, discussed, *infra*.[60] The Division is empowered to determine whether a violation has been committed and to apply the appropriate sanction.[61]

To survive scrutiny in a CAS hearing, a sport governing body's rules regulating PEDs, like sports governing body eligibility rules, must be unambiguous and they must also provide athletes notice of prohibited conduct.[62] In addition, a sports governing body may only impose a penalty on an athlete who violates its doping rules if the penalty is authorized as a sanction for the violation in question.[63] Doping in international sport is addressed in greater detail, *infra*, in subsection [C] of this chapter.

[2] Precedential Value

Unlike appellate decisions in many judicial systems, including those in the United States, CAS decisions and arbitration awards have no precedential value.[64] Therefore, the impact of CAS decisions beyond the parties to a case is unclear. The combination

---

58. *Id.*

59. *See, e.g.*, Arbitration CAS ad hoc Division (O.G. Sydney 2000) 005, Perez v. IOC, award of 19 Sept. 2000, in COURT OF ARBITRATION FOR SPORT, CAS AWARDS — SYDNEY 2000, 53, 62 (2000) (CAS will resolve sports governing body eligibility rules in favor of the athlete "[i]f a text may be interpreted in two ways").

60. Arbitration Rules for the CAS Anti-Doping Division, A1; see *infra* note 94 and accompanying text.

61. *Id.*

62. *See, e.g.*, Arbitration CAS ad hoc Division (O.G. Nagano 1998) 002, R. v. IOC, award of 12 Feb. 1998 in Vol. 1 DIGEST OF CAS AWARDS 1986–1998 419 (Matthieu Reeb 2004) (agreeing with the sanctioned athlete that marijuana-related doping violation be overturned because the international skiing federation ("FIS") doping rules did not clearly prohibit marijuana use).

63. *See, e.g.*, USOC and Athletes v. IOC & IAAF, Arbitration CAS 2004/A/725, award of 20 July 2005 (determining that disqualification of a relay team's results post-race because one team member was ineligible to compete due to a doping violation was not an authorized sanction under the International Amateur Athletic Federation's rules); Arbitration CAS ad hoc Division (O.G. Salt Lake City 2002) 001, Prusis v. IOC, award of 5 Feb. 2002 in Vol. 3 DIGEST OF CAS AWARDS 2001–2003 573 (Matthieu Reeb 2004) (rejecting the IOC's extension of a bobsledder's suspension beyond the three months authorized by the International Bobsleigh and Tobogganing Federation because "an athlete has a legitimate expectation that, once he has completed the punishment imposed on him, he will be permitted to enter and participate in all competitions absent some new reason for refusing his entry.").

64. *See* Mitten, *supra* note 23, at 27.

of *de novo* review and non-binding precedent leaves CAS arbitrators with considerable discretion in rendering decisions. That said, in issuing their arbitration awards, CAS arbitrators generally try to avoid inconsistencies with previous CAS decisions.[65] Moreover, under Article R59 of the CAS Code "[b]efore the award is signed, it shall be transmitted to the CAS Director General"[66] who assesses it for form as well as unjustified inconsistencies with previous CAS decisions made "under the same or similar conditions."[67] So, while previous CAS decisions are not dispositive, they often serve as persuasive authority. Over the years, a substantial volume of CAS arbitral awards has been published so as to produce a body of international sports law, known as *lex sportiva*.[68] As the body of law continues to develop, its persuasive power will likely increase.

[3] Appeal from CAS Decisions

If a party is displeased with a CAS arbitration award, the party may appeal to the Swiss Federal Tribunal ("SFT"). The SFT has made clear that it "does not review whether the arbitration court applied the law, upon which it based its decision, correctly."[69] The grounds for SFT review are quite limited, and chances for success on appeal are extremely slim.[70] Under Swiss law, appeals can only be granted for one or more of the following reasons:

1) The appealing party was effectively denied the right to be heard before the arbitral tribunal;

2) The arbitral panel was constituted irregularly;

3) The arbitral panel lacked impartiality;

4) The arbitral panel erred in finding that it had jurisdiction over the matter decided;

5) The arbitral panel's award exceeded its authority as submitted to it; and

6) The panel's award contravened public policy.[71]

Due in part to the limited grounds upon which to file an appeal with the SFT, few CAS arbitration awards are appealed. And of the awards that are ultimately appealed, the appeals are rarely successful. The *Caster Semenya* case, discussed in Chapter 5 of this book, is illustrative. In that case, Semanya, the 800-meter track

---

65. *See* Mitten, *supra* note 23, at 27–28; Arbitration CAS 2004/A/628, IAAF v. USA Track and Field & Jerome Young, award of 28 June 2004 (stating that "a CAS Panel will obviously try, if the evidence permits, to come to the same conclusion on matters of law as a previous CAS Panel.").

66. CAS Code, *supra* note 22, at art. R59.

67. Despina Mavromati & Matthieu Reeb, The Code of the Court of Arbitration for Sport — Commentary, Cases, and Materials 367 (Wolters Kluwer Int'l 2015).

68. *See generally* James A.R. Nafziger, International Sports Law 48–61 (2d. ed 2004).

69. Azerbaijan Field Hockey Federation. v. Fédération Internationale de Hockey, 4A_424/2008 (1st Civil Ct., 22 January 2009) at 6.

70. Article 190(2) of Swiss Private International Law Act ("PILA").

71. *Id.*

and field champion at the 2012 and 2016 Olympic Games, challenged a CAS award that upheld the World Athletics' Eligibility Regulations for the Female Classification.[72] Under the award, Semanya, who has hypoandrogenism, was prohibited from competing in the 800 meters in international competition unless she medically suppressed her hormone production.[73] In granting the award, CAS acknowledged that the World Athletics regulations were discriminatory but concluded the discrimination was necessary to ensure an even playing field for female competitors.[74] Semenya argued before the SFT that the award contravened public policy.[75] Specifically, she argued that the regulations "violate essential and widely recognized public policy values, including the prohibition against discrimination, the right to physical integrity, the right to economic freedom, and respect for human dignity."[76] The SFT did not dispute that public policy was implicated, but it concluded the CAS award did not contravene it. The SFT wrote that "it is above all up to the sports federations to determine to what extent a particular physical advantage is likely to distort competition and, if necessary, to introduce legally admissible eligibility rules to remedy this state of affairs."[77] As such, the SFT rejected Semenya's appeal. Even identifiable mistakes on the part of the CAS arbitration panel in the *Semenya* case would not likely have produced a different outcome. The SFT has held that "the manifestly wrong application of a rule of law or the obviously incorrect finding of a point of fact is still not sufficient to justify revocation for breach of public policy of an award made in international arbitration proceedings."[78]

Although CAS decisions are rarely successfully appealed to the SFT, the SFT has opposed attempts to close the appellate path. In 2007, in *Canas v. ATP Tour*,[79] the SFT declined to enforce an Association of Tennis Professionals ("ATP") Tour contractual clause stating, "[t]he decision of CAS shall be final and binding on all parties and no right of appeal will lie from the CAS decision."[80] In that case, the ATP found that the urine sample Argentinean tennis player Guillermo Canas provided as a part of ATP drug testing protocols contained a prohibited substance and suspended him for two years.[81] CAS upheld the suspension but reduced its length to 15 months.[82] Canas then petitioned the SFT to annul the award on grounds that "both his own

---

72. Caster Semenya v. Athletics South Africa & International Association of Athletics Federations (IAAF), Executive Summary, Court of Arbitration and Sport, 1, 1–2 (Jan. 5, 2019, 15:42).

73. *Id.*

74. *Id.* at 3–4.

75. *Id.* at 3.

76. Associated Press, *Semenya Appeals Against Testosterone Ruling*, ESPN (May. 29, 2019).

77. Bundesgericht [BGer] [Federal Supreme Court] Aug. 25, 2020, 4A_248/2019 4A_398/2019 (Switz.); Olympic Channel, *Caster Semenya loses Swiss Supreme Court appeal*, OLYMPICS (Sep. 8, 2020), https://olympics.com/en/news/caster-semenya-loses-swiss-supreme-court-appeal-cas-defeat.

78. N., J., Y., W. v. FINA, 5P.83/1999 (2d Civil Court, Mar. 31, 1999) at 779.

79. 4P.172/2006, 1 (1st Civ. Law Ct., Mar. 22, 2007).

80. *Id.*

81. *Id.* at 2.

82. *Id.*

right to a fair hearing and Swiss public policy had been violated."[83] The ATP responded that "the appeal was inadmissible" because of the contractual waiver of the right to appeal.[84] The SFT rejected the ATP's argument.[85] It emphasized the importance of athletes having the right to appeal CAS awards to "the supreme judicial authority of the state in which the arbitral tribunal is domiciled" and went on to dispose of the case.[86]

[C] The World Anti-Doping Agency

It is generally agreed that the use of PEDs threatens the integrity of sport. Doping scandals involving decorated and then disgraced world-class athletes — such as American cyclist Lance Armstrong and Chinese swimmer Sun Yang — are prime examples. To prevent such scandals and protect the integrity of sport, institutions such as the IOC have established mechanisms that seek to eliminate or at least reduce the prevalence of PED use. To assist in accomplishing this goal, WADA was founded in 1999.[87] Its mission is to create and maintain uniformity in PED testing and enforcement.[88] Although initially a product of the IOC, WADA now extends beyond the Olympic Movement, touching all manner of sports around the globe.[89]

Prior to WADA's existence, efforts to stymie the use of PEDs were piecemeal as different organizations and nations imposed different testing standards and eligibility thresholds.[90] Most nations accept WADA's authority and have established a national organization responsible for PED testing in keeping with WADA's rules.[91] The United States Anti-Doping Agency ("USADA") fulfills this function in the United States.[92] WADA's rules are set out in the WADA Code ("WADC"), first established in 2003 and revised periodically, most recently in 2021.[93] The WADC is extensive, providing detailed guidance for national anti-doping agencies. The WADC sets forth which substances are banned, the manner in which athletes should be tested, and the appropriate punishments for a PED violation.[94]

---

83. *Id.* at 3.

84. *Id.*

85. *Id.*

86. *Id.* at 9. The *Canas* case is a rare example of a successful CAS appeal to the SFT. The SFT found that "the right to a fair hearing was infringed by CAS" and annulled the award. *Id.* at 13.

87. Matthew Hard, *Caught in the Net: Athletes' Rights and the World Anti-Doping Agency*, 19 S. CAL. INTERDISC. L.J. 533, 541–42 (2010).

88. *Who We Are*, WORLD ANTI-DOPING AGENCY, https://www.wada-ama.org/en/who-we-are.

89. *Id.*

90. *See id.* at 538 (describing the fragmented nature and high variability of anti-doping policy).

91. *Code Signatories*, WORLD ANTI-DOPING AGENCY, https://www.wada-ama.org/en/code-signatories (listing sports organizations that have accepted the Code).

92. 21 U.S.C. § 2001(b)(1).

93. *The Code*, WORLD ANTI-DOPING AGENCY, https://www.wada-ama.org/en/what-we-do/the-code (describing the history of the Code).

94. *See generally* World Anti-Doping Code (2021) [hereinafter WADC].

A controversial feature of the WADC is its strict liability posture. Under the WADC, an athlete's intent is irrelevant to a determination of guilt. If an athlete's urine or blood test reveals the presence of a banned substance in an amount above the WADC-established threshold, the athlete has committed a violation.[95] No claim of accident or mistake will avoid a finding that the athlete committed a doping violation.[96] This has proven frustrating to athletes who have argued that a compound in food, medicine, or some other consumable — rather than purposeful use of a banned substance — triggered a positive test.[97] Although the standard is seemingly harsh, the theory is that anything less than a strict liability standard would be insufficient to control what at times has been rampant PED use in the sports world.[98]

An athlete's intent, however, may be relevant to the sanction imposed for the violation.[99] Under Article 10.2 of the WADC, the presumed penalty for a doping violation is a four-year period of ineligibility.[100] Mitigating circumstances may, however, reduce or even eliminate the period of ineligibility.[101]

- WADC Article 10.5 states that if an athlete establishes "No Fault or Negligence, then the otherwise applicable period of Ineligibility shall be eliminated."[102]

- WADC Article 10.6 states that if an athlete establishes "No *Significant* Fault or Negligence, then the period of Ineligibility shall be, at a minimum, a reprimand and no period of ineligibility, and at a maximum, two years of ineligibility, depending on the [athlete's] degree of Fault."[103]

CAS arbitrators who hear doping disputes attempt to determine whether an athlete can establish "no fault or negligence" or "no significant fault or negligence" with respect to a positive PED test. A finding of "no fault or negligence" and an accompanying elimination of the presumed ineligibility period, imposes a burden on the athlete to show they "did not know or suspect, and could not reasonably have known or suspected even with the exercise of utmost caution" that the athlete committed an anti-doping violation.[104]

CAS made such a finding in *Pobydeonostev v. IIHF*,[105] a case in which the International Ice Hockey Federation ("IIHF") suspended Ukrainian ice hockey player Alexander Pobydeonostev for two years after he tested positive for norandrosterone,

---

95. *Id.* at art. 2.1.

96. *Id.*

97. *See, e.g.,* Hard, *supra* note 87, at 553 (providing examples of athletes who unknowingly ingested supplements).

98. *Id.* at 552.

99. WADC, *supra* note 94, at art. 10.2.

100. *Id.*

101. *Id.*

102. *Id.* at art. 10.5.

103. *Id.* at art. 10.6.

104. *Id.* at 172.

105. Pobydeonostev v. IIHF, CAS 2005/A/990, Arbitral Award, 1 (2005).

a prohibited substance, during the 2005 IIHF Senior Ice Hockey Championship.[106] Pobydeonostev appealed the suspension to CAS.[107] In his appeal, he noted that after suffering a severe in-game injury a month earlier, he underwent emergency surgery, during which he was treated with a drug called Nandrolone while under anesthesia.[108] He further noted that the Nandrolone, unbeknownst to him, contained the banned substance that later triggered his positive test.[109] Moreover, Pobydeonostev explained in his submission to the CAS panel that when he arrived at the hospital, "he was in a very bad physical and mental condition which made it impossible for him to monitor or even ask questions about the treatment which was going to be applied."[110] Compounding matters, the team physician failed to accompany Pobydeonostev to the hospital (which resulted in the physician's termination), and was therefore not present to monitor Pobydeonostev's treatment.[111] The CAS panel found that under these circumstances, Pobydeonostev "had no reason to suspect that he was treated with a [banned] substance."[112] Consequently, it concluded that he "was without fault or negligence" with respect to the substance's presence in his system, and it annulled the IIHF's imposed suspension.[113]

A finding of "no significant fault or negligence" requires a showing that the athlete's "fault or negligence, when viewed in the totality of the circumstances ... was not significant in relationship" to the anti-doping rule violation.[114] The less significant the fault or negligence, the lighter the penalty. While a "no significant fault or negligence" determination means the ineligibility period cannot exceed two years, it can be reduced to any length shorter than that — and even replaced with a simple reprimand, as set forth in Article 10.6.[115]

Nado Italia v. Errani and ITF,[116] illustrates CAS's "no significant fault or negligence" analysis, which is deeply fact-intensive.[117] That case involved Italian tennis player Sara Errani, who tested positive for a prohibited substance in February 2017 while

---

106. *Id.* at 2.
107. *Id.*
108. *Id.*
109. *Id.*
110. *Id.*
111. *Id.*
112. *Id.* at 6.
113. *Id.* Although the paradigmatic "no fault or negligence" case involves emergency medical treatment, CAS has found that athletes have established no fault of negligence in other circumstances. For instance, in *ITF and WADA v. Gasquet*, CAS 2009/A/1926 & 1930, a CAS panel found that a French tennis player, Richard Gasquet, was without "fault or negligence" for a positive test that the panel concluded "more likely than not" resulted from kissing a previously unknown woman in a nightclub. The CAS panel reasoned that "even if [Gasquet] exercised the utmost caution, he could not have been aware of the consequences of kissing a girl who he had met in a totally unsuspicious environment." *Id.* at 21.
114. WADC, *supra* note 94, at 172.
115. *Id.* at art. 10.6.
116. National Anti-Doping Organisation (Nado) Italia v. Sara Errani and ITF, CAS 2017/A/5302, Arbitral Award, 1 (2017).
117. *Id.* at 10.

staying at her parents' home a day after competing in the Federation Cup.[118] Errani did not dispute the test results, but denied intentionally ingesting anything containing the substance. She argued that her mother's medication must have fallen into food her mother was cooking and that she must have ingested the medication, which contained the prohibited substance, along with her meal.[119] The International Tennis Federation referred the matter to an Independent Tribunal, which in August of 2017 found Errani was at fault, but that her fault was "at the lower end of the scale."[120] Pursuant to that finding, the ITF suspended Errani for two months and disqualified all of her results between February 16 and June 7, 2017 (the date on which the ITF submitted that testing indicated the prohibited substance was no longer in Errani's system).[121] Both Errani and Nado Italia, the Italian Anti-Doping Organization, appealed to CAS.[122] Errani challenged the disqualification of her results, and Nado Italia challenged the suspension length, asserting that the suspension length should have been two years rather than two months.[123] Each party made arguments as to degree of fault.[124] Nado Italia noted that an "express doping warning" was printed on Errani's mother's medicine package and questioned the likelihood of "a single pill flying into the filling of a single tortellino."[125] Errani asserted that her mother kept her medicine on the counter where she cooked to remind her to take it daily and that on past occasions when taking her medicine, her mother had accidentally dispensed more than one pill and dropped it onto the counter.[126]

Considering all of the facts, the CAS panel concluded that Errani bore "no significant fault or negligence" with respect to ingestion of the prohibited substance.[127] It found that Errani established, "by a balance of probability, but only just, that the source of letrozole found in her sample was the Femara medication of her mother that found its way into the family meal."[128] Still, it held Errani to an obligation to control her environment as both an objective and subjective matter.[129] The panel explained, "the objective element relates to what standard of care could have been expected from a reasonable person in the athlete's situation while the subjective element describes what could have been expected from that particular athlete, in the light of [her] particular capacities."[130] Finding that Errani had failed to sufficiently control her environment, the panel concluded she bore "light" fault.[131] Having done so, it

---

118. *Id.* at 9.
119. *Id.*
120. *Id.* at 3.
121. *Id.* at 4.
122. *Id.*
123. *Id.* at 8.
124. *Id.*
125. *Id.*
126. *Id.* at 9.
127. *Id.* at 17.
128. *Id.* at 40.
129. *Id.* at 35.
130. *Id.* at 11.
131. *Id.* at 40.

upheld the disqualification.[132] It also upheld the suspension, but determined it should last for ten months, an increase from the initial two months, but short of the maximum two years.[133]

The responsibility for administering actual drug tests falls not upon WADA but upon the organization charged with overseeing each nation's anti-doping efforts.[134] The WADA regime is, therefore, only as strong as the various national anti-doping programs' commitment to eliminating the use of PEDs. For this reason, global public confidence in anti-doping efforts suffered a major blow in advance of the 2016 Rio Olympic Summer Games when the Russia Anti-Doping Agency ("RUSADA") was revealed to have coordinated and enabled athlete doping.[135] Years of investigation followed, dozens of Russian athletes were stripped of medals, and in December 2019, WADA banned Russia from participating in major international sporting events for a period of four years (later reduced to two years).[136] Still, the scandal underscored the importance of strong, non-corrupt, national anti-doping bodies in the effort to stymie PED use in sport and the damage to the integrity of sports that can result from a corrupt anti-doping agency.

Although, as noted above, WADA and the WADC have great reach throughout sport, one powerful collection of sports entities has opted out. America's major professional sports leagues, such as the NFL, the NBA, and MLB, do not accept WADA's authority and are not signatories to the WADC, choosing to employ their own anti-doping approaches as negotiated with their players' unions.[137] Former WADA president Craig Reedie, before his term concluded at the end of 2019, forcefully criticized the leagues for their non-participation.[138] He urged "harmonization with the rest of the world," but those leagues remain outside of WADA's ambit.[139]

§ 3.03 Scope of Olympic Governing Body Authority in the United States

Although the USOPC is responsible for coordinating and supervising the United States' participation in the Olympics, it does not have unfettered authority.[140] Similarly,

---

132. *Id.*

133. *Id.*

134. *Id.* at art. 5.2.

135. *WADA Welcomes Independent Commission's Report into Widespread Doping in Sport,* WORLD ANTI-DOPING AGENCY, https://www.wada-ama.org/en/media/news/2015-11/wada-welcomes-independent-commissions-report-into-widespread-doping-in-sport.

136. Tariq Panja, *Russia's Doping Ban Is Cut to a Largely Symbolic Two Years,* NY TIMES (Dec. 17, 2020), https://www.nytimes.com/2020/12/17/sports/olympics/russia-doping-wada.html.

137. Hard, *supra* note 87, at 542.

138. Rob Harris, *WADA President Turns Criticism to U.S. Sports Leagues,* ASSOCIATED PRESS (Nov. 1, 2018), https://apnews.com/article/5451ac4813984b9f84009279817c2f4c.

139. *Id.*

140. 36 U.S.C. § 220505(c).

the authority of the NGBs is limited.[141] The Ted Stevens Olympic and Amateur Sports Act (Amateur Sports Act) cordons that authority by articulating the rights to which athletes are entitled as they strive to compete for the United States in international competition.[142]

[A] The Amateur Sports Act

In 1978, the United States Congress passed the Amateur Sports Act.[143] The Amateur Sports Act creates the charter for the USOC.[144] The USOC creates the charters for U.S. NGBs in the various sports.[145] And the NGBs create the rules and eligibility criteria for selecting members of the United States Olympic Team.[146] The Amateur Sports Act, therefore, frames the entire system, and athletes aggrieved by the system's operation have utilized the Act in seeking recourse.

[1] Athlete Recourse

The Amateur Sports Act empowers athletes in several ways. As a structural matter, it requires that athletes who currently represent the United States in athletic competition or who have done so within the past ten years must comprise 20 percent of any NGB's governing board.[147] In addition, it affords athletes the right to appeal with respect to adverse eligibility determinations.[148] Further, to ensure athletes are aware of, and able to effectuate, their rights, the Act created an Ombudsman's Office to provide athletes independent counsel.[149] The scope of the Amateur Sports Act's athlete protections has expanded since its passage in 1978 — particularly through a 1998 revision to the statute — but athletes have turned to it for support since its inception.[150]

[a] Athlete Recourse Regarding United States
Participation in International Competition

Importantly, the Amateur Sports Act does not guarantee athletes the right to represent the United States in international athletic competition. *DeFrantz v. U.S. Olympic Committee*,[151] decided in 1980, illustrates the limited protections the Amateur Sports

141. *See* 36 U.S.C. § 220523.
142. *See* 36 U.S.C. §§ 220501–220543.
143. *See* Ted Stevens Olympic and Amateur Sports Act of 1978 (codified at 36 U.S.C. §§ 220501–220543).
144. 36 U.S.C. § 220502(a).
145. *Id.* at § 220505(c).
146. *Id.* at §§ 220523–220524.
147. *Id.* at § 220522(11).
148. *Id.* at § 220509(b).
149. *Id.* at § 220509(b).
150. *See* Olympic and Amateur Sports Act Amendments of 1998, S. Rep. No. 105-325.
151. 492 F. Supp. 1181 (D. D.C. 1980).

Act provides, as well as the USOC's power vis-a-vis athletes. In that case, 25 American athletes (one of whom, Anita DeFrantz, was also a member of the USOC's Executive Board (the USOPC was then called the USOC)) unsuccessfully challenged the USOC's decision to refrain from sending a team to compete in that summer's Olympic Games in Moscow.[152]

The USOC decided not to send a delegation after the Soviet Union invaded Afghanistan and U.S. President Jimmy Carter condemned the aggression and "strenuously urged" an Olympic boycott.[153] The Carter administration felt American participation in the Games "would be taken by the Soviets as evidence that their invasion had faded from memory or was not a matter of great consequence or concern to [the United States]."[154] The United States House of Representatives and the United States Senate expressed agreement with the administration, voting in favor of resolutions to boycott the Games.[155] Notwithstanding the strong political sentiment opposing participation, many athletes wanted to compete, complaining that otherwise they would "lose a once-in-a-lifetime opportunity to participate in the Olympic Games, and the honor and prestige that such participation affords."[156] The USOC was unmoved, and the athletes sued under the Amateur Sports Act, arguing that the Act does not authorize the USOC to refrain from sending a team to the Olympics for non-sports related reasons and that not sending the team violated the athletes' constitutional rights to liberty, self-expression, personal autonomy, and privacy.[157]

The court found for the USOC in a decision that established the balance of power between the governing body and athletes. The court determined first that the USOC has the authority to decide against sending athletes into international competition even if the reasons are unrelated to sports.[158] It further determined that athletes do not have a right to participate in the Olympic Games and that the USOC's decision not to send a delegation to the Games did not violate athletes' constitutional rights.[159] The court wrote, "Ordinarily, talent alone has determined whether an American would have the privilege of participating in the Olympics. This year, unexpectedly, things are different."[160] That difference — the geo-political tumult — was a key factor in the athletes' lawsuit being unsuccessful. And if, hypothetically, the 2020 Tokyo summer Olympic Games had been held in 2020 (rather than postponed to 2021), but the USOPC had declined to send a team for national public health reasons related

152. DeFrantz v. U.S. Olympic Comm., 492 F. Supp. 1181 (D. D.C. 1980).
153. *Id.* at 1184–85.
154. *Id.* at 1184.
155. *Id.*
156. *Id.* at 1186.
157. *Id.* at 1185.
158. *Id.* at 1189.
159. *Id.* at 1194.
160. *Id.* at 1195.

to COVID-19, any American athlete's suit against the USOPC would have likely been unsuccessful. The Amateur Sports Act simply does not bestow upon athletes a right to engage in international athletic competition.[161]

[b] Athlete Recourse Regarding Selection for Team Membership

With respect to team selection—the decision to place one athlete rather than another on a United States team slated for international competition—the Amateur Sports Act provides athletes robust process.[162] NGBs determine which athletes are selected to participate on a U.S. national team, but inevitably, some athletes are aggrieved when left off of a team. The Amateur Sports Act requires that the USOPC put in place a procedure to ensure the "swift and equitable resolution" of such disputes.[163]

Section 9 of the USOPC Bylaws establishes that an aggrieved athlete must file a formal complaint with the USOPC stating "the factual and legal basis upon which the claimant alleges that his or her opportunity to participate has been denied."[164] Once the complaint is filed, a USOPC designee and an athlete's ombudsperson will review the complaint and pursue a resolution satisfactory to all parties.[165] If the athlete is dissatisfied with the resolution, the athlete may file a claim for "final and binding arbitration."[166] While legal representation is not required, both the athlete and the NGB typically choose to have lawyers represent them in arbitration proceedings. The arbitrator is required to provide a reasoned written decision which, in the absence of extraordinary circumstances, is non-reviewable.[167]

The requirement that an athlete establish a "factual and legal basis" for disputing exclusion from a team prevents the overturning of all but the most objectively unfair

---

161. The same holds true for participation in domestic competitions operated under the auspices of the USOPC, such as the National Track and Field Championships. Consider *Slaney v. Int'l Amateur Athletic Union*, 244 F.3d 580 (7th Cir. 2001), which involved former world-class runner Mary Decker Slaney's failed lawsuit against the USOPC and the International Amateur Athletic Union (IAAF), now known as World Athletics. Slaney sued after she was found to have impermissibly used performance enhancing drugs and was suspended from competition. The district court concluded it had no jurisdiction to entertain Slaney's suit, and the Seventh Circuit affirmed, finding that Slaney's claims "were preempted by Congress's grant of exclusive authority [in the Amateur Sports Act] to the USOC to determine the eligibility of American athletes." *Id.* at 601.

162. 36 U.S.C. § 220522(4)(b).

163. *Id.* at § 220509(a).

164. Bylaws of the United States Olympic & Paralympic Committee, § 9.3 (2021) [hereinafter USOPC Bylaws].

165. *Id.* § 9.6.

166. *Id.* § 9.7.

167. *Id.* § 9.7; *see also* Pliuskaitis v. U.S.A. Swimming, Inc., 243 F. Supp. 3d 1217, 1225 (D. Utah 2017), *aff'd*, 720 Fed. Appx. 481 (10th Cir. 2018) (explaining that an association clearly breaking its own rules, which results in imminent and irreparable harm to the plaintiff, constitutes "extraordinary circumstances").

omissions.[168] An omitted soccer midfielder, for instance, who claims she is simply better than a selected midfielder will almost surely be unsuccessful. This would be the likely outcome even if the player documents her dominance on the field. Coaches and others who make subjective roster decisions are afforded considerable deference. An athlete would have a better chance of success where the facts demonstrate an objective failure by a decision maker to comply with established selection criteria. Such a circumstance arose when a judoka athlete, Alex Hyatt, placed second in her weight division at the United States qualifying event for the 2014 International Judo Federation Junior World Championships.[169] Under competition rules, only the first place finisher in each weight division qualified for the USA Judo National Team, meaning Hyatt did not qualify.[170] Hyatt, however, filed a grievance with USA Judo (the Judo NGB).[171] She alleged that the winner was given an impermissible amount of time to meet the weight threshold prior to the match and that USA Judo should have consequently disqualified her, giving Hyatt first place.[172] USA Judo denied the grievance.[173] Hyatt then filed a Section 9 Complaint with the USOPC challenging the denial, which was similarly unsuccessful.[174] Arbitration followed, and the arbitrator found for Hyatt, determining that USA Judo breached its "approved and published Athlete Selection Procedures" by extending the period of time the first-place winner had to get her weight under the threshold.[175] As such, the arbitrator ordered that Hyatt, rather than the first place winner, be appointed to the United States Junior World Team scheduled to compete in the World Championships.[176] The other grounds for such an order are an NGB's inconsistent application of standards to similarly situated athletes, bad faith or bias, and violation of federal or state law.[177]

[2] Right to Use the Name "Olympics"

The Amateur Sports Act gives the USOPC the exclusive right to leverage the name "Olympics" in the United States in obtaining sponsorships and in other regards.[178] As such, the USOPC "may authorize contributors and suppliers of goods or services to use the [name 'Olympics'] ... to advertise that the contributions, goods, or services were" used by the United States Olympic team.[179] Notwithstanding its exclusive right,

---

168. USOPC Bylaws, *supra* note 164, at § 9.3(b).
169. *See, e.g.,* Hyatt v. U.S. Judo, Inc., AAA Case Number: 01-14-0000-7635 (2014).
170. *Id.* at 2.
171. *Id.* at 8.
172. *Id.*
173. *Id.* at 9.
174. *Id.*
175. *Id.* at 10.
176. *Id.* at 12.
177. *See* MATTHEW J. MITTEN, TIMOTHY DAVIS, N. JEREMI DURU & BARBARA OSBORNE, SPORTS LAW AND REGULATION: CASES, MATERIALS, AND PROBLEMS 266–73 (5th ed. 2020).
178. 36 U.S.C. § 220506(a)(4).
179. *Id.* at § 220506(b).

the USOPC sometimes permits other entities to leverage the name "Olympics" as well. For instance, the USOPC has granted such permission to the Special Olympics — a multi-event athletic completion for individuals with intellectual disabilities.[180] In other cases, however, the USOPC has enforced its authority to limit use of the name. It did so in 2011 when it threatened legal action against Henry Brooks, a Maine resident and business owner, who organized an event in Hebron, Maine that was titled the "Redneck Olympics."[181] The event, which attracted thousands of attendees, engaged participants in several competitions, including "a greased watermelon haul, a wife-carrying race, toilet seat horseshoes, and bobbing for pig's feet."[182] The Amateur Sports Act's goal in granting the USOPC the exclusive right to use "Olympics" within the U.S. is to maintain the name's "extraordinary and unique" mystique.[183] As the USOPC asserted in its cease-and-desist letter to Brooks, otherwise, "the Olympic Games might end up as just another sporting competition."[184] The USOPC argued that Brooks' use of "Olympics" was particularly damaging because of the association it created. As the USOPC stated, "we believe using the name 'Redneck Olympics' for a competition that involves toilet-seat horseshoes and bobbing for pigs' feet tends to denigrate the true nature of the Olympic Games."[185] Brooks ultimately relented and ceased to use "Olympics" in conjunction with his event.[186]

Although the Amateur Sports Act grants authority to the USOPC to control the use of "Olympics," it does not give it authority over the concept of a summer or winter multi-event championship or the names "Summer Games" and "Winter Games." Consequently, the USOPC has not been able to challenge organizers of a similar event held in East Dublin, Georgia called the "Summer Redneck Games." The Georgia event features a ceremonial pseudo-Olympic torch and involves many of the same competitions featured in the "Redneck Olympics," but its omission of the word "Olympics" in its name has spared its organizers legal scrutiny.[187]

---

180. *A Joyful New Movement Gains Momentum*, SPECIAL OLYMPICS, https://www.specialolympics.org/about/history/a-joyful-new-movement-gains-momentum?locale=en.

181. Matt Brooks, *Redneck Olympics under Fire from U.S. Olympic Committee*, WASH. POST (Aug. 10, 2011), https://www.washingtonpost.com/blogs/early-lead/post/redneck-olympics-under-fire-from-us-olympic-committee/2011/08/10/gIQAnfS16I_blog.html.

182. Staci Zaretsky, *The 'Redneck Olympics' Try to Jump the Hurdle of Law*, ABOVE THE LAW (Aug. 10, 2011), https://abovethelaw.com/2011/08/the-redneck-olympics-try-to-jump-the-hurdle-of-law/.

183. Tony Reaves, *U.S. Olympics Committee: Redneck Olympics Disrespects Athletes*, SUN J. (Aug. 16, 2011), https://www.sunjournal.com/2011/08/16/us-olympics-committee-redneck-olympics-disrespects-athletes/#.

184. *Id.*

185. *Id.*

186. Tony Reaves, *Redneck Blank Back for Third Year*, BANGORDAILYNEWS.COM (Apr. 16, 2013), https://bangordailynews.com/2013/04/16/sports/redneck-blank-back-for-third-year/. The USOPC has exercised authority over use of the name "Olympics" in other instances, filing lawsuits to prevent its unauthorized use. *See, e.g.,* San Francisco Arts & Athletics v. U.S. Olympic Comm., 483 U.S. 522 (1987).

187. Brooks, *supra* note 181.

[B] United States Center for Safe Sport

In 2018, Congress passed the Protecting Young Victims from Sexual Abuse and Safe Sport Authorization Act ("Safe Sport Act"), which established the United States Center for Safe Sport (the "Center") and charged it with creating national policies, procedures, and best practices "to prevent the emotional, physical, and sexual abuse of amateur athletes."[188] Importantly, the Center is an independent body, overseeing, rather than reporting to, the USOPC.[189] It has exclusive authority to investigate and respond to allegations of sexual misconduct, harassment, and abuse within the USOPC, NGBs, and other related organizations.[190]

The legislation was spurred by the discovery that former USA Gymnastics ("USAG") physician, Larry Nasser, had sexually abused hundreds of athletes over two decades and that both the USOPC and USAG, the gymnastics NGB, had failed to stop the abuse. The USOPC insisted it "did the right thing at every turn" with respect to addressing the abuse, and USAG insisted it "acted without hesitation," but Congress was convinced greater oversight was necessary.[191]

Prior to passage of the Safe Sport Act, the USOPC and the USAG routinely handled allegations of sexual abuse internally without ever referring them to the criminal justice system. Under the Safe Sport Act, however, such allegations must be reported to law enforcement within 24 hours.[192] In addition to creating the reporting mandate, the Safe Sport Act established strict protocols for sports organizations' internal investigation processes. The protocols require that an allegation of sexual assault triggers an arbitration procedure to "resolve [the] allegation[] of sexual abuse."[193] To protect the alleged victim and other athletes from sexual abuse, the accused may be suspended on an interim basis while the allegation is being resolved.[194] An accused, however, has the right to challenge the interim suspension, which an arbitrator can overturn if the arbitrator deems it not necessary to safeguard the health, safety, or well-being of other athletes.[195]

---

188. *The Safe Sport Act,* U.S. CENTER FOR SAFE SPORT, https://uscenterforsafesport.org/about/safesport-act/; *see also* 36 U.S.C. § 220541(a)(1) (listing the duties of the U.S. Center for Safe Sport).

189. 36 U.S.C. § 220541(a)(1)(A)–(B).

190. *Id.*

191. Will Hobson, *USOC, USA Gymnastics Did Not Protect Athletes After Larry Nassar Complaints, Report Shows,* WASH. POST (Dec. 10, 2018, 6:17 PM), https://www.washingtonpost.com/sports/olympics/usoc-usa-gymnastics-did-not-protect-athletes-from-larry-nassar-report-shows/2018/12/10/5f3fc2fa-fcb7-11e8-862a-b6a6f3ce8199_story.html; *Statement from USA Gymnastics Board Chairman Paul Parilla and CEO Steve Penny,* USA GYMNASTICS (Feb. 19, 2017), https://usagym.org/pages/post.html?PostID=19765&prog=h.

192. 36 U.S.C. § 220505(d)(1)(A); 36 U.S.C, § 220542(a)(2)(A); *see also* Victims of Child Abuse Act of 1990 § 226, 34 U.S.C. 20341 (defining "immediately" as within 24 hours).

193. 36 U.S.C. § 220541(c)(1).

194. *See* 36 U.S.C. § 220542(b).

195. U.S. Center for Safe Sport, Safe Sport Code, XII(A)(4), 28 (2019).

§ 3.04 International Athletes in American Sports Leagues

[A] Agreements between Leagues

Many of the sports popular in the United States are also popular elsewhere in the world, and competitive leagues featuring these sports exist internationally. In some sports, like soccer, many of those other leagues are generally regarded as stronger than the premier American domestic league (Major League Soccer).[196] In other sports, such as baseball and basketball, the premier American domestic leagues (Major League Baseball and the National Basketball Association, respectively) are considered dominant.[197] Consequently, non-American athletes sometimes seek to leave sports leagues in their countries to play in the United States. In some cases, such moves trigger substantial processes and legal issues that involve more than an athlete leaving one club to play with another.

The "posting" agreement that binds MLB and Japan's Nippon Professional Baseball ("NPB") illustrates the legal processes and issues that arise when a player on an NPB team wants to play on a MLB team. Under NPB rules, a player becomes a free agent after accruing nine years of service with an NPB club.[198] This restriction on player mobility gives NPB considerable power over players who desire to play in MLB. Therefore, MLB clubs desiring to sign NPB players must pay a steep price.

Assume that an NPB player wants to play in MLB; under the posting system, the player's NPB club may post the player, between November 1 and December 5,[199] by notifying the MLB Commissioner's Office of the player's availability.[200] The Commissioner's Office then alerts MLB clubs of the posting.[201] Any MLB club that wants to sign the player must pay the player's NPB club a handsome sum for the privilege of negotiating with the player.[202] The amount of that fee depends on the nature of the deal ultimately struck between the player and the MLB club. For instance, if the MLB club signs the player to a contract with guaranteed compensation of $25 million

---

196. *See* Joe Tansey, *Statistically Ranking the World's Top 10 Football Leagues,* BLEACHER REPORT (Jan. 14, 2014), https://bleacherreport.com/articles/1922780-statistically-ranking-the-worlds-top-10-football-leagues (ranking Major League Soccer as the tenth best soccer league in the world based on various statistics).

197. *See The 5 Most Important Baseball Leagues Around the Globe,* BASEBALL IN GREECE (Oct. 13, 2020), https://baseballgreece.com/the-5-most-important-baseball-leagues-around-the-globe/; *Basketball Leagues,* THE FIRST BASKET, https://www.thefirstbasket.com/basketball-leagues/.

198. *Japanese Posting System,* MLB, https://www.mlb.com/glossary/transactions/japanese-posting-system.

199. *Id.*

200. Keiji Kawai & Matt Nichol, *Labor in Nippon Professional Baseball and the Future of Player Transfers to Major League Baseball,* 25 MARQ. SPORTS L. REV. 491, 502 (2015).

201. *Id.*

202. *Id.* at 503.

or less, the MLB club must pay the NPB club the equivalent of twenty percent of the contract's total guaranteed value.[203] More expensive guaranteed contracts and contracts including salary escalators or bonus provisions implicate more complex posting-fee formulas.[204] The MLB club is only liable for the posting fee if it successfully negotiates with the player.[205] If the MLB club and the player do not reach an agreement, no posting fee must be paid.[206]

MLB has a similar agreement in place with the Korean Baseball Organization ("KBO"), generally viewed to be the world's third strongest baseball league, behind MLB and NPB.[207] These are only two examples, but they illustrate the global interplay involved in high level professional sport in the twenty first century. The details of all such posting and transfer agreements between American sports leagues and leagues in other nations are beyond the scope of this book.

[B] Athlete Recruitment

In many cases, professional American sports teams recruit amateur athletes from other countries. Such athletes are typically minors, and their recruitment may raise questions of illegality and exploitation. The pipeline of baseball players from the Dominican Republic to the United States is illustrative. The Dominican Republic has a population of just ten million people, yet Dominican baseball players comprise ten percent of MLB players and thirty percent of minor league baseball players.[208] Moreover, Dominican players, such as Fernando Tatis, Jr., Vladimir Guerrero, Jr., Manny Machado, and Albert Pujols are among MLB's brightest stars. In hopes of finding and signing the game's future greats, MLB clubs systematically mine the Dominican Republic for prospects, creating a shadowy legal and ethical landscape. Roughly thirty percent of Dominicans live below the poverty line, and "[m]any young boys and their families see baseball as their only way out,"[209] which sets the stage for potential exploitation. Indeed, the Caribbean island has been described as MLB's "puppy mill."[210]

---

203. *Japanese Posting System, supra* note 198.

204. *Id.*

205. *Id.*

206. *See* Kawai & Nichol, *supra* note 200, at 503.

207. *Korean Posting System,* MLB, https://www.mlb.com/glossary/transactions/korean-posting-system; *see also* Kyle Glaser, *How Good are the KBO and CPBL? Scouts and Front Office Officials Weigh In,* BASEBALL AMERICA (May 5, 2020), https://www.baseballamerica.com/stories/how-good-are-the-kbo-and-cpbl-scouts-and-front-office-officials-weigh-in/ (discussing the relative strength of the Korean Baseball Organization).

208. Rob Ruck, *The Tropic of Baseball: Dominican Talent and the MLB,* AUSTRALIAN INSTITUTE OF INTERNATIONAL AFFAIRS REPORT (Feb. 27, 2020), https://www.internationalaffairs.org.au/australian outlook/the-tropic-of-baseball-dominican-talent-and-the-mlb/.

209. Ryan Sharp, *Dominican Players Face Difficulties on the Road Out of Poverty and Into MLB,* GLOBAL SPORT MATTERS (Mar. 26, 2019), https://globalsportmatters.com/culture/2019/03/26/dominican-players-face-difficulties-on-the-road-out-of-poverty-and-into-mlb/.

210. Sean Gregory, *Baseball Dreams: Striking Out in the Dominican Republic,* TIME (July 26, 2010), http://content.time.com/time/magazine/article/0,9171,2004099,00.html.

Every MLB club has a youth academy in the Dominican Republic at which the club trains prospective professional players from the age of sixteen years old.[211] To catch the eye of an MLB team, however, players often begin full time training as young as thirteen years old with a "buscon," often dropping out of school to do so.[212] "Buscon"—derived from the Spanish word "buscar," meaning "to search"—is a broad term used to describe the more than one thousand scouts/agents/handlers/ trainers in the Dominican Republic who groom children for professional baseball careers.[213] While some buscone genuinely care for the young athletes—feeding and housing them and helping them develop as players—many others steal from them, involve them in fraud (such as altering a birth certificate to make a player appear younger), or inject them with performance-enhancing drugs seeking to increase the players' market value.[214] And if a player lands a contract with a major league club, the buscon may take up to 50% of the signing bonus.[215]

While some buscone have certainly proven to be bad actors, "MLB's craving for talent" has set the stage for the exploitation, spawning what one commentator describes as, "a profitable youth market that at times is akin to trafficking children."[216] Amid calls for reform, MLB has attempted self-regulation through various initiatives. It has implemented rules: (1) mandating that players receive Spanish-language versions of contracts so that no third-party is required to translate;[217] (2) providing financial literacy training to athletes;[218] (3) requiring that signing bonuses be wired directly to players' accounts in Dominican banks;[219] (4) educating players on the dangers of performance-enhancing drugs;[220] and (5) substantially increasing drug testing at Dominican academies.[221] MLB attempts to create an "MLB-controlled player development system," which would have eliminated the influence of buscones, have been unsuccessful. Buscones have proved too powerful and entrenched to be sidelined.[222]

With MLB self-regulation unable to reduce buscones' influence, legal efforts to protect the young players have emerged. For instance, the Dominican Government

---

211. Jackeline Pou, *Dominican Teens Keep Baseball Hopes Alive, But Not Without Risks*, NBC News (June 26, 2020), https://www.nbcnews.com/news/latino/dominican-teens-keep-baseball-hopes-alive-not-without-risks-n1062061.

212. *See* Ruck, *supra* note 208.

213. *Id.*

214. *Id.*

215. *See* Gregory, *supra* note 210.

216. *See* Ruck, *supra* note 208.

217. *See* Arturo J. Marcano & David P. Fidler, Stealing Lives: The Globalization of Baseball and the Tragic Story of Alexis Quiroz 181 (2002).

218. *See* Barry Svrluga, *Baseball's Coming of Age in the Dominican Republic*, Wash. Post (Mar. 9, 2009), https://www.washingtonpost.com/wp-dyn/content/story/2009/03/08/ST2009030802175.html.

219. *See id.*

220. Bryan Llenas, *Dominican Republic's 'Desperate' Baseball Culture Fuels Steroid Use, Experts Say*, Fox News Latino, Aug. 9, 2013, https://www.foxnews.com/sports/dominican-republics-desperate-baseball-culture-fuels-steroid-use-experts-say.

221. *Id.*

222. *See* Ruck, *supra* note 208.

passed a law capping buscones' profit, allowing them "to take just 15 percent for players they [have] been involved with for more than a year, and 10 percent for players they [have] coached for less than a year."[223] Notwithstanding this legislation, the United States Department of Justice in 2018 launched a long-running investigation into MLB's recruitment of foreign players, citing "dossiers detailing agent criminality" and "emails documenting shady dealings."[224]

MLB's experience with foreign-athlete recruitment teaches that, with respect to such matters, league self-regulation may be insufficient and legal regulation may be a necessity.

---

223. *See* Llenas, *supra* note 220.

224. Jon Wertheim, *Exclusive: The Evidence That Persuaded U.S. Department of Justice to Investigate MLB Recruitment of Foreign Players*, Sports Illustrated (Oct. 2, 2018), https://www.si.com/mlb/2018/10/02/fbi-investigation-mlb-atlanta-braves-los-angeles-dodgers.

Chapter 4

Coaching: Legal Issues and Relationships

§ 4.01 Introduction

As is true in other areas of sports, contract law plays a central role in regulating the relationships between coaches and the entities that employ them. Thus, the parties' contract is the point of departure when disputes arise regarding matters such as the scope of a coach's duties and whether those duties are competently executed, the termination of the relationship, a coach's entitlement to compensation, the components of compensation, and post-termination rights. In defining and adjusting the rights and obligations of coaches and their employers, courts often consult regulations and principles external to the parties' contract, including NCAA regulations, state statutes, and constitutional law principles. The materials that follow focus on contract law doctrine and intersecting principles that sculpt the coach and employer relationship. The discussion primarily focuses on coaching contracts at the amateur level which implicate not only contractual but also constitutional law issues. Where appropriate, there is also discussion of issues at the professional level.

§ 4.02 Representative Terms of Contractual Relationships

[A] Introduction

The competitive market for coaches, the potential revenues generated by successful college revenue-producing sports programs, the rapid turnover rate of coaches, and the ever-increasing compensation paid for coaching services, are among the factors that underscore the importance of contractual provisions in defining the coach's relationship with her or his professional team or university.[1] Coaches and their institutions often engage in tough contract negotiations as each seeks to incorporate

---

1. *See* Martin J. Greenberg, *College Coaching Contracts Revisited*, 12 MARQ. SPORTS L. REV. 127, 128–30 (2001); *see also* Randall S. Thomas & Lawrence Van Horn, *College Football Coaches' Pay and Contracts: Are They Overpaid and Unduly Privileged*, 91 IND. L.J. 189, 217–18 (2016) (showing an increase of fixed compensation for Division I football coaches).

contractual provisions that further their often disparate interests. For example, a university must balance the high costs of acquiring and keeping a successful coach and protecting its investment in the coach against the coach's desire for job security and the flexibility to pursue even more lucrative coaching opportunities before the expiration of the contract's term of duration.[2] This chapter identifies contractual provisions that are often included in coaching contracts as parties seek to include provisions to further their respective interests. It begins with a discussion of provisions that typically are incorporated into coaching contracts before shifting focus to compensation, termination, reassignment, and liquidated damages provisions.

[B] Representative Terms

As an initial matter, it is prudent that the parties, particularly a coach, memorialize their agreed upon understanding in a signed writing. A written agreement removes doubt as to the parties' respective obligations, the term of the agreement, and the agreement's enforceability. *Price v. University of Alabama*[3] is instructive. There, the court held that the parties' failure to execute a draft written agreement or a summary of the draft agreement rendered the head football coach's multi-year contract unenforceable by virtue of the statute of frauds.[4] The court further stated that the parties' partial performance of the contract did not constitute an effective exception to the statute of fraud's writing requirement.[5]

Assuming a written agreement, it will typically include language delineating a coach's duties[6] and requiring the coach to exercise good faith and reasonable or best efforts in performing those duties.[7] The specificity of these responsibilities varies from contract to contract. During the negotiations, however, a university will seek to include an extensive list of specific duties to enhance its right to terminate for cause a coach pursuant to a contract's termination provision.[8] On the other hand, a coach will seek more generally defined responsibilities to better insulate herself or himself from a university's accusations of a material breach.[9]

The duration of the contractual relationship is ordinarily a term of the parties' agreement. In addition to defining the length of the employment relationship to avoid disputes over its duration, language establishing a specified duration also negates the existence of an at-will employment relationship and the consequences that flow

---

2. Richard T. Karcher, *The Coaching Carousel in Big-Time Intercollegiate Athletics: Economic Implications and Legal Considerations*, 20 FORDHAM INTELL. PROP. MEDIA & ENT. L.J. 1, 54 (2009) (noting costly litigation and prolonged negative public relations as reasons why universities avoid litigation and leaving breaching coaches "able to leave their employment").

3. 318 F. Supp. 2d 1084 (N.D. Ala. 2003).

4. *Id.* at 1092.

5. *Id.* at 1093.

6. *See* Greenberg, *supra* note 1, at 151–52.

7. *Id.* at 152–55.

8. *Id.* at 155.

9. *Id.* at 155–56

therefrom.[10] For successful coaches, agreements are often extended pursuant to rollover clauses that extend the term of the agreement while keeping the original term of the contract as the remaining term of the contract.[11]

Coaching contracts frequently include provisions: (1) granting a coach authority to hire and fire assistant coaches as well as articulating an institution's promises regarding future salary increases and other benefits for assistant coaches;[12] (2) affording the coach input into the scheduling of games; 3) articulating a university's commitment to the development of an athletic program, including providing support for the athletic and educational development of student-athletes;[13] 4) providing that coaching services for the university constitute the coach's primary professional endeavor;[14] and 5) governing reassignments, buyouts, opt outs, and liquidated damages which are discussed *infra*.[15]

[C] Compensation

The compensation of most coaches consists of a fixed salary (*i.e.*, base compensation), fringe benefits, and bonuses — performance-based pay — conditioned on on-field as well as off-field events.[16] While bonuses have always been present in coaching contracts,[17] the increase in universities' athletically related revenue has made bonuses a much larger component of coaches' overall compensation.[18]

The base salary is the amount a university agrees to pay the coach for her or his coaching services.[19] This component of a coach's salary may also compensate a coach for attending or participating in public relations events such as radio and television interviews, giving speeches, and making alumni event appearances.[20] A coach may

---

10. *See* discussion *infra* § 4.03[A]; *see also* Kingsford v. Salt Lake City Sch. Dist., 247 F.3d 1123 (10th Cir. 2001) (stating that coach's failure to sign a written agreement for a specified term merely created an at-will employment relationship undermining the plaintiff's argument that he possessed a property interest in his job); Kish v. Iowa Cent. Comty. Coll., 142 F. Supp. 2d 1084 (N.D. Iowa 2001).

11. Greenberg, *supra* note 1, at 160–63 (illustrating the operative effect of a rollover provision as follows: "Coach Jones has a five-year contract with a rollover provision. At the end of each season, the university, with Coach Jones' consent, has a right to extend the contract an additional year, provided the university is pleased with the performance of the coach. Thus, if the university continues to exercise its rollover provision, Coach Jones will have at all times a five-year contract. Coach Jones may want the rollover provision to state that if the university does not extend the contract for two consecutive years, the coach has a right to terminate the contract without needing to comply with the release or buy-out provision.").

12. *Id.* at 255–56.

13. *Id.* at 254–56.

14. Greenberg, *supra* note 1, at 191–93.

15. *See* discussion *infra* § 4.02[F].

16. Thomas & Van Horn, *supra* note 1, at 217–27.

17. Jasmine Harris, *How Bonuses for Winning Coaches Became a Tradition in College Football*, HigherEdJobs (Dec. 24, 2018).

18. Thomas & Van Horn, *supra* note 1, at 217–18.

19. *Id.* at 217.

20. *Id.*

also receive pay for participating in summer camps either by direct payment from the university or by receiving the net income generated by the camp.[21] Coaches may also enter into endorsement contracts with third parties.[22]

Coaching contracts usually entitle coaches to fringe benefits.[23] This popular form of compensation includes but is not limited to insurance, paid vacations, housing benefits, use of a luxury car, tickets to professional and collegiate sporting events, and country club memberships.[24] While the existence and extent of fringe benefits varies on a case-by-case basis, coaches are generally entitled to such benefits in the event that the university breaches the employment agreement, reassigns a coach, or otherwise relieves a coach of coaching responsibilities but continues to pay a coach.[25]

Finally, coaching contracts frequently include bonuses conditioned on the occurrence of specified on-field and off-field events.[26] Coaches are entitled to receive on-field benefits when the coach's team accomplishes achievements identified in the contract, including the coach's team winning a conference title, competing in conference playoff, bowl, and championship games, and winning a championship.[27] In addition, a coach may be entitled to receive bonus payments if his or her team reaches academic benchmarks relating to academic progress rates, grade point averages, and graduation rates.[28]

The contract that Brian Kelly signed to become the head football coach at Louisiana State University offers a glimpse into the payment structure of prominent college football coaching contracts. The 10-year contract, which is valued at $95 to $100 million, includes base annual salary of $400,000 and annual supplemental income that "begins at an annual rate of $8.6 million, and a $500,000 'longevity' payment that he will receive if he is on the job each July 1."[29] In addition to provisions allowing for potential increases in Kelly's annual supplemental income, the contract includes the following bonuses:

- $50,000 if the football team meets certain academic benchmarks
- $75,000 if LSU reaches the SEC title game

---

21. *Id.*

22. *Id.*

23. Greenberg, *supra* note 1, at 174–75.

24. *Id.*; Thomas & Van Horn, *supra* note 1, at 226–27.

25. *See* Rodgers v. Ga. Tech Athletic Ass'n., 303 S.E.2d 467 (Ga. Ct. App. 1983) (holding that although question of fact remained as to whether coach was entitled to continue receiving certain fringe benefits provided by the university and third parties following termination, coach was not entitled to receive fringe benefits with sole purpose of fulfilling duties or to continue receiving gifts he had received during tenure).

26. Thomas & Van Horn, *supra* note 1, at 219–22.

27. *Id.* at 219–20. *But see also* O'Brien v. Ohio State Univ., 859 N.E.2d 607 (Ohio Ct. Cl. 2006), *aff'd*, 2007 WL 2729077 (Ohio Ct. App. Sept. 20, 2007) (holding coach was not entitled to on-field performance-based bonuses where NCAA vacated championship seasons and bonuses were conditioned on on-field performance during those seasons).

28. Thomas & Van Horn, *supra* note 1, 221–22.

29. Tom Schad & Steve Berkowitz, *Brian Kelly's 10-year deal with LSU football includes $1.2M loan for residence, eye-popping bonuses*, USA TODAY (Dec. 1, 2021); Glen West, *A Deeper Look into the Details of Brian Kelly's LSU Contract*, SI.COM (Dec. 1, 2021).

- $75,000 if LSU wins the SEC title game
- $125,000 if Kelly is named coach of the year
- $200,000 if LSU is in a national football championship semi-final game
- $200,000 if LSU is in a national football championship final game
- $500,000 if LSU wins the national championship[30]

Additional provisions include one providing Kelly with an interest free loan (not exceeding $1.2 million) to cover the purchase of Kelly's primary residence (to be located within 30 miles of the LSU campus) and two cars, and another allowing 50 hours of use by Kelly of a private jet for personal use.[31] With respect to outside income, coaching contracts frequently include a framework for coaches to earn such income in a way that complies with NCAA bylaws.[32] Contracts include language by which a coach stipulates an intention to annually report to the institution's president or chancellor, as required by NCAA bylaws, "athletically related income or benefits from a source outside the institution."[33]

[D] Termination

Due to a university's significant investment in coaches, and the high turnover rate in the field, termination provisions are a very important component of a coaching contract for both coaches and universities.[34] Coaching contracts usually include "termination for cause" and "termination without cause" provisions which define the events granting a university the right to terminate the agreement.[35] A "termination for cause" provision lists causes for which a coach can be terminated without the university committing a breach of contract.[36] The "termination without cause" provision generally entitles the coach to all or a portion of her or his compensation if a coach is dismissed for any reason not enumerated in the "termination for cause" provision.[37]

[1] Termination Based on Team Performance

Due to the uncertain nature of every sport, coaching contracts that stipulate a coach can only be fired for cause generally do not include team performance as a just cause for termination. Therefore, a university usually cannot terminate a coaching contract

---

30. Schad & Berkowitz, *supra* note 29; West, *supra* note 29.

31. Schad & Berkowitz, *supra* note 29; West, *supra* note 29.

32. Greenberg, *supra* note 1, at 191–93.

33. Nat'l Collegiate Athletic Ass'n, 2021–22 NCAA Division I Manual 50 (2021) [hereinafter NCAA Manual] (bylaw 11.2.2).

34. *See* Greenberg, *supra* note 1, at 128–30, 209.

35. Martin J. Greenberg, *Termination of College Coaching Contracts: When Does Adequate Cause to Terminate Exist and Who Determines its Existence?*, 17 Marq. Sports L. Rev. 197, 205, 210 (2006) [hereinafter *Termination of College Coaching Contracts*].

36. *Id.*

37. *Id.*

because of a team's poor record without incurring some form of liability. However, where a contract broadly defines what constitutes just cause, a court may interpret a contract's termination provisions as permitting such action.[38] In *Cole v. Valley Ice Garden*,[39] the Montana Supreme Court held that a contract's termination provision allowed the defendant employer to terminate the plaintiff's coaching contract for poor team performance. The plaintiff, who was employed as a head coach of a junior hockey team, was fired prior to the expiration of the term of employment when the team had a losing record despite the owner having made substantial investments.[40] The employment contract entitled the plaintiff to certain payments if he was fired without cause but did not define what constituted cause.[41] In reversing the district court's grant of summary judgment in favor of the plaintiff on his breach of contract action, the court relied on Montana's Wrongful Discharge from Employment Act to broadly interpret cause as "a reason logically related to the needs of the business."[42] The court therefore held that the defendant had adequate cause entitling it to terminate the coach's employment without incurring liability under the contract.[43]

[2] Termination Based on Coaches' Conduct

In the interest of protecting itself from potential liability and negative publicity, universities will also seek to include contractual language relating to a coach's conduct as a basis for a just cause termination.[44] These clauses are akin to morality clauses and seek to deter certain behaviors by coaches.[45] Like many of the terms discussed above, the inclusion and import of these terms varies on a case-by-case basis but plays a major role in defining a university's right to terminate. Moreover, "[t]he question of whether a morality clause correctly triggers termination is one of fact, premised upon the clause's language and whether the allegedly offending behavior falls within its ambit."[46] For example, Bobby Petrino was terminated in 2012 from his position as the University of Arkansas's head football coach after it was revealed that he had an affair with an employee.[47] Several coaches lost their jobs for their involvement in a scheme in which the coaches' false portrayals of applicants as high-caliber athletes were instrumental in the applicants gaining admission into several highly-selective universities.[48]

---

38. *Id.* at 226.

39. 113 P.3d 275 (2005).

40. *Id.* at 277–78.

41. *Id.* at 278.

42. *Id.* at 279–80.

43. *Id.* at 280–81.

44. *See* Patricia Sánchez Abril & Nicholas Greene, *Contracting Correctness: A Rubric for Analyzing Morality Clauses*, 74 Wash. & Lee L. Rev. 3, 12–19 (2017).

45. *See id.* at 5.

46. *Id.* at 40.

47. Tom Weir, *Petrino Dumped by Arkansas*, USA Today (Apr. 11, 2012).

48. Matthew J. Mitten, Timothy Davis, N. Jeremi Duru & Barbara Osborne, Sports Law and Regulation: Cases, Materials, and Problems 344 (5th ed. 2020) (identifying the coaches and universities implicated).

[3] Termination for Violation of NCAA Regulations

Contract language may provide a coach's violation of NCAA rules as a basis for a just cause termination.[49] A university may also attempt to justifiably terminate a coach based on NCAA rules violations committed by members of her or his coaching staff.[50] The specificity of contract language combined with the coach's conduct will ultimately determine a university's right to terminate a coach for NCAA rules violations.[51] Imprecise contract language nullified a university's attempt at a just cause termination of a coach for NCAA infractions in *O'Brien v. Ohio State Univ.*[52] In that case, the Ohio Court of Appeals held that a coach was terminated without cause after he violated NCAA rules. The plaintiff coach, who was hired to coach the university's men's basketball team,[53] violated NCAA regulations including prohibitions on making improper inducements to recruited athletes.[54] The university asserted that the contract afforded it the discretion to terminate the coach for cause for a material breach or violation of NCAA rules leading to an investigation resulting in: (1) a finding of a lack of institutional control over the program or (2) a sanction against the university.[55] Even though the coach's violation of rules ultimately resulted in the NCAA imposing severe sanctions on the university's basketball program, the court ruled the coach's conduct did not constitute a material breach.[56] The court reasoned that the university's termination of the coach was without cause because it was based on the university's own interpretation of NCAA rules rather than on the *results* of the NCAA's investigation—the events upon which "termination for cause" was actually conditioned.[57] Therefore, the university breached the parties' contract entitling the coach to damages established by the contract's liquidated damages provision.[58]

[4] Termination for Abusive Conduct

Termination for cause provisions in coaching contracts frequently contain clauses prohibiting abusive conduct by a coach.[59] As is true with other matters addressed in termination for cause provisions, the contractual language and subsequent judicial

---

49. *See, e.g., Termination of College Coaching Contracts, supra* note 35, at 210–21 (listing college coaching contracts with similar clauses).

50. *See generally* Joshua Lens, *NCAA Head Coach Responsibilities Legislation*, 14 DePaul J. Sports L. 33 (2018); *see also* NCAA Manual, *supra* note 33 (bylaw 11.1.1) (creating a rebuttable presumption of a head coach's responsibility of NCAA infractions committed by coaching).

51. *See* Abril & Greene, *supra* note 44, at 40; *see also Termination of College Coaching Contracts, supra* note 35, at 210–21 (analyzing termination provisions of different college coaching contracts and discussing the import of their language).

52. 2007 WL 2729077 (Ohio Ct. App. Sept. 20, 2007).

53. *Id.* at *3.

54. *Id.* at *5–11.

55. *Id.* at *4–5.

56. *Id.* at *7.

57. *Id.* at *13–15.

58. *See O'Brien*, 859 N.E.2d 607.

59. *See, e.g.,* Martin J. Greenberg, *supra* note 1, at 211–13 (providing an example of a termination provision containing similar clauses).

interpretation of it will determine a university's right to terminate for abusive con-duct.[60] *Board of Directors v. Cullinan*[61] involved the termination of a head high school basketball coach with a history of having been reprimanded for threatening and in-timidating treatment of players.[62] The coach's termination stemmed from the board's investigation of an allegation that the coach had intimidated a player during a one-on-one postgame meeting despite having received a directive from his employer to not hold one-on-one meetings.[63] Under sections of a relevant Iowa statute, teaching and coaching contracts could only be terminated for just cause, and while the statute did not define just cause, Iowa case law had defined it as conduct "which directly or indirectly significantly and adversely affects what must be the ultimate goal of every school system: high quality education for the district's students."[64] The court first reasoned that the coach's entire employment history was relevant to a just cause analysis[65] before holding that the one-on-one incident was sufficient to trigger ter-mination proceedings.[66] Further, because the court granted deference to the board's finding that the meeting was a violation of previous directives, the defendant had just cause to terminate the plaintiff.[67] It is also worth noting that an employer with a right to terminate because of a coach's abusive conduct may be held liable for the manner in which an otherwise valid termination decision is conducted.[68]

[E] Reassignment Provisions

Colleges and universities often include reassignment provisions in contracts with their coaches.[69] Reassignment provisions allow universities to transfer a coach from a contracted-for coaching position to another position within a university without the institution breaching its contract with a coach.[70] Thus, such clauses afford uni-versities leverage over coaches, which can be used to negotiate the coach's departure from a program in exchange for a payment that is less than what the coach would be entitled to receive under her contract.[71]

---

60. *See* Abril & Greene, *supra* note 44, at 5–12 (distinguishing between bad behavior morality clauses containing prohibitions on certain behavior and reputational impact morality clauses forbidding a coach from engaging in actions that are offensive).

61. 745 N.W.2d 487 (Iowa 2008).

62. *Id.* at 489–92.

63. *Id.* at 492–93.

64. *Id.* at 493–94 (citing Briggs v. Bd. of Dirs., 282 N.W.2d 740, 743 (Iowa 1979)).

65. *Id.* at 494–96.

66. *Id.* at 496–97.

67. *See id.* at 497–98.

68. *See* Campanelli v. Bockrath, 100 F.3d 1476 (9th Cir. 1996) (holding terminated plaintiff coach sufficiently pled deprivation of liberty interest although defendant had not breached he contract by terminating the coach's employment).

69. Martin J. Greenberg & Brandon Leibsohn, *The Disappearance of a Dinosaur: Reassignment Clauses Are Losing Their Footing in College Coaches' Contracts*, 25 MARQ. SPORTS L. REV. 39, 42 (2014).

70. *Id.*; WALTER T. CHAMPION, JR., FUNDAMENTALS OF SPORTS LAW § 16:8 (2020).

71. *See* Greenberg & Leibsohn, *supra* note 69, at 62–63.

In practice, a reassignment clause may contain language that prohibits an institution from assigning a coach to a position that is inconsistent with his or her education and experience.[72] Moreover, the language of the contract may incorporate by reference applicable statutes, regulations, and university policies.[73] Taken together, the foregoing may limit a university's ability to reassign a coach and mandate procedures to which the institution must adhere in making a reassignment.[74] Courts uphold, however, the enforceability of an institution's reassignment of a coach that is conducted in accordance with the language of the contract.[75] Note, however, that coaches may also challenge the propriety of a transfer from a coaching position, notwithstanding a contractual reassignment provision, pursuant to theories of constructive discharge or deprivation of constitutional rights.[76]

As illustrated in *Monson v. State*,[77] a university has the right to terminate a coach who refuses to accept a properly executed reassignment.[78] There, the university notified the head coach of the university's men's basketball team, who had two years remaining on his contract, that he would be reassigned to coach the men's golf team.[79] Believing that accepting the reassignment would be "professional suicide," the coach refused to accept the offer.[80] The university subsequently offered Monson the position of compliance coordinator for NCAA rules and regulations. After the coach failed to accept either position, the university terminated his employment without paying any compensation. After the trial court denied the defendant's motion for directed verdict, a jury found for the plaintiff and awarded him almost $300,000 in damages.[81]

The Oregon Court of Appeals reversed the trial court's denial of the state's motion for directed verdict based on the reassignment clause in the parties' contract.[82] The court reasoned that, by its terms, the contract incorporated an Oregon administrative rule, which authorized "personnel [to] be transferred or reassigned within [the Uni-

72. *See, e.g., id.* at 61–62.

73. *See* Dennison v. Murray State Univ., 465 F. Supp. 2d 733, 744–46 (W.D. Ky. 2006); Monson v. State, 901 P.2d 904, 905 (Ore. Ct. App. 1995); Greenberg & Leibsohn, *supra* note 69, at 43–47 (providing a list of reassignment provisions in college coaching contracts).

74. *E.g., Dennison*, 465 F. Supp. 2d at 744–46 (ruling contract which by its terms employed plaintiff as "Athletics Director" but also stating "this contract is subject to all applicable statutes and decisional law, and to all rules, policies and regulations of University and may be terminated in accordance therewith" allowed defendant, in accordance with university policy, to reassign plaintiff to different position at the same pay grade).

75. *See e.g.*, Greenberg, *supra* note 1, at 164–71.

76. *See* Greenberg & Leibsohn, *supra* note 69, at 43–49, 56 ("The case law demonstrates that universities subject themselves to potential liability regarding any reassignment that they make regardless of the language used to create the clauses.").

77. 901 P.2d 904 (Ore. Ct. App. 1995).

78. WALTER T. CHAMPION, JR., *supra* note 70.

79. *Monson*, 901 P.2d at 904–07.

80. *Id.* at 906.

81. *Id.* at 907.

82. *Id.* at 910–11.

versity of Oregon] in accordance with the staff needs of the institution."[83] The court then broadly defined the operative term, "staff needs," to mean, "those things that are necessary, useful, or desirable with regards to the group of staff members on which the university depends for its general operations."[84] The court held that the university properly exercised the deference arising by virtue of the incorporated rule, and despite the differences between plaintiff's coaching position and the offered positions, the university's attempted reassignment and termination of plaintiff's employment did not breach the parties' contract.[85]

[F] Liquidated Damages Provisions

It is common for college coaching contracts to include liquidated damages provisions that stipulate an aggrieved parties' exclusive remedy in the event of a breach of contract.[86] A liquidated damages provision is enforceable if it is reasonable in that it is neither punitive nor unreasonably disproportionate to an aggrieved parties' actual damages arising from a breach.[87] In assessing the reasonableness of such a clause, the party seeking enforcement of the provision has the burden of demonstrating that: (1) the stipulated damages are a reasonable estimation of compensatory damages in light of the anticipated or actual loss caused by breach and; (2) the actual damages in the event of a breach were uncertain or difficult to determine at the time of contract formation.[88]

In the context of collegiate coaching, courts have validated the reasonableness of liquidated damages provisions when either party breaches because of the uncertainty or difficulty the aggrieved party would likely encounter in determining its actual damages. In *Fleming v. Kent State Univ.*,[89] the court emphasized the parties' difficulty at the time of contract formation in anticipating a coach's actual damages because they could not predict whether the team's performance would entitle a coach to bonus-related income or reasonably foresee the coach's future collateral business opportunities.[90]

When the institution is the aggrieved party, courts have focused on the parties' difficulty in ascertaining actual damages because of the uncertainty associated with

---

83. *Id.* at 908.

84. *Id.* at 909–10.

85. *Id.* at 909–11. *But see* Greenberg & Leibsohn, *supra* note 69, at 56–57 (arguing that a modern court would come to a different conclusion about plaintiff's reassignment based on the difference in positions).

86. *See*, Martin J. Greenberg & Djenane Paul, *Coaches' Contracts: Terminating a Coach Without Cause and the Obligation to Mitigate Damages*, 23 MARQ. SPORTS L. REV. 339, 345–46 (2013).

87. WILLISTON ON CONTRACTS § 65:1 (4th ed. 2020); *See also* Restatement (Second) of Contracts § 356 (Am. Law Inst. 1981) ("A term fixing unreasonably large liquidated damages is unenforceable on grounds of public policy as a penalty").

88. *See* Greenberg & Paul, *supra* note 86, at 348; Joe Meyer, Comment, *Paying to Play (Somewhere Else): An Examination of the Enforceability of Athletic Conferences' Liquidated Damages Provisions*, 20 JEFFEREY S. MOORAD SPORTS L.J. 107, 113–114 (2013).

89. 17 N.E.3d 620 (Ohio Ct. App. 2014).

90. *Id.* at 626–28.

the costs of replacing a coach and other negative effects to an athletics program when a coach departs before expiration of the parties' contract. In *Vanderbilt Univ. v. Di-Nardo*,[91] the court upheld the enforcement of a liquidated damages provision, stating: "It is impossible to estimate how the loss of a head football coach will affect alumni relations, public support, football ticket sales, contributions, etc."[92] Similarly, in *Kent State Univ. v. Ford*,[93] the court recognized the following impediments to quantifying the harm to the institution resulting from a coach's premature departure:

> [T]he departure of a university's head basketball coach may result in a decrease in ticket sales, impact the ability to successfully recruit players and community support for the team, and require a search for both a new coach and additional coaching staff. Many of these damages cannot be easily measured or proven.[94]

The court in *O'Brien v. Ohio State Univ.*, discussed *supra*, relied on these factors in enforcing a liquidated damages provision benefitting the plaintiff coach.[95]

§ 4.03 Constitutional Law Issues

[A] Termination and Entitlement to Procedural Due Process

[1] A Property Interest — The Source of Due Process Rights

The Fourteenth Amendment precludes state actors (*i.e.*, public entities) from depriving any citizen of property without due process of the law.[96] A plaintiff seeking redress for procedural due process violations must establish a protectible property interest of which she or he was deprived without sufficient procedural protection, including adequate notice and a fair hearing.[97] In order to prevail on a claim that her or his coaching position was terminated in violation of due process, a coach must possess a constitutionally protected property interest and have a "legitimate claim of entitlement" to continued employment[98] derived from contract or state statutory

---

91. 174 F.3d 751 (6th Cir. 1999).

92. *Id.* at 756.

93. 26 N.E.3d 868 (Ohio Ct. App. 2015).

94. *Id.* at 874.

95. 859 N.E.2d 607 (Ohio Ct. Cl. 2006), *aff'd*, 2007 WL 2729077 (Ohio Ct. App. Sept. 20, 2007) (holding liquated damages provisions expressed the parties' understanding that damages — the value of lost collateral business opportunities and the amount of possible incentives — were difficult to predict at the time of contracting).

96. U.S. CONST. amend. XIV.

97. Bd. of Regents of State Colleges v. Roth, 408 U.S. 564, 569–70 (1972); *see also* Jacobeit v. Rich Twp. High Sch. Dist. 227, 673 F. Supp. 2d 653, 665 (N.D. Ill. 2009); Kish v. Iowa Cent. Cmty. Coll., 142 F. Supp. 2d 1084, 1096 (N.D. Iowa 2001).

98. Kingsford v. Salt Lake City Sch. Dist., 247 F.3d 1123, 1128 (10th Cir. 2001); Price v. Univ. of Ala., 318 F. Supp. 2d 1084, 1090–91 (N.D. Ala. 2003).

law,[99] or customs, practices, and policies that create an implied contractual promise to only terminate a coach for cause.[100] In other words, a property interest is not created by the Constitution but arises from an independent source of law.[101]

[2] A Property Interest Arising from Express Contract

A coach hired by a public school or state university for a specified period of time has a legitimate claim of entitlement that limits the circumstances under which the school can terminate the coach's employment without providing adequate notice and a fair hearing.[102] In contrast, a coach hired for an indefinite term is considered an at-will employee and has no protectible property interest in a coaching position.[103] An at-will employment relationship was present in *Kish v. Iowa Cent. Cmty. Coll.*,[104] where the court ruled as a matter of law that a contract stating "'this contract is not continuing in nature and may be terminated at the pleasure of the Board'" created no legitimate claim of entitlement to continued employment.[105]

Coaches possess a protected property interest in continued employment if, by the terms of their contract, they may only be terminated for cause. In *Barkauskie v. Indian River Sch. Dist.*,[106] the court held that contract language stating that the plaintiff coach could not be fired for "arbitrary and capricious reasons" and guaranteed "full constitutional protection of due process" created a protected property interest in continued employment. Similarly, in *Kelly v. Independent Sch. Dist. No. 12 of Oklahoma City*,[107] the Tenth Circuit sided with a plaintiff coach who was terminated without notice. Relying on language in the parties' contract requiring that the coach be given 30-day notice when terminated without cause, the court stated that the coach's contract created "a legitimate claim of entitlement to thirty days of continued employment ... and that, unless and until the School District gave the required thirty days prior notice and the thirty-day period expired, [his] coaching assignments could be terminated only for cause."[108]

A cognizable property interest is not likely to arise, however, where an agreement is rendered unenforceable for reasons including the failure of the contract to satisfy a state's statute of frauds unless circumstances give rise to an exception that removes

---

99. *E.g., Kingsford*, 247 F.3d at 1128–31.
100. Perry v. Sindermann, 408 U.S. 593, 601–02 (1972); *Kingsford*, 247 F.3d at 1131–32.
101. *Roth*, 408 U.S. at 577.
102. *See, e.g., Jacobeit*, 673 F. Supp. 2d at 666; *Kingsford*, 247 F.3d at 1128–30.
103. Smith v. Bd. of Educ. of Urbana Sch. Dist. No. 116 of Champaign Cty., 708 F.2d 258, 263–65 (7th Cir. 1983) (stating that under Illinois law, oral promises for indefinite employment are unenforceable absent sufficient reliance); *see, e.g., Kish*, 142 F. Supp. 2d at 1097.
104. 142 F. Supp. 2d at 1098.
105. *Id.; see also* Ludwig v. Bd. of Trs. of Ferris State Univ., 123 F.3d 404 (6th Cir. 1997) (holding that coach had no property interest in continued pay during suspension where contract authorized university to suspend coach for a maximum of thirty days and did not oblige university to provide notice or pay coach during the suspension).
106. 951 F. Supp. 519, 529 (D. Del. 1996).
107. 80 F. App'x 36 (10th Cir. 2003).
108. *Id.* at 38, 41.

the statute of frauds as a bar to enforcement. In this regard, *Price v. Univ. of Alabama*,[109] is instructive. There, the court held that the parties' failure to execute a draft written agreement or a summary of the draft agreement rendered the head football coach's multi-year contract unenforceable by virtue of the statute of frauds.[110] The court further stated that the parties' partial performance of the contract did not constitute an effective exception to the statute of fraud's writing requirement.[111]

[3] Other Sources of a Property Interest

State law governing implied-in-fact contracts can serve as a source of a coach's property interest.[112] This occurred in *Kingsford v. Salt Lake City Sch. Dist.*,[113] where the Tenth Circuit remanded a case to decide the factual question of whether an implied-in-fact promise existed to only terminate coaches from their coaching positions for cause.[114] The plaintiff coach's written contract with the school district was for his teaching position and did not mention the additional coaching duties he performed for the school throughout his employment.[115] After being terminated from his coaching position but not his teaching position, the plaintiff filed suit.[116] The record revealed statements from both the plaintiff and defendants that coaches were only fired from their position for cause and not for any "arbitrary or capricious" reason.[117] Notwithstanding substantial evidence that coaches worked on an at-will basis, the court held that under Utah law, the existence of an implied contract is a question of fact for the jury.[118] If the jury were to find that an implied contract existed, then the coach would have a property interest in his coaching position that would require procedural protection before termination.

State statutory law can serve as a source of a coach's protected property interest.[119] In such instances, courts generally require a statute to place substantive limits on a state actor's discretion in terminating covered employees.[120] For example, in *Wallace*

---

109. 318 F. Supp. 2d 1084 (N.D. Ala. 2003).

110. *Id.* at 1092.

111. *Id.* at 1093. *But see* Vail v. Bd. of Educ. of Paris Union Sch. Dist. No. 95, 706 F.2d 1435, 1440 (7th Cir. 1983), *aff'd*, 466 U.S. 377 (1984) (holding that partial performance as well as reasonable reliance served as an exception to the statute of frauds one-year provision and took oral promise to renew a one-year contract out of the statute of frauds).

112. *E.g., Jacobeit*, 673 F. Supp. 2d at 665–67 (holding that under Illinois law, plaintiff coach had sufficiently alleged enough facts to challenge presumption of at-will employment). *See generally Perry*, 408 U.S. at 602 ("Explicit contractual provisions may be supplemented by other agreements implied from 'the promisor's words and conduct in the light of the surrounding circumstances.'").

113. 247 F.3d at 1123.

114. *Id.*

115. *Id.* at 1126–27.

116. *Id.*

117. *Id.* at 1132.

118. *Id.*

119. *E.g.*, Wallace v. DeSoto Cty. Sch. Dist., 768 F. App'x 233 (5th Cir. 2019).

120. Kentucky Dep't of Corr. v. Thompson, 490 U.S. 454, 462 (1989) (ruling that statutes create a property interest by establishing "substantive predicates" to govern official decision-making or by mandating an outcome be reached upon the finding that certain criteria are met). *But see* McGuire

v. DeSoto Cty. Sch. Dist.,[121] the Fifth Circuit ruled that a Mississippi statute vested a property interest in applicable employees.[122] A former teacher and coach at a high school was terminated from his positions for "immoral conduct" stemming from the discovery of an online nude photograph of him.[123] Following the cancellation of a scheduled hearing to contest his termination, the plaintiff brought a due process claim against the school district alleging that it had deprived him of a property interest arising out of a Mississippi statute.[124] The statute provided covered employees the right to continued employment so long as they engaged in good behavior and mandated that before any "licensed employees" could be dismissed or suspended for cause, the employee was entitled to a public hearing.[125] The court held that, if the plaintiff had a valid contract that brought him within the scope of a "licensed employee," the statute created and defined a protected property interest in his coaching and teaching positions and therefore entitled him to procedural protections before termination.[126] However, where the scope of a statute only covers employees working in their teaching capacity, a coach working as a teacher and coach will only possess a property interest in the teaching position.[127]

[B] A Coach's Reputational Liberty Interest

The Fourteenth Amendment also precludes a state actor from depriving any citizen of their liberty without due process of the law.[128] In the context of public high schools and colleges, courts have held that coaches possess an occupational liberty interest in their good name and reputation.[129] Damage to a coach's reputation is not constitutionally protectible, however, unless it is coupled with the denial of a more tangible interest.[130] Therefore, where a coach is stigmatized by comments made in the course

---

v. Indep. Sch. Dist. No. 833, 863 F.3d 1030, 1035 (8th Cir. 2017) (holding that a statute prohibiting parental complaints from being sole reason for non-renewal created no property interest for the coach because it placed single substantive limit on employer's discretion and only gave employee a mere subjective expectancy of continued employment).

121. 768 F. App'x at 238.

122. *Id.*

123. *Id.* at 234.

124. *Id.*

125. *Id.* at 236 (citing Miss. Code. Ann. § 37-9-59 (West)).

126. *Id.* at 238.

127. *Smith*, 708 F.2d at 262–63 (rejecting plaintiffs' argument that, because they were hired as teachers and coaches, a statute creating a property interest in tenured teaching positions extended to coaching positions); Hill v. Silsbee Indep. Sch. Dist., 933 F. Supp. 616, 625–26 (E.D. Tex. 1996) (holding the same).

128. U.S. Const. amend. XIV.

129. *See generally* Wisconsin v. Constantineau, 400 U.S. 433, 437 (1971) ("Where a person's good name, reputation, honor, or integrity is at stake because of what the government is doing to him, notice and an opportunity to be heard are essential.").

130. Brewer v. Purvis, 816 F. Supp. 1560, 1575–76 (M.D. Ga. 1993), *aff'd*, 44 F.3d 1008 (11th Cir. 1995).

of adverse employment action, she has a cognizable liberty interest that entitles her to an opportunity to refute the charges and clear her name even if she does not have a property interest in her position.[131]

Generally, a plaintiff seeking to successfully assert a due process claim alleging deprivation of a liberty interest must show that the defendant (1) made a false statement (2) of a stigmatizing nature (3) in connection with a governmental employee's discharge (4) made public (5) by the governmental employer (6) without a meaningful opportunity for an employee name clearing hearing.[132] In addition, the plaintiff must show that the statement resulted in the tangible loss of other employment opportunities in the plaintiff's chosen profession.[133]

For example, in *Isler v. New Mexico Activities Ass'n*,[134] a federal district court held that a coach had not been deprived of a cognizable liberty interest.[135] The plaintiff in the case was a coach who was accused of violating a state law prohibiting coaches from communicating with a student and parent in a way that could be construed as recruiting.[136] After being suspended from his coaching duties by his employer, the plaintiff sued and alleged, *inter alia*, that the New Mexico Activities Association ("NMAA") had deprived him of his liberty interest in his good name and reputation without due process of law.[137] The district court held that the plaintiff had not been deprived of a liberty interest, first, because the NMAA did not employ him and could not terminate him.[138] Therefore, any comments the NMAA made were not in connection with his discharge or made public by his employer.[139] Second, the district court found that the plaintiff had not suffered a tangible loss of employment opportunities because he had been rehired to the same position at his school and subsequently accepted an offer for another coaching position at a University.[140] Therefore, the plaintiff did not have a valid due process claim for deprivation of a liberty interest.

---

131. Puchalski v. Sch. Dist. of Springfield, 161 F. Supp. 2d 395, 406 (E.D. Pa. 2001) (citing *Roth*, 408 U.S. at 573); *Brewer*, 816 F. Supp. at 1575.

132. *Brewer*, 816 F. Supp. at 1576 (citing Buxton v. Plant City, 871 F.2d 1037, 1042 (11th Cir.1989)); *Price*, 318 F. Supp. 2d at 1094; *see also* Schul v. Sherard, 102 F. Supp. 2d 877, 890–91 (S.D. Ohio 2000) (holding that plaintiff coach had not been deprived of liberty interest where there was no evidence that defendant was the source of negative publicity surrounding plaintiff's termination).

133. *See* Isler v. N.M. Activities Ass'n, 893 F. Supp. 2d 1145, 1156 (D. N.M. 2012), order vacated in part on reconsideration, 2013 WL 12328907 (D. N.M. Sept. 25, 2013); Bryant v. Gardner, 545 F. Supp. 2d 791 (N.D. Ill. 2008) (holding that plaintiff coach sufficiently pled claim for deprivation of liberty interest with allegations that defendant's comments substantially interfered with his ability to secure another coaching position although he retained his gym teacher position).

134. 893 F. Supp. 2d 1145.

135. *Id.* at 1156–57.

136. *Id.* at 1148.

137. *Id.* at 1148–49.

138. *Id.* at 1156.

139. *Id.*

140. *Id.* 1156–57.

[C] Substantive Due Process

As discussed in Chapter 2, substantive due process prohibits a state from taking actions against individuals that are "unreasonable, arbitrary, or capricious" and infringe upon their fundamental rights or liberty interests.[141] In the context of public employment, substantive due process precludes state actors from taking adverse employment actions against an employee because the employee exercises a fundamental constitutional right.[142] The scope of these fundamental rights is limited to those found in the U.S. Constitution and does not include substantive rights created by state law.[143] Additional fundamental rights protected by substantive due process include the right for an employee to not be terminated based on race, gender, or pregnancy, or in a manner which violates other civil rights legislation.[144] An employer is justified, however, in terminating an employee for reasons including an employee's violation of existing regulations or contractual provisions.[145]

While coaches have brought substantive due process claims in response to adverse employment actions, courts have held that the right to coach a team is not a fundamental right.[146] Even where a coach's fundamental right has been infringed upon by a state actor by way of an adverse employment action, a substantive due process claim will fail if the termination of the coach's employment was justified. This principle was illustrated in *Patria v. East Hartford Bd. of Educ.*[147] There, the court granted the defendant state employer's motion for summary judgment on the plaintiff's procedural and substantive due process claims.[148] The plaintiff, who was a high school teacher and coached both the girls' and boys' volleyball teams, was terminated from her position after failing to notify her supervisors of an inappropriate and potentially illegal relationship between a player and a team volunteer.[149] In ruling on the plaintiff's substantive due process claims, the court held the plaintiff had no property interest in continued employment. Without discussing whether a fundamental right had been implicated, the court also ruled that the school district was entitled to summary judgment on the plaintiff's substantive due process claim.[150] The court reasoned that plaintiff's substantive due process claim was deficient as a matter of law because her failure to notify her supervisors or dismiss the volunteer gave rise to the defendants'

---

141. 16C C.J.S. *Constitutional Law* § 1821 (2020) ("A claim of violation of Fourteenth Amendment substantive due process requires proof that a defendant's conduct shocks the conscience or interferes with rights implicit in the concept of ordered liberty, or offends judicial notions of fairness, or is offensive to human dignity, or is taken with deliberate indifference to protected rights.").

142. *Id.* at § 2107.

143. *Id.*

144. *Id.*

145. *Id.*

146. *E.g.*, Schneeweis v. Jacobs, 771 F. Supp. 733, 738 (E.D. Va. 1991), *aff'd*, 966 F.2d 1444 (4th Cir. 1992) ("The law does not recognize a fundamental right to coach basketball.").

147. 2009 WL 840667 (D. Conn. Mar. 31, 2009).

148. *Id.* at *6–9.

149. *Id.* at *1–5.

150. *Id.* at *8–9.

rational belief that the plaintiff had exposed the school system to liability and placed a student in danger.[151] The court further held that termination of plaintiff's employment served a legitimate governmental objective — disciplinary action taken in response to the plaintiff's unprofessional conduct.[152]

A coach's substantive due process claim will fail where the allegations implicate nothing more than contractual rights arising under state law.[153] For example, in *Holthaus v. Bd. of Educ.*,[154] the plaintiff entered into a one-year contract with a high school to serve as its head football coach.[155] Following a full evidentiary hearing, the defendant board of education terminated the coach's employment because of his use of a racial slur during a team practice.[156] In granting the defendants' motion for summary judgment on plaintiff's substantive due process claim, the district court framed the primary due process issue as whether the defendants had deprived the plaintiff of a fundamental right.[157] Noting that substantive due process only protects interests "implicit in the concept of ordered liberty" and that such interests do not include contractual rights, the court held that the plaintiff's contractual right to coach was not a fundamental right.[158] Therefore, the plaintiff had not alleged a cognizable substantive due process claim as a matter of law.[159] The same result will ensue when a coach alleges a substantive due process claim premised only on a right arising out of state tort law.[160]

§ 4.04 Coaches, Privacy, and Free Speech

[A] A Coach's Privacy Rights

The privacy rights of public employees arise out of the Constitution and create a confidentiality interest in avoiding disclosure of certain personal information.[161] While the U.S. Constitution sets a ceiling on the privacy rights it affords individuals,

---

151. *Id.* at *9.

152. *See id.*

153. Wallace v. Bd. of Regents of the Univ. Sys. of Ga., 967 F. Supp. 1287, 1294 (S.D. Ga. 1997) (quoting McKinney v. Pate, 20 F.3d 1550, 1556 (11th Cir.1994)) (rejecting plaintiff coaches' substantive due process claims following termination of contracts because "[s]tate created rights can be 'rescinded so long as the elements of procedural — not substantive — due process are observed.'").

154. 1992 WL 457285 (S.D. Ohio Mar. 31, 1992), *aff'd*, Holthaus v. Bd. of Educ., Cincinnati Pub. Sch., 986 F.2d 1044 (6th Cir. 1993).

155. *Id.* at *1.

156. *Id.*

157. *Id.* at *2.

158. *Id.* at *2–3.

159. *Id.*

160. *See* Daniel v. Hancock Sch. Dist., 626 F. App'x 825 (11th Cir. 2015) (holding that coach whose remedies consisted of those arising out of state tort law had not asserted a legally viable substantive due process claim).

161. James Baird et al., American Bar Association, Public Employee Privacy § 1.II.A (1995).

state constitutions may provide greater privacy protections.[162] Federal and state statutes provide additional protection for coaches employed in the private and public sectors.[163] Whether a coach has a privacy interest in information turns on whether it is within an individual's reasonable expectation of privacy.[164] The more personal the information, the greater the reasonable expectation of privacy.[165]

The foregoing principles were on display in *Hill v. Halford*,[166] where a Mississippi district court held that the plaintiff had alleged a cognizable claim for violation of privacy.[167] The plaintiff, a teacher and coach, was forced to undergo testing for sexually transmitted diseases and report the results to the school district in the aftermath of allegations of inappropriate conduct.[168] Although the tests results were negative, the plaintiff alleged his right to privacy was violated when the school's athletic director disclosed the information to at least one student.[169] The court held that because the defendant allegedly told plaintiff that the investigation was confidential, the plaintiff had a legitimate expectation of privacy creating a right to privacy.[170] The court also found that the plaintiff's privacy interest outweighed the public's interest in disclosure because the test results were negative and the investigation had been closed.[171]

[B] The Scope of a Coach's Free-Speech Rights

The First Amendment limits federal and state governments' power to regulate citizens' expression.[172] In the context of public employment, coaches "'do not surrender all of their First Amendment rights by reason of their employment'.... Rather, they retain the right 'in certain circumstances[] to speak as a citizen addressing matters of public concern.'"[173] Therefore, a coach suing an employer alleging retaliation based

---

162. *Id.* § 1.II.B (listing different states' constitutional provisions).

163. *Id.* § 1.III.A–B; *see, e.g.,* Associated Chino Teachers v. Chino Valley Unified Sch. Dist., 241 Cal. Rptr. 3d 732 (Ct. App. 2018) (granting petition made by teacher association on behalf of coach to prevent release of personnel documents when statute mandated disclosure of personnel documents but exempted documents where the public's interest in disclosure was outweighed by an individual's privacy interest).

164. *See* LaRose v. Chichester Sch. Dist., 2010 WL 1254305, at *4–5 (E.D. Pa. Mar. 31, 2010) (quoting C.N. v. Ridgewood Bd. of Educ., 430 F.3d 159, 179 (3d Cir. 1980)) ("The more intimate or personal the information, the more justified is the expectation that it will not be subject to public scrutiny"); *see also* O'Connor v. Pierson, 426 F.3d 187 (2d Cir. 2005) (holding that a teacher and coach had privacy interest in not disclosing medical information to a school district and board of education where such a disclosure was a condition of returning to work).

165. *Ridgewood Bd. of Educ.,* 430 F.3d at 179.

166. 2012 WL 141145 (N.D. Miss. Jan. 18, 2012).

167. *Id.*

168. *Id.* at *1.

169. *Id.* at *7.

170. *Id.*

171. *Id.*

172. U.S. Const. amend. I.

173. Kennedy v. Bremerton Sch. Dist., 869 F.3d 813, 822 (9th Cir. 2017) (quoting Garcetti v. Ceballos, 547 U.S. 410, 417 (2006)).

on her exercise of expressive speech protected by the First Amendment must show that: (1) she spoke as a private citizen; (2) on a matter of public concern; and (3) the relevant speech was a motivating factor in the adverse employment action.[174] Whether a coach's statements were spoken in her capacity as a public employee or private citizen presents a question of fact as to the coach's scope of employment and a question of law as to what constitutional significance the scope of employment has on the speech.[175] Speech made pursuant to an employee's duties or speech that owes its existence to a public employee's position is generally unprotected.[176] Where a coach speaks independently of her duties in a manner similar to that of any member of the general public, however, she is deemed to speak as a private citizen, and the speech cannot provide a justifiable basis supporting the adverse governmental action.[177] The determination of whether the speech relates to a matter of public concern requires an analysis of the content, form, and context of the speech.[178]

[C] Freedom of Religious Expression

Courts recognize that a coach's free speech includes the freedom to express religious views.[179] While such speech is constitutionally protectible speech, the coach's right is not unlimited, especially when the speech is exercised by the coach while working as a public employee.[180] Thus, courts have upheld an institution's efforts to circumscribe a coach's freedom of religious expression when doing so enables the institution to avoid violating the United States Constitution's Establishment Clause.[181] For example, in *Borden v. Sch. Dist. of Twp. of East Brunswick*,[182] the Third Circuit addressed the constitutionality of a school district's policy prohibiting its employees from participating in student prayers. During his twenty-three years of employment, the plaintiff coach had engaged in two prayer activities with students on his team; one during team dinners and one immediately before games.[183] In response to a parental complaint, the superintendent told the plaintiff that any student-involved prayer must

---

174. *Id.* at 822.

175. *Id.* at 823–24.

176. *Id.* at 823.

177. *Id.* (citing Pickering v. Bd. of Educ. of Twp. High Sch. Dist. 205, 391 U.S. 563, 573–74 (1968)).

178. Borden v. Sch. Dist. of Twp. of East Brunswick, 523 F.3d 153, 169 (3d Cir. 2008) (quoting Connick v. Myers, 461 U.S. 138 (1983)); Richardson v. Sugg, 325 F. Supp. 2d 919, 942 (E.D. Ark. 2004) (same). Even if these elements are established, however, a defendant may avoid liability by showing that it was justified in treating the coach differently than public citizens or that it would have taken the adverse employment action in the absence of the speech. *Kennedy*, 869 F.3d at 822.

179. *See* Bobby Bramhall, *An Employment Stance on Taking a Knee*, 27 J. LEGAL ASPECTS SPORT 109, 111–13 (2017).

180. *Id.*

181. *Kennedy*, 869 F.3d at 832 (Smith, J., concurring) (citing Good News Club v. Milford Cent. Sch., 533 U.S. 98, 112 (2001)). *See generally* U.S. CONST. amend. I ("Congress shall make no law respecting an establishment of religion") (applied to the states through the 14th Amendment).

182. 523 F.3d 153 (3d Cir. 2008).

183. *Id.* at 159–60.

be student initiated and that employees could not participate.[184] The plaintiff successfully argued before the district court that the policy was unconstitutional under the First Amendment and the New Jersey State Constitution.[185]

In reversing the district court's ruling, the Third Circuit held that the coach's speech was not protected because the prayer was not a matter of public concern.[186] The court reasoned that the plaintiff's stated purpose of promoting team solidarity by bowing his head and kneeling during prayer was neither a broad social statement nor a comment on the school's operations made in a way that would be important to the public.[187] The court further stated that the plaintiff's participation constituted a violation of the Establishment Clause under a theory of endorsement.[188] The court reasoned that the plaintiff's long history of leading prayer with the students would make a reasonable observer conclude that the plaintiff, as an arm of the state, was endorsing a religious practice by bowing his head and taking a knee during the prayer sessions.[189] Consequently, the school was constitutionally justified in regulating the coach's speech by prohibiting his participation.[190]

[D] Defamation

[1] General Considerations

While the First Amendment protects citizen's speech from governmental intrusion, courts have held that free speech rights are not unlimited and individuals as well as organizations can be held liable under state law for defamatory speech.[191] Generally, a plaintiff asserting a defamation claim must prove "(1) the defendant made a defamatory statement concerning the plaintiff; (2) the defendant published the defamatory statement by communicating it to a third person; (3) the defamatory statement was false; and (4) the defendant acted with the degree of fault required in the circumstances of the case."[192] Where a plaintiff is deemed either a public official or public figure, the Supreme Court requires the plaintiff to prove with clear and convincing evidence that the defendant published material with "actual malice," defined as acting with knowledge that a statement is false or with reckless disregard of the statement's

---

184. *Id.* at 160–61.
185. *Id.* at 162–63.
186. *Id.* at 168–71.
187. *Id.* at 170–71.
188. *Id.* at 174–79.
189. *Id.* at 177–78.
190. *Id.* at 174.
191. U.S. CONST. amend. I; *see* Gertz v. Robert Welch, Inc., 418 U.S. 323, 341 (1974) ("The legitimate state interest underlying the law of libel is the compensation of individuals for the harm inflicted on them by defamatory falsehood.").
192. Rebecca E. Hatch, *Cause of Action for Defamation Involving Plaintiff's Profession, Trade, or Business, in* 44 CAUSES OF ACTION 2d § 5 (2010); *see also* 128 Am. Jur. *Trials*, 339 at § 5 (Dec. 2021 Update).

truth.[193] In contrast, if the plaintiff is a private figure, states are free to establish a standard of liability allowing for the recovery of compensatory damages.[194]

[2] Defamation and Coaches as Public Figures

Coaches of teams at various levels of competition can be considered public officials or public figures for purposes of defamation claims. In determining whether a coach employed by a government entity is a public official, courts generally consider, *inter alia*, "(1) the extent to which the inherent attributes of a position define it as one of influence over issues of public importance; (2) the position's special access to the media as a means of self-help; and (3) the risk of diminished privacy assumed upon taking the position."[195] Even if a court finds that a coach is not a public official, coaches of collegiate and professional teams are generally considered public figures — individuals "involved in issues in which the public has a justified and important interest."[196] Courts distinguish between "all-purpose public figures" and "limited purpose public figures." The latter is considered a public figure only with respect to defamatory statements connected to public controversies in which they have chosen to involve themselves. In both contexts, however, a court may require that plaintiffs meet the "actual malice" standard as established in *New York Times Co. v. Sullivan*[197] to succeed on a defamation claim.[198]

---

193. Harte-Hanks Commc'ns, Inc. v. Connaughton, 491 U.S. 657, 665–67 (1989) (citing *Gertz*, 418 U.S. 323) (rejecting the standard announced in Curtis Publishing Co. v. Butts, 388 U.S. 130 (1967), that public figures only need to establish "highly unreasonable conduct").

194. *Gertz*, 418 U.S. at 339.

195. 14D MASS. PRAC., *Summary of Basic Law* § 16:230 (5th ed.); *see also* O'Connor v. Burningham, 165 P.3d 1214 (Utah 2007) (holding that coach of public high school basketball team was not public official because the "policies and actions of the coach of any high school athletic team does not affect in any material way the civic affairs of a community — the affairs most citizens would understand to be the real work of government").

196. *Butts*, 388 U.S. at 134; *see also* Turner v. Wells, 879 F.3d 1254, 1272 (11th Cir. 2018) (citing multiple cases supporting holding that coaches of professional and collegiate sports teams are considered public figures); Marcone v. Penthouse Int'l Magazine for Men, 754 F.2d 1072, 1083 (3d Cir. 1985) ("[S]ports figures are generally considered public figures because of their position as athletes or coaches."). *But see* Joyner v. www.socalsoccertalk.com, 2007 WL 1697486 (Cal. Ct. App. June 13, 2007) (holding that statements about local soccer coach on public forum website with 600 members was not sufficiently significant to be matter of public interest).

197. 376 U.S. 254, 279–80 (1964).

198. *See* Time, Inc. v. Johnston, 448 F.2d 378 (4th Cir. 1971) (holding statement in magazine that Bill Russel psychologically destroyed plaintiff, who was a former NBA player and current Wake Forest basketball coach at the time of publication, was not defamatory because statement was an accurate quote of Russell's coach and therefore was not malicious); Mahoney v. Adirondack Pub. Co., 71 N.Y.2d 31 (N.Y. 1987) (holding false statements published in newspaper about plaintiff coach's conduct during a game were not proven to have been made with actual malice where reporter viewed events from 30 feet away and defendant's false account was similar to plaintiff's and witnesses' accounts). *See generally* 14D MASS. PRAC., *supra* note 195.

An Illinois appellate court remanded a coach's defamation action against a football player's parent in *Myers v. Levy*.[199] The plaintiff coach was dismissed from his position as football coach after the defendant communicated several defamatory statements to a high school principal and athletic director.[200] The plaintiff conceded he was required to prove actual malice by the defendant in order to prevail. Therefore, the coach's status as public official or public figure was not relevant to the court's analysis.[201] The evidence in the record revealed that the defendant had praised the plaintiff's coaching ability prior to making his communications with the principal and athletic director, and that the defamatory communications were made a short time after the defendant's and plaintiff's sons began competing for the team's quarterback position.[202] Additionally, the record contained allegations that the defendant had misrepresented the number of parents who signed his petition letter calling for the removal of the coach.[203] The court ruled that summary judgement in favor of the defendant was improper because the unusual timing of the new communications created a question of fact as to whether the defendant acted with actual malice, that is, with knowledge that the statements about the plaintiff's coaching performance were false or made with reckless disregard for the statements' truth.[204]

[3] Defamation and Coaches as Private Individuals

Where a coach is not considered a public official or public figure, the coach is generally categorized as a private individual.[205] In defamation actions brought by plaintiffs deemed private individuals, states are free to fashion standards of liability without proof of actual malice if they comport with First Amendment rights and require some level of fault.[206] Most jurisdictions generally require plaintiffs to show that the defendant acted negligently with regard to the truth, but others require proof of actual malice or gross irresponsibility.[207]

In *Moss v. Stockard*,[208] the D.C. Circuit upheld a ruling that the coach of a women's basketball team was a private figure.[209] The plaintiff coach was terminated from her position as a result of the athletic director's dissatisfaction with her handling of university funds during a team trip.[210] Following the coach's termination, the school's athletic director made multiple statements to members of the basketball team and coaching staff that the plaintiff was fired for "misappropriation of funds" which those

---

199. 808 N.E.2d 1139 (Ill. Ct. App. 2004).

200. *Id.* at 1144–45.

201. *Id.* at 1148–49.

202. *Id.* at 1145, 1150.

203. *Id.* at 1145.

204. *Id.* at 1152.

205. *See* 14D Mass. Prac., *supra* note 195.

206. *Gertz*, 418 U.S. at 339.

207. *See generally* 53 C.J.S. *Libel and Slander; Injurious Falsehood* § 80 (listing different standards adopted by jurisdictions).

208. 580 A.2d 1011 (D.C. Cir. 1990).

209. *Id.*

210. *Id.* at 1014–16.

hearing the statement interpreted as stealing from the team.[211] Notwithstanding a dispute regarding the extent to which the coach had deviated from the university's policy of money distributions, the district court ruled that the plaintiff was a private figure.[212] In upholding this ruling, the circuit court reasoned that the plaintiff was not a public official because her coaching duties gave her neither "substantial responsibility for [n]or control over the conduct of governmental affairs," nor was she in a position of "apparent public importance."[213] Additionally, the court held she was not an all-purpose or limited public figure because she coached a basketball team that was not sufficiently prominent and she had not attempted to influence or insert herself into the outcome of any public controversy.[214] Because she was a private figure, the court ruled she was not required to prove actual malice with clear and convincing evidence.[215] In short, the status of a coach determines the quantum of proof required to succeed on a defamation claim.

211. *Id.* at 1016.
212. *Id.* at 1015–16, 1029–30.
213. *Id.* at 1029–30.
214. *Id.* at 1030–33.
215. *Id.* at 1033.

Part II

Sport and Society

Chapter 5

Gender and Sex Discrimination Issues in Sports

§ 5.01 Introduction

This chapter examines gender and sex discrimination in sports. After providing historical context, the chapter focuses on the impediments that historically limited opportunities for girls and women to participate in sports. It then explores constitutional and statutory principles relied on by female athletes to assist them in overcoming these barriers. In this regard, the chapter discusses the contours and application of Title IX of the Education Amendments of 1972 ("Title IX") and the Equal Protection Clause of the Fourteenth Amendment which converged to increase female sports participation opportunities and enhance equity and fairness relating to benefits and treatment. The chapter also explores constitutional challenges brought principally by male athletes in response to institutional efforts to achieve gender equity. In addition, the materials examine other gender-related issues including: sexual violence and harassment in sport, equal pay claims of female coaches and athletes, and legal issues arising from transgender athletes' participation and hyperandrogenism in sport.

§ 5.02 Historical Context

Prior to passage of Title IX and the statute's eventual implementation, girls and women faced persistent institutional barriers to interscholastic and intercollegiate athletic competition, which were byproducts of societal norms and pressures.[1] Adhering to Victorian ideals, women's sport began as an exercise for instilling balance and grace. Activities were structured carefully to avoid "detract[ion] from the[] ability to reproduce."[2] Societal structures and medical myths led male and female academic

---

1. *See, e.g.*, Cohen v. Brown Univ., 101 F.3d 155 (1st Cir. 1996), *cert. denied*, 520 U.S. 1186 (1997); *see also* ASSOCIATION OF AMERICAN COLLEGES, *What Constitutes Equality for Women in Sport?: Federal Law Puts Women in the Running* 1, 3 (April 1974) [hereinafter *Sports Report*] ("Myths die slowly.... The attitudes that people have about women in sport influence the total athletic opportunities available to women — the funding of their program, the adequacy of their facilities and equipment, the employment conditions of their teachers and coaches, etc.").

2. Vassar College, *Athletics, 1865–1945*, VASSAR ENCYCLOPEDIA (2005), https://www.vassar.edu/vcencyclopedia/student-organizations/athletics/athletics-1865-1945.html.

leaders to relegate women's athletics to non- (or less) strenuous and noncompetitive activities.[3] Women were prevented from marathons based on the belief that women were "not physiologically able to run a marathon."[4] Women's basketball was played in a half-court model to avoid increased stress on the body[5] and contact sports generally were thought to place women's supposedly weaker bones at risk.[6]

Competition as a female athlete for a majority of the twentieth century came with "joys and indignities,"[7] rooted in deference to boys' and men's athletics. In intercollegiate competition, this translated to institutions allowing opportunities for women only in the form of "Play Days" consisting of noncompetitive intercollegiate activities once a year,[8] non-school based programs, or intramurals.[9] Women's athletics were not simply underfunded, but administratively disapproved of, resulting in women receiving the cast-offs of what college administrators reserved for the men.[10]

Societal barriers came down slowly following the enactment of Title IX.[11] The gradual societal response began when Billie Jean King's tennis victory over Bobby Riggs "convinced skeptics that a female athlete [could] survive pressure-filled situations."[12] Financial models in higher education had to respond as well, as schools scrambled to equalize their offerings during Title IX's three-year implementation period.[13] For instance, the University of Washington had to equalize a $2.48 million budget disparity between their men's and women's athletics programs in the 1974 fiscal year.[14] Moreover, Washington's experience was not anomalous.

---

3. Elizabeth A. Gregg & Vanessa H. Gregg, *Women in Sport: Historical Perspectives*, 36 CLIN. SPORTS MED. 603, 605 (2017); Deborah Brake & Elizabeth Catlin, *The Path of Most Resistance: The Long Road Toward Gender Equity in Intercollegiate Athletics*, 51 DUKE J. OF GENDER L. & POL'Y 52 (1996); *see also Sports Report, supra* note 1, at 2–3.

4. Alisa Ross, *The Woman who Crashed the Boston Marathon*, JSTOR DAILY (March 18, 2018), https://daily.jstor.org/the-woman-who-crashed-the-boston-marathon/.

5. Patricia A. Cain, *Women, Race and Sports: Life Before Title IX*, 4 J. GENDER, RACE & JUSTICE 337, 340–42 (2001).

6. *See Sports Report, supra* note 1, at 7.

7. Manisha Aggarwal-Schifellite, *How They Leveled the Playing Field*, THE HARVARD GAZETTE (Nov. 19, 2020), https://news.harvard.edu/gazette/story/2020/11/what-it-was-like-to-be-a-female-athlete-before-title-ix/.

8. Gregg & Gregg, *supra* note 3, at 605.

9. Vassar College, *supra* note 2.

10. *See* Aggarwal-Schifellite, *supra* note 7; *see also Sports Report, supra* note 1, at 7.

11. As late as 1972, the year Title IX was enacted, researchers reported "recent evidence" indicating that differences in male and female athletic opportunities "may be more of an artifact of societal or cultural restrictions imposed on the female … rather than a result of true biological differences." *Sports Report, supra* note 1, at 6.

12. THE LEARNING NETWORK, *Sept. 20, 1973: Billie Jean King Wins the 'Battle of the Sexes,'* N.Y. TIMES (Sept. 20, 2011), https://learning.blogs.nytimes.com/2011/09/20/sept-20-1973-billie-jean-king-wins-the-battle-of-the-sexes/.

13. *See* Julia Lamber, *Gender and Intercollegiate Athletics: Data and Myths*, 34 U. MICH. J. L. REFORM 151, 155 (2000).

14. Radcliffe Institute for Advanced Study, *Playing Fair? Title IX at 45*, HARVARD UNIV. (2017), https://www.radcliffe.harvard.edu/schlesinger-library/exhibition/playing-fair-title-ix-45.

U.S. Department of Education policy interpretations and legal decisions applying Title IX facilitated marked increases in sports participation opportunities for girls and women.[15] The year before Title IX's enactment, 31,852 women participated in intercollegiate athletics.[16] By the 2019–20 academic year, this number had increased to 221,042.[17] Although female college athletic participation has increased dramatically, women still lag behind men.[18] As a percentage of total participants at the collegiate level, women have closed the gap from being 15.5% of the intercollegiate student-athlete population in 1971 to being 43.7% of the student-athlete population in 2019.[19] When compared to overall enrollment, male student-athletes remain a constant 3.3% of the male undergraduate student population, while women still lag behind at 1.9% of the female undergraduate student population.[20]

Statistics for high school participation show an even greater increase in access for women since Title IX's passage. Female high school athletic participation has increased eleven-fold, from just shy of three hundred thousand in 1971 to over three million in 2019.[21] Since Title IX's passage, high school participation rates for female athletes increased from less than 10% in 1972 to 42.8% of all high school athletes in 2018.[22] Current female participation on the high school level mirrors female participation on the collegiate level, hovering at just over 40% of total athletic participants.[23]

Notwithstanding Title IX's enactment and the progress it has catalyzed, female athletes across the country continue to endure a lack of equal access to participation and inequitable benefits and treatment (*e.g.*, inferior facilities and equipment compared to men).[24] Girls and women remain behind boys and men in participation at the high school and collegiate level, and social, political, and legal issues continue to place

---

15. *See* A Policy Interpretation: Title IX and Intercollegiate Athletics, 44 Fed. Reg. 71413-23 (Dec. 11, 1979) (to be codified at 45 C.F.R. pt. 26) [hereinafter *Policy Interpretation*]; *Cohen,* 101 F.3d at 163; Biediger v. Quinnipiac Univ., 691 F.3d 85 (2d Cir. 2012).

16. *See* DEPARTMENT OF EDUCATION, *Title IX: 25 Years of Progress* (June 1997), https://www2.ed. gov/pubs/TitleIX/part5.html [hereinafter *1997 Report*]; *see also* Erin Irick, *Student-Athlete Participation 1981-1982 — 2018-19: NCAA Sports Sponsorship and Participation Rates Report,* NAT'L COLLEGIATE ATHLETIC ASS'N 82-83 (2019), https://ncaaorg.s3.amazonaws.com/research/sportpart/2018-19RES_ SportsSponsorshipParticipationRatesReport.pdf [hereinafter *NCAA Participation Report*].

17. *See 1997 Report, supra* note 16; *NCAA Participation Report, supra* note 16, at 82-83.

18. *NCAA Participation Report, supra* note 16, at 82-83.

19. *See id.; see also 1997 Report, supra* note 16.

20. *See NCAA Participation Report, supra* note 16; *see also* NAT'L CTR FOR EDUC. STAT., TABLE 303.10: TOTAL FALL ENROLLMENT IN DEGREE-GRANTING POSTSECONDARY INSTITUTIONS, BY ATTENDANCE, STATUS, SEX OF STUDENT, AND CONTROL OF INSTITUTION: SELECTED YEARS 1947 THROUGH 2029 (2019), https://nces.ed.gov/programs/digest/d19/tables/dt19_303.10.asp [hereinafter *Postsecondary Enrollment 2019*].

21. THE NAT'L FED'N OF STATE HIGH SCH. ASS'NS, 2018–2019 HIGH SCHOOL ATHLETICS PARTICIPATION SURVEY, 50, 54–55 (2019), https://www.nfhs.org/media/1020412/2018-19_participation_survey.pdf.

22. *Id.*

23. *See id.*

24. *See Sports Report, supra* note 1, at 7; Aggarwal-Schifellite, *supra* note 7.

pressure on equality in sport.[25] Women have yet to meet the participation numbers men had in the year Title IX was enacted.[26] The social pressures that have long disadvantaged female athletic participants[27] persist today with layers of complexity. Barriers such as anti-LGBTQ+ attitudes, cultural impediments for immigrant families, racial disparity, and religious tensions about female sport participation have been identified as impediments to fully equitable treatment for female participation in sport.[28]

The slow pace of progress was evident at the 2021 NCAA Division I women's and men's basketball tournaments. A national uproar ensued after a video revealed the gross inequities in the men's and women's weight room facilities at the tournament site.[29] In response to severe criticism, the NCAA elevated the quality of the women's facilities.[30] The NCAA's men's basketball tournament is commonly referred to as "March Madness." Following the recommendation of an external gender-equity review of the women's tournament undertaken following the weight room controversy, the NCAA decided to extend the March Madness label to the women's basketball tournament beginning in 2022.[31] This change assisted in marketing the women's tournament.[32] The progress wrought by Title IX as well as some of the remaining impediments are discussed *infra*.

---

25. "In order to gain a full appreciation of the gender gaps that exist for girls and women in the U.S. sport system, it is important to consider those gaps within the larger context of other aspects of the human condition that contribute to the ways in which girls and women live in the world, the way they view themselves and the way others view them. In effect, not all female experience is the same, shaped as it is by cultural, ethnic, gender, political, national, racial, and religious identities as well as socio-economic status and sexual orientation, as examples. As a consequence, policy designed to encourage greater access to sport among U.S. girls and women needs to take the complexity of girls' and women's lives into account." Deborah Antonine, *Chasing Equity: The Triumphs, Challenges and Opportunities in Sports for Girls and Women*, Women's Sports Found. Rsch. Rep., 29–35 (Jan. 2020) (internal citations omitted).

26. *1997 Report, supra* note 16; THE NAT'L FED'N OF STATE HIGH SCH. ASS'NS, *supra* note 21.

27. *See Sports Report, supra* note 1, at 6.

28. Antonine, *supra* note 25 at 34. Additional barriers to female participation in athletics include mandatory sport fees following No Child Left Behind, the increased financial demand of the youth-sports elite club system, lack of safety in low-income neighborhoods placing girls with the choice of safety or participation, and sexual abuse of female athletes. *See id.*

29. Rachel Bachman, *The NCAA's 'March Madness' Basketball Brand will now Include Women*, WALL STREET J. (Sept. 29, 2021).

30. *Id.*

31. *Id.*

32. *Id.*

§ 5.03 Title IX — Participation
Opportunities and Equitable Treatment

[A] Overview of Title IX

Title IX, which was passed by Congress in 1972,[33] prohibits sex discrimination in educational programs. The statutory language provides: "[N]o person in the United States shall, on the basis of sex, be excluded from participation in, be denied the benefits of, or be subjected to discrimination under any education program or activity receiving Federal financial assistance...."[34] Educational institutions at all levels (*i.e.*, grade school and colleges) are subject to Title IX if any program within the educational institution receives federal funding.[35] Although Title IX prohibits sex discrimination in three areas within educational institutions — employment, treatment of students, and admissions — the statute is most commonly associated with prohibiting sex discrimination in athletics programs.

An injured person alleging Title IX discrimination can file a complaint with the Department of Education ("DOE") which will trigger a mandatory investigation by the agency.[36] The DOE is also authorized to periodically conduct compliance reviews of institutions without a complaint having been filed.[37] If the DOE finds that either the complaint has merit or its investigation reveals that an institution is noncompliant, it will inform the institution and attempt to informally resolve the matter.[38] If no resolution is reached, the agency may terminate federal funding after an administrative hearing.[39]

In *Cannon v. University of Chicago*,[40] the Court recognized an implied private right of action pursuant to which individuals can sue institutions for discrimination in violation of Title IX. Individuals exercising this implied right of action may seek injunctive relief and monetary damages.[41] Withholding federal funds facilitates Title

---

33. Title IX refers to that Title of the Higher Education Amendments Act, 20 U.S.C. §§ 1681–1688 (1972).

34. 20 U.S.C. § 1681(a).

35. The applicability of Title IX does not depend on the level of education but whether an educational institution is the recipient of federal funding. 20 U.S.C. § 1681(a). *See* Ollier v. Sweetwater Union High Sch. Dist., 768 F.3d 843, 855 (2014) (stating Title IX does not specifically refer to high schools but does not exclude them).

36. *See* Brust v. Regents of Univ. of Cal., 2007 WL 4365521 at *5 (E.D. Calif. Dec. 12, 2007); 34 C.F.R. § 100.7(b).

37. *Brust*, 2007 WL 4365521, at *5; 34 C.F.R. § 100.7(b).

38. *Brust*, 2007 WL 4365521, at *5.

39. *Id.* at *5; 34 C.F.R. § 100.8. *See also* 20 U.S.C. § 1682; Fitzgerald v. Barnstable Sch. Comm., 555 U.S. 246, 247 (2009). The right of an administrative agency to revoke federal funds is a consequence of Title IX's promulgation pursuant to the Spending Clause of the U.S. Constitution. *See* Equity in Athletics, Inc. v. Dep't of Educ. 675 F. Supp. 2d 660, 674 (W.D. Va. 2009).

40. 441 U.S. 677, 717 (1979).

41. Franklin v. Gwinnett Cty. Pub. Schs., 503 U.S. 60, 76 (1992).

IX's goal of preventing the use of federal funds for discriminatory purposes.[42] Title IX's other purpose, protecting individuals against discrimination, is facilitated by the private right of action.[43] Because Title IX does not have an exhaustion of administrative remedies requirement, an individual can file suit directly in court pursuant to the implied private right of action.[44]

The DOE's Office of Civil Rights ("OCR") promulgated regulations establishing the requirements with which educational institutions must comply to avoid violating Title IX.[45] OCR's 1979 Intercollegiate Athletics Policy Interpretation, commonly known as the *Policy Interpretation*, specifies that Title IX regulates institutional conduct in three areas: (1) accommodating the interests and abilities of athletes (*i.e.*, sports participation opportunities); (2) athletic financial assistance (*i.e.*, scholarships); and, (3) other program areas (*i.e.*, benefits and treatment such as equipment, supplies, and facilities).

The use of Title IX in athletics was initially limited because it was interpreted as applying only to specific programs within a school or college that received federal funding.[46] Congress's passage of the Civil Rights Restoration Act of 1987, which established that Title IX applies on an institution-wide basis (if any program within an educational institution receives federal funds), spurred the use of Title IX to achieve greater gender equity in athletics.[47] As alluded to above, the increased use of the statute as an enforcement mechanism to increase athletic opportunities for female students was further facilitated by a U.S. Supreme Court decision, *Franklin v. Gwinnett County Public Schools*,[48] which permitted plaintiffs to recover monetary damages and to be awarded attorney's fees for intentional violations of Title IX.[49]

---

42. *Fitzgerald*, 555 U.S. at 247.

43. *Cannon*, 441 U.S. at 704.

44. *Fitzgerald*, 555 U.S. at 247.

45. *Policy Interpretation, supra* note 15, at 71414. The promulgation of the *Policy Interpretation* was considered a dire necessity:

> The three-year transition period for compliance with the regulations expired in July of 1978. HEW's Office for Civil Rights (OCR) had received nearly one hundred complaints alleging discrimination in athletics programs. Based on these comments, the OCR determined the need for further guidance "so as to provide a framework within which complaints [could] be resolved and to provide institutions of higher education with additional guidance on the requirements of compliance with Title IX." On December 11, 1978, the OCR issued a proposed policy interpretation which would become the *1979 Policy Interpretation*.

Brake & Catlin, *supra* note 3, at 56.

46. Grove City College v. Bell, 465 U.S. 555, 556 (1984).

47. *See* NCAA v. Smith, 525 U.S. 459, 466 (1999) ("'a program or activity' includes 'all of the operations of ... a college, university, or other postsecondary institution'") (citing 20 U.S.C. § 1687(2)(A)).

48. 503 U.S. 60, 75 (1992).

49. *Id.*; Pederson v. Louisiana State Univ., 213 F.3d 858, 879–80 (5th Cir. 2000) (regarding whether Louisiana State University's conduct was intentional, the court stated: "If an institution makes a decision not to provide equal athletic opportunities for its female students because of paternalism and stereotypical assumptions about their interests and abilities, that institution intended to treat women differently because of their sex. Moreover, Appellees' ignorance about whether they are violating Title IX does not excuse their intentional decision not to accommodate effectively the interests of their female students by not providing sufficient athletic opportunities.").

Title IX claims in athletics can be categorized as involving "effective accommodation," which focuses on athletic participation opportunities, or "equal treatment," which focuses on benefits and treatment.[50] We turn first to effective accommodation claims.

[B] Effective Accommodation

[1] The OCR's 1996 Clarification and the Three-Prong Test

The OCR's *Policy Interpretation* is complemented by its 1996 *Clarification of Intercollegiate Athletics Policy Guidance: The Three-Part Test* ("*1996 Clarification*").[51] Together, these interpretations establish guidelines for determining whether an institution is accommodating the athletics interests and abilities of female and male students. The *1996 Clarification* establishes a three-pronged test on which courts rely in making this determination:[52]

(1) Whether intercollegiate level participation opportunities for male and female students are provided in numbers substantially proportionate to their respective [undergraduate] enrollments; or

(2) Where the members of one sex have been and are underrepresented among intercollegiate athletes, whether the institution can show a history and continuing practice of program expansion which is demonstrably responsive to the developing interests and abilities of the members of that sex; or

(3) Where the members of one sex are underrepresented among intercollegiate athletes, and the institution cannot show a history and continuing practice of program expansion, as described above, whether it can be demonstrated that the interests and abilities of the members of that sex have been fully and effectively accommodated by the present program.[53]

The *1996 Clarification* is structured to provide educational institutions with the flexibility to determine how to comply with Title IX.[54] Accordingly, each prong of the test can independently serve as a "safe harbor" for an institution.[55] By way of example and as detailed, *infra*, if an institution's athletics opportunities for women are not substantially proportionate (Prong 1) to the rate of full-time undergraduate female enrollment, an institution may nevertheless comply with Title IX if it can establish

---

50. *Pederson*, 213 F.3d at 864–65.

51. Norma Cantu, Assistant Sec'y for Civil Rights, *Clarification of Intercollegiate Athletics Policy Guidance: The Three-Part Test*, Office for Civil Rights, U.S. Dep't of Ed. (Jan. 16, 1996) [hereinafter *1996 Clarification*].

52. *Cohen*, 101 F.3d at 166; *see also* Biediger v. Quinnipiac Univ., 928 F. Supp. 2d 414, 436 (D. Conn. 2013).

53. *1996 Clarification, supra* note 51.

54. *See* Kelly v. Bd. of Trustees, 35 F.3d 265, 271 (1994) (acknowledging Title IX regulations do not simply require an equivalent women's sport for each male sport).

55. *Biediger*, 691 F.3d 93 (2012).

a history and continuing practice of expanding athletic opportunities for women (Prong 2).[56]

[2] Prong 1: Substantial Proportionality

The First Circuit's application of Prong 1 of the three-prong standard in *Cohen v. Brown University*[57] is representative of the approach adopted by other courts. In *Cohen*, the university, as a cost cutting measure, demoted two women's and two men's teams from university- to donor-funded status. The women on the two demoted women's teams sued the university alleging that it discriminated against them by operating its athletics program in violation of Title IX.[58]

The *Cohen* court adopted the *Policy Interpretation* and *1996 Clarification* in analyzing Brown University's compliance with Title IX.[59] In so doing, the court set the stage for subsequent courts to defer to the OCR's (as an administrative agency) interpretation of Title IX.[60] The court also stated principles subsequently adopted by other courts, including the notion that Title IX is neither an affirmative action nor a quota-based statute mandating "strict numerical equality between the gender balance of a college's athletics program and the gender balance of its student body."[61] Rather, the court characterized Title IX as an antidiscrimination statute that permits gender conscious remedies to redress discrimination in athletics programs.[62] According to the court, Title IX is a remedial statute concerned with balancing opportunities between the underrepresented gender and the predominate gender.[63] The court also noted that each Title IX case is a fact-based matter, and the three-pronged test is merely a starting point rather than a conclusion regarding an institution's liability.[64] Noting that Title IX protects both men and women against gender discrimination, the court acknowledged that the past history of discrimination against women in the institution's athletics program had resulted and would likely continue to result in women turning more frequently to the statute to remediate proscribed discriminatory conduct.[65]

The *Cohen* court began its analysis of the substantial proportionality prong by examining male and female athletes' respective intercollegiate athletics participation levels and undergraduate enrollments. At the time of the lawsuit, it found that there was a 13.1% disparity between women's athletic participation opportunities and

56. Boucher v. Syracuse Univ., 1998 WL 167296, at *4 (N.D. N.Y Apr. 3, 1998); *1996 Clarification*, *supra* note 51.

57. 101 F.3d 155 (1st Cir. 1996).

58. *Id.* at 161.

59. *Id.* at 166–67.

60. This approach is consistent with the Supreme Court's mandate in *Chevron, U.S.A., Inc. v. Nat. Res. Def. Couns., Inc.*, 467 U.S. 837, 865 (1984).

61. *Cohen*, 101 F.3d at 164.

62. *Id.* at 170.

63. *Id.* at 175.

64. *Id.* at 171.

65. *Id.* at 155.

women's full-time undergraduate enrollment. The court concluded this rendered Brown incapable of successfully invoking Title IX's substantial proportionality safe harbor as a defense to plaintiffs' discrimination claims.[66]

Recognizing the notion of institutional control and the flexibility Title IX affords institutions to achieve substantial proportionality, the court suggested the means pursuant to which the University could fall within the substantial proportionality safe harbor. The court stated Brown "may eliminate its athletics program altogether, it may elevate or create the requisite number of women's positions, it may demote or eliminate the requisite number of men's positions, or it may implement a combination of these remedies."[67] Consistent with the notion that institutions are ultimately in control of the operation of their athletics programs, the court accepted the lower court's interpretation of Title IX's policies, yet reversed the specific relief granted by the district court.[68] The district court's order required Brown to promote certain women's sports to university-funded status rather than allowing the university to cut men's teams to satisfy the substantial proportionality prong. In contrast, the circuit court noted that cutting men's teams in an effort to reach proportionality is "a permissible means of effectuating compliance with the statute."[69]

The substantial proportionality prong of the three-prong standard has spawned other issues to which the discussion will now turn.

[a] Defining Participation Opportunities

The *1996 Clarification* provides that the first step in assessing substantial proportionality is to determine the number of athletic opportunities afforded female and male athletes. Integral to this approach is making two determinations: what counts as a participation opportunity and what types of activities constitute sports for Title IX purposes.[70] As for what constitutes a countable participation opportunity, certain generalizations can be drawn from the *1996 Clarification* and Title IX caselaw. The *1996 Clarification* provides that countable participation opportunities for determining substantial proportionality means "actual athletes," not "unfilled slots."[71] Applying this interpretation, the *Cohen* court rejected Brown's attempt to use predetermined yet unfilled roster spots to measure their women's athletic participation.[72] The court stated that Title IX counts "actual participants on intercollegiate teams...."[73] In accord with this view, a court held that the "mere opportunity to try out for a team ... is

---

66. *Id.* at 163, 180.
67. *Id.* at 185.
68. *Id.* at 187.
69. *Id.*
70. *Ollier,* 768 F.3d at 855–56.
71. *1996 Clarification, supra* note 51.
72. *Cohen,* 101 F.3d at 167. Brown University's assertion in *Cohen* that if a sport permitted twenty individuals on the roster, yet only eighteen women participated in that academic year, it could use the number twenty for its participation numbers was rejected. *See id.* at 164.
73. *Id.* at 173.

not determinative of the question of 'previously limited' athletic opportunities under Title IX. 'Athletic opportunities' means real opportunities, not illusory ones."[74] Therefore, opportunities to try out for a team will not be considered unless such opportunities produce athletes participating on teams. At the collegiate level, participation in intercollegiate varsity-level sports can be counted in contrast to participation on junior varsity or club teams.[75] Moreover, participation numbers must be measured through assessment of the entire athletic department, not simply focusing on specific individual sports.[76] Finally, Title IX considers the number of participation opportunities rather than the number of female and male teams.[77]

[b] Countable Activities (Sports)

Courts have also considered what constitutes a sport for purposes of determining whether to count female participants when considering substantial proportionality. An *OCR 2008 Dear Colleague Letter*[78] states an activity counts for determining substantial proportionality if the activity: has support (*e.g.*, budget, support staff, recruiting opportunities); affords opportunities for competition against intercollegiate or interscholastic competitors from like institutions;[79] is recognized and thus sponsored by a national organization such as the NCAA or NAIA;[80] and has a defined season with consistent competition rules governed by a uniform body.[81]

The NCAA defines "sport" as "an institutional activity ... involving physical exertion for the purpose of competition against teams or individuals within an intercollegiate competition structure [which] operate[s] under standardized rules with rating/scoring systems ratified by at least one official regulatory agency and/or governing body."[82] Assuming a sport is not recognized by a national organization like the NCAA or is not an NCAA-sanctioned emerging sport, the OCR relies on elements of the NCAA's definition of "sport" in its analysis of the activity.[83] The OCR employs a holistic analysis that assesses the activity's program structure and administration, team preparation and competition, and national governing body oversight.[84]

---

74. Williams v. Sch. Dist. of Bethlehem, 998 F.2d 168, 175 (3d Cir. 1993); *see also* Horner v. Ky. High Sch. Athletic Ass'n, 43 F.3d 265 (6th Cir. 1994).

75. *Cohen*, 101 F.3d at 186.

76. *Williams*, 998 F.2d at 176.

77. *Id.*

78. Stephanie Monroe, Assistant Sec'y for Civil Rights, *Dear Colleague Letter: Athletic Activities Counted for Title IX Compliance*, Office for Civil Rights, U.S. Dep't of Ed. (Sept. 17, 2008) [hereinafter *2008 Dear Colleague Letter*].

79. *Id.*

80. *Id.*; *Biediger*, 928 F. Supp. at 442.

81. *2008 Dear Colleague Letter*, *supra* note 78.

82. National Collegiate Athletic Association Committee on Women's Athletics, *NCAA Emerging Sports for Women Process Guide*, 1–2, https://ncaaorg.s3.amazonaws.com/inclusion/emsports/INC_EmergingSportsForWomen-ProcessGuide.pdf.

83. *2008 Dear Colleague Letter*, *supra* note 78.

84. The structure and administration of the activity evaluates operating budgets, benefits, services, coaching staff, facilities, length of season, off-campus recruiting, number of competition opportunities,

In *Biedeger v. Quinnipiac University*,[85] the defendant eliminated NCAA-recognized women's sports and added cheerleading.[86] Using the steps outlined by the OCR, the court refused to recognize cheerleading as a sport.[87] The court acknowledged that certain changes moved cheerleading in the direction of recognition as a sport, but pointed to a lack of the following as reasons to refuse recognition: off-campus recruiting, a uniform set of rules applicable to competitive cheerleading, a "progressive playoff system leading to a championship game," recognition by the NCAA as a sport or an emerging sport, and Quinnipiac's team not facing varsity intercollegiate competitive cheerleading teams.[88] Thus far, the issue raised in *Biedeger* has largely been restricted to cheerleading, but other emerging activities could prompt similar analysis.

[c] Evaluating the Numerical Disparity

The statistical basis for a determination of substantial proportionality resides in the gap between the athletic participation opportunities for the unrepresented sex, typically women, and that sex's undergraduate enrollment as a percentage of the whole. In *Cohen*, the 13.01% disparity between Brown's female undergraduate enrollment and the number of women participating in intercollegiate varsity athletics fell far short of substantial proportionality in athletics opportunities for women and men.[89] Although there is no "magic number at which substantial proportionality is achieved,"[90] OCR regulatory interpretations and judicial decisions offer guidance. The Department of Education states that "there is no set ratio that constitutes substantially proportionate."[91] The *1996 Clarification* further provides that "substantial proportionality is determined on a case-by-case basis" in light of "the institution's specific circumstances and the size of its athletic program."[92] Moreover, the *1996 Clarification* instructs courts "that substantial proportionality generally requires that 'the number of additional participants ... required for exact proportionality' be insufficient 'to sustain a viable team.'"[93]

These principles and judicial decisions give rise to both certainty and uncertainty. A two percent or lower disparity in women's participation opportunities and enroll-

nature of competition, existence of a uniform set of rules that govern competition, and nature of playoff/championship. Team preparation and competition evaluate a team's practice time, regime, venues, length of competitive season, and minimum number of competitive opportunities. *Biediger*, 691 F.3d at 94, 103–04.

85. *Id.*
86. *Id.* at 91.
87. *Id.* at 103.
88. *Id.* The court ruled that the NCAA's recognition of an activity as an "emerging sport" creates a presumption that it should be counted as a sport for Title IX purposes. *See NCAA Emerging Sports, supra* note 82.
89. *Cohen*, 101 F.3d at 163.
90. *Equity in Athletics*, 639 F.3d at 110.
91. Valerie Bonnette & Daniel Lamar, *Title IX Athletics Investigator's Manual*, Dep't. of Educ. (1990), available at: https://files.eric.ed.gov/fulltext/ED400763.pdf.
92. *1996 Clarification, supra* note 51.
93. *Ollier*, 768 F.3d at 856 (quoting *Biediger*, 691 F.3d at 94) (internal quotation marks omitted).

ment will likely be sufficient to establish substantial proportionality, as recognized by the court in *Equity in Athletics, Inc. v. Department of Education*.[94] On the other hand, gaps of 10% or greater, such as the 10.6% and 10.8% disparities in *Roberts v. Colorado State Bd. of Agriculture*[95] and *Bryant v. Colgate University*,[96] respectively, will invariably fail to demonstrate substantial proportionality in athletic participation opportunities.

Uncertainty arises in those instances where the disparity is in excess of two and less than ten percent. Within this range, courts are mindful to state that determining substantial proportionality is to be made through a fact specific inquiry. Circumstances that courts consider include whether the numerical disparity is of such magnitude to allow the defendant institution to field a new girls' or women's sport, and whether the participation gap arises, or is increased, as a result of institutional conduct.[97]

In *Ollier v. Sweetwater Union High School Dist.*,[98] the court found that a 6.7% disparity in girls' athletics participation and enrollment was too large for a school district to fall within the substantial proportionality safe harbor. A finding that the gap amounted to forty-seven athletes was instrumental to the court's decision. That number of athletes would have been sufficient for a new sport for girls, the underrepresented sex. Similarly, in *Brust v. Regents of the University of California*,[99] the court rejected defendant's motion to dismiss based on its assertion that a 6% disparity brought it within the substantial proportionality safe harbor. Acknowledging that the substantial proportionality inquiry is inherently a question of fact, the court stated that substantial proportionality determinations could only be made in light of the size of the University's enrollment and athletic program.[100]

The Second Circuit's decision in *Biedeger* offers additional insight. The court considered whether a 3.62% gap — amounting to thirty-eight participation opportunities — brought the University within the substantial proportionality safe harbor. It observed that this gap created a "borderline case."[101] Nevertheless, the "specific circumstance" supporting the court's conclusion that a lack of substantial proportionality existed, included the University's elimination of a viable women's athletic team, which only required fourteen individuals to compete.[102]

---

94. 639 F.3d 91, 110 (4th Cir. 2011).

95. 998 F.2d 824 (10th Cir. 1993).

96. 1996 WL 328446 (N.D. N.Y. 1996).

97. *See Ollier*, 768 F.3d at 857; *Biediger*, 691 F.3d at 95.

98. *Ollier*, 768 F.3d at 856–57.

99. 2007 WL 4365521, at *4 (E.D. Cal. 2007).

100. *Id.*

101. *Biediger*, 691 F.3d at 95.

102. *Id.* at 107; *see also* Cohen v. Brown University, 16 F.4th 935, 941 (1st Cir. 2021) (discussing the 1998 indefinite settlement agreement arising from *Cohen*, 101 F.3d 155, requiring a balance of between 2.5% and 3.5%).

[3] Prong 2: History and Continuing Practice of
Program Expansion

Prong 2 of the *1996 Clarification* provides that an educational institution unable to establish substantial proportionality can nevertheless comply with Title IX by showing "a history and continuing practice of program expansion that is demonstrably responsive to the developing interest and abilities of the members of the underrepresented sex."[103] In addressing this affirmative defense, the *Cohen* court stated that Title IX compliance is achieved "so long as a university is continually expanding athletic opportunities in an ongoing effort to meet the needs of the underrepresented gender, and persists in this approach as interest and ability levels in its student body and secondary feeder schools rise."[104] The *1996 Clarification* further provides that compliance under Prong 2 will be determined by assessing whether the institution can demonstrate a history of expanding participation opportunities for the underrepresented gender and a continuing practice of expanding such opportunities in response to its student body's "interest and abilities."[105]

A history of program expansion examines the following factors:

(1) an institution's record of adding intercollegiate teams, or upgrading teams to intercollegiate status, for the underrepresented sex;

(2) an institution's record of increasing the numbers of participants in intercollegiate athletics who are members of the underrepresented sex; and

(3) an institution's affirmative responses to requests by students or others for addition or elevation of sports.[106]

An institution's contention that it has a continuing practice of expanding opportunities considers: "(1) an institution's current implementation of a nondiscriminatory policy or procedure for requesting the addition of sports ...[107] and the effective communication of the policy or procedure to students; and, (2) an institution's current implementation of a plan of program expansion that is responsive to developing interests and abilities."[108]

These factors were adopted and examined in *Boucher v. Syracuse University*.[109] In addressing Syracuse University's history of program expansion, the court found that over the ten-year period following Title IX's enactment, Syracuse added sports that

---

103. *Cohen*, 101 F.3d at 166; *Boucher*, 1998 WL 167296 at *3; *Bryant*, 1996 WL 328446 at *10.

104. *Cohen*, 991 F.2d at 898.

105. *1996 Clarification, supra* note 51; *see also Boucher*, 1998 WL 167296 at *3.

106. *1996 Clarification, supra* note 51; *see also Boucher*, 1998 WL 167296 at *5.

107. *1996 Clarification, supra* note 51; *see also Boucher*, 1998 WL 167296 at *3. The addition of sports need not be the creation of a team from "scratch" but can also include the elevation of a high-performing or high-interest club or intramural team to varsity status. *Id.*

108. *1996 Clarification, supra* note 51; *see also Boucher*, 1998 WL 167296 at *3.

109. *Boucher*, 1998 WL 167296 at *3–5.

increased the number of participation opportunities for women.[110] Although the University failed to add any women's sports between 1982 and 1995, the court found it had increased the financial and operational resources for women's sports programs and had increased the number of participants in women's sports by 47 percent.[111] Moreover, the institution added two women's athletic teams between 1995 and 1998 and planned to add a third new women's sport in 1999.[112] When assessing if a demonstrated continuing practice was present, the court pointed to the addition of women's sports teams, the University's increased financial support (*e.g.*, athletic scholarships, upgraded facilities, and support services) for women's athletics, and the institution's monitoring in order to be "responsive to the abilities and interests of the student body."[113] The court added that while it is preferable that an institution have a formal policy to demonstrate its continuing practice, the court concluded the University's actual practice was sufficient evidence.[114]

Prong 2 also focuses on whether an institution is attentive to student interests. The *Cohen* court stated: "So long as a university ... persists in this approach as interest and ability levels in its student body and secondary feeder schools rise, benchmark two is satisfied."[115] The failure of an institution to be attentive to student interests resulted in a court's rejection of Colgate University's argument that it fell within the Prong 2 safe harbor. The court's conclusion was supported by the University's refusal to add a women's sport when the opportunity arose.[116] Moreover, an institution is unlikely to sustain its burden under Prong 2 when it engages in remedial efforts such as adding sports while at the same time decreasing actual female participation opportunities. This occurred in *Mansourian v. Board of Regents of University of California*,[117] where the court held that a finding of continued expansion would be incongruous when considering the decrease in participation numbers, regardless of the aggressive remedial efforts taken by the University of California, Davis to add sports.[118] An institution is unlikely to sustain its burden if it is inattentive to the growing interests of the underrepresented sex in particular sports as evidenced by women's increased participation in certain club sports sufficient to sustain a varsity-level team.[119] A court is likely to arrive at the same conclusion where an institution is inattentive to sports participation offerings for girls and women in feeder-school popu-

---

110. *Id.* at *4.
111. *Id.*
112. *Id.*
113. *Id.*
114. *Id.*
115. *Cohen*, 991 F.2d at 898.
116. *Bryant*, 1996 WL 328446, at *11.
117. 816 F. Supp. 2d 869, 924 (E.D. Cal. 2011).
118. *Id.*; *see also* Favia v. Indiana Univ. of Pennsylvania, 812 F. Supp. 578, 585 (W.D. Pa. 1993) (factors contributing to the court's conclusion that the university failed to carry the burden of proof required under Prong 2 included the elimination of women's sports).
119. *See Bryant*, 1996 WL 328446 at *9.

lations[120] or where an institution eliminates women's participation opportunities even if it provides nondiscriminatory reasoning for doing so.[121]

[4] Prong 3: Fully Accommodating Interests and Abilities

The final avenue by which an institution can show that it complies with its Title IX duty to provide gender equality in athletic participation opportunities is if it has adequately fulfilled the needs and interests of its student population.[122] This prong determines if the "gender imbalance in athletics is the product of impermissible discrimination or merely the genders' varying levels of interest in sports."[123] The *1996 Clarification* advises consideration of whether there is: (a) unmet interest in a particular sport;[124] (b) sufficient ability to sustain a team in the sport;[125] and (c) a reasonable expectation of competition for the team.[126]

To measure interest, a school should periodically conduct surveys of its student body to determine whether members of the underrepresented sex have unmet interests.[127] As the OCR factors suggest, the interest of the underrepresented sex must be

---

120. *See Boucher*, 1998 WL 167296 at *4.

121. Portz v. St. Cloud State Univ., 401 F. Supp. 3d 834, 860 (D. Minn. 2019); *see* Mayerova v. Eastern Mich. Univ., 346 F. Supp. 3d 983, 996 (E.D. Mich. 2018).

122. *Cohen*, 101 F.3d at 174.

123. *Ollier*, 768 F.3d at 858 (stating that a school with a gender imbalance does not violate Title IX if interest is satisfied).

124. The *1996 Clarification* lists the following as relevant to determining unmet interest among students of the underrepresented gender: requests by current and admitted students that a sport be added; requests that a club team be elevated to intercollegiate status; the levels of participation in club or intramural sports; and results of questionnaires/surveys soliciting student interest in a particular sport. *1996 Clarification*, *supra*, note 51, at 9–10.

125. Specific factual circumstances relevant to this determination include: the athletic experiences of students in club and intramural sports and the opinions of athletic personnel and students regarding the potential of students to sustain a varsity team, and whether the team has competed at the intramural or club levels. *Id.* at 10.

126. Relevant factors in making this determination include: the existence of competitive opportunities in the sport offered by teams against which the school competes and competitive opportunities in the sports at schools in the institution's geographic region. *Id.* at 10–11.

127. *See* Portz v. St. Cloud State Univ., 401 F. Supp. 3d 834, 861 (D. Minn. 2019). For a brief period, the OCR in a "controversial move" permitted surveys as the exclusive means for measuring interest, regardless of the response rate of survey participants. James F. Manning, Assistant Sec'y of Civil Rights, *Additional Clarification of Intercollegiate Athletics Policy: Three-Part Test — Part Three*, Office of Civil Rights, U.S. Dep't of Ed. (March 17, 2005); *see also* Robb v. Lock Haven Univ. of Pennsylvania, 2019 WL 2005636 at *10, n.67 (M.D. Pa. May 7, 2019) (relying on a 17% response rate as a demonstration of sufficient interest); Barrett v. West Chester Univ. of Pennsylvania, 2003 WL 22803477, at *9 (E.D. Pa. Nov. 12, 2003) (relying on a 39% response rate, ignoring NCAA guidance that 60% is necessary). After five years, the OCR withdrew this directive and now requires the review of several factors, including survey results, formal requests, club and intramural participation, and interscholastic sports in which admitted students compete. Russlyn Ali, Assistant Secretary of Civil Rights, Dear Colleague Letter, Office for Civil Rights, U.S. Dep't of Ed. (Apr. 20, 2010), https://www2.ed.gov/about/offices/list/ocr/letters/colleague-20100420.pdf [hereinafter *2010 OCR Letter*]; Paul Anderson & Barbara Osborne, *A Historical Review of Title IX Litigation*, 18 MARQ. SPORTS L. REV. 127 (2008).

significant enough to support a team in a particular sport.[128] Moreover, there must be reasonable prospects of competition for the proposed team within the school's athletic conference and/or geographic region.[129]

Institutions have been largely unsuccessful in arguing that the interests and abilities of women and girls have been met where a school has eliminated or threatened to eliminate an existing women's team.[130] In *Ollier*, the school cut its field hockey team in response to a coaching vacancy and difficulty encountered in hiring a new coach.[131] Because team members' interest in playing the sport did not falter, the court ruled that their interests had not been fully accommodated.[132] Similarly, in *Roberts*, the continued interest of roster members of an eliminated softball team created an adequate demonstration of unmet need.[133] In *Horner v. Kentucky High School Athletic Association*,[134] the court determined that evidence showing that seventeen percent of schools in the state-wide high school association were interested in creating a new softball team was sufficient to demonstrate unmet interest and need.[135] On the other hand, an institution is "not required to field a team in response to the pleas of 'one talented player' if sufficient numbers to form a team to compete do not exist."[136]

[C] Equitable Benefits and Treatment

The history of sports in the United States is marked by inequitable treatment of female athletes. In 1976, members of the Yale University's women's rowing team protested the disparity in showers in the men's program versus the women's program by marching naked into the athletic director's office to assert the right for their bodies to be treated equally.[137] This incident demonstrated that the inequitable treatment of women in athletics was not restricted to disproportionately fewer athletic participation opportunities for women but extended to inequities in other aspects of athletics. The OCR's *1979 Clarification* established Title IX's second mandate, to achieve

128. *Biediger*, 691 F.3d at 107.
129. *Bryant*, 1996 WL 328446, at *10.
130. *Biediger*, 691 F.3d at 91; *Roberts*, 998 F.2d 824; *2010 OCR Letter, supra* note 127 (stating that the recent elimination of a team creates a presumption of noncompliance).
131. 768 F.3d at 858.
132. *Id.* at 859.
133. 998 F.2d at 831.
134. 43 F.3d 265 (6th Cir. 1994).
135. *Id.* at 269. While "significant" falls somewhere between one interested athlete and enough for a full team roster, for conferences it presumptively falls somewhere in the low teens. *Id.*
136. *Horner*, 43 F.3d at 275, n.9 (quoting *Roberts*, 998 F.2d 831, n.10).
137. *See* New York Times Archives, *Yale Women Strip to Protest a Lack of Crew's Showers*, N.Y. TIMES (March 4, 1976), https://www.nytimes.com/1976/03/04/archives/yale-women-strip-to-protest-a-lack-of-crews-showers.html#:~:text=NEW%20HAVEN%2C%20March%203%E2%80%94Nineteen, fa%20cilities%20at%20Derby%2C%20Conn; *see also* Steven Wulf, *Title Waves*, ESPN (May 29, 2012), https://www.espn.com/espnw/title-ix/story/_/id/7985418/espn-magazine-1976-protest-helped-define-title-ix-movement.

gender equity regarding financial aid (*i.e.*, athletic scholarships)[138] and the operational elements of athletics.[139]

[1] Athletic Financial Assistance (Scholarships)

In regard to financial assistance, the OCR's *Policy Interpretation* requires that scholarships be awarded in proportion to the participation opportunities afforded to female and male athletes.[140] Assume that 40% of student-athletes are women even though they compromise 55% of an institution's undergraduate population. The university will be in compliance regarding athletic financial assistance if women receive 40% of the total athletic scholarships awarded by the institution. Thus, an institution can be noncompliant with Title IX regarding athletic participation opportunities while being compliant regarding athletic scholarships.[141]

[2] Equivalence in Athletic Benefits and Treatment

The OCR's *Policy Interpretation* requires an equivalency of benefits and opportunities in matters including: the provision of equipment and supplies; scheduling of games and practice times; travel and per diem; opportunities for coaching and academic support; assignment of coaches and tutors; provision of locker rooms and facilities; provision of medical and training services; provision of housing and dining facilities; and publicity.[142] Issues that have emerged from courts' application of this aspect of the *Policy Interpretation* include: whether equivalency is to be measured on a program-wide or sport-specific basis; the circumstances under which a disparity is substantial; when a substantial disparity results in a violation of Title IX; whether identical benefits or treatment is required; and what amounts to nondiscriminatory reasons for a lack of equivalency.

Several of the foregoing issues were addressed by the court in *McCormick v. School District of Mamaroneck*.[143] There, the scheduling of girls' high school soccer in the spring was inconsistent with 99.1% of other schools in the state of New York, which scheduled boys' and girls' soccer in the fall. The defendant school district's out-of-season scheduling of girls' soccer deprived plaintiffs of the ability to compete for the regional and state championships. Boys, who played soccer in the fall, were not deprived of these competitive opportunities.[144] The court found that the scheduling of girls' soccer created a substantial disparity that denied plaintiffs equality of athletic opportunities.[145] The court reasoned that: "scheduling of soccer in the spring, ...

---

138. 34 C.F.R. § 106.37.

139. 34 C.F.R. § 106.41(c)(2)–(10).

140. "[Institutions] must provide reasonable opportunities for such award of financial assistance for members of each sex in proportion to the number of students of each sex participating in intercollegiate athletics." *Policy Interpretation, supra* note 15, at 71415.

141. *See id.*

142. 34 C.F.R. § 106.41(c)(2)–(10).

143. 370 F.3d 275, 292 (2d Cir. 2004).

144. *Id.* at 280.

145. *Id.* at 294; 34 C.F.R. § 106.41(c).

place[d] a ceiling on the possible achievement of the female soccer players that they cannot break through no matter how hard they strive. The boys are subject to no such ceiling."[146]

In reaching the foregoing conclusion, the court provided a roadmap for assessing whether a disparity in benefits and treatment warrants granting relief to plaintiffs. First, disparities in benefits and treatment are to be assessed on program-wide versus a sport-specific basis.[147] Therefore, Title IX did not require that boys' and girls' soccer be scheduled identically. Consequently, the scheduling of girls' soccer out-of-season would not have violated Title IX if it had been offset by a comparable disadvantage in the boys' athletics program.[148] According to the court,

> [T]he *Policy Interpretation* makes clear that identical scheduling for boys and girls is not required.... "Under this standard, identical benefits, opportunities, or treatment are not required, provided the *overall effect* of any difference is negligible".... [C]ompliance should not be measured by a "sport-specific comparison" but rather by examining "program-wide benefits and opportunities...."[149]

Thus, a disparity in equipment for the soccer teams — with men having better equipment — may be balanced by an inverse disparity in locker room facilities for the swim teams — with women having a better locker room.

In *McCormick*, because the evidence failed to establish any areas of the athletics program in which girls received comparatively better treatment than boys, the court moved to the next stage of analysis, which considers whether the disparity is substantial and denies equality of athletic opportunity.[150] The court concluded that treating girls differently regarding a matter so fundamental to the experience of sports — the chance

---

146. *McCormick*, 370 F.3d at 293.

147. *Id.*; *see also Williams*, 998 F.2d at 176 (compliance in the area of equal treatment and benefits is assessed based on an overall comparison of the male and female athletic programs); 34 C.F.R. § 106.41(c).

148. *McCormick*, 370 F.3d 275 ("any difference favoring, for example, men's teams, should be offset by differences favoring women's teams in other sports") (citation omitted); *see also* Parker v. Franklin Cnty. Cmty. School Corp., 667 F.3d 910, 922 (7th Cir. 2012) ("disadvantaging one sex in one part of a school's athletic program can be offset by a comparable advantage to that sex in another area").

149. *McCormick*, 370 F.3d at 293; *accord* Clemons v. Shelby Cnty. Bd. of Educ., 818 F. App'x 453, 462 (6th Cir. 2020); *Portz*, 401 F. Supp. at 864 (stating that determining whether several inequities in equipment and facilities violate Title IX must be made holistically, examining the entire athletic program); *Parker*, 677 F.3d at 922 (stating, in light of *McCormick*, that "[t]he court should look to the overall effect of any differences, on a program-wide, not sport specific basis.").

150. *See McCormick*, 370 F.3d at 293; *Parker*, 667 F.3d at 922. When evaluating a scheduling disparity, the court must determine "whether a difference in scheduling has a negative impact on one sex, and then determine whether that disparity is substantial enough to deny members equality of athletic opportunity." The *Parker* court concluded that the scheduling of women's basketball competitions in non-primetime time slots disadvantaged female athletes who were also sent the message that they were "subordinate to their male counterparts." *Id.*; *see also* Communities for Equity v. Michigan High Sch. Athletic Ass'n, 178 F. Supp. 2d 805 (W.D. Mich. 2001) (concluding playing sports in the non-traditional season disproportionately affects girls).

to be champions — is "inconsistent with Title IX's mandate of equal opportunity for both sexes."[151]

Assuming that the foregoing questions are answered affirmatively, the analysis then shifts to whether nondiscriminatory reasons support the disparity.[152] Disparities in benefits will not violate Title IX if they are a consequence of nondiscriminatory justifications such as those related to factors that are inherent to a sport, including: rules of play; nature/replacement of equipment; rates of injury resulting from participation; nature of facilities required for competition; and the maintenance/upkeep requirements of those facilities.[153] Additional nondiscriminatory factors may arise from management of a sport or event which requires a different level of expenditure, such as crowd management at football and men's basketball competitions, which often draw the largest spectator crowds.[154] The *Policy Interpretation* acknowledges that this may be most likely to occur where a school sponsors football.[155]

The *McCormick* court rejected defendant's proffered justifications: administrative difficulties relating to hiring a new coach, a lack of field space on which the girls could practice, and a shortage of officials. The court specifically stated that the "fact that money needs to be spent to comply with Title IX is obviously not a defense to the statute."[156] Due to an absence of data supporting defendant's contentions, the court also rejected arguments that moving soccer would hurt girls because it would force them to choose between playing soccer and other fall sports and that there might not be a sufficient number of girls to make a soccer team if the sport was moved to the fall.[157]

Other courts have explicitly and implicitly adopted the *McCormick* court's analysis to find disparities advantaging male athletes over female athletes in violation of Title IX.[158] In *Ollier*, the court found that the "quality, size and location of the locker rooms

151. *McCormick*, 370 F.3d at 295. *See Parker*, 667 F.3d at 923–24 (stating that systematic disparate scheduling "creates a cyclical effect that stifles ... and discourage[s] females from participating" in athletics. The impact of the "obvious disparity" can be substantial.); *but see* Clemons *ex rel* T.W. v. Shelby Cnty. Bd. of Educ., 818 F. App'x 453, 463 (6th Cir. 2020) (stating that holding tryouts — and therefore cuts — for girls' tennis team but not boys' tennis team because more girls wanted to play tennis than boys was not a "systemic" deprivation of girls' opportunity to participate).

152. *McCormick*, 370 F.3d at 297; *Parker*, 667 F.3d at 922–23 (stating that "[i]f an institution reserves primetime for boys ... the institutions would be expected to provide a nondiscriminatory justification for the difference in treatment." Elaborating with an example that adherence to "tradition" or "scheduling practices" would be an insufficient justification).

153. *McCormick*, 370 F.3d at 292 (citing the *Policy Interpretation*, *supra* note 15, at 71415–16).

154. *See Policy Interpretation*, *supra* note 15, at 71416. The *Policy Interpretation* adds, however, that the "variation in kind and degree" of event management must be done in a manner that does not hinder other sports from attracting larger crowds. *Id.*

155. *McCormick*, 370 F.3d at 292.

156. *Id.* at 297.

157. *Id.* at 298; *see Parker*, 667 F.3d at 922 (rejecting defendant's contention that scheduling that favored boys over girls was necessary to adhere to tradition was a non-discriminatory justification for scheduling that favored boys over girls).

158. *See, e.g.*, Landow v. Sch. Bd. of Brevard Cnty., 132 F. Supp. 2d 958, 964 (M.D. Fla. 2000) (finding numerous disparities that favored boys with respect to facilities, which collectively *signaled* "to the girls that they are not as important as the boys").

were better for male athletes than female athletes."[159] Male athletes were also provided with better "quality equipment and supplies than those provided to female athletes,"[160] more favorable scheduling such as the number and quality of practices, and better publicity and promotional support.[161] Courts have addressed disparities regarding alleged inequities in a range of benefits and treatment including: equipment and athletic facilities;[162] housing and dining options;[163] academic services such as tutoring;[164] coaching resources — experience and workload;[165] medical treatment and facilities;[166] and recruitment budgets and scheduling.[167]

In *Daniels v. School Board of Brevard County*,[168] inequities in facilities and equipment resulted from disparate funding; the baseball-team boosters raised more money than the softball-team boosters. The court rejected the defendant's argument that it was permissible for the school to allow boosters to supplement the funding for athletics teams provided by the school. It also stated, however, that because the school had "acquiesced" to that financial structure, the "defendant is responsible for the consequences of that approach" and must ensure equal athletic opportunities despite variations in fundraising capabilities.[169]

The court in *Haffer v. Temple University*[170] found no discrimination resulting from alleged inequities in scheduling and facilities,[171] because several men's and women's teams equitably shared facilities[172] and the men's and women's basketball teams each had an equal number of hours per week in the main basketball arena.[173] In response to plaintiffs' argument that evidence that the men's tennis team played more contests

---

159. 858 F. Supp 2d at 1111 (finding Title IX violation where boy's facilities were better maintained and protected from damage than girls' facilities).

160. *Id.*

161. *Id.* at 1112.

162. Daniels v. Sch. Bd. of Brevard Cnty., 985 F. Supp. 1458 (M.D. Fla. 1997) (inequalities consisted of dedicated field for baseball and a shared field for softball, better baseball scoreboards, batting cages, press boxes, dugouts); *Landow*, 132 F. Supp. 2d 958 (boys' baseball team had multiple batting cages and girls' softball team had none); *Ollier*, 858 F. Supp. 2d at 1111 ("disparities in the provision of equipment, uniforms and storage denied girls opportunities and benefits that boys enjoy, and that denial of opportunities and benefits was not negligible").

163. Lopez v. Regents of Univ. of California, 5 F. Supp. 3d 1106, 1122 (N.D. Cal. 2013).

164. *Landow*, 132 F. Supp. 2d at 963–64.

165. *Ollier*, 858 F. Supp. 2d at 1111–12 (noting that when coaching resources are unequal, it is not enough of a defense to say that women's teams, with inadequate coaching, still outperform the men's teams); Haffer v. Temple Univ. of the Commonwealth System of Higher Education, 678 F. Supp. 517, 531 (E.D. Pa. 1988) ("[T]he quality of coaching cannot be measured by simply evaluating win-loss records, and ... compensation is a factor in evaluating the quality of a coaching staff.").

166. *Ollier*, 858 F. Supp. 2d at 1112.

167. *See Ollier*, 858 F. Supp. 2d 1110–11; *Haffer*, 678 F. Supp. at 530.

168. 985 F. Supp. 1458 (M.D. Fla. 1997).

169. *Id.* at 1462.

170. 678 F. Supp. at 553.

171. *Id.*

172. *Id.* at 532.

173. *Id.*

than the women's team was discriminatory, the court stated: "the disparity of a handful of tennis matches, in the context of an athletic program that sponsors approximately 400 intercollegiate competitions each year does not raise a genuine issue."[174]

It should be noted that inequitable treatment regarding benefits and services are not the exclusive province of Title IX.[175] Gender-based inequitable benefits and treatment may also give rise to Fourteenth Amendment equal protection claims.[176] To prevail on such a claim, a plaintiff must demonstrate that the school district or municipal entity's inequitable treatment was a consequence of municipal custom, policy, or practice.[177]

§ 5.04 Single-Sex Teams — Title IX and Constitutional Dimensions

Female and male athletes denied the right to participate on a sports team restricted to the other sex have pursued Title IX and both federal and state constitutional law claims.[178] In the Title IX context, three factors figure prominently in an individual's likelihood of success: whether the sport at issue is a contact or noncontact sport; whether the person seeking the right to participate is a member of an underrepresented gender; and whether the institution provides a team in the sport for those of the plaintiff's gender. The factors impacting the plaintiff's likelihood of success on federal and state constitutional claims are discussed in section 5.04[B], *infra*. We begin with a discussion of Title IX in subsection A before turning to constitutional claims in subsection B.

[A] Title IX

[1] Noncontact Sports

Title IX's regulations articulate the circumstances under which an institution will be required to permit the members of one sex to try out for a single-sex team of the other sex:

---

174. *Id.* at 533.

175. *Fitzgerald*, 555 U.S. at 257 (distinguishing what a plaintiff must prove to prevail on a Title IX versus an equal protection claim).

176. *Communities for Equity*, 178 F. Supp. 2d 850–51 (finding that scheduling women's competition in the non-advantageous season, the Michigan High School Athletic Association violated the Fourteenth Amendment because the disadvantage in scheduling disparately impacted girls as a whole); *Parker*, 667 F.3d at 929 (holding Title IX is not the exclusive vehicle for pursing unequal benefits and treatment claims, and the school district could be liable pursuant to a § 1983 equal protection analysis).

177. Monell v. New York City Dept. of Social Servs., 436 U.S. 658, 694 (1978); *Fitzgerald*, 555 U.S. at 258 (distinguishing what a plaintiff must prove to prevail on a Title IX versus an equal protection claim).

178. *See* Force *ex rel.* Force v. Pierce City R-VI School Dist., 570 F. Supp. 1020, 1025 (W.D. Mo. 1983).

[W]here a recipient operates or sponsors a team in a particular sport for members of one sex but operates or sponsors no such team for members of the other sex, and athletic opportunities for members of that sex have previously been limited, members of the excluded sex must be allowed to try out for the team offered unless the sport is a contact sport.[179]

Reserving momentarily the discussion of whether a sport is a contact sport, courts have addressed interpretative issues arising from the regulatory language, including what constitutes an athletic opportunity and when such opportunities have previously been limited at the institution for members of the plaintiff's sex. As previously discussed in section 5.03[B][2][a], *supra*, athletic opportunities consist of genuine opportunities for athletic participation and not merely the opportunity to try out for a team.[180]

In determining whether athletic opportunities have previously been limited for the plaintiff's gender, courts examine the entire athletics program and not a specific sport. In *Williams v. School District of Bethlehem*,[181] a boy sought to compel a school district to permit him to try out for his high school's field hockey team. The court rejected the plaintiff's sport-specific argument that athletic opportunities previously had been limited because boys had not been permitted to play on the girls' field hockey team.[182] Thus, the court held that for noncontact sports, determinations of whether opportunities have been previously limited for the plaintiff's gender should be made on a program-wide and not a sport-specific basis.[183]

In the case of a noncontact sport in which athletic opportunities have previously been limited for members of the plaintiff's gender, Title IX requires that the plaintiff be permitted to try out for a single-sex team if there is no team in the sport for members of the plaintiff's sex.[184] When there is a team in a sport for the plaintiff's sex, the defendant institution is not required to permit the plaintiff to try out for the team in the same sport reserved for the other gender. Thus, a plaintiff's argument that the team for the other gender will provide better competition leading to better skills development will be of no avail.[185]

---

179. 34 C.F.R. § 106.41(b).

180. *Williams*, 998 F.2d at 174–75 ("'Athletic opportunities' means real opportunities, not illusory ones.").

181. *Id.*

182. *Id.*

183. *Id.* at 175.

184. *See Force*, 570 F. Supp. at 1024; 34 C.F.R. § 106.41(b).

185. "It may have once been that requiring the superior female athlete to play on the girls' or women's team was to remove all possibility of developing her skills to the highest level attainable. However, with the advent of Title IX, it may be that required participation on the female team is not always unequal treatment. Indeed, with more attention being paid to women's sports in general and with a nearer approach to equality as provided in 45 C.F.R. § 86.41(c), the opportunities for the outstanding female athlete to excel are enhanced. Separate teams may to a large extent aid in this equalization not only because they provide more opportunities but also because they make monitoring of the opportunities provided easier." Yellow Springs Exempted Village Sch. Dist. Bd. of Educ. v. Ohio High Sch. Ath. Ass'n, 647 F.2d 651, 657 (6th Cir. 1981).

[2] Contact Sports and the Title IX Exception

Title IX's regulations create a contact sport exception, under which an institution has the discretion to allow or disallow the members of one sex to try out for a single-sex contact-sport team reserved for members of the other sex even if no team is offered in the sport for members of the plaintiff's sex.[186] Thus, Title IX neither prohibits nor requires an institution to permit the members of one sex to try out for a team of the other sex in a contact sport. Title IX's regulations create a contact sport exception rather than an exemption. In *Mercer v. Duke University*,[187] a woman kicker gained a roster spot on the men's football team. The plaintiff asserted after making the team that she was subjected to discriminatory conduct in violation of Title IX. The university argued that Title IX created an exemption that operated as a complete defense to Title IX gender-discrimination claims if the sport involved was a contact sport. The court rejected this argument in holding that even though Duke was not required to permit the plaintiff to try out for the football team, once "an institution has allowed a member of one sex to try out for a team operated by the institution for the other sex in a contact sport, ... the institution is subject to the general anti-discrimination provision" of Title IX's regulations.[188]

The OCR's Title IX regulations identify the following as contact sports: "boxing, wrestling, rugby, ice hockey, football, basketball and other sports the purpose or major activity of which involves bodily contact."[189] Disputes arise in regard to sports that are not explicitly defined as contact sports, particularly where some level of contact is inherent in playing the game. In *Williams*, which involved field hockey, the court analyzed the level of contact inherent in game play and determined that acts involving "advancing the ball, checking, shooting, and blocking . . . inevitably involve bodily contact."[190] The court also concluded that rules penalizing certain types of contact could provide a basis for finding that a sport is a contact sport.[191] Contact that is incidental to playing a sport yet occurs frequently may also provide a basis for defining a sport as a contact sport for Title IX purposes.[192]

[B] Constitutional Claims

Plaintiffs have also turned to the Equal Protection Clause as a basis for arguing unconstitutional gender discrimination when seeking the opportunity to try out for a single-sex team of the other gender. Before examining the constitutional basis for such a claim, a preliminary matter must be addressed. Prior to the U.S. Supreme Court's decision in *Fitzgerald v. Barnstable*,[193] circuit courts were split on whether

---

186. *Id.* at 656.
187. 190 F.3d 643 (4th Cir. 1999).
188. *Id.* at 648.
189. 34 C.F.R. § 106.41(b)
190. *Williams*, 998 F.2d at 181.
191. *Id.*
192. Kleczek v. Rhode Island Interscholastic League, 768 F. Supp. 951 (D.R.I. 1991).
193. 555 U.S. 246 (2009).

Title IX foreclosed a claimant's right to pursue a constitutionally-based claim asserting gender discrimination.[194] The *Fitzgerald* Court held that the structure of Title IX, including its lack of a remedial scheme or requirement for administrative exhaustion, allows a plaintiff to pursue both Title IX and equal protection claims. Specifically, the Court held that under Title IX, "[Section] 1983 suits based on the Equal Protection Clause remain available to plaintiffs alleging unconstitutional gender discrimination in schools."[195] In light of *Fitzgerald*, plaintiffs have both statutory and constitutional avenues for pursuing gender discrimination claims.

Moreover, an equal protection claim may succeed even if a Title IX claim fails because of the latter's contact sport exception.[196] An equal protection analysis does not draw a distinction between contact and noncontact sports as the sole basis for determining the unconstitutionality of an institution's conduct.[197]

[1] Fourteenth Amendment Equal Protection Claims

Several generalized observations can be made regarding Equal Protection Clause challenges to rules prohibiting the members of one gender from trying out for single-sex teams restricted to the other gender: (1) the same sports participation opportunities must be provided to both genders unless an exclusionary policy or rule serves an important government interest;[198] (2) courts apply an intermediate level of scrutiny — an exceedingly persuasive justification — in assessing the constitutionality of gender-based classifications; (3) justifications based on concerns for plaintiff's safety and health are legitimate governmental objectives but they must be supported by evidence; (4) a plaintiff is entitled to an individualized determination rather than broad, often stereotypic assumptions, regarding a plaintiff's suitability and capability to compete for a position on a single-sex team; (5) the existence of separate but equal teams is a legitimate basis for denying members of one gender an opportunity to participate on a team comprised only of members of the other gender; and (6) equal protection only requires a fair opportunity to compete for a position but does not guarantee a roster spot given that there is no constitutional right to athletic participation.

Force v. Pierce City R-VI School District,[199] addresses most of the above-referenced issues and reflects the approach many courts have adopted in assessing plaintiffs' Fourteenth Amendment Equal Protection Clause challenges. In *Force*, school board officials based their rejection of an eight-grade girl's effort to try out for the football team on a state interscholastic athletic association policy preventing members of one gender from trying out for a single-sex team involving a contact sport.[200]

---

194. *Id.* at 247.

195. *Id.* at 258.

196. *See Force*, 570 F. Supp. at 1032.

197. *Id.* at 1023–24.

198. Clark *ex rel.* Clark v. Arizona Interscholastic Ass'n, 695 F.2d 1126, 1130 (9th Cir. 1982) ("[D]enial of an opportunity in a specific sport, even when overall opportunities are equal, can be a violation of the equal protection clause").

199. 570 F. Supp. 1020 (W.D. Mo. 1983).

200. *Id.* at 1024.

Turning first to the level of scrutiny, the court found that because the interscholastic rule discriminated among applicants on the basis of gender, it was subject to an intermediate level of scrutiny under the Equal Protection Clause of the Fourteenth Amendment.[201] A classification based on gender is assessed under "intermediate scrutiny," which falls somewhere between minimal and strict scrutiny.[202] This level of scrutiny involves a showing that the gender-based classification is related to an important governmental objective[203] and that the justification for the classification is exceedingly persuasive.[204] Moreover, the discriminatory means employed must be substantially related to achieving these objectives.[205]

The *Force* court rejected defendant's argument that the exclusionary policy was justified by the objective of protecting the safety of female athletes. The court concluded that Title IX's goal to "maximize educational athletic opportunities for all students, regardless of gender," requires a substantial reason for excluding one gender from an opportunity.[206] The court acknowledged that such a "substantial reason" for excluding one gender could be linked to safety or equipment requirements.[207] It added, however, that "those instances would [] be relatively rare."[208] In rejecting the school district's safety argument, the court reasoned that the safety concerns were only applicable to female students.[209] According to the court, any male, regardless of his ability to safely play football, could try out for the football team. Therefore, preventing a girl from trying out on the assumption that she could not safely play the sport created an impermissible distinction based on gender.[210] The court further observed that generalized assumptions do not justify exclusionary rules that limit a student's opportunity to participate in a sport based solely on gender.[211] Moreover, an individualized determination is required in assessing whether a state actor's interests

---

201. *Id.* (citing Reed v. Reed, 404 U.S. 71 (1971)).

202. *Clark*, 695 F.2d at 1129.

203. *Force*, 570 F. Supp. at 1023–24; *see also Equity in Athletics*, 639 F.3d at 104 (an institution's efforts to comply with Title IX serves an important governmental objective); Communities for Equity v. Michigan High Sch. Ath. Ass'n, 459 F.3d 676, 693 (6th Cir. 2006); Kelley v. Bd. of Trustees, 35 F.3d 265, 272 (7th Cir. 1994) (remediating sexual discrimination in athletics in educational institutions constitutes an important governmental objective); J.S. v. Laurel Cnty. Bd. of Educ., 2018 WL 5892355, at *2 (E.D. Ky. Nov. 11, 2018).

204. *Force*, 570 F. Supp. at 1024; *Communities for Equity*, 459 F.3d at 693; *Laurel Cnty. Bd. of Educ.*, 2018 WL 5892355 at *2.

205. *Force*, 570 F. Supp. at 1024; *Communities for Equity*, 459 F.3d at 693.

206. *Force*, 570 F. Supp. at 1028.

207. *Id.*; Kleczek v. R.I. Interscholastic League, Inc., 612 A.2d 734, 739 (R.I. 1992) (promoting and preserving safety and preserving interscholastic athletic competition for boys and girls are important government interests).

208. *Force*, 570 F. Supp. at 1028.

209. *Id.* When the assessment is on an individual level, however, the important government interest is not inappropriate Federal fund allocation but "promoting safety, increasing competition, redressing past discrimination, and providing more athletic opportunities for female athletes." D.M. *ex rel.* Bao Xiong v. Minnesota State High School League, 917 F.3d 994, 1003 (8th Cir. 2019).

210. *Force*, 570 F. Supp. at 1030.

211. *Force*, 570 F. Supp. at 1030, n. 14.

warrant excluding a participant from playing on a team restricted to members of the other gender.[212]

Courts have also addressed the circumstances under which efforts made by an institution to remediate past gender discriminatory practices will withstand an Equal Protection challenge. In *D.M. by Bao Xiong v. Minnesota State High School League*,[213] three teen boys were prevented from participating on their school's all-girl dance teams.[214] The defendant argued that prohibiting boys from trying out advanced the important governmental interest of providing opportunities to women to remedy past discrimination.[215] In rejecting the defendant's argument, the court stated the classification favoring one sex to remedy past discrimination is permissible but only under limited circumstances:

> Such circumstances exist when the classification "intentionally and directly assists members of the sex that is disproportionately burdened...." However, a government actor may "evoke a compensatory purpose to justify an otherwise discriminatory classification only if members of the gender benefited by the classification *actually suffer* a disadvantage related to the classification...." In other words, for a government actor to classify individuals based on gender for the purpose of remedying a prior lack of opportunities, the individuals must continue to lack opportunities or the classification is not constitutionally justified.[216]

Similarly, an institution's compliance with Title IX is an important government interest, but it too will run afoul of the Equal Protection Clause unless the gender-based classification is substantially related to achieving the statute's objectives.[217]

Two other principles—a cognizable equal protection claim does not guarantee a roster spot, and separate but equal is constitutionally acceptable in the context of a gender-based classification—emerge from cases addressing equal protection claims. These equal protection cases adhere to the principle that there is no right to athletic participation. The Equal Protection Clause only requires that an individual be given "an equal opportunity to compete for such a position,"[218] but does not guarantee a position on a team.[219]

---

212. *Mansourian*, 816 F. Supp. at 937.
213. 917 F.3d 994 (6th Cir. 2019).
214. *Id.* at 1003.
215. *Id.*
216. *Id.* at 1002 (emphasis in the original) (citations omitted).
217. *Force*, 570 F. Supp. at 1024; *Communities for Equity*, 459 F.3d at 693; *Laurel Cnty. Bd. of Educ.*, 2018 WL 5892355 at *3.
218. *Force*, 570 F. Supp. at 1031; Lantz v. Ambach, 620 F. Supp. 663, 665 (S.D.N.Y. 1985).
219. *Mansourian*, 816 F. Supp 2d at 930–31 (citing to numerous cases adopting this proposition); *see also* Croteau v. Fair, 686 F. Supp 552, 554 ("there is no constitutional or statutory right to play any position on any athletic team. Instead, there is only the right to compete for such a position on equal terms."); *Lantz*, 620 F. Supp. at 666 (stating plaintiff has "no legal entitlement to a starting position" yet does have a "chance ... to display those abilities" and a "right to try").

In addition, because an equal protection claim is evaluated pursuant to an intermediate level of scrutiny, having separate girls' and boys' teams in the same sport is an acceptable way to address athletic opportunities.[220] Accordingly, if a team has a boys' team and a girls' team in the same sport, the members of the other gender will not be permitted to try out for the team.[221] While having separate teams in the same sport for females and males is constitutionally permissible, creating separate standards for females and males trying out for the same team is not. Noted one court, "the consistent holding of the body of law in this area is that women should be entitled to a right to *compete* for a spot on a men's team *under equal terms*" when there is no comparable female team.[222]

[2] State Constitutional Claims

The segregation of males and females in athletics may violate state constitutional provisions such as an Equal Rights Amendment. In this regard, the court in *Williams* stated that a classification that segregates teams based on gender is permissible only if there are "any real physical differences between boys and girls that warrant[s] different treatment."[223] Therefore, gender classifications "based on impermissible assumptions and stereotypes about the comparative characteristics or abilities of boys and girls," will likely violate state constitutional law.[224] As is true of Fourteenth Amendment equal protection claims, the applicable level of scrutiny will impact the viability of such claims.[225]

[3] "Reverse" Discrimination Claims

Plaintiffs have met with little success in asserting Equal Protection claims premised on an institution's efforts to comply with Title IX's substantial proportionality requirement through eliminating or reducing sport opportunities for male student-athletes. In *Neal v. Board of Trustees of the California State Universities*,[226] plaintiffs asserted a denial of equal protection after the defendant imposed size limits on men's teams, including its wrestling team, as a part of a consent decree to resolve claims that women's athletics opportunities were substantially disproportionate with their undergraduate enrollment.[227] Rejecting plaintiffs' claim that the substantial proportionality prong of the OCR's three-part test violates the Equal Protection Clause, the court adopted the reasoning employed by the First and Seventh Circuits:

---

220. *Yellow Springs*, 647 F.2d at 663.
221. *Id.* at 658 ("required participation on the female team is not always unequal treatment").
222. *Mansourian*, 816 F. Supp. 2d at 939.
223. *Williams*, 998 F.2d at 179.
224. *Id.* at 177.
225. *Haffer*, 678 F. Supp. at 536; *see Laurel Cty. Bd. of Educ.*, 2018 WL 5892355 at *2 (stating the level of scrutiny under the relevant state constitutional provisions mirrors that applied in Fourteenth Amendment Equal Protection cases).
226. 198 F.3d 763 (9th Cir. 1999).
227. *Id.* at 765–66.

Cohen II noted that the *Policy Interpretation* furthered the "clearly important" objectives of "avoid[ing] the use of federal resources to support discriminatory practices, and provid[ing] individual citizens effective protection against those practices." Moreover, it found that "judicial enforcement of federal anti-discrimination statutes is at least an important governmental objective." ... Along the same lines, the Seventh Circuit held that "the remedial scheme established by Title IX and the applicable regulation and policy interpretation are clearly substantially related to" the objective of prohibiting "educational institutions from discriminating on the basis of sex." We adopt the reasoning of *Cohen I*, *Cohen II*, and *Kelley* and hold that the constitutional analysis contained therein persuasively disposes of any serious constitutional concerns that might be raised in relation to the OCR *Policy Interpretation*.[228]

[4] *Freedom of Association and Freedom of Assembly*

Plaintiffs have asserted Title IX is unconstitutional based on their rights to freedom of association and assembly under the First Amendment. In *Equity in Athletics*, male student-athletes, inter alia, asserted that the university's elimination of certain men's teams without the elimination of the corresponding women's teams infringed upon the male athletes' First Amendment right to freedom of association. According to the plaintiffs, the university's conduct violated their right to intimate relationships because without the "reciprocal teams" they could not "compete together and 'help to train each other.'"[229] In rejecting plaintiffs' claim, the court defined "intimate association" for constitutional purposes as "highly personal relationships" such as those involving family (*e.g.*, marriage, childbirth).[230] It concluded the plaintiffs failed to establish that the relationships between members of the identified men's and women's athletics team constituted intimate relationships.[231]

§ 5.05 Other Gender and Sex Discrimination Issues in Sports

[A] Introduction

As the following discussion reveals, sex-based discrimination in sport is not restricted to participation opportunities and unequal benefits and treatment. Indeed,

---

228. *Neal*, 198 F.3d at 772 (emphasis in original) (internal citations omitted) (citing *Kelly*, 35 F.3d 265 and *Cohen*, 101 F.3d 155); *see also* Miami Univ. Wrestling Club v. Miami Univ., 302 F.3d 608, 614 (6th Cir. 2002) (rejecting attack by male athletes on teams eliminated as part of university's efforts to achieve substantial proportionality); *Equity in Athletics*, 675 F. Supp. 660; *Mansourian*, 816 F. Supp. 2d at 869; Gonyo v. Drake Univ., 879 F. Supp. 1000, 1006 (S.D. Iowa 1995); *Roberts*, 998 F.2d at 830 ("[f]inancially strapped institutions may still comply with Title IX by cutting athletic programs").
229. *Equity in Athletics*, 675 F. Supp. 2d at 673.
230. *Id.*
231. *Id.*

it covers sex-related issues in sport including those relating to sexual harassment and violence in sports. We turn first to another matter, employment discrimination in sports.

[B] Employment Discrimination

Plaintiffs have resorted to Title IX, the Equal Pay Act, and constitutional theories in seeking redress from alleged employment-related inequities in sports. This section explores the legal theories advanced by plaintiffs including coaches, athletes, and athletic administrators and the judiciary's receptiveness to these theories. It begins with a discussion of Title IX-based employment discrimination claims.

[1] Title IX Claims

[a] Gender-Based Unequal Pay

College coaches have sought relief under Title IX for alleged pay inequities and for retaliation in response to their efforts to achieve gender equity for their female athletes. A coach's Title IX pay discrimination claim will succeed only if evidence establishes that compensation and other inequitable treatment, "assignment policies or practices deny male and female athletes coaching of equivalent quality, nature, or availability."[232] Thus, an institution will be held liable not based on the harm to the coach but the impact of the unequal treatment of the coach on the institution's athletes.

In *Deli v. University of Minnesota*,[233] a female head coach of a university's women's gymnastics team alleged she was improperly paid less than head coaches of several men's athletics teams. According to the plaintiff, the alleged pay inequity was a result of gender discrimination in violation of the Equal Pay Act, Title VII, and Title IX. In regard to the Title IX claim, the court concluded it must fail on the merits.[234] The court first noted that courts have afforded the OCR's interpretations of Title IX substantial discretion. Although the court found that plaintiff's Title IX action was barred by the statute of limitations, the court nevertheless turned to the *Policy Interpretation* in finding that plaintiff's claim failed because the complaint failed to assert that "the athletes she supervised received lesser quality coaching as a result of the difference between plaintiff's salary and salaries paid to coaches of the men's football, hockey and basketball teams."[235]

[b] Gender-Based Retaliation

In *Jackson v. Birmingham Board of Education*,[236] the Supreme Court recognized that coaches have a private right of action under Title IX for retaliation for the coach's

---

232. *Policy Interpretation, supra* note 15, at 71416.
233. 863 F. Supp. 958 (D. Minn. 1994).
234. *Id.* at 959.
235. *Id.* at 963.
236. 544 U.S. 167, 168 (2005).

conduct in speaking out against gender discrimination in their athletes' programs. There, a coach of a girls' basketball team alleged that after he complained to his supervisors of inequities in athletic equipment and facilities provided to his players, the school board retaliated by terminating his position as head coach.[237] Although the Court had previously ruled that there is an implied private right of action for monetary damages in cases involving intentional discrimination under Title IX, it had not considered whether this right extended to retaliation claims.

In ruling that such a private right of action arises, the Court first explained that retaliation against a person complaining about discrimination in violation of Title IX is by its very nature a form of intentional discrimination. It added that retaliation constitutes intentional sex discrimination "because the complainant is being subjected to differential treatment."[238] The Court reasoned that reporting incidents of discrimination is integral to Title IX enforcement and would be discouraged if retaliation against those who report went unpunished. Indeed, if retaliation were not prohibited, Title IX's enforcement scheme would unravel.[239] The Court also stated that a cognizable Title IX retaliation claim arises even if the plaintiff was not a victim of the gender discrimination that was the subject of the discriminatory treatment of which the plaintiff originally complained.[240] Title IX retaliation actions "only cover[] conduct protected [by] Title IX."[241] Finally, to present a prima facie retaliation claim, a plaintiff must establish "(1) that she engaged in protected activity,[242] (2) that the funding recipient took a materially adverse action against her,[243] and (3) that there was a but-for causal 'connection between her protected activity and the materially adverse action.'"[244]

[2] Equal Pay Act Claims

Female coaches have also asserted that the lower compensation they received when compared to that of male coaches violates the Equal Pay Act ("EPA"). The EPA proscribes paying wages to an employee at a lower rate than that paid to the opposite sex "on the basis of sex ... for equal work, on jobs the performance of which requires equal skill, effort, and responsibility, and which are performed under similar working

---

237. *Id.* at 171.

238. *Id.* at 173–74.

239. *Id.* at 180.

240. *Id.* at 179.

241. Lowrey v. Texas A & M Univ. Systems, 11 F. Supp. 2d 895, 911 (S.D. Tex. 1998). Therefore, "a plaintiff may only recover under Title IX when the defendant retaliated against her 'solely as a consequence of complaints alleging noncompliance with the substantive provisions of Title IX.'" *Id.*

242. Bryant v. Gardner, 587 F. Supp. 2d 951, 964 (N.D. Ill. 2008) (stating that a plaintiff must offer sufficient evidence to show that they presented a complaint concerning prohibited practices to the institution); Weaver v. Ohio St. Univ., 71 F. Supp. 2d 789, 793 (S.D. Ohio 1998).

243. *Bryant*, 587 F. Supp. 2d at 951 (adverse action in the form of termination); *Lowrey*, 11 F. Supp. 2d at 901 (finding adverse action through demotion and removal of responsibilities).

244. DuBois v. Bd. of Regents of Univ. of Minnesota, 439 F. Supp. 3d 1128, 1136 (D. Minn. 2020); *see also Bryant*, 587 F. Supp. 2d at 964–65 (stating that a "causal link may be shown when the adverse action occurred" in close proximity to the protected action).

conditions."[245] In order to prevail, a plaintiff need not establish that her job and the comparative employees' jobs were identical, only that the jobs are substantially equal. Moreover, the comparison must be individualized in that the "the male comparator must be a particular individual employed by the defendant, not some hypothetical composite male."[246] In addition, an EPA claim must be premised on the gender of the coaches and not on the gender of the players that the plaintiff coaches.[247]

Courts consider the following factors in determining whether the difference in pay was a consequence of gender discrimination: team size, number of assistant coaches, recruiting responsibilities, community notoriety, community involvement expectation, spectator attendance and revenue generation, media relations expectations, and the importance of the sport in the athletic department.[248] In *Deli v. University of Minnesota*,[249] the comparator coaches were in sports different from the sports coached by the plaintiff. The court was persuaded by evidence presented by the defendants that differences including the male coaches having larger teams, supervising more employees than plaintiff, and their teams drawing greater spectator attendance (which generates more revenue) supported a conclusion that the male coaches' and plaintiff's jobs were not substantially similar.[250]

In *Stanley v. University of Southern California*,[251] the former women's head basketball coach was unable to show substantial similarity between her position and the men's head basketball coach's position. The court relied on the substantial difference in the public relations and revenue generation of the men's basketball team when compared to the women's team.[252] It also recognized that the men's basketball coach had different requirements for his position, including a mandatory number of press conferences each year, participation in donation or fundraising activities, and other mandatory public appearances.[253] The court held that these additional responsibilities, which were not required of the women's coach, rendered these positions substantially unequal.[254] The court also found that the men's head coach also had more seniority

---

245. 29 U.S.C. § 206(d)(1).

246. Bartges v. Univ. of North Carolina at Charlotte, 908 F. Supp. 1312, 1322 (W.D. N.C. 1995).

247. *Deli*, 863 F. Supp. at 961 ("the EPA prohibits discrimination based on the gender of the claimant only and does not reach compensation differentials based on the gender of student-athletes coached by a claimant"); *see also* Arceneaux v. Vanderbilt Univ., 25 F. App'x 345, 348 (6th Cir. 2001) (finding a discrimination claim based on "association with members of a protected class" was not sufficient to establish a prima facia case). Conversely, courts have observed cases where a female coach and her male counterpart in a comparable sport each receive funds from different sources.

248. *Weaver*, 71 F. Supp. 2d at 799; *see* EEOC v. Madison Cmty Sch. Dist. No. 12, 818 F.2d 577, 582 (7th Cir. 1987) (applying a list of factors to consider in determining whether female and male comparator's coaching positions were substantially similar).

249. *Deli*, 863 F. Supp. at 962.

250. *Id.*; *see also Bartges*, 908 F. Supp. 1312 (holding that greater public relations, supervision responsibilities, and larger rosters negate claims that coaching positions are substantially the same).

251. 13 F.3d 1313 (9th Cir. 1994).

252. *Id.* at 1321–22.

253. *Id.*

254. *Id.* at 1322.

and increased pressure to succeed.[255] The court rejected plaintiff's argument that the fact that women's teams bring in less revenue and have less pressure, which are a consequence of societal pressure and a preference for men's sports, should not be held against her.[256]

Express contract terms also impact the viability of an Equal Pay Act claim. In *Morgan v. United States Soccer Federation, Inc.*,[257] members of the United States Women's National Team ("USWNT") disputed their pay structure, asserting they were paid less than their male counterparts.[258] The court analyzed the wage structure, finding the USWNT received annual salaries determined by contract, while the men's team pay was based on a "pay-to-play" structure.[259] Under the latter structure, players are not compensated unless they participate in a training camp or make a particular roster.[260] The court summarized the USWNT's arguments as follows:

> Plaintiffs make two primary arguments. First, Plaintiffs focus on the CBAs' bonus provisions, arguing that the WNT CBA provides for lower bonuses than the MNT CBA for friendlies, World Cup-related matches, and other tournaments. Second, Plaintiffs point to what WNT players *would have received* had they been compensated under the terms of the MNT CBA. Plaintiffs' expert opines that had WNT players been compensated under the MNT CBA, they would have received more money over the class period than they did under the WNT CBA, even when all fringe benefits are considered.[261]

The court found that although the USWNT might receive less in bonuses, their wage compensation is equal to — if not greater than — the men's.[262] The court reasoned:

> One of the defining features of the WNT CBA is its guarantee that players will be compensated regardless of whether they play a match or not. This

---

255. *Id.* at 1323; *see also* Harker v. Utica College of Syracuse Univ., 885 F. Supp. 378, 390 (N.D.N.Y. 1995) (stating that stronger educational background, previous coaching experience, and seniority negate a similar skill, effort, or working conditions).

256. *Stanley*, 13 F.3d at 1322.

257. 445 F. Supp. 3d 635 (C.D. Cal. 2020). The case has been appealed with oral arguments scheduled for March 2022. On appeal, appellants argued that the district court erred by, among other issues: (1) failing to account for performance; (2) improperly utilizing a "total compensation" standard; and (3) using a revenue-based calculations demonstrates women and men are paid an unequal "rate." *See* Reply Brief for Plaintiffs-Appellants, Morgan v. United States Soccer Federation (2021), No. 22-55356, 2021 WL 6071082. The United States Soccer Federation, meanwhile, argued, among other things, that: (1) the men's team's higher earning potential gave rise to higher bonuses; (2) the pay structure was negotiated at a time when the men were more successful; and (3) the pay structure was negotiated and agreed to by the women's team to prioritize guarantees over bonuses. *See* Answering Brief for United States Soccer Federation, Morgan v. United States Soccer Federation 2021 WL 4466512 (9th Cir. Sept. 22, 2021).

258. *Morgan*, 445 F. Supp. 3d at 641.

259. *Id.* at 655.

260. *Id.* at 641.

261. *Id.* at 652–53 (emphasis in original).

262. *Id.* at 654.

stands in stark contrast to the MNT CBA, under which players are only compensated if they are called into camp to play and then participate in a match. It is difficult to attach a dollar value to this "insurance" benefit, and neither party attempts to do so here. However, there is indisputably economic value to this type of "fixed pay" contract, as compared to a "performance pay" contract.... Indeed, the WNT clearly attached significant economic value to this contractual arrangement because it was willing to agree to lower bonuses in exchange for higher fixed payments in its 2017 CBA. Merely comparing what WNT players received under their own CBA with what they would have received under the MNT CBA discounts the value that the team placed on the guaranteed benefits they receive under their agreement, which they opted for at the expense of higher performance-based bonuses.[263]

[3] Title VII Claims

Coaches have also pursued Title VII claims premised on the statute's prohibition against an employer discriminating against any employee with respect to her "compensation, terms, conditions, or privileges of employment, *because of* such individual's ... sex[.]"[264] Under the *McDonnell Douglas Corp. v. Green*[265] framework, a plaintiff must establish a prima facie case, which must be done by demonstrating "(1) she belongs to a protected class; (2) she was performing her job adequately; (3) she suffered an adverse employment action; and (4) similarly situated individuals outside of her protected class were treated more favorably, or other circumstances surrounding the adverse employment action give rise to an inference of discrimination."[266] Assuming that the plaintiff establishes a prima facie case, "the burden of production, but not persuasion ... shifts to the employer to articulate some legitimate, nondiscriminatory reason for the challenged action."[267] At this stage, the defendant must merely present evidence that there is a material issue of fact as to whether it discriminated against the plaintiff.[268] The employer's articulation of a legitimate nondiscriminatory reason then shifts the burden to the plaintiff to show, through direct or circumstantial evidence, "that the legitimate reasons offered by the defendant were not its true reasons, but were a pretext for discrimination."[269]

In *Deli*, discussed above, the court rejected plaintiff's Title VII claim that was premised on her assertion that she was paid less because she coached female athletes. The court stated that a plaintiff cannot prevail on a Title VII claim based on the gender of the athletes the coach supervises.[270] To fall within the scope of Title VII,

---

263. *Id.* at 655–56.
264. 42 U.S.C. § 2000e-2(a)(1); *Morgan*, 445 F. Supp. 3d at 659.
265. 411 U.S. 792 (1973).
266. *Morgan*, 445 F. Supp. 3d at 659.
267. *Id.* (quoting Chuang v. Univ. of Cal. Davis, Bd. of Trs., 225 F.3d 115, 1123 (9th Cir. 2000)).
268. *Morgan*, 445 F. Supp. 3d at 660.
269. *Id.* (quoting Texas Dept. of Cmty Affairs v. Burdine, 450 U.S. 248, 253 (1981)).
270. 863 F. Supp. at 960.

the discrimination must be on account of the plaintiff's gender. It should also be noted that a plaintiff will not be able to allege a cognizable Title VII claim for retaliation based on the plaintiff's complaints regarding the institution's noncompliance with Title IX.[271] Title VII encompasses retaliation that is connected to the plaintiff's opposition to discriminatory employment practices or complaints regarding such practices.[272] A court also rejected a plaintiff's Title VII claim in *Lamb-Bowman v. Delaware State University*,[273] where a former coach alleged she was terminated in violation of Title VII not because she complained about employment practices but because of the school's lack of compliance with Title IX.

When assessing the merits of a Title VII claim, the court will look to similarly situated individuals and address if they are treated more favorably than members of the protected class. In *Mehus v. Emporia State University*,[274] the district court analyzed a female volleyball coach's claim that she was treated unfairly and paid less than her similarly situated male counterparts — some of whom also coached women's athletics. Addressing issues including recruiting calendars, coaching requirements (such as media broadcast duties), and coaching experience prior to hiring, the court found that the factual determination necessary to make a comparison between employees warranted denying the university's motion for summary judgement.[275] Additionally, the court based its denial of summary judgment on genuine issues of material fact pertaining to whether the coaching skill required and the structure of the program (*i.e.*, higher profile and more media coverage) imposed greater responsibility on the comparator male coaches.[276] The *Mehus* decision appears to conflict with other courts' determinations. In *Bartges v. University of North Carolina at Charlotte*,[277] the court found that a male coach was required to supervise more athletes, had larger public relations duties, and more extensive recruiting requirements. Unlike in *Mehus*, the *Bartges* court found these differences entitled the university to summary judgement.[278] Similarly, in *Stanley*,[279] the women's basketball coach was unable to show that her job was similar to that of the men's basketball coach, who was required to participate in substantially more media events and coached a team which generated much higher revenues.[280] Finally, in *Jacobs v. College of William and Mary*,[281] the court found that the absence of recruiting responsibilities for the female coach made her position substantially unequal to the male coach's position.

271. *Weaver*, 71 F. Supp. 2d at 793.
272. *Lowery*, 117 F.3d at 254.
273. 152 F. Supp. 2d 553, 560 (D. Del. 2001).
274. 222 F.R.D. 455 (D. Kan. 2004).
275. *Id.* at 475.
276. *Id.* at 475–76.
277. 908 F. Supp. 1312, 1323–24 (W.D.N.C. 1995).
278. *Id.*
279. 13 F.3d 1313, 1321 (9th Cir. 1994).
280. *Id.*
281. 517 F. Supp. 791 (E.D. Va. 1980).

[C] Sexual Harassment in Sports

[1] Liability of Educational Institutions under Title IX

Increasingly, plaintiffs have turned to Title IX as a means of redress for acts of sexual harassment. The two primary contexts in which this arises in sports are where an athlete sexually harasses another student (student-to-student sexual harassment) or where a coach sexually harasses a student-athlete (teacher-to-student sexual harassment). The U.S. Supreme Court has recognized the viability of each of these claims under Title IX.[282] A plaintiff's basis for redress under Title IX is that the sexual harassment deprived her/him of her/his ability to "access an educational opportunity or benefit."[283] In the context of sexual harassment, such claims are an outgrowth of behavior creating a sexually hostile environment leading to the deprivation. As more fully explored *infra*, institutional liability under Title IX is premised not on the sexual harassment perpetrated by the harasser but on the educational institution's knowledge that the harasser posed a substantial threat of sexual harassment or the institution's response after it becomes aware of the harassment.[284] As a predicate to the discussion, sexual harassment is defined broadly to include "unwelcome sexual advances, requests for sexual favors, and other verbal or physical harassment of a sexual nature."[285]

Even after a plaintiff establishes that sexual harassment occurred and the defendant educational institution is a recipient of federal funding, there are other requisites to the imposition of liability. *Davis ex rel. LaShonda D. v. Monroe County Board of Education*[286] and *Gebser v. Lago Vista Independent School District*[287] articulate those requisites: (1) the funding recipient had actual notice (*i.e.*, actual knowledge) of the sexual harassment;[288] (2) the funding recipient was "deliberately indifferent" to the sexual harassment; and (3) the harassment was "so severe, pervasive, and objectively

---

282. Gebser v. Lago Vista Indep. Sch. Dist., 524 U.S. 274 (1998); Davis *ex rel.* LaShonda D. v. Monroe Cty. Bd. of Educ., 526 U.S. 629, 633 (1999) (recognizing student-to-student sexual harassment claims under Title IX).

283. *See Davis*, 526 U.S. at 650.

284. *See* Williams v. Bd. of Regents of the Univ. Sys. of Ga., 447 F.3d 1282 (11th Cir. 2007); Simpson v. Univ. of Col. Boulder, 500 F.3d 1170 (10th Cir. 2007); Doe v. Sch. Bd. of Broward Cty., 604 F.3d 1248, 1258 (11th Cir. 2010).

285. *See* 29 C.F.R. § 1604.11(a). The designation "sexual harassment" includes sexual assault. Office on Violence Against Women, *Sexual Assault*, Dept. of Justice (2021), https://www.justice.gov/ovw/sexual-assault ("any nonconsensual sexual act proscribed by Federal, tribal, or State law, including when the victim lacks capacity to consent.").

286. 526 U.S. 629 (1999).

287. 524 U.S. 274 (1998).

288. An educational institution receiving federal funding can only be liable for its actions, including its failure to act. *Davis*, 526 U.S. at 640 (private actions of an individual cannot be imputed to the institution unless the institution had the ability to act, and such action is impossible without notice that action is required); *but see* Escue v. Northern Oklahoma College, 450 F.3d 1146, 1154 (10th Cir. 2006) ("Although *Gebser* makes clear that actual notice requires more than a simple report of inappropriate conduct by a teacher ... the actual notice standard does not set the bar so high that a school district is not put on notice until it receives a clearly credible report of sexual abuse from the plaintiff-student").

offensive" that it "deprive[d] the [plaintiff] of access to the educational opportunities or benefits provided by the school."[289]

[a] Actual Notice (*i.e.*, Knowledge) by an Appropriate Person

Title IX claims alleging student-to-student or teacher-to-student sexual harassment are enforceable by an implied private right of action for damages against educational institutions.[290] Enforcement of Title IX's mandate requires that an agency that disburses funds to the educational institution must provide "notice to an appropriate person and an opportunity to rectify the violation."[291] Thus, the notice requirement set forth in *Davis* and *Gebser* is a product of Title IX's mandate and tied to the plaintiff's ability to recover monetary damages. Case authority defines actual notice as equivalent to the recipient's "actual knowledge of discrimination in the recipient's programs."[292]

The actual knowledge must be possessed by an appropriate person, which is defined as an official of the defendant institution "with authority to take corrective action to end the discrimination."[293] There also must be a connection between the knowledge and the alleged sexual misconduct.[294] Although the previous inappropriate behavior need not be the same as the behavior at issue to impute knowledge to an institution, similar incidents may be sufficient to establish actual notice to authority figures of the threat posed by the perpetrator.[295] Accordingly, less severe past harassment than the harassment at issue may nonetheless provide actual notice of sexually violent conduct, for it is the "risk of such conduct that the Title IX recipient has the duty to deter."[296] Actual knowledge can arise from formal reports, the reports of parents[297] and other students,[298] and previous incidents involving the perpetrator of the sexual harassment.[299]

---

289. *Davis*, 526 U.S. at 650; *see also* Bostic v. Smyrna Sch. Dist., 418 F.3d 355, 360 (3d Cir. 2005).

290. *Davis*, 526 U.S. at 656; *Gebser*, 524 U.S. at 290–91.

291. *Gebser*, 524 U.S. at 290.

292. *Id.* at 290. The court stated the recipient must possess actual notice before it "could be liable for the conduct at issue." *Davis*, 526 U.S. at 640.

293. *Gebser*, 524 U.S. at 290; *see Bostic*, 418 F.3d at 361 (noting that whether individuals, such as school principals, should be deemed appropriate persons as a matter of law requires a factual analysis).

294. *See Gebser*, 524 U.S. at 279 (stating that notice of a teacher's sexually suggestive comments in the classroom are too attenuated to actual sexual intercourse with a student to have provided the administration with notice); *see also* Turner v. McQuarter, 79 F. Supp. 2d 911, 915 (1999) (noting that a head coach having the same address on school records as student that the coach is sexually abusing is not enough to grant notice of sexual abuse); *but see Sch. Bd. of Broward Cty.*, 604 F.3d at 1258 ("[L]esser harassment may still provide actual notice of sexually violent conduct, for it is the risk of such conduct that the Title IX recipient has the duty to deter.").

295. *See Williams*, 477 F.3d at 1282.

296. *Sch. Bd. of Broward Cty.*, 604 F.3d at 1258.

297. Warren *ex rel.* Good v. Reading Sch. Dist., 278 F.3d 163, 168–69 (3d Cir. 2002).

298. Hill *ex rel.* B.H.J. v. Cundiff, 797 F.3d 948 (11th Cir. 2015); J.K. v. Arizona Bd. of Regents, 2008 WL 4446712, at *14 (D. Ariz. Sept. 30, 2008).

299. *Simpson*, 500 F.3d at 1170.

Based on the foregoing principles, courts have found that an appropriate person possessed actual knowledge of discrimination where such a person: had preexisting knowledge of the harasser's past sexual misconduct[300] that sufficiently indicated "substantial danger to a student so that the institution [could] reasonably be said to [have been] aware of the danger";[301] was aware that the perpetrator committed acts of sexual misconduct against persons other than the plaintiff[302] that created a substantial risk of the potential for sexual misconduct;[303] and had knowledge that sexual harassment had occurred or was occurring at the institution.[304]

[b] Deliberate Indifference

In addition to showing actual knowledge, a plaintiff must also proffer evidence establishing that the educational institution acted with deliberate indifference. This is a factual determination that courts are generally unwilling to dispose of summarily.[305] In *Davis*, the Court stated that proof of deliberate indifference requires a showing that a school's response or nonresponse was "clearly unreasonable in light of the known circumstances."[306] Similarly, the crux of deliberate indifference was stated by the *Gebser* Court as "the purposeful failure of an official with actual knowledge of an employee's discrimination and the authority to remedy the misconduct to adequately respond is tantamount to 'an official decision by the [institution] not to remedy the violation.'"[307] In *Davis*, the Court added that deliberate indifference on behalf of the school must "cause students to undergo harassment or make them liable or vulnerable to it."[308] Once a recipient of federal funding has actual knowledge of the sexual harassment, they cannot "turn a blind eye to the harassment."[309]

Courts have cited the potential for deliberate indifference where: a head coach facilitated an assailant basketball player's return to the university and placed him in the same dorm as the victim for more than three weeks without any special monitoring

---

300. *Williams*, 447 F.3d at 1293.

301. *Bostic*, 418 F.3d at 360.

302. *J.K.*, 2008 WL 4446712, at *14.

303. *See Williams*, 447 F.3d at 1282; *J.K.*, 2008 WL 4446712; *but* see Ross v. Corp. of Mercer Univ., 506 F. Supp. 2d 1325, 1348 (M.D. Ga. 2007) (finding that a university's knowledge of student likelihood of developing substance abuse issues is not enough to foreshadow sexual assault behavior).

304. *See, e.g., Simpson*, 500 F.3d at 1170.

305. *J.K.*, 2008 WL 4446712 at *16.

306. *Davis*, 526 U.S. at 630.

307. Ericson v. Syracuse, 35 F. Supp. 2d 326, 328 (S.D.N.Y. 1999) (quoting *Gebser*, 524 U.S. at 290). While deliberate indifference does not require a subsequent assault to occur, some courts have found that matters unrelated to the victim becoming an assault victim may not present a cognizable Title IX claim. *See* Doe *ex rel.* Doe v. North Allegheny Sch. Dist., 2011 WL 3667279, at *9 (stating that allegations of deliberate indifference by the school district were related to incidents before Doe became a sexual assault victim, causing Doe's claim to fail); *see also Ross*, 506 F. Supp. 2d at 1356.

308. *Davis*, 526 U.S. at 644–45 or 648–49; *see also* Doe *ex rel.* Doe v. Dallas Indep. Sch. Dist., 153 F.3d 211, 219 (5th Cir. 1998).

309. Farmer v. Kansas State Univ., 918 F.3d 1094, 1104 (10th Cir. 2019).

or supervision;[310] a university allowed alleged student assailants — unchecked and without the school investigating alleged rapes — to continue to attend the university with alleged victims who were left vulnerable to further sexual harassment;[311] a university's recruitment of a student-athlete with a known history of sexual misconduct without informing the athlete of the institution's sexual misconduct policy, its failure to take steps to adequately supervise the athlete, and the institution's response after sexual assault;[312] and an institution's failure to provide adequate training or guidance.[313] On the other hand, "[a]ctions and decisions by officials that are merely inept, erroneous, ineffective or negligent do not amount to deliberate indifference...."[314]

[c] Severity of the Discrimination

Institutional liability under Title IX for student-on-student or teacher-on-student sexual harassment is premised on harassment that is "so severe, pervasive, and objectively offensive that it effectively bars the victim's access to an educational opportunity or benefit."[315] Although a victim's "physical exclusion from an institution is not a prerequisite to demonstrating deprivation of education opportunities,"[316] a single instance of harassment can be sufficiently severe, on its own, to give rise to liability under Title IX.[317] On the other hand, a "mere decline in grades" is unlikely by itself to be sufficient to "establish denial of access to education."[318] Moreover, a plaintiff must allege more than a general fear of their attacker.[319] Illustrations of a severe impact include: the plaintiff's inability to return to the educational institution

---

310. *J.K.*, 2008 WL 4446712, at *17 (denying defendant's motion for summary judgment and finding the defendant may have acted with deliberate indifference).

311. *Farmer*, 918 F.3d at 1104.

312. *Williams*, 477 F.3d at 1296.

313. *See Gebser*, 524 U.S. at 296.

314. *Dallas Indep. Sch. Dist.*, 153 F.3d at 219.

315. *Davis*, 526 U.S. at 633; *see also* Timothy Davis & Keith E. Smith, *Eradicating Student-Athlete Sexual Assault of Women: Section 1983 and Personal Liability Following* Fitzgerald v. Barnstable, 2009 MICH. ST. L. REV. 629, 643 (2009) (observing that the harassment must have created a hostile environment that interferes with a student's ability to benefit from a school's educational program). As it relates to potential Title IX liability, two distinct forms of sexual harassment are recognized. Quid pro quo sexual harassment occurs when "a teacher or other employee conditions an educational decision or benefit on the student's submission to unwelcome sexual conduct." *Id.* Hostile environment sexual harassment occurs when "conduct is sufficiently serious to deny or limit a student's ability to participate in or benefit from the school's program based on sex." *Id.*; *see also* U.S. DEP'T OF EDUC., OFFICE FOR CIVIL RIGHTS, REVISED SEXUAL HARASSMENT GUIDANCE: HARASSMENT OF STUDENTS BY SCHOOL EMPLOYEES, OTHER STUDENTS, OR THIRD PARTIES: TITLE IX 5 (2001). *See also* Hunter *ex rel.* Hunter v. Barnstable Sch. Comm., 456 F. Supp. 2d 255, 263 (D. Mass. 2006) (defining quid pro quo and hostile environment sexual harassment).

316. Davis & Smith, *supra* note 315, at 643.

317. *Id.* at 972; *but see Ross*, 506 F. Supp. 2d at 1358 ("[T]he Court must conclude that a single incident, however traumatic to its victim, is not likely to be pervasive, or to have a systemic effect on educational activities").

318. *Davis*, 526 U.S. at 652; *Farmer*, 918 F.3d at 1105

319. *Farmer*, 918 F.3d at 1105.

where the sexual harassment occurred and participate in extracurricular activities;[320] the plaintiff's inability to engage with campus programming at the institution where the incident occurred;[321] and self-destructive or depressive behavior by the plaintiff that leads to decreased engagement in the educational process.[322]

[d] Illustrative Cases

An institution's deliberate indifference and the severity of the impact of the discrimination, two of the elements discussed above, were the focus of the court's discussion in *S.S. v. Alexander*.[323] A female student and employee in the University of Washington's athletic department alleged the actions of UW officials, following her report of having been raped by a member of UW's football team, "deprived her of [the] right to be free from sex discrimination in [an] educational program[]" in violation of Title IX.[324] Applying an approach incorporating the essential elements of the *Davis* test, the court found that plaintiff had proffered sufficient evidence of a Title IX sexual harassment case to survive dismissal.

The court ruled that determining deliberate indifference is a "fact-based question, for which bright line rules are ill-suited."[325] The court then concluded that evidence of the following post-harassment conduct by the university supported the plaintiff's allegations of deliberate indifference:

> A lack of appropriate discipline of [the plaintiff's] rapist, minimizing the effects of her rape, treating the victim equally with the rapist in the mediation process, allowing her rapist's denial of wrong-doing to be accepted at face value at the mediation, keeping the matter out of the public eye to avoid negative publicity, offering only a repeated mediation as an alternative remedial measure, discouraging [the plaintiff] from filing a police report, top administrators not notifying the UW's own police force of the report of a violent sex crime, repeatedly suggesting that [the plaintiff] leave her job with the football program while her rapist would remain, wearing [the plaintiff] down until she believed that further complaints would be futile, a decision not to investigate — or cause to be investigated — her rape report, and — in the absence of a proper investigation — questioning her truthfulness when she expressed dissatisfaction with the results of the mediation....[326]

---

320. *See Williams*, 477 F.3d 1282 (finding concern for future attack by actual perpetrators or like students causing a student to withdraw creates an adverse educational impact).

321. *Farmer*, 918 F.3d at 1105.

322. Jennings v. University of North Carolina at Chapel Hill, 240 F. Supp. 2d 492, 511 (2002) ("Interfering with a student's education and participation in sports may deprive a student of an educational opportunity or benefit in violation of Title IX."). *See also* Davis & Smith, *supra* note 315, at 643 (discussing the impact of the harassing behavior).

323. 177 P.3d 724 (Wash. Ct. App. 2008).

324. *Id.* at 728.

325. *Id.* at 738 (quoting Doe v. Derby Bd. of Educ., 451 F. Supp. 2d 438, 447 (D. Conn. 2006)).

326. *Id.* at 740.

The court emphasized that the university is not responsible for the rape itself, but for its actions after the plaintiff reported the rape.[327] Finally, the court found that the negative effect on the plaintiff's studies resulting from the "distress, anxiety, and emotional hurt" flowing from the university's post-harassment conduct could be sufficient to demonstrate that she was "denied the full benefit of her educational experience."[328]

Williams v. Board of Regents of the University System of Georgia[329] is representative of a case in which a court applied a broad interpretation of the actual knowledge and deliberate indifference requirements. There, the plaintiff, a student at the University of Georgia, alleged she was sexually assaulted and raped by three student-athletes.[330] The plaintiff also alleged that university personnel, including the head basketball coach, athletic director, and university president, were aware of a high risk of sexual assault being perpetrated by one of her alleged assailants.[331] According to the plaintiff, this stemmed from the officials' recruitment and admission of one of the athletes, notwithstanding their knowledge of his past history of "disciplinary and criminal problems, particularly those [relating to the athlete's] harassment of women, at other colleges."[332] Williams also alleged that the university failed to act on student-athletes' suggestions that they be informed of the university's sexual harassment policy.[333] The court ruled that these factors, along with the recipient's response to the sexual harassment, could amount to allegations of deliberate indifference sufficient to survive defendant's motion to dismiss.[334] Thus, *Williams* concludes that it may be appropriate to consider "before-the-fact" as well as "after-the-fact" harassment in ascertaining the required deliberate indifference. The court ruled that the university's response following the incident, including waiting several months to conduct a hearing and its failure to take action to prevent further attacks by the players, also amounted to deliberate indifference.[335] With respect to the severity of the harassment, the court articulated the following standard:

> Whether gender-oriented conduct rises to the level of actionable "harassment" thus "depends on a constellation of surrounding circumstances, expectation, and relationships," including, but not limited to, the ages of the harasser and the victim and the number of individuals involved. [T]o have a "systemic effect" of denying the victim equal access to an educational program or activity … gender discrimination must be more widespread than a single instance of one-on-one peer harassment.[336]

---

327. *Id.* at 743.
328. *Id.* at 745.
329. 477 F.3d 1282 (11th Cir. 2007).
330. *Id.* at 1288.
331. *Id.* at 1289–90.
332. *Id.*
333. *Id.* at 1290.
334. *Id.* at 1297.
335. *Id.* at 1296–97.
336. *Id.* at 1297 (quoting *Davis*, 526 U.S. at 651, 652–53 (internal quotations omitted)).

Another student-to-student sexual harassment case in which a court adopted a broad interpretation of the actual knowledge and deliberate indifference standards is *Simpson v. University of Colorado Boulder*.[337] Leading cases applying the *Davis* and *Gebser* elements in teacher-to-student harassment arising in the athletic context include *Jennings v. University of North Carolina at Chapel Hill*,[338] *Bostic v. Smyrna School District*,[339] and *Ericson v. Syracuse University*.[340]

[2] Professional Sports

The major professional sports leagues in conjunction with players associations have implemented policies to address sexual violence in sports.[341] League domestic violence policies were enacted in the aftermath of high-profile incidents,[342] and a U.S. Senatorial Committee recognizing that "[due to] the high-profile nature of professional sports, when a celebrity athlete is charged with committing domestic violence, it uniquely reverberates through our society in fascinating ways."[343] The committee also encouraged professional sports leagues to better respond to issues of domestic violence.[344]

---

337. 500 F.3d 1170; *see also J.K.*, 2008 WL 4446712, at *5.

338. 482 F.3d 686 (4th Cir. 2007) (in reversing lower and three judge appellate court panel, court finds coach's persistent comments degrading women constituted sufficient facts on which a jury could find the existence of a hostile and abusive environment).

339. 418 F.3d 355 (3d Cir. 2005) (concluding plaintiff failed to establish the school possessed actual knowledge of coach's sexual relationship with a high school student).

340. 35 F. Supp. 2d 326 (S.D.N.Y. 1999) (stating plaintiffs alleged facts giving rise to a cognizable Title IX claim); *see also* Diane Heckman, *Title IX and Sexual Harassment Claims Involving Educational Athletic Department Employees and Student-Athletes in the Twenty-First Century*, 8 VA. SPORTS & ENT. L.J. 233 (2009) (providing overview of Title IX claims against coaches).

341. *See* National Football League, *National Football League Players Association Collective Bargaining Agreement* (Mar. 5, 2020), https://nflpaweb.blob.core.windows.net/media/Default/NFLPA/CBA2020/NFL-NFLPA_CBA_March_5_2020.pdf [hereinafter *National Football League CBA*]; National Basketball Association, *National Basketball Players Association Collective Bargaining Agreement* (Jan. 19, 2017), https://cosmic-s3.imgix.net/3c7a0a50-8e11-11e9-875d-3d44e94ae33f-2017-NBA-NBPA-Collective-Bargaining-Agreement.pdf [hereinafter *National Basketball Association CBA*]; Major League Baseball, *Major League Baseball Collective Bargaining Agreement* (2017), https://d39ba378-ae47-4003-86d3-147e4fa6e51b.filesusr.com/ugd/b0a4c2_95883690627349e0a5203f61b93715b5.pdf [hereinafter *Major League Baseball CBA*].

342. Paul Skribina, *When Pro Athletes Are Accused of Abuse, How Often Does Punishment Follow?*, THE TENNESSEAN (Sept. 19, 2018, 10:17 am), https://www.tennessean.com/story/sports/nhl/predators/2018/09/19/nfl-domestic-violence-sexual-assault-child-abuse-nba-mlb-nhl/1335799002/; *see also* Tate Martin, Comment, *Wake-up Call: How the Ray Rice Incident Opened the Public's Eyes to Domestic Violence in Professional Sports and the Need for Change*, 24 SPORTS LAW. J. 183, 187 (2017); Bethany P. Withers, Note, *The Integrity of the Game: Professional Athletes and Domestic Violence*, 1 HARV. J. SPORTS & ENT. L. 145, 149, 166, 171 (2010).

343. *Addressing Domestic Violence in Professional Sports: Hearing before the Committee on Commerce, Science, and Transportation*, 113th Cong., Second Session, 1, 1 (2014) (Statement of Hon. John D. Rockefeller, IV).

344. *Id.*

[a] League Policies

The NFL's standard player contract permits termination of the agreement if the "[p]layer has engaged in personal conduct reasonably judged by [the NFL] to adversely affect or reflect on [the NFL]."[345] While vaguely referencing any conduct bringing adverse media or judicial attention to the NFL as grounds for termination, the body of the contract itself does not provide specific domestic violence related terms.

The NFL's Personal Conduct Policy defines "detrimental to the integrity of and public confidence in" the NFL as including: "illegal, violent, dangerous, or irresponsible [action which] puts innocent victims at risk, damages the reputation of others in the game, and undercuts public respect and support for the NFL."[346] Illegality encompasses a judicial finding of guilt and circumstances where a player is "subject to a disposition of a criminal proceeding."[347] Conduct prohibited under the policy includes physical violence, domestic violence, sexual assault of any kind, and intimidation.[348] The policy's domestic violence provision encompasses "actual or threatened violence against another person, including dating violence, domestic violence, child abuse, or other forms of family violence."[349]

In addition to "conduct detrimental" provisions,[350] MLB's and NBA's respective CBAs include personal conduct policies.[351] The NBA defines domestic violence as violence or attempted violence, yet also includes: "stalking, harassment, ... behavior that intimidates, manipulates, humiliates, isolates, frightens, terrorizes, coerces, threatens, injures, or places another person in fear of bodily harm."[352] MLB's broad definition encompasses: "physical or sexual violence, emotional and/or psychological intimidation, verbal violence, stalking, economic control, harassment, physical intimidation, or injury."[353] MLB and the NBA policies state that domestic violence can be a single

---

345. *See National Football League CBA, supra* note 341, at 339.

346. *See* National Football League, *Personal Conduct Policy: League Policies for Players* 1 (2018), https://nflcommunications.com/Documents/2018%20Policies/2018%20Personal%20Conduct%20 Policy.pdf [hereinafter *NFL Conduct Policy*].

347. *Id.* at 2.

348. *Id.*

349. *Id.* The NFL's policy does not include forms of relationship violence such as intimidation, control, and emotional abuse, all of which can be forms of domestic violence. Vera E. Mouradian, *Abuse in Intimate Relationships: Defining the Multiple Dimensions and Terms,* National Violence Against Women Prevention Research Center at Wellesley College (2000), https://mainweb-v.musc. edu/vawprevention/research/defining.shtml.

350. *See National Basketball Association CBA, supra* note 341, at A-4, A-24; *Major League Baseball CBA, supra* note 341, at 52.

351. *See National Basketball Association CBA, supra* note 341, at F-1; *Major League Baseball CBA, supra* note 341, at 308. The presence of a domestic violence policy within a CBA arguably creates an inherently stronger policy than one existing as a separate document, or one which is non-existent. *See* Al Neal, *Which of the Big 4 Has the Best Domestic Violence Policy,* Grand Stand Central (Aug. 4, 2018), https://grandstandcentral.com/2018/society/best-domestic-violence-policy-sports/.

352. *National Basketball Association CBA, supra* note 341 at F-1.

353. *Major League Baseball CBA, supra* note 341, at 308. *See* Kristy Candela, *Protecting the Invisible Victim: Incorporating Coercive Control in Domestic Violence Statutes,* 54 Family Ct. Review, 112 (2016) (arguing that "[l]imiting the definition of abuse to purely physical acts or threats of physical acts does not address the unforgiving realities of domestic abuse").

act or a pattern of behavior[354] and acknowledge that domestic violence can occur between same-sex partners.[355] Although the NHL does not have a domestic violence policy, the league maintains that the commissioner's authority to impose sanctions for players' off-ice conduct detrimental to the NHL also governs domestic violence and allows for a case-by-case analysis of such incidents.[356]

[b] Education and Treatment

MLB, the NBA, and the NFL each provide educational resources and programming for players who are disciplined for domestic violence or who seek assistance with respect to domestic violence.[357] The NHL lacks a specific program.[358] The NFL designates the team clinician as the party "responsible for implementing the mental health education programming," which addresses[359] issues including depression and violent behaviors.[360] Under the NFL's policy, the team clinicians are assigned to create mental health networks for use by players.[361] MLB and NBA's Joint Policy Committee is responsible for implementing the Leagues' education program.[362] The Committee, which is required to have at least one member with expertise in "domestic violence, sexual assault, and child abuse,"[363] determines the staffing, content, and frequency of educational programming for players.[364] Finally, MLB makes domestic violence education available to players' families.[365]

---

354. *See National Basketball Association CBA, supra* note 341 at F-1; *Major League Baseball CBA, supra* note 341, at 308.

355. *See National Basketball Association CBA, supra* note 341, at F-1; *Major League Baseball CBA, supra* note 341, at 308.

356. "The NHL has failed to move in the direction of creating a policy regarding domestic violence and sexual assault." Chelsea Augelli & Tamara L. Kuennen, *Domestic Violence & Men's Professional Sports: Advancing the Ball,* 21 U. Denv. Sports & Ent. L.J. 27, 63 (2018). *See* National Hockey League, *National Hockey League Players Association Collective Bargaining Agreement,* 1, 124 (Sept. 16, 2012), https://cdn.nhlpa.com/img/assets/file/NHL_NHLPA_2013_CBA.pdf [hereinafter *National Hockey League CBA*]; *see* Lindsey Munchauser, *Is the NHL Skating on Thin Ice without a Domestic Violence Policy?,* U. Buff L. Sports & Ent. F. (2018), https://ublawsportsforum.com/2018/10/11/is-the-nhl-skating-on-thin-ice-without-a-domestic-violence-policy/; *see also* Stephen Whyno, *NHL Suspends Voynov for 2019–20 Season for Domestic Violence,* Associated Press (Apr. 09, 2019, 2:35 PM), https://www.chicagotribune.com/sports/ct-spt-slave-voynov-suspended-domestic-violence-20190409-story.html.

357. *See NFL Conduct Policy, supra* note 346, at 3; *National Basketball Association CBA, supra* note 341, at F-3–F-5; *Major League Baseball CBA, supra* note 341, at 319.

358. *See National Hockey League CBA, supra* note 356, at 123, 189.

359. *See National Football League CBA, supra* note 341, at 233.

360. *Id.* at 231.

361. *Id.* at 233.

362. *National Basketball Association CBA, supra* note 341 at F-3; *Major League Baseball CBA, supra* note 341, at 318.

363. *See, e.g., National Basketball Association CBA, supra* note 341, at F-2.

364. *Id.* at F-3; *Major League Baseball CBA, supra* note 341, at 318.

365. *Major League Baseball CBA, supra* note 341, at 324.

Under the leagues' respective policies, NFL, NBA, or MLB players arrested or charged with violent conduct must participate in a formal clinical evaluation and follow up treatment.[366] The NFL Player Conduct Policy requires services for any player "arrested or charged" with violent behavior.[367] MLB's domestic violence policy offers treatment to players who "committed or are alleged to have committed" an act within the MLB definition of domestic violence.[368] The NBA policy offers education and treatment for any player when there is "reasonable cause to believe" the player engaged in "off-court violent conduct."[369] The NBA also provides treatment for domestic violence upon a conduct violation or criminal conviction.[370]

[c] Sanctions and Appeals

The Leagues' sanctions for players' domestic violence differ. The NFL sanctions include "fines, suspension without pay," and "banishment from the league with an opportunity to reapply."[371] The threshold sanction is a minimum six-game suspension[372] with aggravating factors likely to increase the magnitude of the punishment.[373] MLB's policy places its players on a mandatory seven-day administrative leave subject to extension.[374] The NBA's policy imposes an immediate ten-game suspension on any player convicted of a violent felony.[375] In domestic violence cases, governed by the specific policy and distinct from the NBA's handling of other violence, there is no minimum-game suspension or duration for administrative leave.[376] The MLB,[377] NFL[378] and NBA[379] policies each impose penalties on players' failure to comply with treatment protocols.

NBA, NHL, and MLB players may appeal disciplinary sanctions to an impartial arbitrator, and appeals are processed like other grievance arbitrations.[380] NFL Personal

---

366. See *NFL Conduct Policy*, *supra* note 346, at 3; *National Basketball Association CBA*, *supra* note 341 at F-4; *Major League Baseball CBA*, *supra* note 341, at 319.

367. *NFL Conduct Policy*, *supra* note 346, at 3.

368. See *Major League Baseball CBA*, *supra* note 341, at 240, 318.

369. See *National Basketball Association CBA*, *supra* note 341, at 119.

370. *Id*. at F-4.

371. See *NFL Conduct Policy*, *supra* note 346, at 6.

372. *Id*. at 7.

373. *Id*. Aggravating factors include repeated behavior, use of a weapon, and the vulnerability of the victim (*e.g.*, pregnancy). *Id*.

374. See *Major League Baseball CBA*, *supra* note 341, at 309.

375. See *National Basketball Association CBA*, *supra* note 341, at 119.

376. *Id*. at F-7. Unlike MLB and the NFL, administrative leave is not the NBA's default. The NBA's policy states, "administrative leave should be applied in only those cases in which a balancing of all relevant factors clearly establishes that it is reasonable to do so under the totality of the circumstances." *Id*.

377. See *Major League Baseball CBA*, *supra* note 341, at 320.

378. See *NFL Conduct Policy*, *supra* note 346, at 8.

379. See *National Basketball Association CBA*, *supra* note 341, at F-5.

380. See *Major League Baseball CBA*, *supra* note 341, at 45, 310; *National Basketball Association CBA*, *supra* note 341, at 392, F-8. The NHL's disciplinary appeals are for conduct not related to domestic violence, as this league does not have a domestic violence policy. *National Hockey League CBA*, *supra* note 356, at 109.

Conduct Policy violations are heard by a hearing officer. The Commissioner has the discretion to serve as the hearing officer, but he can appoint a different person to the role.[381]

[d] Same-Sex Domestic Violence

Domestic violence is not restricted to male-on-female conduct. The NBA and MLB recognize in their domestic violence provisions that domestic violence can occur in same-sex relationships.[382] Domestic violence can also be perpetrated by women, whether in same-sex or different-sex relationships.[383] Domestic violence incidents involving high-profile women's athletes[384] influenced the WNBA to develop a domestic violence policy modeled on the NBA's policy.[385] The WNBA provides a sweeping definition of domestic violence that includes all sexual orientations, current and former intimate relations, and violence as well as intimidation or other emotionally manipulative behaviors.[386] Like the NBA's policy, the WNBA's policy requires the development of educational initiatives and has no baseline timeframe for disciplinary administrative leave or sanctions.[387]

§ 5.06 Transgender Issues in Sport

[A] Introduction

Legal issues pertaining to sport participation opportunities of transgender, non-gender, and cisgender athletes have emerged at all levels of athletic competition. Con-

---

381. *NFL Conduct Policy, supra* note 346, at 6. Should the arbitrator rule adversely to the player, he may appeal to the appropriate federal district court. *See, e.g.,* National Football Players Association on behalf of Adrian Peterson v. National Football League, 831 F.3d 985, 993 (8th Cir. 2016).

382. *See National Basketball Association CBA, supra* note 341, at F-1; *Major League Baseball CBA, supra* note 341, at 308.

383. *See* Benjamin Hine, et al., *"I Have Guys Call Me and Say 'I Can't Be the Victim of Domestic Abuse'": Exploring the Experiences of Telephone Support Providers for Male Victims of Domestic Violence and Abuse,* J. OF INTERPERSONAL VIOLENCE 1, 3 (2020).

384. *See* Ray Sanchez, *Soccer Star Hope Solo Arrested on Domestic Assault Charges,* CNN (June 21, 2014, 10:27 PM), https://www.cnn.com/2014/06/21/us/hope-solo-domestic-assault-charge/index.html; *see also* Victor Mather, *Brittney Griner and Glory Johnson Suspended 7 Games in Domestic Violence Case,* N.Y. TIMES (May 15, 2015), https://www.nytimes.com/2015/05/16/sports/basketball/wnba-suspends-brittney-griner-and-glory-johnson-in-domestic-violence-case.html; Alexandria R. Chase, *"Equal Opportunity Violence": Hope Solo and the Rhetoric of Domestic Violence in Sports Media,* 42 WOMEN'S STUDIES IN COMMUNICATION 241 (2019).

385. *See* Women's National Basketball Association, *Women's National Basketball Association Players Collective Bargaining Agreement,* 1, 329 (2020), https://wnbpa.com/wp-content/uploads/2020/01/WNBA-WNBPA-CBA-2020-2027.pdf [*hereinafter WNBA CBA*]. Due to ongoing litigation regarding the United States Women's National Team Collective Bargaining Agreement, the document is not accessible to the general public. *See Morgan,* 445 F. Supp. 3d 635 (C.D. Cal. 2020), *cert. denied,* No. 219CV01717RGKAGR, 2020 WL 4390368 (C.D. Cal. June 23, 2020).

386. *See WNBA CBA, supra* note 385, at 329.

387. *Id.* at 322.

troversy most frequently revolves around the fear of an unfair competitive advantage when a male athlete, who transitions to female, wants to engage in athletic competition against girls and women, and where female athletes with naturally occurring high levels of testosterone want to compete against other females.[388] The latter of these two circumstances was at issue in two high-profile cases, to which we now turn.

[B] Olympic Sports and CAS Determinations

[1] Dutee Chand

Dutee Chand is a sprinter with hyperandrogenism, a condition that causes her body to naturally produce an amount of testosterone that placed her at the "male" hormonal level according to international track and field standards.[389] Pursuant to the International Association of Athletics Federation's ("IAAF" — which is now called World Athletics) "Regulations Governing Eligibility of Females with Hyperandrogenism to Compete in Women's Competition," the Indian affiliate ("AFI") suspended Chand's eligibility to compete against women in her event, the 100 meters.[390] The aforementioned IAAF regulations went into effect in 2014, and placed restrictions on the eligibility of female athletes with high levels of naturally occurring testosterone to participate in competitive athletics.[391]

Chand brought proceedings before the Court of Arbitration for Sport ("CAS") challenging the regulation. The CAS upheld her challenge finding that Chand had established that it was discriminatory to require female — but not male — athletes to undergo testing for levels of endogenous testosterone, and to restrict eligibility based on natural physical characteristics.[392] The CAS suspended IAAF's regulations to permit the organization to gather and present evidence regarding the extent of any sustained advantageous athletic performance hyperandrogenic female athletes possess over non-hyperandrogenic female athletes as a result of the former's higher levels of

---

388. Juliet Macur, *Fighting for the Body She Was Born With*, N.Y. TIMES (Oct. 6, 2014), https://www.nytimes.com/2014/10/07/sports/sprinter-dutee-chand-fights-ban-over-her-testosterone-level.html; Juliet Macur, *What Qualifies a Woman to Compete as a Woman?: An Ugly Fight Continues*, N.Y. TIMES (Aug. 4, 2017), https://www.nytimes.com/2017/08/04/sports/olympics/gender-dutee-chand-india.html; Anna North, *"I am a woman and I am fast": What Caster Semenya's story says about gender and race in sports*, VOX (May 3, 2019, 7:30 a.m.), https://www.vox.com/identities/2019/5/3/18526723/caster-semenya-800-gender-race-intersex-athletes; Dutee Chand v. Athletics Federation of India & IAAF, CAS 2014/A/3759 (July 24, 2015).

389. Juliet Macur, *Fighting for the Body She Was Born With*, N.Y. TIMES (Oct. 6, 2014), https://www.nytimes.com/2014/10/07/sports/sprinter-dutee-chand-fights-ban-over-her-testosterone-level.html.

390. *Dutee Chand v. AFI*, at 5–6; Juliet Macur, *What Qualifies a Woman to Compete as a Woman?: An Ugly Fight Continues*, N.Y. TIMES (Aug. 4, 2017), https://www.nytimes.com/2017/08/04/sports/olympics/gender-dutee-chand-india.html.

391. *Chand v. AFI*, at 12–13.

392. *Id.* at 89.

testosterone.[393] In 2018, the IAAF adopted new regulations, the Differences of Sex Development Regulations ("DSD Regulations").

The IAAF-commissioned study in response to the *Chand* case concluded that high testosterone levels in female sprinters did not create an advantage equal to the standard 10–12% advantage of males over females.[394] The study also found, however, higher testosterone levels advantaged female athletes greatest in the 400m, 800m, and 1500m events.[395] The study provided a basis for the IAAF's decision prohibiting Caster Semenya from competing in the women's 800-meter event.[396]

[2] Caster Semenya

The importance of the *Chand* decision, permitting her to compete in the 100 meter dash, would not be fully realized until the Caster Semenya case in 2019. The research study which permitted Chand to compete found an advantage for women with higher levels of testosterone[397] in the events in which Caster Semenya, a South African with hypoandrogenism, competed.[398] Chand, therefore, won a battle to compete using a research study that created the Athletes with Differences of Sex Development Restricted Events List.[399] The list that benefitted her yet barred Semenya.[400]

Like Chand, Semenya challenged the competition ban she faced. In examining Semenya's challenge to the DSD Regulations, the CAS adopted an analytical approach similar to the *McDonnell-Douglas* framework applied in Title VII cases.[401] The CAS began by analyzing whether the plaintiff had established a prime facie case of discrimination.[402] It unanimously concluded that the DSD Regulations were prima facie discriminatory because "they impose differential treatment based on protected characteristics. In particular, the DSD Regulations establish restrictions that are targeted to a subset of the female/intersex athlete populations, and do not impose any equivalent restrictions on male athletes."[403] The CAS also concluded that the DSD Regulations created restrictions targeting individuals with "immutable biological characteristics" which did not apply to individuals without such characteristics.[404]

The CAS then considered whether IAAF established a legitimate reason to support upholding the DSD and whether the means selected to achieve any such objectives

---

393. *Id.* at 104, 108.

394. Macur, *supra* note 389.

395. *See* Caster Semenya v. Athletics South Africa & International Association of Athletics Federations (IAAF): Executive Summary, Court of Arbitration and Sport, 1, 1–2 (Jan. 5, 2019, 15:42), https://www.tas-cas.org/fileadmin/user_upload/CAS_Executive_Summary__5794_.pdf.

396. *Id.*

397. *See id.*

398. *Id.*

399. *Id.* at 1.

400. *Id.* at 4.

401. *See id.*

402. *See id.*; *see also* McDonnell Douglas Corp. v. Green, 411 U.S. 792 (1973).

403. Semenya, *supra* note 395, at 3.

404. *Id.*; Dutee Chand v. Athletics Federation of India & IAAF, CAS 2014/A/3759 (July 24, 2015).

were reasonable and proportionate.[405] The IAAF argued "that once it is recognized that it is legitimate to have separate categories of male and female competition, it inevitably follows that it is necessary to devise an objective, fair and effective means of determining which individuals may, and which may not, participate in those categories."[406] Relying on expert evidence, the CAS found that "androgen sensitive female athletes" with levels of testosterone falling within the adult male range possess a significant performance advantage over other female athletes. The CAS then concluded that the DSD Regulation was necessary to maintain fair competition in female athletics "by ensuring that female athletes who do not enjoy significant performance advantage caused by exposure to levels of circulating testosterone in the adult male range do not have to compete against female athletes who enjoy that performance advantage."[407] The CAS also found that the DSD Regulations were a reasonable and proportionate means of achieving this objective.[408]

[3] The 2020 [2021] Olympics

The 2020 Tokyo Olympics, held in July and August of 2021, hailed a new level of inclusion that was widely applauded and widely contested. Laurel Hubbard, a weightlifter from New Zealand, became the first transgender athlete in the history of the games.[409] Hubbard, who once competed under the name Gavin Hubbard,[410] began transitioning in 2012 and qualified for the Olympics under the International Weightlifting Federation's Transgender Guidelines.[411] The transgender policy published by the International Olympic Committee ("IOC") in 2015 required Hubbard to have been under hormone therapy for at least a year.[412] Hubbard was the first athlete to have completed transition to compete in the games, but not the only transgender athlete. Hubbard was joined by Quinn, the first openly transgender and non-binary Olympic Gold Medalist (Canada, Women's Soccer), and Chelsea Wolfe, an alternate for the United States' BMX team.[413]

---

405. *Sumenya, supra* note 395, at 4.

406. *Id.*

407. *Id.* at 5.

408. *Id.*

409. Jo Yurcaba and Reuters, *With Olympics' backing, Laurel Hubbard will be first trans athlete in Games' history*, NBC NEWS (July 19, 2021), https://www.nbcnews.com/feature/nbc-out/olympics-backing-laurel-hubbard-will-first-trans-athlete-games-history-rcna1454.

410. *Weightlifting: Transgender lifter Laurel Hubbard wins first International Outing*, NZ HERALD (Mar. 19, 2017), https://www.nzherald.co.nz/sport/weightlifting-transgender-lifter-laurel-hubbard-wins-first-international-outing/QXF5IUS6ROJ6274ACLFUYPFUNY/.

411. Leigh McManus, *What records did Laurel Hubbard break? Athlete becomes first transgender Olympian*, THE FOCUS (July 2021), https://www.thefocus.news/sports/laurel-hubbard-records/.

412. International Olympic Committee, Meeting Minutes: IOC Consensus Meeting on Sex Reassignment and Hyperandrogenism (Nov. 2015), available at https://stillmed.olympic.org/Documents/Commissions_PDFfiles/Medical_commission/2015-11_ioc_consensus_meeting_on_sex_reassignment_and_hyperandrogenism-en.pdf.

413. The Associated Press, *First openly Transgender athletes are competing in Tokyo*, NBC NEWS (July 26, 2021), https://www.nbcnews.com/nbc-out/out-news/first-openly-transgender-olympians-are-competing-tokyo-rcna1507.

During the Games, the IOC announced it would rewrite the transgender policies published in 2016,[414] citing the need to balance safety with inclusivity, and stating that "[t]he other important thing to remember is that trans women are women. You have got to include all women if you possibly can."[415] The new policy was released in November of 2021.[416] The policy places responsibility on sports organizations to establish eligibility criteria for the inclusion of competitors.[417] It also explicitly bans the exclusion of individuals from competition based on the competitor's "unverified, alleged, or perceived unfair competitive advantage."[418] Exclusion from competition or certain events is permitted, however, if robust peer reviewed research "demonstrates consistent, unfair, disproportionate competitive advantage" or "a risk to the physical safety of other athletes."[419] Competitors excluded due to advantage or risk should be accommodated as reasonable and permitted to compete in other events that do not present the same statistically supported advantage.[420]

Joining the IOC in policy development and lobbying initiatives are organizations such as the Women's Sports Policy Working Group, a bipartisan group of former elite female athletes seeking to include transgender females without disadvantaging cisgender female athletes.[421] The organization has drafted a model state statute that includes provisions permitting transgender females to compete with and against cisgender females if they have not experienced male puberty, or if they have experienced all or part of male puberty, only after they have demonstrated "that they have mitigated their sex linked performance advantages."[422] The model statute notes that mitigated performance advantages occur when testosterone levels are within the "normal range" found in cisgender females.[423] As a result, the model provision does not account for intersex athletes.

---

414. See International Olympic Committee, *supra* note 412.

415. Sean Ingle, *IOC admits guidelines for transgender athletes are not fit for purpose*, THE GUARDIAN (July 30, 2021), https://www.theguardian.com/sport/2021/jul/30/ioc-admits-guidelines-for-transgender-athletes-are-not-fit-for-purpose.

416. International Olympic Committee, *OC Framework on Fairness, Inclusion, and Non-Discrimination on the Basis of Gender Identity and Sex Variations*, available at https://stillmed.olympics.com/media/Documents/News/2021/11/IOC-Framework-Fairness-Inclusion-Non-discrimination-2021.pdf?_ga=2.195521836.1048075235.1637092563-834742310.1637092563.

417. *Id.*

418. *Id.*

419. *Id.*

420. *Id.*

421. Women's Sports Policy Working Group, available at https://womenssportspolicy.org/about-us/#mission.

422. Women's Sports Policy Working Group, *Inclusion of Transgender Girls and Women in Girl's and Women's Sports: Model State Statute* at 3 (Apr. 15, 2021), available at https://womenssportspolicy.org/wp-content/uploads/2021/04/WSPWG-Model-State-Statute.pdf.

423. *Id.* at 4, n.5.

[C] Other Levels of Competition

[1] Title IX Regulations

The issue of competition when testosterone levels are naturally higher, or when previously high testosterone levels allowed the athlete's body to develop differently than their gender-conforming peers, are not unique to the elite or Olympic level. Biological testing was at issue under New York Human Rights Law in 1978 when Dr. Renee Richards sought to play in the U.S. Open Masters Tennis Tournament.[424] Richards was a biological male who, following sex reassignment surgery, sought to compete in the women's division.[425] Richards was permitted to compete as a woman.[426] The court determined that a chromosomal test "is not and should not be the sole criterion [to compete] where, as here, the circumstances warrant consideration of other factors."[427]

While lawsuits by transgender individuals are rare, litigation and administrative interpretations have weighed in on the competitive rights of transgender and gender-nonconforming athletes, as well as cisgender athletes.[428] At the high school level, litigation in the United States has raised issues of access to competition, equal rights, and Title IX concerns.[429] Such litigation has been impacted by politics. In 2016, the Obama administration published a "Dear Colleague" letter, stating that transgender students were included in the "on the basis of sex" umbrella of Title IX protections.[430] The Obama administration acknowledged that excluding a class of students (here transgender students) was inappropriate and violated Title IX.[431] This letter was, however, quickly rescinded by the Trump administration in 2017.[432] The revocation of the 2016 Dear Colleague letter emphasized that the Obama-era decision that "on the basis of sex" encompassed gender identity was not "consistent with the express language of Title IX."[433]

Under the Trump administration's guidance, access for transgender athletes in sport was further restricted in an August 2020 administrative action warning letter to the State of Connecticut.[434] The Department of Education considered a case in

---

424. Richards v. United States Tennis Assn, 93 Misc. 2d 713 (Sup. Ct. N.Y. Cty. 1973).

425. *Id.* at 713–14.

426. *Id.* at 722.

427. *Id.*

428. *See, e.g.*, Alliance Defending Freedom, *Title IX Discrimination Complaint on Behalf of Minor Children Selina Soule, [Second Complainant], and Alanna Smith* (June 17, 2019), http://www.adfmedia. org/files/SouleComplaintOCR.pdf; Pat Eaton-Robb, *Girls Sue to Block Participation of Transgender Athletes*, Associated Press (Feb. 12, 2020) https://apnews.com/article/8fd300537131153cc44e0cf2ad e3244b.

429. *See* Alliance Defending Freedom, *supra* note 428.

430. Catherine E. Lhamon & Vanita Gupta, Dear Colleague Letter on Transgender Students, Dept of Justice and Dept. of Educ. 1, 2 (May 13, 2016).

431. *Id.*

432. Sandra Battle & T.E. Wheeler, Dear Colleague Letter, Dept of Justice and Dept. of Educ., 1 (February 22, 2017).

433. *Id.*

434. Kimberly M. Richey, Revised Letter of Impending Enforcement Action: Connecticut Interscholastic Athletic Conference, No. 01-19-4025 (Aug. 31, 2020).

which cisgender females competing in high school girls track in Connecticut claimed a denial of equal opportunity to compete.[435] Their claim arose out of state championship competitions in which male-to-female transgender student athletes placed higher than the complainant cisgender athletes.[436] The cisgender athletes claimed that a deprivation of their right to compete was demonstrated by their lower individual and team standing, and alleged lower college recruitment opportunity based on those standings.[437] The Department of Education agreed, finding that allowing transgender athletes to compete removed opportunity from gender-conforming students, which is "inconsistent with Title IX's mandate of equal opportunity for both sexes."[438] It warned that Connecticut high schools risked losing federal funding if they failed to correct the situation.[439] That lawsuit has since been dismissed.[440]

The pendulum swung the other direction in January of 2021 when President Biden signed Executive Order 13988, which stated in part that "sex" in Title IX included sexual orientation and gender identity.[441] This stance was reinforced by the Department of Education in June of 2021, which reiterated and adopted the statements of EO 13988.[442]

The nation's high schools have differing polices addressing sports participation by transgender students.[443] The Connecticut policy at issue in the DOE case is similar to that of approximately twenty states that allow transgender individuals to compete without having to undergo any medical diagnosis or treatment to begin a gender-identity conforming transition.[444] Approximately fifteen states require either some level of medical treatment or a case-by-case assessment to determine the appropriate athletic team for the high school student.[445] Other states have restrictive policies that permit participation based on birth sex, or require gender confirmation surgery for participation.[446]

Recently, high school athletic association policies have taken a back seat to state statutes banning transgender athletes from athletic participation on teams aligning with their gender identity. Under various other titles, states across the country began

---

435. *Id.*

436. *Id.*

437. *Id.*

438. *Id.* at 37.

439. *Id.* at 48–49.

440. Soule *ex rel.* Stanescu v. Connecticut Ass'n of Schools, Inc., 2021 WL 1617206 (D. Conn. April 21, 2021). In the order to dismiss, the judge noted that the plaintiffs were no longer high school athletes, lack of redressability, and holding that plaintiff's claims for monetary damages were barred. *Id.*

441. Exec. Order No. 13,988, 86 Fed. Reg. 7023 (Jan. 20, 2021).

442. Susane B. Goldberg, *Notice of Interpretation: Enforcement of Title IX of the Education Amendments of 1972 with Respect to Discrimination Based on Sexual Orientation and Gender Identity in Light of* Bostock v. Clayton County, DEP'T OF EDUC. (June 16, 2021).

443. Christin Flynn Lal, Note, *Inclusion is Necessary to Protect the Health and Safety of Transgender Student-Athletes: Are Recent Legal Challenges Enough to Move the Goalposts?*, 16 J. HEALTH & BIO-MEDICAL L. 231, 242–45 (2020).

444. *Id.*

445. *Id.*

446. *Id.*

enacting "Save Women's Sports Act[s]" which ban male-to-female athletes from competition in K-12 sports.[447] These laws are being hotly contested across the country and challenged by interest groups (such as the ACLU) and the Department of Justice alike.[448]

At the collegiate level, between 2011 and early January 2022, the NCAA recognized that after one year of hormonal treatment, the perceived competitive advantage that someone born male may have over female teammates dissipates.[449] The NCAA retained policies specific to the first year of transition.[450] For example, a male participating on a female team reclassified the team as a "mixed" team, and makes the athlete ineligible for women's intercollegiate athletic championship competition.[451] A trans male (FTM), however, could immediately compete on a men's team,[452] or continue to compete on a women's team. Doing the latter, however, would qualify the women's team as "mixed" for the remainder of the time the FTM athlete was on the team, barring the team from championship competition.[453] A trans female (MTF) could compete on a men's team.[454] They could also compete on a women's team, and would qualify a women's team as "mixed" only in the first year of hormonal treatment, and thereafter could compete on a women's team without the team being classified as a mixed team.[455] Additionally, testosterone was considered a performance enhancing substance which required a medical exemption within NCAA drug testing protocols.[456]

Competition at the collegiate level following transition reached heightened debate in 2021 when Lia Thomas began shattering women's swimming records at the University of Pennsylvania — having previously earned second team all-Ivy League dis-

447. *See* Okla. Engrossed House Amend. to Engrossed Senate Bill No. 2 (Apr. 20, 2021); Alabama H.B. 391 (Apr. 20, 2021); Arkansas S.B. 450, 93 Gen. Ass. (Apr. 1, 2021); Florida H.B. 1475 (2021); Idaho H.B. 500, 65 Leg. Sess. (2020); Mississippi S.B. 2536 (2021); Montana H.B. 112, 67 Leg. Sess. (2021); North Dakota H.B. 1298, 67 Leg. Sess. (2021); Tennessee Pub. Ch. No. 40, S. Bill. No. 228 (March 22, 2021). Some governors have taken action. *See* S. Dak. Exec. Order. 2021-05 and 2021-06 (2021). Other states began the legislative process yet bills failed to pass prior to the end of session. *See* Tex. S.B. 29 (postponed on May 25, 2021); *see also* Georgia S.B. 266 (sent to committee on Feb. 25, 2021); N.C. H.B. 358 (sent to committee on Apr. 26, 2021).

448. *See, e.g.*, Complaint for Declaratory and Injunctive Relief *in* D.N. *ex rel.* Jessica N. v. Desantis, et al, 0:21-cv-61344-XXXX (filed June 29, 2021), (Florida); B.P.J. v. West Virginia State Board of Education, 2021 WL 3081883 (S.D. W.Va. 2021) (granting a preliminary injunction and finding that transgender female B.P.J. would suffer irreparable harm from being forced to compete on the boys team when a girls team is available, and stating that there is no doubt B.P.J. was excluded from athletic competition based on sex).

449. Pat Griffin & Hellen Carrol, *NCAA Inclusion of Transgender Student Athletes*, National Collegiate Athletic Association, 1, 8 (2011), https://www.ncaa.org/sites/default/files/Transgender_Handbook_2011_Final.pdf.

450. *Id.* at 12–13.

451. *Id.*

452. *Id.*

453. *Id.*

454. *Id.*

455. *Id.*

456. *Id.*

tinction for the University of Pennsylvania Men's Swimming team during the 2018–2019 season.[457] In winter 2021, Thomas was recording slower times than they did in the 2018 and 2019, but demolishing competitors in their new field of competition.[458] In response to the IOC guidelines announced in October of 2021 — and facing heightened need for response following Thomas' media attention — the NCAA unveiled a new competition policy for transgender athletes in January 2022.[459] The policy, which took immediate effect, aligned NCAA policy with IOC policy by placing responsibility on each sport's national governing body to establish participation policies for transgender athletes. If a sport does not have a national governing body, the international governing body's policy controls, and if no such organization exists, IOC policy controls.[460] The NCAA retains the ability to "review and recommend" policy to each national governing body.[461]

The judiciary has struggled with the application of gender identity and sexual orientation to the phrase "on the basis of sex" for years. In *Videckis v. Pepperdine University*,[462] the court held that the distinction between gender identity and biological sex "is illusory and artificial, and that sexual orientation discrimination is not a category distinct from sex or gender discrimination. Thus, claims of discrimination based on sexual orientation are covered by Title VII and IX."[463] The Western District of Pennsylvania has held, however, that discrimination is linked only to sex at birth, and barring a transgender student from the bathroom that conformed to their gender identity did not violate Title IX or the Equal Protection Clause.[464] While some additional federal cases side with the view adopted in *Videckis* and equate gender identity and sex within Title IX, such analyses are based on harassment and bathroom access, not athletics participation.[465]

The Supreme Court's recent interpretations have incorporated sexual orientation and transgender status in the definition of "sex" within the phrase "on the basis of sex" as included in the employment discrimination statute, Title VII.[466] This expansion of the definition of sex in *Bostock v. Clayton Cty., Georgia*, has been interpreted by

---

457. John Kinsey, *Second Female Penn Swimmer Steps Forward, Describes Teammates in Tears,* FOXNEWS (Dec. 10, 2021); Phil Mushnick, *Inequality Created by Transgender Swimmer Lia Thomas is Antithesis of Far Play,* N.Y. POST (Dec. 24, 2021).

458. Kinsey, *supra* note 457.

459. National Collegiate Athletic Association, Press Release, *Board of Governors Updates Transgender Participation Policy* (Jan. 19, 2022), available at https://www.ncaa.org/news/2022/1/19/mediacenter-board-of-governors-updates-transgender-participation-policy.aspx.

460. *Id.*

461. *Id.*

462. 150 F. Supp. 3d 1151 (C.D. Cal. 2015).

463. *Id.* at 1159.

464. Johnston v. Univ. of Pittsburgh, 97 F. Supp. 3d 657 (W.D. Pa. 2015).

465. Whitaker *ex rel.* Whitaker v. Kenosha Unified Sch. Dist. No. 1, 858 F.3d 1034 (7th Cir. 2017). *See also* Grimm v. Gloucester Cty. Sch. Bd., 972 F.3d 586, 612–13 (4th Cir. 2020) ("being transgender is as natural and immutable as being cisgender" and transgender discrimination is therefore discrimination based on sex).

466. Bostock v. Clayton Cty., Georgia, 140 S. Ct. 1731 (2020).

lower courts as also applying to Title IX.[467] At present, the Department of Education, Department of Justice, and Office of the President are in agreement that Title IX protects against discrimination based on gender identity.[468] The conflict with state law, as outlined above, will require consistent attention from the NCAA and state high school athletic associations to ensure compliance until a judicial interpretation from the Supreme Court provides clarity.

---

467. *See* Adams *ex rel.* Kasper v. Sch. Bd. of St. Johns Cnty., 968 F.3d 1286, 1305 (11th Cir. 2020) (applying *Bostock*'s definition of sex to Title IX); *but see* DuBois v. The Board of Regents of the Univ. of Minnesota, 439 F. Supp. 3d 1128, 1138 (D. Minn. 2020) ("The fact that Du Bois has to rely on Title VII in arguing that she has a cause of action under Title IX highlights the problem with her argument: Title VII and Title IX are different statutes."). This debate is also occurring at the state court level. *See* Clark Cnty. Sch. Dist. v. Bryan, 478 P.3d 344, 354 (Nev. 2020).

468. Exec. Order No. 13,988, 86 Fed. Reg. 7023 (Jan. 20, 2021); Susane B. Goldberg, Notice of Interpretation: Enforcement of Title IX of the Education Amendments of 1972 with Respect to Discrimination Based on Sexual Orientation and Gender Identity in Light of Bostock v. Clayton County, DEP'T OF EDUC. (June 16, 2021).

Chapter 6

Race and Racial Discrimination Issues in Sports

§ 6.01 Introduction

Just as racial discrimination and discord exist in society in general, they exist in sport. When studying the intersection of race, sports, and law, it is important to study it with an eye toward the impact of sport on issues of race in society. The law, and how it is applied, largely determines whether the impact is positive or negative. This chapter begins by exploring foundational racially discriminatory structures and systems in American law and society. It then addresses the modern context and the legal tools available to challenge racial discrimination in the sports industry. In doing so, the chapter touches on the structural impediments facing such challenges and the consequent development of extra-judicial means of countering racial discrimination in the industry. The chapter has a particular focus on racial discrimination and exploitation in collegiate athletics, a context which — as outlined in Chapter 2 — is in substantial flux. Finally, the chapter addresses the controversy and the state of the law regarding the use of Native American names and mascots in professional and amateur sports.

§ 6.02 Exclusion Based on Race

[A] Early Exclusion

[1] Reconstruction Era African American Athletic Achievement

After the Civil War, during the Reconstruction Era, African Americans began to experience limited opportunities to participate and achieve in various forms of American life, sports included.[1] The opportunities were tenuous, and often fraught with risk, but those African Americans with the chance to engage in sports at the highest level often excelled, and they did so across the sporting landscape.[2] Isaac Murphy, born into slavery in 1861, dominated horse racing in the late nineteenth century,

---

1. WILLIAM C. RHODEN, FORTY MILLION DOLLAR SLAVES: THE RISE, FALL, AND REDEMPTION OF THE BLACK ATHLETE (2006).
2. *See id.* at 69.

winning the Kentucky Derby three times.[3] Major Taylor dominated cycling during the same time period, setting world records at different distances, and winning elite events in the United States, Europe, and Australia.[4] Numerous African American boxers also achieved success during the Reconstruction Era.[5] At the time, horse racing, cycling, and boxing were wildly popular, making these athletes' achievements all the more notable. The most popular team sport of the day, baseball, also featured several African Americans.[6] These athletes' successes, of course, threatened the national narrative of black inferiority, and just as the post-Reconstruction Era's heightened racial repression purged successful African Americans from other realms of American life, it essentially eliminated African American participation in mainstream sports.[7]

[2] Exclusion under Law

The United States Supreme Court's segregationist decision in *Plessy v. Ferguson*[8] and the widespread proliferation of racially exclusionary legislation known as "black codes" swiftly cratered the promise of the Reconstruction Era by force of law.[9] These repressive legal doctrines created a foundation for state and municipality mandated racial exclusion specific to sport.

A 1932 Georgia statute prohibited "any amateur colored baseball team [from playing] baseball in any vacant lot or baseball diamond within two blocks of any playground devoted to the white race."[10] A similarly specific Texas statute targeted combat sports. That statute, enacted in 1933, prohibited any "boxing, sparring or wrestling contest or exhibition between any person of the Caucasian or 'White' race and one of the African or 'Negro' race...."[11] Other laws were extremely broad, legislating separation of the races in many regards, including sports. For example, a 1958 Louisiana statute decreed:

> All persons, firms and corporations are prohibited from sponsoring, arranging, participating in, or permitting on premises under their control any dancing, social functions, entertainment, athletic training, games, sports or contests and other such activities involving personal and social contacts, in which the participants or contestants are members of the white and negro races.[12]

Other laws were slightly more cordoned, applying only to sports and games, not to other social activities. A Birmingham, Alabama ordinance, for instance, proclaimed

---

3. *Id.* at 63, 66–67.

4. *Id.* at 85–90.

5. *Id.* at 60.

6. *Id.* at 47–48.

7. Timothy Davis, *Race and Sports in America: An Historical Overview*, 7 VA. SPORTS & ENT. L.J. 291, 293–94 (2008) [hereinafter Davis, *Race and Sports in America*].

8. 163 U.S. 537 (1896).

9. Davis, *Race and Sports in America, supra* note 7, at 294.

10. Danielle Conway-Jones, *The Perpetuation of Privilege and Anti-Affirmative Action Sentiment in Rice v. Cayetano*, 3 ASIAN-PAC. L. & POL'Y J. 371, 376 n.11 (2002); *see also* National Park Service, https://www.nps.gov/malu/learn/education/jim_crow_laws.htm (last visited Sept. 25, 2021).

11. TEX. CRIM. STAT. § 614-11(f) (1933).

12. LA. STAT. ANN. § 4:451 (1958).

"[i]t shall be unlawful for a Negro and a white person to play together, or [be] in [the] company with each other, in any games of cards, dice, dominoes, checkers, baseball, softball, football, basketball, or similar games."[13]

While exclusionary laws such as these were widespread, the absence of such laws did not mean African Americans were treated equally. Informal, extra-judicial discrimination was virtually ubiquitous.

[3] "Gentlemen's Agreements" to Exclude

Much of the exclusion African American athletes suffered was not legally mandated. In horse racing, for instance:

> African American jockeys disappeared because of a confluence of powerful forces — owners and trainers who stopped hiring them, white jockeys who ganged up on them, and the Jockey Club that systematically denied the reenlisting of blacks. Black riders became victims of the Jockey Syndrome, or changing the rules to fit a need — the need to maintain control in the face of a perceived challenge to white supremacy.[14]

Similar informal exclusion drove African Americans, as well as dark-skinned Latinos, out of professional baseball. In 1887, six of the ten member clubs of the International League — one of several professional baseball leagues at the time — voted to bar African Americans from participation in the league.[15] The International League's purge of African Americans, which sparked a league-wide "Gentlemen's Agreement,"[16] "set a precedent for all levels of organized baseball," and soon, African Americans were driven out of leagues throughout the industry.[17] Spectators, teammates, and opposing players increasingly abused African American players physically and verbally, and other stakeholders such as club executives and media members derided them.[18] By 1891, even though no formal segregationist rule existed, organized American baseball was entirely White.[19] Years later, when questioned about the game's racial homogeneity, baseball's first Commissioner, Judge Kennesaw Landis, was quick to assert "there is no rule, formal or informal, or any understanding — unwritten, subterranean, or sub-anything — against the hiring of Negro players by the teams of organized baseball."[20] In fact, the "Gentlemen's Agreements" carried the force of formal contracts. Together with the certain harassment African Americans would face upon attempting to play, the "Gentlemen's Agreements" created an absolute bar. Indeed,

---

13. Timothy Davis, *The Myth of the Superspade: The Persistence of Racism in College Athletics*, 22 FORDHAM URB. L.J. 615, 625 n.40 (1995) [hereinafter Davis, *The Myth of the Superspade*].

14. RHODEN, FORTY MILLION DOLLAR SLAVES, *supra* note 1, at 68.

15. Davis, *Race and Sports in America*, *supra* note 7, at 296.

16. *Id.*

17. Timothy Davis, *Breaking the Color Barrier*, *in* COURTING THE YANKEES: LEGAL ESSAYS ON THE BRONX BOMBERS 337 (Ettie Ward ed., 2003).

18. *Id.*

19. *Id.*

20. *Id.*

as one author at the time explained, "[p]robably in no other business in America is the color line so finely drawn as in baseball. An African who attempts to put on a uniform and go in among a lot of white players is taking his life into his hands."[21]

Similar forces drove African Americans out of a new sport gaining popularity in the United States in the early twentieth century: football. Although few African Americans played during the National Football League's early years, they were consistently brutalized on the field through intentionally injurious tackles and late hits.[22] Even those few were expelled from the league in 1934 when the league's owners entered a "Gentlemen's Agreement" to segregate.[23]

Informal "Gentlemen's Agreements" and racially exclusive norms also often precluded African Americans from competing on the collegiate level.[24] African Americans desiring to play collegiate sports in the early and mid-twentieth century were restricted to historically black colleges and universities as well as a few northern predominately-white institutions.[25] Predominantly white southern schools were out of the question.[26] And when playing predominantly white southern schools, predominantly white northern schools often, by custom, held their African American players out the game.[27] Moreover, many predominantly white northern schools adhered to the "superspade" requirement, meaning they imposed informal quotas and only rostered one or two truly exceptional African American players.[28] Other African Americans, who were not superstars but would certainly have made teams were they White, were rejected.[29]

---

21. J. Gordon Hylton, *American Civil Rights Laws and the Legacy of Jackie Robinson*, 8 MARQ. SPORTS L.J. 387, 391 (1998) (citation omitted). In response to this exclusion, African Americans founded their own baseball leagues, known collectively as the Negro Leagues, or played in Latin America where racism was generally not as virulent. *Negro Leagues History,* NEGRO LEAGUES BASEBALL MUSEUM, https://nlbm.com/negro-leagues-history/ (last visited Sept. 25, 2021).

22. Ben Collins, *NFL: Fritz Pollard's Pioneering Role in American Football History*, BBC SPORT (Oct. 2, 2020), https://www.bbc.com/sport/american-football/54342296. The threat of such attacks was so substantial that Fritz Pollard, a star player in the early 1920s (and the NFL's first African American head coach), developed a method of self-defense he employed whenever he was knocked to the ground. N. JEREMI DURU, ADVANCING THE BALL: RACE, REFORMATION, AND THE QUEST FOR EQUAL COACHING OPPORTUNITY IN THE NATIONAL FOOTBALL LEAGUE 126 (2011) [hereinafter DURU, ADVANCING THE BALL]. Upon hitting the turf, he immediately flipped onto his back and began cycling his legs in the air as if riding a bicycle so as to kick any player trying to injure him. *Id.* When the coast was clear, he would quickly rise to his feet and join the huddle. *Id.*

23. Collins, *supra* note 22.

24. Davis, *The Myth of the Superspade*, *supra* note 13.

25. *Id.* at 629.

26. *Id.* at 627–28.

27. *Id.* at 628–29.

28. Davis, *Race and Sports in America, supra* note 7, at 298.

29. *Id.*

[B] Desegregation in the Sports Industry

As the twentieth century wore on, sport throughout the nation began to desegregate.[30] Many factors propelled this desegregation. The hypocrisy of Americans pursuing democratic ideals in fighting World War II abroad while racially oppressing citizens on home soil was certainly one.[31] In addition, the civil rights movement, which increased African American participation in electoral politics (and consequently political power), together with the United States Supreme Court's *Brown v. Board of Education*[32] school desegregation decision also turned the tide against segregation in society generally, thus impacting sport.[33]

In addition, self-interest played a role. Many universities and professional clubs realized that by artificially limiting their talent pool, they were forsaking a potential competitive advantage. This was ever more important as athletics became increasingly commercialized and potentially lucrative.[34] And as some universities and clubs desegregated, others followed to avoid being at a competitive disadvantage, creating a cascading effect.[35] Most famously, the Brooklyn Dodgers in 1947 placed Jackie Robinson on its Major League roster, desegregating MLB and incentivizing other clubs to follow suit.[36] By 1959, MLB's final holdout, the Boston Red Sox, added its first African American player to its roster.[37] The march toward desegregation was slower in collegiate athletics. A watershed moment, however, occurred in 1966 when the legendary University of Kentucky basketball team, which was entirely white, played for the national championship against a Texas Western University team with an entirely African American starting lineup.[38] Texas Western won, convincing even the most segregationist university athletic programs that race-based roster restrictions were disadvantageous.[39]

[C] Positional Stacking on Desegregated Teams

Even after college and professional sports teams were desegregated, widespread discrimination often continued within teams in the form of positional segregation — or stacking — a phenomenon that involved informally reserving certain positions

---

30. *Id.* at 301. Northern universities and professional sports leagues tended to precede those in the south, but not always. (The Boston Red Sox were famously the last Major League Baseball team to add an African American player to its roster.) *See* Tyler Kepner, *Thomas Yawkey, the Red Sox Owner Who Resisted Integration*, N.Y. TIMES (Aug. 18, 2017), https://www.nytimes.com/2017/08/18/sports/baseball/red-sox-thomas-yawkey-integration.html.

31. ARTHUR ASHE, A HARD ROAD TO GLORY (1988).

32. 347 U.S. 483 (1954)

33. ASHE, *supra* note 31, at 6.

34. Davis, *Race and Sports in America, supra* note 7, at 301.

35. *Id.*

36. ASHE, *supra* note 31, at 16.

37. *See* Kepner, *supra* note 30.

38. Dana Hunsinger Benbow, *What Texas Western's Black Players and White Coach Did in 1966 Continues to Ripple*, INDIANAPOLIS STAR (Feb. 12, 2021), https://www.indystar.com/story/sports/college/2021/02/12/they-were-the-first-all-black-starting-five-to-win-ncaa-title/4285930001/.

39. *Id.*

largely for Whites.[40] African Americans were generally steered away from pitcher and catcher in baseball, point guard in basketball, and center, middle linebacker, and — most famously — quarterback in football.[41] These were deemed "thinking positions," and team decision makers harboring old stereotypes of African American intellectual inferiority routinely barred African Americans from occupying them.[42] Quarterback, perhaps the most glamourous position in American sports, is where position stacking manifested most clearly. Successful African American high school and collegiate quarterbacks were often forced to play other positions in college and the National Football League ("NFL"), respectively.[43]

Such positional stacking was deeply ingrained. For more than twenty years after the NFL desegregated in 1946, no African American started an NFL game at quarterback. In 1968, however, Marlin Briscoe, a star quarterback in college who the Denver Broncos drafted to play defensive back, turned to the power of contract to resist positional stacking.[44] He refused to sign with the club unless his contract guaranteed him a three-day quarterback tryout during training camp, which he knew would be open to the press and fans and would give him a chance to show off his skills.[45] With the tryout clause in place, Briscoe secured a roster spot at quarterback. When the starting quarterback was injured during the season, Briscoe took over the job, becoming the first African American starting quarterback in modern NFL history.[46] Briscoe excelled at quarterback for the remainder of the season, earning second place in rookie of the year voting and setting multiple Broncos passing records, but stacking rendered his grip on the position tenuous.[47] Going into the 1969 season, Briscoe learned that fans were disgruntled about the team having an African American quarterback and his coaches and the Broncos' other quarterbacks were meeting without him. Ultimately, he would not be welcomed back as a quarterback.[48] He was released and never played quarterback again, settling for roster spots as a wide receiver for the remainder of his career.[49]

Beyond the possibility of contracting for an opportunity, as Briscoe did, African Americans had little recourse against being positionally stacked or otherwise deprived of employment opportunities in sport. Opportunities for African Americans have

40. RHODEN, FORTY MILLION DOLLAR SLAVES, *supra* note 1.

41. *Id.*

42. *See* RICHARD LAPCHICK, SMASHING BARRIERS: RACE AND SPORT IN THE NEW MILLENNIUM 229 (2001).

43. *Id.*

44. Jason Reid, *The Rise and Fall and Resurgence of Marlin Briscoe*, ESPN.COM (Aug. 25, 2016), https://theundefeated.com/features/the-rise-and-fall-and-resurgence-of-marlin-briscoe/.

45. *Id.*

46. *Id.* At the time, the Denver Broncos played in the AFL. *Denver Broncos*, COLORADO PRESS (2017), https://www.coloradopress.net/denver-broncos/. In 1970, the AFL joined the NFL as part of a merger. *Id.*

47. Reid, *The Rise and Fall and Resurgence of Marlin Briscoe*, *supra* note 44.

48. *Id.*

49. *Id.*

widely expanded in the post-civil rights era,[50] yet substantial inequity remains, particularly with respect to coaching and administration, but for athletes as well. And legal recourse in instances of discrimination remains limited. Anti-employment discrimination legislation exists, but the context of American sport makes it difficult to deploy in a lawsuit, particularly in the professional and high-profile collegiate ranks.[51] Two principal factors contribute to the difficulty: 1) potential plaintiffs' fear of the damage legal action would do to their career prospects; and 2) challenging standards of proof they face under the law.

[D] Challenging Racial Discrimination in Post-Civil Rights Era Sport

[1] The Statutory Framework

Professional athletics is a glamourous and profitable industry, and many professional athletes, coaches, and executives in professional sports leagues are celebrities and are handsomely remunerated. They are, however, employees who fall under the ambit of anti-employment discrimination law just as America's millions of other employees do. The two federal statutes of greatest relevance in this regard are Title VII of the Civil Rights Act of 1964 (42 U.S.C. § 2000e et seq.) and 42 U.S.C § 1981.

The Civil Rights Act of 1964 is generally regarded as modern America's most powerful civil rights legislation.[52] The Act contains eleven titles, prohibiting discrimination in a variety of realms.[53] Among these titles, Title VII, which addresses employment, "has emerged as having the most significant impact in helping to shape the legal and policy discourse on the meaning of equality."[54] Title VII makes it unlawful for an employer, whether in the public or private sector, "to fail or refuse to hire or to discharge any individual, or otherwise to discriminate against any individual with respect to his compensation, terms, conditions, or privileges of employment, because of such individual's race, color, religion, sex, or national origin...."[55] The statute requires a complainant to file a charge with the United States Equal Employment Opportunity Commission (EEOC) as a prerequisite to filing a lawsuit. An employee dissatisfied with the EEOC's resolution of a complaint can move forward with a federal claim.

---

50. Despite the general expansion of opportunity, racial inequity among professional athletes still exists, nowhere as starkly as among quarterbacks. MITTEN, DAVIS, DURU & OSBOURNE, SPORTS LAW AND REGULATION: CASES, MATERIALS, AND PROBLEMS 714–15 (2020).

51. DURU, ADVANCING THE BALL, *supra* note 22, at 35–36.

52. STEFFEN W. SCHMIDT ET AL., AMERICAN GOVERNMENT AND POLITICS TODAY 164 (2001–2002 ed., 2001); N. Jeremi Duru, *Fielding a Team for the Fans: The Societal Consequences and Title VII Implications of Race-Considered Roster Construction in Professional Sport*, 84 WASH. U. L. REV. 375 (2006).

53. *Id.*

54. Robert Belton, *Title VII at Forty: A Brief Look at the Birth, Death, and Resurrection of the Disparate Impact Theory of Discrimination*, 22 HOFSTRA LAB. & EMP. L.J. 431, 432–33 (2005).

55. 42 U.S.C. § 2000e-2(a) (2000).

Section 1981 is a much older statute. It was initially enacted as part of the Civil Rights Act of 1866, which was designed to protect newly emancipated slaves from racial oppression and discrimination.[56] The text of § 1981 does not specifically mention employment, guaranteeing instead the right "to make and enforce contracts,"[57] and for decades it was deemed applicable only to governmental, rather than private, action.[58] It has long been recognized, however, that the statute's language prohibits employment discrimination. The United States Supreme Court's decisions in *Johnson v. Ry. Express Agency, Inc.*,[59] and *Runyon v. McCrary*,[60] in 1975 and 1976, respectively, made clear that the statute applies to the private sector as well as the public sector.[61]

Title VII is limited in one way that § 1981 is not: it applies only to employers with 15 or more employees.[62] But in that virtually all sports clubs employ well over 15 employees, this limitation does not generally impact the statute's efficacy in the sports industry. Because Title VII and § 1981 have similar applicability with respect to racial discrimination in the sports world, plaintiffs who choose to sue may generally do so under both statutes simultaneously.

State statutes provide an alternative or additional means of challenging race-based employment discrimination in the sports industry. Nearly every state has enacted an employment discrimination law, and most are modeled closely after Title VII.[63] Some expand protected categories beyond the five that Title VII enumerates while others reduce the number of employees necessary to be considered an employer under the statute; virtually all prohibit discrimination based on race.[64] State anti-discrimination statutes, therefore, provide another option for sports industry professionals alleging racial discrimination.

[2] Reluctance to Sue

Despite the existence of these statutes, the particularities of the professional sports industry render them largely ineffective. The major sports leagues in the United States are insular, and alleging racial discrimination risks alienating that community and

---

56. *See* Angela M. Ford, *Private Alienage Discrimination and the Reconstruction Amendments: The Constitutionality of 42 U.S.C. § 1981*, 49 U. Kan. L. Rev. 457, 460–62 (2001).

57. 42 U.S.C. § 1981.

58. N. Jeremi Duru, *Exploring Jethroe's Injustice: The Impact of an Ex-Ballplayer's Legal Quest for a Pension on the Movement for Restorative Racial Justice*, 76 U. Cin. L. Rev. 793, 804 (2008).

59. 421 U.S. 454 (1975).

60. 427 U.S. 160 (1976).

61. *See* Duru, *Exploring Jethroe's Injustice*, *supra* note 58, at 808. It is arguable that the text and legislative history of the 1866 Act established from the beginning the statute's applicability to private actors. *Id.* at 805–08.

62. 42 U.S.C. § 2000e(b).

63. *Discrimination and Harassment in the Workplace*, Nat'l Conference of State Legislatures (Mar. 18, 2019), https://www.ncsl.org/research/labor-and-employment/employment-discrimination. aspx.

64. *Id.*

hampering future job prospects not just with one's current club, but with all clubs.[65] Although both Title VII and § 1981 provide causes of action for retaliation against challenges to or concerns expressed about allegedly discriminatory employment regimes,[66] such causes of action do not assure a plaintiff — whether a player, coach, or team executive — continued employment in the sports industry. As such, racial discrimination challenges have been so exceedingly rare in high profile athletics[67] that employers in the industry largely discount them as a possibility, thus gutting the anti-employment discrimination statutes' power. Indeed, Mike Florio, a longtime labor and employment lawyer turned NFL commentator, noted in 2020 that the league's hiring system for coaches and executives is deeply inequitable. Florio attributes the inequity largely to the justifiable fear NFL professionals of color have of challenging the system: "given the unique nature of the industry — 32 teams bound together by a league office — no one has been willing to trade his future NFL career by taking a stand in court against one of its teams."[68] The same holds for other leagues and high-profile collegiate athletic programs. Former Miami Dolphins head coach Brian Flores' 2022 racial discrimination lawsuit against the NFL,[69] if successful, may change this dynamic, but that has to be seen.

Lower-level collegiate athletics and high school athletics present a different context. Whereas no major professional sports league has more than 32 clubs and there are approximately only 60 schools in the NCAA's five highest-resource conferences (the "Power Five"), lower-level college programs and high school programs number in the tens of thousands. Consequently, coaching and administrative opportunities at that level are far more numerous and far less coveted. Perhaps for this reason, coaches and administrators at high schools and non-Power 5 colleges have shown slightly greater willingness to risk challenging their employers or potential employers with racial discrimination lawsuits than those at higher levels of sport. Those few who have sued, however, have generally met with little success.

---

65. DURU, ADVANCING THE BALL, *supra* note 22, at 70–71.

66. 42 U.S.C. § 2000(e)(3)(a); CBOCS West Inc. v. Humphries, 553 U.S. 442, 445 (2008).

67. It bears noting that on occasion such actions are brought. In 2009, Elgin Baylor, longtime Los Angeles Clippers general manager, sued the club for racial discrimination, but later dropped his claims. *Baylor: I'm putting Clips behind me,* ESPN.COM, June 11, 2014, https://www.espn.com/los-angeles/nba/story/_/id/11069206/former-los-angeles-clippers-gm-elgin-baylor-says-limited-opportunities-were-reasons-working-donald-sterling. More recently, the Houston Texans' security coordinator sued the Texans for racial discrimination. Aaron Wilson, *Ex-Texans security coordinator Jeff Pope files lawsuit against team,* CHRON.COM, Aug. 23, 2019, https://www.chron.com/sports/texans/article/Ex-security-Jeff-Pope-files-lawsuit-vs-Texans-14373756.php. The case was dismissed in favor of mandatory contractual arbitration as required in Pope's employment agreement with the club. *See* Pope v. Houston NFL Holdings, L.P., 2021 WL 4096551 (S.D. Tex. 2021). Still, these actions are the rare exception.

68. Mike Florio, *NFL's "Broken System" of Hiring Can Be Fixed in Only Two Ways,* NBCSPORTS. COM (May 25, 2020), https://profootballtalk.nbcsports.com/2020/05/25/nfls-broken-system-of-minority-hiring-can-be-fixed-in-only-two-ways/.

69. *See* Flores v. National Football League et al., 1:22-CV-00871 (S.D.N.Y.) (filed 2/01/2022).

[3] General Inefficacy of Litigation

Two theoretical approaches are available to aggrieved sports industry professionals who choose to pursue a legal remedy for alleged employment discrimination: disparate treatment and disparate impact. A disparate treatment claim alleges that an employer purposely discriminated on the basis of a protected characteristic.[70] A disparate impact claim, on the other hand, does not allege purposeful discrimination. Rather, it alleges that an employer's facially neutral rule or policy resulted in a disproportionate impact on people who share a protected characteristic.[71]

Title VII provides prospective plaintiffs a cause of action under both theories,[72] whereas § 1981 permits only disparate treatment claims.[73] This is one reason Title VII is deemed the more powerful anti-discriminatory tool. Under both the disparate treatment and disparate impact theories, sports industry plaintiffs struggle to survive summary judgment.

[a] Disparate Treatment Theory

Direct evidence of intentional discrimination such as an admission is, of course, sufficient to survive summary judgment, but such direct evidence rarely exists with respect to employment discrimination allegations in sports.[74] In the absence of direct evidence, disparate treatment analysis at the summary judgment stage involves a burden-shifting framework between the plaintiff and the defendant.[75] The framework, first applied to Title VII claims in the United States Supreme Court's decision in *McDonnell Douglas Corp. v. Green*,[76] is now recognized as applying to claims brought under § 1981 as well.[77] Under the framework, the plaintiff must first make out a prima facie case, which involves establishing: (1) membership in a protected class; (2) qualification for the position in question; (3) an adverse employment action (*e.g.*, failure to hire, demotion, or reduced compensation); and (4) circumstances

---

70. Martha Chamallas, Principles of Employment Discrimination Law 19 (1st ed. 2018).

71. *Id.* at 89.

72. *Id.* at 19.

73. *Id.* at 98.

74. *See* Duru, *Fielding a Team for the Fans, supra* note 52, at 404. Interestingly, in 2020, as the NFL struggled against allegations made in the press about clubs racially discriminating against aspiring head coaches and general managers of color, NFL Executive Vice President of Football Operations Troy Vincent, an African American, was startlingly candid about the league's failures with respect to equal opportunity. He stated: "The facts are, we have a broken system.... [S]itting in these meetings [with those responsible for hiring at NFL clubs], listening, hearing people give different excuses.... Those are the same words that they told people in my community in the fifties, the forties, about integration of school systems, housing — but not giving us any solutions." *See* Florio, *NFL's "Broken System," supra* note 68. If an aspiring head coach or general manager of color were to file a race-based employment discrimination claim against the league or one of the league's clubs and this or a similar statement were to be deemed an admission, it could constitute direct evidence, substantially improving the plaintiff's likelihood of litigation success.

75. Chamallas *supra* note 70, at 26.

76. 411 U.S. 792 (1973).

77. Mark A. Rothstein et al., Employment Law 124 (6th ed. 2019).

creating an inference of discrimination.[78] Second, if the plaintiff successfully makes out a prima facie case, the defendant may present a legitimate non-discriminatory rationale for its employment action.[79] Finally, if the defendant presents such a rationale, the plaintiff must show that the defendant's rationale is, in fact, pretext for discrimination.[80]

This framework has proven quite difficult for sports industry professionals to successfully navigate, largely because courts are generally deferential to defendants' subjective assessments of employees or prospective employees. This is particularly the case in the sports industry, with respect to which courts often admit a lack of expertise.[81] Judicial deference comes into play most notably at the second prong of the prima facie test (determining qualification for the position in question) and when a court considers whether a defendant's rationale for the employment decision is, indeed, legitimate and non-discriminatory as well as non-pretextual. *Jackson v. Univ. of New Haven*,[82] *Flowers v. Troup County, Ga. School Dist*,[83] and *Banks v. Pocatello Sch. Dist. No. 25*[84] provide helpful illustrations.

Jackson involved the University of New Haven's head football coach search in 1999.[85] James Jackson, an African American, was one of 36 applicants for the job. He was not among the six applicants to progress to the interview stage of the search process and was therefore excluded from the candidate pool.[86] All six of the candidates receiving interview invitations were White, and all six had college coaching experience, which Jackson did not have.[87] Jackson asserted a disparate treatment claim against the university under Title VII and § 1981 as well as Title VI of the Civil Right Act of 1964 (which is not employment-specific but prohibits organizations that receive federal funds from racially discriminating). He argued that the university racially discriminated against him in excluding him from consideration.[88] The university denied the allegation and ultimately moved for summary judgement.[89] At the prima facie stage of the analysis, both parties agreed that Jackson was a member of a protected class, but they disagreed as to whether he was qualified.[90] Jackson insisted that his stellar record as a professional minor league football coach qualified him for the job.[91] The university, on the other hand, insisted Jackson was not qualified regardless of his professional minor league

78. CHAMALLAS *supra* note 70, at 25.
79. *Id.* at 26.
80. *Id.*
81. Cole v. NCAA, 120 F. Supp. 2d 1060, 1071 (N.D. Ga. 2000).
82. 228 F. Supp. 2d 156 (D. Conn. 2002).
83. 1 F. Supp. 3d 1363 (N.D. Ga. 2014).
84. 429 F. Supp. 2d 1197 (D. Idaho 2006).
85. *Jackson*, 228 F. Supp. 2d at 157.
86. *Id.* at 157–58.
87. *Id.* at 158.
88. *Id.*
89. *Id.* at 159.
90. *Id.* at 160.
91. *Id.* at 161.

success, because he had no college coaching experience, which the university listed in the job posting as a critical requirement for the job.[92]

The court sided with the university. In doing so, it noted that employers are afforded "considerable latitude in selecting employment qualifications" and that the university was not required to, and would not, balance the merits of minor league professional success against college coaching experience.[93] From the court's perspective, if Jackson were the nation's best minor league coach and the six white coaches who received interviews had been substandard college coaches, it would not have mattered. Concluding that the university was entitled to broad deference, the court stated "[a]bsent a showing by the plaintiff that the employer's demands were made in bad faith ... an employer ... is not compelled to submit the reasonableness of its employment criteria to the assessment of either judge or jury."[94] As such, the court found Jackson was unable to meet his burden of establishing a *prima facie* case of racial discrimination and granted the university's summary judgment motion on Jackson's disparate treatment claim.[95]

Had Jackson somehow succeeded in establishing a prima facie case, he would have faced another substantial obstacle when the burden shifted to the defendant. Courts across the nation require very little from a defendant with respect to articulating a legitimate, non-discriminatory reason for its decision and do not lightly deem such reasons pretextual.[96] As Judge Wisdom of the Eleventh Circuit has written, Title VII does not "require the employer to have good cause for its decisions. The employer may [take an employment action] for a good reason, a bad reason, a reason based on erroneous facts, or for no reason at all, as long as its action is not for a discriminatory reason."[97]

Flowers v. Troup County, Ga. School Dist., a federal district court case litigated in Georgia, is also illustrative of the challenge plaintiffs have in discrediting a defendant's proffered legitimate non-discriminatory rationale for an employment action. That case involved Charles Flowers, who in 2020, became the first African American head football coach in Troupe County High School history.[98] Early in Flowers' tenure as head coach, Cole Pugh, the Troup County School District superintendent, received a complaint that Flowers was recruiting players from other districts in violation of Georgia State High School Association bylaws.[99] Pugh launched an investigation and ultimately terminated Flowers,[100] who responded with an employment discrimination

92. *Id.*
93. *Id.*
94. *Id.* (quoting Thornley v. Peton Publ'g, 104 F.3d 26 (2d Cir. 1997)).
95. *Id.* at 162.
96. Duru, *Fielding a Team for the Fans, supra* note 52.
97. Nix v. WLCY Radio/Rahall Comms, 738 F.2d 1181, 1187 (11th Cir. 1984).
98. *Flowers*, 1 F. Supp. 3d at 1367.
99. *Id.* at 1367–68.
100. *Id.* at 1369.

suit.[101] When the school district moved for summary judgment, the court applied the *McDonnell Douglas* burden-shifting framework.[102] There was no dispute that Flowers established a prima facie case. Therefore, the court proceeded to assess whether the school district's reason for terminating Flowers — the alleged recruiting violations — was legitimate and non-discriminatory.[103] Flowers argued that he did not impermissibly recruit and that racism was at the root of his firing.[104] Despite evidence that Pugh was mistaken in his belief that Flowers impermissibly recruited, the court granted the school district's motion, finding pretext did not exist. "To be blunt," the court wrote, "Pugh's belief can be dead wrong, but so long as it was honestly held, then Flowers's race-discrimination claims cannot succeed."[105]

It is, of course, not impossible for sports industry professionals to proceed beyond summary judgment with racial employment discrimination claims, but their claims must be strong to survive dismissal. Consider *Banks v. Pocatella Sch. Dist. No. 25*, in which John Banks, an African American, was successful in moving his employment discrimination claim beyond summary judgment to trial. Over the course of five years, Banks had applied for seven football coaching positions at two high schools in the Pocatello, Idaho School District.[106] He was rejected each time and ultimately sued the school district for, among other things, racial employment discrimination.[107] After Banks established a prima facie case, the school district discharged its burden of proffering a legitimate non-discriminatory reason for rejecting Banks, asserting that Banks had poor communication and organizational skills.[108] Banks, however, had been a teacher in the school district for years before applying for the coaching positions and had consistently received positive evaluations from his supervisors with respect to both communication and organization.[109] Indeed, the court found that, "[t]he evaluations described Banks's teaching style as 'very well organized,' 'systematic[],' 'clear,' and 'well planned.' They also consistently assessed his communication skills with parents and students favorably."[110] Moreover, two administrators who sat on some of the committees rejecting Banks as a coaching candidate wrote the majority of the laudatory teaching evaluations.[111] Banks argued that this evidence proved both that he possessed the skills at issue and that the school district *knew* he possessed the skills at issue, calling into question the legitimacy of the school district's proffered reasons for rejecting his candidacy.[112] The court agreed. In denying summary judgment, it concluded that

101. *Id.*
102. *Id.* at 1370.
103. *Id.* at 1371.
104. *Id.*
105. *Id.* at 1374.
106. *Banks*, 429 F. Supp. 2d at 1198–99.
107. *Id.* at 1199.
108. *Id.* at 1201–02.
109. *Id.* at 1203.
110. *Id.*
111. *Id.*
112. *Id.* at 1203–04.

"[t]he positive evaluations of [Banks'] organizational and communication skills ... as a teacher raise doubt about the ... proffered reasons for not hiring him as a coach."[113]

Considering the deference courts generally grant employment discrimination defendants — particularly defendants making employment decisions in the sports context — sports industry professionals asserting racial discrimination require very strong facts, such as those *Banks* was able to marshal, to succeed in their disparate treatment claims.

[b] Disparate Impact Theory

Although the disparate impact theory offers plaintiffs a path to establishing liability without having to establish intentional discrimination, it presents its own challenges for sports industry professionals. Like disparate treatment analysis, disparate impact analysis involves a burden-shifting framework, but it is a different burden-shifting framework. The disparate impact burden shift was set forth in the Civil Rights Act of 1991.[114] A cognizable prima facie case requires a showing that the defendant's hiring process produces selections in a pattern that substantially differs from the racial composition of the applicant pool.[115] Specifically, the plaintiff must: "(1) identify [an employer's] policy or practice, (2) demonstrate that a disparity exists, and (3) establish a causal relationship between the two."[116] Assuming the plaintiff establishes a prima facie case, the burden shifts to the employer to show the policy or practice has "'a manifest relationship to the employment in question.'"[117] If the employer can do so, the plaintiff can only prevail by showing that alternative policies or practices would reduce or eliminate the racial disproportionality while still meeting the employer's needs.[118]

Disparate impact suits are generally not a promising path for sports industry professionals, because the industry's unique characteristics make establishing a prima facie case extremely difficult. A successful prima facie case generally requires statistically significant evidence that the employer's practice or policy, rather than random chance, resulted in the disparity.[119] Statistical significance requires a large enough sample size to rule out the possibility of coincidence.[120] Jobs in the sports industry are generally specialized with small applicant pools, rarely providing sample sizes from which statistical significance can be drawn. *Jackson v. University of New Haven,* discussed above, is illustrative here as well, as the plaintiff Jackson asserted a disparate

---

113. *Id.* at 1204.

114. CHAMALLAS, *supra* note 70, at 90.

115. *Id.* at 92.

116. Robinson v. Metro-North Commuter R.R., 267 F.3d 147, 160 (2d Cir. 2001) (citing 42 U.S.C. § 2000e-2(k)(1)(A)(I)).

117. NAACP, Inc. v. Town of East Haven, 70 F.3d 219, 225 (2d Cir.1995).

118. *Id.*

119. CHAMALLAS, *supra* note 70, at 101–02.

120. *Robinson,* 267 F.3d at 160.

impact claim in addition to a disparate treatment claim against the University of New Haven.[121]

In seeking to establish his *prima facie* disparate impact case, Jackson argued that the university's college coaching experience requirement disproportionately disadvantaged African Americans.[122] To support his argument, he presented statistics showing that, of the head coaching candidates who disclosed their race, 50% of the African Americans had no college coaching experience and only 10% of the Caucasians had no college coaching experience.[123] The court indicated that this substantial disparity might be probative with a large enough sample size, but that in this case the sample size was too small.[124] Only 14 (of the 36) candidates disclosed their race, 10 being Caucasian and four being African American, meaning the 10% of Caucasians with no college coaching experience represented one out of 10 and the 50% of African Americans with no college coaching experience represented two out of four.[125] The court concluded, "this statistical evidence fails to establish a sufficient causal link between the defendants' employment criterion and its impact on African-Americans.... [T]he relevant sample size is only 14 ... which is too small to yield a statistically significant result."[126]

The challenge in establishing statistical significance at the *prima facie* stage of a disparate impact racial discrimination lawsuit often renders suits under this theory ineffective, and they are therefore only marginally more likely to yield success than disparate treatment suits.

[E] Extra-Legal Approaches to Incentivizing Equal Opportunity in the Sports Industry

Fear of being professionally shunned for alleging racial discrimination together with a low likelihood of success in court conspire to generally discourage aggrieved sports industry professionals from filing lawsuits. In the absence of the disincentive to discriminate that the threat of civil litigation produces, racial equity activists have stepped into the void with extra-judicial approaches seeking to spur diversity.

For instance, The Institute for Diversity and Ethics in Sport ("TIDES") at the University of Central Florida issues annual Racial and Gender Report Cards ("Report Cards") for America's major professional sports leagues as well as collegiate athletic programs.[127] The Report Cards assign letter grades for organizational diversity, granting "A" grades to the most diverse organizations and lower grades to organizations

---

121. *Jackson*, 228 F. Supp. 2d at 158.
122. *Id.* at 163.
123. *Id.* at 165.
124. *Id.*
125. *Id.*
126. *Id.*
127. Richard Lapchick, *The Racial and Gender Report Card*, TIDES (2021), https://www.tidesport.org/racial-gender-report-card.

with less diversity.[128] The Report Cards also include grades for subcategories such as players, coaches, and executives.[129] Well-respected sports media outlets, such as ESPN and the Sports Business Journal, routinely publish TIDES' grades, nationally broadcasting sports organizations' successes and failures on diversity. The impact on these sports organizations of the grades they receive is unclear, but the report cards are potentially incentivizing.[130]

Another extra-judicial initiative designed to increase diversity is the Rooney Rule ("the Rule"), which was proposed in 2003 to the National Football League by civil rights lawyers dissatisfied with the League's hiring practices.[131] The lawyers, Johnnie Cochran and Cyrus Mehri, were frustrated with what they deemed to be discrimination facing African American coaches in the NFL who aspired to become head coaches.[132] They commissioned a study from a University of Pennsylvania labor economist to analyze and compare the win-loss records of African American and White head coaches over the previous 15 years.[133] The study concluded: "No matter how we look at success, black coaches are performing better. The data are consistent with blacks having to be better coaches than the whites in order to get a job as a head coach in the NFL."[134] Armed with this study, Cochran and Mehri contemplated a lawsuit. Understanding, however, that African American coaches would be reluctant to step forward as plaintiffs and aware of courts' general deference to defendants' subjectivity — particularly in sports matters — the lawyers approached the league with a legal threat but a cooperative posture.[135] The NFL ultimately adopted the rule, mandating that every club searching for a head coach or general manager interview at least one person of color for the job.[136] The Rule initially propelled substantial diversity increases.[137] By 2018, however, the league's diversity numbers had returned to where they had stood fifteen years earlier when the Rule was implemented, prompting the

---

128. *Id.*

129. *Id.*

130. No industry-wide studies of the report cards' impact exist, but leagues routinely respond in the press to the grades, indicating, at the very least, their awareness and attention. *See, e.g.,* Liz Mullen, *NFL Scores B– in Latest Racial, Gender Diversity Report Card,* Sports Business Journal (Dec. 10, 2020), https://www.sportsbusinessjournal.com/Daily/Issues/2020/12/10/Leagues-and-Governing-Bodies/NFL-Tides.aspx; John Lombardo, *NBA Again Leads Other Leagues in Racial, Gender Hiring Efforts,* Sports Business Journal (June 24, 2019), https://www.sportsbusinessdaily.com/Journal/Issues/2019/06/24/Ratings-and-Research/NBA report-card.aspx.

131. N. Jeremi Duru, *The Fritz Pollard Alliance, The Rooney Rule, and the Quest to "Level the Playing Field" in the National Football League,* 7 Va. Sports & Ent. L.J. 179, 186–88 (2008).

132. *Id.*

133. *Id.* at 186.

134. *Id.* (quoting Johnnie L. Cochran, Jr. & Cyrus Mehri, Black Coaches in the National Football League: Superior Performance, Inferior Opportunities 1 (2002)).

135. N. Jeremi Duru, *When the Law Won't Work: The National Football League's Extra-Judicial Approach to Addressing Employment Discrimination in Coaching, in* Race, Ethnicity and Racism in Sports Coaching (Routledge, 2020).

136. *Id.*

137. *Id.*

NFL to begin a process of revamping and attempting to strengthen the Rule.[138] In 2020 and 2021, the league expanded the Rule in multiple ways. Under the new Rule, each club must interview at least two candidates of color for head coaching positions, general manager positions, and offensive, defensive, and special teams coordinator positions. In addition, each club must interview at least one person of color and at least one women for senior-level executive openings on the business side of the organization (*e.g.*, president and CEO).[139]

Notably, the Rooney Rule concept has gained traction outside of the NFL, both in the United States and abroad. For instance, Oregon legislation now requires that the state's public universities interview at least one candidate of color for all head coaching and athletic director positions.[140] The Football Association, England's governing body for soccer, has adopted a similar rule with respect to all managerial openings in both the men's and women's soccer programs.[141] The Rooney Rule has also found adherents outside of sport, exemplifying the impact sport and developments in sport can have on broader society. Several municipalities, including Portland, Oregon and Pittsburgh, Pennsylvania, have instituted Rooney Rule-like interviewing procedures for certain city jobs.[142] Some in federal government have imported the concept as well. Indeed, Democrats in both the House of Representatives and the Senate have resolved to interview diverse slates of candidates for staff positions.[143] In addition, many leading corporations, including Microsoft, Xerox, Intel, and Facebook, and many of the nation's largest banks, including JP-Morgan Chase, Bank of America, and Citigroup have also adopted forms of the Rule.[144]

The extent to which the Rooney Rule will further impact diversity in the NFL and whether it will be effective in expanding opportunities in these other arenas is to be determined.

[F] The Particular Problem of Discriminating in Roster Construction

The above discussion with respect to challenging racial discrimination in post-civil rights era sport focuses principally on coaches, administrators, and executives rather than players. Although such discrimination is not as widespread as it once

---

138. Jason Reid, *NFL Creates List to Strengthen Rooney Rule*, ESPN.COM (Dec. 12, 2018), https://www.espn.com/nfl/story/_/id/25518202/nfl-creates-list-strengthen-rooney-rule.

139. Kevin Patra, *NFL instituting changes to Rooney Rule*, NFL.COM, May 18, 2020, https://www.nfl.com/news/nfl-instituting-changes-to-rooney-rule.

140. Duru, *When the Law Won't Work*, *supra* note 135.

141. *Id.*

142. *Id.*

143. *Id.*

144. *Id.*; Ben Eisen, *Biggest U.S. Banks Embrace 'Rooney Rule' Policies in Diversity Hiring Push*, WALL STREET JOURNAL (Jan. 26, 2021), https://www.wsj.com/articles/biggest-u-s-banks-embrace-rooney-rule-policies-in-diversity-hiring-push-11611686889.

was, racial inequity still exists among players. A prime example is the quarterback position in the NFL. Opportunity for African Americans at the position has certainly increased since 1968 when star college quarterback Marlin Briscoe, discussed *supra*, was drafted as a defensive back and had to contract for an opportunity to tryout at quarterback. As of 1992, roughly 8% of the league's quarterbacks were African American, which represented substantial progress.[145] Ten years later, that percentage had more than doubled to over twenty percent, representing still further progress.[146] But sixteen years later, in 2018, the percentage of African American quarterbacks in the NFL still hovered around twenty percent even though African Americans made up roughly 70% of the league's players.[147] An open market for quarterbacks would likely not reflect such gross disproportionality. Moreover, among the league's African American quarterbacks, a disproportionate number are starters and stars, suggesting the stubborn persistence of the "superspade" requirement, at least with respect to quarterbacks.

In isolation, such inequitable opportunity in rostering players is certainly concerning, but when a roster is substantially more homogenous than others in a league or conference, it produces a concerning dynamic that is unique to sport. This is because professional sports organizations are unique among employers. They have fans: people who follow, and in some cases, obsess, about their teams' successes and failures. For many, supporting a team is not a hobby, it is a way of life. These ardent fans view themselves as a part of the team and use the pronoun "we" when speaking of the team.[148] Indeed, many such fans connect so closely with their teams that while watching the teams compete, "they experience hormonal surges and other physiological changes" just like the athletes they are supporting.[149] Because of this strong connection between fan and team, when "a professional sports organization engages in discriminatory employment practices and creates a racially imbalanced or homogeneous team, it risks fans' identification not only with that team, but also with the team's racial imbalance or homogeneity."[150] This can imbue fan rivalries with a racial element, spurring predictably disastrous consequences.

The most infamous example of such consequences playing out in the post-civil rights era occurred at the University of Massachusetts, Amherst ("UMass") after the New York Mets defeated the Boston Red Sox to win the 1986 World Series. The Red Sox roster was disproportionately White and had been so essentially since MLB's de-

---

145. David Meggyesy, *Let Players Decide Who Coaches Will Be*, SPORTS BUSINESS JOURNAL (Oct. 21–27, 2002), https://www.sportsbusinessjournal.com/Journal/Issues/2002/10/21/Opinion/Let-Players-Decide-Who-Coaches-Will-Be.aspx.

146. *Id.*

147. MITTEN ET AL., *supra* note 50, at 714.

148. N. Jeremi Duru, *For Fear of the Fans: An Argument for Holding Sports Teams Accountable for Fans' Post-Match Conduct*, 20 TEX. REV. ENT. & SPORTS L. 1, 3 (2019).

149. Paul C. Bernhardt et al., *Testosterone Changes During Vicarious Experiences of Winning and Losing Among Fans at Sporting Events*, 65 PHYSIOLOGY & BEHAVIOR 59, 61 (1998), https://www.science direct.com/science/article/abs/pii/S0031938498001474.

150. Duru, *Fielding a Team for the Fans*, *supra* note 52, at 378.

segregation, and its fan base was almost exclusively White as well.[151] As disappointed Red Sox fans left their dorms in the game's aftermath, they began to riot, first targeting Mets fans, but soon attacking African American students randomly.[152] Two independent investigations followed — one conducted by the district attorney with jurisdiction and the other conducted by the Massachusetts Commission Against Discrimination — and both concluded the violence was racially motivated.[153] The Red Sox fan group viewed their team as the White team and the far more diverse Mets team as the Black team, and as they roamed the campus, the Black students they encountered "all became Mets fans" whether they supported the club or not.[154] In short, the Red Sox fans were "focusing in on a surrogate target against which to take revenge for the Sox loss and that surrogate target ... became [B]lack students."[155] In all, roughly 3,000 students were involved in the riot, and ten students were seriously injured, one of whom was beaten unconscious with sticks and poles.[156]

In light of how closely and passionately fans identify with their favorite teams, the UMass riot illustrates the danger of that identification being race-associated and the consequences of discriminatory roster construction that creates racial disproportionality. Although the riot occurred in 1986, racial tension continues to simmer in the United States. In 2019, the Pew Research Center reported that "about six-in-ten Americans (58%) say race relations in the U.S. are bad, and of those, few see them improving."[157] A year after that study came out, the racial justice-inspired protests occurring in the aftermath of George Floyd's murder highlighted the continued virulent racial tension and discord in the United States. As such, the possibility of a contemporary racially catalyzed sports-related riot cannot be ruled out, counseling continued attention to racial discrimination in roster construction.

§ 6.03 Race in Modern Collegiate Athletics

[A] African American Disproportionality in Revenue-Producing Collegiate Sports

As discussed in Chapter 2, collegiate athletics is a multi-billion dollar industry. Most college sports, however, produce little or no revenue and lose money annually.[158]

---

151. *Id.*

152. *Id.*

153. *Id.* at 387–88.

154. FREDERICK A. HURST, REPORT ON UMASS INVESTIGATION 1, 14 (1987).

155. *Id.* at 13.

156. Duru, *Fielding a Team for the Fans, supra* note 52, at 387–89.

157. Julianna Menasce Horowitz, Anna Brown & Kiana Cox, *Race in America 2019: Public has negative views of the country's racial progress; more than half say Trump has made race relations worse,* PEW RESEARCH CENTER (April 9, 2019), https://www.pewresearch.org/social-trends/2019/04/09/race-in-america-2019/.

158. Jo Craven McGinty, *March Madness Is a Moneymaker. Most Schools Still Operate in Red,* WALL STREET JOURNAL (March 12, 2021), https://www.wsj.com/articles/march-madness-is-a-moneymaker-most-schools-still-operate-in-red-11615545002.

The two highest revenue-producing collegiate sports are football and basketball, both of which feature a disproportionate number of African Americans athletes.[159] In 2021, 48% of NCAA Division I football players, 56% of NCAA Division I men's basketball players, and 46% of NCAA Division I women's basketball players were African American, whereas African Americans comprised only 13.4% of Americans generally and only 13.2% of college students in America.[160] African Americans make up an even larger proportion of athletes in the nation's top grossing collegiate football and basketball programs.[161]

The NCAA's amateurism rules largely prevent these athletes from sharing in the revenues, which has driven commentators to describe collegiate athletics as a racially exploitative system.[162] Such commentators have identified two additional phenomena as supportive of this position. The first is the racial disproportionality among those who do profit, in many cases handsomely, from NCAA athletics: head coaches, administrators and conference commissioners, who are overwhelmingly White.[163] The second is what New York Times columnist Bill Rhoden describes in his award winning book, *Forty Million Dollar Slaves: The Rise, Fall, and Redemption of the Black Athlete*, as the "conveyor belt" that carries African American athletes from childhood through adolescence to young adulthood with little regard for academics and other pursuits and that, Rhoden contends, inures to the benefit of collegiate athletic programs.[164]

---

159. *Id.*

160. *See NCAA Demographics Database*, NCAA (2021), www.ncaa.org/about/resources/research/ncaa-demographics-database [hereinafter Data visualization dashboard]; *United States Census Bureau*, CENSUS.GOV, https://www.census.gov/quickfacts/fact/table/US/PST045219; *Undergraduate Enrollment*, NCES (2019), https://nces.ed.gov/programs/coe/indicator/cha.

161. *See* Jemele Hill, *It's Time for Black Athletes to Leave White Colleges*, THE ATLANTIC (Oct. 2019), https://www.theatlantic.com/magazine/archive/2019/10/black-athletes-should-leave-white-colleges/596629/ ("[B]lack men make up only 2.4 percent of the total undergraduate population of the 65 schools in the so-called Power Five athletic conferences. Yet black men make up 55 percent of the football players in those conferences, and 56 percent of basketball players.").

162. *See* Brandi Collins-Dexter, *NCAA Amateurism Rule Exploits Black Athletes as Slave Labor*, THE UNDEFEATED (Mar. 27, 2018), https://theundefeated.com/features/ncaas-amateurism-rule-exploits-black-athletes-as-slave-labor/. It bears noting that despite the NCAA's amateurism rules, student-athletes are now able to profit from their names, images, and likenesses. Dan Murphy, *Everything You Need to Know About the NCAA's NIL Debate*, ESPN (Jul. 14, 2021), https://www.espn.com/college-sports/story/_/id/31086019/everything-need-know-ncaa-nil-debate. In 2019, the California legislature passed the Fair Pay to Play Act, which allows student-athletes at California colleges and universities to receive sponsorships and endorsements without losing their NCAA eligibility. *Id.* Other state legislatures followed, prompting the NCAA to waive its name, image, and likeness restrictions. *Id.* See Chapter 2, *supra*, for a more detailed discussion of NCAA eligibility rules.

163. Christopher Ingraham, *NCAA Rules Allow White Students and Coaches to Profit Off Black Ones, Study Finds*, WASHINGTON POST (Sept. 7, 2020), https://www.washingtonpost.com/business/2020/09/07/ncaa-student-athletes-pay-equity/ (citing Craig Garthwaite, et al., *Who Profits From Amateurism? Rent-Sharing in Modern College Sports*, National Bureau of Economic Research (Aug. 2020)).

164. RHODEN, FORTY MILLION DOLLAR SLAVES, *supra* note 1, at 169.

[B] Issues of Race in Collegiate Admission and Eligibility

Together, these various dynamics — the "conveyor belt," the disproportionate involvement of African American athletes in revenue producing collegiate athletics, the prohibition on collegiate athletes sharing in the revenue, and the scarcity of African Americans among those who financially profit most from collegiate athletics — inject a racial subtext into many legal disputes in collegiate athletics, including those involving admission and eligibility. *Ross v. Creighton*,[165] discussed in Chapter 2 is illustrative. Although Ross did not assert race-based claims, he was an African American student-athlete basketball player alleging exploitation at a predominantly white institution. The racial undertones in the case are inescapable.

Ross played on the Creighton University varsity basketball team from 1978–1982.[166] He hailed from "an academically disadvantaged background," and his entering academic credentials fell well below Creighton University's admission standards.[167] Specifically, "he scored in the bottom fifth percentile of college-bound seniors taking the American College Test (ACT), while the average freshman admitted to Creighton with him scored in the upper twenty-seven percent."[168] Ross was, in essence, illiterate. Nonetheless, Creighton admitted him.[169] Ross alleged Creighton guaranteed he would have sufficient tutoring to ensure he received a "meaningful education" while at Creighton, but instead of providing him tutoring, employed a secretary to "read his assignments and prepare and type his papers."[170] He also alleged that Creighton's athletic department instructed him to take non-rigorous courses that did not count towards a degree.[171] During his four years at Creighton, Ross compiled a D average and earned far fewer credits than were needed to graduate, and upon leaving Creighton, he had "the overall language skills of a fourth grader."[172]

Ross believed that Creighton admitted him to exploit his basketball talent with the expectation that he would fail academically, and Ross therefore sued. He asserted both contract claims and novel tort claims — educational malpractice and negligent admission — against the university in federal court.[173] Creighton filed a motion to dismiss for failure to state a claim for which relief can be granted, and the district court granted the motion and dismissed the case.[174] The United States Court of Appeals for the Seventh Circuit affirmed in part and reversed in part,[175] illustrating the way in which courts generally address such claims. The Seventh Circuit affirmed

---

165. 957 F.2d 410 (7th Cir. 1992).
166. *Id.* at 412.
167. *Id.* at 411.
168. *Id.*
169. *Id.*
170. *Id.* at 411, 412.
171. *Id.* at 412.
172. *Id.*
173. *Id.*
174. *Id.* at 412–13.
175. *Id.* at 417.

the district court's dismissal of the tort claims, noting that courts disapprove of such claims on policy grounds.[176] Educational malpractice claims, the court noted, involve "inherent uncertainties" with respect to "the cause and nature of damages," turning on factors such as the student's motivation, temperament, and past experiences, which makes proving that a teacher proximately caused the educational deficiency a "practical impossibility."[177] The court described negligent admission claims as problematic as well, because "if universities and colleges faced tort liability for admitting an unprepared student, schools would be encouraged to admit only those students who were certain to succeed in the institution. The opportunities of marginal students to receive an education therefore would likely be lessened."[178] Although the court agreed with the district court's assessment that these tort claims failed to state a claim for which relief could be granted, it reversed the district court's dismissal of the contract claims — claims alleging failure to keep specific promises, such as to provide tutoring.[179] The court emphasized that the contract claims may not ultimately be successful, but that they were justiciable claims.[180] After securing reversal on the contract claims, Ross entered settlement negotiations with Creighton and the parties ultimately settled.[181]

Ross was impactful for two reasons. First, although Ross' negligent admission and educational malpractice claims failed, the facts underlying them shone an unflattering spotlight on university admission and educative practices with respect to athletic recruits. Second, the case suggested contract claims offer a better path forward than tort claims for student-athletes concerned that their educations have been undermined. These two impacts will be addressed in turn.

The circumstances of Ross' college admission in 1978 and subsequent college career were not anomalous, and the prevalence of such stories prompted substantial concern, leading the NCAA to revise student-athlete eligibility standards.[182] Some of their changes, however, created new challenges, bringing the racial subtext in cases such as *Ross* to the fore.

In 1992, the NCAA's Division I colleges and universities adopted an athletic eligibility standard called Proposition 16, which modified a previous athletic eligibility standard called Proposition 48.[183] Proposition 16 established an eligibility formula that combined a student athlete's SAT or ACT score with his or her grade point av-

---

176. *Id.* at 414–15.

177. *Id.* at 414.

178. *Id.* at 415.

179. *Id.* at 417.

180. *Id.*

181. William Grady, *Ross Settles Lawsuit with Creighton*, CHICAGO TRIBUNE (Apr. 28, 1992), https://www.chicagotribune.com/news/ct-xpm-1992-04-28-9202070837-story.html.

182. Timothy Davis, *A Thirty-Year Retrospective of Legal Developments Impacting College Athletics*, 30 MARQ. SPORTS L. REV. 309, 312–14 (2020).

183. Michael Mondello, *An Historical Overview of Student-Athlete Academic Eligibility and the Future Implications of* Cureton v. NCAA, 7 VILL. SPORTS & ENT. L.J. 127, 131 (2000).

erage in certain core high school courses.[184] The NCAA's purported goal with Proposition 16 was to make eligibility requirements more rigorous in an effort to ensure African American student-athletes were prepared for a collegiate academic experience and to consequently improve African American student-athlete graduation rates.[185] African American student-athletes, however, sued, alleging in *Pryor v. NCAA*[186] that Proposition 16 disproportionately denied African American student-athletes eligibility and that the NCAA intended that outcome.[187] They did so under Title VI of the Civil Rights Act of 1964 (42 U.S.C. § 2000e, et seq.), which prohibits entities that receive Federal financial assistance from racially discriminating, and 42 U.S.C. § 1981, which prohibits racial discrimination in contract formation.[188]

Although the facts plaintiffs asserted with respect to the Proposition's disproportionate impact on African Americans would have been well-suited for a disparate impact claim (*see* § 6.02[D][3][b], *supra*, for a discussion of the disparate impact theory), such a claim would have failed. Section 1981 has long been understood to offer no disparate impact avenue.[189] Although the availability of a disparate impact claim under Title VI was once deemed a possibility, the United States Supreme Court's decision in *Alexander v. Sandoval*[190] ruled out that possibility.[191] Plaintiffs had access only to disparate treatment theory, and they argued that in enacting Proposition 16, the NCAA intentionally discriminated against African Americans.[192]

The district court dismissed the plaintiffs' lawsuit for failure to state a claim for which relief could be granted.[193] The Third Circuit, however, reversed[194] and established that it could only affirm the lower court's decision if it appeared "beyond doubt that no set of facts would entitle Plaintiffs to relief." The court found that doubt existed — that the NCAA may, indeed, have instituted Proposition 16 in an effort to discriminate against African Americans.[195] Just months after the *Pryor* decision, the NCAA passed legislation revamping its initial eligibility rules.[196] The new legislation eliminated the standardized test score eligibility threshold that Proposition 16 established, creating a more comprehensive sliding scale between grade point average and

---

184. *Id.* at 135–36.
185. *Id.* at 127–28.
186. 288 F.3d 548 (3d Cir. 2002).
187. Mondello, *supra* note 183, at 127–28.
188. *Id.*
189. CHAMALLAS, *supra* note 70, at 98.
190. 532 U.S. 275 (2001).
191. *Alexander*, 532 U.S. at 293.
192. *Pryor*, 288 F.3d at 554.
193. *Id.*
194. *Id.*
195. *Id.*
196. Jerome Pandell, *New NCAA Eligibility Rules Won't Affect NU*, THE DAILY NORTHWESTERN (Nov. 7, 2002), https://dailynorthwestern.com/2002/11/07/archive-manual/new-ncaa-eligibility-rules-wont-affect-nu/.

standardized test score.[197] In subsequent years, the NCAA has further tweaked its initial eligibility rules.

Nevertheless, concerns that NCAA member institutions continue to exploit student athletes — and African American student-athletes in particular — persist. The University of North Carolina's ("UNC") academic scandal that erupted in 2014 sparked several such lawsuits against UNC, most notably, *McAdoo v. University of North Carolina*.[198] In 2014, the law firm of Cadwalader, Wickersham, and Taft issued a 136-page report that detailed eighteen years of academic fraud at UNC.[199] The report, titled *Investigation of Irregular Classes in the Department of African and Afro-American Studies at the University of North Carolina at Chapel Hill*, uncovered rampant and systemic academic improprieties occurring between 1993 and 2011, centered around:

> a "shadow curriculum" within the [Afro and African-American Studies] Department that provided students with academically flawed instruction through the offering of "paper classes." These were classes that involved no interaction with a faculty member, required no class attendance or course work other than a single paper, and resulted in consistently high grades that [an office secretary and administrator] awarded without reading the papers or otherwise evaluating their true quality.[200]

The report further found that academic counselors working in UNC's Academic Support Program for Student-Athletes ("ASPSA") systematically referred student-athletes in revenue-producing sports to these classes.[201] The academic counselors did so, the report concluded, because they "were always under pressure to maintain student-athlete eligibility and saw these classes — and their artificially high grades — as key to helping academically-challenged student-athletes remain eligible and on the playing field."[202] UNC's Chancellor acknowledged the improprieties within the institution, explaining after the report's release, "I believe very strongly that we have to hold each other accountable."[203]

Led by Michael McAdoo, a former UNC football player, several African American football and basketball student athletes sued UNC, alleging they were recruited with promises of a high caliber education and then pressured into non-rigorous classes

---

197. *Test Scores*, NCAA, https://www.ncaa.org/student-athletes/future/test-scores (last visited Sept. 25, 2021).

198. 248 F. Supp. 3d 705 (2017).

199. KENNETH L. WAINSTEIN ET AL., INVESTIGATION OF IRREGULAR CLASSES IN THE DEPARTMENT OF AFRICAN AND AFRO-AMERICAN STUDIES AT THE UNIVERSITY OF NORTH CAROLINA AT CHAPEL HILL, Cadwalader Wickersham & Taft (Oct. 16, 2014), https://carolinacommitment.unc.edu/wp-content/uploads/sites/350/2014/10/UNC-FINAL-REPORT.pdf [hereinafter Cadwalader Report].

200. *Id.* at 3.

201. *Id.* at 2.

202. *Id.*

203. Jake New, *Two Decades of "Paper Classes,"* INSIDEHIGHERED.COM (Oct. 23, 2014), https://www.insidehighered.com/news/2014/10/23/report-finds-academic-fraud-u-north-carolina-lasted-nearly-20-years.

through the "shadow curriculum."[204] Influenced by the *Ross* court's dismissal of Ross' novel tort claims, the *McAdoo* plaintiffs avoided claims such as "education malpractice" and instead hinged their suit on contract and fraud claims.[205] The compelling evidence of fraud laid bare by the Wainstein report — which would have otherwise required contentious discovery to acquire — formed the foundation of a strong substantive case, but the lawsuit did not reach the merits. UNC successfully argued for dismissal, claiming sovereign immunity from suit and noting that plaintiffs, who had graduated from or otherwise left UNC years earlier, were time barred from bringing their claims.[206] Plaintiffs did not appeal and instead opted to settle the matter.

Although the *McAdoo* case did not proceed to trial, UNC's academic scandal became national news and prompted calls for widespread academic reform at institutions competing in intercollegiate athletics.[207] Indeed, both an internal NCAA working group and the Division I Presidential Forum recommended that the NCAA pass a bylaw that would give it "broader authority to punish institutions that engage[d] in academic fraud."[208] The NCAA's Board of Directors, however, declined to do so.[209] Whether such broad-based reforms will come to pass going forward, and if so, whether they will have an impact that prevents future African American student-athletes from feeling the need to bring suit alleging exploitation at the hands of their universities is uncertain. If such additional claims do come to pass, *Ross* and *McAdoo*, taken together, suggest that plaintiffs with the highest likelihood of success would be current (or recently graduated) student-athletes at private universities (to avoid a sovereign immunity defense) alleging contract and fraud — rather than novel tort — claims.

§ 6.04 Native American Names, Mascots, and Images

Many American sports teams use Native American mascots, names, and images. Examples in collegiate and professional athletics include the Kansas City Chiefs, Atlanta Braves, Chicago Blackhawks, University of Florida State Seminoles, and University of Utah Utes. Hundreds of high schools throughout the United States also use Native American mascots, names, and images.[210] This practice of sports teams using Native American mascots, names, and images has long caused substantial con-

---

204. *McAdoo*, 248 F. Supp. 3d at 709.

205. *Id.*

206. *Id.*

207. Jeremy Bauer-Wolf, *Keeping the Status Quo*, INSIDEHIGHERED.COM (Sept. 5, 2019), https://www.insidehighered.com/news/2019/09/05/ncaa-does-not-move-forward-new-academic-reform-rules.

208. *Id.*

209. *Id.*

210. Hope Allchin, *Hundreds of Schools Are Still Using Native Americans as Team Mascots*, FIVE THIRTY EIGHT (Oct. 12, 2020), https://fivethirtyeight.com/features/hundreds-of-schools-are-still-using-native-americans-as-team-mascots/.

troversy.[211] Many view such use as non-offensive and harmless, and in some cases celebratory of Native American heritage. Others view such use as degrading and dehumanizing and as a catalyst for fans to insultingly mimic Native Americans with stereotypical dances and chants while cheering for teams. Passions run high on the issue and have triggered organizational policy initiatives, litigation, and legislation meriting discussion.

[A] NCAA Policy

In 2005, the NCAA instituted a policy regarding its member institutions' use of Native American mascots, names, and images.[212] The policy takes aim at "hostile and abusive" use through disincentives.[213] Although the policy does not prevent schools from using "hostile and abusive" mascots, names, and images, it prevents schools from displaying them at NCAA championship events, whether on their uniforms or elsewhere in venues.[214] This outcome would be impractical and would damage the school in question's branding. Championship events are the lifeblood of collegiate athletic programs, so the disincentive is a strong one, leaving schools two choices: abandon the name, mascot, and image or convince the NCAA's Executive Committee that the name, mascot, and imagery are not "hostile and abusive."

Many schools chose to adopt new names, mascots, or imagery. Some schools, however, argued their names, mascots, and imagery were not "hostile and abusive" and petitioned the NCAA for continued use. To succeed, the petitioning school must present evidence that the namesake tribe or local Native American population approves of the name, mascot, or imagery in question.[215] Several schools, including Catawaba College (Indians), Central Michigan University (Chippewas), Florida State University (Seminoles), Mississippi College (Choctaws), and University of Utah (Utes), were successful in their arguments.[216] The University of North Dakota which used the name Fighting Sioux, on the other hand failed to secure approval from local Sioux tribes.[217] Rather than forsake participation in NCAA championships, the university ultimately retired its name in favor of the Fighting Hawks.[218]

---

211. *See* Stephanie Bollinger, *Between a Tomahawk and a Hard Place: Indian Mascots and the NCAA*, 2016 B.Y.U. Educ. & L.J. 73, 73–75 (2016).

212. *NCAA Executive Committee Issues Guidelines for Use of Native American Mascots at Championship Events*, NCAA (Feb. 5, 2005), http://fs.ncaa.org/Docs/PressArchive/2005/Announcements/NCAA%2BExecutive%2BCommittee%2BIssues%2BGuidelines%2Bfor%2BUse%2Bof%2BNative%2BAmerican%2BMascots%2Bat%2BChampionship%2BEvents.html.

213. *Id.*

214. *Id.*

215. Bollinger, *supra* note 211, at 79–80.

216. *Id.* at 80.

217. Pat Borzi, *The Sioux Nickname Is Gone, but North Dakota Hockey Fans Haven't Moved On*, N.Y. Times (Mar. 1, 2016), https://www.nytimes.com/2016/03/03/sports/hockey/with-sioux-nickname-gone-north-dakota-hockey-fans-are-fighting-change.html.

218. *Id.*

[B] Native American Names, Mascots, and Images in Professional Sports

Professional sports has no NCAA analogue; no single administrative body with broad-based oversight. Instead, professional sports leagues are entirely independent of each other. Moreover, the clubs in most leagues are individually owned, and while league commissioners likely have authority to issue league-wide regulations with respect to the use of Native American names, mascots, and images, none have done so. Potentially offensive Native American names, mascots, and images are consequently more prevalent in professional sports than in collegiate sports. Indeed, some professional teams' current and past names, mascots, and images — were they used in college — would certainly have been deemed "hostile and offensive" under the NCAA Policy. MLB's Cleveland Guardians (until 2021 called the Cleveland "Indians") and the NFL's Washington Commanders (before 2020, called the Washington Redskins, and from 2020 to 2022, called the Washington Football Team) are prime examples. The Cleveland Indians' name would not likely run afoul of the policy (as Catawaba College, referenced above, successfully petitioned to continue using the name "Indians"). Its longtime logo — a caricatured red-faced Native American with an exaggerated nose, oversized teeth, and a feather in its hair named Chief Wahoo — certainly would. As would the Washington Football Team's former name — the "Redskins" — which dictionaries define variously as "disparaging" and "offensive."[219] Because the NCAA policy has no application in professional sports, however, those opposing such names and mascots have had to resort to legal challenges.

"Cleveland Indians"

Since the Cleveland Indians (now, the Guardians) began using the Chief Wahoo logo in the mid-twentieth century, opponents of its use have challenged it through grass roots efforts and — as early 1972 — through the courts.[220] Although legal action was not successful in forcing a logo change, it did, together with the grass roots activism, raise awareness and bring attention to the concern. The team's 2016 run through the playoffs to the World Series, however, brought the issue to a head. After defeating the Boston Red Sox in the Wild Card round of the playoffs, the Indians faced the Toronto Blue Jays in the American League Championship Series (ALCS). In advance of Game 3, the first game of the series to be played in Toronto, a Canadian

---

219. *See, e.g.,* the definition of "Redskin" in the following dictionaries:
Merriam-Webster Dictionary: "*Offensive* — used as an insulting and contemptuous term for an American Indian"
American Heritage Dictionary: "*Offensive Slang.* Used as a disparaging term for a Native American"
Dictionary.Com: "*Disparaging and Offensive.* A contemptuous term used to refer to a North American Indian"
220. Jack Guggenheim, *The Indians' Chief Problem: Chief Wahoo as State Sponsored Discrimination and a Disparaging Mark*, 46 CLEV. ST. L. REV. 211, 214–15 (1998); Glenn George, *Playing Cowboys and Indians*, 6 VA. SPORTS & ENT. L.J. 90, 93 (2006).

citizen and member of the Blackfoot Tribe named Douglass Cardinal brought suit against the Indians and MLB. The suit in an Ontario Court sought to enjoin the Indians from using their name or the Chief Wahoo logo on their uniforms while playing in Canada.[221] He alleged the team's use of its name and logo constituted racial discrimination against indigenous Canadians under both Ontario provincial and national human rights legislation, causes of action not available under United States law.[222] The suit elevated to the international level concerns activists had long raised. Although the injunction was denied,[223] controversy around the name and mascot clouded the ALCS as well as the World Series, to which the Indians advanced but ultimately lost. Moreover, Cardinal continued to press his case, which despite jurisdictional challenges, progressed through the Canadian legal system and increased pressure on MLB and the team.[224] At the same time, local activists, including a coalition called the Cleveland American Indian Movement (CAIM), intensified protests against the team's name and logo.[225]

In 2018, under mounting pressure, MLB Commissioner Rob Manfred persuaded the team's owner Paul Dolan to remove the Chief Wahoo logo from team uniforms for the 2019 season.[226] Dolan had long resisted doing so, trumpeting the logo's nostalgic pull: "You can't help but be aware of how many of our fans are connected to Chief Wahoo. We grew up with it. I remember seeing the little cartoon of The Chief in the paper each day, showing if the Indians won or lost."[227] Although Dolan acceded to strip the uniforms of the Chief Wahoo logo, the team continues to welcome fans' use of the logo in cheering the team at home games.[228] CAIM continued to protest the team, arguing that the team name, continued prevalence of the logo, and culture surrounding them both will continue to inspire the "racism that happens at the stadium with the red-face and the people dressing up as natives and the hooping and hollering."[229] In 2020, with pressure intensified by the nationwide protests against systemic racial

---

221. Cardinal v. Cleveland Indians Baseball Co., 2016 Ont. Superior Ct. of Just. 6929 (2018).

222. *Id.*

223. *Id.*

224. Peter Edwards, *Challenge to Cleveland Indians Name Proceeds*, TORONTO STAR (June 5, 2017), https://www.thestar.com/news/gta/2017/06/05/challenge-to-cleveland-indians-name-proceeds.html.

225. A.J. Perez, *Rob Manfred, Indians Have Had Talks on 'Transitioning Away' from Chief Wahoo*, USA TODAY (Apr. 12, 2017), https://www.usatoday.com/story/sports/mlb/2017/04/12/rob-manfred-indians-chief-wahoo/100369802/.

226. Bill Shaikin, *Cleveland Indians to Retire Chief Wahoo Logo*, LOS ANGELES TIMES (Jan. 29, 2018), https://www.latimes.com/sports/mlb/la-sp-indians-wahoo-20180129-story.html.

227. *Id.*

228. Marisa Saenz, *Cleveland Indians Fans Will Still Be Able to Wear Chief Wahoo Gear to Games, Despite New Ban on Headdresses and Face Paint*, WKYC (Apr. 1, 2021), https://www.wkyc.com/article/sports/mlb/indians/ban-headdresses-face-paint-cleveland-indians-fans-chief-wahoo-gear/95-87e8bec4-0253-4048-9ff2-f41d4ab06370.

229. Kevin Barry, *Cleveland Indians Start Home Opener without Chief Wahoo, but Will Continue to Sell Wahoo Merchandise*, NEWS 5 CLEVELAND (Apr. 1, 2019), https://www.news5cleveland.com/sports/baseball/indians/cleveland-indians-start-home-opener-without-chief-wahoo-but-will-continue-to-sell-wahoo-merchandise.

discrimination that summer, Dolan finally relented and committed to changing the name.[230] In 2021, the club announced its new name: the Cleveland Guardians.

The challenge to the Chief Wahoo logo illustrates the power of lawsuits in challenging the use of Native American names, mascots, and images, even if not initially — or ever — successful in court. Cardinal's initial goal of preventing the Indians from wearing the team name and Chief Wahoo logo during the 2016 American League Championship Series failed, but his continued litigation operated as an activist tool, raising awareness and applying pressure.

"Washington Redskins"

The legal attack on the Washington Redskins' name — the most intense and sustained legal challenge to a Native American name, mascot, or image in United States history — also raised awareness despite failing to compel the club to change.

Two sets of plaintiffs, one after the other, sued Pro-Football, Inc. (Pro-Football), which owns the Washington Redskins football team, over the course of twenty years in an effort to make Pro-Football change the team's name.[231] They took a novel legal approach, petitioning the United States Patent and Trademark Office's Trademark Trial and Appeal Board ("TTAB") to cancel Pro-Football's trademarks of the term "Redskins" and several derivations thereof pursuant to Section 2(a) of the Lanham Trademark Act of 1946, which prohibits trademarks on words or phrases that are "scandalous" or "may disparage" a person or group of people.[232] Trademark cancellation would not force Pro-Football to change the name, but it would mean Pro-Football could not prevent other entities from using the name in producing and selling merchandise.[233] This would economically disadvantage the club, and, it would seem, incentivize a name change.[234]

The first group of plaintiffs, in *Harjo v. Pro-Football. Inc.*,[235] petitioned the TTAB in 1992 to cancel the trademarks.[236] The TTAB agreed that the trademarked term "Redskins" "may disparage Native Americans" and ordered that the trademarks be cancelled.[237] Pro-Football appealed, and the United States District Court for the District of Columbia (the court to which TTAB appeals typically go) reversed on two grounds.[238] First, it determined the TTAB's finding of disparagement was unwar-

---

230. Perez, *supra* note 225.

231. Doori Song, *Blackhorse's Last Stand?: The First Amendment Battle Against the Washington "Redskins" Trademark After* Matal v. Tam, 19 WAKE FOREST J. BUS. & INTELL. PROP. L. 173, 174–78 (2019).

232. *Id.*

233. Casey Leins, *Washington Redskins Lose 6 Trademarks in Landmark Case*, U.S. NEWS (June 18, 2014), https://www.usnews.com/news/articles/2014/06/18/washington-redskins-lose-6-trademarks-in-landmark-case.

234. *Id.*

235. 50 U.S.P.Q.2d 1705 (T.T.A.B. 1999).

236. *Id.* at *1.

237. *Id.* at *48.

238. Pro-Football, Inc. v. Harjo, 284 F. Supp. 2d 96, 145 (D.D.C. 2003).

ranted.[239] Second, it determined plaintiffs unreasonably delayed in asserting their claim under the laches doctrine.[240] Harjo then appealed, and the United States Court of Appeals for the D.C. Circuit affirmed the district court's decision on laches grounds and therefore never reached the disparagement issue.[241]

The *Harjo* case, over the course of its long pendency, inspired substantial opposition to the "Redskins" name in Washington, D.C. as well as in other parts of the country.[242] In 2006, while *Harjo* was pending, a second group of younger plaintiffs, to whom the laches defense would be inapplicable, filed an essentially identical lawsuit, *Blackhorse v. Pro-Football*.[243] As in *Harjo*, the TTAB ordered that the trademarks be cancelled.[244] Unlike in *Harjo*, however, the district court affirmed the TTAB's decision,[245] presenting the possibility that, with the laches argument inapplicable on appeal, the Circuit Court would concur. But in 2017, during the appeal's pendency, the United States Supreme Court decided *Matal v. Tam*,[246] a case that also involved the trademarking of a potentially disparaging term. In *Matal*, the Court declared that Section 2(a) of the Lanham Act — the precise provision on which both the *Harjo* and *Blackhorse* plaintiffs relied — violates the First Amendment right to free speech.[247] This cratered the *Blackhorse* plaintiffs' position, and their district court victory was summarily vacated, leaving Pro-Football's trademarks on "Redskins" and related terms in place.[248]

The team's owner, Dan Snyder, was adamantly opposed to changing the name throughout the litigation, at one point resolutely telling reporters, "we'll never change the name.... It's that simple. NEVER — you can use caps."[249] But even having won in court, Snyder finally buckled and agreed to change the name in 2020 when sponsors — responding to increasing public consciousness of systemic racism in the United States in the aftermath of George Floyd's killing — threatened to disassociate from the team.[250] The team went by the generic moniker, "Washington Football Team" for the 2020 and 2021 football seasons and in February 2022 became the Washington

239. *Id.*
240. *Id.*
241. Pro-Football, Inc. v. Harjo, 565 F.3d 880, 881 (D.C. Cir. 2009).
242. Ken Belson, *Redskins' Name Change Remains Activist's Unfinished Business*, N.Y. TIMES (Oct. 9, 2013), https://www.nytimes.com/2013/10/10/sports/football/redskins-name-change-remains-her-unfinished-business.html; Tom Geoghegan, *Washington Redskins: Time to Change the Name?*, BBC (Sept. 14, 2013), https://www.bbc.com/news/magazine-24027457.
243. 111 U.S.P.Q.2d 1080 (T.T.A.B. 2014).
244. *Id.* at *34.
245. Pro-Football, Inc. v. Blackhorse, 112 F. Supp. 3d 439, 490 (E.D. Va. 2015).
246. 137 U.S. 1744 (2017).
247. *Id.* at 1765.
248. Pro-Football, Inc. v. Blackhorse, 709 F. App'x 182, 183–84 (4th Cir. 2018).
249. Erik Brady, *Daniel Snyder Says Redskins Will Never Change Name*, USA TODAY (May 9, 2013), https://www.usatoday.com/story/sports/nfl/redskins/2013/05/09/washington-redskins-daniel-snyder/2148127/.
250. Ken Belson & Kevin Draper, *FedEx Made a Demand Dan Snyder Couldn't Afford to Miss*, N.Y. TIMES (July 10, 2020), https://www.nytimes.com/2020/07/10/sports/football/dan-snyder-washington-redskins-name-fedex.html.

Commanders.[251] Although the litigation failed, the goal of the litigation, which was to force a name change through applying financial pressure, came to pass via other means.

[C] Individual Sports Governing Bodies

In 2019, US Lacrosse took a strong stance on the use of Native American names, mascots, and images. Noting that lacrosse was invented by Native Americans, US Lacrosse issued an official statement reading: "US Lacrosse believes that the misuse of Native American nicknames, logos, and mascots reflect and promote misleading stereotypes that are degrading and harmful to Native Americans."[252] As such, US Lacrosse banned "offensive or stereotypical mascots and logos" at all events and competitions under US Lacrosse's control.[253]

US Lacrosse's position is unprecedented among sports governing bodies in the United States, but its ultimate impact is yet to be seen. Because US Lacrosse controls neither of the nation's most prominent professional lacrosse leagues — Premier Lacrosse League and Major League Lacrosse — its mandate will not apply at the game's highest levels. Moreover, US Lacrosse does not control lacrosse on the collegiate level. The manner in which US Lacrosse determines what constitutes "offensive or stereotypical" is unclear, but even if its standard is one that would prohibit, for instance, the "Seminole" name, mascot, and imagery that the NCAA permits Florida State University to use, US Lacrosse's prohibition would have no bearing on matches Florida State plays.

[D] Individual States' Policies

In 2019, Maine became the first state to enact a ban on sports teams using Native American names and imagery.[254] The law requires that no public educational institution on any level — from elementary school through university — "have or adopt a name, symbol or image that depicts or refers to a Native American tribe, individual, custom or tradition and that is used as a mascot, nickname, logo, letterhead or team

---

251. Ken Belson, *With Commanders, the Washington N.F.L. Franchise Moves Past Old Name*, N.Y. Times (Feb. 2, 2022), available at https://www.nytimes.com/2022/02/02/sports/washington-football-team-commanders.html.

252. Paul Ohanian, *US Lacrosse Position Statement on Native American Mascots*, US LACROSSE (Feb. 7, 2019), https://www.uslacrosse.org/blog/us-lacrosse-position-statement-on-native-american-mascots.

253. *Id.*

254. *See* David Williams, *Maine to Become First State to Ban Native American Mascots in Public Schools*, CNN (May 17, 2019), https://www.cnn.com/2019/05/17/us/maine-bans-native-american-mascots/index.html. In 2021, Colorado became the second state to pass such legislation. Derek Draplin, *Colorado Public Schools Banned from Having American Indian Mascots under New Law*, THE DAILY SENTINEL (June 29, 2021), https://www.gjsentinel.com/news/colorado/colorado-public-schools-banned-from-having-american-indian-mascots-under-new-law/article_bfbabe70-d6f2-53de-bc74-b69e82e871d2.html.

name of the school."[255] Notably, the statute does not allow for subjectivity, short-circuiting any argument that uses may be harmless, non-offensive or celebratory. It is an absolute ban, which makes it more stringent than both the NCAA Policy and the US Lacrosse prohibition. For example, if a Maine school's Native American team name or logo were to survive NCAA or US Lacrosse scrutiny, it would still be unusable as a matter of state law.

Other states including Washington and Colorado have followed suit.[256] Illinois has pending legislation that takes a nuanced approach to the issue, falling short of an absolute ban but going well beyond what the NCAA Policy requires. If passed, the Illinois legislation "would prohibit [Illinois] schools from using Native American logos, mascots or other imagery unless they:

1) receive written permission from a tribe within 500 miles of the school, which would have to be renewed every five years;

2) conduct a schoolwide program on Native American culture at least twice a year;

3) offer a course on Native American contributions to society; and

4) file an annual report with the state on the academic programs they offer about Native Americans."[257]

These states' legislative efforts reveal a desire to eradicate or substantially limit sports teams' use of Native American names, mascots, and images. The legislation, however, applies only to public schools in those states, and has no effect on private schools and other private entities, such as professional sports leagues. Whether the legislative trend will impact policy choices made by organizations outside the legislation's ambit is to be determined.

---

255. ME Rev. Stat. Ann. tit. 20-A, § 12 (2019).

256. *Washington Legislature Approves Ban on Native American Mascots at Schools*, The Seattle Times (Apr. 12, 2021), https://www.seattletimes.com/seattle-news/politics/washington-legislature-approves-ban-on-native-american-mascots-at-schools/; Draplin, *supra* note 254.

257. Harmeet Kaur, *Illinois Lawmakers Have Introduced a Bill to Ban Native American Mascots*, CNN (Feb. 27, 2020), https://www.cnn.com/2020/02/27/us/illinois-native-american-mascots-ban-trnd/index.html.

Part III

Legal Issues in Professional Leagues

Chapter 7

League Governance, Commissioner Authority, and Antitrust

§ 7.01 Introduction

Professional sports leagues in the United States follow a common competitive format. Teams play each other in a lengthy regular season at the end of which the teams with a win-loss record above an established threshold qualify for postseason play. Those qualifying teams compete in successive rounds of playoffs until two teams meet in a championship game or series, with one team emerging as the league champion. For the most part, these leagues also share similar governance structures. Most notably, they are all headed by a commissioner with extensive authority over league operations. In addition, with one exception (Major League Soccer ("MLS"), which is discussed below), they consist of many individually-owned franchises operating under the league's umbrella. This structure has generally proven successful and profitable and remains the gold standard in American professional team sports. This chapter explores league governance in American sport with an emphasis on the scope and contours of commissioner authority. The chapter also focuses on antitrust (and other) restrictions on league governance.

§ 7.02 Origins of American Professional Sports Leagues

Founded in 1876, the National League of Professional Base Ball Clubs was America's first professional sports league.[1] Prior to its founding, professional baseball teams existed and competed against one another, but they did so in an informal and disorganized manner.[2] Teams played schedules of different lengths, on-the-field rules were inconsistent or inconsistently applied, and the quality of play varied wildly.[3] The National League instituted a structure that had never before been seen in Amer-

---

1. Marc Edelman, *Why the "Single Entity" Defense Can Never Apply to NFL Clubs: A Primer on Property-Rights Theory in Professional Sports*, 18 FORDHAM INTELL. PROP. MEDIA & ENT. L.J. 891, 899 (2008).
2. *Id.* at 897–99.
3. *Id.* at 898.

ican sports.[4] The league included eight member clubs whose owners drafted a constitution that created a process for appointing a board of directors to govern the league's affairs.[5] In 1901, a similar baseball league, the American League, was founded. Two years later, the National League and American League formed an affiliation.[6] Although the leagues remained separate entities, they came to be known collectively as Major League Baseball.[7]

The National League and the American League created the organizational template that other American professional sports leagues would adopt over the course of the following several decades. The National Hockey League ("NHL") was founded in 1917,[8] the National Football League ("NFL") was founded in 1920,[9] and the National Basketball Association ("NBA") was founded in 1946.[10] MLB, the NHL, the NFL, and the NBA are the nation's oldest continuously operating leagues and have come to be known as the "big four" American sports leagues. In 1996, however, the American professional sporting landscape expanded with the emergence of the Women's National Basketball Association (founded with support from the NBA)[11] and MLS.[12] Both leagues have substantially strengthened since their founding. In 2012, the National Women's Soccer League formed,[13] and it, too, has strengthened, though it stands on more precarious financial footing than MLS and the WNBA. Other leagues, such as Major League Lacrosse, also exist — and still others like the XFL and the Alliance of American Football have come and gone — but the "big four" remain America's largest sports leagues as judged by annual revenue.[14] Regardless of their size and

---

4. Ron McCulloch, Baseball Roots: The Fascinating Birth of America's Game and the Amazing Players That Were its Champions 11–51 (2000).

5. *Id.* at 24–26.

6. *Id.* at 62–63.

7. *Id.*

8. *NHL History*, NHL Records, https://records.nhl.com/history (last visited Aug. 30, 2021).

9. *1920 — American Professional Football Conference is Formed*, Pro Football Hall of Fame, https://www.profootballhof.com/football-history/history-of-football/1869-1939/1920-american-professional-football-conference-is-formed/ (last visited Aug. 30, 2021). At its founding, the NFL was called the American Professional Football Conference and then the American Professional Football Association before settling in 1922 on its current name. *1922 — American Professional Football Association Changes Name to National Football League*, Pro Football Hall of Fame, https://www.profootballhof.com/football-history/history-of-football/1869-1939/1922-american-professional-football-association-changes-name-to-national-football-league/ (last visited Aug. 30, 2021).

10. *History Season Review: 1946–47*, NBA History, https://www.nba.com/history/season-recap/1946-47 (last visited Aug. 30, 2021).

11. *History*, Official Site of the WNBA, https://www.wnba.com/history/ (last visited Aug. 31, 2021).

12. *About Major League Soccer*, MLS Soccer, https://www.mlssoccer.com/news/about-major-league-soccer (last visited Aug. 31, 2021).

13. *NWSL*, Just Women's Sports, https://justwomenssports.com/wiki/nwsl/ (last visited Aug. 31, 2021).

14. *See Major Professional Sports Leagues: The US & Canada*, The Daily Gazette (Aug. 31, 2021), https://dailygazette.com/major-professional-sports-leagues-the-us-canada/; Premier Lacrosse League, https://premierlacrosseleague.com/ (last visited Aug. 31, 2021); XFL, https://www.xfl.com/ (last visited Aug. 31, 2021).

scope, all of these leagues have adopted a similar structure: a closed league in which only member clubs participate, and they all maintain that basic structure today.

§ 7.03 The Commissioner

[A] Origin of the Office of the Commissioner

All American professional sports leagues also share an additional feature: an overarching authoritative league administrator called a commissioner. The Office of the Commissioner was a Major League Baseball ("MLB") innovation. The National League and the American League existed for decades without a commissioner, but a crisis that erupted in 1919 convinced the leagues that greater oversight was necessary. In that year, members of the Chicago White Sox baseball club allegedly played poorly intentionally in exchange for payoffs from gamblers betting on their opponent, the Cincinnati Reds.[15] Because predetermined or fixed outcomes cut against the very core of competitive athletics, the scandal threatened to doom professional baseball in the United States.

Major League Baseball responded in 1920 by appointing Judge Kenesaw Mountain Landis as Commissioner of the Major Leagues and endowing him with robust authority to govern the game.[16] In doing so, it granted him the authority to penalize any "act," "transaction," or "practice" deemed not "in the best interests of baseball."[17] The players accused of throwing the World Series were all criminally prosecuted, and they were all found not guilty in a trial that many observers described as less than rigorous.[18] Landis was undaunted by the outcome, famously stating:

> Regardless of the verdict of juries, no player that throws a ball game; no player that undertakes or promises to throw a ball game; no player that sits in a conference with a bunch of crooked players and gamblers where the ways and means of throwing ball games are planned and discussed and does not promptly tell his club about it, will ever play professional baseball.[19]

Landis made good on his threat, banning eight Chicago White Sox players from baseball for life.[20] Landis' action following the 1919 World Series concretized the breadth of his power and established that the standard for meting out league discipline need not parallel the judicial system's standards if more exacting standards are "in the best interests of baseball."

---

15. ROBERT C. COTTRELL, BLACKBALL, THE BLACK SOX, AND THE BABE 258 (2002).

16. *Id.* at 251.

17. *Id.*

18. *Id.* at 259. When the not guilty verdicts were read in the courtroom, the presiding judge and the bailiffs reportedly appeared pleased. *See id.* at 258–59. That evening, the exonerated players and jury members celebrated together at an Italian restaurant in Chicago. J.G. TAYLOR SPINK, JUDGE LANDIS AND TWENTY-FIVE YEARS OF BASEBALL (revised ed. 1974).

19. COTTRELL, *supra* note 15, at 259–60.

20. *Id.* at 261.

[B] General Scope of Commissioner Authority

Predictably, disgruntled stakeholders in baseball challenged Landis' authority. Courts, however, were reluctant to restrict it, and they have been reluctant to restrict commissioners' authority since. *Milwaukee American Ass'n v. Landis*[21] offers an early illustration of courts' reticence in this regard. The case involved Commissioner Landis' 1930 declaration affording free agency for Fred Bennett, a player the St. Louis Browns baseball club had assigned to multiple minor league clubs (one of which was the Milwaukee club).[22] Landis reached his decision after concluding that the owner of the Browns, Phil Ball, had secret ownership stakes in the minor league clubs and manipulated the assignments in a way that prevented other clubs from retaining Bennett's services. Landis viewed Ball's machinations as detrimental to baseball.[23] The Milwaukee club, which was slated to receive Bennett's services under a contract with the Browns, sued to enjoin Landis from declaring Bennett a free agent.[24]

The court began its analysis by emphasizing that the Major League Agreement — between all 16 members of the two Major Leagues in professional baseball — granted the Commissioner the power to:

> [I]nvestigate, either upon complaint or upon his own initiative, any act, transaction or practice charged, alleged or suspected to be detrimental to the best interests of the national game of baseball ... [and t]o determine, after investigation, what preventive, remedial or punitive action is appropriate....[25]

The court went on to note that other affiliate agreements among the stakeholders in professional baseball, which together with the Major League Agreement are known collectively as the "code governing organized baseball" ("the baseball code"), were consistent in signaling broad commissioner authority.[26] The various agreements, the court stated, "disclose a clear intent upon the part of the parties to endow the commissioner with all the attributes of a benevolent but absolute despot and all the disciplinary powers of the proverbial pater familias."[27] The court cautioned that the Commissioner has no right to exercise authority in an illegal, fraudulent, or arbitrary manner, but short of that, has "almost unlimited discretion" both in determining what constitutes action that damages baseball and in issuing discipline.[28]

As other professional American sports leagues adopted organizational structures headed by commissioners, they granted their commissioners similarly broad authority.

---

21. 49 F.2d 298 (N.D. Ill. 1931).
22. *Id.* at 300–02.
23. *Id.* at 303.
24. *Id.* at 299.
25. *Id.*
26. *Id.*
27. *Id.*
28. *Id.* at 303.

Other leagues do not use the "best interests" language, but their language reflects MLB's general approach. Consider the following provisions granting commissioners authority.

- The NBA Commissioner has power to "promulgate and enforce reasonable rules governing the conduct of players on the playing court" or conduct that is harmful to the "preservation of the integrity of, or the maintenance of public confidence in, the game."[29]

- The NFL Commissioner has power to "resolve disputes" and to take action against a person connected with the league when the person engages in "conduct detrimental to the league."[30]

- The NHL Commissioner has the power to do what is necessary to "protect[] the integrity of the game of professional hockey and preserv[e] public confidence in the league."[31]

Though expressed in different ways, each of these articulations grants the commissioners of the respective leagues substantial power. Over the years, various courts, like the *Milwaukee American Ass'n* court, have declined to substantially circumscribe a commissioner's authority. *Finley v. Kuhn*[32] is a leading case in this regard. There, the Oakland Athletics's owner, Charles Finley, sought to sell three players to other clubs.[33] However, MLB's Commissioner Bowie Kuhn, objected.[34] Kuhn believed that the transaction would diminish the Oakland franchise and compromise the league's competitive balance.[35] As such, he utilized his "best interests" authority to prevent the transaction.[36] Finley sued, challenging Kuhn's authority to void the deal.[37] He argued that Kuhn's action was, among other things, "arbitrary, capricious, unreasonable, [and] discriminatory."[38] In finding for Kuhn, the court emphasized the breadth of the commissioner's authority under the "best interests" clause, but noted the commissioner only enjoys that authority while operating in good faith.[39] Because Finley made his decision in good faith, the court found in his favor. It concluded that "whether he was right or wrong" was beyond its "competence and the jurisdiction ... to decide."[40] Although commissioners must operate in good faith, as established in

---

29. 2011 NBA CBA, art. VI, §12; 2011 NBA CBA, art. XXXI, §9. *See also* NBA Const. & By-Laws, §2.01 (2019) (stating that "the commissioner shall have the right to disqualify a player if the commissioner finds the player does not possess the requisite qualities of character and morality").

30. NFL Const. art VIII, §8.3 (2006).

31. NHL Const. art. 6 (1993).

32. 569 F.2d 527 (7th Cir. 1978).

33. *Id.* at 531.

34. *Id.*

35. *Id.*

36. *Id.*

37. *Id.*

38. *Id.* at 535.

39. *Id.* at 539.

40. *Id.*

Finley, and cannot take actions motivated by bias or ill will,[41] they are extremely powerful forces in operating their leagues.

No major sports league commissioner, however, enjoys the breadth of authority Commissioner Landis enjoyed. Not even the current MLB Commissioner's "best interests" authority measures up to the authority Landis wielded. Landis ruled over MLB at a time when players were largely powerless. Players in all major American professional sports leagues are now unionized, and those unions (discussed in detail in Chapter 8) provide a check on commissioner power that did not previously exist. The extent and nuances of a commissioner's authority, therefore, depend on the terms the union and the league reach in the collective bargaining agreement that binds them. Courts today are loath to look behind commissioner authority granted in a CBA — even if extreme — just as courts during the Landis era were loath to look behind the commissioner's authority as set out in the Major League Agreement.

One of the most controversial episodes in recent professional sports history — known colloquially as "Deflategate" and resolved in a case called *National Football League Management Council v. National Football League Players Assn.*[42] — is illustrative. The case involved an equipment dispute that grew out of the NFL's 2015 AFC championship game. The dispute dominated newspaper headlines, the league's arbitral system, and court dockets for years, and ultimately reaffirmed NFL Commissioner Roger Goodell's considerable power. Under NFL rules, each NFL club provides the footballs it uses on offense, and league rules require that the balls be inflated to a pressure of between 12.5 pounds per square inch and 13.5 pounds per square inch.[43] During that game, however, the Indianapolis Colts believed the New England Patriots were using under-inflated balls, which then-Patriots quarterback Tom Brady explicitly preferred.[44] The Colts reported their suspicion to NFL officials who tested the Patriots' balls and found them all to be under the 12.5 pounds per square inch threshold.[45]

The following week, the league commissioned an independent investigation, which concluded that Brady was "at least generally aware" that Patriots equipment managers likely deflated the balls.[46] The investigators also reported that Brady purposely impaired the investigation.[47] Exercising his power under Article 46 of the CBA between the NFL and the NFL Players Association, Commissioner Goodell issued Brady a four game suspension for "conduct detrimental to the integrity of and public confidence in the game of professional football."[48] Brady appealed the suspension, and Goodell

---

41. *See* Atlanta Nat'l League Baseball Club, Inc. v. Kuhn, 432 F. Supp. 1213, 1222 (N.D. Ga 1977).
42. 820 F.3d 527 (2d Cir. 2016).
43. *Id.* at 532–33.
44. *Id.*
45. *Id.*
46. *Id.* at 533.
47. *Id.* at 534.
48. *Id.*

appointed himself — as was his right under the CBA — to hear the appeal.[49] Goodell predictably upheld the suspension he had imposed.[50]

Federal litigation followed, and the district court vacated the suspension, finding that Goodell exceeded his authority.[51] On appeal, however, the United States Court of Appeals for the Second Circuit reversed, outlining the breadth of Goodell's authority, as granted him in the CBA. The Second Circuit first found that Goodell did not abuse his authority in suspending Brady, because the CBA "empowers the Commissioner to take disciplinary action against a player whom he 'reasonably judge[s]' to have engaged in 'conduct detrimental to the integrity of, or public confidence in, the game of professional football.'"[52] The Second Circuit then rejected the NFLPA's argument that the Commissioner was evidently partial in serving as the hearing officer who "adjudicate[d] the propriety of his own conduct."[53] The court acknowledged that the CBA provision giving the Commissioner unchecked authority at all levels of the disciplinary process was "especially broad," but emphasized that the parties agreed to it:

> In their collective bargaining agreement, the players and the League mutually decided many years ago that the Commissioner should investigate possible rule violations, should impose appropriate sanctions, and may preside at arbitrations challenging his discipline. Although this tripartite regime may appear somewhat unorthodox, it is the regime bargained for and agreed upon by the parties, which we can only presume they determined was mutually satisfactory.[54]

Having agreed as such, the court continued, all parties knew "full well that the Commissioner had the sole power of determining what constitutes 'conduct detrimental,' and thus kn[ew] that the Commissioner would have a stake both in the underlying discipline and in [the appeal]."[55] This being the case, the court refused to step in to

---

49. *Id.* Commissioner Goodell may have been influenced to exercise his right to hear the appeal by the outcome of what was, until "Deflategate," the most notable scandal to beset the league during Goodell's tenure. In 2012, Commissioner Goodell had suspended several New Orleans Saints players for participating in an alleged scheme to purposely injure opposing players ("Bountygate"). The players appealed, and although Goodell had the right under the CBA to hear and decide the appeal of his decision, he instead appointed former commissioner Paul Tagliabue to hear the appeal. In his role as hearing officer, Tagliabue vacated the suspensions. *See* Jesse Reed, *Reviewing the Complete Timeline of NFL, Saints Bountygate Scandal*, BLEACHER REPORT (Dec. 11, 2012), https://bleacherreport.com/articles/1441646-reviewing-the-complete-timeline-of-nfl-saints-bountygate-scandal. This dealt Goodell's authority an ostensible blow, but in fact Goodell had short circuited his own authority by delegating the hearing officer role. Goodell decided against such delegation in the "Deflategate" matter, consolidating his power.

50. *Nat'l Football League Mgmt. Council*, 820 F.3d at 535.

51. Nat'l Football League Mgmt. Council v. Nat'l Football League Players Ass'n, 125 F. Supp. 3d 449, 474 (S.D.N.Y. 2015).

52. *Nat'l Football League Mgmt. Council*, 820 F.3d at 537.

53. *Id.* at 548.

54. *Id.* at 532.

55. *Id.* at 548. Before and after the Deflategate case, the NFLPA was roundly criticized in the media for granting the Commissioner so much power through the 2011 CBA. *See, e.g.*, Ben Volin, *Now More*

cordon the Commissioner's authority, concluding that even if the Commissioner "made mistakes of fact or law, we may not disturb [the decision] so long as he acted within the bounds of his bargained-for authority."[56]

The "Deflategate" case reinforces the extent to which courts defer to commissioner authority, whether granted through league foundational documents such as the Major League agreement or through a CBA. If league stakeholders, such as players, coaches, or owners wish to restrict commissioner authority, they would be advised to do so through contract. Prevailing upon courts to divest a commissioner of his or her authority in the absence of illegality, ill will, bias, or *ultra vires* action is generally a losing battle.

[C] Commissioner Authority: Personal Conduct

The above-described commissioner disciplinary action involved an incident occurring during athletic competition. Commissioners, however, have generally taken the position that a player's or other league stakeholder's actions away from competition can also be "detrimental" to a league or not in the league's "best interest" and therefore trigger discipline. Domestic violence is a prime example.

Domestic violence has long been a societal scourge, and athlete involvement in domestic violence is certainly not new. A 2014 incident, however, served as an inflection point in the way professional sports leagues respond to their players' perpetrating domestic violence. In February of that year, Baltimore Ravens star running back Ray Rice argued with his with fiancée in an Atlantic City elevator and then knocked her unconscious with a powerful punch to her face.[57] The elevator's camera recorded the attack, and the video, which was aired repeatedly in the media, appalled the nation.[58] Although the NFL had a policy in place since 1997 that addressed off-field player conduct, the owners of all 32 NFL clubs agreed that a stronger and more targeted policy was needed. In December 2014, they unanimously passed a new "Personal Conduct Policy," which reaffirmed commissioner authority over players' off-field conduct and expanded the league's attention to the issue. The new policy focuses not just on punishment but also on education, counseling, and treatment around

Than Ever, We Realize Owners Won, Boston Globe (July 21, 2013), https://www.bostonglobe.com/sports/2013/07/20/nfl-owners-destroyed-players-cba-negotiations/ia3c1ydpS16H5FhFEiviHP/story.html (noting that the 26% revenue increase released in the 2013 Green Bay Packers' annual financial statements emphasized how much revenue and benefits the players lost). Although the NFLPA entered CBA renegotiations in 2019 with an eye toward limiting that power, the renegotiated CBA — agreed to in 2020 — limits it only marginally. Although the NFL and NFLPA must now jointly agree on the disciplinary officer who presides over the disciplinary hearings (meaning Commissioner Goodell can no longer simply appoint himself), Commissioner Goodell handles all appeals and can affirm, reduce, increase, or vacate the terms of discipline. Moreover, Commissioner Goodell's decision is binding and "constitute[s] [a] full, final[,] and complete disposition of the dispute." *See* 2020 NFL CBA, art. XLVI, § 1(e)(v). Commissioner Goodell, therefore, retains substantial control over player discipline.

56. *Nat'l Football League Mgmt. Council*, 820 F.3d at 532.

57. Tate Martin, *Wake Up Call: How the Ray Rice Incident Opened the Public's Eyes to Domestic Violence in Professional Sports and the Need for Change*, 24 Sports Law. J. 183, 188–91 (2017).

58. *Id.* at 191.

domestic violence issues.[59] In 2015, MLB announced a Domestic Violence, Sexual Assault & Child Abuse Policy,[60] and in 2017, the NBA reasserted its commitment to addressing these issues with an updated domestic violence and sexual assault policy as well.[61] In 2020, the WNBA established its "Policy on Domestic/Intimate Partner Violence, Sexual Assault, and Child Abuse."[62] All of these policies are the product of negotiation and ultimate agreement — through collective bargaining — between the leagues and their corresponding players unions. They grant varying degrees of commissioner authority in doling out punishments for violations. The NHL has no analogous policy, as the league and the NHLPA have not come to agreement on the matter. Their collective bargaining agreement, however, does include a provision titled "Commissioner Discipline for Off-Ice Conduct," which sets forth the bounds of the NHL commissioner's authority in this realm.[63]

[D] Protecting the Reputation of the Game

The lure of competitive sports is that they are, indeed, *competitive*. The idea is that no participant has an unfair advantage over any other participant and that no outcome is predetermined. If players cheat to gain an advantage or if they purposely play poorly, that ideal is shattered and the reputation of the league in question falters. As such, commissioners have historically viewed the maintenance of fair competition as a paramount priority and have striven mightily against any actions that potentially undermine it. The two realms in which these issues have most forcefully come to the forefront are gambling and the use of performance enhancing drugs. They will be addressed in turn.

[1] Gambling

While gambling in and of itself does not denote wrongdoing in competition, commissioners have long viewed it as incentivizing wrongdoing. As noted above, concern about players being paid by gamblers to lose games on purpose spurred MLB to appoint the first commissioner in American professional sports.[64] And the commissioner

---

59. Tom Pelissero, *NFL Owners Pass New Personal Conduct Policy*, USA TODAY (Dec. 10, 2014), https://www.usatoday.com/story/sports/nfl/2014/12/10/roger-goodell-nfl-owners-personal-conduct-policy/20199033/.

60. Gabe Lacques, *MLB Announces Domestic Violence, Assault and Child Abuse Policy*, USA TODAY (Aug. 21, 2015), https://www.usatoday.com/story/sports/mlb/2015/08/21/mlb-announces-domestic-violence-sexual-assault-child-abuse-policy/32140129/.

61. Diana Moskovitz, *The NBA's New Policy on Domestic Violence, Sexual Assault, and Child Abuse Is Here*, DEADSPIN (May 24, 2017), https://deadspin.com/the-nbas-new-policy-on-domestic-violence-sexual-assaul-1795378340.

62. *See* Women's National Basketball Association, *Women's National Basketball Association Players Collective Bargaining Agreement*, 1, 321 (2020), https://wnbpa.com/wp-content/uploads/2020/01/WNBA-WNBPA-CBA-2020-2027.pdf.

63. *See* National Hockey League, *National Hockey League Players Association Collective Bargaining Agreement*, art. 18-A (Sept. 16, 2012), https://www.nhlpa.com/the-pa/cba.

64. COTTRELL, *supra* note 15, at 251.

they hired, Kennesaw Mountain Landis, sent a strong message by imposing a lifetime ban on several players who allegedly intentionally lost games.[65]

Notably, as sports gambling evolved, so too did the opportunities to assist gamblers in more nuanced ways than losing on purpose. Using the "point spread" gambling technique, for example, a gambler can bet on a team to win, but by only a certain number of points. A player helping a gambler could, therefore, try to limit scoring — called "point shaving" — without sacrificing a victory. Concerns about gambling's impact on sport, through incentivizing point shaving or purposeful losing, persisted through the twentieth century, with professional sports leagues lobbying against expansion of legal sports gambling beyond the state of Nevada (which first permitted sports gambling in 1931 and has permitted it ever since) and league commissioners imposing harsh punishment on players found to have gambled on their sport.

For instance, in 1963, then-NFL Commissioner Pete Rozelle suspended Green Bay Packers star Paul Hornung and Detroit Lions star Alex Karras indefinitely for gambling on football.[66] Neither player was implicated in throwing a game or shaving points, but Rozelle felt the league needed to send a strong message to all players about the dangers of sports gambling.[67] Both players were reinstated the next year and are enshrined in the Hall of Fame.[68]

MLB player Pete Rose fared much worse. After a legendary playing career during which he amassed more base hits than anyone in MLB history, Rose became a manager.[69] As a manager, he was long suspected of gambling on MLB games, but he denied doing so.[70] During the spring of 1989, while Rose was managing the Cincinnati Reds, MLB's then-Commissioner Bart Giamatti, pursuant to his "best interests" authority, launched an investigation into allegations that Rose bet on baseball.[71] MLB hired Washington, D.C.-based lawyer John Dowd to lead the investigation.[72] Dowd produced a 225-page report, which concluded that Rose had bet on baseball.[73] Giamatti set a hearing on the matter, but Rose sued in state court for a temporary restraining order to prevent Giamatti from holding the hearing.[74] After two months of litigation,

---

65. *Id.* at 259–60.
66. Michael E. Lomax, *Detrimental to the League: Gambling and the Governance of Professional Football, 1946–1963*, 29 J. Sport Hist. 289, 303 (Summer 2002).
67. *Id.*
68. *Id.* at 304. *See* Justin Rogers, *Finally In! Detroit Lions Great Alex Karras Selected to Pro Football Hall of Fame*, The Detroit News (Jan. 15, 2020), https://www.detroitnews.com/story/sports/nfl/lions/2020/01/15/detroit-lions-great-alex-karras-elected-pro-football-hall-fame/4476406002/; Cody Benjamin, *Hall of Famer Paul Hornung, Packers and Notre Dame Legend, Dies at 84*, CBS Sports (Nov. 13, 2020), https://www.cbssports.com/nfl/news/hall-of-famer-paul-hornung-packers-and-notre-dame-legend-dies-at-84/.
69. Kendall Howell, *You Can Bet On It: The Legal Evolution of Sports Betting*, 11 Harv. J. Sports & Ent. L. 73, 76 n.13 (2020).
70. *Id.* at 76–78.
71. *Id.* at 77–78.
72. *Id.* at 76.
73. *Id.* at 76–77.
74. Rose v. Giamatti, 721 F. Supp. 924 (S.D. Ohio 1989).

which involved removal of the case to federal court and ever-mounting evidence against Rose, Rose opted to be placed on MLB's "permanently ineligible" list in exchange for MLB making no formal liability finding.[75] Over a decade later, in 2003, Rose admitted to gambling on baseball but denied betting on his team to lose; he argued, therefore, that he had no incentive to manage poorly or impede his players' success.[76] Nonetheless, Rose has not been reinstated and has been banned from consideration for the Hall of Fame.[77]

While all major sports leagues continue to prohibit players from gambling on their sport, leagues' perspectives on sports gambling have softened substantially. In this regard, a key development was the 2018 United States Supreme Court case, *Murphy v. NCAA*.[78] That case centered on a 1992 federal statute titled Professional and Amateur Sports Protection Act ("PASPA"), which outlawed sports gambling throughout the nation, with the notable exception of Nevada and sports lottery systems in Delaware, Oregon, and Montana.[79] The New Jersey legislature, hoping to add sports gambling to the attractions at Atlantic City casinos, enacted a state law that cleared the way for legalized sports gambling in New Jersey.[80] The big four sports leagues — the NFL, the NBA, the NHL, and MLB — true to historical form opposed any expansion of legalized sports gambling. These leagues joined the NCAA in suing New Jersey's governor and other state officials, arguing that sports gambling in New Jersey would violate PASPA.[81] The plaintiffs won at the district and appeals court levels, and New Jersey sought certiorari from the United States Supreme Court.[82] New Jersey argued that PASPA violated the "anticommandeering" provisions of the United States Constitution's Tenth Amendment.[83] In short, New Jersey asserted that, in passing PASPA, the federal government unconstitutionally commandeered power reserved

---

75. Howell, *supra* note 69, at 78.

76. *Id.* at 78–79. Critics counter that although Rose may not have had incentives to lose, he may have been so incentivized to win that he made decisions that could have harmed his team and players. *See* Geoffrey Rapp, *Betting on Your Own Team, in the World of Baseball and the Corporate World: Is Pete Rose Really as Evil as Ken Lay?*, FINDLAW (Dec. 16, 2002), https://supreme.findlaw.com/legal-commentary/betting-on-your-own-team-in-the-world-of-baseball-and-the-corporate-world.html (comparing Rose's betting on himself to corporate law in the context of incentivizing optimal performance); *see also* Barry M. Bloom, *Pete Rose Swears Off Betting on Baseball as Gambling Millions Roll in*, SPORTICO (Apr. 16, 2021), https://www.sportico.com/leagues/baseball/2021/pete-rose-baseball-gambling-1234627492/ (quoting Pete Rose as having said that he "bet on every game for the Reds to win because I needed the extra incentive, the extra kick."). For instance, critics argue, Rose may have chosen to play a pitcher on short rest or for more innings than he otherwise would have so as to get the best possible short-term outcome at the potential expense of the pitcher's long-term health. *See* Rapp, *supra*.

77. Howell, *supra* note 69, at 78–79.

78. 138 S. Ct. 1461 (2018).

79. *History of Sports Betting in the USA*, LEGAL SPORTS BETTING, https://www.legalsportsbetting.com/history-of-sports-betting-in-the-usa/ (last visited Aug. 31, 2021).

80. *Murphy*, 138 S. Ct. at 1471.

81. *Id.*

82. *Id.* at 1471–72.

83. *Id.* at 1472.

for the states by prohibiting them from permitting sports gambling.[84] The Court agreed and invalidated PASPA. In doing so, the Court paved the way for states to legalize sports betting as a means of increasing revenue.[85] At the time of this writing, dozens of states and the District of Columbia have legalized sports gambling, and nine more states are on the verge of doing so.[86]

Despite professional sports leagues' public opposition to sports gambling and its potentially corrupting influence on players, sports gambling undeniably keeps spectators interested in sporting events and drives revenue to the leagues.[87] All of the major sports leagues' rules continue to prohibit players and team personnel from betting on their sports. Moreover, all of the major sports leagues' commissioners would certainly use their authority to punish those who violate those rules. At the same time, leagues and their clubs have quickly pivoted to accepting, and in some cases, embracing sports gambling.

For decades, all major sports leagues viewed Las Vegas, Nevada — which, under PASPA, had a virtual monopoly on full-service sports betting — as strictly off-limits for franchise location. In 2017, however, as *Murphy* was working its way through the courts, the NHL placed the first major league sports team in Las Vegas: the Las Vegas Knights. In 2019, the NFL's Raiders followed suit, relocating to Las Vegas. And in spring 2021, when MLB gave the Oakland Athletics permission to seek out a new home city, rumors immediately began to swirl that Las Vegas would be their new home.

---

84. *Id.*

85. *Id.* at 1484–85.

86. States vary in the format through which sports gambling is legalized. Some states only permit in-person sports wagering (Delaware, Mississippi, North Carolina, New Mexico, Arkansas, New Hampshire, and Montana); others permit only online sports wagering (New Hampshire, Tennessee, Wyoming, Connecticut, and North Dakota); and still others permit wagering in either format (Nevada, Arizona, New Jersey, West Virginia, Pennsylvania, Rhode Island, New York, Iowa, Oregon, Indiana, Illinois, Michigan, Colorado, Washington D.C., and Virginia). The states of Washington and South Dakota follow a mixed model allowing online sports wagering only when on site at a licensed casino. Some states that allow in-person sports wagering only permit such sports wagering at tribal casinos (North Dakota, Connecticut, South Dakota, Arizona, Washington, and North Carolina). Further, some states have placed restrictions on the type of sport for which gambling is permitted. Maryland, Louisiana, Florida, and Nebraska were moving toward enacting such legislation in late 2021 and early 2022. Idaho, Wisconsin, and Utah are the only states that, as of this writing, have not moved toward legalization. *See* ESPN, *United States of Sports Betting: An Updated Map of Where Every State Stands*, ESPN.COM (last visited Feb. 6, 2022) (last updated Dec. 2, 2021), available at https://www.espn.com/chalk/story/_/id/19740480/the-united-states-sports-betting-where-all-50-states-stand-legalization. *See also* Will Yakowicz, *Where is Sports Betting Legal? A Guide to All 50 States*, FORBES (Jan. 7, 2022), available at https://www.forbes.com/sites/willyakowicz/2022/01/07/where-is-sports-betting-legal-america-2022/?sh=765255ef2342.

87. *See* Hilary Russ, *U.S. Sports Leagues Could Reap $4.2 Billion a Year from Legal Betting: Survey*, REUTERS (Oct. 18, 2018), https://www.reuters.com/article/us-usa-gambling-sports/u-s-sports-leagues-could-reap-4-2-billion-a-year-from-legal-betting-survey-idUSKCN1MS1CT.

Moreover, leagues and clubs have begun forming partnerships directly with organizations in the gambling space. The NBA and WNBA were the first major American sports leagues to move aggressively in this space, naming MGM Resorts International as the league's official gaming partner in 2018.[88] MLB, MLS, and the NHL followed suit within a year, partnering with various gaming organizations.[89] The NFL, the longest holdout against joint ventures with gaming organizations, eventually did the same, naming Caesars Entertainment Corporation, FanDuel and DraftKings as official NFL betting partners.[90] Individual teams have formed gaming partnerships as well. Perhaps most notably, Monumental Sports — the parent company of the NBA's Washington Wizards, the WNBA's Washington Mystics, and the NHL's Washington Capitals — partnered with global sports gambling giant William Hill in 2021 to open the nation's first in-arena sports gambling facility (known colloquially as a "sports book") in Capital One Arena, where the Wizards and Capitals play.[91] Although in-arena sports books are common in other nations such as England and Australia, they were, until recently, unthinkable in the United States. As American sports organizations continue to gain comfort with sports gambling and the revenues it can produce, additional in-arena sports books are likely to open.

[2] Performance Enhancing Drugs

Athletic excellence is the foundation of professional sports. Extraordinary athletic feats and intense competition between elite athletes draw the spectators, advertisement dollars, and general societal interest that buoy the sports industry. When athletes use impermissible performance enhancing drugs, however, the integrity of that competition is called into question. Consequently, league commissioners often take action against the offending athlete in order to further the "best interests" of the game.

As early as the nineteenth century, athletes have been known to use performance enhancing drugs ("PED").[92] French cyclists of that era often ingested a mixture of

---

88. David Purdum, *What You Need to Know About the NBA's New Gambling Partnership*, ESPN (July 31, 2018), https://www.espn.com/chalk/story/_/id/24248120/gambling-need-know-nba-sports-betting-partnership.

89. *See MLB, MGM Announce Gaming Partnership*, MLB NEWS (Nov. 27, 2018), https://www.mlb.com/news/mlb-mgm-announce-gaming-partnership-c301163068#:~:text=The%20new%20multiyear%20agreement%20designates,Official%20Entertainment%20Partner%20of%20MLB.%22; *MLS Announces Multi-Year Gaming Partnership with MGM Resorts International*, MLS SOCCER NEWS (Mar. 19, 2019), https://www.mlssoccer.com/news/mls-announces-multi-year-gaming-partnership-mgm-resorts-international; Carol Schram, *The NHL Adds William Hill US as Its Third Sports Betting Partner*, FORBES (Mar. 29, 2019), https://www.forbes.com/sites/carolschram/2019/03/29/the-nhl-adds-william-hill-us-as-its-third-sports-betting-partner/?sh=6fc8690d45e2.

90. Darren Rovell, *NFL Announces Only Official Sports Betting* Partnerships, CHICAGO TRIBUNE (Apr. 17, 2021), https://www.chicagotribune.com/gambling/ct-aud-actnet-nfl-sports-betting-partnership-20210417-endtjelkuvax3pnwaaf4ccvhmm-story.html.

91. Adam Kilgore, *Capital One Arena Just Knocked Down the Final Wall Between Gambling and U.S. Pro Sports*, WASHINGTON POST (May 26, 2021), https://www.washingtonpost.com/sports/2021/05/26/capital-one-arena-sportsbook-william-hill/.

92. Phillip D. Harvey, *A Long History of Athletes Using Performance-Enhancing Drugs*, MIAMI HERALD (Feb. 9, 2018), https://www.miamiherald.com/living/health-fitness/article199386654.html.

wine and coca leaves (from which cocaine is derived) to boost endurance and stamina.[93] Performance enhancing drug use was not widely exposed in American professional sports, however, until 1960. In that year, a Sports Illustrated journalist wrote an article titled *Our Drug-Happy Athletes* exposing the widespread use of amphetamines, cocaine, and other drugs in professional sport.[94] Several years later, the Los Angeles Dodgers' team physician, Robert Kerlan, publicly predicted that "[t]he excessive and secretive use of drugs is likely to become a major athletic scandal, one that will shake public confidence in many sports...."[95] Although athletes generally insisted performance enhancing drug use was aberrant in professional sports, former New York Yankees pitcher Jim Bouton wrote openly in his groundbreaking 1970 baseball expose, *Ball Four*, about the rampant use of performance enhancing drugs — principally amphetamines, also known as "greenies" — in his team's clubhouse before games.[96] He has since explained that the drug use went well beyond the Yankees: "In the 1970s, half of the guys in the big leagues were taking greenies, and if we had steroids, we would have taken those, too."[97] Once steroids became available, baseball players did indeed turn to them. By the 1990s, MLB entered into what is now widely recognized as "The Steroids Era," during which time offensive production exploded across the league.[98] MLB, however, did not institute its random steroid testing program until 2003.[99] As the problem worsened and superstar players were implicated in doping allegations, MLB Commissioner Bud Selig in 2006 used his "best interests"

---

93. *Id.*

94. George Walsh, *Our Drug-Happy Athletes*, Sports Illustrated (Nov. 21, 1960), https://vault. si.com/vault/1960/11/21/our-drughappy-athletes.

95. *How We Got Here*, Sports Illustrated (Mar. 11, 2008), https://www.si.com/more-sports/ 2008/03/11/steroid-timeline.

96. Jim Bouton, Ball Four 81, 212 (1970).

97. *10 Burning Questions for Jim Bouton*, ESPN, http://www.espn.com/page2/s/questions/bouton. html.

98. *The Steroids Era*, ESPN (Dec. 5, 2012), https://www.espn.com/mlb/topics/_/page/the-steroids-era.

99. *Id.* Some commentators argue Commissioner Selig and other MLB officials were well aware of the growing PED pandemic gripping baseball. They theorize that MLB tolerated the PED use, because it fueled exciting play that thrilled fans and increased revenues. *See, e.g.*, Craig Calcaterra, *Bud Selig Is Still, Laughably, Pleading Ignorance About the Steroid Era*, NBC Sports (Dec. 6, 2016), https:// mlb.nbcsports.com/2016/12/06/bud-selig-is-still-laughably-pleading-ignorance-about-the-steroid-era/. For instance, during the 1998 season, St. Louis Cardinals player Mark McGwire and Chicago Cubs player Sammy Sosa both broke the MLB single-season home run record by a substantial margin and dueled to determine who would be first in the record books and who would be second. *The Steroids Era*, ESPN (Dec. 5, 2012), https://www.espn.com/mlb/topics/_/page/the-steroids-era. Selig celebrated the home run race, which drew tremendous national interest, despite allegations that both players were doping. *See* Scott Detrow, *In 'For the Good of the Game,' Bud Selig Tells of the MLB Steroid Era*, NPR (July 9, 2019), https://www.npr.org/2019/07/09/739505827/in-for-the-good-of-the-game-bud-selig-tells-of-the-mlb-steroid-era. That year, McGwire admitted to steroid use, but Sosa continues to deny it (despite the Cubs owner's refusal to invite Sosa to alumni events until he admits his steroid use). *Id.*

authority in appointing former United States Senator and prosecutor George Mitchell to investigate the use of performance enhancing drugs in MLB.[100]

After a 20-month investigation, Mitchell released his *Report to the Commissioner of Baseball of an Independent Investigation into the Illegal Use of Steroids and Other Performance Enhancing Substances by Players in Major League Baseball* (the "Mitchell Report").[101] The Mitchell Report established that a doping crisis existed in MLB. It named 89 players — including superstars such as Roger Clemens and Barry Bonds — alleged to have used performance enhancing drugs and suggested that a culture of doping existed throughout MLB.[102] Though no players were disciplined, the Mitchell Report supported Commissioner Selig's increased scrutiny with respect to performance enhancing drugs. That scrutiny bore substantial fruit when MLB identified Anthony Bosch, the founder of a Florida-based "anti-aging" clinic, as a major supplier of performance enhancing drugs to MLB players.[103] Bosch provided MLB with a "cache of material" that strongly suggested MLB players were doping, and Commissioner Selig imposed long-term suspensions on over a dozen players, including superstar Alex Rodriguez.[104]

MLB is not alone in its battle against performance enhancing drugs. All major American sports leagues have contended with performance enhancing drugs, and they all have policies banning their use. Each policy is collectively bargained between the league and the players' association. In the NBA, performance enhancing drug detection in the first instance triggers a 25-game suspension,[105] whereas in the WNBA, the first violation triggers a ten-game suspension.[106] In the NFL, a first-violation suspension ranges from two games to eight games depending on the nature of the violation;[107] in the NHL, a first-violation suspension is 20 games;[108] and in MLB, a first-violation suspension is 80 games.[109] In all of the leagues, repeated violations trigger longer suspensions and possible expulsion.

---

100. Andrew Brandt, *Where to Draw the Line: The Endless Search for a (Legal) Competitive Edge*, 28 Jeffrey S. Moorad Sports L.J. 319, 323 (2021).

101. *Id.*

102. *Id.*

103. Barry Boss & Rebecca Brodey, *Immaculate Suspension: Non-Analytical Positive Doping Violations from USADA to MLB*, 30 Ent. & Sports Law. 3 (2014).

104. *Id.* Rodriguez was initially suspended for 211 days, but he challenged the suspension with the MLBPA's help. At arbitration, his suspension was reduced to 162 days, which is the length of one MLB season. MLBPA v. Office of the Commissioner of Baseball, MLB Arbitration Panel Decision No. 131, 32–34 (Jan. 13, 2014).

105. NBA CBA, art. XXXIII, Sec. 9(b)(A).

106. WNBA CBA, Exhibit 2 WNBA Anti-Drug Program, Sec. 9(b)(A).

107. NFLPA, *Policy on Performance-Enhancing Substances*, at 8–9 (2020), https://nflpaweb.blob. core.windows.net/website/Departments/Salary-Cap-Agent-Admin/2020-Policy-on-Performance-Enhancing-Substances.pdf.

108. NHL CBA, art. 47, Sec. 7(a)(i).

109. MLB, *Joint Drug Prevention and Treatment Program*, 37–38 (2017), https://d39ba378-ae47-4003-86d3-147e4fa6e51b.filesusr.com/ugd/b0a4c2_df9222b1bea34634a60f154499aedcff.pdf.

§ 7.04 Antitrust Restrictions on League Governance

Although, as discussed throughout this chapter, commissioners typically have great authority in running their leagues, league governance is not entirely unchecked. Two realms of law are most relevant in this regard: labor law and antitrust law. Labor law and the collective bargaining agreements it gives rise to certainly play a role, which although touched on here, is more fully explored in Chapter 8. The following sections of this chapter will primarily explore antitrust law restrictions on league governance.

[A] Antitrust Law Basics

The purpose of antitrust law is to preserve economic competition in business.[110] The premise underlying this purpose is that "competition leads to the best economic, political, and social outcomes."[111] In the absence of competition, the theory goes, commercial entities can increase prices and reduce the quality of goods and services to the consuming public's detriment.[112] Antitrust principles, which have been embedded in American law for over 120 years, serve to prevent this outcome and promote consumer welfare. In 1890, the United States Congress passed the Sherman Antitrust Act,[113] and this statute remains perhaps the nation's most important antitrust legislation. Notably, the Sherman Act only applies to alleged anticompetitive activities that are connected to interstate commerce.[114]

The Sherman Act contains two principal sections: Section 1, which prohibits any "contract, combination … or conspiracy in restraint of trade or commerce"; and Section 2, which prohibits any "monopoliz[ation] or attempt to monopolize … trade or commerce."[115] Together, these sections create the core of American antitrust law and have been employed to challenge anticompetitive and monopolistic corporate behavior in scores of industries.

[B] The Unique Case of Commercial Competition in Sport

Each major professional sports league in the United States consists of many member clubs that work together to ensure unrivaled dominance in each league's respective

---

110. Jeremy Ulm, Comment, *Antitrust Changeup: How a Single Antitrust Reform Could Be a Home Run for Minor League Baseball Players*, 125 Dick. L. Rev. 227, 230 (2020).

111. *Id.*

112. *Id.*

113. Sherman Antitrust Act, 15 USC § 1, *et seq.* (1890).

114. *Id.* at § 1.

115. *Id.* at §§ 1–2.

sport.[116] As a result, each major league wields substantial market power in the multi-billion dollar sports industry.[117] This is the sort of monopolistic dominance antitrust law typically serves to check. Professional sports leagues, however, constitute a unique case.[118] In order to produce an attractive and sustainable product that appeals to fans, a league's clubs must work cooperatively.[119] This creates an unavoidable tension. One sports law scholar states, "[p]rofessional sports are built around competition, but the industry would not exist without collusion."[120] Consequently, antitrust law does not apply seamlessly in the professional sports industry.[121]

In most industries, a company would benefit from its rival going out of business. For instance, personal computing manufacturer Hewlett Packard executives would be pleased if the high quality of their products forced rivals Dell and Lenovo out of business. This is not the case with professional sports clubs. Consider one of the NFL's biggest rivalries: The Baltimore Ravens and the Pittsburgh Steelers. Each seeks to be more successful than the other on the field of play. The Ravens, however, would be *displeased* if league competition resulted in the Steelers going out of business. For the Ravens to stay in business, the club needs rivals against which to play. Without other clubs to play against, the Ravens would be out of business themselves. So, while professional sports clubs engage in unbridled competition on the field (or the court or the ice), they engage in restrained competition as a business necessity. As a federal district court judge explained, "On the playing field, of course, [professional sports clubs] must compete as hard as they can all the time. But it is not necessary and indeed it is unwise for all the teams to compete as hard as they can against each other in a business way."[122]

This restrained economic competition takes two principal forms. First, leagues often attempt to restrain clubs from moving into the geographic area in which an existing club is based so as to avoid either dividing a fan base or one club pilfering another club's fans. Second, leagues attempt to ensure some level of parity among member clubs even where some clubs are financially stronger than others. If the Ravens were able to acquire all of the league's best talent, and the Steelers and other clubs were so weak that the Ravens never lost a game for seasons on end, interest in NFL football would likely dwindle, and the Ravens, together with the league's other teams, would suffer economic decline.

In short, professional sports leagues have an interest in limiting economic competition among clubs so as to ensure competition on the playing surface. Antitrust

---

116. Nathaniel Grow, *Regulating Professional Sports Leagues*, 72 WASH. & LEE L. REV. 573 (2015).

117. *Id.* at 575.

118. *Id.* at 581.

119. *Id.*

120. Leah Farzin, *On the Antitrust Exemption for Professional Sports in the United States and Europe*, 22 JEFFREY S. MOORAD SPORTS L.J. 75, 75 (2015).

121. *Id.*

122. United States v. Nat'l Football League, 116 F. Supp. 319, 323 (E.D. Pa. 1953).

law, however, exists to prevent such limitation, creating a strange and dynamic relationship between antitrust law and sport.

[C] MLB's Antitrust Exemption

Major League Baseball is unique among professional sports leagues in that it enjoys antitrust immunity. This immunity is one of sports law's most notable quirks. It was born of case law in the early twentieth century and has persisted over the course of many decades despite its underlying reasoning being questioned and other professional sports leagues being denied the exemption.

The exemption took root in *Federal Baseball Club of Baltimore, Inc. v. National League of Professional Baseball Clubs*,[123] a 1922 United States Supreme Court case that ruled the Sherman Act did not apply to baseball.[124] The case involved the Federal League, a one-time rival of the American League and National League. The Federal Baseball Club of Baltimore, which had been part of the Federal League, alleged the American League and National League violated antitrust law by conspiring to destroy the Federal League, leaving the Baltimore Club as a team without a league.[125]

To determine whether the Sherman Act applied to professional baseball, the Court had to first determine whether professional baseball involved interstate commerce. Despite acknowledging that professional baseball competitions "must be arranged between clubs from different cities and States," the Court concluded that professional baseball did not constitute interstate commerce.[126] Rather, the Court concluded, "exhibitions of baseball ... are purely state affairs" and "the transport is a mere incident, not the essential thing."[127] As such, the Court held professional baseball was exempt from antitrust law.

In 1953, the United States Supreme Court had the opportunity in *Toolson v. New York Yankees*[128] to end the exemption. It elected not to do so, despite professional baseball having grown even more interstate in nature than it was when *Federal Baseball* was decided. The *Toolson* Court did not insist, as the *Federal Baseball* Court had, that professional baseball did not concern interstate commerce. Indeed, the Court drew no conclusion on that matter. Rather, the Court noted that the ruling had existed undisturbed for 30 years, and during that time, the baseball industry had developed "on the understanding that it was not subject to existing antitrust legislation."[129] The Court wrote that although Congress had ample opportunity to legisla-

---

123. 259 U.S. 200 (1922).
124. *Id.* at 208.
125. *Id.* at 207.
126. *Id.* at 208–09.
127. *Id.* at 208.
128. 346 U.S. 356 (1953).
129. *Id.* at 357.

tively overrule *Federal Baseball* during those 30 years, it had not done so, signaling Congress's satisfaction with the Court's determination.[130]

In the years following *Toolson*, the Supreme Court heard antitrust actions against leagues and organizing bodies in other sports, including boxing,[131] football,[132] and basketball.[133] In each of those cases, the Court found that the entities engaged in activities impacting interstate commerce and that the antitrust laws applied to their activities. In doing so, the Court established that MLB's antitrust exemption was a unique exemption applying only to that one league in that one sport and not to similarly situated leagues in other sports. The Court explicitly did so in *Flood v. Kuhn*,[134] a 1972 Supreme Court case in which MLB player Curt Flood challenged the "reserve clause" system, which bound players to the teams holding their rights.

In October of 1969, the Cardinals traded Flood to the Philadelphia Phillies, but he was not consulted about the trade and did not want to play for the Phillies.[135] He opposed the trade, and when the Commissioner would not void it, Flood filed an antitrust suit alleging baseball's policies, which prevented player movement among teams, were anticompetitive.[136] A federal district court dismissed Flood's suit, and both the Second Circuit and the United States Supreme Court affirmed. In its opinion, the Supreme Court acknowledged what it refused to acknowledge in *Federal Baseball* and *Toolson*: that "professional baseball . . . is engaged in interstate commerce."[137] The Court went on to hold that, nonetheless, baseball should remain exempt from antitrust scrutiny even though other sports similarly engaged in interstate commerce were not so exempt.[138] In doing so, it emphasized that Congress had allowed *Federal Baseball* and *Toolson* to stand for 50 years and expressed reluctance to overturn them judicially, given that the baseball industry had developed and expanded under the exemption "unhindered" for so long.[139] The Court recognized that some might regard this baseball-only exemption as "inconsistent, or illogical," and described it as an aberration, but ultimately insisted the "aberration is an established one."[140]

[1] An Unprincipled Approach?

From the start, the *Flood* case seemed like one in which the underlying goal was to protect the baseball industry at the expense of players and perhaps at the expense of a reasonable interpretation of the law. Professor Brad Snyder argues in his book,

---

130. *Id.*
131. United States v. Int'l Boxing Club of N.Y., Inc., 348 U.S. 236 (1955).
132. Radovich v. Nat'l Football League, 352 U.S. 445 (1957).
133. Haywood v. Nat'l Basketball Ass'n, 401 U.S. 1204 (1971).
134. 407 U.S. 258 (1972).
135. *Id.* at 265.
136. *Id.*
137. *Id.* at 282.
138. *Id.* at 284.
139. *Id.* at 283.
140. *Id.* at 282.

A Well-Paid Slave: Curt Flood's Fight for Free Agency in Professional Sports, that the general consensus at the time was that a Flood victory would weaken, and maybe destroy, professional baseball, and that the courts hearing the case were committed to not letting that happen.[141] Snyder notes that the District Court Judge who presided over the trial, Irving Ben Cooper, was a big baseball fan, making him a terrible draw for Flood. Cooper made his fandom for the game clear during the trial, at one point announcing a recess by saying "The Court announces a seventh-inning stretch" and at another point — at the end of a hearing — saying "You have thrown the ball to me. I hope I don't muff it."[142] Justice Blackmun, who wrote the Supreme Court's majority decision in the *Flood* case, was no less enamored of the game. Indeed, in one passage of his opinion, he listed, for no apparent reason, the names of dozens of former MLB players he described as having "provided tinder for recaptured thrills, for reminiscence and comparisons, and for conversation and anticipation in-season and off-season."[143] For many sports law scholars, this list symbolized commitment to protecting the sport no matter the merits. Indeed, sports law professor Roger Abrams devoted an entire law review article, titled *Blackmun's List*, to his criticism of the opinion.[144] Abrams writes that "although Blackmun took considerable time in his opinion to celebrate the national game, he could not have considered how the reserve system, which the Court's opinion upheld, affected the lives of the men he memorialized."[145]

Despite being roundly criticized as an unprincipled decision in which sport was elevated above law, the *Flood* case has never been overruled, and MLB still enjoys its antitrust immunity.

[2] The Curt Flood Act of 1998 and its Scope

Seventy-six years after the *Federal Baseball Club of Baltimore* decision and twenty-six years after the *Flood* decision reaffirming it, Congress stepped in to limit the expanse of MLB's antitrust immunity with the Curt Flood Act of 1998. The limitation is, however, in and of itself, limited. The Act permits MLB players to challenge MLB under antitrust law, but only with respect to matters "directly relating to or affecting employment of major league baseball players to play baseball at the major league level."[146] As such, it does not limit MLB's immunity to challenges against employment practices in the broad network of MLB-affiliated minor league clubs.

The 2017 case of *Miranda v. Selig*[147] is illustrative. There, a class of minor league baseball players sued MLB Commissioner Bud Selig and all MLB clubs, alleging that

---

141. Brad Snyder, A Well-Paid Slave: Curt Flood's Fight for Free Agency in Professional Sports (2007).

142. *Id.* at 129, 130.

143. *Flood*, 407 U.S. at 261.

144. Roger I. Abrams, *Blackmun's List*, 6 Va. Sports & Ent. L.J. 181 (2007).

145. *Id.* at 189.

146. Curt Flood Act, Pub. L. No. 105-297, 112 Stat. 2824 (1998).

147. 860 F.3d 1237 (9th Cir. 2017).

MLB's hiring and employment policies violate federal antitrust laws by "'restrain[ing] horizontal competition between and among' the MLB franchises and 'artificially and illegally depressing' minor league salaries."[148] Each MLB club employs minor league players under a uniform contract that binds each player to his club for seven seasons, precluding the player from joining another club of his own volition.[149] Plaintiffs contended that this restriction substantially depressed minor league salaries.[150] Defendants moved to dismiss, and the district court granted the motion.[151] The court reasoned that precedent had long established the "business of baseball" as exempt from federal antitrust laws and noted that "Congress specifically declined to take minor league baseball out of the scope of the exemption."[152] The Ninth Circuit affirmed, explaining that the employment of minor league players is "precisely the type of activity that falls within the antitrust exemption."[153] The court went on to emphasize that in passing the Curt Flood Act, Congress clearly intended to maintain the baseball exemption for the "employment of minor league players ... and the relationship between major and minor league baseball."[154]

Baseball's antitrust exemption has generally survived challenge outside of the minor league context as well.[155] For instance, in *City of San Jose v. Office of the Commissioner of Baseball*,[156] the City of San Jose ("San Jose") unsuccessfully alleged that MLB violated federal and state antitrust laws by delaying the Oakland Athletics' requested relocation from Oakland, California to San Jose, California. Under the MLB constitution, no club can move into another club's "designated operating territory" unless three-fourths of MLB's 30 clubs approve.[157] San Jose falls within the San Francisco Giants' territory, meaning the Athletics needed the approval to move.[158] Rather than hold a timely vote on whether to approve the relocation, MLB spent four years studying the implications of the proposed move.[159] San Jose sued, claiming the "delay was MLB's attempt to stymie the relocation and preserve the Giants' local monop-

---

148. *Id.* at 1239.
149. *Id.*
150. *Id.*
151. *Id.*
152. *Id.*
153. *Id.* at 1242.
154. *Id.* at 1243.
155. *See, e.g.*, Wyckoff v. Off. of Comm'r of Baseball, 705 F. App'x 26 (2d Cir. 2017) (holding because professional baseball scouts are involved in the business of baseball, their antitrust claim that MLB conspired to decrease competition in the labor market must be dismissed); Major League Baseball v. Crist, 331 F.3d 1177 (11th Cir. 2003) (prohibiting the Florida Attorney General from proceeding with an investigation of an alleged antitrust violation and holding that contraction of teams in baseball leagues is not subject to antitrust enforcement); Major League Baseball v. Butterworth, 181 F. Supp. 2d 1316 (N.D. Fla. 2001) (holding that a proposed contraction from 30 to 28 clubs for the 2002 season was within the "business of baseball" exemption from antitrust law).
156. 776 F.3d 686 (9th Cir. 2015).
157. *Id.* at 688.
158. *Id.*
159. *Id.*

oly."[160] The Office of the Commissioner moved to dismiss based on the antitrust exemption.[161] In attempting to escape the exemption's application, San Jose argued that the Supreme Court's *Flood* decision was limited to the facts of the case and applied only to the "reserve clause."[162] The court, however, rejected San Jose's argument and granted the motion to dismiss, writing that such a "drastic limitation on *Flood*'s scope is foreclosed by [] precedent" and that baseball's antitrust exemption extends beyond the reserve clause.[163] Indeed, the court held that "antitrust claims against MLB's franchise relocation policies are in the heartland of those precluded by *Flood*'s rationale."[164] Specifically, it noted that because Congress was "aware of the possibility that the baseball exemption could apply to franchise relocation ... declined to alter the status quo ... [and chose] to overturn the exemption in other areas," the baseball exemption necessarily applied to franchise relocation.[165]

While a minority of courts interpret baseball's antitrust exemption more narrowly,[166] the exemption broadly insulates baseball from antitrust challenge.[167]

[D] Sherman Act Section 1 and Concerted Action

Section 1 of the Sherman Antitrust Act, which prohibits "combinations" and "conspiracies" that restrain trade, requires concerted action to establish liability.[168] A single entity's actions do not qualify, because, by definition, a single entity alone cannot work in combination or conspire. As such, sports leagues that have not enjoyed MLB's antitrust immunity have long argued that they constitute single entities, legally incapable of violating antitrust laws.[169] Thus, courts tasked with adjudicating antitrust lawsuits against sports leagues have had to determine whether a league, made up of different clubs, is: 1) a collection of separate entities engaged in a joint venture; or 2) a single economic entity comprising multiple components.

---

160. *Id.*

161. *Id.*

162. *Id.* at 689.

163. *Id.*

164. *Id.* at 691.

165. *Id.*; *but see* Piazza v. Major League Baseball, 831 F. Supp. 420 (E.D. Pa. 1993) (holding that baseball's antitrust exemption "is limited to baseball's 'reserve system'" and is "inapplicable" to franchise sale and relocation disputes); Morsani v. Major League Baseball, 663 So. 2d 653 (Fla. Dist. App. Ct. 1995) (finding that decisions regarding sales of baseball franchises are not immune from antitrust scrutiny).

166. *See, e.g.,* Laumann v. NHL, 56 F. Supp. 3d 280, 297 (S.D. N.Y. 2014) (finding television broadcast contracts are not "central to the business of baseball" and opting not to apply the exemption in this realm); Postema v. National League of Professional Baseball Clubs, 799 F. Supp. 1475 (S.D. N.Y. 1992) (declining to grant antitrust immunity regarding relations with baseball umpires).

167. Matthew J. Mitten, Timothy Davis, N. Jeremi Duru & Barbara Osborne, Sports Law and Regulation: Cases, Materials, and Problems 400 (5th ed. 2020).

168. Sherman Antitrust Act, 15 U.S.C. § 1 (1890).

169. Nathaniel Grow, *There's No "I" in "League": Professional Sports Leagues and the Single Entity Defense*, 105 Mich. L. Rev. 183, 185 (2006).

[1] The Single-Entity Defense to Antitrust Challenges

The single-entity defense was first pressed in the sports context by the National Hockey League in the 1974 *San Francisco Seals, Ltd. v. NHL* case.[170] In that case, the court concluded the NHL was a single entity.[171] In subsequent litigation, district courts reached different decisions, sometimes accepting the single-entity defense and sometimes rejecting it.[172] At the Circuit level, however, courts have generally rejected the single-entity defense.[173] In *American Needle, Inc. v. NFL*,[174] the United States Supreme Court emphatically did so as well, unanimously holding that the NFL is not a single entity.[175] The Court made clear that clubs comprising the NFL are distinct economic entities, each with "its own name, colors, logo ... and intellectual property ... well known to millions of sports fans."[176] The Court framed the relevant issue as follows:

> The relevant inquiry [in this case] ... is whether there is a "contract, combination ... or conspiracy" amongst "separate economic actors pursuing separate economic interests" such that the agreement "deprives the marketplace of independent centers of decisionmaking" and therefore of "diversity of entrepreneurial interests," and thus of actual or potential competition.[177]

Answering the inquiry in the affirmative, the Court concluded that, although NFL clubs certainly share some interests and engage in joint ventures, such cooperation does not "transform[] concerted action into independent action."[178] While the decision applied only to the NFL, it dampened the prospects of any league with a traditional NFL-like operating structure — involving separately owned and operated clubs — sheltering from Sherman Act § 1 scrutiny under a single-entity argument.

---

170. 379 F. Supp. 966 (C.D. Cal. 1974). *See* Clifford Mendelsohn, *Fraser v. Major League Soccer: A New Window of Opportunity for the Single-Entity Defense in Professional Sports*, 10 SPORTS L.J. 69, 74 (2003).

171. *San Francisco Seals*, 379 F. Supp. at 970.

172. *See, e.g.*, Los Angeles Mem'l Coliseum Comm'n v. Nat'l Football League, 519 F. Supp. 581 (C.D. Cal. 1981) (rejecting the single-entity defense for the NFL); Chicago Pro. Sports Ltd. P'ship v. Nat'l Basketball Ass'n, 874 F. Supp. 844, 850 (N.D. Ill. 1995) (finding the NBA is a joint venture and not a single entity); Fraser v. Major League Soccer, L.L.C., 97 F. Supp. 2d 130 (D. Mass. 2000) (finding the MLS's single-entity defense valid).

173. *See, e.g.*, Am. Needle, Inc. v. Nat'l Football League, 560 U.S. 183 (2010) (denying the NFL's single-entity defense); Los Angeles Mem'l Coliseum Comm'n v. Nat'l Football League, 726 F.2d 1381 (9th Cir. 1984) (holding the NFL is not a "single entity" for the purposes of federal antitrust law). *But see* Fraser v. Major League Soccer, L.L.C., 284 F.3d 47 (1st Cir. 2002) (affirming the lower court decision that MLS is a single entity); Chicago Pro. Sports Ltd. P'ship v. Nat'l Basketball Ass'n, 95 F.3d 593 (7th Cir. 1996) (vacating the lower court decision while stating that NBA teams may not need complete unity of interest in broadcasting rights for it to be treated as a single entity).

174. 560 U.S. 183 (2010).

175. *Id.*

176. *Id.* at 187.

177. *Id.* at 195.

178. *Id.* at 199.

Leagues with a more centralized structure in which the league has a controlling stake in its clubs present a different circumstance. In that context, leagues can be legally recognized as single entities. Major League Soccer ("MLS") is one such league. Founded in 1995, MLS is America's premier professional soccer league. It was born long after the nation's other major professional sports leagues and adopted a different operating structure. The following description identifies many of MLS's distinctive characteristics:

> MLS retains significant centralized control over both league and individual team operations. MLS owns all of the teams that play in the league (a total of 12 prior to the start of 2002), as well as all intellectual property rights, tickets, supplied equipment, and broadcast rights. MLS sets the teams' schedules; negotiates all stadium leases and assumes all related liabilities; pays the salaries of referees and other league personnel; and supplies certain equipment.[179]

This organizational structure, in which "operator/investors" rather than "owners" run the clubs, allowed MLS to shelter from Sherman Act § 1 applicability in *Fraser v. Major League Soccer*.[180] In that case, eight players sued MLS asserting numerous claims including that "MLS and its operator/investors violated Sherman Act section 1 by agreeing not to compete for player services."[181] MLS defended against the suit with the single entity defense. Finding for MLS, the district court concluded that "MLS and its operator/investors were uniquely integrated and did comprise a single entity."[182] On appeal, the First Circuit drew a slightly different conclusion. It noted that although MLS' operator/investors are in many ways like traditional professional sports club owners, they "comprise a hybrid arrangement, somewhere between a single company ... and a cooperative arrangement between existing competitors."[183] After drawing that conclusion, however, the court noted that it did not need to solve the "single entity problem" in order to resolve the case and therefore left undisturbed the district court's conclusion that MLS is a single entity.[184]

---

179. 284 F.3d 47, 53 (1st Cir. 2002).

180. *Id.*

181. *Id.* at 54–55.

182. *Id.* at 56.

183. *Id.* at 58.

184. *Id.* at 59. To date, no court has concluded that MLS in not a single entity, but several commentators have questioned whether MLS will ultimately be able to retain single-entity status. *See, e.g.*, Brendan H. Ewing, *MLS Promotion! Can MLS's Single Entity Status Protect It from "Pro/Rel"?*, 25 JEFFREY S. MOORAD SPORTS L.J. 359, 360 (2018) (arguing that "given a proper plaintiff, MLS would no longer enjoy the single entity defense upon which its structure was based when it was founded."); Daniel S. MacMillan, *Is MLS Inherently Anticompetetive? The Strange Single-Entity Structure of Major League Soccer in Order to Legitimize American Professional Soccer*, 28 MARQ. SPORTS L. REV. 503, 504 (2018) (exploring "the nature of the single-entity status of MLS, the relationship that players have with teams and their owners, and the basis for a lawsuit that could potentially overturn the MLS single-entity structure for good").

[2] *Unreasonable Restraint of Trade Analysis*

Another key question in determining liability under section I of the Sherman Act is whether the challenged league rule *unreasonably* restrains trade.[185] In *NCAA v. Board of Regents*,[186] the United States Supreme Court recognized that professional sports leagues are unique and that creating athletic competition and maintaining a modicum of competitive balance requires some cooperation.[187] The Court explained that sports leagues produce and market competition and that "this would be completely ineffective if there were no rules on which the competitors agreed to create and define the competition to be marketed."[188] As such, when courts analyze Sherman Act § 1 antitrust claims against professional sports leagues, they apply a Rule of Reason analysis to determine whether the challenged restraint (*i.e.,* the league rule or policy at issue) amounts to a reasonable or unreasonable restraint.[189] The Rule of Reason analysis involves a case-by-case, factually intensive inquiry that compares the league rule's anti-competitive consequences with its business benefits and concludes whether the rule is reasonable notwithstanding those consequences.[190] On balance, if a restraint's procompetitive benefits outweigh its anticompetitive harm, the legal challenge fails unless demonstrably less restrictive means could have produced those benefits. A variety of league rules have triggered Sherman Act § 1 challenges and Rule of Reason analysis. These include rules regarding sales and purchases of clubs, geographical relocation of clubs, and clubs' rights over players. The latter category — clubs' rights over players — involves labor law considerations, which add a degree of complexity to the analysis. These cases will be discussed in Chapter 8 (Labor Law and Labor Relations) of this book. Let us, at this point, focus on cases applying the Rule of Reason analysis in disputes among clubs, which do not materially implicate player rights.

The NFL's Oakland Raiders' move to Los Angeles in 1982 produced one of the league's most intense antirust battles. In *Los Angeles Memorial Coliseum Commission v. NFL (Raiders I)*,[191] the Ninth Circuit's decision in the matter provides a helpful illustration of Rule of Reason analysis. As of 1977, the NFL's Rams franchise was based in Los Angeles, California, and its Raiders franchise was based in Oakland, California. In 1978, however, the Rams' owner, Carroll Rosenbloom, moved his team to Anaheim, California, roughly thirty miles away.[192] This left the stadium in which the Rams had been playing, the Los Angeles Coliseum, without a tenant.[193] The Raiders' owner, Al

---

185. Ryan M. Rodenberg, *The NBA's Latest Three Point Play*, 25 ENT. & SPORTS L. 14 (2008).
186. 468 U.S. 85 (1984).
187. *Id.* at 101.
188. *Id.*
189. *Id.* at 113.
190. James T. McKeown, *The Economics of Competitive Balance: Sports Antitrust Claims After American Needle*, 21 MARQ. SPORTS L. REV. 517, 529 (2011).
191. 726 F.2d 1381 (9th Cir. 1984).
192. *Id.* at 1384.
193. *Id.*

Davis, subsequently agreed to lease the Coliseum and attempted to move the Raiders to Los Angeles, which triggered Rule 4.3 of Article IV of the NFL Constitution.[194] That provision reads as follows:

> The League shall have exclusive control of the exhibition of football games by member clubs within the home territory of each member. No member club shall have the right to transfer its franchise or playing site to a different city … without prior approval by the affirmative vote of three-fourths of the existing member clubs of the League.[195]

As required by Article IV, NFL owners considered Davis' proposed move and unanimously voted (22–0) against approving the move.[196] Davis filed a lawsuit against the NFL alleging that Rule 4.3 created an illegal restraint on trade in violation of Sherman Act § 1.[197] The trial court agreed with Davis, and the NFL appealed.[198] On appeal, the NFL argued that Rule 4.3 is a reasonable restraint of trade and therefore lawful.[199] In engaging in a Rule of Reason analysis, the court noted, "NFL teams are not true competitors, nor can they be."[200] Consequently, it explained, "this lawsuit requires us to engage in the difficult task of analyzing the negative and positive effects of a business practice in an industry which does not readily fit into the antitrust context."[201] The court also explained that even if Rule 4.3's benefits for competition outweighed the Rule's harm to competition, the Rule would likely not pass muster if those benefits could be achieved through a less restrictive intervention.[202]

Balancing the procompetitive and anticompetitive effects of Rule 4.3, the appellate court concluded the trial court was correct in finding for Davis.[203] It recognized the NFL's proffered justifications for Rule 4.3, including that it aids the league in maintaining geographical balance and provides a check against a club moving into another club's home territory and siphoning off fans, thereby damaging the club that was first in the market.[204] It then weighed those proffered benefits against the Rule's competitive harms, chief among them, empowering owners to "insulate each team from competition within the NFL market, in essence allowing clubs to set monopoly prices to the detriment of the consuming public."[205] The court acknowledged that "NFL football requires some territorial restrictions in order both to encourage participation

---

194. *Id.* at 1385.
195. *Id.* at 1385 n.1.
196. *Id.* at 1385.
197. *Id.*
198. *Id.* at 1387.
199. *Id.* at 1390–94.
200. *Id.* at 1391.
201. *Id.*
202. *Id.* at 1396.
203. *Id.* at 1395.
204. *Id.*
205. *Id.*

in the venture and to secure each venturer the legitimate fruits of that participation."[206] It noted, however, that "the same goals can be achieved in a variety of ways which are less harmful to competition," and that substantial evidence therefore existed for the jury to conclude Rule 4.3 was not reasonably necessary to the production and sale of the NFL product.[207]

The Ninth Circuit's decision — which sets forth the paradigmatic Rule of Reason analytical framework still used today — gave Davis the victory. In 1982 Davis moved his club to Los Angeles. It bears noting that in making its decision, the Court assumed the Los Angeles market was large enough to support two professional football clubs, but history suggests that assumption may have been faulty. Within 15 years of the Raiders moving to Los Angeles, both clubs abandoned the area — the Raiders returned to Oakland, and the Rams moved to St. Louis. The Rams returned to Los Angeles in 2016, and the San Diego Chargers moved to Los Angeles the following year, once again situating two clubs in the area.

In 2020, the Raiders left Oakland for a second time, this time for Las Vegas. Like the Raiders' move to Los Angeles, their move to Las Vegas was proceeded by an antitrust suit. In *City of Oakland v. Oakland Raiders (Raiders III)*,[208] the City of Oakland sued the Raiders and the rest of the league, alleging that the club's decision to move, and the league's assent, violated § 1 of the Sherman Act.[209] The district court dismissed the complaint, and the Ninth Circuit affirmed.[210] The Circuit Court determined plaintiff had failed to allege a group boycott under the statute.[211] The court acknowledged that the vast majority of the NFL's 32 clubs voted to approve the Raiders' relocation to Las Vegas, but emphasized that the near-unanimous vote did not constitute a boycott.[212] The court held that the boycott was Oakland's alone, and "[c]ollective action in support of an individual boycott is not the same as a group boycott."[213] The decision cleared the path for the club's third relocation in 40 years.

[E] Sherman Act Section 2 and the Phenomenon of Upstart Leagues

Whereas Sherman Act § 1 regulates concerted action, Sherman Act § 2 regulates unilateral action and monopolization. As such, in the sports industry, Sherman Act § 2 comes into play most often when an upstart league accuses an established league of exercising monopoly power. Monopolization under Sherman Act § 2 requires:

---

206. *Id.* at 1396.
207. *Id.*
208. 445 F. Supp. 3d 587 (N.D. Cal. 2020).
209. *Id.* at 591.
210. City of Oakland v. Oakland Raiders, 20 F.4th 441 (9th Cir. 2021).
211. *Id.* at 448.
212. *Id.* at 454.
213. *Id.* at 453.

"1) the possession of monopoly power in the relevant market and (2) the willful acquisition or maintenance of that power as distinguished from growth or development as a consequence of a superior product, business acumen, or historic accident."[214]

Over the past 50 years, the most significant Section 2 antitrust challenge involved the United States Football League's attempt in the 1980s to join the NFL as a force on the American professional football landscape. The USFL was founded in 1981 as a spring football league.[215] USFL organizers did not initially intend to directly challenge the NFL (which plays in the fall) for viewers but ultimately established a major league that competed with the NFL for football playing talent. The USFL's first season of competition, 1983, produced mixed results. The league showcased some of the previous college football season's brightest stars, attracted substantial media attention, and, at least early in the season, enjoyed television rating similar to the NFL's fall ratings.[216] The league's second season revealed instability with several clubs moving to new cities and some club owners selling their clubs to new investors.[217] Some new club owners advanced an aggressive business strategy to pressure the NFL into a merger.[218] The plan involved establishing franchises in non-NFL cities, playing in the fall, and directly challenging the NFL in hopes that the NFL would choose to merge rather than fight.[219] In 1984, while pursuing this business strategy, the USFL sued the NFL under Sherman Act § 2 for illegal monopolization of the professional football market.[220]

At trial, the jury found for the USFL in some regards, noting that the NFL increased roster sizes, drafted USFL players, and attempted to "'co-opt' USFL club owners."[221] The jury, however, rejected the claims "'at the heart of the [USFL's] case'" — that the NFL unlawfully arranged with the three major television networks, ABC, CBS, and NBC, to only broadcast professional football games if they were NFL games, thus excluding all competitors.[222] In doing so, it rejected the USFL's requested injunctive relief: membership in the NFL and separation of the NFL into two leagues each of which would be limited to being shown on one network.[223] The USFL appealed. The Second Circuit, faced with determining whether the district court erred in not finding that the NFL's alleged "three-network 'tie-up'" violated Sherman Act § 2,[224] concluded the district court did not err.[225]

---

214. United States v. Grinnell Corp., 384 U.S. 563, 570–71 (1966).

215. United States Football League v. NFL, 842 F.2d 1335, 1350 (2d Cir. 1988).

216. *Id.* at 1351.

217. *Id.*

218. *Id.*

219. *Id.* at 1351–52.

220. *Id.* at 1352.

221. *Id.* at 1353.

222. *Id.* at 1341.

223. *Id.* Notably, the jury did award the USFL $1 in nominal damages (the $1 was trebled to $3, as is the norm with antitrust awards), which the court matter-of-factly noted was "no consolation for the USFL." *Id.*

224. *Id.* at 1348.

225. *Id.* at 1380.

With respect to the networks, the Second Circuit affirmed the trial court's determination that no monopolization occurred.[226] It also emphasized that at the time of the trial, the NFL's contracts with each of the networks had expired, meaning there was "free competition between the NFL's and the USFL's respective products."[227] Each network was free to contract with the league of their choice, and their decisions to contract with the NFL — whether because they believed the NFL's product to be superior, as a consequence of historical accident, or for other reasons — did not, in the court's view, support a Sherman Act § 2 claim.[228] In 1985, the USFL folded after having been unsuccessful in forcing a merger with the NFL through either its business practices or its Sherman Act § 2 lawsuit.

---

226. *Id.* at 1379.
227. *Id.*
228. *Id.* at 1380.

Part IV

Professional Athletes

Chapter 8

Labor Law, Labor Relations and Collective Bargaining

§ 8.01 Introduction

The sports industry, like any other industry, relies on labor. In the sports industry, the principal laborers are the athletes, without whom the industry could not exist. In the early days of professional sports, like in the early days of American labor, workers received few protections and were often exploited. In 1935, however, Congress intervened with the National Labor Relations Act ("NLRA"), which along with several amendments affords workers protections that did not previously exist.[1] NLRA § 7 sets forth the statute's key provisions with respect to workers' rights: 1) the right to unionize; 2) the right to bargain as a collective; and 3) the right to engage in concerted activities, such as strikes.[2] The National Labor Relations Board ("NLRB") enforces the NLRA's provisions and prohibits employers from engaging in unfair labor practices that interfere with workers' rights guaranteed by those provisions.[3] Importantly, the NLRA protects employers as well, empowering them, among other things, to lock employees out under certain circumstances.[4] The NLRA's provisions, taken together, are designed to encourage and incentivize collective bargaining.

This chapter explores the origins and scope of collective bargaining under the NLRA as well as employer and employee rights in the collective bargaining context. In addition, this chapter discusses labor arbitration in sports. The chapter also examines the statutory and non-statutory labor exemptions from antitrust law.

---

1. 29 U.S.C. §§ 151–169 (1935).

2. Benjamin J. Hogan, *Awakening the Spirit of the NLRA: The Future of Concerted Activity Through Social Media*, 118 W. Va. L. Rev. 841, 848 (2015).

3. *What We Do*, National Labor Relations Board, https://www.nlrb.gov/about-nlrb/what-we-do (last visited May 4, 2022).

4. *See, e.g.*, CII Carbon, LLC, 331 N.L.R.B. 1157 (2000) (finding lockout appropriate when imposed to prevent possible sabotage of equipment and contamination of products); Boehringer Ingelheim Vetmedica, Inc., 350 N.L.R.B. 678 (2007) (finding lockout appropriate to safeguard public safety).

§ 8.02 The Origin of Collective Bargaining in Professional Sports

Federal labor law is triggered by interstate activity. That is, the NLRB will only exercise jurisdiction over employers that engage in interstate commerce that "exceeds a minimal level."[5] For decades after the NLRB was established in 1935, it did not explicitly recognize professional sports as interstate activity meriting regulation. That changed, however, in 1969 when umpires employed by the American League of Professional Baseball Clubs sought to unionize. In *The American League of Professional Baseball Clubs and Ass'n of National Baseball League Umpires*,[6] the NLRB began its opinion by acknowledging that its jurisdiction is based on the United States Constitution's Commerce Clause.[7] It then noted that, although the United States Supreme Court in the 1922 *Federal Baseball Club of Baltimore v. National League of Professional Baseball Clubs*[8] case found that professional baseball was not interstate in nature, subsequent cases clearly assumed the interstate nature of baseball and other professional sports.[9] The NLRB noted that "millions of dollars of interstate commerce are involved in [professional baseball's] normal business operations" and that future disputes in the industry "will be national in scope, radiating their impact far beyond individual State boundaries."[10] The defendant argued that professional baseball's "internal self-regulation" was sufficient to address any disputes between umpires and the league. The NLRB found otherwise, writing that asserting jurisdiction over professional baseball would "best effectuate the mandates of the [NLRA], as well as national labor policy."[11] In reaching this conclusion, the NLRB paved the way for umpires to unionize and further strengthened the ground upon which the then-recently founded unions of professional athletes — the NBPA, NFLPA, MLBPA, and NHLPA — stood.

Once athletes were granted the right to unionize and enter collective bargaining agreements with their respective leagues, players' power dramatically increased vis-a-vis their leagues. With the ability to bargain collectively, athletes were able to make demands that had previously been out of reach. While the benefits of collective bargaining to athletes are varied, as discussed *infra*, the power of unionization is perhaps best illustrated by juxtaposing Major League Baseball players with minor league baseball players with respect to compensation. In the years since MLB players unionized,

5. *About NLRB*, NATIONAL LABOR RELATIONS BOARD, https://www.nlrb.gov/about-nlrb/rights-we-protect/the-law/jurisdictional-standards (last visited Sept. 9, 2021).

6. Am. League of Pro. Baseball Clubs & Ass'n of Nat'l Baseball League Umpires, 180 N.L.R.B. 190 (1969).

7. *Id.* at 190.

8. 259 U.S. 200 (1922).

9. 180 N.L.R.B. at 190.

10. *Id.* at 192.

11. *Id.* at 191.

minimum MLB salaries have increased by over 5,000%.[12] During that same timespan, minimum salaries for minor league players have increased by a relatively miniscule 100%.[13] MLB players' gains did not come all at once, and their gains stretch well beyond money, but this comparison between unionized athletes and non-unionized athletes in the same sport highlights the importance of labor law protections and employees' ability to collectively bargain.

§ 8.03 Exclusive Bargaining Unit

No union can impose itself on a group of athletes. Rather, athletes must choose to unionize, by majority vote. Under NLRB § 9(a), once a group of athletes selects a union, the union can serve as the "exclusive representative[] of all the employees in [the] unit for the purposes of collective bargaining...."[14] The union that serves as the "exclusive representative" for a group of employees enjoys a great deal of power, and with this power comes a duty of fair representation.[15] In *Steele v. Louisville & N.R. Co.*,[16] the United States Supreme Court concluded the NLRA demands that any union represent all members.[17] It may not advance some members' interests at the expense of others.

This duty of fair representation is critically important, because the agreements a union forges take precedence over any individual agreements a particular employee enters with an employer. Indeed, as the United States Supreme Court explained in 1944 in *J.I. Case Co. v. NLRB*:[18]

> The very purpose of providing by statute for the collective agreement is to supersede the terms of separate agreements of employees with terms which reflect the strength and bargaining power and serve the welfare of the group. Its benefits and advantages are open to every employee of the represented unit, whatever the type or terms of his pre-existing contract of employment.[19]

In most industries, unions eliminate individual employee bargaining altogether, which as noted above they are empowered to do under NLRB § 9(a). The sports industry, however, is different. In the sports industry, collective bargaining agreements ("CBA") create baselines applicable to all players, but they also allow for individual players to negotiate separate agreements provided those agreements do not conflict

---

12. MITTEN, DAVIS, DURU & OSBOURNE, SPORTS LAW AND REGULATION: CASES, MATERIALS, AND PROBLEMS 479 (5th ed., 2020).

13. *Id.*

14. 29 U.S.C. § 159(a).

15. Lee M. Modjeska, *The Supreme Court and the Duty of Fair Representation*, 7 OHIO ST. J. DISP. RESOL. 1, 2–3 (1991).

16. 323 U.S. 192 (1944).

17. *Id.* at 207.

18. 321 U.S. 332 (1944).

19. *Id.* at 338.

with terms of the CBA. For instance, the NFL's 2021 minimum rookie salary, as established in the CBA, is $660,000.[20] No rookie may receive a salary lower than that, but under the CBA, every rookie is permitted to negotiate for a salary higher than that, and sought-after rookies do so. For instance, the first selection in the 2021 NFL draft, quarterback Trevor Lawrence, negotiated for a four-year contract worth $36.8 million with the NFL's Jacksonville Jaguars — well above the rookie minimum.[21]

Although individual players have a limited right to negotiate contractual terms that do not conflict with the CBA, the players' union — vested with exclusive bargaining authority — is generally responsible for negotiating the terms that govern players' employment relationships with their club.[22]

§ 8.04 Scope of Collective Bargaining

Not all issues that may conceivably arise between an employer and employees are subject to negotiation under labor law, but many are. Most notably, "wages, hours, and other terms and conditions of employment" are subject to negotiation.[23] The NLRA identifies these topics as mandatory subjects of bargaining.[24] This means that if either an employer or employees request to bargain over wages, hours, or working conditions, the other party must agree to bargain over them and must do so in good faith.[25] If the other party refuses or fails to do so, it is deemed as having engaged in an unfair labor practice in violation of NLRA § 8.[26]

Unsurprisingly, labor and management often disagree on what exactly is encompassed by the terms "wages," "hours," and "working conditions." The term "wages" is generally understood to be broader than the amount of money received for a period of work and includes items such as bonuses and fringe benefits.[27] And the term "working conditions" is generally understood to include elements impacting the work environment such as safety rules.[28] Moreover, courts tend to consider leagues' overarching policies bearing on "wages, hours, and other terms and conditions of

---

20. Joel Corry, *Agent's Take: 2021 NFL Rookie Contract Projections for Key Round 1 Picks, Plus a Rookie Wage Scale Explainer*, CBS SPORTS (May 7, 2022), https://www.cbssports.com/nfl/news/agents-take-2021-nfl-rookie-contract-projections-for-key-round-1-picks-plus-a-rookie-wage-scale-explainer/.

21. *Id.*

22. Gabe Feldman, *Collective Bargaining in Professional Sports: The Duel Between Players and Owners and Labor Law and Antitrust Law*, THE OXFORD HANDBOOK OF AM. SPORTS L. (Sept. 2017), https://www.oxfordhandbooks.com/view/10.1093/oxfordhb/9780190465957.001.0001/oxfordhb-978 0190465957-e-10?print=pdf.

23. 29 U.S.C. § 158(d).

24. *Id.*

25. *Id.*

26. *Id.*

27. *Basic Guide to the National Labor Relations Act*, NAT'L LAB. REL. BOARD (1997), https://www.nlrb.gov/sites/default/files/attachments/basic-page/node-3024/basicguide.pdf.

28. *Id.*

employment" to constitute mandatory subjects of collective bargaining. *Wood v. National Basketball Association*[29] is illustrative. In that case, involving standout college basketball player Leon Wood's lawsuit against the NBA, the Second Circuit found that matters that do not regard particular players' contracts but instead frame the economic context in which players are employed qualified as mandatory subjects of collective bargaining.[30] For instance, it held that revenue sharing policies and policies regarding the amateur draft are mandatory subjects, as:

> [e]ach of them is intimately related to "wages, hours, and other terms and conditions of employment." Indeed, it is precisely because of [these policies'] direct relationship to wages and conditions of employment that such matters are so controversial and so much the focus of bargaining in professional sports.[31]

The court in *Silverman v. Major League Baseball Player Relations Committee*,[32] which involved allegations that Major League Baseball violated its duty to bargain in good faith with the MLBPA, similarly viewed "wages, hours, and other terms and conditions of employment" expansively. It found that the league's free agency system, which set out the rules involving player movement among clubs, impacted player "wages, hours, and other terms and conditions of employment" and was therefore a mandatory subject of collective bargaining.[33]

While mandatory subjects of collective bargaining must be bargained over if at least one party desires it, illegal subjects of bargaining may not be bargained over, *even if both parties desire it*.[34] For instance, suppose an employer and employees sought to bargain about the structure of a compensation system that provided perks based on skin color. Because racial employment discrimination is illegal, this would be an illegal subject of bargaining under the NLRA. Subjects of bargaining that are neither mandatory nor illegal are known as permissive subjects of bargaining.[35] An employer and employees may choose to negotiate over permissive subjects of bargaining, but neither side is required to do so.[36]

§ 8.05 Principal Subjects of Collective Bargaining

Over the years, professional sports leagues and their respective unions have collectively bargained over both mandatory and permissive subjects. During the early

---

29. 809 F.2d 954 (2d Cir. 1987).
30. *Id.* at 962.
31. *Id.*
32. 880 F. Supp. 246 (S.D.N.Y. 1995).
33. *Id.* at 257.
34. *Basic Guide to the National Labor Relations Act, supra* note 27.
35. *Id.*
36. *Id.*

days of collective bargaining, negotiations tended to focus largely on baseline protections, such as job security, health benefits, minimum compensation thresholds, and pensions.[37] Those issues remain critical to collective bargaining negotiations, but as the sports industry has evolved, collective bargaining has increasingly involved discussions regarding *maximum* salaries and players' ability to determine the clubs for which they play. Indeed, maximum salaries and player mobility are now pivotal to collective bargaining negotiations, and the manner in which leagues and unions generally address these issue demands brief exploration.

[A] Maximum Salaries

Once players became able, through collective bargaining, to establish minimum salaries and as those salaries began to rise, club owners grew increasingly concerned. Higher salaries meant lower profit margins and potential financial instability. In addition, it created the possibility that the wealthiest owners might be able, through lavish spending, to purchase the best talent and create competitive imbalance within a league. Such competitive imbalance could, ultimately, result in some clubs being driven out of the league and the league as whole, therefore, suffering. In 1984, the NBA and NBPA were the first major American sports league and union to institute any sort of maximum spending salary threshold through collective bargaining, and they did so in the form of a salary cap.[38] The NBPA was reluctant, but when presented with the league's troubling financial picture, it agreed with the NBA to put a limit on salaries.[39] This NBA salary cap was — understandably, as it was the first of its kind — relatively porous, which allowed for manipulation.[40] The NBA's subsequent iterations of its salary cap have been more rigid, but exceptions and workarounds exist.[41]

A decade after the NBA implemented its salary cap, the NFL implemented a salary cap based on the same basic principles: restraining salaries to maintain profit margins and competitive balance.[42] MLB has opted against implementing a salary cap, but has instead instituted a tax — first called a "luxury tax" and now called a "competitive balance tax" — on clubs that exceed a certain threshold for salary spending.[43] The

---

37. *See* C. Peter Goplerud III, *Collective Bargaining in the National Football League: A Historical and Comparative Analysis*, 4 JEFFREY S. MOORAD SPORTS L.J. 13, 13–16 (1997) (detailing the early days of NFL collective bargaining).

38. Paul D. Staudohar, *Salary Caps in Professional Team Sports*, U.S. BUREAU OF LABOR STATISTICS (Spring 1998), https://www.bls.gov/opub/mlr/cwc/salary-caps-in-professional-team-sports.pdf.

39. *Larry Coon's NBA Salary Cap FAQ*, http://www.cbafaq.com/salarycap.htm#Q5 (last visited Sept. 10, 2021).

40. *Id.*

41. *Id.*

42. Aaron Tallent, *The NFL Salary Cap Turns 25: How It Began and Where It Is Now*, ATHLON SPORTS (Aug. 9, 2019), https://athlonsports.com/nfl/nfl-salary-cap-turns-25-matter-survival-standard-operating-procedure.

43. *Competitive Balance Tax*, MLB, https://www.mlb.com/glossary/transactions/competitive-balance-tax (last visited Sept. 10, 2021). The MLB tax has not dissuaded clubs willing to pay the tax,

NHL held out against a maximum salary spending threshold longer than any major American professional sports league, but after a nearly year-long work stoppage after the 2004 season, the NHL and NHLPA agreed to a salary cap as a part of a new CBA between the parties.[44] MLS, the newest league on the major American professional sports landscape, also employs a salary cap, which resulted from collective bargaining with the MLSPA.

[B] Player Freedom of Movement

From the earliest days of professional sport in the United States and for decades going forward, players had very little say in where and for whom they played. Clubs held a player's rights through various means, including the "reserve system."[45] This system was first established in 1879 in the National League (which would merge with the American League in 1903 to become Major League Baseball).[46] Prior to the reserve system's enactment, there was little stability in the National League, with players freely moving from team to team throughout a season in pursuit of higher pay.[47] The reserve system thwarted this practice by way of contract. All of the league's teams agreed to utilize the same standard contract in signing players, and the contract included a "reserve clause," which reserved for the club the rights to a player.[48] Specifically, the clause provided that upon the contract's expiration, the club had an option to renew the contract, and because the previous contract included the reserve clause, the new one did as well, essentially obligating a player to a club in perpetuity.[49]

In 1901, Nap Lajoie, one of the best players in MLB history, famously challenged the reserve clause when his five-year contract with the Philadelphia Phillies came to an end. Lajoie wanted to play for the cross-town Philadelphia Athletics rather than

---

such as the New York Yankees and Boston Red Sox, from outspending financially weaker clubs by a three to one or four to one margin. This extreme disparity has presented a great challenge for the financially weaker clubs, but in confronting that challenge, one such club, the Oakland Athletics, created innovations that changed baseball and all of professional sports. Athletics general manager Billy Beane began aggressively leveraging statistics to exploit inefficiencies in the market for players, allowing him to identify and sign players who other clubs undervalued. With this guiding philosophy, Beane constructed competitive rosters for a fraction of what the most freely spending MLB clubs spent. Bestselling author Michael Lewis popularized Beane's approach in the book *Moneyball*, and other MLB clubs soon began using his methods. Player evaluation in all sports is now far more statistically driven, thanks in large part to Beane's innovations.

44. Jodi Kaufman, *The NHL Salary Cap — History and a Refresher from Jodi Kaufman*, LIGHTNING INSIDER (Dec. 3, 2020), https://lightninginsider.com/index.php/locker-room/commentary/1245-the-nhl-salary-cap-history-and-a-refersher-from-jodi-kaufman.

45. Staudohar, *supra* note 38.

46. Edmund P. Edmonds, *Arthur Soden's Legacy: The Origins and Early History of Baseball's Reserve System*, 5 ALB. GOV'T L. REV. 38, 48 (2012); *Nat'l League of Baseball is Founded*, HISTORY.COM (Jan. 30, 2020), https://www.history.com/this-day-in-history/national-league-of-baseball-is-founded.

47. Edmonds, *supra* note 46, at 43.

48. *Id.* at 49–50.

49. *Id.*

the Phillies and signed a contract with that club.[50] The Phillies owner, however, sought an injunction to prevent Lajoie from playing for the Athletics, citing the reserve clause in Lajoie's contract.[51] The trial court denied the injunction, but the Pennsylvania Supreme Court, in *Philadelphia Ball Club, Ltd. v. Lajoie*,[52] ultimately reversed, finding "the provisions of the contract reasonable" and prohibiting Lajoie from playing for the Athletics.[53] This proved to be a landmark decision, cementing the validity of the reserve system in professional baseball. Under the system, although clubs could trade or release players, players were largely powerless to chart their own paths.[54] This consequently frustrated market competition and artificially capped player salaries. The system obviously inured to the economic benefit of club owners, and as other professional sports leagues were founded and developed, club owners in those leagues adopted similarly restrictive employment systems.[55]

In their efforts to reduce restrictions on mobility, players in some leagues eventually turned to antitrust lawsuits to extricate themselves from reserve clauses and had mixed success, as discussed at length in Chapter 7.[56] MLB players had no such option due to MLB's longstanding antitrust exemption, reinforced in the United States Supreme Court's 1972 *Flood v. Kuhn*[57] decision (also discussed in Chapter 7).[58] In 1976, however, two MLB players — Andy Messersmith and Dave McNally — successfully challenged the reserve system on contract grounds in an arbitration, paving the way for free agency in baseball.[59] Messersmith and McNally completed the 1974 MLB season with the Los Angeles Dodgers and Montreal Expos (which have since become the Washington Nationals), respectively.[60] Both players, however, refused to execute new contracts with their respective clubs for the 1975 season, and argued that because they did not sign new contracts, their clubs' right to their services would lapse after that 1975 season.[61] MLB, on the other hand, argued that the previously signed contract containing the "right of renewal" language entitled the club to "renew the contract in successive years ... so long as the Player is alive and the Club has duly discharged

50. Philadelphia Ball Club, Ltd. v. Lajoie, 202 Pa. 210 (Pa. 1902).

51. *Id.* at 215.

52. 202 Pa. 210 (Pa. 1902).

53. *Id.* at 222.

54. *Id.*

55. *See, e.g.,* Alvin Dominique, *NFL History: The Road to Free Agency,* BLEACHER REPORT (Apr. 17, 2018), https://bleacherreport.com/articles/18183-nfl-history-the-road-to-free-agency (stating that the NFL initially used a "reserve" system similar to the MLB).

56. *Staudohar, supra* note 38.

57. 407 U.S. 258 (1972).

58. *Id.*

59. National & American League Professional Baseball Clubs v. MLBPA, 66 Lab. Arb. Rep. (BNA) 101 (1976).

60. Mike Axisa, *On This Date 40 Years Ago: Free Agency Comes to MLB,* CBS SPORTS (Dec. 23, 2015), https://www.cbssports.com/mlb/news/on-this-date-40-years-ago-free-agency-comes-to-mlb/.

61. *See* Joseph Durso, *Arbitrator Frees 2 Baseball Stars,* N.Y. TIMES (Dec. 24, 1975), https://www.nytimes.com/1975/12/24/archives/arbitrator-frees-2-baseball-stars-arbitrator-frees-mcnally-and.html.

all conditions required of it."[62] Arbitrator Peter Seitz sided with the players, explaining that he found great difficulty in assuming such perpetual obligation "in respect of a contract providing for the rendition of personal services in which one would expect a more explicit expression of intention."[63]

While the outcome of the Messersmith and McNally arbitration was historic and momentous, the most robust tools at the disposal of MLB players as well as players in other major American sports leagues in securing freedom of movement have been collective bargaining agreements. Collective bargaining has provided players the opportunity to negotiate the contours of free agency as well as the potential to make mobility-related concessions in exchange for gains in other realms of their employment arrangement. As such, player mobility has become a key component of collective bargaining negotiations.[64] All of the major American professional sports leagues have free agency rules that have been collectively agreed to by the owners and the players.[65] Similarly, leagues have draft processes, resulting from collective bargaining, through which clubs select amateur players.[66]

§ 8.06 The Uniform Player Contract

Through collective bargaining, players and owners generally agree to a set of provisions that constitute required elements of every contract binding a player to a club. Taken together, these provisions constitute a league's Uniform Player Contract. The Uniform Player Contract contains mandatory clauses that cannot be eliminated from any particular individual contract between a club and a player.[67] For instance, Uniform Player Contracts generally regulate the use of both recreational drugs and performance enhancing drugs.[68] As such, an individual player and an individual club may not agree to a drug-use provision of their own making that is not in keeping with the Uniform Player Contract.

---

62. National & American League Professional Baseball Clubs v. MLBPA, 66 Lab. Arb. Rep. (BNA) 101 (1976).

63. *Id.*

64. *See* Jon Shelton, *How Free Agency Changed the Course of Baseball's Labor History*, IN THE TIMES (Dec. 23, 2015), https://inthesetimes.com/article/todays-baseball-salaries-are-the-result-of-a-labor-struggle.

65. *See, e.g.*, 2020 NFL CBA, art. 9; 2017 NBA CBA, art. XI; 2017 MLB CBA, art. XX; 2012 NHL CBA, art. 10.

66. *Id.*

67. *See, e.g.*, 2017 NBA CBA, art. II; 2017 MLB CBA, art. III, appendix A.

68. *See, e.g.*, 2017 NBA CBA, art. II, sec. 4 (permitting termination of a player's contract for use of any Prohibited Substance or controlled substance); 2017 MLB CBA, art. III, appendix A (requiring the club and the player to agree to "abide by and comply with" all rules and regulations, including those regarding the prohibited substances).

That which is not established in the Uniform Player Contract, however, is left to individual negotiation.[69] For example, as long as a salary is within the bounds of any collectively bargained salary restrictions (whether with respect to a floor or a ceiling), an individual player and club can mutually agree to what they deem acceptable. Thus, 2021 rookie quarterback Trevor Lawrence was able to negotiate for his aforementioned $36.8 million dollar contract with the Jacksonville Jaguars, even though it far exceeded the CBA's rookie minimum salary. Specific bonus arrangements, no-trade clauses, and restrictions on personal conduct (beyond what the Uniform Player Contract requires) are also generally fair game for individual negotiation.[70]

§ 8.07 Concerted Action

Collective bargaining does not always seamlessly result in a collective bargaining agreement. There are often substantial obstacles along the way, and parties sometimes reach a negotiating impasse, the nuances of which are discussed in § 8.11, *infra*. When collective bargaining fails, the parties are permitted under NLRA § 7 to engage in concerted action as a means of exerting economic pressure.[71] Such concerted action often takes the form of strikes (by the players) or lockouts (by the clubs). The following subsections of this chapter describe both strikes and lockouts and discuss means through which players and owners brace financially for a work stoppage.

[A] Strikes and Lockouts

A strike in the professional athletics context involves unionized players refusing to participate in team activities, including games, until they obtain concessions from their employing clubs. A variety of player grievances can motivate a strike, but the grievances generally revolve around economic terms. For instance, MLB players have gone on strike five times in league history, and money has been at the heart of each strike. The strikes twice involved pensions and binding salary arbitration, twice involved free agent compensation, and once involved a proposed salary cap.[72] The threat of strike is an important tool that sports unions can use in getting club owners to the negotiating table. Importantly, however, the right to strike does not free players from the obligation to bargain in good faith leading up to a strike.[73] Indeed, even

---

69. *See Contract Types*, CBA BREAKDOWN, https://cbabreakdown.com/contract-types (last visited Sept. 10, 2021) (describing various types of NBA contracts and the ability for players to negotiate terms beyond the Uniform Player Contract).

70. *See* Corry, *supra* note 20.

71. 29 U.S.C. § 157.

72. *Pro Sports Lockouts and Strikes Fast Facts*, CNN.COM (Dec. 4, 2021), https://www.cnn.com/2013/09/03/us/pro-sports-lockouts-and-strikes-fast-facts/index.html.

73. *See Collective Bargaining (Section 8(d) & 8(b)(3))*, Nat'l Lab. Rel. Board, https://www.nlrb.gov/about-nlrb/rights-we-protect/the-law/collective-bargaining-section-8d-8b3 (last visited May 7, 2022).

during a strike, players must bargain in good faith.[74] It is also important to note that unionized athletes' right to strike is not absolute. They can forfeit the right to strike if they pursue an unlawful objective or if they engage in unlawful means of pursuing a lawful objective (such as, for instance, bombing a club's practice facility).[75] While players do not lose their employee status during the course of a strike, clubs can sanction them and withhold pay.[76]

Just as unionized athletes can force a work stoppage through striking, club owners can force a work stoppage through imposing a lockout. In locking players out, club owners refuse to allow the players to practice or play games and consequently deprive the players of income. In some cases, lockouts involve a club shutting down all operations, and in other cases, they involve partially shutting down by preventing players from participating. Major American sports leagues have locked players out over a dozen times since collective bargaining began in the industry,[77] and lockouts often lead to litigation. For instance, the NFL's most recent lockout, in 2011, sparked *Brady v. National Football League*,[78] discussed *infra* in § 8.11[D] of this chapter. Lockouts are used to force players to resume negotiations after an impasse or to move off of positions the owners feel are unacceptable.[79]

In that both strikes and lockouts result in players not receiving salaries, players' ability to withstand the lack of income is a critical factor in the decision to strike or, if owners impose a lockout, decisions as to whether to cede to owners' demands. This generally gives owners a negotiating advantage. Athletes' careers tend to be short, as elite athletic ability quickly (and ultimately always) fades.[80] This means even a short work stoppage period can have a substantial impact on a player's overall career earnings. In addition, among a group of unionized athletes, there are always some players with high salaries and others with league minimum salaries; some with promises of long careers and others with hopes of lasting just a few years in the

74. *See id.*; Textile Workers Union of Am., CIO v. N.L.R.B., 227 F.2d 409, 410 (D.C. Cir. 1955) (affirming the NLRB's determination that a union calling a strike does not create an inference that union members have failed to negotiate in good faith); Gen. Elec. Co. v. N.L.R.B., 412 F.2d 512, 521 (2d Cir. 1969) (finding that the obligation to bargain continues during a strike).

75. *See The Right to Strike*, Nat'l Lab. Rel. Board, https://www.nlrb.gov/strikes (last visited Nov. 24, 2021).

76. *See id.*

77. *Pro Sports Lockouts and Strikes Fast Facts*, *supra* note 72.

78. 644 F.3d 661 (8th Cir. 2011).

79. Feldman, *supra* note 22 at 3–4.

80. *See* Seth Sandler, *NFL, MLB, NHL, MLS & NBA: Which Leagues and Players Make the Most Money?*, BLEACHER REPORT (Mar. 18, 2012), https://bleacherreport.com/articles/1109952-nfl-mlb-nhl-mls-nba-which-leagues-and-players-make-the-most-money (reporting the average span of professional athletes are 3.5 years for the NFL, 4.8 years for the NBA, 5.6 years for the MLB, and 5.5 years for the NHL).

league. As such, it can be difficult for a players' union to establish consensus on whether to agree to terms that a league offers or, on the other hand, risk a work stoppage.[81] This dynamic can reduce players' leverage vis-a-vis club owners.

[B] War Chests

While players are generally more vulnerable in the case of a work stoppage than club owners, both players and owners face substantial financial losses when work stops. To maintain negotiating strength in the event of such loses, it is customary for both sides to try to strengthen their financial positions as much as possible when a work stoppage appears likely. Major League Baseball first took this approach in 1981, purchasing strike insurance in anticipation of a players' strike.[82] The players ultimately did strike, and the owners' $50 million dollar insurance payout buttressed the owners' coffers during the month and a half long strike.[83]

Unionized players, like club owners, have attempted to stockpile funds in advance of potential work stoppages, both through purchasing insurance and other means. For instance, as the NFL's CBA neared termination in 2011 and as a lockout appeared increasingly likely, the NFLPA launched a campaign to increase players' financial literacy and emphasize the value of saving.[84] Specifically, the NFLPA suggested that all players save three game checks worth of salary to build a personal finance cushion in case of work stoppage.[85] In addition, however, the NFLPA purchased insurance policies designed to produce enough money that every union member would receive a low six-figure payout if a work stoppage prevented regular season games from

---

81. For instance, as the NFLPA negotiated a new CBA with the NFL in early 2020, the NFL's players were divided with respect to accepting the proposed deal. *See* Christian Red, *How likely is an NFL work stoppage? Fears grow after marquee players announce opposition*, NBC NEWS (March 1, 2020), https://www.nbcnews.com/news/sports/how-likely-nfl-work-stoppage-fears-grow-after-marquee-athletes-n1146001. A key element of the proposed deal involved expanding the season from sixteen to seventeen games. *Id.* Superstar quarterbacks, including Aaron Rodgers and Russell Wilson, were the most vocal opponents of the expansion. *Id.* They were concerned about the added toll an extra game would take on their bodies and those of their fellow players, and they seemed willing to risk a work stoppage over it. *Id.* Other players who were younger, had accrued less wealth and fame, and had more to lose from every week, month, or year of a work stoppage, felt differently about the season expansion, notwithstanding the potential health consequences. *Id.* In the end, the players agreed to a new CBA including the expanded season by a narrow 1,019 to 959 margin. Grant Gordon, *NFL player vote ratifies new CBA through 2030 season*, NFL.COM (March 15, 2020), https://www.nfl.com/news/nfl-player-vote-ratifies-new-cba-through-2030-season-0ap3000001106246.

82. *See This Day in MLBPA History: The 50-Day Strike in 1981 Ends with Compromise*, MLB NEWS (July 31, 2016), https://www.mlb.com/news/this-day-in-mlbpa-history-the-50-day-strike-in-1981-ends-with-compromise-c192452.

83. *See id.*

84. *NFLPA to Players: Save Your Pay for Possible 2011 Lockout*, NFL NEWS (Dec. 4, 2010), https://www.nfl.com/news/nflpa-to-players-save-your-pay-for-possible-2011-lockout-09000d5d81ca0a43.

85. *Id.*

being played.[86] That same year, when the NBPA faced a lockout at the hands of the NBA, the NBPA stressed the importance of securing income, and indeed nearly half of the league's players took out individual work stoppage insurance policies.[87] The NBPA also encouraged players to play in overseas basketball leagues during the lockout in order to continue earning money and to signal self-sufficiency and independence from the NBA.[88]

All of these tactics, though designed to economically damage the other party to the collective bargaining relationship, are lawful under the NLRA. Parties are, however, prohibited under the Act from negotiating in bad faith and from engaging in unfair labor practices.[89]

§ 8.08 Unfair Labor Practices

Congress clearly expressed its intent in the NLRA that for labor law to operate effectively neither employees nor employers may sabotage the process, and courts have reinforced the message.[90] NLRA Section 8 requires that both employers and the unions that employees authorize to negotiate with them must not engage in unfair labor practices.[91] Unfair labor practices can take various forms, including failure to bargain in good faith, restraining or interfering with workers' right to unionize, retaliation against union members, discrimination against striking workers upon a strike's conclusion, and failure to acknowledge the union as the employees' collective bargaining representative.[92] Several of these contexts are explored below.

Both the union and the league must bargain in good faith.[93] Failure to do so is unlawful. This does not mean that the parties must necessarily compromise or agree. Rather they must "meet at reasonable times and confer in good faith" during negotiations.[94] If the parties are not able to agree, either party can apply economic pressure on the other, and such pressure does not violate the duty to bargain in good faith.[95] As noted above, such pressure can include strikes, lockouts, and creating war chests.

---

86. Jim Trotter, *Players' Secret Lockout Insurance Could Have Sparked Talks*, Sports Illustrated (July 15, 2011), https://www.si.com/.amp/more-sports/2011/07/15/secret-lockout-fund (noting the insurance would pay each player roughly $200,000).

87. *See* Dave Williams, *NBA Lockout May Leave Players in Financial Trouble*, Atlanta Bus. Chron. (Sept. 30, 2011), https://www.bizjournals.com/atlanta/print-edition/2011/09/30/nba-lockout-may-leave-players-in.html.

88. *See id.*

89. *See Collective Bargaining (Section 8(d) & 8(b)(3)), supra* note 73.

90. *See, e.g.*, Nordstrom d/b/a Seattle Seahawks, 292 N.L.R.B. 899 (1989); In re Karch, 314 N.L.R.B. 482 (1994). *See also Basic Guide to the National Labor Relations Act, supra* note 27.

91. 29 U.S.C. § 158.

92. 29 U.S.C. § 158(a).

93. 29 U.S.C. § 158(a)(5).

94. *Id.* at § 158(d).

95. *Id.*

While these tactics are legally sanctioned, conduct engaged in by players and employers can constitute an unfair labor process.

The NFL's actions in advance of the aforementioned 2011 lockout are illustrative. Years earlier, in 2008, the NFL began preparing for labor unrest. Among other prophylactic measures the league took, it structured television broadcasting deals designed to provide revenue for the league in the fall and winter of 2011 whether or not any games were played.[96] The broadcasting deals were back-loaded, providing the most substantial revenue in the period after the work stoppage (during which players would not receive a share) and relatively less revenue in the period before the work stoppage (during which players would receive a share).[97] In all, the deals produced a $4 billion dollar war chest for the league. The NFLPA and the NFL had resolved a previous labor dispute by, among other things, entering a Stipulation and Settlement Agreement that included a good faith provision stemming from the NLRA's good faith obligation. In 2011, citing the back-loaded broadcasting deals, the NFLPA sued the NFL claiming it operated in bad faith.[98] The court, in *White v. National Football League*,[99] sided with the NFLPA.[100] It found that "the NFL is not entitled to obtain leverage by renegotiating shared revenue contracts ... to advance its own interests and harm the interests of the Players" and that doing so here "constitutes 'a design ... to seek an unconscionable advantage' and is inconsistent with good faith."[101] The case highlights the good faith dealing that courts expect from parties to a collective bargaining relationship.

As noted above, any effort aimed at preventing employees from effectuating the right to unionize is an unfair labor practice.[102] The Arena Football League drew NLRB scrutiny on this front in 2000 when it recognized the Arena Football League Players Organizing Committee ("AFLPOC") rather than the Arena Football League Players Association ("AFLPA") as the players' collective bargaining unit. That year, a number of players sued the league's clubs' owners alleging collusion and also formed the AFLPA to represent their collective interests. In response, the owners threatened to cancel the season. Then, before the AFLPA acquired union status, the owners reportedly threatened and coerced players to join the AFLPOC. The NLRB filed an unfair labor practices complaint against the AFL alleging that the AFL interfered with the players' right to unionize by essentially forming the AFLPOC as a management-friendly entity whose existence was designed to damage the AFLPA. The AFL ultimately settled the matter, agreeing to withdraw its recognition of the AFLPOC as the players' collective bargaining unit as well as to pay the players $5 million in damages.

---

96. *See* White v. Nat'l Football League, 766 F. Supp. 2d 941, 945–48 (D. Minn. 2011).
97. *Id.*
98. *Id.* at 944.
99. 766 F. Supp. 2d 941 (D. Minn. 2011).
100. *Id.* at 951.
101. *Id.*
102. 29 U.S.C. § 158(a)(2).

Retaliating against employees for union membership or union-related activism is also an unfair labor practice,[103] as evidenced by the NLRB's disposition in *Seattle Seahawks v. NFLPA & Sam McCullum*.[104] McCullum was a Seahawks wide receiver who in 1982 was cut from the team.[105] Less than a year earlier, McCullum had been elected by his teammates to serve as the Seahawks' representative to the NFLPA.[106] Upon being elected, McCullum became deeply involved in union affairs and player advocacy, and he worked to build bonds among players on different NFL teams.[107] His most notable act in this regard was to create a "solidarity handshake among players during the 1982 preseason.[108] This act, together with McCullum's general player advocacy, angered Seahawks head coach Jack Patera.[109] Before the regular season commenced, the Seahawks traded for a new wide receiver and subsequently terminated McCullum's employment.[110] McCullum responded by filing an unfair labor practice charge under NLRA § 8(a)(3) against the Seahawks.[111] In determining whether an employee's termination constitutes an unfair labor practice, the NLRB asks whether the union activity was a motivating factor for the termination, and if the answer is yes, it allows the employer to defend by arguing that the employee would still have been terminated absent the union activity.[112] In *McCullum*, the NLRB concluded McCullum's union activity motivated the club to terminate his employment. It wrote that the club made the decision to trade for a new wide receiver so it could "rid itself of [McCullum,] the most visible team symbol of the [Union's] solidarity."[113]

Even after labor war has erupted, employers are prohibited under the NLRA from engaging in unfair labor practices. Indeed, the NLRB has determined that "the right to strike includes the right to full and complete reinstatement upon unconditional application to return."[114] The NLRB made this clear in its decision, regarding the NFL's conduct in response to a 1987 players' strike, captioned *National Football League Management Council and NFLPA and Steve Fuller*.[115] That case arose from long simmering tension between the NFL and NFLPA during the 1970s and early 1980s. The parties had entered a five-year CBA in 1977, and by 1982, as the CBA's term was coming to the end, NFL revenues had increased substantially.[116]

---

103. *Id.*
104. 292 N.L.R.B. 899 (1989).
105. *Id.* at 909–10.
106. *Id.* at 910–11.
107. *Id.*
108. *Id.* at 913–15.
109. *Id.* at 910–16.
110. *Id.*
111. *Id.* at 906.
112. NLRB v. Transportation Management Corp., 462 U.S. 393, 400–03 (1983).
113. *Seattle Seahawks*, 292 N.L.R.B. at 902.
114. Nat'l Football League Mgm't Council and NFLPA, 309 N.L.R.B. 78, 84 (1992).
115. *Id.*
116. Tommy Craggs, *Fate of the Union: What the NFLPA Can Learn from the Fight of '77*, Sports Illustrated (June 18, 2019), https://www.si.com/nfl/2019/06/18/nflpa-players-union-cba-negotiations-work-stoppage-ed-garvey-free-agency-1977.

In light of the increase, when negotiations began on a new CBA, the players argued they were entitled to a larger share of revenues going forward.[117] Owners refused the demand, players threatened to strike, owners threatened to lock the players out, and the season was almost lost.[118] In the end, the parties agreed to a new five-year CBA, and a shortened nine-game season commenced.[119] The players, however, remained displeased with the revenue split. In 1987, with no progress made toward a new CBA, the players applied economic pressure against the owners by going on strike two games into the season.[120] The owners responded with their own economic pressure, by hiring replacement players, which, like the players' decision to strike, did not constitute an unfair labor practice.[121]

The alleged unfair labor practice did not arise until the players capitulated and unconditionally agreed to end the strike and return to work on October 15, 1987, after the league had played games for three weeks with replacement players.[122] The players noted that league rules permitted a club to sign a player who had not previously been on an NFL roster as late as Saturday in advance of the following Sunday's game but required that formerly striking players report to their teams by Wednesday.[123] Because October 15, 1987 was a Thursday, this rule meant that strikers would be prohibited from playing the following Sunday (and getting paid for the game), while non-strikers would be eligible to play and earn a game check.[124]

The NFLPA sued, and the NLRB held in its favor, finding that the NFL's return to play protocols — which did not provide "full and complete reinstatement upon unconditional application to return" — discriminated against striking players and constituted an unfair labor practice.[125] So, while labor law permits fierce economic pressure as a means of persuasion as between a players' union and a league, it prohibits rubbing salt in the proverbial wound through discriminatory treatment once resolution is achieved.

§ 8.09 Labor Arbitration

Most CBAs, including those in the sports industry, contain arbitration clauses to facilitate dispute resolution. In the sports industry, these negotiated labor arbitration systems have been fundamental to the relations between leagues and players. Different approaches, however, exist. In the NBA, NFL, and NHL contexts, the parties have generally agreed that a sole arbitrator will serve the role. The MLB and the MLBPA,

---

117. *Id.*
118. *Id.*
119. *Nat'l Football League Mgmt. Council*, 309 N.L.R.B. at 78.
120. *Id.* at 79.
121. *Id.*
122. *Id.* at 79–80.
123. *Id.* at 79.
124. *Id.* at 79–80.
125. *Id.* at 80–81.

on the other hand, have often utilized a three-person arbitral panel, consisting of one union-selected member, one league-selected member, and one mutually acceptable member to serve as panel chair.

Historically, unions and leagues have engaged in arbitration to resolve various types of disputes, including disputes regarding discipline, salaries, and CBA language interpretation, and arbitrators and arbitration panels have come to different conclusions based on the differing facts and contexts.[126] Whatever the outcomes, however, arbitral decisions tend to be the final word, as judicial review of arbitral decisions is extremely limited in scope.[127] The United States Supreme Court's 1960 resolution of *United States of America v. Enterprise Wheel & Car Corp.*,[128] a non-sports related case, made clear that courts should not substitute their judgment for the judgment of arbitrators with respect to the merits of arbitrators' decisions.[129] The *Enterprise Wheel* Court found that while a court may certainly vacate an arbitral award, it may do so only if the arbitrator essentially abandoned their duties, not if the court simply disagrees with the conclusions the arbitrator drew on the substance.[130] The United States Supreme Court later addressed this issue in the sports realm, in *MLBPA v. Garvey*,[131] and reached the same conclusion.

The *Garvey* case involved an All-Star Major League first baseman named Steve Garvey who alleged collusion among MLB clubs resulting in his contract with the San Diego Padres not being extended beyond the 1987 season.[132] Other players also alleged such collusion. These disputes resulted in a settlement under which the MLBPA established a framework through which to assess individual players' claims.[133] Garvey submitted a roughly $3 million damages claim to the MLBPA under the framework, but the MLBPA rejected the claim.[134] Garvey objected and sought arbitration, and the arbitrator, after reviewing the evidence, denied Garvey's claim.[135] Garvey then brought an action in federal district court to vacate the arbitrator's award.[136] The district court denied the motion, and the court of appeals reversed and remanded,[137] catalyzing a tortured procedural history that culminated with the case in the United States Supreme Court. The Supreme Court's task was to determine whether the lower courts granted the arbitrator's decision appropriate deference, and

---

126. *See* James B. Gessford, *Arbitration of Professional Athletes' Contracts: An Effective System of Dispute Resolution in Professional Sports*, 55 NEB. L. REV. 362 (1975).

127. Joseph C. Sweeney, *Judicial Review of Arbitral Proceedings*, 5 FORDHAM INT'L L.J. 253, 254 (1981).

128. 363 U.S. 593 (1960).

129. *Id.* at 599.

130. *Id.* at 597.

131. 532 U.S. 504 (2001).

132. *Id.* at 506.

133. *Id.* at 505–06.

134. *Id.* at 506.

135. *Id.* at 506–07.

136. *Id.* at 507.

137. *Id.* at 508.

the Supreme Court concluded that they did not, forcefully emphasizing the limited scope of judicial review of arbitral decisions.[138] The Court wrote:

> Courts are not authorized to review the arbitrator's decisions on the merits despite allegations that the decision rests on factual errors or misinterprets the parties' agreement.... It is only when the arbitrator strays from interpretation and application of the agreement and effectively "dispenses his own brand of industrial justice" that his decision may be unenforceable. When an arbitrator resolves disputes regarding the application of a contract, and no dishonesty is alleged, the arbitrator's "improvident, even silly, fact-finding" does not provide a basis for a reviewing court to refuse to enforce the award.[139]

Given an arbitrator's authority, the decision as to who serves as arbitrator or who comprises the arbitral panel is critical. As noted *infra*, the NFL, NBA, NHL, and MLB all have arbitrator selection procedures that require agreement between the league and the union. The NFL and NFLPA agreement in this regard, however, has caused tremendous controversy.[140] Although the parties agreed in their CBA to an arbitration selection procedure, that procedure permits NFL Commissioner Roger Goodell to appoint himself as arbitrator with respect to certain disciplinary matters.[141] Goodell has utilized this authority to consolidate power through the arbitrator role in conjunction with the broad deference arbitrators receive from courts. Consequently, NFL players facing discipline have often had scant success in challenging Goodell's decisions.[142] Future Hall of Fame Quarterback Tom Brady, who was embroiled in the NFL's infamous "Deflategate" scandal, is perhaps the most notable player in this regard. In 2015, Brady was accused of having his team's equipment managers release air from footballs so they would be softer and easier for him to throw accurately.[143] The NFL investigated and concluded that Brady, indeed, was culpable.[144] Goodell suspended Brady for four games, and Brady appealed, claiming among other things, that Goodell was evidently partial.[145] Goodell — who appointed himself as arbitrator

---

138. *Id*. at 509–10.

139. *Id*. at 509.

140. Many legal scholars have engaged this issue, emphasizing the one-sided nature of the agreement. *See, e.g.*, Jeffrey F. Levine, Ian P. Gunn & Anita M. Moorman, *Peterson, Brady, Elliot: Analyzing "The Trilogy" in Light of the NFL Commissioner's Discipline Authority*, 29 J. Legal Aspects Sport 223 (2019); Kara Crawford, *NFL 3–0 in Federal Appellate Court Challenges to Player Suspensions: A Pattern of "Substantial Deference" to the NFL Creates an Uphill Battle for Players*, 26 Jeffrey S. Moorad Sports L.J. 39 (2019); Josh Mandel, *Deflategate Pumped Up: Analyzing the Second Circuit's Decision and the NFL Commissioner's Authority*, 72 U. Mia. L. Rev. 827 (2018); Eric. L. Einhorn, *Between the Hash Marks: The Absolute Power the NFL's Collective Bargaining Agreement Grants Its Commissioner*, 82 Brook. L. Rev. 393 (2016).

141. *Einhorn*, *supra* note 140, at 402.

142. *See id*. at 416–19.

143. National Football League Management Council v. National Football League Players Ass'n, 820 F.3d 527, 532–33 (2d Cir. 2016).

144. *Id*. at 533–34.

145. *Id*. at 534.

to hear the appeal of the discipline he meted out — upheld the suspension.[146] Federal litigation followed, and the district court found that Goodell exceeded his authority and vacated the suspension.[147] The Second Circuit, however, reversed. In doing so, it made clear that the district court had not afforded sufficient deference to Goodell, the arbitrator.[148] The appellate court acknowledged that the district court may reasonably have viewed Goodell's power to hear appeals of his own decisions as "unorthodox,"[149] but concluded that "[the court] may not disturb [Goodell's determination on appeal] so long as he acted within the bounds of his bargained-for authority."[150]

Although Goodell has the right under the CBA to appoint himself as arbitrator in the disciplinary context, he is not required to do so. In a 2014 disciplinary matter involving NFL running back Adrian Peterson, for instance, Goodell appointed former longtime NFL executive Harold Henderson to the role.[151] Peterson had been indicted for physically abusing his son, and after pleading no contest, the NFL suspended him for violating the league's personal conduct policy.[152] Peterson appealed, and Henderson issued an arbitration award upholding the suspension.[153] Peterson then filed a federal lawsuit to vacate the arbitration award, and although the district court vacated the award, the Eighth Circuit reversed.[154] Peterson's arguments that Henderson was "evidently partial" and that the arbitration was "fundamentally unfair" were unavailing. The Eight Circuit concluded, as the Second Circuit had concluded in the "Deflategate" case, that it could not disturb the arbitrator's award, writing, "the parties bargained to be bound by the decision of the arbitrator, and the arbitrator acted within his authority."[155]

These cases reasserted the limitations courts face when reviewing arbitrators' decisions. It is important that both league and union leadership understand these limitations and craft their arbitration selection procedures recognizing the power that arbitrators wield in light of courts' reluctance to intervene.

§ 8.10 Labor Management Relations Act Preemption

Section 301(a) of the Labor Management Relations Act ("LMRA") provides potential plaintiffs a cause of action for breach of a CBA. Courts have long read this

---

146. *Id.* at 534–35.

147. *Id.* at 535–36.

148. *Id.* at 532.

149. *Id.*

150. *Id.*

151. National Football League Players Association on behalf of Peterson v. National Football League, 831 F.3d 985, 990 (8th Cir. 2016).

152. *Id.*

153. *Id.* at 990–91.

154. *Id.* at 999.

155. *Id.* at 989.

provision to preempt state law claims when resolution of the claims would require the court to interpret a CBA's provisions. Whether CBA interpretation is necessary in the case of a particular state claim obviously depends on the contours of the claim and the nature of the CBA in question. Consequently, LMRA § 301 preemption analysis is factually intensive, and "'[a]s one would expect in case-by-case analysis, in some situations preemption is found, and in others, it is not.'"[156]

In *Dent v. National Football League*,[157] the Ninth Circuit found that LMRA § 301 did not preempt former NFL players' state law tort claims against the league, because resolution of those claims did not require CBA interpretation.[158] In that case, the players alleged that the NFL systematically provided them narcotic painkilling injections and pills so they would be able to continue playing despite injury, that the NFL did not inform them of the drugs' long term health consequences, and that the drugs substantially damaged their health.[159] Specifically, the players claimed that the NFL violated state law by administrating controlled substances without proper labels and warnings and without prescriptions.[160] The Ninth Circuit agreed with the players that the NFL had a duty to use reasonable care in distributing controlled substances, and the duty was not born of the CBA but was rather inherent in the distribution of such items.[161] Having determined that the duty at issue was independent of the CBA, the court then asked, "whether litigating the state law claim nonetheless requires interpretation of a CBA."[162] The court found that it did not; it found that determining whether the NFL failed in its duty to properly prescribe the narcotic painkillers was a pure question of fact and that its resolution did not require CBA interpretation.[163] Preemption, therefore, was inappropriate.

By contrast, in *Atwater v. National Football League Players Association*,[164] which involved former NFL players bringing negligence claims against the NFL and NFLPA, the Eleventh Circuit affirmed preemption of the plaintiffs' claims. The players alleged that the defendants breached their duty under Georgia law by insufficiently vetting financial advisors who provided financial services to players through the NFLPA's Financial Advisors Program.[165] Defendants moved for summary judgment on preemption grounds, asserting that they conducted background checks on financial advisors as a

---

156. Duerson v. Nat'l Football League, 2012 WL 1658353, at *5 (N.D. Ill. May 11, 2012) (quoting In re Bentz Metal Products Co., Inc., 253 F.3d 283, 289 (7th Cir. 2001)).

157. 902 F.3d 1109 (9th Cir. 2018).

158. *Id.* at 1126.

159. *Id.* at 1114.

160. Second Amended Complaint at 81–83, Dent v. NFL, No. 14-02324-WHA (N.D. Cal. Dec. 17, 2014).

161. *Dent*, 902 F.3d at 1119.

162. *Id.* at 1116 (quoting Alaska Airline, Inc. v. Schurke, 898 F.3d 904, 921 (9th Cir. 2018)).

163. *Id.* at 1119–20.

164. 626 F.3d 1170 (11th Cir. 2010).

165. *Id.* at 1174.

part of their obligations under the CBA's Career Planning Program and arguing that any assessment of plaintiffs' claims would require interpreting the CBA.[166] The district court granted the motion and, as noted above, the Eleventh Circuit affirmed.[167] The court explained that LMRA § 301 preempts a state claim when the "claim either arises out of a CBA or is dependent upon the meaning of a CBA."[168] Applying that standard, the court concluded that preemption was appropriate. It found that the defendants' duty to investigate prospective financial advisers with reasonable care arose from the CBA, and even if it did not, the court "would still have to consider the CBA's Career Planning Program provision in determining the scope of any duty the NFLPA owed Plaintiffs."[169]

In some circumstances, certain claims in a lawsuit are preempted while others are not. Latrell Sprewell's suit against the NBA and its Golden State Warriors franchise is illustrative. That case, *Sprewell v. Golden State Warriors*,[170] stemmed from an altercation at practice between Sprewell, who at the time played for the Warriors, and the club's head coach, P.J. Carlesimo. During the practice, Carlesimo criticized the manner in which Sprewell passed the ball to a teammate, and the two engaged in a heated argument.[171] Sprewell then grabbed Carlesimo's neck, threatened his life, and began to choke him.[172] The Warriors subsequently terminated Sprewell's contract, and the NBA suspended Sprewell for the remainder of the season.[173] Sprewell brought multiple state claims against the defendants.[174] These included an unfair business practices claim related to his termination and suspension, and tortious interference claims alleging defendants damaged his business relations with third parties by vilifying him in the press.[175] The court found that LMRA § 301 preempted the unfair business practices claim, but not the tortious interference claims.[176] It concluded that the unfair business practices claim "require[d] an interpretation of the disciplinary provisions of the CBA," and therefore could not go forward.[177] The court, however, viewed the tortious interference claims differently.[178] It concluded that although the same incident at the Warriors' practice session spawned both the unfair business practice claim and the tortious interference claims, the latter claims did not require CBA interpretation.[179] It found that those claims were born entirely of California law

---

166. *Id.* at 1179–81.
167. *Id.* at 1185.
168. *Id.* at 1176–77.
169. *Id.* at 1181–82.
170. 266 F.3d 979 (9th Cir. 2001).
171. *Id.* at 984.
172. *Id.* at 984–85.
173. *Id.* at 985.
174. *Id.*
175. *Id.* at 990–92.
176. *Id.* at 991–92.
177. *Id.* at 992.
178. *Id.*
179. *Id.*

and that resolving them required applying that California law to the facts at issue, but did not require interpreting the CBA.[180]

Although LMRA § 301 preemption analysis is factually intensive and courts have gone in different directions, the key inquiry is whether resolving the claim in question requires the presiding court to interpret a CBA.

§ 8.11 The Labor Exemption from Antitrust Law

As discussed in this chapter, labor law exists to protect employees through allowing them to form multi-employee bargaining units, known as unions, that can negotiate with employers or multi-employer bargaining units, such as sports leagues. As discussed in Chapter 7, antitrust law exists to promote competition among buyers and sellers of services. In the employment realm, this would seemingly prohibit employees and employers from forming groups that might collude and stifle competition for employees' services, which would create an unavoidable tension with the aims of labor law.

[A] The Statutory Labor Exemption

Recognizing this tension, over a century ago Congress passed legislation — the Clayton Act of 1914 — to insulate labor unions from antitrust liability with regard to the unions' actions designed to further their members' economic interests.[181] The Clayton Act, which amended the Sherman Antitrust Act, reads, in relevant part:

> The labor of a human being is not a commodity or article of commerce. Nothing contained in the antitrust law shall be construed to forbid the existence and operation of labor ... organizations ... or to forbid or restrain individual members of such organizations from lawfully carrying out the legitimate objects thereof.[182]

Notwithstanding the broad scope of the Clayton Act's apparent carve-out, the United States Supreme Court initially seemed willing to restrict the labor exemption from antitrust law to what it described as a union's "normal and legitimate objects" and not apply it in the case of strikes and boycotts.[183] In 1932, however, Congress followed up the Clayton Act with the Norris-LaGuardia Act to confirm that members of labor organizations are, indeed, protected from antitrust scrutiny when engaging in such employee self-help just as they are during the course of other union activities.[184] Notably, multi-employer bargaining units are also spared antitrust scrutiny under certain

---

180. *Id.*
181. 15 U.S.C. § 17 (1914).
182. *Id.*; *see* Sherman Act, 15 U.S.C. § 1 (1890).
183. *See* Duplex Printing Press Co. v. Deering, 254 U.S. 443, 469 (1921).
184. 29 U.S.C. §§ 101–115 (1932).

circumstances when pursuing their members' collective interests.[185] The Clayton Act and the Norris-LaGuardia Act, taken together, create what is known as the statutory labor exemption from antitrust law, or simply, the statutory labor exemption.[186]

[B] The Non-Statutory Labor Exemption

Importantly, the statutory labor exemption bears only on a union's unilateral conduct.[187] It does not apply to the union's involvements with management.[188] As such, the statutory labor exemption does not protect collective bargaining agreements from antitrust scrutiny.[189] Consequently, the statutory labor exemption protects striking employees from antitrust liability, but it does not protect from antitrust liability agreements made between labor and management that might result from that strike.[190] Courts recognized that this incongruity was antithetical to the statutory labor exemption's premise and through case law created the non-statutory labor exemption, which extends protection from antitrust scrutiny to collective bargaining agreements.[191] The contours of the non-statutory labor exemption, however, have never been entirely clear, and the United States Supreme Court has struggled over the years to articulate a cogent and consistent test to apply when assessing antitrust challenges to CBA provisions.[192]

When professional athletes began to unionize and enter into CBAs with league management in the late 1960s, the non-statutory labor exemption became an important concept in the sports industry. And in 1976, in *Mackey v. NFL*,[193] the Eighth Circuit created a test that has framed the manner in which many courts apply the exemption. Under *Mackey*, the non-statutory labor exemption is only potentially applicable when: 1) the restraint on trade primarily affects just the parties to a collective bargaining agreement; 2) the issue or agreement sought to be exempted concerns a mandatory subject of collective bargaining (*i.e.*, wages, hours, and other terms and conditions of employment);[194] and 3) the agreement sought to be exempted is the

---

185. *See* Kennedy v. Long Island R. Co., 319 F.2d 366 (2d Cir. 1963).

186. Christopher Smith, *A Necessary Game Changer: Resolving the Legal Quagmire Surrounding Expiration of the Nonstatutory Labor Exemption in Sports*, 14 U. Pa. J. Bus. L. 1191, 1195 (2012).

187. *Id.*

188. *Id.*

189. *Id.*

190. *Id.*

191. *Id.* at 1195–96.

192. *See, e.g.*, Allen Bradley Co. v. Loc. Union No. 3, Int'l Bhd. of Elec. Workers, 325 U.S. 797 (1945); United Mine Workers of Am. v. Pennington, 381 U.S. 657 (1965); Connell Const. Co. v. Plumbers & Steamfitters Loc. Union No. 100, 421 U.S. 616 (1975).

193. 543 F.2d 606 (8th Cir. 1976).

194. With respect to what constitutes a mandatory subject of collective bargaining, the court explained that "[w]hether an agreement concerns a mandatory subject depends not on its form but on its practical effect," and as such found that the rule in question's impact in "depress[ing] player salaries" qualified it as a mandatory subject. *Id.* at 615.

product of bona fide arms-length bargaining.[195] If any of the three elements is not met, the restraint on trade is not exempt from antitrust law, and it is subject to antitrust scrutiny, which triggers Rule of Reason analysis. Under the Rule of Reason, a restraint on trade may be permissible if it is "justified by a legitimate business purpose, and is no more restrictive than necessary."[196]

Although the *Mackey* test remains a widely used test for assessing the applicability of the non-statutory labor exemption in professional sports,[197] it is not the only such standard. The Second Circuit adopted a more amorphous, free-flowing test in 2004 in *Clarett v. NFL*.[198] Under this test, the court generally assesses whether subjecting the NFL's eligibility rules to antitrust scrutiny would "subvert fundamental principles of our federal labor policy.'"[199] The case involved All-American Ohio State University running back Maurice Clarett's antitrust challenge to the NFL's age eligibility threshold. After an historically successful freshman year at Ohio State in 2002, Clarett was accused of having violated NCAA's amateurism rules and was subsequently suspended from the school's football team for the 2003 season.[200] When it became clear that he might be barred from playing during the 2004 season as well, Clarett set his sights on the NFL, but was ineligible due to the league's age requirements.[201] Clarett sued the NFL, arguing that the age eligibility threshold violated antitrust law.[202] The NFL responded with the non-statutory labor exemption, arguing that "federal labor law favoring and governing the collective bargaining process precludes the application of the antitrust laws to its eligibility rules...."[203]

A federal district court found the eligibility rule failed to satisfy the three factors of the *Mackey* test and therefore concluded that the non-statutory labor exemption did not apply.[204] The Second Circuit, however, reversed, explaining that it had "never regarded the Eighth Circuit's test in *Mackey* as defining the appropriate limits of the non-statutory exemption."[205] Instead, it assessed whether scrutinizing the age eligibility rule under antitrust law would subvert the fundamentals of labor policy, ultimately concluding that it would.[206] In reversing the district court's order declaring Clarett eligible for the draft, the Second Circuit stressed that the eligibility rule was collectively bargained for and that:

---

195. *Id.* at 614.

196. *Id.* at 620.

197. *See* Abraham Spira, Comment, *Almost Three Decades Later, Is Mackey Still Viable?*, 17 FORDHAM INTEL. PROP. MEDIA & ENT. L.J. 805, 827–34 (2007) (explaining the various cases that followed the *Mackey* decision).

198. 369 F.3d 124 (2d Cir. 2004).

199. *Id.* at 138 (quoting Wood v. Nat'l Basketball Ass'n, 809 F.2d 954 (2d Cir. 1987)).

200. *Id.* at 125–26.

201. *Id.* at 126.

202. *Id.*

203. *Id.* at 130.

204. *Id.* at 129.

205. *Id.* at 133.

206. *Id.* at 138 (quoting Wood v. Nat'l Basketball Ass'n, 809 F.2d 954 (2d Cir. 1987)).

> In the context of collective bargaining ... federal labor policy permits the NFL teams to act collectively as a multi-employer bargaining unit in structuring the rules of play and setting criteria for player employment. Such concerted action is encouraged as a matter of labor policy and tolerated as a matter of antitrust law.[207]

The *Mackey* test remains persuasive in some jurisdictions,[208] but as *Clarett* illustrates, other jurisdictions use less formulaic approaches when considering the non-statutory labor exemption's applicability.[209] Either way, courts — most notably the Eighth Circuit in *Powell v. NFL*[210] and later the Supreme Court in *Brown v. Pro Football*[211] — have established that the non-statutory labor exemption extends beyond the point of impasse, strengthening management's defense against players' antitrust actions.

[C] Navigating the Nexus of Antitrust and Labor

In *Powell*, the court found that league management has the right after impasse to "make unilateral changes that are reasonably comprehended within its pre-impasse proposals."[212] This essentially means that as long as a union remains players' bargaining representative, the league is insulated from antitrust suit with respect to those changes under the non-statutory labor exemption. If, however, players terminate a union's role as their collective bargaining representative, they may sue under antitrust law as individuals.

The approach NFL players took to challenging a restrictive free agency scheme in 1990 is illustrative.[213] The clubs' player representatives to the NFLPA voted to terminate the NFLPA's status as their union and the NFLPA disclaimed its authority to represent the players in collective bargaining, rendering the NFLPA as nothing more than a voluntary professional association.[214] Several players, led by New York Jets running back Freeman McNeil, then sued the NFL, claiming that the scheme — which gave clubs the right of first refusal to re-sign certain of their players with ex-

---

207. *Id.* at 142.

208. *See, e.g.*, Int'l Longshore & Warehouse Union v. ICTSI Oregon, Inc., 863 F.3d 1178 (9th Cir. 2017); Loc. Union 257, Int'l Bhd. of Elec. Workers, AFL-CIO v. Sebastian Elec., 121 F.3d 1180 (8th Cir. 1997); McCourt v. California Sports, Inc., 600 F.2d 1193 (6th Cir. 1979); Grinnell Corp. v. Rd. Sprinkler Fitters Loc. Union No. 669, 1997 WL 311498, at *1 (D. Md. June 3, 1997).

209. *See, e.g.*, U.S. Football League v. Nat'l Football League, 842 F.2d 1335 (2d Cir. 1988); Wood v. Nat'l Basketball Ass'n, 809 F.2d 954, 962 n. 6 (2d Cir. 1987); Dickey v. Nat'l Football League, 2020 WL 6819135, at *1 (1st Cir. Feb. 13, 2020).

210. 930 F.2d 1293 (8th Cir. 1989).

211. 518 U.S. 231 (1996).

212. *Powell*, 930 F.2d at 1302.

213. Sean W.L. Alford, *Dusting Off the AK-47: An Examination of NFL Players' Most Powerful Weapon in an Antitrust Suit Against the NFL*, 88 N.C. L. Rev. 212, 226–227 (2009); Benjamin C. Block & Cyril Djoukeng, *A Short History of NFL Labor Disputes*, 30 Del. Law. 8, 10 (2012).

214. *Id.*

piring contracts — violated antitrust law.[215] In *McNeil v. NFL*,[216] the court concluded that the NFLPA's disclaimer of its authority to serve as the players' collective bargaining unit nullified the non-statutory labor exemption.[217] This allowed the *McNeil* plaintiffs to assert their antitrust claim, and they prevailed on the merits.[218] Other NFL players, having observed the *McNeil* plaintiffs' success, soon thereafter — and with the NFLPA's support — filed a class action suit, *White v. National Football League*,[219] on many of the same grounds the *McNeil* plaintiffs asserted.[220] Without access to the non-statutory labor exemption, the NFL had no defense and no choice but to settle the matter for $115 million.[221]

As a part of the settlement, the NFLPA reestablished as a union and as the players' collective bargaining unit.[222] Though it was part of the settlement, this immediate reestablishment of the union as the players' bargaining representative suggested that the NFLPA's disclaimer was, in essence, a sham intended to allow players to file individual antitrust suits while not altering the NFLPA's role in substance.[223] The NFL made this argument, insisting that an actual decertification of the union would have required substantial process, including an NLRB-supervised vote (rather than the more informal and easily reversible disclaimer), and would truly have evinced an intent to terminate the collective bargaining relationship.[224] The NFL asserted that disclaimer, on the other hand, was a smokescreen. The NFL's argument was not successful, but the extent of formality required to terminate a union's collective bargaining authority after impasse and sue under antitrust remains unresolved.[225] As such, when collective bargaining agreements near termination and renewal negotiations reach impasse, unions will likely continue to pursue disclaimer. Moreover, leagues and players will spar about whether disclaimer is sufficient to dissolve the non-statutory labor exemption and open the gates to players' antitrust lawsuits.

In 1996, the United States Supreme Court took up *Brown v. Pro Football, Inc.*[226] to address the question of whether the non-statutory labor exemption can survive

---

215. McNeil v. Nat'l Football League, 790 F. Supp. 871, 875 (D. Minn. 1992).
216. *Id.*
217. *Id.* at 886–87, n.20.
218. *Id.* at 896–97.
219. 836 F. Supp. 1458 (1993).
220. *Id.* at 1462.
221. *Id.* at 1479, 1505.
222. Chris Deubert, Glenn Wong & John Howe, *All Four Quarters: A Retrospective and Analysis of the 2011 Collective Bargaining Process and Agreement in the National Football League*, 19 UCLA Ent. L. Rev. 1 (2012).
223. Block & Djoukeng, *supra* note 213, at 10 (noting that the presiding judge rejected the NFL's "sham" argument "notwithstanding considerable testimony from player leaders that the sole purpose of the disclaimer was to pursue antitrust litigation to accomplish their bargaining objectives regarding free agency").
224. *Id.*
225. This question was presented in *Brady v. NFL*, 644 F.3d 661 (8th Cir. 2011), discussed *infra*, but the court disposed of the matter on jurisdictional grounds, and therefore failed to reach the issue.
226. 518 U.S. 231 (1996).

beyond impasse, and the Court confirmed that it could. That case involved CBA negotiations between the NFL and the NFLPA in 1989.[227] During negotiations, the NFL proposed Resolution G-2, which would allow each club to establish a "developmental squad" and place on that squad as many as six rookie players who did not make the club's regular roster.[228] The proposed Resolution G-2 further provided that each developmental squad player would receive a $1,000 per week salary.[229] The NFLPA opposed Resolution G-2 and demanded that developmental squad players be permitted to negotiate their salaries.[230] After months of negotiation, the parties reached an impasse, after which the NFL "unilaterally implemented the developmental squad program."[231] A group of developmental squad players subsequently sued the NFL, alleging that the league's $1,000 salary requirement violated the Sherman Antitrust Act.[232] The NFL responded that the non-statutory labor exemption shielded the salary provision from antitrust scrutiny.[233] The district court found the exemption did not apply, and the D.C. Circuit reversed, finding that it did.[234] The Supreme Court affirmed the D.C. Circuit's decision, concluding that the non-statutory labor exemption encompassed the developmental squad scheme: "an agreement among several employers bargaining together to implement after impasse the terms of their last best good-faith offer."[235] The court noted that employer bargaining groups are not free to act with impunity post-impasse. Rather, as the *Powell* court stated, any new terms must have been "reasonably comprehended" in the pre-impasse proposals and, in addition, the pre-impasse collective bargaining must not have involved unfair labor practices.[236]

[D] Federal Jurisdiction over Labor Disputes

The Norris-LaGuardia Act, mentioned above, prevents federal courts from prohibiting a lockout during a labor dispute. This issue has arisen most notably in *Brady v. National Football League*,[237] a case that grew out of NFL labor discord in 2011. As the 1993 CBA neared expiration in 2011, the NFL and NFLPA were unable to agree on the terms of an extension, and league management made it known that if the CBA expired, the league would lock the players out.[238] The union, anticipating the league would threaten a lock out, opted to terminate its status as the players' collective bargaining unit through disclaimer, just as it had in 1990.[239] And just as McNeil along

---

227. *Id.* at 234.
228. *Id.*
229. *Id.*
230. *Id.*
231. *Id.* at 235.
232. *Id.*
233. *Id.*
234. *Id.*
235. *Id.* at 238.
236. *Id.* at 238–39.
237. 644 F.3d 661 (8th Cir. 2011).
238. *Id.* at 663.
239. *Id.*

with other players filed an antitrust suit on the heels of the 1990 disclaimer, Tom Brady along with other players filed an antitrust suit on the heels of the 2011 disclaimer, arguing that the league's planned lockout would be an illegal group boycott.[240] The next day, the league implemented the lockout, and the players moved for a preliminary injunction in United States District Court for the District of Minnesota, asking the court to enjoin the lockout because it constituted an unlawful group boycott which was causing players irreparable harm.[241] The court granted the preliminary injunction, but the league appealed to the Eight Circuit, which reversed, holding that the district court lacked jurisdiction to grant the injunction.[242] Specifically, the court held "the Norris-LaGuardia Act deprives a federal court of power to issue an injunction prohibiting a party to a labor dispute from implementing a lockout of its employees."[243]

240. *Id.*
241. *Id.*
242. *Id.*
243. *Id.* at 680–81.

Chapter 9

Agents (Representing Athletes)

§ 9.01 Introduction

Prior to the emergence of the sports agent industry, players would directly negotiate with sports teams.[1] Over the past several decades, however, the number, role, and use of sports agents has grown as a result of multiple factors affecting sports as a component of the broader entertainment industry.[2] One of the more important functions of today's athlete-agent is providing a "level of parity" in negotiations between athletes and sports organizations more experienced in negotiations.[3] In addition to athletes relying on agents to negotiate athlete-team contracts to "protect athletes' interests in relation to those of owners,"[4] many agents handle: "tax planning, financial planning, money management, investments, estate planning, income tax preparation, incorporating the client, endorsements, sports medicine consultations, physical health consultations, post-career development, career and personal development counseling, legal consultations, and insurance matters."[5]

Given agents' expanded role within the sports industry, the legal principles that shape the contours of their relationships with athletes take on greater significance. This chapter examines the layers of private and public law that regulate the athlete-agent relationship. It begins with a discussion of the common law principles that govern the relationship and the parties' respective rights and obligations arising from these principles. The chapter also examines the multiple internal and external mechanisms, including players associations regulations and the Revised Uniform Athlete Agents Act, which regulate the athlete-agent relationship. What we see is that common law agency principles, complemented by players association regulations (in the case of major professional sports leagues), largely regulate the relationship as supplemented by state and federal laws. These multiple levels of regulation serve as the backdrop

---

1. William Rothstein, *The Business of Sports Representation: Agent Evolution in the Industry*, 9 Va. Sports & Ent. L.J. 19, 21–23 (2009).

2. *Id.*; Matthew J. Mitten, Timothy Davis, N. Jeremi Duru & Barbara Osborne, Sports Law and Regulation: Cases, Materials, and Problems 427 (5th ed. 2020) (listing multiple reasons for the proliferation in the number and use of sports agents).

3. *Id.* at 25.

4. Rothstein, *supra* note 1, at 24.

5. Walter T. Champion, Jr., *Attorneys Qua Sports Agents: An Ethical Conundrum*, 7 Marq. Sports L.J. 349, 351–52 (1997).

against which athlete-agent disputes and agent-to-agent disputes are examined. The chapter concludes with a discussion of the unique ethical issues that arise given that some agents are lawyers, but other agents are non-lawyers. Although it is not addressed in detail herein, legal issues also may arise when players represent themselves rather than using the services of agents.[6]

§ 9.02 Agency Principles: Defining the Athlete-Agent Relationship

[A] The Agent as a Fiduciary: Common Law Agency Principles

In sports, the athlete-agent relationship typically arises out of an express contract between the athlete and agent.[7] Like other principal-agent relationships, the athlete-agent relationship is governed by common law agency principles.[8] A key agency law principle is that "the agent shall act on the principal's behalf and subject to the principal's control."[9] As a consequence, the athlete, as the principal, has final decision-making authority in all matters and the agent must act in accordance with their athlete's directives even if they conflict with the agent's own judgment.[10] Additionally, the agent assumes a fiduciary duty when providing services for a principal (*i.e.*, an athlete).[11] Because a fiduciary acts primarily for the benefit of its principal,[12] agency law mandates that the agent must be loyal to the athlete's interests when acting on the athlete's behalf.[13] The fiduciary obligation also imposes on agents a duty to use reasonable care and skill in performing tasks.[14] As discussed *infra*,[15] although the rules regulating agents may vary depending on the agent's status as a lawyer or non-lawyer, either is subject to the duty of reasonable care and skill.[16]

---

6. Although the vast majority of professional athletes hire agents to represent them, in 2021, it was reported that seventeen NFL players, including high-profile players such as Lamar Jackson, Josh Allen, and Dak Prescott, elected to forgo traditional representation by sports agents. Ken Belson, *Lamar Jackson's Bold Play: A Contract Without an Agent*, N.Y. TIMES (Sept. 29, 2021). For a discussion of legal issues emerging from athlete self-representation, see Jodi Balsam, *"Free My Agent": Legal Implications of Professional Athletes' Self-Representation*, 16 WAKE FOREST J. BUS. & INTELL. PROP. L. 510 (2015–16).

7. Timothy Davis, *Regulating the Athlete-Agent Industry: Intended and Unintended Consequences*, 42 WILLAMETTE L. REV. 781, 792 (2006).

8. *See* MITTEN, ET AL., *supra* note 2, at 428–29.

9. RESTATEMENT (THIRD) OF AGENCY § 1.01 (Am. Law Inst. 2006).

10. *See* MITTEN, ET AL., *supra* note 2, at 428–29.

11. Rothstein, *supra* note 1, at 28–29.

12. *Id.* at 29

13. RESTATEMENT (THIRD) OF AGENCY § 1.01 cmt. e.

14. Davis, *supra* note 7, at 793.

15. *See* Section 9.06, Ethical Considerations, *infra*.

16. Rothstein, *supra* note 1, at 26–27 (arguing that although attorneys may possess a competitive advantage due to legal education and experience, attorneys are also subjected to the rules of legal ethics and required to comply with additional regulations).

As the foregoing discussion reveals, agents assume multiple obligations by virtue of the fiduciary duty they owe to their athlete clients.[17] In summary, agents must always act in their clients' best interests and in accordance with the duties of loyalty, good faith, and honest and fair dealing.[18]

[B] Breaches of Fiduciary Obligations

The following discussion examines legal disputes between athletes and agents that emerge from alleged breaches of their obligations arising from their contractual relationship. The cases examined focus on conduct that allegedly violated obligations arising from agents' fiduciary duties beginning with the agent's duty to use reasonable care and to act in good faith in performing services for athletes.

[1] Duty of Reasonable Care and Good Faith

Conduct resulting in players suing their agents can grow out of an agent's failure to competently provide services for their athlete clients. Such conduct ranges from an agent's failure to meet critical deadlines in negotiating a player-team contract to an agent's financial mismanagement of an athlete's assets.[19] In seeking redress from agents, athletes assert claims sounding in breaches of fiduciary duty and contract, and fraud.[20] Agents frequently defend against claims by asserting their work conformed to the standard of care and the athlete is simply attempting to avoid paying the agent for services rendered.

In performing services on behalf of an athlete, an agent possesses the fundamental obligation to exercise reasonable care and good faith.[21] The athlete has a corresponding duty to compensate the agent, usually in the form of a commission, for services the agent performed. Both of these issues arose in *Zinn v. Parrish.*[22] There, an agent sued an athlete to recover 10% commission owed to him under their management contract.[23] The athlete argued he was not obligated to pay because Zinn failed adequately to perform contractually agreed upon services. The parties' contract obligated the agent to use "reasonable efforts" when procuring pro-football employment for the athlete. The contract was silent, however, as to the applicable standard regarding the agent's other services (*e.g.*, business and tax advice and procuring endorsements and off-season employment for the athlete).[24] After the agent represented the client in

---

17. Kenneth L. Shropshire, Timothy Davis & N. Jeremi Duru, The Business of Sports Agents 91–92 (3d ed. 2016).

18. *Id.*

19. Davis, *supra* note 7, at 782.

20. Athletes also seek a judicially mandated accounting of assets and the return of funds misappropriated by agents.

21. Champion, *supra* note 5, at 350–51.

22. 644 F.2d 360 (7th Cir. 1981).

23. *Id.* at 360.

24. *Id.* at 361

negotiating a series of lucrative contracts with the team over the course of several years, the athlete terminated his contract with the agent.

The Seventh Circuit adopted a reasonable efforts standard, which was stipulated in the parties' contract, in concluding that the agent competently performed services in negotiating the athlete's contract with his team. The court held that the plaintiff's efforts to secure employment for the athlete with a pro-football team were reasonable because the defendant was never a "free agent," so the plaintiff was barred by NFL rules from negotiating with any other team.[25] With respect to the other services, the court applied a good faith standard. The court said there was no breach by the agent in performing the other duties because he had made good faith efforts to obtain what his client had sought, notwithstanding unsuccessful attempts.[26] The court rejected the athlete's argument that the good faith standard required the agent to be successful in securing off-season employment for the athlete.[27]

[2] Loyalty and the Avoidance of Conflicts of Interests

Another basic obligation derived from the fiduciary character of the agent-athlete relationship is the duty of loyalty, which precludes an agent from engaging in conduct antithetical to the principal's interests.[28] Thus, "an agent is subject to a duty not to act ... during the period of his agency for persons whose interests conflict with those of [their] principal."[29] A potential conflict of interest arises when there is a substantial risk that the agent's representation of a client would be materially and adversely affected by the agent's own interests or by the agent's duties to another client.[30] While an agent with a potential conflict of interest may be able to continue representing his or her clients, the agent is required to obtain informed consent from such clients to avoid breaching his or her duties.[31] As stated by the court in a leading case, *Detroit Lions, Inc. v. Argovitz*,[32] which is discussed below, "[a]n agent's duty of loyalty requires that he not have a personal stake that conflicts with the principal's interest in the transaction in which he represents the principal."[33] Consequently, an agent who breaches this duty by failing to sufficiently disclose their own self-interest will lose the right to receive compensation and may make some transactions voidable by the athlete.

The paradigmatic case of a conflict of interest occurs when an agent fails to disclose his or her financial interest in a transaction that also involves the athlete. This scenario

---

25. *Id.* at 365.

26. *Id.* at 366.

27. *Id.*

28. RESTATEMENT (THIRD) OF AGENCY § 8.03.

29. RESTATEMENT (SECOND) OF AGENCY § 394 (Am. L. Inst. 1958).

30. *See* RESTATEMENT (THIRD) OF THE LAW GOVERNING LAWYERS § 121 (Am. L. Inst. 2000).

31. *See generally* RESTATEMENT (SECOND) OF AGENCY § 394 cmt. b.

32. 580 F. Supp. 542 (E.D. Mich. 1984).

33. *Id.* at 548; *see also* Scott R. Rosner, *Conflicts of Interest and the Shifting Paradigm of Athlete Representation*, 11 UCLA ENT. L. REV. 193, 91–92 (2004) (listing multiple examples of conflicts of interests arising out of consolidation); Joshua Lens, *When a College Coach's Agent Recruits the Coach's Players: Potential Legal and NCAA Ramifications*, 26 JEFFREY S. MOORAD SPORTS L.J. 1, 7 (2019).

occurred in *Argovitz*,[34] in which former NFL running back Billy Sims sought to rescind a contract he signed with the Houston Gamblers. Sims had been under contract with the NFL's Detroit Lions. While representing Sims in his negotiations with the Lions, agent Jerry Argovitz sought and obtained an ownership interest in the Houston Gamblers of the United States Football League.[35]

After Argovitz secured his ownership interest, he continued negotiations with the Lions on behalf of Sims. At the same time, however, Argovitz decided to seek an offer for Sims from the Gamblers, and the agent had one of his partners handle the negotiations.[36] Armed with information provided by Argovitz, the Gamblers made a satisfactory offer to Sims which Sims instructed Argovitz to accept.[37] While Sims did not instruct Argovitz to seek a final offer from the Lions, Sims was operating on information provided by Argovitz that made him incorrectly believe that the Lions were negotiating in bad faith or dragging their feet.[38] Argovitz ultimately did not contact the Lions despite the fact that it is a customary practice for an agent to do so and Argovitz had done so in the past for other clients in similar positions.[39] When the full extent of Argovitz's representation came to light, Sims signed a subsequent contract with the Lions and filed suit to rescind his agreement with the Gamblers.[40]

The court ruled that the sequence of conduct engaged in by Argovitz constituted an egregious breach of the fiduciary duties he owed to Sims. Specifically, the court found that although Argovitz told Sims that he had applied for and received an ownership interest in the Gamblers, the agent failed to disclose the extent of his ownership interest. This nondisclosure amounted to an especially egregious breach of his fiduciary duties. "Where an agent has an interest adverse to that of his principal in a transaction in which he purports to act on behalf of his principal, the transaction is voidable by the principal unless the agent disclosed all material facts within the agent's knowledge that might affect the principal's judgment."[41]

According to the court, Argovitz had a "duty to telephone the Lions, receive its final offer, and present the terms of both offers to Sims," so that Sims could make a fully informed decision.[42] The court rejected Argovitz's argument that he was simply following Sims's instruction to not contact the Lions.[43] It reasoned that although an agent is generally "not liable for the losses occurring as a result of following [a] principal's instruction, [that] rule of law is not applicable when the agent has placed

---

34. *Detroit Lions, Inc.*, 580 F. Supp. at 545.
35. *Id.* at 544.
36. *Id.* at 545.
37. *Id.*
38. *Id.* at 544–45.
39. *Id.* at 545–46.
40. *Id.* at 543.
41. *Id.* at 548.
42. *Id.*
43. *Id.*

himself in a position adverse to that of his principal."[44] Finally, the court acknowledged that contacting the Lions would have allowed Argovitz to use the Gamblers' offer as a "wedge" to leverage the Lions into making a better offer to Sims.[45]

Other situations that present potential conflicts of interest include an agent's representation of multiple clients on the same team in a league and an agent's representation of both an athlete and a coach or other management personnel.[46] In the former circumstance, a conflict arises out of the fact that teams in leagues with salary caps have a limited fund from which they pay their players, so the athletes on the team are essentially competing to secure limited team resources.[47] This leads to a zero-sum game, because "a high salary for one player may lead to a lower salary for another."[48] Because multiple clients are competing to obtain "the maximum share of a limited budget, the conflict may not be eliminated," and the representation of both clients by attorney agents "may not be undertaken regardless of informed consent."[49] Even in the absence of a salary cap, a potential conflict arises where an agent represents two players on the same team who play the same position. Roster limits create the possibility that one of the players may not make the team. Nevertheless, these situations create only potential conflicts of interest and as such are not prohibited by player association regulations. Consequently, players' association regulations do not expressly prohibit an agent's representation of multiple players on the same team.[50]

Where an agent represents a player as well as a coach or general manager with the player's team, a conflict arises because a player seeks to maximize earnings whereas coaches and management personnel seek to lower a player's compensation.[51] This concern is reflected in the NBPA's regulations banning such representation. It is

---

44. *Id.*

45. *Id.* at 546. The court also criticized Argovitz for persuading Sims to sign a waiver absolving the agent from liability for breaches of his fiduciary duties. *Id.*

46. Lens, *supra* note 33, at 14–22.

47. *Id.* at 15.

48. *Id.*

49. *Id.*; *see also* Jamie E. Brown, *The Battle the Fans Never See: Conflicts of Interest for Sports Lawyers*, 7 GEO. J. LEGAL ETHICS 813, 816 (1994) (explaining why the actual conflict of interest in this type of situation may not be eliminated pursuant to Model Rule of Professional Conduct 1.7).

50. *See* Darren A. Heitner & Jason B. Belzer, *An Offer They Should Refuse: Why Conflicts of Interest Raised by Dual Representation Among Player Agents is a Major Threat to the NCAA and Professional Leagues*, 2 ARIZ. ST. SPORTS & ENT. L.J. 1, 5–9 (2012) (arguing that despite player associations' efforts, agents' use of loopholes in NFLPA, NBPA, MLBPA, and NHLPA rules and regulations has caused conflicts of interests to continue). *See generally* NFLPA Regulations Governing Contract Advisors § 3 (as amended through August 2016) [hereinafter NFLPA Regulations], *available at* https://nflpaweb. blob.core.windows.net/media/Default/PDFs/Agents/RegulationsAmendedAugust2016.pdf; NBPA Regulations Governing Player Agents § 5 (as amended through June 2019) [hereinafter NBAPA Regulations], *available at* https://cosmic-s3.imgix.net/fec8eea0-dbdc-11e9-a097-0b637a5431fa-Agent-Regulations-Final-2019.pdf § 3(b); MLBPA Regulations Governing Player Agents § 5(B)(12) (as amended through December 2019) [hereinafter MLBPA Regulations], *available at* http://reg.mlbpaagent.org/Documents/AgentForms/Agent%20Regulations.pdf.

51. Heitner & Belzer, *supra* note 50, at 19–20; *see also* Lens, *supra* note 33, at 19–20.

worth noting, however, that larger sports agencies have the capacity to "circumvent[] the rules by having different agents within the same agency represent individual talent, which is enough to 'prove compliance.'"[52]

For agents who are also attorneys, professional standards governing attorneys (*e.g.*, The American Bar Association's Model Rules of Professional Conduct ("MRPC")) also mandate that such agents avoid conflicts of interest. For example, consider *Sports Management Network v. Busch*,[53] where a representation agreement between a race car driver and his agents resulted in multiple conflicts of interest that tainted their representation efforts. The agency in the case concurrently represented multiple parties with interests adverse to the driver including teams that employed him. In fact, the agent went as far as to say that he didn't see himself as having clients, but rather that he was only "facilitating the meeting of minds." The lack of loyalty shown to Busch ultimately led the court to render the representation agreement unenforceable.

[3] Fiduciary Obligations:
Duty of Honesty and Fair Dealing

Athletes have sued and will likely continue to sue their agents for misconduct ranging from misappropriation and negligent use of athletes' funds to agents failing to keep athletes informed of the status of their finances. These lawsuits sound in substantive causes of action including breach of fiduciary duty, fraud, and breach of contract. The actions arise from agents failing to abide by obligations owed to their principals, including "act[ing] loyally for the principal's benefit,"[54] refraining from conduct injurious to the principal,[55] exercising due care when acting on the principal's behalf, providing information[56] and an accounting of the principal's property,[57] and refraining from using the principal's property for the agent's benefit.[58]

Williams v. CWI, Inc.[59] illustrates an athlete's successful fraud action against his agent. An agent, who was hired by the athlete to provide financial and tax advice, persuaded the athlete to invest $1 million in a project without disclosing that the project was in financial trouble and was operated and controlled by the agent.[60] After the athlete made a $50,000 down payment, the defendant appropriated the money for his own use and caused the plaintiff to suffer serious tax penalties.[61] The court found that plaintiff was entitled to recover the $50,000 paid and the expenses incurred as a result of the agent's fraudulent conduct, including the cost to amend his tax re-

---

52. Heitner & Belzer, *supra* note 50, at 19–20.
53. 2019 WL 1057314 (E.D. Mich. March 6, 2019).
54. RESTATEMENT (THIRD) OF AGENCY §8.01, cmt. (a).
55. *Id.* §8.10.
56. *Id.* at 8.11.
57. *Id.* at 8.12.
58. *Id.* at 8.05.
59. 777 F. Supp. 1006 (D. D.C. 1991).
60. *Id.* at 1007–08.
61. *Id.* at 1008.

turns, attorneys fees, and penalties and interest owed to the government.[62] The court also awarded plaintiff punitive damages because the defendant's conduct put the plaintiff at risk of committing tax fraud.[63]

Another example is found in *Hilliard v. Black*,[64] in which several athletes alleged, *inter alia*, breach of fiduciary duty, conversion and negligence claims against William Black and the agency he was Chairman and CEO of, Professional Management, Inc. (PMI). PMI "provide[d] its clients with financial services that include[d] investment and retirement planning."[65] Plaintiffs' claims arose out of two stock-related ponzi schemes.[66] Black and PMI employees did not disclose to the athletes the extent of the investment's risk exposure, how the funds were to be used, or defendant's financial interest in the investment.[67] The scheme ultimately resulted in all of plaintiffs' investment returns being misappropriated and diverted by the defendants rather than being reinvested or distributed to the plaintiffs.[68]

Following these events, the plaintiffs brought suit and asserted multiple claims based in tort law.[69] In particular, the plaintiffs alleged that the defendants breached their fiduciary duty by inducing them to invest millions of dollars in the two financial scams.[70] The main issue before the court was whether the economic loss rule barred the plaintiffs from bringing such claims.[71] The economic loss rule bars a plaintiff from maintaining "a tort action to recover economic damages that arise from a contract unless the claims are for physical injury or property damage."[72] The court held that when the law imposes a fiduciary duty on a party, liability can arise when such duties are breached even if there is an underlying written or oral contract.[73] Therefore, Florida's economic loss rule, as articulated by the court, did not bar the plaintiffs' breach of fiduciary duty or conversion claims because the plaintiffs alleged that the defendants' intentional conduct was independent of any acts that may have breached the contract.[74]

---

62. *Id.* at 1008–09.

63. *Id.* at 1009.

64. 125 F. Supp. 2d 1071 (N.D. Fla. 2000).

65. *Id.* at 1074.

66. *Id.*

67. *Id.* at 1075–77.

68. *Id.*

69. *Id.* at 1074.

70. *Id.* at 1077.

71. *Id.*

72. *Id.* at 1077–78.

73. *Id.* at 1078–80.

74. *Id.* ("where [a] defendant's acts were 'not merely a failure to perform, but an affirmative and intentional act of converting the funds to his own use by allegedly stealing the monies to which he was entrusted, there is not merely a breach of contract but a separate and independent tort'").

In contrast to the forgoing cases, a different result was reached in *Gordon v. Vitalis Partners*.[75] The plaintiff athlete entered into an agreement with the defendant pursuant to which the athlete was to pay a fixed fee in exchange for financial services.[76] After he performed under the original agreement for two years, the agent informed the plaintiff that the fee structure was changing to a percentage-based model.[77] Although the plaintiff never expressly agreed to the change, he never objected to it and paid the invoices sent to him over the following 14 months.[78] In addition to this, while being represented by the defendant, the plaintiff loaned money in an apparent real estate transaction that resulted in the borrowers defaulting.[79] Following these events, the plaintiff filed suit alleging that the defendant breached its fiduciary duty in changing the fee structure and inducing the plaintiff to make the loan to the borrowers.[80]

In regard to the fee structure, the court held that the defendant had not breached its fiduciary duty because the plaintiff's conduct in paying the invoices indicated his assent to the new percentage-based model.[81] In regard to the loan transaction, the court emphasized that the plaintiff received a promissory note memorializing the agreement, read the note, and consulted with a different financial advisor before agreeing to its terms.[82] The court then held that because the plaintiff, as principal, was the final decision maker with respect to the loan, the defendant could not be deemed to have breached its fiduciary duty.[83]

§ 9.03 Legislation Governing Agent Conduct

[A] Pre-UAAA State Legislation

Before the enactment of the Uniform Athlete Agents Act ("UAAA"), agent-specific state legislation and generally applicable criminal statutes were relied on to regulate agent conduct. Pre-UAAA agent-related legislation sought to protect universities from the financial penalties that could result from improper relationships between agents and athletes. It also protected athletes against improper agent conduct, including misappropriation of athlete funds. Many states granted universities a statutory private cause of action to seek damages from agents. Although Pre-UAAA legislation

---

75. 2010 WL 381119 (N.D. Ill. Jan. 27, 2010).
76. *Id.* at *1.
77. *Id.*
78. *Id.*
79. *Id.* at *1–2.
80. *Id.* at *2.
81. *Id.* at *3.
82. *Id.*
83. *Id.*

varied, there were similarities including: registration, registration fees, and the posting of surety bonds in order to act as agents.[84]

[B] Federal Regulation

In 2004, President George W. Bush signed The Sports Agents Responsibility Trust Act ("SPARTA"), the first federal legislation specifically enacted to regulate sports agents.[85] Modeled after the UAAA, SPARTA supplements but does not preempt state law.[86] SPARTA, like the UAAA, prohibits agents from providing improper inducements and misleading information in their recruitment of student-athletes. It includes a requirement that agents disclose to the parents of student-athletes under 18 and to the athletic director of the student-athlete's school that entering into an agency contract may result in a loss of eligibility to compete in athletic competition as an amateur.[87] SPARTA also prohibits the pre- or post-dating of agency contracts.[88] Agent conduct violative of SPARTA constitutes an unfair and deceptive act or practice under the Federal Trade Commission Act and is subject to enforcement by the FTC or a state attorney general, and is punishable by fines of up to $10,000 per incident. If the FTC initiates an action against an agent, a state attorney general may not bring an action during the pendency of the FTC's action.

Agents are also subject to criminal liability pursuant to non-agent specific federal laws, including RICO or mail fraud statutes.[89] One of the more celebrated of these cases is *United States v. Piggie* in which federal prosecutors relied on, *inter alia*, mail and wire fraud and tax statutes to secure a criminal conviction. The defendant, Myron Piggie, paid elite high school basketball players. The court stated: "The payments were designed to retain top athletes on his [AAU] team, gain access to sports agents, obtain profitable sponsorship contracts, and forge ongoing relationships with players to his benefit when athletes joined the [NBA]."[90] The wire and mail fraud occurred, in part, when the athletes falsely certified to their colleges, including Duke University and the University of California at Los Angeles, that "they had not previously received payment to play basketball. The athletes delivered through the U.S. Postal Service signed letters of intent asserting their eligibility."[91]

Non-agent specific federal laws proscribing wire fraud and conspiring to commit wire fraud[92] were instrumental in the conviction of Christian Dawkins for his involvement in a scheme under which Dawkins and other defendants made cash pay-

---

84. *See* SHROPSHIRE ET AL., *supra* note 17, at 154–155.

85. Sports Agent Responsibility and Trust Act, 15 U.S.C. §§ 7801–7807 (2004).

86. Davis, *supra* note 7, at 653.

87. 15 U.S.C. § 7802.

88. *Id.*

89. *See, e.g.,* United States v. Piggie, 303 F.3d 923 (8th Cir. 2002); United States. v. Walters, 997 F.2d 1219 (7th Cir. 1993).

90. *Piggie*, 303 F.3d at 924.

91. *Id.* at 925.

92. U.S. v. Dawkins, 2019 WL 1313711 (S.D.N.Y. Mar. 15, 2019).

ment to college basketball coaches in exchange for the coaches using their influence to persuade college athletes to enter into representation agreements with certain agencies.[93] The scheme also involved Dawkins and other individuals funneling cash obtained from Adidas to make payments to the families of high school basketball players in exchange for family members using their influence to persuade the players to attend colleges sponsored by Adidas.[94]

Prosecutors used federal securities law and money laundering statutes to successfully prosecute Nevin Shapiro, a University of Miami booster, who owned a sports management agency and used cash he obtained as a part of a Ponzi scheme to recruit college athletes to the university.[95] Yet another case involved Fairron Newton who was convicted of violating federal tax and money laundering statutes.[96]

[C] The Uniform Athlete Agents Act (UAAA)

The Uniform Athlete Agents Act ("UAAA") was promulgated by the Uniform Law Commission ("ULC") in 2000.[97] It's stated purpose was to achieve greater uniformity of state laws regulating sports agents. The ULC states: "[the] Act governs relations among student-athletes, athlete agents, and educational institutions, protecting the interests of student-athletes and academic institutions by regulating the activities of athlete agents."[98] As of August 15, 2021, 42 states, territories and Washington, D.C. had adopted the UAAA.[99]

In 2015, the UAAA was revised. The ULC states that "[t]he purposes of the [Revised UAAA ("RUAAA")] include providing enhanced protection for student-athletes and educational institutions, creating a uniform body of agent registration information for use by the state agencies registering agents, and simplifying the registration process for agents."[100] It further states that the RUAAA makes "changes to the original act, including expanding the definition of 'athlete agent'"; "simplifying the registration process for agents"; adding new requirements to the signing of an agency contract; and "enhancing notification obligations."[101] In 2019, the RUAAA was revised in order to be in alignment with NCAA rule changes that now permit elite basketball players to hire agents to assist the athletes in determining whether

---

93. U.S. Dept. of Justice, *Aspiring Manager and Former Adidas Consultant Sentenced to Prison Terms for Bribing NCAA Division I Men's College Basketball Coaches,* Attorney's Office, S.D. N.Y. (Oct. 4, 2019), https://www.justice.gov/usao-sdny/pr/aspiring-manager-and-former-adidas-consultant-sentenced-prison-terms-bribing-ncaa.

94. *Id.*

95. *See* SHROPSHIRE, ET AL., *supra* note 17, at 69–70.

96. *Id.* at 72–73.

97. *2000 Athlete Agents Act,* UNIF. L. COMM'N, https://www.uniformlaws.org/committees/community-home?CommunityKey=86324d0a-17fe-4325-85bc-17d11b46f84d.

98. *Id.*

99. *Id.*

100. *2015 Athlete Agents Act,* UNIF. L. COMM'N, https://www.uniformlaws.org/committees/community-home?CommunityKey=4d46906c-2d24-4ede-84ab-a57b40fa5c37.

101. *Id.* at *7–8.

to enter the NBA draft or continue to play college sports.[102] Recent state legislation and NCAA rules changes that permit student-athletes to be represented by agents in relation to the athletes' names, images, and likenesses will require further amendments to the RUAAA.

Section 2 of the RUAAA contains important definitions. Section 2(1) defines an "Agency contract" as "an agreement in which a student-athlete authorizes a person to negotiate or solicit on behalf of the athlete a professional-sports-services contract or endorsement contract."[103] This and two additional definitions are critical to determining if a contract between an agent and athlete falls within the scope of the RUAAA. The expanded definition of agent includes "an individual who, *inter alia*, for compensation or the anticipation of compensation, serves the athlete in an advisory capacity on a matter related to finances, business pursuits, or career management decisions or manages the business affairs of the athlete...."[104] A student-athlete is defined as "an individual who is eligible to attend an educational institution and engages in, is eligible to engage in, or may be eligible in the future to engage in, any interscholastic or intercollegiate sport."[105]

The scope of the UAAA was recently contested in *Williamson v. Prime Sports Marketing LLC*.[106] NBA rising star Zion Williamson sued a marketing agency seeking a declaratory judgment that their contract was void under North Carolina's version of the UAAA.[107] The defendants' primary argument against Williamson was that he wasn't considered a "Student-Athlete" as defined in the UAAA and its provisions were, therefore, inapplicable.[108] The court found, however, that the defendants only made conclusory statements that Williamson engaged in conduct which would result in the revocation of his student-athlete status and that such conclusory statements were insufficient to create a genuine issue of material fact. From this, the court voided the contract, because it failed to include language required by the UAAA.[109]

Other key provisions of the RUAAA include the following: (1) an athlete agent must be registered in the state in which an agency contract is signed; (2) an agency contract entered into between a student-athlete and an unregistered agent is void;[110] (3) agents must notify the institution at which an athlete is enrolled before contacting the athlete; (4) under certain circumstances, an agent with a preexisting relationship with a scholarship athlete must notify the institution at which the athlete is enrolled of the relationship; (5) as a part of the application process, registration applicants

---

102. *2019 Athlete Agents Act*, Unif. L. Comm'n, https://www.uniformlaws.org/committees/community-home?CommunityKey=cef8ae71-2f7b-4404-9af5-309bb70e861e.

103. Revised Uniform Athlete Agents Act § 2(1) (Unif. L. Comm'n last amended 2019).

104. *Id.* § 2(2).

105. *Id.* § 2(19).

106. 2021 WL 201255 (M.D.N.C. Jan. 20, 2021).

107. *Id.* at *1.

108. *Id.* at *6–8.

109. *Id.* at *6–9.

110. Revised Uniform Athlete Agents Act § 4(c).

are required to provide information relating to their personal and business affairs, and past or present matters that reflect on their capacity to faithfully carry out their fiduciary obligations, and any communications between the applicant and student-athletes;[111] (6) the grounds pursuant to which a secretary of state may refuse to issue a registration,[112] revoke or refuse to renew a registration.[113]

The RUAAA also provides for the required form of an agency agreement and notification requirements. An agency contract must: (1) be in a record that is signed by both parties;[114] (2) contain a statement by the agent that they are registered in the state in which the contract is signed and a list of other states in which the agent is registered;[115] (3) provide the amount and method for calculating the compensation the athlete is to pay the agent and the duration of the agency contract; (4) include a conspicuous notice warning that the athlete by signing the agreement may lose eligibility to compete as an amateur, and that the athlete and agent must notify, within 72 hours of signing the contract or before the next competitive event, the athletic director at the institution in which the athlete is enrolled of the signing of an agency contract;[116] (5) contain a conspicuous warning that the athlete may cancel the contract within 14 days but doing so may not restore the athlete's amateur eligibility;[117] and (6) include a separate signed record by the athlete (and parents or guardians for minor athletes) acknowledging having seen the warning.[118] An agency contract that does not follow the required form is voidable by the athlete, and the athlete is not required to return any consideration received from the agent to induce the athlete to sign the contract.[119] The athlete and the parents or guardians of a minor have the right to cancel the agency contract within 14 days.[120] Within 72 hours after the signing of the agency contract or the next athletic event, both the agent and athlete are required to inform the institution of the agency agreement.[121]

Under the RUAAA, prohibited conduct that may result in a criminal violation[122] includes: making misrepresentations to induce the signing of a contract; providing anything of value to induce the signing of a contract; pre- or post-dating an agency contract; and failing to notify the athlete or the athlete's parents/guardians that the athlete's signing of the agreement may result in a loss of amateur eligibility.[123] Finally, an athlete or the educational institution adversely impacted by the acts or omissions

---

111. *Id.* § 5.
112. *Id.* § 6.
113. *Id.* § 7.
114. *Id.* § 10(a).
115. *Id.* § 10(b).
116. *Id.* § 10(c).
117. *Id.*
118. *Id.*
119. *Id.* § 10(e).
120. *Id.* § 12.
121. *Id.* § 11.
122. *Id.* § 15
123. *Id.*

of the agent and suffering financial losses is granted a private right of action against the agent.[124]

§ 9.04 Player Association Regulations

As discussed in Chapter 8 *supra*,[125] player associations are an essential actor in the collective bargaining process, which in turn, plays a prominent role in establishing the respective rights and obligations arising among players, teams, and professional sports leagues. In the major U.S. team sports, players associations are unions and as such are the exclusive bargaining representatives of athletes in negotiating contracts with teams. Players associations delegate, however, their exclusive right to negotiate player-team contracts to third parties. This delegation is accompanied by the right of players associations to regulate the individuals (*i.e.*, agents) who can negotiate player-team contracts.

In fulfilling responsibilities to their athlete members, players associations have promulgated regulations governing player-agent relationships. These regulations set forth the criteria with which prospective agents must comply in order to obtain certification as contract advisors (*i.e.*, agents). Although the authority of players associations only extends to determine which individuals can represent players with respect to what falls within the collective bargaining process — negotiation of players' contracts with the teams — these associations can nevertheless consider conduct of agents unrelated to player-team contract negotiation when evaluating an agent's qualifications to be certified. Players associations' agent regulations also include provisions permitting the union to sanction agents who violate the rules set forth in their respective regulations.[126]

In addition, by affirming the authority of players associations to regulate agents, courts have given legal effect to association regulations. In a leading case, *Collins v. National Basketball Players Association*,[127] a former agent of Kareem Abdul-Jabbar challenged the NBPA's authority to deny his certification for conduct unrelated to negotiating player contracts.[128] Specifically, he argued that the denial was improper due to the fact that it was based on a breach of fiduciary duty claim asserted against him as an investment agent and money manager.[129] In response to this argument, the Tenth Circuit first explained the history and purpose of the NBPA and NBA collective bargaining agreements. It noted that agent regulations were enacted "in response to a growing number of player complaints about agent abuses — including violations of various fiduciary duties."[130] The court then affirmed the district court's

---

124. *Id.* § 16. For a discussion of actions brought against agents see MITTEN, ET AL., *supra* note 2, 670–71.

125. *See* Section 8.03, Exclusive Bargaining Unit, *supra*.

126. Davis, *supra* note 7, at 815–16.

127. 1992 U.S. App. LEXIS 24069 (10th Cir. Sept. 21, 1992) (unpublished).

128. *Id.*

129. *Id.* at *2.

130. *Id.* at *1.

ruling, reasoning that "[t]he integrity of a prospective negotiating agent is well within the NBPA's legitimate interest in maintaining the wage scale and working conditions of its members."[131]

A more recent challenge to a players union's authority to regulate agents arose in *Dickey v. Natl. Football League.*[132] An NFLPA-certified agent challenged the union's decertification of his registration because Dickey had failed to comply with the union's "Three Year Rule." The "rule provides for automatic expiration of an agent's certification if the agent is unable to negotiate an individual contract on behalf of a football player to an NFL club's active fifty-three-man roster within three years."[133] Dickey alleged, *inter alia*, that the Three Year Rule unreasonably restrained "fair and equitable competition" between agents by creating an artificial barrier to new agents representing athletes in violation of Section I of the Sherman Act.[134]

The court stated that Dickey's antitrust claim was subject to dismissal pursuant to the statutory exemption to antitrust laws "[s]o long as a union acts in its self-interest and does not combine with non-labor groups."[135] The court found that the Three Year Rule promotes the NFLPA's legitimate self-interest because it is an integral part of the NFLPA's standards seeking to assure that agents provide "fair, reasonable, and uniformly applicable rates to players," because the rule "requires agents to demonstrate their qualifications to represent NFLPA members by either (1) successfully negotiating at least one contract or (2) obtaining recertification."[136] The court also concluded that by enforcing its own regulations, the NFLPA had not combined with a non-labor group.[137]

In the major professional team sports, players associations' agent regulations mandate the use of standardized form contracts that establish the express contractual agreement between agents and athletes.[138] Generally, the athlete will agree to pay an agent fees in exchange for a set of services defined in the contract.[139] Thus, the provisions of these standardized representation agreements combine with agency principles to define the athlete-agent relationship and the duties arising therefrom.

---

131. *Id.* at *2; *see also* White v. Nat'l Football League, 92 F. Supp. 2d 918 (D. Minn. 2000) (holding that agents are bound by the NFL collective bargaining agreement and stipulation and settlement agreement); Black v. Nat'l Football League Players Ass'n, 87 F. Supp. 2d 1, 6 (D.D.C. 2000) (upholding arbitration agreement in collective bargaining agreement where agent was "aware of and freely agreed to the arbitration terms").
132. 2018 WL 4623061 (D. Mass. Sept. 26, 2018).
133. *Id.* at *1.
134. *Id.* at *5.
135. *Id.*
136. *Id.* at *6.
137. *Id.*
138. *See, e.g.*, NFLPA Regulations § 4(A) (invalidating agreements between agents and players that are not in writing in the pre-printed form provided by the National Football League Players Association).
139. Champion, *supra* note 5, at 351.

§ 9.05 Agent-to-Agent Legal Disputes

[A] "Client Stealing"

Disputes within the sports agent industry also frequently arise due to conflicts between competing agents.[140] Fierce competition for clients has been fueled by factors including increases in player salaries and the increase of competing agents despite a stable pool of potential athlete-clients.[141] Moreover, standard agent representation agreements augment the industry's competitive environment because they allow players to terminate their representation contracts and switch agents with ease.[142] These factors along with the consolidation of agencies has resulted in smaller firms struggling to compete with much larger firms that employ aggressive recruiting tactics to acquire or "steal" clients from other agents.[143]

Under the current system, which lacks standard industry ethical rules, agents are incentivized to utilize these aggressive tactics or "risk being pushed out of the business by more unethical or nefarious agents, and thus risk losing their clients to other agents."[144] In fact, courts have avoided intervening to regulate the athlete-agent industry. Thus, while agents who engage in aggressive recruiting tactics could potentially face liability for tortious interference with contractual relations, agents have met with little success in suing other agents for alleged client stealing.[145]

To illustrate, in *Speakers of Sport, Inc. v. Proserv, Inc.*,[146] the Seventh Circuit ruled in favor of the defendant agency, which had convinced a baseball player to terminate his representation contract with the plaintiff. The athlete in the case, Ivan Rodriguez, was a successful catcher for the Texas Rangers and had entered into a series of one-year at-will contracts with the plaintiff agency, Speakers of Sport.[147] The defendant agency, Proserv, approached Rodriguez and promised to obtain significant endorsement deals for him if he switched agencies.[148] As a result, Rodriguez terminated his agreement with Speakers and entered into a contract with Proserv to be his new agent.[149] After Proserv was unable to fulfill its promise to Rodriguez by failing to secure major endorsements, he terminated his agreement with Proserv and signed with a new agency that successfully negotiated a five-year $42 million contract with the Rangers.[150]

---

140. Davis, *supra* note 7, at 793.

141. MITTEN ET AL., *supra* note 2, at 643.

142. *Id.*

143. *Id.*

144. Stacey B. Evans, *Sports Agents: Ethical Representatives or Overly Aggressive Adversaries?*, 17 VILL. SPORTS & ENT. L.J. 91, 107–08 (2010).

145. *See, e.g.*, Bauer v. The Interpublic Group of Companies, Inc., 255 F. Supp. 2d 1086 (N.D. Cal. 2003).

146. 178 F.3d 862 (7th Cir. 1999).

147. *Id.* at 864.

148. *Id.*

149. *Id.*

150. *Id.*

Following these events, Speakers filed suit against Proserv alleging tortious interference with a contractual relationship.[151] On appeal, the Seventh Circuit affirmed summary judgment in favor of Proserv.[152] The court first reasoned that client stealing is a natural result of competition and that competition serves as a defense to a tortious interference claim when the competing agent does not induce a breach of contract.[153]

> There is in general nothing wrong with one sport agent trying to take a client from another if this can be done without precipitating a breach of contract. That is the process known as competition, which though painful, fierce, frequently ruthless, and sometimes Darwinian in its pitilessness, is the cornerstone of our highly successful economic system. Competition is not a tort, ... but on the contrary provides a defense (the "competitor's privilege") to the tort of improper interference.... It does not privilege inducing a breach of contract ... — conduct usefully regarded as a separate tort from interfering with a business relationship without precipitating an actual breach of contract — but it does privilege inducing the lawful termination of a contract that is terminable at will.[154]

Consequently, the court held that Proserv had not improperly interfered with Speaker's contractual relationship with Rodriguez, and Proserv could therefore not be held liable for its conduct.[155] Noting that the competitor's privilege does not encompass a "right to get business from a competitor by means of fraud,"[156] the court examined ProServ's alleged fraudulent promises to secure endorsements for Rodriquez. It noted that in Illinois, like most other jurisdictions, promissory fraud is actionable only where the fraudulent promise is a "part of a scheme to defraud, that is, unless it is one element of a pattern of fraudulent acts."[157] Finding no such scheme, the court rejected the fraud claim. It added that Proserv's statements to Rodriguez were puffery akin to a sales pitch rather than an actual promise.

Another point to consider is that agents face additional hurdles when pursuing claims of client stealing. For one, players often have little incentive to testify against a poaching agent, "especially when the poaching agent has treated them to fancy dinners and lavish gifts."[158] Moreover, agents themselves are also hesitant to report their peers out of fear of the consequences of such actions.[159] While a reported agent might face immediate repercussions for improper behavior in the form of a suspension or tort liability, the same agent might retaliate to being "ratted out" by leaving his agency

---

151. *Id.* at 865
152. *Id.*
153. *Id.* at 865–66.
154. *Id.*
155. *Id.* at 867.
156. *Id.*
157. *Id.* at 866.
158. Evans, *supra* note 144, at 108.
159. *Id.* at 108–09.

and taking many of the agency's clients in the process.[160] This is what happened with agent David Dunn and, although he ultimately lost a lawsuit for stealing approximately 50 clients from his agency, his actions essentially destroyed a prominent professional football representation firm.[161]

Along similar lines, in *Total Econ. Athletic Mgmt. of Am., Inc. v. Pickens*,[162] the plaintiff agency, TEAM, received an unsatisfying judgment that was upheld by the Missouri Court of Appeals. TEAM used potentially illicit methods to persuade former University of Nebraska cornerback, Bruce Pickens, to sign an NFLPA standard representation agreement prior to declaring for the draft.[163] Pickens ultimately decided to sign with agent Tom Condon, a former NFL player and NFLPA President.[164] Condon successfully negotiated five multimillion dollar one-year contracts on behalf of Pickens.[165]

While TEAM was able to receive a $20,000 verdict in its favor against Pickens, it appealed, arguing that such damages were inadequate.[166] The thrust of TEAM's argument was that it was entitled to damages determinable by the formula in its representation contract as applied to the ultimate value received in the contracts negotiated by Condon.[167] The court countered TEAM stating, "[i]n the context of professional sports, the player's breach of an agency agreement does not necessarily entitle the agent to commission. Technically, the agent is only entitled to damages for breach of contract, *i.e.*, the value of the promised performance reduced by any expenses saved."[168] Thus, TEAM "was not entitled to commissions based solely on the contracts negotiated by others."[169]

[B] Regulation of Fees

In team sports, players association regulations include provisions detailing the manner in which agents are to be compensated for their services. For example, the NBPA agent regulations and its standard player-agent contract specify that the maximum fee an agent may earn is 4 percent of the compensation negotiated for the player for each playing season.[170] A two percent maximum applies to representation of players who only receive the minimum salary.[171] The NFLPA's agent regulations set 1.5 percent as the default fee but permit a player and agent to agree to a fee of up

---

160. *Id.*
161. *Id.*
162. 898 S.W.2d 98 (Mo. Ct. App. 1995).
163. *Id.* at 101–02.
164. *Id.* at 102–03.
165. *Id.* at 103.
166. *Id.* at 106–09.
167. *Id.* at 108.
168. *Id.* at 108–09.
169. *Id.* at 109.
170. NBAPA Regulations § B(2).
171. *Id.* § B(1)

to 3 percent with lower limits for franchise and transition players.[172] The WNBPA sets a 5 percent maximum fee.[173] Neither the MLBPA nor the NHLPA agent regulations generally contain fee maximums. Taking a hands-off approach, the MLBPA's website states "just as the [MLBPA] endorses a free market system for its players in negotiating contracts with Club owners, the agent fee is negotiated freely between the player and his agent."[174] The MLBPA regulations, however, forbid agents from charging a fee if the player's salary does not exceed the applicable minimum.[175]

Players association regulations also define compensation. The NBPA regulations state: "the term 'compensation' shall include base salary, signing bonus and any performance bonus actually received by the player, no other benefits negotiated on behalf of the individual player shall be taken into consideration — including, but not limited to, the value of a personal loan, an insurance policy, an automobile, or a residence...."[176] The NFLPA regulations define compensation to "include only salaries, signing bonuses, reporting bonuses, roster bonuses, Practice Squad salary in excess of the minimum Practice Squad salary ... and any performance incentives earned by the player during the term of the contract (including any option year) negotiated by the Contract Advisor."[177] Player association regulations also address when agents are entitled to receive their fee. Generally, a player agent shall not be entitled to receive any fee for services until the player receives the compensation upon which the fee is based.[178] Allowance is made, however, for the agent to receive payments in regard to deferred compensation and other circumstances.[179]

§ 9.06 Mandatory Arbitration

[A] Agent-Player Disputes

Players associations' agent regulations and the accompanying standardized representation agreements now include mandatory arbitration provisions that encompass disputes between an agent and an athlete.[180] For example, the NFLPA regulations

---

172. NFLPA Regulations § 4(B)(1).

173. WNBAPA Regulations Governing Player Agents § 4(B) [hereinafter WNBAPA Regulations], *available at* http://wnbpa.wpengine.com/wp-content/uploads/2017/08/WNBPAAgentRegulations. pdf.

174. Frequently Asked Questions, MLB Players, https://www.mlbplayers.com/faq; *see also* NHLPA Regulations Governing Agent Certification § 4(B).

175. Frequently Asked Questions, MLB Players, https://www.mlbplayers.com/faq.

176. NBAPA Regulations § B.

177. NFLPA Regulations § 4(b)(3).

178. NBAPA Regulations § B.

179. NBAPA Regulations § B; *see also* NFLPA Regulations § 4(B); NHLPA Regulations § 4(B); WNBAPA Regulations, § 4(B); MLBPA Regulation § 6(G).

180. Mitten, *supra* note 2, at 629; *see* Wasserman Media Croup, Inc. v. Bender, 2011 WL 1886460 (S.D.N.Y. May 16, 2011) (upholding arbitration award in favor of player and against his agent); Octagon, Inc. v. Richards, 2010 WL 3932272 (E.D. Va. Oct. 5, 2010) (validating arbitration clause in representation agreement between athlete and agent); Dye v. Sexton, 2017 WL 7615571 (N.D. Ga.

state that arbitration shall be the exclusive method for resolving disputes between Agents and NFL players as well as disputes over an agent's application certification.[181] Similarly, NBPA regulations require arbitration for all "disputes that may arise from denying certification to an applicant or from the interpretation, application or enforcement of [NBPA] Regulations and the resulting [contracts] between Player Agents and individual Players."[182]

Agents and athletes may challenge an adverse arbitration award but are unlikely to succeed because of the limited grounds on which an arbitration award may be vacated or modified.[183] In *Adams v. Barnes*,[184] a court refused to vacate an arbitrator's ruling in favor of an NFL agent. The agent and player's dispute fell within the scope of the NFLPA's agent regulations mandating arbitration as the exclusive method for resolving certain disputes between players and agents.[185] The player argued that the award should be set aside because the arbitrator had presided over a previous dispute between the parties and was therefore partial.[186] In rejecting this argument, the court stated that the parties should have reasonably expected this because the arbitrator was the only one employed by the NFLPA.[187] Before ruling in favor of the agent, the court stated the principle that even manifest disregard for the law is not sufficient to vacate an arbitration award.[188] In *Wichard v. Suggs*,[189] the court also refused to vacate an arbitration award because the arbitrator's decision was neither irrational nor in manifest disregard of the law.[190] From this, it is clear that athletes and agents who are parties to a mandatory arbitration will generally be bound to the ultimate decision of an arbitrator.

[B] Agent-to-Agent Disputes

As is true for conflicts between athletes and agents in the major professional sports leagues, players associations' regulations require arbitration of disputes between agents.[191] For example, the NBPA's regulations state that its arbitration process "shall

---

Dec. 13, 2017) (validating NFLPA mandatory arbitration provision in dispute between athlete and agent).

181. NFLPA Regulations § 5(A).

182. NBAPA Regulations § 5.

183. *See, e.g.*, Bender, 2011 WL 1886460 (confirming arbitration award in favor of agency). *See generally* 9 U.S.C. § 10–11 (listing grounds for vacating, modifying, and correcting an arbitration award under the Federal Arbitration Act).

184. 2010 WL 2484251 (N.D. Tex. June 17, 2010).

185. *Id.* at *1.

186. *Id.* at *2.

187. *Id.* at *3–4.

188. *Id.*

189. 95 F. Supp. 3d 935 (E.D. Va. 2015).

190. *Id.* at 942–47.

191. Dye v. Sexton, 2017 WL 7615571 (N.D. Ga. Dec. 13, 2017); Smith v. IMG Worldwide, Inc., 360 F. Supp. 2d 681, 685 (E.D. Pa. 2005); Rosenhaus v. Star Sports, Inc., 929 So. 2d 40, 411 (Fla. Dist. Ct. App. 2006) (court holds "All parties are members of the NFLPA and are 'Contract Advisors,' as defined by that organization.... [A]s contract Advisors, they are bound by the Agent Regulations promulgated by the NFLPA which detail the obligations, rights, and liabilities of Contract Advisors ...

be the exclusive method for resolving any and all disputes that may arise from ... [a] dispute ... between two or more Player Agents with respect to their individual entitlement to fees owed, whether paid or unpaid, by a Player who was jointly represented by such Player Agents."[192] Similarly, the NFLPA's regulations state that arbitration "shall be the exclusive method for resolving any and all disputes that may arise from ... A dispute between two or more Contract Advisors with respect to whether or not a Contract Advisor interfered with the contractual relationship of a Contract Advisor and player...."[193] The MLBPA agent's regulations also include similar language.[194]

Dye v. Sexton[195] illustrates the breadth of players association regulations mandating arbitration of disputes between agents. There, the court granted an agent's motion to compel arbitration in a case involving alleged solicitation of clients of the agency at which the defendant agent had been employed before he went to work for a competitor agency.[196] This prompted the plaintiff to sue the agent asserting multiple state claims including the solicitation of clients of the agent's former agency.[197]

When Sexton moved to compel arbitration, Dye argued that the dispute was not subject to mandatory arbitration proceedings because his partnership agreement with Sexton did not contain an arbitration agreement.[198] In rejecting this argument, the court noted that both parties were "Contract Advisors" bound by the NFLPA regulations and "by agreeing to the NFLPA Regulations, each agreed that any covered dispute between himself and another Contract Advisor would be subject to arbitration."[199] Therefore, in effect, the court held that the arbitration agreement as contained in the NFLPA regulations governing Contract Advisors mandated arbitration notwithstanding the partnership agreement between the parties.[200]

Similarly, in *France v. Bernstein*,[201] a district court denied an agent's attempt to vacate an arbitration award on the basis that it was either secured by fraud or that the arbitrator refused to consider pertinent evidence in the form of deposition testimony. Regarding the first argument, the court emphasized that the agent simply

---

[and] contain a provision requiring certain disputes between Contract Advisors to be resolved through arbitration"); Branion v. Wallace, WL 11633674 (C.D. Cal. Jan. 18, 2017) (holding that a dispute between two agents was subject to arbitration). *But see* Dogra v. Griffin, 2020 WL 5411187 (E.D. Mo. Sept. 9, 2020) (dismissing agency's claim for unpaid marketing commission fees despite arbitration award in its favor due to the lapse of two-year statute of limitations period).

192. NBAPA Regulations § 5.

193. NFLPA Regulations § 5(A)(5).

194. *See* MLBPA Regulations § 7 (stating that the association's arbitration process shall be the exclusive method for resolving "all disputes between or among Player Agents, Applicants, Agencies, affiliated persons or entities and Expert Agent Advisors").

195. 2017 WL 7615571 (N.D. Ga. Dec. 13, 2017).

196. *Id.* at *3.

197. *Id.*

198. *Id.*

199. *Id.*

200. *Id.* at *4.

201. 2020 U.S. Dist. LEXIS 202838 (M.D. Pa. Oct. 30, 2020).

had not met the "demanding evidentiary standard necessary to vacate an arbitration award on the basis of fraud." Moreover, the court dismissed the second argument as being meritless considering that arbitrators have no ability to compel witness testimony. This case exemplifies judicial reluctance to review final arbitration awards.

§ 9.07 Ethical Considerations

The American Bar Association's MRPC provide ethical standards and govern attorneys in almost every state. Despite agents attempts to skirt these rules by arguing that they serve their clients in business but not legal matters, many courts have held that attorney agents who are admitted to a state bar hold themselves out as having legal expertise and are bound by the MRPC's rules.[202] Therefore, "[a]s long as a lawyer is engaged in the practice of law, he is bound by ethical requirements of [the legal] profession, and he may not defend his actions by contending that he was engaged in some other kind of professional activity."[203]

In addition to agency law principles and player associations' regulations, MRPC Rule 1.7 governs conflicts of interest faced by attorney agents.[204] MRPC 1.7(a) provides:

> Except as provided in [MRPC 1.7(b)], a lawyer shall not represent a client if the representation involves a concurrent conflict of interest. A concurrent conflict of interest exists if:
>
> (1) the representation of one client will be directly adverse to another client; or
>
> (2) there is a significant risk that the representation of one or more clients will be materially limited by the lawyer's responsibilities to another client, a former client or a third person or by a personal interest of the lawyer.

MRPC 1.7(b) provides:

> Notwithstanding the existence of a concurrent conflict of interest under [MRPC 1.7(a)], a lawyer may represent a client if:

---

202. Melissa Neiman, *Fair Game: Ethical Considerations in Negotiation by Sports Agents*, 9 TEX. REV. ENT. & SPORTS L. 123, 129–30 (2007) (citing Cuyahoga County Bar Ass'n v. Glenn, 649 N.E.2d 1213 (Ohio 1995)).

203. Rothstein, *supra* note 1, at 26; *see also* Neiman, *supra* note 202, at 129 ("[U]pon admission to a state bar, the attorney agrees to abide by the professional responsibility rules set out by that state bar; if the attorney's general business practices violate these ethics rules, the attorney may be sanctioned by the state bar authorities.").

204. Neiman, *supra* note 202, at 128–30.

(1) the lawyer reasonably believes that the lawyer will be able to provide competent and diligent representation to each affected client;

(2) the representation is not prohibited by law;

(3) the representation does not involve the assertion of a claim by one client against another client represented by the lawyer in the same litigation or other proceeding before a tribunal; and

(4) each affected client gives informed consent, confirmed in writing.

MRPC 1.7(a) sets out the general principle that an attorney agent may not represent a client if there is a concurrent conflict of interest and defines when such a conflict exists, while MRPC 1.7(b) provides an exception to MRPC 1.7(a) and defines when the exception is satisfied. From this, it is first worth noting that MRPC 1.7(a)'s mandate not only prohibits actual conflicts of interest (*i.e.*, where an agent's client has interests directly adverse to another client) but also prohibits potential conflicts of interest (*i.e.*, where there is a *"significant risk"* that an agent's representation of one client will materially limit the attorney's representation of another client). Secondly, despite the provisions listed in MRPC 1.7(b)'s exception, the official comments flesh out the requirements of informed consent as well as situations when representations are nonconsensual.[205] Accordingly, to avoid liability or state bar sanctions, attorney agents should be aware of these rules even when working on general business matters.

To illustrate, *Sports Management Network v. Busch*[206] provides a rather blatant example of conflicts of interests being "sufficiently egregious [so as to] infect the entire [representation agreement]."[207] There, a federal district court held that a representation agreement between race car driver Kurt Busch, his agent, his agents' sports agency, and his agents' law firm was unenforceable as a matter of law.[208] The court noted that Busch's agent, who owed business-motivated fiduciary duties to his own agency as acting CEO, violated Michigan's Rules of Professional Conduct by "representing [Busch] in a manner that could be materially limited 'by the lawyer's own interests.'"[209] Such representation ran counter to the policy of lawyers being "free to exercise independent professional judgment regarding whether to represent the customer and what legal services the customer should have, without being influenced by whatever the nonlaw business has recommended."[210] The court also cited the fact that the agency represented multiple adverse parties, without Busch's knowledge, including sponsors and driving

---

205. Model Rules of Prof'l Conduct R. 1.7 cmt. 7–11 (2018).
206. 2019 WL 1057314 (E.D. Mich. March 6, 2019).
207. *Id.* at *5.
208. *Id.*
209. *Id.* at *4.
210. *Id.*

teams that employed Busch during his career.[211] These simultaneous representations led the court to conclude that while the attorney "billed himself as Busch's agent and attorney, ... when Busch's interests were adverse to his other clients, the best he could provide was facilitation, not the loyalty that is the lodestone of Rule 1.7."[212]

---

211. *Id.* at *5.

212. *Id.*; *see also* Matter of Henley, 478 S.E.2d 134 (Ga. 1996) (holding agent's failure to disclose financial interests to former NFL player "illustrate[d] one of the most blatant appearances of impropriety."); Cuyahoga Cty. B. Assn. v. Glenn, 649 N.E.2d 1213 (Ohio 1995) (expanding disciplinary panel's recommended sanction against agent for receiving and retaining unauthorized payment of proceeds during MLB player's renegotiations).

Part V

Health and Safety

Chapter 10

Health, Safety and Disability Issues in Sport

§ 10.01 Introduction

This chapter examines tort liability issues that arise in sport. The chapter begins with an exploration of the duties owed by participants in sports to their fellow participants and the circumstances under which courts determine that coparticipant liability is appropriate. We then examine the standards courts apply in assessing claims spectators make against facility owners and operators for injuries suffered on premises. The chapter also examines the circumstances that warrant holding educational institutions liable in tort for injuries to their student-athletes. It then explores the common law principles and statutes on which courts rely in addressing disability issues in sport. The chapter concludes with discussion of sovereign and qualified immunity as well as the effect of pre-injury liability waivers.

§ 10.02 Coparticipant Liability

[A] Introduction

Participating in a sport exposes an athlete to risks. Indeed, many activities that are accepted and indeed required during the course of sport participation would likely amount to a tort or a crime if the activity occurred outside of a sport. Examples abound, but consider a tackle in football, a slide tackle in soccer, a body check in hockey, and a hard box-out in basketball. Each of these actions, occurring off the field of play would likely constitute tortious battery if the conduct resulted in an injury to another participant. In sports and recreational activities, however, the standard adopted by most courts absolves alleged tortfeasors of liability ensuing from all but the most extreme conduct.

The following discussion addresses the standards that govern the liability of one participant to another and the policy reasons that justify the most frequently adopted standard: an athlete is not liable to a coparticipant for injuries resulting from conduct that is a risk inherent in playing a sport.[1] Only when a participant increases the risk

---

1. John Inazu, *Beyond Unreasonable*, 99 NEB. L. REV. 375, 410 (2020).

associated with a particular sport will liability likely ensue. The following discussion necessarily examines what constitutes an inherent risk as well as when an athlete's sport participation crosses the line into reckless and intentional behavior. It also briefly discusses the minority rule — a negligence standard — and the policy rationales that have prompted a few courts to adopt it.

[B] The Majority Approach — An Elevated Standard of Care

[1] The Reckless and Intentional Conduct Standard

In 1973, an on-the-field incident during a game between the NFL's Denver Broncos and Cincinnati Bengals provided an opportunity for courts to adopt a standard for determining the liability of one participant to another. The matter, *Hackbart v. Cincinnati Bengals, Inc.*, produced a federal district opinion[2] favoring the defendant, and a circuit court opinion[3] favoring the plaintiff and articulating a coparticipant liability standard that many courts would later adopt.

Hackbart played safety for Denver, and Clark played fullback for Cincinnati. With Denver winning 21–3, Hackbart fell down while attempting to block Clark.[4] As Hackbart watched the play move away from him, Clark approached Hackbart from behind and, "out of anger and frustration," forcefully hit Hackbart in the helmet with his forearm, knocking Hackbart to the ground.[5] Hackbart suffered a neck injury that allegedly resulted in Denver ultimately releasing him from the team.[6]

Hackbart sued Clark and the Cincinnati club, alleging reckless misconduct and negligence.[7] The district court stated that Clark's liability would turn on whether he acted as a "reasonably prudent professional football player" would have acted under the circumstances.[8] After a detailed examination of professional football's norms and culture, which the court described as imbued with frequent disabling injuries[9] and "the spectacle of savagery,"[10] the court concluded "[i]t is wholly incongruous to talk about a professional football player's duty of care for the safety of opposing players."[11] Consequently, it found that Clark had not acted unreasonably.[12]

The Tenth Circuit disapproved of the liability standard fashioned by the district court and reasoned that "there are no principles of law which allow a court to rule

---

2. 435 F. Supp. 352 (D. Colo. 1977).
3. 601 F.2d 516 (10th Cir. 1979).
4. *Hackbart*, 435 F. Supp. at 353.
5. *Id.*
6. *Id.* at 354.
7. *Id.* at 355.
8. *Id.*
9. *Id.*
10. *Id.*
11. *Id.* at 356.
12. *Id.*

out certain tortious conduct by reason of general roughness of the game."[13] It found that the legal system cannot allow sport to abandon civility altogether. In line with this reasoning, the Tenth Circuit established recklessness as the standard for assessing the liability of one sport participant to another. Applying the recklessness standard, the court added that a plaintiff need not prove a specific intent to injure. Rather, a plaintiff need only prove the defendant intended the allegedly tortious act and recognized it as potentially harmful.[14]

The standard adopted by the Tenth Circuit in *Hackbart* articulates the majority approach, although courts in subsequent decisions have refined its contours. Like the Tenth Circuit, some courts frame the governing standard with an emphasis on a defendant's reckless behavior and the inherent risks of a sport. Other courts use the terminology of primary assumption of the risk, which also requires identifying the risks inherent to a sport and assessing whether the defendant's conduct (*e.g.,* recklessness) increased those risks. Notwithstanding the terminology that the majority of courts use, those adopting the majority approach invariably address: (1) whether the defendant owed a duty to a coparticipant; (2) what risks are inherent in the particular sport; and (3) whether the defendant's conduct crossed the line into reckless, willful or intentional conduct. Finally, a distinct minority of jurisdictions have adopted an ordinary negligence standard.

Gauvin v. Clark[15] illustrates the approach of courts that frame coparticipant liability in terms of the defendant's recklessness. In that case, a varsity high school hockey player was injured after being struck with the back end of hockey stick wielded by a player on the opposing team. The court stated that "participants in an athletic event owe a duty of care to other participants to refrain from reckless misconduct and liability may result from injuries caused a player by reason of the breach of that duty."[16] Similarly in *Nabozny v. Barnhill,*[17] the court stated, "a player is liable for injury in a tort action if his conduct is such that it is either deliberate, wilful [sic] or with a reckless disregard for the safety of the other player so as to cause injury to that player, the same being a question of fact to be decided by a jury." In another case in which a court adopted a recklessness standard, it also spoke of risks inherent to the game,

---

13. *Id.* at 520.

14. *Id.* at 521.

15. 537 N.E.2d 94 (Mass. 1989).

16. *Id.* at 95; *accord* Mohney v. USA Hockey, 5 F. App'x 450, 456 (6th Cir. 2001); Ritchie-Gamester v. City of Berkley, 597 N.W.2d 517, 525 (Mich. 1999) (adopting a recklessness standard); Hoke v. Cullinan, 914 S.W.2d 335 (Ky. 1995) (rejecting a negligence standard in favor of recklessness standard); Thompson v. McNeill, 559 N.E.2d 705, 706–07 (Ohio 1990) (in adopting recklessness standard, court holds that coparticipant owed no duty to plaintiff for conduct resulting in an injury that was a customary part of the game); Grady v. Chenango Valley Central Sch. Dist., 141 N.Y.S.3d 513, 515 (N.Y. 2021) (participant in sporting activity accepts the risks that are commonly encountered in, or are inherent to, the sport); Dunagan v. Coleman, 427 S.W.3d 552, 558 (Tex. Ct. App. 2014) ("Although a defendant cannot be held liable for ordinary negligence committed in the course of participating in a sports activity, participants are not immunized from all liability for their conduct.").

17. 334 N.E.2d 258, 261 (Ill. Ct. App. 1975).

stating that "the duty of care is such that each participant assumes the risks ordinarily incident thereto ... including 'the risk of an obvious danger or of one that is a matter of common knowledge.'"[18] The court added that the plaintiff, a softball player who was injured when an opposing player slid into her at second base, assumed the risk that such an injury might occur because it was an inherent risk of playing softball.[19] A 2021 Ohio appellate court decision adhering to the precedent established by the Ohio Supreme Court in *Thompson v. McNeil*,[20] likewise emphasized the nature of the defendant's conduct. "'Thus, a participant who injures another participant in the course of a sporting activity ... cannot be held liable for negligence because no duty is owed to protect the victim from that conduct.'"[21]

[2] The Primary Assumption of the Risk Doctrine

Other courts adopt the functional equivalent of the recklessness standard, but couch their standard in the terminology of the primary assumption of the risk doctrine and whether the injury results from an inherent risk of the sport. In a leading case, *Knight v. Jewett*,[22] a player suffered a severe injury to her finger after another player stepped on it during an informal touch football game. After her finger was amputated, the plaintiff sued the coparticipant for negligence, assault, and battery.[23] The California Supreme Court stated that the pertinent question under primary assumption is whether a defendant owes a duty to "protect the plaintiff from a particular risk of harm."[24] Secondary assumption of the risk assumes the defendant owed a duty to the plaintiff, and the salient issue is whether the "plaintiff knowingly encounters a risk of injury caused by the defendant's breach of that duty."[25] The court added that if no duty arises pursuant to a primary assumption of the risk analysis, then the defendant is absolved of liability to the plaintiff.[26] Turning to the duty that one athletic participant owes to another, the court held:

> Although defendants generally have no legal duty to eliminate (or protect a plaintiff against) risks inherent in the sport itself, it is well established that defendants generally do have a duty to use care not to increase the risks to a participant over and above those inherent in the sport.... In some situations ... the careless conduct of others is treated as an "inherent risk" of a

---

18. Kiley v. Patterson, 763 A.2d 583, 586 (R.I. 2000) (quoting Ogden v. Rabinowitz, 134 A.2d 416 (R.I. 1957)).

19. *Id*. at 587.

20. 559 N.E.2d 705 (Ohio 1990).

21. Kumar v. Sevastos, 174 N.E.3d 398, 490 (Ohio Ct. App. 2021) (quoting Barakat v. Pordash, 842 N.E.2d 120 (Ohio Ct. App. 2005)).

22. 834 P.2d 696 (Cal. 1992).

23. *Id*. at 698.

24. *Id*. at 704. *See* Ochall v. McNamer, 79 N.E.3d 1215, 1229 (Ohio Ct. App. 2016) (stating the primary assumption of the risk doctrine involves the question of duty); Mark v. Moser, 746 N.E.2d 410, 420 (Ind. Ct. App. 2001) (adopting the primary assumption of risk doctrine and providing an excellent summary of different judicial approaches to coparticipant liability).

25. *Knight*, 834 P.2d at 703.

26. *Id*. at 708.

sport, thus barring recovery by the plaintiff. For example, numerous cases recognize that in a game of baseball, a player generally cannot recover if he or she is hit and injured by a carelessly thrown ball ... and that in the game of basketball, recovery is not permitted for an injury caused by a carelessly extended elbow.[27]

The court elaborated that the:

> overwhelming majority of cases, both within and outside of California, that have addressed the issue of coparticipant liability in ... a sport, have concluded that it is improper to hold a sports participant liable to a co-participant for ordinary careless conduct committed during the sport ... and that liability properly may be imposed on a participant only when he or she intentionally injures another player or engages in reckless conduct that is totally outside the range of the ordinary activity involved in the sport.[28]

Following the *Knight* approach, other courts identify the critical inquiries as whether a duty arose pursuant to a primary assumption of the risk analysis, which invariably involves an analysis of the inherent risks of a sport.[29]

[3] The Contact Sport Exception

Courts in some jurisdictions examine coparticipant liability by distinguishing contact and noncontact sports. This approach also, however, requires a determination of whether the defendant's conduct went beyond simple negligence. In *Pfister v. Shusta*,[30] the court stated that in noncontact sports, a negligence standard determines the liability of one participant to another. It then stated another standard applies to contact sports. "[V]oluntary participants in contact sports are not liable for injuries caused by simple negligent conduct; however, they owe each other a duty to refrain from willful and wanton or intentional misconduct and are liable for injuries caused by willful and wanton misconduct."[31] The court reasoned as follows:

---

27. *Id.*

28. *Id.* at 710.

29. *See, e.g., Ochall*, 79 N.E.3d at 1228; Daly v. McFarland, 812 N.W.2d 113, 120 (Minn. 2012) (stating the primary assumption of the risk doctrine applies to coparticipants in sports and approving of *Schneider* ex rel. *Schneider v. Erickson*, 654 N.W.2d 144, 151 (Minn. Ct. App. 2002), in which court adopted the primary assumption of the risk approach to coparticipant liability); Yoneda v. Tom, 133 P.3d 796, 808 (Haw. 2006) (applying primary assumption of risk doctrine to golfer hit in head by golf ball of another participant).

30. 657 N.E.2d 1013 (Ill. 2001).

31. *Id.* at 1015. *See also* Feld v. Borkowski, 790 N.W.2d 72 (Iowa 2010) (adopting contact sport exception); Jaworski v. Kiernan, 696 A.2d 332, 338 (Conn. 2008) (adopting contact sport exception); Ludman v. Davenport Assumption Sch., 805 N.W.2d 902, 911 (Iowa 2017) (acknowledging applicability of contact sport exception in cases involving coparticipant liability); Laughman v. Girtakovskis, 374 P.3d 504, 507–08 (Colo. Ct. App. 2015) (approving of the *Knight* approach but also noting that liability will not ensue for risk inherent in a contact sport such as martial arts and ultimately appearing to adopt a standard that focuses on whether the injury-causing activity was inherent to the sport).

Participants in team sports, where physical contact among participants is
inherent and virtually inevitable, assume greater risks of injury than non-
participants or participants in noncontact sports.... Recovery will be granted
for injuries sustained by participants in contact sports only if the injuries
are caused by willful and wanton or intentional misconduct of co-participants.... The contact sports exception strikes the appropriate balance between
society's interest in limiting liability for injuries resulting from physical contact inherent in a contact sport and society's interest in allowing recovery
for injuries resulting from willful and wanton or intentional misconduct by
participants. Those who participate in soccer, football, softball, basketball,
or even a spontaneous game of can kicking, choose to play games in which
physical contact among participants is inherent in the conduct of the game.
Participants in such games assume a greater risk of injury resulting from the
negligent conduct of co-participants.[32]

Thus, the contact sport exception entails a two-step process: (1) determining whether
a sport is a contact sport; and (2) determining whether the defendant's behavior resulting in a coparticipant's injury is willful, wanton, or reckless.

Some courts, however, have expressly or impliedly rejected the contact sport distinction as the standard governing coparticipant liability. *Thompson v. McNeil*[33] illustrates this approach. There, the Ohio Supreme Court reasoned that the reckless
or intentional conduct standard:

reveals the awareness of the court below that there are different duties and
risks appropriate to different sports, but the contact-non-contact distinction
does not sufficiently take into account that we are dealing with a spectrum
of duties and risks rather than an either-or distinction. Is golf a contact sport?
Obviously, a golfer accepts the risk of coming in contact with wayward golf
shots on the links, so golf is more dangerous than table tennis, for instance,
but certainly not as dangerous as kickboxing. Analyzing liability for injuries
inflicted in sports in terms of a continuum along which the standard of care
rises as the inherent danger of the sport falls is more useful than distinguishing
sports by applying a black-and-white distinction between contact and noncontact sports.[34]

As discussed *infra*, other courts also reject the contact/noncontact distinction as the
basis for assessing a coparticipant's liability.

Such was the case in *Nixon v. Clay*.[35] In that case, the Utah Supreme Court expressly
rejected the contact versus noncontact sport distinction.[36] The court expressed concern
that basing coparticipant liability on the contact/noncontact sport distinction could

---

32. *Pfister*, 657 N.E.2d at 1017–18.
33. 559 N.E.2d 705 (Ohio 1990).
34. *Id.* at 708–09.
35. 449 P.3d 11 (Utah 2019).
36. *Id.* at ¶¶ 3, 39.

result in arbitrary line drawing, which would often hinge on the extent of contact typically "anticipated by the sport as a whole."[37] Adopting the primary assumption of the risk doctrine, the *Nixon* court held that participant is not liable to a coparticipant in a sport for injuries resulting from risks inherent in the sport.[38]

In *Shin v. Ahn*,[39] a golfer "inadvertently 'pulled' a tee shot," striking the plaintiff in the head with a golf ball.[40] The court noted that in *Knight* and subsequent cases, it had left open the question of whether *Knight*'s primary assumption of the risk standard should apply to noncontact sports.[41] Reversing the court of appeals decision that primary assumption of the risk did not apply, the California Supreme Court concluded that primary assumption of the risk applies to golf regardless of its classification as a contact or noncontact sport.[42] It noted that although golf may not present the physical demands of other sports, there are risks that are inherent in the sport.[43] After examining numerous other decisions in which courts have applied the primary assumption of the risk doctrine rather than the contact sport exception to golf,[44] the court approvingly quoted *Allen v. Donath*.[45] "While the genteel game of golf can hardly be described as 'a competitive contact sport,' we believe the recklessness and intentional standard is every bit as appropriate to conduct on the links as it is on the polo field."[46]

[4] The Rationale for the Majority Rule

The forgoing cases predicate their rejection of a negligence standard on concerns that such a standard could "alter fundamentally the nature of the sport by deterring participants from vigorously engaging in activity that falls close to, but on the permissible side of, a prescribed act."[47] Courts have also expressed concern that a negligence standard would lead to a flood of litigation.[48] Given these reasons, courts prefer to leave the imposition of sanctions to the internal mechanisms established by sport governing bodies.[49]

It is notable that courts have also held that a player's violation of a sport's safety rule will not necessarily result in coparticipant liability.[50] Again, liability will ensue

---

37. *Id.* at ¶ 31.

38. *Id.* at ¶ 3.

39. 165 P.3d 581 (Cal. 2007).

40. *Id.* at 583.

41. *Id.* at 582–83.

42. *Id.* at 584.

43. *Id.* at 586.

44. *Id.* at 588–89.

45. 875 S.W.2d 438, 440 (1994).

46. *Shin*, 165 P.3d at 589.

47. *Id.* at 585; Nixon v. Clay, 449 P.3d 11, at ¶ 20 (Utah 2019); *Hoke*, 914 S.W.2d at 338–39; *Knight*, 834 P.2d at 318; *Gauvin*, 537 N.E.2d at 96; *Kiley*, 763 A.2d at 586; *Nabozny*, 334 N.E.2d at 260.

48. *Kiley*, 763 A.2d at 586; *accord Nixon*, 449 P.3d at ¶ 20.

49. *Knight*, 834 P.2d at 318–19.

50. *Gauvin*, 537 N.E.2d at 97; Karas v. Strevell, 884 N.E.2d 122, 137 (Ill. 2008) (stating rules violations are an inherent part of the game); *Moser*, 746 N.E.2d at 420 (holding a coparticipant's violation

only if the rule's violation increased the inherent risk of a sport because, for example, the defendant acted recklessly.[51]

[5] Inherent Risk

Determining what constitutes an inherent risk is a critical aspect of the majority approach, whether a court employs the language of primary assumption of the risk or recklessness. The Utah Supreme Court adopted the following definition: "Under a primary assumption of the risk analysis, the question is not necessarily whether a skier would 'wish' to encounter a certain risk, but whether a risk is inherent or essential to the sport of skiing and therefore whether the risk is one that a skier reasonably expects to encounter when participating in the sport."[52] In *Nixon v. Clay*,[53] the same court suggested several factors to consider in determining whether a risk is inherent to a sport, including: (1) how frequent the injury-causing conduct occurs in the sport; (2) whether such conduct is a regular part of the strategy of a sport; and (3) the severity of the sanctions imposed if the conduct violates a rule of the sport.

In *Joseph v. New York Racing Ass'n, Inc.*,[54] the court stated that an inherent risk does not require the injured plaintiff to have "foreseen the exact manner in which the injury occurred 'so long as he or she is aware of the potential for injury of the mechanism from which the injury results.'" In *Morgan v. State*,[55] the court held that:

> a participant consents to those commonly appreciated risks which are inherent in and arise out of the nature of the sport generally and flow from such participation. Thus, the risks of becoming injured due to fatigue..., being bumped by a horse during a race or exhibition ... or being struck by a ball or bat during a baseball game ... are risks which various participants are legally deemed to have accepted personal responsibility for because they commonly inhere in the nature of those activities....[56]

In short, an injury resulting from an inherent risk of a sport is unlikely to result in coparticipant liability.

---

of a rule of the game is evidence of recklessness but does not "*per se*" establish reckless or intentional conduct).

51. *Gauvin*, 537 N.E.2d at 97.

52. Rutherford v. Talisker Canyons Finance Co, LLC, 445 P.3d 474, 498 (Utah 2019).

53. 449 P.3d at ¶ 29. *Accord* Bertin v. Mann, 918 N.W.2d 707, 717 (Mich. 2018) (stating inherent risks "are those that are reasonably foreseeable under the circumstances of the case." The court added: "[i]t is not enough that participant could foresee being injured in general; the participant must have been able to foresee that the injury could arise though the 'mechanism' it resulted from.").

54. 809 N.Y.S.2d 526, 528 (N.Y. App. Div. 2006); *see also*, W.R. Habeeb, Annotation, *Liability for Injury to or Death of Participant in Game or Contest*, 7 A.L.R.2d 704 (1949) ("Where a person voluntarily participated in a lawful game or contest, he assumes the ordinary risks of such game or contest...."); Grady v. Chenango Valley Central Sch. Dist., 141 N.Y.S.3d 513, 516 (N.Y. App. Div. 2021) (batter being hit in face by pitched ball was an inherent risk of playing baseball).

55. 685 N.E.2d 202 (N.Y. 1997).

56. *Id.* at 207–08.

[C] The Minority Approach:
A Negligence Standard

A minority of courts apply a negligence standard in resolving disputes involving coparticipant liability.[57] These courts reject the above-mentioned rationale for an elevated standard of care. *Allen v. Dover Co-Recreational Softball League*[58] is illustrative. In that case, Carol Allen, a recreational softball player who was not wearing a helmet, was hit in the head by a thrown softball as she ran to first base during a game in a recreational softball league.[59] Allen, who "suffered head and brain injuries that caused cognitive deficiencies including impaired speech,"[60] sued the league,[61] arguing it was negligent in, among other things, using unsafe softballs and not requiring all players to wear helmets.[62] The defendant league asserted that "recreational athletic activities would be chilled without a recklessness standard." Adopting a negligence standard,[63] the court stated liability is not appropriate for "a participant, sponsor, or organizer 'who creates only risks that are normal or ordinary to the sport,'" because that person has acted "as a reasonable person of ordinary prudence under the circumstances."[64] The court nevertheless found for the defendant, concluding that the plaintiff failed to allege facts necessary to show that the league "unreasonably created a new risk outside the ordinary risks ... that [she] would be injured when struck by a softball" during the game.[65]

The court in *Pfenning v. Lineman*[66] took a similar approach. There, the plaintiff, who was driving a golf cart, was hit in the mouth by an errant golf ball. She sued several persons including the operators of the golf course who argued that "participants and spectators in sporting events are precluded from recovery for injuries that result from the sport's inherent dangers" which include being struck by a golf ball.[67] The court rejected the primary assumption of the risk standard the defendant sought.[68] It nevertheless adopted a similar standard in holding that "in negligence claims against a participant in a sports activity, if the conduct of such participant is within the range of ordinary behavior of participants in the sport, the conduct is reasonable as a matter of law and does not constitute a breach of duty."[69] The court

---

57. Erica K. Rosenthal, *Inside the Lines: Basing Negligence Liability in Sports for Safety-Based Rule Violations on the Level of Play*, 72 FORDHAM L. REV. 2631, 2648 (2004).

58. 807 A.2d 1274 (N.H. 2002).

59. *Id.* at 1278.

60. *Id.* at 1279.

61. *Id.*

62. *Id.*

63. *Id.* at 1284.

64. *Id.*

65. *Id.* at 1288; *cf.* Estes v. Tripson, 932 P.2d 1364, 1367 (1997) (finding that a player running from third base to home plate in an ordinary manner was not liable for breaking a catcher's leg, because the runner did not unreasonably "increase or exacerbate the inherent risks" the catcher faced).

66. 947 N.E.2d 392 (Ind. 2011).

67. *Id.* at 397.

68. *Id.* at 402–03.

69. *Id* at 404.

added that a participant's intentional or reckless behavior is beyond the range of ordinary behavior of a participant.[70]

§ 10.03 Criminal Law's General Abstention from Sport

[A] Introduction

As discussed *supra*, regulated violence is integral to some sports. This is certainly true of combat sports, such as boxing and mixed martial arts ("MMA"), as well as collision sports, such as football, rugby, and hockey. What might be an impressive maneuver in these sports — a punch in boxing, a chokehold in MMA, or a full body tackle in football — would likely constitute criminal battery if it occurred outside of sport participation. This is because criminal battery statutes (which vary by state) tend to require a touching to which the victim does not consent.[71] Sport participants generally grant consent. A boxer's jab that hits the boxer's opponent in the nose during a typical boxing match, therefore, will not trigger criminal liability. The same holds true for an NFL defensive lineman's heavy tackle of a running back. But when violence strays too far beyond a sport's norms and is intentionally inflicted with the goal of causing serious injury,[72] the notion of consent is undermined. Thus, while the criminal justice system generally defers to a sports league's internal mechanisms for adjudicating player injury-causing behavior,[73] the possibility of criminal prosecution increases when a player's conduct is so egregious that it is antithetical to the competitive spirit of a sport.[74]

A 2017 Arizona case exemplifies conduct that sometimes prompts prosecution. Christopher Crawford, an Arizona State University rugby player, was prosecuted for aggravated assault.[75] Play had stopped, and while the victim was on one knee tying

---

70. *Id. See also* Lestina v. West Bend Mutual Ins. Co., 501 N.W.2d 28, 33 (Wis. 1993) (adopting a negligence standard).

71. *See* McDonald v. Lipov, 13 N.E.3d 179, 187 (Ill. Ct. App. 2014) (noting that "[i]t is not the hostile intent of the defendant but rather the absence of consent by the plaintiff that is at the core of an action for battery.").

72. A 1986 boxing match between Luis Resto and Billy Collins, Jr. in New York City provides an example of such violence. Before the match, Resto and his trainer, Panama Lewis, wrapped Resto's hands in plaster-hardened cloth and then removed the padding from Resto's gloves before putting them on. With gloves that felt like stone, Resto pummeled Collins for ten rounds, permanently blurring his vision and ending his boxing career. Both Resto and Lewis were prosecuted and convicted of assault in the second degree, reckless assault, criminal possession of a weapon in the fourth degree, and conspiracy to assault. *See* Collins v. Resto, 746 F. Supp. 360, 363 n.2 (S.D.N.Y. 1990).

73. *See* Dionne L. Koller, *Putting Public Law into Private Sport*, 43 PEPP. L. REV. 681, 696 (2016).

74. For a discussion of the merits of substantially increasing the frequency of criminal prosecution in cases of violence during sports competition, see Jeff Yates & William Gillespie, *The Problem of Sports Violence and the Criminal Prosecution Solution*, 12 CORNELL J.L. & PUB. POL'Y 145 (2002).

75. Christopher Crawford, *ASU Rugby Player Who Kicked a UA Player in the Face Pleads Guilty*, TUCSON.COM (Apr. 25, 2018), https://tucson.com/sports/arizonawildcats/asu-rugby-player-who-kicked-a-ua-player-in-the-face-pleads-guilty/article_22affb68-48a6-11e8-91ed-8fdf301f10c6.html.

his shoe, Crawford approached him and kicked him in the face with full force.[76] The victim was knocked unconscious, hospitalized, and underwent facial reconstructive surgery.[77] Crawford pled guilty and was sentenced to one day in jail and three years of probation.[78]

Because Crawford pled guilty, the court did not explore the standards governing violence during sports competitions. The few cases of alleged criminal activity during sporting events that have gone to trial, however, have established the variables that courts consider in determining criminal culpability. These factors include whether the defendant intended to cause an injury, the extent of physicality permitted under the formal and informal rules of the game, and the severity of the victim's injury.[79]

[B] Prosecuting Athletes for In-Game Conduct

Regina v. Bradshaw,[80] an 1878 case adjudicated in England, represents one of the first recorded prosecutions for in-game conduct. In that case, prosecutors charged William Bradshaw with the manslaughter of Herbert Dockery.[81] During a soccer match, Dockery dribbled toward Bradshaw's team's goal when Bradshaw ran at him with "considerable speed."[82] Dockery kicked the ball past Bradshaw at which point Bradshaw "jumped in the air and struck [Dockery] with his knee in the stomach."[83] The impact ruptured Dockery's intestines, and he died the next day.[84] In determining Bradshaw's innocence or guilt, the court focused on the extent to which: 1) Bradshaw's conduct "was contrary to the rules and practices of the game"; and 2) Bradshaw intended to seriously injure the victim or was "indifferent and reckless as to whether he would produce serious injury."[85] Though the court weighed the evidence, its verdict seemed to unduly focus on preserving and protecting sport. Notwithstanding the evidence of atypically "rough" play, the court ruled that Bradshaw was not guilty.[86] It was "unwilling to decry the manly sports of [England], all of which were no doubt attended with more or less danger."[87]

---

76. *Id.*

77. *Id.*

78. Angie Forburger, *ASU Rugby Player Sentenced to One Day in Jail for Aggravated Assault,* THE REPUBLIC (July 24, 2018), https://www.azcentral.com/story/news/local/tempe/2018/07/24/asu-rugby-player-sentenced-one-day-jail-aggravated-assault/828657002/.

79. *See* Allison v. United States, 927 F. Supp. 2d 550, 554 (C.D. Ill. 2013) (noting that "participants in contact sports may be held liable for injuries to coparticipants caused by willful and wanton or intentional misconduct, but they are not liable for injuries caused by ordinary negligence.").

80. 14 Cox Crim. Cases 83 (Leicester Spring Assizes 1878).

81. *Id.* at 84–85.

82. *Id.* at 84.

83. *Id.*

84. *Id.*

85. *Id.*

86. *Id.* at 85.

87. *Id.*

Although the *Bradshaw* case is nearly 150 years old, the considerations that influenced the court's analysis and decision continue to impact the outcome of criminal prosecutions arising from sport competition. Courts continue to consider deviations from a sport's rules or norms and the intent to injure. They also acknowledge — and in some cases celebrate, as the *Bradshaw* court did — the inherent danger of many sports.[88] Consequently, defendants are rarely convicted.

Consider *State v. Forbes*,[89] in which David Forbes, a player for the NHL's Boston Bruins, was prosecuted for aggravated assault with a dangerous weapon during a game against the Minnesota North Stars. When Forbes and the North Stars' Henry Boucha were both penalized for rough play, the two sat in their respective penalty boxes and exchanged words. Forbes told Boucha he would shove his stick down Boucha's throat.[90] Following their release from the penalty boxes, Forbes struck Boucha in the face with his stick causing Boucha to drop to the ice.[91] Forbes then beat Boucha until other players pulled Forbes off.[92] Boucha suffered a gash requiring 25 stitches and a fractured eye socket.[93] Fighting is an accepted part of hockey. Yet, then-NHL President Clarence Campbell described the attack as "one of the most vicious incidents that I have ever been called upon to deal with."[94] Nonetheless, the jury deadlocked,[95] and the prosecutor opted not to retry Forbes.[96]

A year later, Dan Maloney, who played for the NHL's Detroit Red Wings, was prosecuted in Canada for an in-game assault on the Toronto Maple Leafs' Brian Glennie.[97] Believing Glennie had been unduly rough with one of Maloney's teammates, Maloney approached Glennie from behind, punched him in the face and threw him to the ice.[98] Maloney then dropped to his knees and repeatedly lifted Glennie's unhelmeted head and slammed it on the ice, knocking Glennie unconscious.[99] Glennie was hospitalized.[100] Although slamming a player's unprotected head repeatedly against the ice violates hockey's rules and norms and would seemingly indicate an intent to injure, Maloney was acquitted.[101]

---

88. *See Allison*, 927 F. Supp. 2d at 555 (explaining that "[c]ourts have expressed a standard of care that balances these concerns and, in particular, acknowledges the risks inherent in certain sports, in various ways.").

89. No. 63280 (D. Minn. Aug. 12, 1975) (ending in mistrial); *see also* Mark Mulvoy, *Hockey is Courting Disaster*, Sports Illustrated (Jan. 27, 1975), https://vault.si.com/vault/1975/01/27/hockey-is-courting-disaster.

90. Mulvoy, *supra* note 89.

91. *Id.*

92. *Id.*

93. *Id.*

94. *Id.*

95. *Id.*

96. *Id.*

97. Regina v. Maloney, 28 C.C.C.2d 323, 324 (Ont. Co. Ct. 1976).

98. *Id.* at 328.

99. *Id.*

100. *Id.*

101. *Id.* at 330.

The *Forbes* and *Maloney* cases illustrate the difficulty prosecutors encounter in securing a conviction for activity during in-game competition. In the history of the NHL, only three players have been convicted for in-game conduct.[102] The most notorious of these incidents, involving the Boston Bruins' Marty McSorely, was comprehensively chronicled in the media and produced an opinion that did little to clarify what constitutes a convictable offense on the ice.

In *Regina v. McSorely*,[103] McSorely was charged with assault with a weapon.[104] The charge stemmed from an incident in a game between the Bruins and the Vancouver Canucks.[105] McSorely and the Canucks' Donald Brashear had been in conflict throughout the game and had engaged in a fight, which Brashear had won.[106] Just before time expired in the game, McSorely hit Brashear in the head with his stick causing Brashear to fall and hit his head against the ice.[107] Brashear suffered a seizure before recovering consciousness and being transported to the hospital.[108] In determining whether McSorely was guilty, the court considered the factors the *Bradshaw, Forbes, and Maloney* courts had considered. The court examined whether McSorely intended to injure Brashear and whether his conduct violated the rules and customs of the game. It recognized, however, the inherent roughness of the game and stated that it would not put the "game of hockey itself" on trial.[109]

In exploring hockey's norms, the court noted that players hitting other players with hockey sticks is an acceptable part of hockey, but that a player striking an opponent's head with a stick is unacceptable.[110] Turning to McSorley's intent, the court concluded McSorely "had an impulse to strike him in the head.... He slashed for the head.... Brashear was struck as intended."[111] Having decided as such, the court found McSorely "guilty as charged."[112]

The variables discussed in the forgoing cases prominently appear in *People v. Schacker*.[113] There, a misdemeanor assault action was filed against a hockey player who struck another player with a hockey stick after play had stopped.[114] The victim sustained serious injuries. It was notable that the league was a non-checking hockey

---

102. *Some Notable On-Ice Incidents that Led to Criminal Charges*, CITY NEWS (Feb. 9, 2016), https://toronto.citynews.ca/2016/02/09/some-notable-on-ice-incidents-that-led-to-criminal-charges/.

103. 2000 British Columbia Provincial Ct. 0116 (Crim. Div. 2000).

104. *Id.*

105. *Id.* ¶¶ 1, 108.

106. *Id.* ¶ 27.

107. *Id.* ¶ 30.

108. *Id.* ¶ 59.

109. *Id.* ¶¶ 6, 60.

110. *Id.* ¶ 18.

111. *Id.* ¶ 108.

112. *Id.* ¶ 109. Although McSorley faced the possibility of up to 18 months in jail, the presiding judge did not sentence him to confinement, opining that the negative stigma of being found guilty was sufficient punishment. *McSorley Found Guilty, Gets Conditional Discharge*, CBC (Oct. 7, 2000), https://www.cbc.ca/news/canada/mcsorley-found-guilty-gets-conditional-discharge-1.252239.

113. 670 N.Y.S.2d 308 (N.Y. Dist. Ct. 1998).

114. *Id.* at 309.

league.[115] The court recognized that hockey players accept the inherent dangers of the sport.[116] Consistent with courts' analyses of cases involving coparticipant civil liability, the court articulated the standard that an injured player does not "assume the risk of reckless or intentional conduct."[117] In articulating the appropriate standard for assigning criminal liability, the court identified the two particularly critical factors. First, it stated "in order to allege a criminal act which occurred in a hockey game, the factual portion of the information must allege acts that show that the intent was to inflict physical injury which was unrelated to the athletic competition."[118] It then held that criminal liability may ensue only if, in addition, "the injuries [are] so severe as to be unacceptable in normal competition, requiring a change in the nature of the game."[119] The court concluded that neither of these factors was present. Employing reasoning similar to that employed by courts in limiting coparticipant civil liability, the court stated.

> The idea that a hockey player should be prosecuted runs afoul of the policy to encourage free and fierce competition in athletic events. The people argued at the hearing that this was a non-checking hockey league. While the rules of the league may prohibit certain conduct, thereby reducing the potential injuries, nevertheless, the participant continues to assume the risk of a strenuous and competitive athletic endeavor. The normal conduct in a hockey game cannot be the standard for criminal activity under the Penal Law, nor can the Penal Law be imposed on a hockey game without running afoul of the policy of encouraging athletic competition.[120]

As stated *supra*, prosecutors rarely file criminal charges against athletes for in-game conduct. A contributing factor is the informal code among athletes to not press charges against other athletes, even for conduct that deviates from acceptable standards for behavior.[121] Consider the 1997 boxing match during which Mike Tyson bit off a portion of Evander Holyfield's left ear. Although boxing is a brutal sport, biting an opponent is outside the sport's norms and the range of activity to which boxers consent. Tyson bit Holyfield on two occasions during the match, ignoring the referee's warning after the first incident.[122] Despite Nevada criminal law that prohibits "depriv[ing] a human being of a member of his body, or disfigur[ing] or render[ing] it useless," the case did not enter the criminal justice system because Holyfield elected

---

115. *Id.* at 310.

116. *Id.* at 309.

117. *Id.*

118. *Id.* at 309–10.

119. *Id.* at 310.

120. *Id.*

121. Yates & Gillespie, *supra* note 74, at 145–46 (2002) (discussing the "underlying and largely unexpressed sentiment of many athletes ... that acts of violence occurring in the context of competitive sports are acceptable and should be exempt from criminal liability.").

122. Chris Bengel, *Mike Tyson Recalls Infamous Evander Holyfield Incident: 'I Bit Him Because I Wanted to Kill Him'*, CBSSPORTS.COM (Nov. 18, 2020), https://www.cbssports.com/boxing/news/mike-tyson-recalls-infamous-evander-holyfield-incident-i-bit-him-because-i-wanted-to-kill-him/.

not to press charges or urge prosecution.[123] The Nevada State Athletic Commission, however, indefinitely revoked Tyson's boxing license.[124]

A recent NFL in-game attack also illustrates athletes' disinclination to seek criminal justice charges. During a 2019 NFL game between the Pittsburgh Steelers and Cleveland Browns, Browns defensive lineman Myles Garrett pulled Steelers' quarterback Mason Rudolph to the ground just as Rudolph was throwing the ball.[125] The two briefly tussled before Garrett ripped Rudolph's helmet off. After both men rose to their feet, Garrett clubbed Rudolph over the head with the helmet.[126] Fortunately, the portion of the helmet that hit Rudolph was padded, otherwise the blow could have more seriously injured Rudolph.[127] A criminal law expert explained after the incident, "[t]hat is assault and battery in every jurisdiction in the United States.... But prosecutor offices and police departments have to exercise discretion."[128] As was true of the Tyson/Holyfield matter, the victim of the assault did not call for prosecution, and the criminal justice system deferred to the NFL to impose appropriate discipline.[129]

When criminal charges are pursued, however, courts generally consider the informal and formal rules of the sport, an athlete's intent to seriously injure, and the severity of the injury.[130]

§ 10.04 Liability for Injuries to Spectators

[A] Introduction

The following discussion addresses the liability of premises owners to spectators in two factual contexts — spectator injuries resulting from projectiles leaving the field of play, and spectator injuries resulting from defects in premises that bear no rela-

---

123. Glenn Jeffers, *Ring Actually Saved Tyson from Charges*, CHICAGO TRIBUNE (July 2, 1997), https://www.chicagotribune.com/news/ct-xpm-1997-07-02-9707020043-story.html.

124. Tim Kawakami, *Tyson License Revoked; He Is Fined $3 Million*, LOS ANGELES TIMES (July 10, 1997), https://www.latimes.com/archives/la-xpm-1997-jul-10-mn-11357-story.html.

125. Dan Bernstein, *Revisiting the Myles Garrett-Mason Rudolph Helmet Incident on 'Thursday Night Football'*, SPORTING NEWS (Oct. 18, 2020), https://www.sportingnews.com/us/nfl/news/myles-garrett-mason-rudolph-helmet/176nas3bm3pgf1gw2br2p61g8h.

126. *Id.*

127. *Id.*

128. Kevin Allen, *Why the Browns' Myles Garrett Likely Won't Face Charges After Hitting Steelers QB Mason Rudolph with Helmet*, USA TODAY (Nov. 15, 2019), https://www.usatoday.com/story/sports/nfl/browns/2019/11/15/myles-garrett-browns-likely-no-charges-hitting-steelers-mason-rudolph/4202749002/.

129. *Id.* The NFL initially suspended Garrett indefinitely, but later reduced the suspension to six games. *Browns' Myles Garrett Reinstated by NFL After 6-Game Suspension*, CHICAGO TRIBUNE, (Feb. 12, 2020), https://www.chicagotribune.com/sports/breaking/ct-cleveland-browns-myles-garrett-suspension-20200212-adpcvtiduvasflzyj7w6wnjunm-story.html.

130. *See* David Horton, *Extreme Sports and Assumption of Risk: A Blueprint*, 38 U.S.F. L. REV. 599, 612 (2004).

tionship to the sport. Regarding the first context, the discussion traces the evolution of the standards adopted by courts for determining the liability of a stadium or arena owner or operator. In the sport of baseball, the evolution is particularly notable given that the "baseball rule" has evolved from an absolute shield protecting owners and operators of sports facilities to standards that borrow from the primary assumption of the risk doctrine and the notion of inherent risks as discussed in Section 10.02, *supra*. In the second context, premises liability unconnected to the sport, stadium owners and operators are subject to the ordinary tort standard of care applicable to possessors of land.

[B] The "Baseball Rule"

Because of the weight and density of baseballs and the velocity at which they travel when pitched, thrown or hit, baseballs leaving the playing field can cause serious injuries to spectators.[131] Well over a thousand incidents of injuries to spectators caused by baseball are reported every MLB season, ranging from minor bruises to cracked skulls.[132] As an investigative report by HBO's Real Sports revealed, spectators up and down the foul lines within 75 feet from home plate are virtually defenseless against hard hit foul balls.[133] Despite this danger, spectators crave the opportunity to catch balls flying into the stands, so that they can take home a souvenir. The sport of baseball, therefore, faces a conundrum: how to provide spectators the experience of catching balls hit into the stands while at the same time protecting them from those balls.

It is against these realities that special rules have been promulgated to govern the liability of owners, occupiers, and operators of sports facilities to spectators for injuries resulting from projectiles such as baseballs and hockey pucks. The uniqueness of the rule is clear if viewed through the prism of the liability standard generally applicable to owners and possessors of land. As a general rule, owners and operators of facilities owe a duty of reasonable care to those who come onto those premises.[134] As noted above, however, courts have sanctioned standards that afford defendants protection against spectator lawsuits.

In *Edward C. v. City of Albuquerque*,[135] the New Mexico Supreme Court provided a detailed overview of the history of this special rule — frequently labeled the baseball rule. The *Edward C.* court noted the differing formulations of the baseball rule as

131. Michelle Tak, *Foul balls hurt hundreds of fans at MLB ballparks. See where your team stands on netting*, NBCNEWS.COM, Oct. 1, 2019, https://www.nbcnews.com/news/sports/we-re-going-need-bigger-net-foul-balls-hurt-hundreds-n1060291.

132. *Id.*; Annette Choi, *We Watched 906 Foul Balls to Find Out Where the Most Dangerous Ones Land*, FIVETHIRTYEIGHT.COM, Jul. 15, 2019, https://fivethirtyeight.com/features/we-watched-906-foul-balls-to-find-out-where-the-most-dangerous-ones-land/.

133. HBO REAL SPORTS: FOUL BALL INJURIES IN MLB (Apr. 19, 2016); *see* Kyle Tanzer, *The Prehistoric Baseball Rule: Outdated for Today's Game*, 16 DEPAUL J. SPORTS L. 147, 148 (2020).

134. MATTHEW J. MITTEN, TIMOTHY DAVIS, N. JEREMI DURU & BARBARA OSBORNE, SPORTS LAW AND REGULATION: CASES, MATERIALS, AND PROBLEMS 882 (5th ed. 2020).

135. 241 P.3d 1086, 1092–95 (N.M. 2010).

well as the varying short-hand language employed to describe the legal effect of the rule. In regard to the second point, language frequently used includes "the no duty rule" or "the limited duty rule."[136] In regard to the differing formulations, the court stated that a common conceptualization of the baseball rule immunizes stadium owners and operators under the following circumstances:

> [W]here a proprietor of a ball park furnish[ed] screening for the area of the field where the danger of being struck by a ball is the greatest and that screening is of sufficient extent to provide adequate protection for as many spectators as may reasonably be expected to desire such seating in the course of an ordinary game, the proprietor fulfills the duty of care imposed by law and, therefore, cannot be liable in negligence.[137]

Under the forgoing formulations, a stadium owner/operator was afforded an absolute defense if it had provided protective screening to spectators.

While noting the variations of the baseball rule, the court in *Akins v. Glens Falls City School District*,[138] adopted a two-pronged formulation of the rule. The court stated, "the owner must screen the most dangerous section of the field — the area behind home plate — and the screening that is provided must be sufficient for those spectators who may be reasonably anticipated to desire protected seats on an ordinary occasion."[139]

Rationales supporting the baseball rule include the belief that stadium owners are not insurers of spectators' safety and the protection of spectator/consumer preference.

---

136. Turner v. Mandalay Sports Entertainment, LLC, 180 P.3d 1172, 1175 (Nev. 2008) (stating that 13 states had adopted the limited duty rule, which absolves an owner/operator of a stadium, when protected seating is provided for spectators who can reasonably be expected to desire such seating in the most dangerous parts of a stadium); Hudson v. Kansas City Baseball Club, 164 S.W.2d 318, 320 (Mo. 1942) (using no-duty language to describe the baseball rule); Lawson v. Salt Lake Trappers, Inc., 901 P.2d 1013,1015 (Utah 1995) (adopting limited duty rule); Reed-Jennings v. Baseball Club of Seattle, L.P., 351 P.3d 887, 890–91 (Wash. Ct. App. 2015) (holding the same); Coomer v. Kansas City Royals Baseball Corp., 437 S.W.3d 184, 194, n. 6 (stating that the baseball rule has been referred to as the "no duty" or "limited duty" rule); Benejam v. Detroit Tigers, Inc., 246 Mich. App. 645, 225 (Mich. Ct. App. 2001) (characterizing as the limited duty rule the doctrine that immunizes owner/operator of stadium from liability to spectators injured by projectiles where owner/operator has provided protecting netting in the most dangerous areas of the stadium; court reasons that projectiles leaving the field of play are an inherent risk of baseball); Arnold v. City of Cedar Rapids, 443 N.W.2d 332, 333 (Iowa 1989) (adopting traditional formulation of baseball rule which court labels as the limited duty rule); Bellezzo v. State, 851 P.2d 847, 850–51 (Ariz. Ct. App. 1992) (discussing differing forms of the baseball rule); Petrongola v. Comcast-Spectacor, LP, 789 A.2d 204, 210–11 (Pa. Super. 2001) (charactering the inherent risk rule as the "no duty rule").

137. *Turner*, 180 P.3d at 1093 (quoting Akins v. Glens Falls Sch. Dist., 424 N.E.2d 531 (N.Y. App. 1981)).

138. 424 N.E.2d 531 (N.Y. App. 1981).

139. *Id.* at 533. The court identified two other formulations of the baseball rule. "Some courts have held that an owner merely has a duty to screen such seats as are adequate to provide its spectators with an opportunity to sit in a protected area if they so desire.... Other courts have stated that a proprietor of a baseball field need only screen as many seats as may reasonably be expected to be applied for on an ordinary occasion by those desiring such protection." *Id.* (citations omitted).

Having defined its approach to the baseball rule, the *Akins* court proceeded to articulate the rationale as follows:

> At the outset, it should be stated that an owner of a baseball field is not an insurer of the safety of its spectators. Rather, like any other owner or occupier of land, it is only under a duty to exercise "reasonable care under the circumstances" to prevent injury to those who come to watch the games played on its field.... The perils of the game of baseball, however, are not so imminent that due care on the part of the owner requires that the entire playing field be screened. Indeed, many spectators prefer to sit where their view of the game is unobstructed by fences or protective netting and the proprietor of a ballpark has a legitimate interest in catering to these desires. Thus, the critical question becomes what amount of screening must be provided by an owner of a baseball field before it will be found to have discharged its duty of care to its spectators.[140]

A North Carolina appellate court recently applied a formulation of the baseball rule that absolved a baseball stadium owner of liability in a case involving an 11-year-old girl. In *Mills v. Durham Bulls Baseball Club, Inc.*,[141] plaintiff sustained injuries after being struck in the head by a foul ball.[142] She was seated in an unscreened area which was the farthest distance from homeplate.[143] Plaintiff argued, *inter alia*, that the baseball rule was inapplicable because she "lacked sufficient knowledge of the game of baseball to understand that foul balls could be hit in the stands and cause injury to unprotected spectators," that she had no choice but to sit in the picnic area (an unprotected area), and that the baseball rule was outdated and should be abandoned.[144]

The court rejected each of the arguments. It first concluded that plaintiff, who had attended and watched numerous baseball games on television and played softball, possessed sufficient ordinary knowledge to "comprehend the danger of balls fouled into the stands...."[145] In rejecting plaintiff's argument that she did not have the option of sitting in a screened area, the court cited North Carolina precedent[146] in concluding that a stadium owner will not be held liable when it provides a "reasonable number of screened seats and ... [a plaintiff chooses] to sit in an unprotected seat with knowledge that he could be injured by a batted ball," even if the protected seats were unavailable to the plaintiff.[147] In rejecting plaintiff's argument that the

140. *Id.*
141. 275 N.C. App. 618 (N.C. Ct. App. 2020).
142. *Id.* at 619–20.
143. *Id.*
144. *Id.* at 622.
145. *Id.* at 622–23.
146. Erickson v. Lexington Baseball Club, 65 S.E.2d 140 (N.C. 1951).
147. *Mills,* 854 S.E.2d at 623.

baseball rule is archaic, the court ruled that it lacked the authority to overturn the North Carolina Supreme Court's adoption of the most protective formulation of the baseball rule.[148]

In sharp contrast to *Mills* is *Rountree v. Boise Baseball, LLC*,[149] in which the court resoundingly rejected the baseball rule. In that case, a spectator located in a minor league baseball stadium's Executive Club, which is at the top of the stadium down the third base line and is conducive to socializing, was hit in the face by a foul ball.[150] The court noted that under the baseball rule, the stadium operator would have been shielded from liability because the injury occurred down the third base line and not behind the plate. The court reasoned, however, that there existed no compelling public policy reason for it to exercise its judicial power to adopt the baseball rule. Deferring to the state legislature, the court stated, "[d]eclining to adopt the Baseball Rule leaves policy formulation to the deliberative body that is better positioned to consider the pros and cons of the issue."[151] The court noted that deferring to the legislature would follow the approach adopted in Colorado, Illinois, and New Jersey,[152] where legislatures have adopted the baseball rule. The court also rejected the primary assumption of the risk doctrine as the standard for assessing an owner/operator's liability to a spectator.[153] Instead, the court opted for a comparative negligence analysis and imposed on the stadium operator a "general duty to exercise ordinary care to prevent unreasonable, foreseeable risks of harm to others."[154]

Increasingly, commentators have questioned the wisdom of adherence to the conceptualization of the baseball rule that absolves stadium owners of liability if they provide protective seating. These critics argue that the baseball rule disincentivizes stadium owners/operators from extending the protected area in baseball stadiums and hockey arenas. Gruesome injuries suffered by spectators, including young chil-

---

148. *Id.* at 625.

149. 296 P.3d 373 (Idaho 2013); *accord* South Shore Baseball, LLC v. DeJesus, 11 N.E.3d 903 (Ind. 2014) (in rejecting the baseball rule, the court follows *Rountree* in holding that the adoption of the baseball rule is a decision best reserved for the legislature rather than by judicial fiat; in such instances, courts adopt the general tort rule governing the liability of possessors of land to invitees); *Pfenning*, 947 N.E.2d at 406–07 (applying the general tort standard to determine the liability of owner of a golf course in suit by plaintiff alleging she was a spectator).

150. *Id.* at 375.

151. *Id.* at 379.

152. COLO. REV. STAT. ANN. § 13-21-120; ILL. COMP. STAT. ANN. 38/10; N.J. STAT. ANN. § 2A:53A-43 to 2A:53A-48; *see* Teneyck v. Roller Hockey Colorado, Ltd., 10 P.3d 707 (Colo. Ct. App. 2000) (finding that the Colorado statute adopting the baseball rule is specific to the sport of baseball, the court refuses to apply statute in a case where a spectator was injured at a roller hockey game).

153. *Id.* at 379–80. The court explained that primary assumption of the risk "essentially means that the defendant was not negligent because there was no duty." It considers the doctrine inconsistent with its comparative negligence standard of liability.

154. *Id.* at 377.

dren, heightened this criticism and prompted action by MLB to enhance the protective features at ballparks.[155] In 2019, MLB Commissioner Rob Manfred announced that in advance of the 2020 season, all clubs would extend protective netting "substantially beyond the end of the dugout."[156] This reform, however, did not provide uniform protection. The distance to which netting extends beyond the dugout as well as the height of the netting remains unregulated.[157] As of August 2021, only six of the thirty MLB ballparks had netting that extends to the foul poles.[158] Moreover, Manfred's proclamation had no effect on minor league baseball clubs. Consequently, dozens of minor league stadiums provide spectators even less protection than the least protective major league stadiums.[159] Forty-two minor league clubs have netting that extends only as far as the end of the dugout.[160]

[C] The Inherent Risk Approach

As discussed *infra,* some courts' formulation of the baseball rule focuses on those risks inherent to a sport as the appropriate standard to determine a stadium or facility operator or owner's liability to a spectator. Some of these courts examine inherent risks within the contours of the primary assumption of the risk doctrine. *Hurst v. East Coast Hockey League, Inc.*[161] is illustrative. In *Hurst,* a spectator, while in the concourse of a hockey arena, was struck by a hockey puck during pregame warmups.[162]

---

155. Tanzer, *supra* note 133. In 2017, a two-year-old girl sitting in a seat along the first base foul line at Yankee Stadium suffered severe brain injury after being hit in the face with a foul ball travelling 105 miles per hour. Dean Balsamini, *Girl's recovery from Yankees foul ball 'nothing short of a miracle,'* *dad says,* NYPOST.COM, Mar. 7, 2020, https://nypost.com/2020/03/07/girls-recovery-from-yankees-foul-ball-nothing-short-of-a-miracle-dad-says/.

156. Andrew Lehren & Michelle Tak, *Every Major League Baseball team will expand netting to protect fans from foul balls,* NBCNEWS.COM, Dec. 11, 2019, https://www.nbcnews.com/news/sports/every-major-league-baseball-team-will-expand-netting-protect-fans-n1100296; Matt Martell, *Crying Foul Over Ballpark Injuries,* SPORTS ILLUSTRATED.COM (Aug. 10, 2021), https://www.si.com/mlb/2021/08/10/crying-foul-mlb-netting-daily-cover. Japanese baseball authorities have taken a more cautious approach. Recognizing the danger of foul balls hit down the line, Nippon Professional Baseball fields have for decades had protective netting that extends all the way to the foul poles. HBO REAL SPORTS: FOUL BALLS IN JAPANESE BASEBALL (Apr. 19, 2016).

157. Lehren & Tak, *supra* note 156.

158. Martell, *supra* note 156.

159. Caroline Klapp, *Campaign urges minor league baseball stadium to extend nets for safety,* WAFF 48, Apr. 29, 2021, https://www.waff.com/2021/04/29/campaign-urges-minor-league-baseball--stadium-extend-nets-safety/; *see also* Martell, *supra* note 156 (noting that "investing in the minors doesn't seem to be a high priority for MLB").

160. Klapp, *supra* note 159; *see also* Matthew Gutierrez, *As more MLB parks extend netting, foul ball victims urge minor league teams to do the same,* WASH. POST (Sep. 6, 2019), https://www.washingtonpost.com/sports/2019/09/06/more-mlb-parks-extend-netting-foul-ball-victims-urge-minor-league-teams-do-same/ (citing financial disparities as a reason why minor league teams have not extended netting).

161. 637 S.E.2d 560 (S.C. 2006).

162. *Id.* at 561.

In finding for the defendant, the court began its analysis by focusing on whether a duty existed. Noting that the primary assumption of the risk doctrine focuses on the question of duty, the court defined the defendant's obligation as not encompassing risks inherent in a game. It stated, "[t]he risk of being struck by a flying puck is inherent to the game of hockey.... Respondents did not have a duty to protect Appellant, a spectator, from inherent risks of the game of hockey."[163]

Hurst is also notable because it rejects the position of some earlier courts, which rejected both the no-duty and inherent risk doctrine as defenses in hockey. In these earlier cases, courts reasoned that the likelihood of pucks leaving the playing area was not sufficiently common.[164] Thus, the court's holding in *Hurst* aligns with recent decisions involving hockey which apply an inherent risk analysis in determining the liability of a facility owner to a spectator.[165] In addition to baseball and hockey, the doctrine that a stadium owner does not possess a duty to protect spectators for risks inherent to a sport has been applied in sports including football,[166] golf,[167] auto racing[168] and horseracing.[169]

Returning to *Edward C.*, the court adopted the inherent risk approach in seeking to balance the burdens imposed on spectators and stadium operators. In that case, plaintiffs, who were attending a "Little League" party at a minor league baseball stadium, were seated beyond the left field fence eating at a picnic table when a batted

---

163. *Id.* at 563.

164. *See, e.g.*, Thurman v. Ice Palace, 97 P.2d 999, 1001 (Cal. Ct. App. 1940) (in finding that baseball rule was inapplicable to ice hockey, the court concluded that it is "not common knowledge that pucks in ice hockey games are liable to be batted into the section occupied by the spectators."); Riley v. Chicago Cougars Hockey Club Inc., 427 N.E.2d 290, 292–93 (Ill. Ct. App. 1940) (refusing to apply baseball rule to hockey because of fundamental differences between hockey and baseball).

165. *See, e.g.*, Nemarnik v. Los Angeles Kings Hockey Club, L.P., 127 Cal. Rptr. 2d 10, 18 (Cal. Ct. App. 2002) (holding hockey arena owners bear no responsibility to protect spectators from risks inherent in the sport); Ingersoll v. Onondaga Hockey Club Inc., 281 N.Y.S. 505, 507–08 (N.Y. App. Div. 1935) (finding a stadium owner was not liable to spectator for risks incidental to attending a hockey game such as pucks flying into the stands); Montminy v. City of Hartford, 2021 WL 5861427, at *5, *9 (Conn. Super. Nov. 10, 2021) (adopting the limited duty rule, the court holds that the risk of hockey puck leaving the field of play and hitting spectator in stands is an inherent risk of the sport).

166. Callinan v. Nat'l Football League, 2021 WL 6081473, *5–6 (Md. Ct. Spec. App. Dec. 23, 2021) (finding that defendants did not owe a duty to protect a spectator against normal risks associated with attending a football game, where a spectator was injured by errant kick during pre-game warmup).

167. Thompson v. Sunset Country Club, 227 S.W.2d 523 (Mo. Ct. App. 1950) (applying limited duty rule to golf).

168. *See* Ochall v. McNamer, 79 N.E.2d 1215, 1228–29 (Ohio Ct. App. 2016) (in an action against owners of go cart facility, the court adopts the primary assumption of the risk doctrine in ruling that owners/operators of recreational facility were not liable for spectator injuries arising from risks inherent in the activity).

169. McCandless v. Ramsey, 211 A.3d 1157, 1162 (Me. 2019) (concluding defendants were not liable because a risk of injury to spectators by horse passing too close to stands is inherent to the sport); Rosales v. Benjamin Equestrian Center, LLC, 597 S.W.3d 669, 678 (Mo. Ct. App. 2020) (although rejecting defendant's motion to dismiss, the court's dictum suggests applicable standard for determining liability is whether the defendant's conduct increased the inherent risks of the sport).

ball struck their son in the head, fracturing his skull.[170] Plaintiffs sued, and the district court applied the baseball rule and found for the defendants.[171] On appeal, however, the New Mexico Supreme Court eschewed the baseball rule, finding that "an owner/ occupant of a commercial baseball stadium owes a duty that is symmetrical to the duty of the spectator."[172] Adopting a standard that examines the inherent risk of the game, the court stated:

> Spectators must exercise ordinary care to protect themselves from the in-
> herent risk of being hit by a projectile that leaves the field of play and the
> owner/occupant must exercise ordinary care not to increase that inherent
> risk. This approach recognizes the impossibility of playing the sport of base-
> ball without projectiles leaving the field of play. This approach also balances
> the competing interests of spectators who want full protection by requiring
> screening behind home plate consistent with the *Akins* approach and allowing
> other spectators to participate in the game by catching souvenirs that leave
> the field of play. In addition, it balances the practical interest of watching a
> sport that encourages players to strike a ball beyond the field of play in fair
> ball territory to score runs with the safety and entertainment interests of the
> spectators in catching such balls.[173]

Although it did not use the terminology of primary assumption of the risk, the court engaged in an analysis akin to that used by courts that expressly adopt the primary assumption of the risk doctrine in spectator liability cases.[174]

The *Edward C.* court reasoned that the shift from the baseball rule to an inherent risk standard was a consequence of: (1) tort law's departure from contributory neg- ligence and assumption of the risk constituting absolute defenses;[175] (2) advances in baseball resulting in injuries caused by events that are not inherent to the sport (*e.g.*, marketing activities that divert spectator's attention from the actual game);[176] and (3) the reality that baseball players are bigger and faster, and hit the ball much faster.[177] The latter of these factors converge to leave spectators less time to react so as to protect themselves.[178] The court also reasoned that the baseball rule does little to in- centivize stadium owners to install safety measures.

---

170. *Edward C.*, 241 P.3d at 1089.

171. *Id.* at 1090.

172. *Id.* at 1097.

173. *Id.* at 1097–98.

174. *Accord* Thurmond v. Prince William Professional Baseball Club, Inc., 574 S.E.2d 246, 250– 51 (Va. 2003) (adopting an inherent risk approach); Romeo v. Pittsburgh Assoc., 787 A.2d 1027, 1031 (Pa. Super. 2001) (although not referring to primary assumption of the risk and using the phrase the "no duty rule," the court concludes facility operator owed no duty to protect spectator against risks that are "'common, frequent, and expected' risks inherent in a baseball game.").

175. *Edward C.*, 241 P.3d at 1093–94.

176. *Id.* at 1094.

177. *Id.*

178. *Id.*

[D] Inherent Risk and the Duty Not to Increase Such Risks

[1] Inherent Risks

As was observed with respect to coparticipant liability, what constitutes an inherent risk of a game is critical to a court's analysis of an owner/occupier's liability to a spectator. In *Loughran v. The Phillies*,[179] the court adopted a broad definition of inherent risk:

> In determining what is a "customary" part of the game, ... we cannot be limited to the rigid standard of the Major League Baseball rule book; we must instead consider the actual everyday goings on that occur both on and off the baseball diamond; we must consider as "customary" those activities that although not specifically sanctioned by baseball authorities, have become as integral a part of attending a games as hot dogs, cracker jack, and seventh inning stretches. Fans routinely arrive early for batting practice in hopes of retrieving an errant baseball as a souvenir, and fans routinely clamor to retrieve balls landing in the stands via home runs or foul balls. Although not technically part of the game of baseball, those activities have become inextricably intertwined with a fan's baseball experience, and must be considered a customary part of the game.[180]

The significance of determining if a spectator injury was the consequence of an inherent risk was evident in *Coomer v. Kansas City Royals Baseball Corp.*[181] There, a spectator attending a baseball game was hit in the eye by a hot dog thrown by a team mascot.[182] The court began its analysis with a reminder of one of the rationales articulated in support of the baseball rule. "The rationale for barring recovery for injuries from risks that are inherent in watching a particular sport under implied primary assumption of the risk is that the defendant team owner cannot remove such risks without materially altering either the sport that spectators come to see or the spectator's enjoyment of it."[183] The court concluded that this rationale would not support including the "hotdog toss" as an inherent risk.[184]

What constitutes an inherent risk has been critical to the outcomes in other cases. In *Jones v. Three Rivers Management Corp.*,[185] the court concluded that the baseball

---

179. 888 A.2d 872 (Pa. Super. 2005).

180. *Id.* at 875–76; *see also* Ochall v. McNamer, 79 N.E.3d at 1230–31 (stating "the risks inherent in an activity are the foreseeable, common, and customary risks of the activity." The court adds that such risks are "so inherent in an activity that they cannot be eliminated, ... which requires a court to focus exclusively upon the activity itself.").

181. 437 S.W.3d 184 (Mo. 2014).

182. *Id.* at 188–89.

183. *Id.* at 202.

184. *Id.*

185. 394 A2d 546, 551–52 (Pa. 1978). *But see* Alwin v. St. Paul Saints Baseball Club, Inc., 672 N.W.2d 570, 573–74 (Minn. App. 2003) (rejecting *Jones* and applying primary assumption of risk to absolve owners of stadium from liability to spectator, who was hit by a ball after he left restroom and

rule did not extend to the concourse area of a baseball stadium because being struck by a ball in that area of the stadium is not an inherent risk of baseball. The notion that the baseball rule's prophylaxis applies only to areas of a stadium "dedicated solely to viewing the game" was addressed in *Masisonave v. Newark Bears Professional Baseball Club, Inc.*[186] There, the court ruled that "public policy and fairness" limited the scope of the baseball rule to injuries occurring while spectators are in the stands and ordinary negligence principles apply to other areas of a stadium including the concourse. The court explained, "[t]o apply the baseball rule to the entire stadium would convert reasonable protection for owners to immunity by virtually eliminating liability for foreseeable, preventable injuries to their patrons even when the fans are no longer engaged in the game."[187]

Courts have also determined whether a spectator injuring other fans is an inherent risk of attending a sports event. In *Telega v. Security Bureau, Inc.*,[188] the court held that "[i]t is not a matter of universal knowledge that an onslaught of displaced fans is a common, frequent or expected occurrence to someone catching a souvenir football."[189] In *Hayden v. University of Notre Dame*,[190] the court applied the general standard of care governing the negligence of owners/operators of facilities.

[2] Duty not to Increase Inherent Risks

Although courts generally rule that an owner/operator of a sports facility need not protect spectators against risks inherent to a sport, courts impose a duty on facility owners and operators not to increase those risks.[191] A circumstance that increases inherent risks arises when a defendant engages in intentional or reckless conduct resulting in injury to a spectator.[192] In *Mayes v. La Sierra University*,[193] the court stated

was near concourse); Gallagher v. Cleveland Browns Football, Co. Inc., 638 N.E.2d 1082, 1090 (Ohio Ct. App. 1994) (in a case in which a cameraman was injured after two football players ran into him when play on field extended to sidelines, court rejects *Jones* because the cameraman being hit was an inherent risk).

186. 881 A.2d 700, 702 (N.J. 2005).
187. *Id.* at 709.
188. 719 A.2d 372 (Pa. Super. 1998).
189. *Id.* at 376.
190. 716 N.E.2d 603 (Ind. Ct. App. 1999).
191. *Edward C.*, 241 P.3d at 1098 (stating the owner/occupant of sport facility owes spectator duty not to increase inherent risks associated with the sport); *Ochall*, 79 N.E.3d at 1237–38; *see* Mayes v. La Sierra Univ., 2022 WL 72038, at *7 (Cal. Ct. App. Jan. 7, 2022) (finding that the defendant has duty not to increase inherent risks; issues of fact remained as to whether defendant increased inherent risk of baseball game to spectators by "failing to install protective netting over and above defendant's dugouts," and not warning spectators there was "no protective netting over and beyond the dugouts"); Rosales v. Benjamin Equestrian Center, LLC, 597 S.W.3d 669, 678 (Mo. Ct. App. 2019) (adopting baseball rule but also stating that owner/operator of a facility has a duty not to increase risks inherent to a sport); Namarnik v. Los Angeles Kings Hockey Club, 127 Cal. Rptr. 2d 10, 13–14 (Cal. Ct. App. 2002) (holding defendant has duty not to increase risks inherent to a sport).
192. WALTER T. CHAMPION, JR., FUNDAMENTALS OF SPORTS LAW, *Participant and Spectator Injuries*, (2d ed. 2004) *6 (Jan. 2022).
193. *Mayes*, 2022 WL 72038 at *8.

that issues of fact remained as to whether defendant increased the inherent risk of a baseball game to spectators by "failing to install protective netting over and above defendant's dugouts," and not warning spectators there was "no protective netting over and beyond the dugouts."[194]

Another circumstance where the defendant's conduct was deemed to enhance the inherent risk of a sport was instrumental in the development of what has been characterized as the distraction exception to the baseball rule. In *Lowe v. California League of Prof. Baseball*, in which a court found that a question of fact existed as to whether a team mascot, which distracted a spectator before he was struck by a foul ball, increased the inherent risk of being struck by a foul ball.[195] It should be noted that some courts have rejected the distraction exception.[196]

[E] Premises Liability Not Involving the Sport

The liability of the owner/operator of a sports facility poses a different issue than that of liability to spectators arising from the sport, such as projectiles leaving the field of play. In *Allred v. Capital Area Soccer League Inc.*,[197] the court appropriately noted that while some courts have intermingled the issues arising from the two scenarios, the issues are separate and require courts to invoke different legal standards. In cases involving injuries to spectators arising from the condition of the premises, courts apply the general negligence standard applicable to owners/operators of facilities. The *Allred* court stated "the owner of a [sport] facility has a duty of reasonable care under the circumstances to invitees."[198] Similarly, the court in *Pryor v. Iberia Parish Sch. Bd.*[199] applied a negligence standard in a case involving allegedly defective bleachers. It stated that "the owner or custodian of property has a duty to keep the property in a reasonably safe condition. The owner or custodian must discover any unreasonably dangerous condition on the premises, and either correct the condition or warn potential victims of its existence."[200] This standard was reiterated by the

---

194. Id. at *11.

195. Lowe v. California League of Prof. Baseball, 65 Cal. Rptr. 2d 105, 111–12 (Cal. Ct. App. 1997); *Namarnik*, 127 Cal. Rptr. 2d at 17–18 (stating that whether a mascot's antics that allegedly distracted a spectator increased the inherent risk of attending a hockey game presents a triable issue of fact); Martinez v. Houston McLean Co. LLC, 414 S.W.3d 219, 230–31 (Tex. Ct. App. 2013) (casting doubt on whether Texas courts would recognize a distraction exception, the court holds the facts failed to establish that the spectator was distracted).

196. Harting v. Dratyon Dragons Prof. Baseball Club, L.L.C., 870 N.E.2d 766, 770 (Ohio Ct. App. 2007) (rejecting the distraction exception and applying primary assumption of the risk to bar tort recovery where spectator had been warned of risk associated with baseball traveling into the stands, particularly given the "prevalence of costumed team mascots at sporting events such as baseball, football, or basketball games, it is perfectly reasonable for a spectator at one of these games to expect to observe those mascots during the normal course of the game.").

197. 669 S.E.2d 777 (N.C. Ct. App. 2008).

198. *Id.* at 779.

199. 60 So. 3d 594 (La. 2011).

200. *Id.* at 596.

court in *DiPietro v. Farmington Sports Arena, LLC*,[201] which involved an allegedly defective playing surface at a soccer facility. The court stated, "[a] business owner owes its invitees a duty to 'keep its premises in a reasonably safe condition.'"[202]

§ 10.05 Liability of Educational Institutions

[A] Introduction

This section examines the liability of high schools and colleges to athletes for injuries sustained during athletes' participation in sports. Much of the discussion centers on the liability of coaches to athletes for alleged negligent instruction and training, failure to provide adequate emergency medical care and equipment, and aggravation of existing injuries. The discussion reveals that courts' adoption of the primary assumption of the risk doctrine severely circumscribes athletes' ability to impose liability on educational institutions. The discussion that follows should also be viewed against the backdrop of defenses available to educational institutions, including sovereign and qualified immunity, and waiver of liability provisions. These defenses are discussed in §§ 10.06 and 10.07, *infra*.

[B] Liability of Coaches and Other Institutional Personnel

[1] Instruction and Training

[a] High Schools

Athletes have sued their high schools and colleges alleging that injuries sustained in practice or competition were a consequence of coaches' negligent instruction and training. The majority of courts seemingly embrace a primary assumption of the risk type standard in determining the responsibility of institutions for a coach's alleged tortious training and instruction. In employing primary assumption of the risk, courts conclude that institutions will be held responsible only when a coach's conduct increases the risks inherent to a sport such as when a coach engages in intentional or reckless behavior. As discussed in § 10.02, *supra*:

> [P]rimary assumption of the risk focuses not on whether the plaintiff voluntarily assumed a known risk, but on the question of duty. Did the defendant possess a duty to protect the plaintiff from the risk of harm resulting in injury? This, in turn, requires an examination of the inherent characteristics of the activity involved. Specifically, did the plaintiff implicitly assume those risks that are an inherent part of the activity allegedly resulting in plaintiff's injury? If the risk causing the injury is an inherent part of the activity, the defendant owed no duty to the plaintiff, and therefore is not liable in negligence.

---

201. 49 A.3d 951 (Conn. 2012).
202. *Id.* at 957 (quoting *Baptiste v. Better Val-U Supermarket, Inc.*, 811 A.2d 687 (Conn. 2002)).

Where such a conclusion can appropriately be reached, primary assumption of the risk operates as a "complete defense." ... [W]hat risks are considered an inherent part of the activity in question is critically important in determining the effect given to primary assumption of the risk in the sports context.[203]

At the high school level, the California Supreme Court embraced the primary assumption of the risk standard in shaping the contours of institutional liability in the leading case of *Kahn v. East Side Union High School*.[204] In *Kahn*, a 14-year-old member of a junior-varsity swim team suffered severe injuries after diving into the shallow area of a pool during a swim meet. The athlete alleged that her coach's failure to provide proper instruction on how to dive into the shallow end of the pool contributed to her injury. The court considered whether to apply the inherent risk standard from *Knight v. Jewett*,[205] which involved coparticipant liability, to the case before it. Acknowledging the differences in the relationship between two coparticipants and the relationships between an athlete and coach, the court nevertheless applied the primary assumption of the risk doctrine.

[B]ecause a significant part of an instructor's or coach's role is to challenge or "push" a student or athlete to advance in his or her skill level and to undertake more difficult tasks, and because the fulfillment of such a role could be improperly chilled by too stringent a standard of potential legal liability, we conclude that the same general standard should apply in cases in which an instructor's alleged liability rests primarily on a claim that he or she challenged the player to perform beyond his or her capacity or failed to provide adequate instruction or supervision before directing or permitting a student to perform a particular maneuver that has resulted in injury to the student. A sports instructor may be found to have breached a duty of care to a student or athlete only if the instructor intentionally injures the student or engages in conduct that is reckless in the sense that it is "totally outside the range of the ordinary activity" involved in teaching or coaching the sport.[206]

While the forgoing represents the majority approach, which requires that a coach not increase the risks inherent to playing a sport,[207] some courts have adopted a negligence standard.[208]

---

203. Timothy Davis, *Avila v. Citrus Community College District: Shaping the Contours of Immunity and Primary Assumption of the Risk*, 17 MARQ. SPORTS L. REV. 259, 270 (2006) (footnotes omitted).

204. 75 P.3d 30 (Cal. 2003).

205. 834 P.2d 696 (Cal. 1992).

206. *Kahn*, 75 P.3d at 32–33.

207. "A plaintiff participating in a sport or recreational activity will not be deemed to have assumed the risks of reckless or intentional conduct or concealed or unreasonably increased risks." Anand v. Kapoor, 942 N.E.2d 295 (N.Y. 2010) (applying the primary assumption of risk approach). *See also* Morgan v. Kent State Univ., 54 N.E.3d 1284 (Ohio Ct. App. 2016) (citing Marchetti v. Kalish, 559 N.E.2d 699 (1990)); Barth v. Blue Diamond, LLC, 2017 WL 5900949, at *2 (Del. Super. Nov. 29, 2017) (citing Helm v. 206 Massachusetts Avenue, LLC, 107 A.3d 1074, 1080 (Del. 2014)); Prejean v. E. Baton Rouge Parish Sch. Bd., 729 So. 2d 686 (La. Ct. App. 1999); City of Miami v. Cisneros, 662 So. 2d 1272, 1275 (Fla. Ct. App. 1997); Kelly v. McCarrick, 841 A.2d 869, 886–87 (Md. Ct. Spec. App. 2004).

208. Wilson v. O'Gorman High Sch., 2008 WL 2571833 at *4 (D.S.D. June 26, 2008); Sherry v. East Suburban Football League, 807 N.W.2d 859, 862 (Mich. Ct. App. 2011).

[b] Colleges and Universities

In *Avila v. Citrus Community College*,[209] the California Supreme Court considered whether to extend the rule adopted in *Knight* and *Kahn* to athlete injuries arising at the college level. In *Avila*, a college baseball player was injured after he was hit in the head by a ball thrown by a pitcher on the opposing team.[210] The court considered whether the defendant's supervisory duty extended to protect players on the opposing team. Extending its precedent in *Knight* and *Kahn*, the court held that in "interscholastic and intercollegiate competition, the host school and its agents owe a duty to home and visiting players alike to, at a minimum, not increase the risk inherent in the sport."[211]

Primary assumption of the risk was successfully asserted by a university to avoid liability in *Bukowski v. Clarkson University*.[212] A pitcher on a college's baseball team sued his baseball coach and university for injuries he suffered after being struck by a ball during practice.[213] Plaintiff alleged that his risk of being hit by a batted ball was enhanced because of the "multicolored pitching backdrop and low lighting at the indoor facility, which made it harder to see the white ball," and the failure to use a protective screen.[214] In rejecting plaintiff's claim, the court stated that "risks which are commonly encountered or 'inherent' in a sport, such as being struck by a ball or bat in baseball, are 'risks [for] which various participants are legally deemed to have accepted personal responsibility....'"[215] It added that the risks inherent to playing a sport include less than optimal playing conditions.[216] The court concluded that the plaintiff, an experienced baseball player, assumed the risk of being hit by a line drive.[217] In *Geiersbach v. Frieje*,[218] the court adopted the same standard in finding that defendant's duty was limited to avoiding "reckless or malicious behavior or intentional injury."[219] The court specially rejected a negligence standard as it relates to injuries arising from the risks inherent to an athlete's participation in a sport.[220]

As alluded to *supra*, the primary assumption of the risk standard does not completely immunize defendants from liability premised on the conduct of coaches. Ac-

---

209. 131 P.3d 383 (Cal. 2006).

210. *Id.* at 385–86.

211. *Id.* at 392; *accord* Trujillo v. Yeager, 642 F. Supp. 2d 86, 91 (D. Conn. 2009) (applying reckless and intentional conduct standard in assessing coach's liability for injury caused by a player on the coach's team to a player on an opposing team); Kavanagh v. Trs. of Boston Univ., 795 N.E.2d 1170, 1179 (Mass. 2003) (adopting an intentional or reckless standard for determining liability of coach when one of his players punched the plaintiff in the face).

212. 971 N.E.2d 849 (N.Y. 2012).

213. *Id.*

214. *Id.* at 850.

215. *Id.* at 851.

216. *Id.*

217. *Id.*

218. 807 N.E.2d 114, 120 (Ind. Ct. App. 2004).

219. *Id.* at 120.

220. *Id.* at 118.

cordingly, coaches will be held liable for injury-causing conduct related to training and instructing athletes that amounts to reckless or intentional behavior. Therefore, where a 13-year-old football player was injured after being slammed by his coach as a part of a demonstration, liability ensued because the coach's conduct "utterly" disregarded the athlete's safety.[221]

[2] Emergency Medical Assistance

At the college and university level, courts have rejected the proposition that a special relationship exists between student-athletes and their teams that gives rise to a general duty of care. In *Orr. v. Brigham Young University*,[222] the plaintiff alleged that his university should be held responsible for injuries he sustained while playing college football. Orr contended that BYU negligently breached a duty of care owed to him in numerous ways including: pressuring players to perform; discouraging players from reporting injuries; employing unqualified personnel to diagnose and treat injuries; misdiagnosing his injuries; and, encouraging him to play even though he was injured.[223] Orr asserted that the basis for his negligence claim was the special relationship that exists between athletes and their colleges.[224] In rejecting Orr's claims, the court stated:

> [T]he court is of the view that acknowledging many of the duties that Orr urges BYU breached is "fundamentally at odds with the nature of the parties' relationship." As the Utah Supreme Court concluded, "society considers the modern college student an adult, not a child of tender years." The court finds nothing different about a student athlete's relationship with a university which would justify the conclusion that a student athlete is a custodial ward of the university while the non-athlete student is an emancipated adult. An athlete's choice to participate in a sport is not coerced. Voluntary association with a collegiate athletic team does not make the student less of "an autonomous adult or the institution more a caretaker."[225]

Notwithstanding the rule articulated in *Orr*, courts have imposed duties on educational institutions to provide emergency medical assistance. They stop short, however, of imposing a duty on colleges and universities for the general welfare of student-athletes. In *Kleinknecht v. Gettysburg College*,[226] a 20-year-old sophomore lacrosse player at Gettysburg College suffered cardiac arrest during lacrosse practice.[227] No athletic trainer was present at the practice. The Third Circuit held that the college "had a duty [of care] to provide prompt and adequate emergency medical services

---

221. Koffman v. Garnett, 574 S.E.2d 258, 261 (Va. 2003); *accord* Patrick v. Great Valley Sch. Dist., 296 F. App'x 258 (3d Cir. 2008); Lemaster v. Grove City Christian Sch., 2017 WL 5157610 (Ohio. Ct. App. Nov. 7, 2017).

222. 960 F. Supp. 1522 (D. Utah. 1994), *aff'd*, 108 F.3d 1388 (10th Cir. 1997).

223. *Id.* at 1525–26.

224. *Id.* at 1526.

225. *Id.* at 1528 (internal citations omitted).

226. 989 F.2d 1360 (3d Cir. 1993).

227. *Id.* at 1362–63.

to [Kleinknecht], one of its intercollegiate athletes, while he was engaged in a school-sponsored athletic activity for which he had been recruited."[228] The court was unwilling to recognize the existence of an all-encompassing special relationship between student-athletes and their colleges and universities. Nevertheless, the court's holding was partially premised on Kleinknecht's status as a student-athlete, which gave rise to the college's duty of care to its athletes to have appropriate medical measures in place given that it is foreseeable that an athlete could experience a life-threatening medical event during participation in intercollegiate athletics.[229]

In *Feleccia v. Lackawanna College*,[230] the Pennsylvania Supreme Court had an opportunity to examine the federal court's ruling in *Kleinknecht*. In *Feleccia*, two members of the college's football team suffered injuries during practice. The court framed the dispositive issue as whether a "Pennsylvania college is required to have qualified medical personnel present at intercollegiate athletic events to satisfy a duty of care to the college's student-athletes."[231] In rejecting *Kleinknecht*, the court stated: "the Superior Court articulated a duty not previously recognized by Pennsylvania Courts: a college has a 'duty of care to its intercollegiate student athletes requir[ing] it to have qualified medical personnel available at [athletic events, including] football try-out ... and to provide adequate treatment in the event that an intercollegiate student athlete suffer[s] a medical emergency."[232]

The court held, however, that it was not necessary for the lower court to have created a new duty, because a duty arose from the affirmative conduct of the college. Relying on § 323 of the Restatement (Second) of Torts,[233] the court stated that the college's affirmative conduct gave rise to "a 'special relationship' with and [sic] increased risk of harm to its student-athletes such that [the defendants] had a duty to 'exercise reasonable care to protect them against an unreasonable risk of harm arising' from that affirmative conduct."[234] The court further stated that defendants undertook a duty to "provide licensed athletic trainers for the purpose of rendering treatment to its student athletes participating in athletic events...."[235] Included among the specific acts that the court identified as giving rise to the athletes' expectation that they would be treated by a certified athlete trainer were: the college's customary employment of licensed trainers; the college requiring student-athletes to sign forms

---

228. *Id.* at 1371.

229. *Id.* at 1367–69.

230. 215 A.3d 3 (Pa. 2019).

231. *Id.* at 11.

232. *Id.* at 12.

233. Section 323 provides that "One who undertakes, gratuitously or for consideration, to render services to another which he should recognize as necessary for the protection of the other's person or things, is subject to liability to the other for physical harm resulting from his failure to exercise reasonable care to perform his undertaking."

234. *Feleccia*, 215 A.3d at 15.

235. *Id.*

consenting to treatment by trainers and physicians in the event of an emergency during practice; trainers treating athletes for their injuries; and the college holding out the trainers as having been certified.[236]

[3] Increasing Inherent Risks

Courts have imposed liability on institutions for conduct viewed as increasing the inherent risk associated with an athlete's participation in a sport. Illustrative circumstances include decisions made by coaches that result in aggravation of an athlete's existing injury.[237] An educational institution may be held liable where a coach either requires or coerces an athlete to return to play resulting in the aggravation of an existing injury.[238] Similarly, a coach permitting or requiring an athlete to return to play without a determination of the athlete's medical condition may expose the institution to liability pursuant to a negligence theory or a coach's decision that increases the inherent risk of a game.[239] Liability may also ensue where a coach fails to supply proper equipment to their athletes.[240]

§ 10.06 Sovereign and Qualified Immunity

[A] Sovereign Immunity — Introduction

Sovereign immunity is a common law doctrine that shields governmental entities from negligence liability.[241] In the United States, the majority rule is that sovereign

---

236. *Id.*; *see also* Davidson v. Univ. N.C. at Chapel Hill, 543 S.E.2d 920 (N.C. App. 2001) (finding college, by virtue of a voluntary undertaking, assumed a duty to "advise and educate cheerleaders regarding safety" that arose independently of any special relationship between the cheerleaders and the college).

237. Limones v. Sch. Dist. of Lee Cty., 161 So. 3d 384, 394 (Fla. 2015); Dugan v. Thayer Academy, 2015 WL 3500385 (Mass. Super. May 27, 2015) (adopting a negligence standard).

238. *See e.g.*, Searles v. Trs. St. Joseph's College, 695 A.2d 1206 (Me. 1997); Morris v. Union High Sch. Dist. A, 294 P. 998 (Wash. 1931); Lamorie v. Warner Pac. Coll., 850 P.2d 401 (Or. Ct. App. 1993).

239. Mayall *ex rel.* H.C. v. USA Water Polo, Inc., 909 F.3d 1055, 1062 (9th Cir. 2018) (holding that while a water polo coach might not have been able to protect athlete from initial injury resulting from a blow to the head, "the player can be protected from a secondary injury from a repeated blow, where 'the greatest danger exists' and was 'reasonably to be expected.' Such secondary injury 'increase[s] the risks to a participant over and above those inherent in the sport'"); Cerny v. Cedar Bluffs Junior/Senior Public Sch., 679 N.W.2d 198 (Neb. 2004) (adopting a negligence standard and finding defendant did not breach the duty); Wattenberger v. Cincinnati Reds, Inc., 33 Cal. Rptr. 2d 732, 736–37 (Cal. 1994) (allowing injured player to continue to play increased inherent risk of the game); Jarreau v. Orleans Parish Sch. Bd., 600 So. 2d 1389 (La. Ct. App. 1992).

240. *See, e.g.*, Henney v. Shelby City Sch. Distr., 2006 WL 747475 (Ohio Ct. App. Mar. 23, 2006); Moose v. Mass. Inst. of Tech., 683 N.E.2d 706 (Mass. Ct. App. 1997); Mone v. Graziadei, 2017 WL 5076472 (N.J. Super. Ct. 2017).

241. Thomas R. Hurst & James N. Knight, *Coaches' Liability for Athletes' Injuries and Deaths*, 13 Seton Hall J. Sport L. 27, 43 (2003).

immunity applies when: (1) the defendant that is a governmental entity or political subdivision, (2) commits a negligent act, (3) within its governmental, not proprietary, function, and (4) no exceptions apply.[242] As it relates to schools, the rationale for sovereign immunity is permitting school boards to function free from fear of litigation that could deplete school funds.[243]

Generally, sovereign immunity is rooted in the following: (1) as a sovereign entity, the state can do no wrong; (2) public agencies have limited funds that should be spent for public purposes; (3) public bodies cannot be responsible for the torts of their employees; and (4) public bodies do not possess the authority to commit torts.[244] Jurisdictions adopting the majority view of sovereign immunity have modeled their statutory language on guidance provided by Section 895C of the Restatement (Second) of Torts § 895C.[245] Some states have abolished sovereign immunity, which exposes governmental entities to negligence liability.[246]

[B] The Basics of the Sovereign Immunity Defense

[1] Governmental Entity Status

Sovereign immunity is available as a defense where: (1) the defendant is a governmental entity or political subdivision; (2) the entity has committed a negligent act; (3) the entity was acting within a governmental function, and not a proprietary function, when the tort occurred; and (4) no exceptions apply to eliminate sovereign immunity as a defense.[247]

A governmental entity is a body that is within, and smaller than, a state which is responsible for governmental activities.[248] "A school board is a political subdivision."[249] In sports-related cases, defendants appear to have encountered little difficulty establishing government-entity status. Although some courts note that there is no dispute

---

242. Schnarrs v. Girard Bd. of Educ., 858 N.E.2d 1258, 1261 (Ohio Ct. App. 2006).

243. Andrew F. Beach, *Dying to Play: School Liability and Immunity for Injuries That Occur as a Result of School-Sponsored Athletic Events*, 10 SPORTS L.J. 275, 292 (2003).

244. Walter T. Champion, Jr., *"At the Ol' Ball Game" and Beyond: Spectators and the Potential for Liability*, 14 AM. J. TRIAL ADVOC. 495, 520 (1991).

245. RESTATEMENT (SECOND) OF TORTS § 895C (Am. L. Inst. 1979).

246. *Id.*; *see also* Ludwig v. Bd. of Educ., 183 N.E.2d 32, 33 (Ill. App. Ct. 1962) (holding that because a school district's conduct amounted to a governmental function, sovereign immunity was a defense to claims of spectator who was injured after falling on football stadium stairs; noting matter rose prior to a decision in which governmental immunity to tort liability was nullified).

247. *Schnarrs*, 858 N.E.2d at 1261.

248. *See* MISS. CODE. ANN. § 11-46-1 (West); *see also* OHIO REV. CODE ANN. § 2744.01 (West).

249. Yanero v. Davis, 65 S.W.3d 510, 521, 526 (Ky. 2001) (quoting Cullinan v. Jefferson Cnty., 418 S.W.2d 407 (Ky. Ct. App. 1967)) (finding that authorizing athletics at school is a governmental function and sovereign immunity is an available defense when athlete alleged the school board should be liable for injuries sustained during batting practice because authorization of such practice was not protected).

regarding the defendant's status as a governmental entity,[250] most courts assume, without discussion, that school boards and districts possess governmental entity status.[251]

Sovereign immunity is related to Eleventh Amendment immunity, but the court in *McCants v. National Collegiate Athletic Association*[252] distinguished the two defenses. In that case, a class action was brought against the NCAA and the University of North Carolina at Chapel Hill alleging claims related to classes of questionable academic value in which former athletes were enrolled.[253] The court distinguished Eleventh Amendment immunity from sovereign immunity. It stated that Eleventh Amendment immunity is a "block on the exercise of [subject matter] jurisdiction."[254] Thus, Eleventh Amendment immunity "addresses whether a state has consented to being sued in a federal court," whereas sovereign immunity addresses whether a state has consented to being sued in any court, state or federal.[254] Although both defenses may be waived, a governmental entity that waives sovereign immunity in state court does not automatically waive Eleventh Amendment immunity in federal court.[256] After Eleventh Amendment immunity is asserted, the defendant has the burden of establishing that it is entitled to sovereign immunity.[257]

[2] Governmental Function

Sovereign immunity is an effective defense only when a governmental entity acts within its governmental rather than proprietary function. An entity acts within its governmental function when it carries out acts authorized or mandated under law, essentially carrying out a function of the state.[258] An act that implicates a proprietary

---

250. Noble v. W. Clermont Local Sch. Dist., 914 N.E.2d 1128, 1132 (Ohio C.P. 2009) (noting there is no dispute about whether or not a school district is a "political subdivision"); Elston *ex rel.* Elston v. Howland Local Schs., 865 N.E.2d 845, 849 (Ohio 2007) (noting there is no dispute about whether or not a school district is a "political subdivision"); Champion, Jr., *supra* note 244, at 520.

251. *See* Brown v. Shepas, 2006 WL 8454004, at *11 (N.D. Ohio 2006) (assuming without discussion that a school district is a governmental entity); *accord* Fowler v. Tyler Indep. Sch. Dist., 232 S.W.3d 335, 337 (Tex. App. 2007); Ward v. Mich. State Univ., 782 N.W.2d 514, 516 (Mich. App. 2010); Schwindel v. Meade Cnty., 113 S.W.3d 159, 165 (Ky. 2003); Repede v. Cmty. Unit Sch. Dist., 779 N.E.2d 372, 375 (Ill. App. Ct. 2002).

252. 251 F. Supp. 3d 952, 956 (M.D. N.C. 2017).

253. *Id.* at 954.

254. *Id.* at 955.

255. *Id.*

256. *Id.*

257. *Id.*

258. *See* Harris v. Univ. of Mich. Bd. of Regents, 558 N.W.2d 225, 228 (Mich. Ct. App. 1996) (concluding money-making activity such as traveling for competitions nevertheless involves a governmental function in case in which athlete alleged a trip to Colorado for competitions in which she suffered injury while sledding was a proprietary activity because it generated revenue); *Yanero*, 65 S.W.3d at 520 (finding that defendant's authorization of interscholastic sports is a governmental function where student was hit in the head by baseball while not wearing a helmet at practice); *Fowler*, 232 S.W.3d at 338 (finding that athletic games are a governmental function); *Schwindel*, 113 S.W.3d at 168 (holding a school board's sponsorship of an athletic tournament at a local park was a governmental function in matter involving spectator's allegations that school board should be liable for injuries sustained when a foot rail on bleachers slipped out of place); Gravely v. Lewisville Indep. Sch. Dist., 701 S.W.2d 956, 957 (Tex. App. 1986) (finding all matters incidental to education—in-

function is one that has a "profit motive" and is not typically supported by taxes.[259] Some courts deem conduct as governmental rather than proprietary where the subject activity is one that the government generally engages in or provides.[260] As stated by the court in *Willett v. Chatham Cnty. Bd. of Educ.*, "If the undertaking of the municipality is one in which only a governmental agency could engage, it is governmental in nature. It is proprietary and 'private' when any corporation, individual, or group of individuals could do the same thing."[261]

Willett[262] illustrates the distinction between a governmental and proprietary function. There, a spectator at a middle school basketball game alleged the school board was negligent in maintaining the school's gymnasium bleachers.[263] The school board asserted sovereign immunity, stating that the board was immune because it acted within its governmental function.[264] The spectator argued sovereign immunity was not an available defense because hosting and charging admission for spectators to attend the game was a proprietary function.[265] The court disagreed stating that a monetary fee to enter a sporting event, especially one that is insubstantial — one dollar for students and two dollars for parents — does not constitute a proprietary act.[266] The court concluded there was no evidence that the money earned through admission fees provided for anything more than the operation of the program. Therefore, the board was not engaged in a proprietary function and sovereign immunity was applicable.[267]

---

cluding sports — are a governmental function thus shielding school district from spectator's claims that alleged the school district was liable for injuries sustained when bleachers collapsed at a basketball game); Couture v. Bd. of Educ. of Town of Plainfield, 505 A.2d 432, 434 (Conn. App. 1986) (citing Winchester v. Cox, 26 A.2d 592 (Conn. 1942)) (finding sporting events are a governmental function in case in which a sideline official alleged the school board should be liable for injuries sustained when a player ran into him); Sch. Bd. of Broward Cnty. v. McCall, 322 So. 3d 655, 659 (Fla. Dist. Ct. App. 2021) (holding security plans for after sporting events are a governmental function when a spectator was injured in the crowd leaving a game).

259. *See* Willett v. Chatham, Cnty. Bd. of Educ., 625 S.E.2d 900, 902 (N.C. Ct. App. 2006); *Ward*, 782 N.W.2d at 519; *Harris*, 558 N.W.2d at 690; Garza v. Edinburg Concol. Indep. Sch. Dist., 576 S.W.2d 916, 918 (Tex. App. 1979).

260. *See Willett*, 625 S.E.2d at 902 (ruling that charging a fee for admission into sporting events is a governmental function when spectator alleged the school board should be liable for injuries sustained in fall on bleachers during a game); *see also Brown*, 2006 WL 8454004 at *11 (concluding that out-of-season sports camps that were not paid for by school board but rather by fund-raising nevertheless amount to board exercising a governmental function).

261. *Willett*, 625 S.E.2d at 920 (quoting Britt v. City of Wilmington, 73 S.E.2d 289, 293 (N.C. 1952)).

262. *Willett*, 625 S.E.2d at 901.

263. *Id.*

264. *Id.*

265. *Id.* at 902.

266. *Id.* at 903.

267. *Id.*; *see also Harris*, 558 N.W.2d. at 230 (citing Adam v. Sylvan Glynn Golf Course, 494 N.W.2d 791 (Mich. App. 1992)) ("a governmental agency may conduct an activity on a self-sustaining basis without being subject to the proprietary function exception").

In *Harris v. University of Michigan Board of Regents*,[268] a student-athlete alleged the school board could not assert sovereign immunity as a defense to her claim that she was negligently injured on a team trip because the purpose of the trip was to "produce profit," thus making it proprietary. Rejecting the athlete's argument, the court emphasized the lack of evidence of a profit motive or that the athletics program was not supported by taxes.[269] Elaborating generally on why athletics at public schools are a governmental function, the court stated: "(1) team sports and competitions are properly a part of a school's overall physical education program, (2) the function of a physical education and related sports program is inherently educational, and (3) because such a program is educational, it is properly considered a governmental function."[270]

In *Brown v. Shepas*,[271] the court's concern was whether the alleged injury-causing activity is one in which a "nongovernmental person[]" typically participates. In *Brown*, an athlete was injured when members of the football team hazed him by attempting to forcibly shave his head.[272] The athlete alleged the team's coaches encouraged the hazing and the school district should be liable.[273] The court first determined whether the alleged injury occurred during a governmental function.[274] It concluded the district acted within its governmental function.[275] The court also addressed whether the team's trip became proprietary because it was voluntary and took place before the start of the season.[276] The court ruled that despite the trip not being funded by the school's athletics program and being voluntary, it was nevertheless within the district's governmental function because students raised the funding "as representatives of the Massillon football team" and the trip was only available to students who were part of the football program.[277]

[3] Exceptions and Waiver

A governmental entity acting within a governmental function may not successfully assert sovereign immunity if an exception applies or the entity waives the defense. Courts recognize exceptions, including: (1) the nuisance exception;[278] (2) the public

---

268. *Harris*, 558 N.W.2d at 226–27.
269. *Id.* at 231.
270. *Id.* at 228.
271. *Brown*, 2006 WL 8454004 at *1.
272. *Id.*
273. *Id.*
274. *Id.* at *10.
275. *Id.*
276. *Id.*
277. *Id.* at *11.
278. *See* RESTATEMENT (SECOND) OF TORTS § 895C (Am. L. Inst. 1979); *see also Couture*, 505 A.2d at 433 (finding the nuisance exception did not apply where plaintiff's alleged injuries did not involve an injury resulting from plaintiff exercising a public right or plaintiff's ownership interest in land).

property or recreational area exception;[279] (3) the negligent act exception;[280] and (4) waiver, such as where the entity has procured liability insurance.[281]

The public property exception — known as the public building exception — was considered by the court in *Ward v. Michigan State University.*[282] There, a spectator attending a college hockey game was injured after she was struck by a hockey puck.[283] The spectator alleged the injury was caused by a building defect — the absence of Plexiglass protecting spectators in the section of the arena where plaintiff sat.[284] In states in which statutes recognize this exception, where an injury results from a building defect, sovereign immunity no longer operates as a shield against negligence liability. In *Ward,* the court acknowledged the existence of a building defect, but found the service of process, which was a precondition to plaintiff's asserting the public building exception to immunity, was improper.[285] Consequently, the exception could not be invoked.[286] At least one jurisdiction recognizes that the public building exception applies even though there is no building defect so long as the injury occurs in a public building.[287]

The nuisance exception is illustrated by *Couture v. Board of Education of the Town of Plainfield,*[288] in which the plaintiff, who arrived at a game as a spectator, was asked to serve as a game official. He agreed and was injured when a player ran into him, pushing him into the stands. The plaintiff alleged the board created a nuisance by "failing to pad the stands or to erect a barrier between the stands and playing field"[289] and by not preventing players from crowding the sideline, which "impair[ed] [his] ability" to get out of the way when players came toward him.[290] The court disagreed, finding there was neither a public nor private nuisance because a public nuisance

---

279. *Noble,* 914 N.E.2d at 1132 (applying the public building exception where the injury occurred on school grounds); Hull v. Weston Indep. Sch. Dist. I 004, 46 P.3d 180, 181, 186 (Okla. Ct. App. 2001) (holding student-athlete's claims that he was injured during a practice football game on school grounds was barred by immunity). *But see Ward,* 782 N.W.2d at 516 (finding that public building exception was inapplicable because of improper service of process); DiVenere v. Univ. of Wyo., 811 P.2d 273, 274 (Wyo. 1991) (concluding public building exception did not apply).

280. Spearman v. Shelby County Bd. of Educ., 637 S.W.3d 719, 733 (Tenn. Ct. App. 2021) (finding that the negligent act exception to the sovereign immunity defense can be invoked when the alleged injury causing act constitutes negligent but not intentional or reckless conduct).

281. *See* RESTATEMENT (SECOND) OF TORTS § 895C (Am. L. Inst. 1979); *see also* Daniel v. City of Morganton, 479 S.E.2d 263, 267 (N.C. App. 1997) (insurance waiver exception did not apply when the injury took place during softball practice and insurance policy excluded injuries sustained at practice or in games); Bowen v. Telfair Cnty. Sch. Dist., 418 F. Supp. 3d 1265, 1271 (S.D. Ga. 2019) (insurance waiver exception did not apply where the applicable statute limited the exception to municipal corporations but not school districts).

282. *Ward,* 782 N.W.2d at 516.

283. *Id.*

284. *Id.*

285. *Id.* at 517–18.

286. *Id.*

287. *Noble,* 914 N.E.2d at 1133–34.

288. *Couture,* 505 A.2d at 433.

289. *Id.*

290. *Id.*

exists when one is injured while exercising a public right and a private nuisance is connected to a plaintiff's "ownership ... interest in land."[291] The court concluded the official was neither injured exercising a public right nor in connection to his ownership interest in property.[292]

The court in *Spearman v. Shelby County Board of Education*[293] recognized the negligent act exception. There, a student, who was trying out for a high school's track team, was severely injured after being struck by a shot-put ball thrown by a coach. The court stated: "[G]overnmental immunity 'is removed for injur[ies] proximately caused by a negligent act or omission of any employee [acting] within the scope of his employment.' In contrast, the intentional torts of assault and battery that are committed by an employee acting within the scope of his employment do not remove governmental immunity."[294] The plaintiff alleged that the coach was negligent and thereby unprotected by sovereign immunity. The defendant claimed sovereign immunity should apply because the plaintiff alleged the defendant engaged in reckless or intentional conduct.[295] The court ruled that defendant's acts were negligent and sovereign immunity was unavailable as a defense.[296]

The Restatement (Second) of Torts § 895C(e) states "the existence of liability insurance has been treated as a waiver of governmental immunity, at least to the extent of the insurance coverage."[297] The insurance exception was explored in *Daniel v. City of Morganton*,[298] where a high school student was injured during a ground ball drill at softball practice. The school board's liability policy covered certain injuries occurring on school grounds or at school events, but not injuries occurring during practice or sports competition.[299] The student alleged the board waived its right to sovereign immunity by obtaining liability insurance.[300] The court offered the following guidance:

[A]ny local board of education is authorized to waive its governmental immunity from liability by securing liability insurance as provided for in the statute. The primary purpose of the statute is to encourage local school boards to waive immunity by obtaining insurance protections while, at the same time, giving such boards the discretion to determine whether and to what extent to waive immunity. The statute makes clear that unless the negligence or tort is covered by the insurance policy, sovereign immunity *has not been waived* by the Board or its agents.[301]

291. *Id.* at 435.

292. *Id.*

293. *Spearman*, 637 S.W. 3d at 725.

294. *Id* at 733. (quoting Hughes v. Metro. Gov't of Nashville & Davidson Cty., 340 S.W.3d 352, 360 (Tenn. 2011)).

295. *Id.* at 731, 733.

296. *Id.* at 725.

297. *See* RESTATEMENT (SECOND) OF TORTS § 895C (Am. L. Inst. 1979).

298. *Daniel*, 479 S.E.2d. at 265–66.

299. *Id.* at 266.

300. *Id.*

301. *Id.* at 267.

Rejecting the student's waiver claim,[302] the court explained that immunity was waived only to the extent that the insurance policy covered the activity in question. Given that the policy specifically excluded sports injuries from coverage, immunity had not been waived.[303] The court added that if the injured party had been a spectator or had not been "practicing for or participating in" a sporting event, the insurance policy would have given rise to a waiver of immunity.[304]

[C] Qualified Immunity

[1] Introduction

When sports-related injuries occur, coaches, athletic trainers, or other public agents may be entitled to the "qualified immunity" defense against tort claims.[305] Sovereign immunity is a common law protection afforded to governmental entities to protect them from negligence claims, and qualified immunity is largely considered a subset of that defense that is instead afforded to public employees.[306] The majority rule in the United States is that public employees are entitled to the qualified immunity defense when: (1) the alleged tortious conduct was committed within the scope of the official's employment; (2) the conduct occurred when the official was "performing a discretionary function"; (3) the tortious conduct amounted to ordinary negligence; and (4) no exception to the qualified immunity doctrine is applicable.[307] Most jurisdictions that have adopted the majority view on qualified immunity have based their statutes on the Restatement (Second) of Torts § 895D.[308]

[2] The Basics of the Qualified Immunity Defense

[a] Within the Scope of the Official's Employment

The four qualified immunity factors outlined above were considered in *Gasper v. Freidel*.[309] In that case, a high school athlete alleged he suffered injuries during a summer football program as a result of his coaches' failure to properly supervise him

---

302. *Id.*

303. *Id.* at 268.

304. *Id.* at 267.

305. Hurst & Knight, *supra* note 241, at 43.

306. *Id.*

307. Yanero v. Davis, 65 S.W.3d 510, 521 (Ky. 2001) (finding that qualified immunity is an available defense where high school athlete alleged the coaches were negligent in not requiring athletes to wear helmets and for not obtaining timely, sufficient medical treatment); Harris *ex rel.* Harris v. McCray, 867 So. 2d 188, 191 (Miss. 2003) (qualified immunity is an available defense where high school athlete alleged coach was negligent in having practices in high temperatures); Pope v. Madison City Sch. Dist. Bd. of Educ., 2004 WL 541121, at *2 (Ohio Ct. App. March 19, 2004) (qualified immunity is available where a middle school athlete alleged the coach was negligent in allowing half-court basketball games); Woods v. Ware, 471 S.W.3d 385, 391 (Mo. Ct. App. 2015) (finding qualified immunity was an available defense where a middle school athlete alleged the coach was negligent in physically participating in practice with the students).

308. RESTATEMENT (SECOND) OF TORTS § 895D (Am. L. Inst. 1979).

309. 450 N.S.2d 226 (S.D. 1990).

during weight training. The student alleged his coaches failed to "provide adequate or proper instruction, supervision, safety devices and facilities," particularly by permitting him to lift weights without a spotter. The coaches had previously expressed the significance of using a spotter during such workouts.[310] The coaches asserted qualified immunity as a defense.

The court first explored whether the coaches were acting in their official capacities as public employees when the injury occurred.[311] The court concluded the injury occurred in the scope of the coaches' employment because their contractual duties subsumed the "pre-school term duties," and the superintendent of the schools authorized "out-of-season conditioning."[312] Similar to *Gasper*, courts have found that conduct was within the scope of defendants' employment in the following circumstances: a coach physically participating in batting practice,[313] coaches not supervising summer weight lifting after instructing the students on proper technique,[314] a coach being in control of determining when practices and breaks from practices take place,[315] a coach making decisions about whether a player's injuries warrant seeing a trainer or returning to practice,[316] coaches allowing high school athletes to compete against middle school athletes at practice,[317] and defendants' role in designing athletic programs.[318]

Wyatt v. Fletcher[319] also involved a coach seeking the protection of qualified immunity. There, it was alleged that the softball coaches at a Texas high school led a student-athlete into the locker room, where they confronted the athlete about a sexual relationship with another woman and disclosed this information to her mother.[320] The mother filed a complaint under the Fourth and Fourteenth Amendments of the Texas Constitution, and the coaches claimed qualified immunity in response.[321] After a lengthy analysis, the court concluded that the coaches were entitled to qualified immunity since the facts failed to show that there was any federal right violated.[322] Thus, a public employee will be entitled to qualified immunity if there is "no violation of a clearly established federal right."[323]

---

310. *Id.*

311. *Id.* at 231.

312. *Id.*

313. *Ex parte* Nall, 879 So. 2d 541, 545 (Ala. 2003) (finding qualified immunity was an available defense where a high school athlete alleged the coach was negligent in conducting practice and supervising the players), as modified on denial of reh'g (Oct. 24, 2003).

314. *Gasper*, 450 N.W.2d at 232.

315. *Harris*, 867 So. 2d. at 189.

316. Prince v. Louisville Mun. Sch. Dist., 741 So. 2d 207, 211 (Ala. 1993).

317. *Woods*, 471 S.W.3d at 388.

318. Jahn v. Bd. of Educ. of Town of Monroe, 99 A.3d 1230, 1236 (Conn. App. 2014) (finding the swim program was designed by a state agent for a public purpose, allowing the coach protection under qualified immunity).

319. 718 F.3d 496 (5th Cir. 2013).

320. *Id.* at 500–01.

321. *Id.* at 502.

322. *Id.* at 510.

323. *See id.*

In contrast to these cases, a public employee has been found to have acted outside the scope of employment generally where there is no connection between the duty the employee is asked to perform and the act that is performed.[324] For example, a coach who committed sexual assault was deemed to have acted outside the scope of his employment.[325]

[b] Discretionary or Ministerial Acts

Qualified immunity is only available as a defense if a public employee can establish the alleged tortious conduct constituted a discretionary act rather than a ministerial act. An act is discretionary if it involves the official using their personal judgment in weighing "competing policies."[326] In contrast to a discretionary act, a ministerial act is one in which the official implements "prescribed" procedures or policies that do not invoke the official's exercise of judgment.[327]

In determining if an act is discretionary or ministerial, courts may consider: (1) the nature of the employee's duties; (2) the extent of judgment required for the act; and (3) the possible consequences of not invoking qualified immunity.[328] "Departmental rules, the orders from superiors" and "the nature of the employee's position"

---

324. 42 TEX. JUR. 3D *Governmental Tort Liability* § 73 (2021).

325. Deborah Brake, *The Struggle for Sex Equality in Sport and the Theory Behind Title IX*, 34 MICH. J.L. REFORM 13, n.399 (2001).

326. *Accord* Bowen v. Telfair Cnty. Sch. Dist., 418 F. Supp. 3d 1265, 1269 (S.D. Ga. 2019) (finding qualified immunity was an available defense where a high school athlete alleged the coach was negligent in allowing the athlete to play after sustaining a concussion); *Harris*, 867 So. 2d. at 190 (stating qualified immunity was an available defense where high school athlete alleged coach was negligent in having practices in high temperatures); Teodoro v. Town of Bristol, 2019 WL 1504003, at *2 (Conn. Super. Ct. Feb. 20, 2019) (holding qualified immunity was an available defense where a high school athlete alleged the coach was negligent in supervising practice); Lennon v. Peterson, 624 So. 2d 171, 173 (Ala. 1993) (finding that qualified immunity was an available defense where a university athlete alleged the coach and athletic director were negligent in misdiagnosing an injury and allowing the athlete to practice through the injury); *Prince*, 741 So. 2d at 211 (applying qualified immunity as an available defense where a high school athlete alleged the coach was negligent in failing to monitor the athlete's health and provide necessary medical care); Elston *ex rel.* Elston v. Howland Local Schs., 865 N.E.2d 845, 847 (Ohio 2007) (finding that determining the use of sporting equipment and facilities is discretionary and qualified immunity is an available defense). *But see* Divia v. S. Hunterdon Reg'l High Sch., 2005 WL 977028, at *4 (N.J. Sup. Ct. App. Div. Apr. 5, 2005) (holding that qualified immunity was not an available defense where a high school athlete alleged the coach was negligent in allowing an athlete to compete without certification required according to the school handbook); Clark Cnty. Sch. Dist. v. Payo, 403 P.3d 1270, 1276 (Nev. 2017) (stating that qualified immunity was not an available defense where middle school student alleged the physical education instructor was negligent in supervising the students during class).

327. *Teodoro*, 2019 WL 1504003 at *3; Karalyos v. Bd. of Educ. of Lake Forest Cmty. High Sch., 788 F. Supp. 2d 727, 731 (N.D. Ill. 2011) (finding qualified immunity unavailable where a swim coach instructed a student to dive despite there being no diving rules).

328. Elias v. Davis, 535 S.W.3d 737, 742 (Mo. Ct. App. 2017) (finding qualified immunity was an available defense where a high school athlete alleged coaches were negligent in physically participating in practice) (citing Southers v. City of Farmington, 263 S.W.3d 603, 611 (Mo. 2008) (en banc)).

all dictate what duties an employee must fulfill.[329] In *Elias v. Davis*,[330] a high school football player alleged his football coaches were negligent in requiring athletes to dress up in full football gear (*i.e.*, shoulder pads and helmets) to practice with the team in a scrimmage that resulted in the student breaking his ankle.[331] One coach lined up as a running back while the student was lined up as a linebacker, and when the student attempted to tackle the coach, his ankle broke.[332]

The coaches asserted qualified immunity, stating that their actions were discretionary given the nature of their duties, the extent that judgment was required, and the consequences of not applying qualified immunity.[333] The court agreed, ruling that the coaches were protected by qualified immunity because their conduct was both within the scope of their employment and discretionary.[334] In finding that the coaches exercised their discretion, the court emphasized that the duties encompassed teaching athletes about the sport and preparing them to execute on the field during games.[335] The court also noted the absence of rules or laws regarding the supervision of practice. It inferred that practice decisions are discretionary as a default in the absence of laws, rules, or regulations, no matter how debatable the decisions may be.[336]

Courts are also mindful of the policy of allowing public employees, acting within their official capacity, to exercise discretion without fear of "retaliatory lawsuits."[337] The court in *Jahn v. Board of Education of Town of Monroe*[338] stated the rationale behind qualified immunity:

> [Qualified immunity] serves the policy goal of avoiding expansive exposure to liability, which would cramp the exercise of official discretion beyond the limits desirable in our society.... [Qualified immunity] reflects a value judgment that — despite injury to a member of the public — the broader interest in having government officers and employees free to exercise judgment and discretion in their official functions, unhampered by fear of second-guessing and retaliatory lawsuits, outweighs the benefits to be had from imposing liability for that injury....[339]

In *Jahn*, a student alleged his swim coach was negligent when the coach left the student and his teammates unsupervised to participate in a practice drill that resulted

---

329. *Elias*, 535 S.W.3d at 742 (citing A.F. v. Hazelwood Sch. Dist., 491 S.W.3d 628, 631 (Mo. App. E.D. 2016)).
330. *Id.* at 740–41.
331. *Id.*
332. *Id.*
333. *Id.* at 742.
334. *Id.* at 743.
335. *Id.*
336. *Id.* at 744.
337. *Jahn*, 99 A.3d at 1236 (finding qualified immunity was an available defense where a high school athlete alleged the coach was negligent in supervising and instructing the team) (citing Edgerton v. Clinton, 86 A.3d 437 (Conn. App. 2014)).
338. 99 A.3d 1236 (Conn. App. 2014).
339. *Id.* at 1236.

in injury.[340] In defense, the swim coach asserted the qualified immunity doctrine.[341] Focusing on whether the coach's conduct involved a discretionary act, the court found that the action allegedly leading to the injury was centered on how to conduct practice — an act that requires the exercise of judgment, making it discretionary.[342]

Divia v. South Hunterdon Regional High School[343] also illustrates the discretionary/ministerial distinction. There, a high school wrestler's arm was fractured after he was slammed to the mat during a match with another student.[344] The student asserted that qualified immunity was not available as a defense for the wrestling coach because the coach failed to fulfill one of his ministerial duties leading up to the match: receiving a minimum weight certification from the student.[345] The coach claimed that the certification was not required by law, so permitting any athlete to compete without it would be an act of discretion.[346] The court stated that the existence of a law adopting the rule in question was not dispositive on whether conduct involves a ministerial act. Rather, an employer may also adopt rules to create a ministerial duty instead of leaving those actions to the discretion of employees.[347]

In some cases, such as *Covington County School District v. Magee*,[348] courts find that only discretionary decisions which invoke public policy should be protected by qualified immunity.[349] There, a high school football player died as a result of heat stroke he suffered at practice.[350] The deceased student's beneficiary asserted that qualified immunity should not apply to the coach's discretionary decision to conduct practice on a hot day — a decision that resulted in the death of the student — because it was not a policy decision.[351] The court disagreed, stating that how to conduct practice does invoke policy because "coaches know their players and must be able to control their teams."[352]

Finally, the discretionary/ministerial distinction arose in *Black v. Town of Westport*.[353] There, a student-athlete was injured during gymnastics practice while attempting to perform a maneuver her coach instructed her to perform.[354] The coach had provided no instruction regarding the technique necessary to perform the ma-

---

340. *Id.* at 1233–34.

341. *Id.*

342. *Id.* at 1236.

343. *Divia*, 2005 WL 977028, at *1 (ruling that ministerial duties are not only prescribed by law but also derived from the policy of the employer).

344. *Id.*

345. *Id.*

346. *Id.* at *4.

347. *Id.*

348. 29 So. 3d 1 (Miss. 2010).

349. *Id.* at 7 (finding that determination as to how to conduct practice invoke public policy and qualified immunity applies); *see also Clark Cnty.*, 403 P.3d at 1276; *Divia*, 2005 WL 977028 at *3.

350. *Covington*, 29 So. 3d at 3

351. *Id.* at 3, 7.

352. *Id.* at 8.

353. Black v. Town of Westport, 2013 WL 3388898 (Conn. Super. Ct. June 17, 2013).

354. *Id.* at *1.

neuver.[355] The athlete sued, alleging violations of ministerial duties and discretionary duties.[356] The court noted that immunity only applies to governmental and not necessarily ministerial acts.[357] The court upheld the lower court decision that summary judgment was inappropriate at this stage because issues of material fact existed as to whether the duties were discretionary or ministerial; these issues of material fact included practice policies.[358]

[c] The Reckless or Intentional Act Exception

Even if an act is discretionary and is committed by a public employee within the scope of their employment, the actor may still be liable for an injury caused when the employee's duty to act — or refrain from acting — in a particular manner is so "clear and unequivocal" that the purpose for qualified immunity is rendered moot.[359] In most jurisdictions, courts recognize a common law exception to qualified immunity. Thus, the doctrine is unavailable as a defense where the injury or harm stems not from ordinary negligence but rather from recklessness, willfulness, wantonness, or intentional conduct.[360] In other jurisdictions, the intentional/wanton conduct exception is provided by a statute. Courts have found that qualified immunity is also unavailable if the alleged tortious conduct subjects an identifiable person or class to imminent harm and the conduct strips a person of some constitutional right.[361] Each of these circumstances involves reckless or intentional conduct.[362]

The court in *Swank v. Valley Christian School*[363] defined gross negligence and recklessness in applying the exception. In *Swank*, an athlete was removed from a

---

355. *Id.* at *2.
356. *Id.* at *3.
357. *Id.*
358. *Id.* at *7–8.
359. Andreozzi v. Town of E. Haven, 2014 WL 2021961, at *2, *4 (Conn. Super. Ct. Apr. 9, 2014) (stating qualified immunity was available as a defense where a high school athlete alleged the coach was negligent in not creating and maintaining a safe environment for the athlete to compete).
360. Barr v. Cunningham, 89 N.E.3d 315, 318 (Ill. 2017) (finding that qualified immunity was an available defense where a high school student alleged the instructor was negligent in failing to require the use of protective eyewear playing floor hockey); *Jahn*, 99 A.3d 1230, 1240 n.3 (Conn. App. 2014) (holding qualified immunity bars claim against coach for alleged negligent supervision and intrusion); *Pope*, 2004 WL 541121, at *2; Radebaugh *ex rel.* Rottier v. Wausau Underwriters Ins. Co., 909 N.W.2d 210 (Wis. App. 2018) (holding that qualified immunity shields negligence liability of coach who did not require middle school score-keeper to wear a helmet); *Yanero*, 65 S.W.3d at 523 (holding the same).
361. *See* Burden v. Wilkes-Barre Area Sch. Dist., 16 F. Supp. 2d 569, 571–72 (M.D. Pa. 1998) (applying qualified immunity where a high school student alleged the school district was violating his constitutional rights by not hiring a certified athletic trainer).
362. *Andreozzi*, 2014 WL 2021961, at *2; *see also Radebaugh*, 909 N.W. 2d at 210; *Jahn*, 99 A.3d at 1237; Bowen v. Telfair Cnty. Sch. Dist., 418 F. Supp. 3d 1265, 1269 (S.D. Ga. 2019).
363. Swank v. Valley Christian Sch., 398 P.3d 1108, 1120 (Wash. 2017) (finding the qualified immunity defense was unavailable where a high school athlete alleged a coach was grossly negligent or reckless in complying with state concussion laws).

football game after suffering a concussion.[364] The athlete was cleared by a doctor to return to play days later but was evidently still dealing with the effects of the concussion during the next game.[365] Nevertheless, his coach kept him in the game until the athlete received another hit to the head, leading to a second concussion from which he collapsed and soon died.[366] The court defined gross negligence as the "failure to exercise slight care, mean[ing] not the total absence of care but care substantially or appreciably less than the quantum of care inhering in ordinary negligence."[367] Recklessness occurs "when [a person] knows of and disregards a substantial risk that a wrongful act may occur and his disregard of such substantial risk is a gross deviation from conduct that a reasonable man would exercise in the same situation."[368] The court determined there was enough evidence of gross negligence and recklessness to create a genuine issue of material fact preventing summary judgment on the grounds of immunity.[369]

Pope v. Trotwood Madison City School Dist. Bd. of Educ.[370] also illustrates the reckless/wanton exception to the qualified immunity defense.[371] There, a middle school student alleged his basketball coach was wantonly and recklessly negligent in permitting students to play half-court basketball games in "open gym" in which the wall was five feet from the court's sideline. The student suffered a neck injury when he hit the wall.[372] The coach asserted qualified immunity as a defense.[373] The court stated that for the coach to have been reckless, the coach and school district actions must have disregarded the risk of injury to the students.[374] The court concluded the that the wall having been covered with protective matting was evidence that the school district and coach were not disregarding the risk of injury but instead taking steps to prevent injury.[375]

In *Barr v. Cunningham*,[376] a plaintiff successfully asserted the willful and wanton exception in a case in which a student, who was playing floor hockey with classmates during his physical education ("P.E.") class, was hit in the eye with the ball the students were using as a puck. The student alleged the P.E. teacher/coach acted willfully and in wanton disregard of the risk of injury to the students by not requiring the students to wear protective eyewear.[377] The coach, who supervised the game to ensure that all the rules were followed, believed eyewear was unnecessary because she had already

---

364. *Id.* at 1113.

365. *Id.*

366. *Id.* at 1114.

367. *Id.* at 1120 (quoting Nist v. Tudor, 407 P.2d 798, 803 (Wash. 1965) (en banc)) (alteration in original).

368. *Id.* (quoting State v. Graham, 103 P.3d 1238, 1242 (Wash. 2005) (en banc)).

369. *Id.*

370. 2004 WL 541121 (Ohio Ct. App. March 19, 2004).

371. *Id.* at *2.

372. *Id.* at *1.

373. *Id.*

374. *Id.* at *3.

375. *Id.* at *4.

376. 89 N.E.3d 315, 317 (Ill. 2017).

377. *Id.* at 316.

modified the equipment used for the game to better protect the students from injury.[378] Agreeing with the coach, the court defined willful and wanton conduct as constituting a conscious disregard for safety.[379] The court determined the coach's modification of the rules of play and the equipment were intended to best protect the students "based on her experience and expertise."[380]

Another exception to qualified immunity was examined in *Andreozzi v. Town of East Haven.*[381] While jogging with his cross country teammates, a middle school student ran into a bench that was left on the track, resulting in several injuries.[382] The injured student argued that qualified immunity was not a defense available to the coach because the school handbook created a ministerial duty for the coach to provide a safe environment for the students; the court was unconvinced.[383] The student also argued that the imminent harm exception deprived the coach of his qualified immunity defense. The court stated this exception applies "when the circumstances make it apparent to the public officer that his or her failure to act would be likely to subject an identifiable person to imminent harm."[384] The court also stated that for harm to be imminent, the risk of harm "must be sufficiently immediate ... The risk of harm must be temporary and of short duration.... 'Imminent harm' excludes risks that might occur, if at all, at some unspecified time in the future."[385]

In *Roventini v. Passadena Independent School District,*[386] a student alleged that his football coach's negligence in holding a strenuous practice in the heat with few breaks led to the student suffering from heat exhaustion, which violated his constitutional rights to life, liberty, health, and safety. In that case, the court noted that to be granted this exception, a plaintiff must allege the violation of a "clearly established law," meaning that it must be apparent that the act is unlawful.[387] According to the court, the student alleged sufficient facts to establish a violation of his constitutional rights because precedent establishes that public officials' indifference to students' bodily integrity and the right to life, liberty, and safety deprives officials of the qualified immunity defense.[388]

---

378. *Id.* at 317.
379. *Id.* at 318.
380. *Id.* at 319.
381. *Andreozzi,* 2014 WL 2021961, at *1.
382. *Id.*
383. *Id.* at *2–3.
384. *Id.* at *3 (quoting Benedict v. Norfolk, 997 A.2d 449, n.1 (Conn. 2010)).
385. *Id.* at *4 (quoting Silberstein v. 54 Hillcrest Park Assocs., LLC, 41 A.3d 1147 (2012)); *see also Jahn,* 99 A.3d at 1240 (determining that the imminent harm exception was inapplicable because the student participated voluntarily in a nonmandatory activity — leaving him out of the identifiable class of school children).
386. Roventini v. Passadena Indep. Sch. Dist., 981 F. Supp. 1013, 1016 (S.D. Tex. 1997), *vacated,* 183 F.R.D. 500 (S.D. Tex. 1998) (holding that coach could not invoke qualified immunity where a high school athlete alleged the coach violated the athlete's constitutional rights to life, liberty, and safety by requiring that the students take part in a strenuous practice in the heat with an insufficient number of breaks).
387. *Id.* at 1023–24.
388. *Id.* at 1019, 1025.

§ 10.07 Enforcing Pre-Injury
Liability Waivers

[A] Introduction

Defendants attempt to protect themselves from tort liability by requiring that participants who engage in sport activities sign liability waivers and releases. These waivers are considered a "defense," yet they are more aptly "characterized as an express assumption of the risk that negates the defendant's duty of care."[389] This section first examines the enforceability of pre-injury waivers signed by parents on behalf of their children. It then discusses the enforceability of pre-injury waivers signed by adults, principally engaged in recreational activities. In each instance, the presence of these contractual provisions has given rise to litigation regarding their enforceability whether agreed to by a parent on behalf of a minor child or by an adult.

[B] The Enforceability of Parental Pre-Injury
Liability Waivers

When a parent signs a waiver for a child to participate in an athletic or recreational activity, the waiver typically includes an exculpatory clause.[390] Courts grapple with whether a parent has the authority to waive a minor's pre-injury claims. While there is a split of authority, a slight majority of courts rule that parents may not bind their children through pre-injury liability waivers.[391] When choosing to adopt or reject the majority rule, courts assess claims on constitutional, state statutory, and public policy grounds.

[1] The Impact of Parental Constitutional Rights

Parents have a constitutionally protectible liberty interest in the care, custody, and control of their child.[392] In *Troxel v. Granville*[393] the Court stated that "the interest of

---

389. Eriksson v. Nunnik, 233 Cal. App. 4th 708 (Cal. Ct. App. 2015).

390. Liability waivers are often accompanied by mandatory arbitration provisions, which courts tend to enforce. *See, e.g.*, Global Travel Marketing, Inc. v. Shea, 908 So. 2d 392 (Fla. 2005). Unlike exculpatory clauses which may create a conflict between parental rights to make decisions for their children and public policy to protect the vulnerable, enforcement of an arbitration clause in itself is considered good public policy. *Id.* at 392.

391. *See, e.g.*, Kelly v. US, 809 F. Supp. 2d 429, 435 (E.D.N.C. 2011); Hojonowski *ex rel.* Hojonowski v. Vans Skate Park, 375 N.J. Super. 568 (2005); Galloway v. State, 790 N.W.2d 252 (Iowa 2010); Kirton v. Fields, 997 So. 2d 349 (Fla. 2008); Rutherford v. Talisker Fin. Co., L.L.C., 445 P.3d 474 (Utah 2019); Miller *ex rel.* E.M. v. House of Boom Ky., 575 S.W.3d 656 (Ky. 2019); Wagenblast v. Odessa Sch. Dist. No. 105-157-166, 758 P.2d 968 (Wash. 1988); *but see* Sharon v. City of Newton, 769 N.E.2d 738 (Mass. 2002); Zivich v. Mentor Soccer Club, Inc., 696 N.E.2d 201 (Ohio 1998); Platzer v. Mammoth Mountain Ski Area, 128 Cal. Rptr. 2d. 885 (Cal. Ct. App. 2002).

392. Troxel v. Granville, 530 U.S. 57 (2000).

393. 530 U.S. 57 (2000).

parents in the care, custody, and control of their children is perhaps the oldest of the fundamental liberty interests recognized by the Court."[394] Relying on *Troxel*, the court in *Saccente v. La Flemme*[395] examined whether a parental waiver protected a horseback riding facility from negligence claims brought by an injured minor. The court held that the parent's waiver bound the child.[396] The court emphasized that "courts must presume that 'fit parents act in the best interests of children.'"[397] The court relied on *Troxel*'s enforcement of the parent's right to make decisions for the child as the exclusive reason to uphold the waiver, noting such enforcement was not against public policy.[398] *Saccente*, however, is an anomaly, given that a majority of courts will look beyond constitutional analysis to assess state contractual provisions.[399]

Parents' right to make decisions for their children is not absolute.[400] Courts refusing to enforce a waiver of liability signed by a parent note that while a parent may have a liberty interest in decision-making regarding the child, the decisions of a parent may place the child at risk of having insufficient care by leaving "the minor in an unacceptably precarious position with no recourse, no parental support, and no method to support himself or care for his injury."[401]

> While a parent's decision to allow a minor child to participate in a particular activity is part of the parent's fundamental right to raise a child, this does not equate with a conclusion that a parent has a fundamental right to execute a pre-injury release of a tortfeasor on behalf of a minor child.[402]

Courts limit parental rights to make decisions for their children citing various public policy concerns. First, courts limiting this parental right fear that accepting parental waivers will create risks of landowner malfeasance. Specifically, courts note a fear that recognizing a waiver will disincentivize a facility to take reasonable precautions.[403] Second, courts differentiate a parent's right to make decisions for their

---

394. *Id.*

395. 2003 WL 21716586 (Conn. Sup. Ct. 2003).

396. *Id.*

397. *Id.* at *6.

398. The "important family decision" made by the injured child's father to have the child participate in a "voluntary, nonessential activity" should be protected by courts' respect for the "fundamental liberty interests of parents in the rearing of children." *Id.; see also Sharon*, 437 Mass. at 109 ("in the circumstance of a voluntary nonessential activity we will not disturb this parental judgement. This comports with the fundamental liberty interest of parents in the rearing of their children.").

399. Blackwell v. Sky High Sports Nashville Operations, LLC, 523 S.W.3d 624, 647 (Tenn. App. 2010).

400. *Id.* at 648; *see also* Kirton v. Fields, 997 So. 2d 349, 353 (Fla. 2008) ("Parental rights are not absolute and the state as *parens patriae* may, in certain situations, usurp parental control."); Woodman *ex rel.* Woodman v. Kera LLC, 785 N.W. 2d 1 (Mich. 2010) (noting in dicta that parental authority related to the care and control of the child, but that this liberty interest does not extend to provide a parent the right to waive a child's rights).

401. Cooper v. Aspen Skiing Co., 48 P.3d 1229, 1235–36 (Colo. 2002).

402. *Kirton*, 997 So. 2d at 357.

403. Hojonowski *ex rel.* Hojonowski v. Vans Skate Park, 187 N.J. 323, 336 (2006).

child and a right to place their child at risk.[404] In making this assessment, a court analyzes whether the parent was acting in the best interests of the child when signing the participation waiver. While it is often presumed that a parent would act in the best interest of their child, courts have noted "that a parent who has decided to voluntarily risk a minor child's physical well-being [cannot be presumed to be] acting in the child's best interest."[405] The court in *Kirton v. Fields*[406] stressed that a parent's willingness to waive the child's right to recovery, the child's right to financial support in medical care, and the child's right to safety and protection cannot be in the child's best interest. Courts invalidating parental rights to waive the child's rights do so in protection of the child, placing the right of the minor ahead of the right of the parent.

[2] Statutory Provisions

State statutes also impact the enforcement of pre-injury liability waivers. Courts will look to whether a statute prohibits the parent from contracting away a child's rights or may uphold a parental waiver. Often the enforceability of the waiver turns on whether the waiver or the activity falls within the scope of the relevant statute. For example, the court in *Platzer v. Mammoth Ski Area*[407] relied, in part, on a state statutory code in enforcing a parental waiver. The statute at issue prohibited common carriers from contracting away their liability for ordinary negligence. Noting that a ski chairlift is not a common carrier but more aptly characterized as part of a recreational pursuit, the court enforced the waiver, which absolved the chairlift operator of negligence.[408]

In *Rutherford v. Talisker Canyons Finance Co.*,[409] the court reinforced its earlier holding in *Hawkins ex rel. Hawkins v. Peart*[410] that a parental release is unenforceable.[411] The *Rutherford* court analyzed whether Utah's Risks of Skiing Act barred claims by parents. Application of the Act hinged on the cause of the injury, which the court held must be caused by an "inherent risk of skiing."[412] The court then analyzed whether skiing into a patch of wet, hard, manmade snow after receiving a warning that snowmaking was in progress qualified as an injury arising from an "integral part of the sport of skiing."[413] Finding that the state statute was silent on negligence liability, the Supreme Court of Utah remanded the case for the lower court to determine if negligence occurred.[414]

---

404. *Kirton*, 997 So. 2d at 357.
405. *Id.*
406. 997 So. 2d 349 (Fla. 2008).
407. 128 Cal. Rptr. 2d 885 (Cal. Ct. App. 2002)
408. *Id.*
409. 445 P.3d 474 (Utah 2019).
410. 37 P.3d 1062 (Utah 2001).
411. *Rutherford*, 445 P.3d at 479 (citing Hawkins *ex rel.* Hawkins v. Peart, 37 P.3d 1062 (2001)).
412. *Id.* at 488.
413. *Id.* at 486.
414. *Id.*

The interplay between a recreational use statute and a liability waiver was at issue in *Johnson v. Rapid City*,[415] which involved injuries suffered during a softball game.[416] The state's recreational use statutes limit landowner liability in order to encourage certain recreational entry onto land.[417] The court noted that because recreational use statutes pertain primarily to hunting, farming, and recreational swimming, immunity for injuries incurred on a softball field did not apply to defendants.[418] The limited nature of the recreational use statute prevented extension of the statute's limited liability to the city's operation of softball fields. As such, the city was not immune under recreational use statutes. Further, because the signed waiver in this case was characterized as a "roster" rather than as a waiver and was not presented to the athletes as a waiver, the athletes could not be held to the release of liability contained in the signed waiver.[419]

[3] Public Policy

Although parents "undoubtedly have a fundamental liberty interest" in rearing their children, "the question whether a parent may release a minor's future tort claims implicates wider public policy concerns and the *parens patriae* duty to protect the best interests of children."[420] With respect to the latter, courts place a public policy boundary on the rights of parents, specifically when the parental decision-making may place a child at risk. In these instances, when a waiver for a minor is involved, courts "stand as guardians of the state's children."[421]

While courts undoubtedly respect the parental liberty provided under the Constitution — and generally employ state statutes in contractual decision-making — courts have held that "an agreement made in the context of sports or recreational programs or services, purporting to release liability for future gross negligence, gen-

---

415. Johnson v. Rapid City Softball Ass'n, 514 N.W.2d 693, 695 (S.D. 1994).

416. *Id.* at 696.

417. *Id.* at 695.

418. *Id.* at 696.

419. *Id.* at 697–98. *See also* Pollock v. Highlands Ranch, 140 P.3d 351, 354–55 (Colo. Ct. App. 2006) (reversing the trial court's retroactive application of a recreational use statute — designed to encourage landowners to allow public recreation, limit a duty of reasonable care, and encourage hunting or other recreation on land — that shielded the defendant from liability, and holding that the waiver was unenforceable because the waiver was signed before the statute became effective).

420. *Hojonowski*, 187 N.J. at 339. The New Jersey Superior Court hearing of *Hojonowski* differentiated public policy from fundamental liberty rights stating:
   we do not read the precedent defining that right ... as encompassing a decision such as this to forego substantial tort remedies, a decision that we find to be different from such fundamental concerns as establishment of a home, upbringing and education, religion, or medical care.
375 N.J. Super. at 584. The *Hojonowski* court agreed with the majority view that a parent cannot waive a child's tort claims. *Id.* Many of these policy grounds are "gleaned from state statutes which provide significant procedural protections for minors in the post-injury context." Saccente v. La Flemme, 2003 WL 21716586, at *5 (Conn. Sup. Ct. July 11, 2003); *Rutherford*, 445 P.3d 474 (stating a parent cannot release a minor's prospective claim for negligence).

421. *Hojonowski*, 187 N.J. at 330.

erally is unenforceable as a matter of public policy."[422] This extends to mere negligence as well, where "stipulations purporting to relieve from liability for negligence are generally held to be invalid."[423] Many courts refusing to accept a waiver of liability signed on behalf of a minor note that a parent cannot release a child's cause of action after the injury has occurred without judicial approval.[424] In accordance with this principle, some courts reason that it is illogical to allow a parent to waive a cause of action pre-injury.[425] As a result, courts hold that a release of liability executed by a parent pre-injury on behalf of the child violates public policy due to the incongruous nature created if the policy were different for pre- and post-injury waivers.[426]

The court in *Galloway v. State*[427] found that public policy restrictions on a parent's ability to enter property and financial contracts for their child are the same public policy restrictions which prevent enforcement of waivers. While parents have a fundamental liberty interest in the care, custody, and control of their children, the child has a right to be protected from the "improvident decisions of their parents."[428] As the court in *Kirton* noted, "it cannot be presumed that a parent who has decided to

---

422. City of Santa Barbara v. Superior Court, 41 Cal. 4th 747, 751 (Cal. 2007).

423. Divia v. South Hunterdon Reg'l High Sch., 2005 WL 977028 (Sup. Ct. N.J. Apr. 5, 2005); *see also Hojonowski*, 375 N.J. Super at 590 (stating that a parent has no right to release a minor's claim).

424. JT *ex rel.* Thode v. Monster Mountain, LLC, 754 F. Supp. 2d 1323 (M.D. Ala. 2010); Kelly v. U.S., 809 F. Supp 2d 429, 434 (E.D.N.C. 2011) ("it is beyond dispute that [minor's] own waiver is unenforceable"); Cooper v. Aspen Skiing Co., 48 P.3d 1229, 1234 (Colo. 2002). This action generally requires prior court approval. *See, e.g.*, Scott *ex rel* Scott v. Pacific West Mountain Resort, 119 Wash. 2d 484 (Wash. 1992).

425. Divia v. South Hunterdon Regional High School, 2005 WL 977028 (Sup. Ct. N.J. Apr. 5, 2005).

426. *Cooper*, 48 P.3d 1229 (holding that a mother's release of liability did not release the claims of her minor child, and that the minor could still bring claims against the ski slope where he incurred injuries); *Scott*, 119 Wash. 2d. at 503–04 (holding that the trial court's grant of summary judgment for defendant ski resort was improper because the child's claims for negligence by the ski lift operator prevailed despite waiver); Woodman *ex rel.* Woodman v. Kera LLC, 486 Mich. 228 (Mich. 2010) (finding a waiver signed by a parent unenforceable against a child). The court in *Saccente* differentiated external pressures of socioeconomic status. 2003 WL 21718586 at *5. Referencing *Fedor v. Mauwehu Council*, 143 A.2d 466 (Conn. Super. Ct. 1958), the court stated that a low-income family desiring opportunity for their child to engage in extracurriculars like Boy Scouts has no choice but to sign a waiver, whereas the parents in *Saccente* did not face the same pressure and had the clear choice to refuse to sign a waiver. *Saccente*, 2003 WL 21716586 at *4; *see also* Harrigan v. New England Dragway, Inc., 2014 WL 12589625, *7 (D. Mass. Jan. 2, 2014).

427. 790 N.W.2d 252 (Iowa 2010).

428. *Id.* at 257. Some courts have noted in dicta that the opposite may be a better approach. In *Divia v. South Henderton Regional High School*, a wrestler signed a waiver that was not as comprehensive as the same waiver he signed to play football a season earlier. The parents contended that the waiver was inadequate and should not bind their child, who was in high school but over the age of majority. The court held that summary judgement was not appropriate in reference to the permission slip and stated in dicta that consideration of the school or community stature may not be as important in New Jersey:

> An exculpatory agreement should not remove all liability from an entity when that entity is
> negligent in its care. This is especially important in the present case where the public entity
> is responsible for the caring and education of our most precious resource, our children.

2005 WL 977028 (Sup. Ct. N.J. Apr. 5, 2005).

voluntarily risk a minor child's physical well-being is acting in the child's best interest."[429] First, a waiver of liability places a benefit in the hands of the tortfeasor.[430] Second, a waiver of liability places a burden on the public to shoulder the cost of care for the child which the parent is unable to carry.[431] Therefore, the protection of minor children is often found to outweigh the parent's constitutional right to the care, custody, and control of the child.[432]

The child's vulnerability and need for protection from an enforceable waiver extends beyond the potential inability of parents to support a child through injury. Courts also have recognized that children may have a different understanding of risk and are therefore less capable of avoiding risks. The *Galloway* court reinforced its refusal to uphold a waiver signed by the parent, noting that a parent signing the waiver understands the risk the child is incurring but the child — the body actually at risk of injury — may be unaware.[433] The court also observed that the parent has "no ability to protect her child once the activity begins," and a child's ability to avoid the risk may vary with respect to: "the age and maturity of the child, the type of activity, ... the personality and competence of the people supervising the activity, and other factors."[434] This reasoning is bolstered by the public policy concern that absolving a program from liability will leave the program less likely to take reasonable protective measures.[435] As it relates to public policy, some courts invoke the six-factor test outlined in *Tunkl v. Regents of the University of California*[436] to determine whether public policy renders a parental pre-injury liability waiver enforceable or unenforceable:

(1) does the release concern an activity generally thought suitable for public regulation; (2) is the party seeking exculpation engaged in performing a serv-

---

429. 997 So. 2d at 357.

430. *Id.* ("[W]hen a parent executes such a release and a child is injured the provider of the activity escapes liability when the parent is left to deal with the financial burden of an injured child.").

431. *Galloway*, 790 N.W.2d at 257; *Kirton*, 997 So. 2d at 358 ("if the parent cannot afford to bear that burden, the parties who suffer are the child, the other family members, and the people of the state who will be called on the bear that financial burden.").

432. *Galloway*, 790 N.W.2d at 257 ("the strong public policy favoring the protection of vulnerable minor children" outweighs the general policy of enforcing a contract or waiver release); *Kirton*, 997 So. 2d at 357 (when a parent signs a liability waiver, the parent "is not protecting the welfare of the child but is instead protecting the interests of the activity provider.").

433. *Galloway*, 790 N.W.2d at 258; *Hojonowski*, 375 N.J. Super. at 590 ("a minor should be afforded protection not only from his own improvident decision to release his possible prospective claims for injury based on another's negligence, but also from unwise decisions made on his behalf by parents who are routinely asked to release their child's claims for liability.").

434. *Galloway*, 790 N.W.2d at 258.

435. City of Santa Barbara v. Superior Court, 41 Cal. 4th 747, 751 (Cal. 2007) (noting a "'public policy to discourage' or at least not facilitate 'aggravated wrongs'" as the basis for refusing to enforce a contract that "removes the obligation to adhere to a minimum standard of care"). *See Kirton*, 997 So. 2d at 358 (relying on the theory of *parens patriae*, the court stated that "the state must assert its role under *parens partiae* to protect the interests of the minor children"); Rosen v. BJ's Wholesale Club, Inc., 206 Md. App. 708, 727 (Md. Ct. Sp. App. 2009) ("the child's welfare is a consideration that is of transcendent importance when the child might ... be in jeopardy").

436. 60 Cal. 2d 92 (Cal. 1963).

ice of great importance to the public; (3) is the service open to any member of the public; (4) is the nature of the service essential; (5) does the party seeking exculpation have superior bargaining power, raising the issue of whether or not the release constitutes an adhesion contract; and (6) does the release place one party under the control of the other.[437]

In California, while *Tunkl* is used to invalidate certain types of waivers, the courts generally refuse to invalidate waivers occurring "in the recreational sports context."[438] Courts use this model to analyze each factor and, if applicable, enforce the waiver if the *Tunkl* factors favor enforcement.[439]

For example, the Supreme Court of Washington invoked *Tunkl* when assessing mandatory waivers for minors' participation in school-sponsored extracurricular activities. In *Wagenblast v. Odessa School District No. 105-107-166J*,[440] the court noted that the more *Tunkl* factors present in a case, the more likely the court will be to declare the agreement invalid on public policy grounds.[441] Beginning with the first factor — regulation — the *Wagenblast* court noted that because the interscholastic sports organizations in question are charged with oversight of high school sport rules and operations, high school sports are clearly a regulated activity.[442] High school sports additionally meet the second *Tunkl* factor of public importance due to the emphasis on sports in school systems, which engenders students to equate sports with schooling.[443] Further, the court noted that because high school sports are available to all students capable of competing and serve as a "monopoly" on the available free recreational activities for high school aged community members, high school sports meet the third and fourth *Tunkl* factors.[444] The noted "monopoly" held by school sponsored activities additionally meets the fifth factor, where the signed waiver serves as an adhesion contract and the student cannot participate without waiving liability.[445] Finally, the control that the school has over athletes and the sole control of the school over the activity, fulfils the final *Tunkl* requirement for exclusive care and control.[446] There-

---

437. *See, e.g., Fischer,* 2002 WL 31126288. In *Fischer,* the court went through each *Tunkl* factor and determined that the injured minor could have stopped playing hockey, participation on the team was not available to anyone in the community, and hockey teams do not provide a public service. These factors, and others, led the court to determine that the signed waiver was enforceable because the public policy goals of the *Tunkl* factors were not met. Even though the organization was a for-profit venture, it received the treatment provided a non-profit (under the majority approach). *Id.*; *see also* Platzer v. Mammoth Mountain Ski Area, 104 Cal. App. 4th 1253 (Cal. App. 2003); Rutherford v. Talisker Canyons Finance Co., LLC., 445 P.3d 474 (Utah 2019) (noting that the *Tunkl* factors are an important assessment).
438. *Platzer,* 104 Cal. App. 4th at 1259.
439. *See, e.g.,* Wagenblast v. Odessa School District No. 105-107-166J, 110 Wash. 2d 845 (1988).
440. 110 Wash. 2d 845 (1988).
441. *Id.* at 853.
442. *Id.*
443. *Id.* at 854.
444. *Id.* at 854–55.
445. *Id.* at 855.
446. *Id.*

fore, under the *Wagenblast* framework, all six *Tunkl* factors are met; a finding which supports holding the waivers invalid on public policy grounds.[447]

[a] The Status of the Defendant

The status of the defendant also influences whether courts will invalidate pre-injury releases signed by parents. When the defendant is a commercial entity, some jurisdictions hold waivers unenforceable as a matter of public policy.[448] These courts reason that "a minor's parent has no right to compromise or settle a minor's claim without court approval."[449] In *Miller ex rel E.M. v. House of Boom*,[450] in which a court held that a waiver of liability signed by a parent did not preclude a minor child from raising claims against a trampoline park, the court stated:

> A commercial entity has the ability to purchase insurance and spread the cost between its customers. It also has the ability to train its employees and inspect the business for unsafe conditions. A child has no similar ability to protect himself from the negligence of others within the confines of a commercial establishment.[451]

Conversely, some courts enforce liability waivers where the defendant is a non-profit, such that the waiver is "executed by parents on behalf of minor children ... [which] involve a minor's participation in school-run or community-sponsored activities."[452] Courts extend protection to these entities because of the public interest in the continued operation of community and school-based programs.[453] Courts fear that

---

447. *Id.*

448. Miller *ex rel.* E.M. v. House of Boom Kentucky, LLC, 575 S.W.3d 656 (Ky. 2019) ("[E]leven out of twelve jurisdictions that have analyzed similar waivers between parents and for-profit entities have adhered to the common law and held such waivers unenforceable"). The common law adhered to in this instance is the ability to sign over a child's property right, and the common law understanding that a parent may not take such action. *Id.*; *see also* Kirton v. Fields, 997 So. 2d 349, 358 (Fla. 2008) ("If pre-injury releases were permitted for commercial establishments, the incentive to take reasonable precautions to protect the safety of minor children would be removed."); Rosen v. BJ's Wholesale Club, Inc., 206 Md. App. 708, 713 (Md. Ct. Sp. App. 2009) ("a parent may not waive by agreement a minor child's claims in negligence against ... a 'commercial enterprise.'").

449. *Miller ex rel. E.M.*, 575 S.W.3d at 661 ("[W]e do not recognize a parent's fundamental liberty interest to quash their child's potential tort claim.").

450. *Id.*

451. *Id.* at 662–63; *see also Rosen*, 206 Md. App. at 728 (stating that an owner of a commercial facility will be more likely to take reasonable safety precautions and have adequate insurance if the waiver is not enforced against the child).

452. Paz v. Lifetime Fitness, Inc., 757 F. Supp. 2d 658, 663 (S.D. Tex. 2010) (finding that a waiver was not enforceable against the minor because the fitness club could not be found to be a community or school program).

453. Plazer v. Mammoth Mountain Ski Area, 104 Cal. App. 4th 1253 (Cal. App. 2003). Therefore, the enforceability of waivers and lack of enforceability are each supported primarily on parallel public policy grounds. JT *ex rel.* Thode v. Monster Mountain, LLC, 754 F. Supp. 2d 1323, 1327 (M.D. Ala. 2010); *Kelly*, 809 F. Supp 2d at 436 (granting an exception "where the liability waiver is in the context of schools, volunteers, or community organizations."); Harrigan v. New England Dragway, Inc., 2014 WL 12589625, *7 (D. Mass. Jan. 2, 2014) (noting the difference between a for-profit venture and a

failing to enforce the waiver may risk losing future offerings of the activity.[454] Activities in which waivers have been enforced include high school athletics,[455] out of school class credit courses,[456] school field trips,[457] and community-based recreation leagues.[458] In *Kelly v. United States*,[459] after lengthy analysis of precedent protecting non-commercial ventures, the court held that a liability waiver to participate in a "school sponsored enrichment program that was extracurricular and voluntary" was enforceable.[460]

In *Zivich v. Mentor Soccer Club*,[461] the Ohio Supreme Court held that parents have the authority to bind their children to this type of waiver contract:

> Parents have the authority to bind their minor children to exculpatory agreements in favor of volunteers and sponsors of nonprofit sports activities where the cause of action sounds in negligence. These agreements may not be disaffirmed by the child on whose behalf they were executed.[462]

The court made this decision pursuant to the constitutional rights afforded parents under the United States Constitution's Due Process Clause.[463] The court added that "invalidation of exculpatory agreements would reduce the number of activities made possible through the uncompensated services of volunteers and their sponsoring organizations."[464]

---

non-profit or government sponsor and holding that a waiver signed by a parent was not enforceable against a for profit entity). In some cases, the public interest is strong enough for this protection to be embodied by state statute. *See* Sharon v. City of Newton, 437 Mass. 99, 109 (Mass. 2002) (citing statutes protecting nonprofits, and managers and coaches of sports programs for minors, from negligence claims).

454. *See Sharon*, 437 Mass. at 110–11 ("the enforcement of the release is consistent with the [state's] policy of encouraging athletic programs for youth"). *See also* Zivich v. Mentor Soccer Club, Inc., 82 Ohio St. 3d. 367, 372 (Ohio 1998) ("faced with the very real threat of a lawsuit, and the potential for substantial damages awards, nonprofit organizations and their volunteers could very well decide that the risks are not worth the effort") (holding that invalidating or failing to enforce waivers signed by parents on behalf of minors may restrict opportunity).

455. *Sharon*, 437 Mass. at 99; *Wagenblast*, 758 P.2d at 973 ("interscholastic sports in public schools are a matter of public importance in this jurisdiction").

456. Gonzalez v. City of Coral Gables, 871 So. 2d 1067, 1067 (Fla. 2004) (Mem).

457. *Galloway*, 790 N.W.2d at 257 ("the strong public policy favoring the protection of children's legal rights must prevail over speculative fears about their continuing access to activities").

458. *Zivich*, 82 Ohio St. 3d. at 367.

459. 809 F. Supp. 2d 429.

460. *Id.* at 437.

461. 82 Ohio St. 3d 367.

462. *Id.* at 375.

463. While outside the scope of this chapter, a corollary note should be made. Case law implies that the constitutional right to the care custody and control of one's child is supported by public policy to protect community and school groups. Conversely, when a commercial entity is involved, the parental right to the care, custody, and control of the child is trumped by the state's public policy interests. This debate becomes, essentially, a battle of public policies: does the public policy to protect the child outweigh the public policy to protect communities, schools, and nonprofits? Or vice versa.

464. *Zivich*, 82 Ohio St. 3d at 372.

Because of precedent in Ohio under *Zivich*, other cases in the state have disaffirmed waivers, not on validity grounds but with respect to the level of intent inherent in the injury. In *Mohney v. USA Hockey*,[465] the court held that the level of wanton or willful misconduct is not present when a severe sports injury occurs.[466] The court stated that regardless of the rarity or severity of the injury (in this case a spinal injury suffered while playing hockey), no reasonable jury could find that failure to specifically warn a minor player of risk of spinal injury was willful when the sport is by nature violent and carries risk of such injury as part of the normal course of the game.[467]

Thus, courts that have held valid a waiver signed by a parent on behalf of their minor child have done so "primarily on the basis that the defendant is a government or non-profit sponsor of the activity."[468] Some courts have also extended this to schools and community-sponsored activities.[469] As it relates to non-commercial entities, courts fear that invalidating pre-injury parental waivers risks loss of the future offerings that these entities make available to children.[470]

[b] Binding Effect on Parents?

Even if a waiver of liability signed by a parent on behalf of their participating minor child may not bind the child, it will likely bind the parent.[471] Some courts have ruled that while a pre-injury parental waiver does not bar the minor from asserting tort claims, it bars the parents' tort claims,[472] while others have found that the waiver does not bar a minor's estate from bringing a cause of action if the plaintiff establishes

---

465. 5 F. App'x 450 (6th Cir. 2001).

466. *Id.*

467. *Id.*

468. *Harrigan*, 2014 WL 12589625, at *7. The court in *Mohney* relied on the public policy support for community organizations as a public policy outweighing the child's claims. The court found that when parents agree to undertake a risk, that decision equally binds the child. 5 F. App'x 450.

469. JT *ex rel.* Thode v. Monster Mountain, LLC, 754 F. Supp. 2d 1323, 1327 (M.D. Ala. 2010); Kelly v. U.S., 809 F. Supp 2d 429, 436 (E.D. N.C. 2011) (granting an exception "where the liability waiver is in the context of schools, volunteers, or community organizations.").

470. "[I]f courts did not enforce this type of exculpatory contract, organizations such as USA Hockey, Inc., little league and youth soccer, and the individuals who volunteer their time as coaches could well decide that the risks of large legal fees and potential judgments are too significant to justify their existence or participation. Thousands of children would then be deprived of the valuable opportunity to play organized sports." Fischer v. Rivest, 2002 WL 31126288, *14 (Conn. Aug 15. 2002); *see also Zivich*, 82 Ohio St. 3d at 372 ("faced with the very real threat of a lawsuit, and the potential for substantial damages awards, nonprofit organizations and their volunteers could very well decide that the risks are not worth the effort") (holding that invalidating or failing to enforce waivers signed by parents on behalf of minors may restrict opportunity).

471. Wethington v. Swainson, 155 F. Supp. 3d 1173, 1179 (W.D. Okla. 2015) (stating that even though a waiver cannot bind the child, if signed by the parent, it may be "conspicuous and clear" enough to prevent the parents from bringing claims).

472. *Wethington*, 155 F. Supp. 3d at 1178; Scott *ex rel.* Scott v. Pacific West Mountain Resort, 119 Wash. 2d 484, 495 (Wash. 1992) ("an otherwise conspicuous and clear exculpatory clause can serve to bar the parent's cause of action based upon injury to the child").

where the injury or death occurred is a commercial entity.[473] In *Eriksson v. Nunnik*,[474] the court noted that a mother's wrongful death and emotional distress claims could survive because the parental waiver on behalf of the participating child only referred to the participant (the child) and there was no mention of the participant's parent (the signatory).[475] The court was unable, however, to rule in favor of the mother because the court reasoned the defendant cannot owe a greater responsibility to the heirs or a third party (such as a parent) than to the decedent or injured participant. A court may find, as it did in *Eriksson*, that a third party cannot have rights exceeding those of the participant, making the waiver of liability a valid defense to both wrongful death and emotional distress claims.[476] Once a participant expressly assumes a risk, that same risk is assumed by the bystanders who observe the risk assumed by the participant.[477]

[c] When the Injury Occurs

Finally, the injury litigated in the athletic context must occur during the course of play. In *Dugan v. Thayer Academy*,[478] a field hockey player was concussed in a game, and then sustained a second concussion in a subsequent game a few days later. The failure of the school to have her injury evaluated was not negligence covered by the participation waiver because the omitted act (failure to evaluate) occurred between contests and therefore between participation opportunities.[479]

[C] Pre-Injury Waivers by Adult Participants

[1] Introduction

As it relates to the enforceability of liability waivers signed by adults, most cases involve waivers that seek to release sports organizers or business owners from future liability resulting from adults participating in recreational activities.[480] Al-

---

473. Kirton v. Fields, 997 So. 2d 349, 358 (Fla. 2008).

474. 233 Cal. App. 4th 708 (Cal. Ct. App. 2015).

475. *Id.* at 721.

476. *Id.* at 726. The court in *Eriksson* feared the option of invoking secondary liability by a third party after the death or injury of a participant risked thwarting instructor involvement in these activities: "to encourage individuals to teach sports, some of which pose a high risk of injury, it is necessary to allow for enforceable releases of liability; otherwise, persons in the Coach's position might not provide the necessary instruction for safe participation in the sport. To then allow the instructor, who has secured an enforceable release from the participant, to be secondarily liable to a nonparticipant for the conduct covered by the release would, in essence, negate the effectiveness of the release and discourage the teaching of the sport. This adversely affects the community as a whole." *Id.*

477. *Id.* (stating that where a participant in a sport has expressly assumed the risk of injury from a defendant's conduct, the defendant no longer owes a duty of care to bystanders with respect to the risk expressly assumed by the participant).

478. 32 Mass. L. Rptr. 657 (Mass. Sup. Ct. May 27, 2015).

479. *Id.* at 11.

480. Matthew S. Thor, *This Is Not Sparta: The Extensive and Unknown Inherent Risks in Obstacle Racing*, 51 VAL. U. L. REV. 251, 262 (2016); Mario R. Arango & William R. Trueba, Jr., *The Sports*

though many courts are reluctant to enforce pre-injury liability waivers involving children, courts generally uphold liability waivers signed by adults on their own behalf.[481]

[2] Waivers Are Strictly Construed

Courts tend to strictly construe pre-injury waivers/releases of liability.[482] To determine the enforceability of liability waivers, courts evaluate whether the provision clearly expresses the intent of the parties and whether the waiver violates public policy.[483] *Jones v. Dressel*[484] illustrates the factors courts often consider: "(1) the existence of a duty to the public; (2) the nature of the service performed; (3) whether the contract was fairly entered into; and (4) whether the intention of the parties is expressed in clear and unambiguous language."[485] A duty to the public often exists when the nature of the business affects the public interest and the services performed are considered essential.[486]

In *Schutkowski v. Carey*,[487] the Supreme Court of Wyoming applied the *Jones* factors in upholding a waiver signed by an adult who suffered injuries while skydiving. However, not all courts use a blanket application of *Jones*. In *Dalury v. S-K-I, Ltd.*,[488] the Vermont Supreme Court acknowledged the *Jones* factors as a potential test but also considered the overall circumstances of the case and societal expectations.[489] Ultimately, the court held that the liability waiver was unenforceable because it was against public policy, finding that the ski resort owed a public duty to its patrons to avoid increasing the risks beyond those reasonably undertaken in the act of skiing.[490]

Chamber: Exculpatory Agreements Under Pressure, 14 U. MIAMI ENT. & SPORTS L. REV. 1, 8 (1997); Brook V. Robertson, *Contract Law — The Use of Waivers, Releases, and Exculpatory Clauses in Extreme Sports* — Tough Mudder, LLC v. Sengupta, 2014 WL 4954657, at *1 (N.D. W.Va. Oct. 2, 2014), 38 AM. J. TRIAL ADVOC. 437, 437 (2014).

481. Bagley v. Mt. Bachelor, Inc., 340 P.3d 27, 33 (Or. 2014); Courbat v. Dahana Ranch, Inc., 111 Hawai'i 254, 265 (2006); *but see* Hanks v. Powder Ridge Rest. Corp., 276 Conn. 314, 326 (2007) (stating that the language in the waiver was clear to a reasonable person but further stating that enforcement of the waiver was unreasonable as against public policy, using the *Tunkl* factors discussed *supra*).

482. B & B Livery, Inc. v. Riehl, 960 P.2d 134, 139 (Colo. 1998); Feleccia v. Lackawanna College, 215 A.3d 3, 17 (Pa. 2019); Heil Valley Ranch, Inc. v. Simkin, 784 P.2d 781, 785 (Colo. 1989); Roberts v. T.H.E. Ins. Co., 367 Wis. 2d 386, 406 (Wis. 2016); Tayar v. Camelback Ski Corp., Inc., 616 Pa. 385, 391 (2012); Turnbough v. Ladner, 754 So. 2d 467, 470 (Miss. 1999).

483. Robertson, *supra* note 480, at 438; Thor, *supra* note 480.

484. 623 P.2d 370 (Colo. 1981).

485. *Id.* at 376; *see also* Brigance v. Vail Summit Resorts, Inc., 883 F.3d 1243, 1250 (10th Cir. 2018); Dalury v. S-K-I, Ltd., 164 Vt. 329, 333 (1995); *Heil Valley Ranch*, 784 P.2d at 784; Milligan v. Big Valley Corp., 754 P.2d 1063, 1066 (Wyo. 1988); Schutowksi v. Carey, 725 P.2d 1057, 1060 (Wyo. 1986).

486. *Milligan*, 754 P.2d at 1066.

487. 725 P.2d 1057 (Wyo. 1986).

488. 164 Vt. 329 (1995).

489. *Id.* at 333–34.

490. *Id.* at 336 (stating that assuming the inherent risk of skiing still requires the ski area to "warn or correct dangers which in the exercise of reasonable [care] ... could have been foreseen and corrected.").

[3] The Required Language

Courts require the intent of the parties be clearly expressed[491] in specific and un-ambiguous terms in order to absolve a party of negligence liability.[492] Thus, courts often require the waiver to explicitly describe and explain the dangers attendant to the particular activity in which a person will engage.[493] This may require clearly describing the risk not in legal terms, but in language a layperson may understand.[494] For example, in *Berlangieri v. Running Elk Corp.*,[495] the New Mexico Supreme Court stressed that a waiver should contain specific language clearly informing the patron of the type(s) of risk(s) being assumed.[496]

Some courts attempt to determine the participant's understanding of the waiver[497] in light of the circumstances that existed when the waiver was signed.[498] Courts assess whether a reasonable person in the participant's position would have known and understood the release of liability.[499] In signing a liability waiver, a reasonable person would understand the waiver if its language "clearly and specifically indicates the intent to release the defendant from liability for personal injury caused by the defendant's negligence."[500] Some courts require the wording of a liability waiver to express as clearly and precisely as possible the extent to which a party intends to be absolved from liability.[501]

A majority of courts, however, do not require a release to specifically state "negligence" or similar words in order to be enforceable.[502] In this regard, courts hold that a waiver need not mention every possible means of negligence that could be potentially committed by an owner or event organizer.[503] In *Douglass v. Skiing Standards, Inc.*,[504] the court upheld a skiing liability waiver even though it did not expressly include the word "negligence," because the waiver evinced the parties' intent

---

491. Tayar v. Camelback Ski Corp., Inc., 616 Pa. 385, 394 (2012); Topp Copy Prods. Inc. v. Singletary, 533 Pa. 468, 471 (1993); Hanks v. Powder Ridge Rest. Corp., 276 Conn. 314, 319 (2007); Hyson v. White Water Mountain Resorts of Conn., Inc., 265 Conn. 636, 643 (2003).

492. Turnbough v. Ladner, 754 So. 2d 467, 470 (Miss. 1999); *see also* Dobratz v. Thomson, 161 Wis. 2d 502, 520 (1991) (stating courts are reluctant to enforce waivers that are stated in broad terms); Roberts v. T.H.E. Ins. Co., 367 Wis. 2d 386, 406 (Wis. 2016) (stating the same).

493. *Roberts*, 367 Wis. 2d at 406; McGrath v. SNH Dev., Inc., 969 A.2d 392, 398 (N.H. 2009); Thor, *supra* note 480, at 263.

494. Berlangieri v. Running Elk Corp, 134 N.M. 341 (2003).

495. 134 N.M. 341 (2003).

496. *Id.* at 351.

497. *Roberts*, 367 Wis. 2d at 406.

498. Turnbough v. Ladner, 754 So. 2d 467, 469 (Miss. 1999).

499. Wright v. Loon Mountain Recreation Corp., 663 A.2d 1340, 1342 (N.H. 1995).

500. *Id.* (quoting Barnes v. New Hampshire Karting Ass'n, Inc., 509 A.2d 151, 154 (1986)).

501. McGrath v. SNH Dev., Inc., 969 A.2d 392, 397 (N.H. 2009).

502. Douglass v. Skiing Standards, Inc., 142 Vt. 634, 637 (1983); Heil Valley Ranch, Inc. v. Simkin, 784 P.2d 781, 781–82 (Colo. 1989); Schutkowski v. Carey, 725 P.2d 1057, 1061 (Wyo. 1986).

503. Arango & Trueba, *supra* note 480.

504. 142 Vt. 634 (1983).

that the ski resort be held harmless for any injuries or damages caused by its negligence.[505] The court stated that it would not be "always necessary to indulge in a
plethora of synonyms and redundancies in order to express the intent of the parties
clearly."[506]

There is some authority, however, that supports the proposition that a waiver
must contain specific language such as "negligence" in order for it to release a defendant from liability.[507] The *Hyson v. White Water Mountain Resorts*[508] court imposed
a requirement that a waiver contain express release language in order to prevent "individuals from inadvertently relinquishing valuable legal rights."[509]

[4] Public Policy

According to the Restatement (Second) of Torts, a liability waiver should be upheld on policy grounds if it is: "(1) freely and fairly made, (2) between parties who
are in an equal bargaining position, and (3) there is no social interest with which it
interferes."[510] Whether a liability waiver contravenes public policy is a matter of law
for the court based on the circumstances of the case.[511] Waivers have been deemed
to contravene public policy where the waiver is "injurious to the interests of the
public, violates some public statute, or tends to interfere with the public welfare or
safety."[512]

An exception to waiver enforceability lies in public policy. A liability waiver affecting the public interest, or giving rise to a public duty, is often one that concerns
a business that performs a "service of great importance to the public."[513] As a result
of the essential nature of the service, the provider has a bargaining advantage against
any member of the public who seeks its services.[514] Most courts find, however, that
voluntary participation in recreational sports or activities does not fall within this
category of public interest. Therefore, it is difficult to prove that a liability waiver for

---

505. *Id.* at 636.

506. *Id.; accord Heil Valley Ranch*, 784 P.2d at 785 (upholding waiver that did not contain word
"negligence").

507. Donahue v. Legends, Inc., 331 P.3d 342, 349 (Alaska 2014) (stating that a release of negligence
is only valid if the release contains the specific waiver of "negligence"); *see also* Hyson v. White Water
Mountain Resorts of Conn., Inc., 265 Conn. 636, 643 (2003) ("the party cannot be released from
liability for injuries resulting from its future negligence in the absence of language that expressly so
provides").

508. 265 Conn. 636, 643 (2003).

509. *Id.*

510. RESTATEMENT (SECOND) OF TORTS § 496B, comment b (1965); Dalury v. S-K-I, Ltd., 164 Vt.
329, 332 (1995).

511. Hanks v. Powder Ridge Rest. Corp., 276 Conn. 314, 327 (2005).

512. McGrath v. SNH Dev., Inc., 969 A.2d 392, 396 (N.H. 2009).

513. *Id.* at 1066; *see also Tunkl*, 383 P.2d at 445–46.

514. *Milligan*, 754 P.2d at 1066–67 (discussing disparity in bargaining power when the service is
essential yet refusing to recognize a public policy reason in the case at hand, finding the waiver valid
and enforceable).

recreational activities is invalid on public policy grounds.[515] In voluntary recreational activities, the signer is not required to participate — much less to sign the liability waiver — because it does not relate to essential services.[516] In *Milligan v. Big Valley Corp.*,[517] the Supreme Court of Wyoming found that voluntary participation in an "Ironman Decathlon" was not essential to any member of the public, but was simply a recreational activity.[518] Therefore, the court upheld the liability waiver as valid under public policy.[519] In *Hanks v. Powder Ridge Rest. Corp.*,[520] however, the court relied on a disparity of bargaining power as the basis for invalidating a liability waiver.[521] The court stated that there is a public policy interest in promoting participation in voluntary recreational activities, such as snowtubing.

[5] Unconscionability

Courts have also found liability waivers to be unenforceable if they are unconscionable. Courts assess unconscionability at the time of contract formation, and the unconscionability must be both procedural and substantive.[522] Procedural unconscionability refers to the conditions of contract formation and focuses on inequity in bargaining power and surprise, such as ambiguous wording.[523] Substantive unconscionability focuses on whether the terms of the liability waiver are against the public interest or public policy.[524] In determining unconscionability, courts will look at the "totality of the circumstances," such as the language of the waiver, the relationship between the parties, the result of enforcing the waiver against one party, and whether the waiver disclaims liability for more than negligence.[525] The party invoking unconscionability as a defense to enforcement of a contractual term must prove lack of meaningful choice and establish that the terms are unreasonably favorable to the other party.[526]

[6] Gross Negligence and Willful Conduct

The majority rule is that public policy dictates that a release only absolve a defendant of negligence liability. Thus, courts hold that it is against public policy to enforce a liability waiver that releases a party for gross negligence or intentional acts.[527] An otherwise valid release also becomes unenforceable where willful and wanton misconduct

---

515. *See, e.g.*, Chepkevich v. Hidden Valley Resort, L.P., 607 Pa. 1, 27 (2010).
516. *Id.* at 29.
517. 754 P.2d 1063 (Wyo. 1988).
518. *Id.* at 1066.
519. *Id.* at 1069.
520. 276 Conn. 314, 326 (2005).
521. *Id.* at 319.
522. Bagley v. Mt. Bachelor, Inc., 340 P.3d 27, 32 (Or. 2014).
523. *Id.* at 35.
524. *Id.* at 36.
525. *Id.* at 38.
526. Bradley v. Nat'l Collegiate Athletic Ass'n, 464 F. Supp. 3d 273, 294 (D. D.C. 2020).
527. Rachael Marvin, *Liability Not Waived for Lackawanna College: Athletic Programs May Not Disregard Minimal Standards of Care and Safety*, 26 JEFFREY S. MOORAD SPORTS L.J. 365, 366 (2019).

is shown.[528] For example, in *Tayar v. Camelback Ski Corp., Inc.*,[529] the Supreme Court of Pennsylvania held that it was against public policy for a pre-injury release to relieve the ski resort of liability for reckless conduct.[530] The court distinguished recklessness as requiring a "conscious action or inaction which creates a substantial risk of harm."[531]

[D] Pre-Injury Liability Waivers in College Athletics

Colleges and universities often require their athletes to sign liability waivers.[532] To evaluate the enforceability of liability waivers signed by collegiate athletes, courts closely follow the reasoning of cases involving recreational activities.[533] At the outset, courts initially determine whether the college or university owed a duty to the athlete. Recently, in *Feleccia v. Lackawanna College*,[534] the Supreme Court of Pennsylvania upheld a liability waiver for negligence by the college.[535] The court found that because the waiver stated it would protect the college from "any and all liability" arising out of "any injury" sustained by student-athletes while playing football, it clearly expressed the parties' intent to bar claims against the college sounding in ordinary negligence.[536] Like the majority of courts, the court also held, however, that a waiver would not protect the college from liability arising from gross negligence or recklessness.[537] The court followed the definition of recklessness as previously described in *Tayar* and recognized that a majority of states, on public policy grounds, do not validate waivers encompassing reckless conduct, even in cases involving voluntary recreational activities.[538]

[E] Pre-Injury Liability Waivers in Professional Sports

Outside of the context of professional race car driving, there is scant authority relating to the presence of liability waivers in the professional sports context.[539] The

---

528. *Milligan*, 754 P.2d at 1068.

529. 616 Pa. 385 (2012).

530. *Id.* at 403.

531. *Id.* at 402.

532. Andrew Manno, *A High Price to Compete: The Feasibility and Effect of Waivers Used to Protect Schools from Liability for Injuries to Athletes with High Medical Risks*, 79 KY. L.J. 867, 870–71 (1991).

533. Bradley v. Nat'l Collegiate Athletic Ass'n, 464 F. Supp. 3d 273 (D.D.C. 2020); Feleccia v. Lackawanna Coll., 215 A.3d 3 (Pa. 2019); Kyriazis v. Univ. of W. Va., 450 S.E.2d 649 (W. Va. 1994); Rachael Marvin, *supra* note 527, at 396; Reed v. Univ. of N.D., 589 N.W.2d 880 (N.D. 1999).

534. 215 A.3d 3 (Pa. 2019).

535. *Id.* at 18.

536. *Id.* at 17.

537. *Id.* at 22.

538. *See Tayar*, 616 Pa. at 385; *Feleccia*, 215 A.3d at 16.

539. Barnes v. Birmingham Int'l Raceway, Inc., 551 So. 2d 929 (Ala. 1989); Mayer v. Howard, 370 N.W.2d 93 (Neb. 1985); Platt v. Gateway Int'l Motorsports Corp., 813 N.E.2d 279 (Ill. 2004); Seaton v. E. Windsor Speedway, Inc., 582 A.2d 1380 (Pa. Super. Ct. 1990).

absence of case law is also likely a result of the comprehensive injury dispute resolution mechanisms set forth in collective bargaining agreements between the major sports leagues in the United States and their players.[540] In evaluating the enforceability of liability waivers signed by those engaged in motorsports, courts generally follow the approach adopted in cases involving recreational activities. *Huckaby v. Confederate Motor Speedway, Inc.*[541] is illustrative. There, the court barred a driver's negligence claim against the Confederate Motor Speedway because the driver had signed a liability waiver.[542] The court reasoned that participation in the race was voluntary and the waiver was enforceable because the language was clear and not against public policy.[543]

§ 10.08 Disability Issues in Sport

[A] Introduction

There exists no general right to participate in sport, but people with disabilities are protected against discriminatory exclusion. Two federal statutes provide that protection: the Rehabilitation Act of 1973 (the "Rehabilitation Act")[544] and the Americans with Disabilities Act of 1990 (the "ADA").[545] The Rehabilitation Act applies to entities receiving federal funds and the ADA applies to private entities. Together, the statutes provide protection against disability discrimination in most amateur and professional sports contexts, and the elements of a claim under the statutes are similar. Under each statute, the plaintiff is required to show that: (1) the plaintiff has or is regarded as having a "disability"; (2) is otherwise qualified to participate in the sport, with or without reasonable accommodations; and (3) was not permitted to participate because of the disability.[546]

Importantly, the statutes apply with respect to both physical and mental disabilities. What precisely constitutes a "disability" has sparked controversy. The ADA deems a person disabled if the person has, has a record of having, or is regarded as having "a physical or mental impairment that substantially limits one or more major life activities."[547] The range of activities accepted as "major life activities" is wide, ranging from walking to concentrating to performance of virtually every bodily function.[548]

---

540. See discussion in Chapter 8.

541. 281 S.E.2d 223 (S.C. 1981).

542. *Id.* at 224.

543. *Id.*

544. 29 U.S.C. §701 *et seq.*

545. 42 U.S.C. §12101 *et seq.*

546. *See* Sandison v. Michigan High Sch. Athletic Ass'n, Inc., 863 F. Supp. 483, 488 (E.D. Mich. 1994), *rev'd in part, appeal dismissed in part,* 64 F.3d 1026 (6th Cir. 1995).

547. 42 U.S.C. §12102(1)(A)–(C).

548. *See, e.g.,* Thomas *ex rel.* Thomas v. Davidson Acad., 846 F. Supp. 611, 617 (M.D. Tenn. 1994) (finding that a plaintiff's disability substantially limited her major life activity of caring for one's self); *see also* Sch. Bd. of Nassau Cty., Fla. v. Arline, 480 U.S. 273, 281 (1987) (finding plaintiff's disability

Title I of the ADA applies particularly to employers, which have an obligation under the statute to not discriminate on the basis of disability and to provide reasonable accommodation in the workplace.[549]

[B] Participation Rights

Lawsuits regarding participation rights for people with disabilities tend to fall into three categories: (1) those involving increased risk to the impaired participant; (2) those involving increased risk that the impaired participant poses to other participants; and (3) those in which accommodating an athlete's disability would arguably force modification of a fundamental aspect of the game. These three categories will be addressed in turn.

[1] Increased Risk to the Impaired Participant

Questions around participation rights are particularly challenging when the athlete at risk of injury is the same athlete who poses the risk. Because nearly every institution of higher education in the United States receives federal funding, the Rehabilitation Act applies widely in collegiate athletics. As such, the Act provides potential recourse for athletes whose institutions argue that allowing the athlete to participate in intercollegiate athletics poses an unacceptable risk to the impaired athlete. *Knapp v. Northwestern University*[550] provides a paradigmatic example of such a case and illustrates the impediments athletes have in succeeding. That case involved Charles Knapp, who in 1994 was considered one of the best high school basketball players in the state of Illinois.[551] At the start of his senior year, Knapp suffered "sudden cardiac death" that required "cardiopulmonary resuscitation, defibrillation (*i.e.*, electric shocks), and injections of drugs to bring Knapp back to life."[552] Upon recovery, Knapp had an internal cardioverter-defibrillator implanted to maintain the rhythm of his heart and then desired to resume his basketball career.[553] Just under two months later, he signed a National Letter of Intent to attend Northwestern University on a basketball scholarship.[554] Not long after he began his freshman year at Northwestern, the university's head team physician declared Knapp medically ineligible for the 1995–1996 season due to his heart condition.[555] After the season, Northwestern and the Big Ten Conference (in which Northwestern competes) declared Knapp permanently ineligible.[556] That same day, Knapp filed a federal lawsuit seeking an

---

to substantially interfere with her bodily function of breathing); Head v. Glacier Nw. Inc., 413 F.3d 1053, 1061 (9th Cir. 2005) (stating that "thinking is a major life activity").

549. 42 U.S.C. § 12112(a)–(b).

550. 101 F.3d 473 (7th Cir. 1996).

551. *Id.* at 476.

552. *Id.*

553. *Id.*

554. *Id.*

555. *Id.* at 476–77.

556. *Id.* at 477.

injunction to bar Northwestern from removing him from the team on grounds of his heart condition.[557]

Knapp brought his suit under the Rehabilitation Act, and the district court found in his favor.[558] The Seventh Circuit, however, reversed.[559] The court acknowledged the challenging paternalism concern raised by the university's decision to exclude Knapp from the team for his own good.[560] Still, the court concluded Knapp had not met the Rehabilitation Act's requirements; that is, he had not proven that he had a physical impairment which substantially limited one or more of his major life activities, was otherwise qualified to play basketball, and had been excluded from doing so solely because of his disability.[561] Knapp asserted that the substantially limited major life activity, in his case, was the activity of learning.[562] He argued that involvement in intercollegiate athletics was critical to his learning and that "his education [would] be substantially limited if he [could] not play on the team."[563] The court rejected Knapp's argument.[564] It acknowledged that "learning" is a major life activity, but rejected Knapp's attempt to particularize "learning" through playing basketball.[565] It found that "any narrowing of what constitutes learning for a particular individual occurs [only] within reasonable limits — coverage of the Rehabilitation Act is not open-ended or based on every dream or desire that a person may have."[566]

The court emphasized that it was not proclaiming Northwestern's decision correct.[567] Rather, it concluded that as long as a school's decision is "reasonably made, and based upon competent medical evidence ... it will be the rare case regarding participation in athletics where a court may substitute its judgment for that of the school's team physicians."[568] The Fourth Circuit drew a similar conclusion in *Class v. Towson University,*[569] deferring to a Towson University team physician who disqualified a football student-athlete, Gavin Class, from participation in football activities.[570] Class had previously suffered heat stroke at football practice, which triggered liver failure and ultimately necessitated a liver transplant.[571] After a long recovery, Class sought to return to the team, but the physician "concluded that allowing Class to participate in the football program presented an unacceptable risk of serious

---

557. *Id.*
558. *Id.*
559. *Id.* at 486.
560. *Id.* at 476.
561. *Id.* at 481–82.
562. *Id.* at 479.
563. *Id.*
564. *Id.* at 481.
565. *Id.*
566. *Id.*
567. *Id.* at 485.
568. *Id.*
569. 806 F.3d 236 (4th Cir. 2015).
570. *Id.* at 239.
571. *Id.*

reinjury or death."[572] Class sued under both the Rehabilitation Act and the ADA.[573] In finding for the university, the court explained that the standard for assessing the physician's judgment as to whether the plaintiff is "otherwise qualified" to participate is "not whether we share that judgment or whether she had a better judgment than some other doctor. Rather, the standard is whether her judgment was reasonable."[574] In that the physician's decision that Class was not "otherwise qualified" to participate "was supported by legitimate health and safety concerns [and] manifested by the medical records ... her decision was not unreasonable."[575]

[2] Increased Risk the Impaired Participant Poses to Other Participants

Courts must balance an impaired athlete's interest in participating in sport against other athletes' interest in avoiding an injury or health risk posed by the impaired athlete.[576] This balance was weighed in *Montalvo v. Radcliffe*,[577] a case in which a 12-year-old HIV-positive boy and his parents sued a karate school for refusing to admit him under Title III of the Americans with Disabilities Act.[578] Title III of the ADA, which prohibits discrimination on the basis of disability by places of public accommodation, reads in relevant part:

> No individual shall be discriminated against on the basis of disability in the full and equal enjoyment of the goods, services, facilities, privileges, advantages, or accommodations of any place of public accommodation by any person who owns, leases (or leases to), or operates a place of public accommodation.[579]

Although the statute's prohibition on discrimination is broad, the statute recognizes a necessary balance between a person's participation rights and the interests of those who might be negatively impacted by the person's participation. To wit, the statute's non-discrimination charge provides an exception when the excluded individual "poses a direct threat to the health or safety of others."[580] The Act defines a direct threat as "a significant risk to the health or safety of others that cannot be eliminated by modification of policies, practices, or procedures or by the provision of auxiliary aides or services."[581] Citing that exception, the district court found in favor of the school, concluding that Montalvo's condition "posed a significant risk to the health or safety of other students and no reasonable modification could suffi-

---

572. *Id.*
573. *Id.*
574. *Id.* at 251.
575. *Id.*
576. Matthew J. Mitten, *Enhanced Risk of Harm to One's Self as a Justification for Exclusion from Athletics*, 8 MARQ. L.J. 189, 215 (1998).
577. 167 F.3d 873 (4th Cir. 1999).
578. *Id.* at 875.
579. 42 U.S.C § 12182(a).
580. 42 U.S.C § 12182(b)(3).
581. *Id.*

ciently reduce this risk without fundamentally altering the nature of the program."[582] The Fourth Circuit affirmed.[583]

In *Doe v. Woodford County*,[584] a case involving a high school student with hepatitis B and hemophilia who sought to join his school's junior varsity basketball team, the Sixth Circuit faced a similar balancing task. Doe's school put the student's roster position on "hold" pending medical clearance, and the student sued under the Rehabilitation Act and the ADA.[585] The court described the defendants as facing a "catch-22" situation: "On the one hand, defendants had to be aware of possibly infringing upon [plaintiff's] civil rights under the Rehabilitation Act and the ADA.... On the other hand, defendants faced potential liability from other students ... [if] another student accidentally became exposed to [hepatitis]."[586] The court ultimately found that the defendants did not violate either statute.[587] It explained, "[i]t is entirely reasonable for defendants to be concerned and arguably were obligated to be concerned with limiting risk of contagion...."[588] The holdings in both *Montalvo* and *Woodford County* are consistent with a general judicial recognition of a legal duty athletic organizations have to use reasonable care to prevent contagion during athletic activity.[589]

[3] Fundamental Modification of the Game

In some cases, a disabled athlete's participation in sport will pose risks to neither the athlete nor other participants, but instead will require an exception to the rules

---

582. *Montalvo*, 167 F.3d at 874. It bears noting that the medical community's understanding of HIV and the manner in which it is transmitted has evolved substantially since *Montalvo v. Radcliffe* was decided. Michael Montalvo sought to join the Bushidokan Karate School just a few years after NBA star Ervin "Magic" Johnson announced he had HIV, which shocked the sports world and stoked fear among NBA players that perhaps they had contracted the virus while competing against him. The concerns regarding transmissibility were so widespread and intense that Johnson — one of basketball's all-time greats — left the game. Francine Uenuma, *Magic Johnson's HIV Disclosure Helped to Shatter Stigmas. But 30 Years Later, Disparities in Treatment Remain*, TIME (Nov. 4, 2021), https://time.com/6113046/magic-johnson-hiv-aids-impact/ (noting that "[i]t also took years of education to reinforce the fact that HIV is not spread through casual contact, a fear that had arisen among other players when Johnson played ... in the 1990s."). In the years since Johnson's announcement and Montalvo's rejection by the Bushidokan Karate School, the medical establishment has come to recognize the virus' fragility and its difficulty in moving from host to host. The public has become less concerned about its transmission. Consequently, sports leagues — professional and amateur, alike — generally do not mandate HIV testing. *See* Mike Holtzclaw, *AIDS in Sports: Focus: Precaution in the Pros*, DAILY PRESS (May 9, 1993), https://www.dailypress.com/news/dp-xpm-19930509-1993-05-09-9305090151-story.html (noting that "[n]o professional sports leagues mandate AIDS tests").

583. *Montalvo*, 167 F.3d at 879.

584. 213 F.3d 921 (6th Cir. 2000).

585. *Id.* at 924.

586. *Id.* at 926.

587. *Id.*

588. *Id.*

589. *See generally*, Joseph E.G. v. E. Irondequoit Cent. Sch. Dist., 708 N.Y.S.2d 537 (N.Y. App. Div. 2000) (assessing whether failure to clean wrestling mats soiled by a competitor's blood constituted negligence); Silver v. Levittown Union Free Sch. Dist., 692 N.Y.S.2d 886 (N.Y. Sup. Ct. 1999) (determining whether wrestler is liable for negligently transmitting a contagious disease during a match).

of the game. Under such circumstances, a disabled athlete's eligibility to participate hinges on whether the requested exception is a reasonable accommodation for the disabled athlete or is one that would fundamentally, and therefore unacceptably, alter the game.[590] The United States Supreme Court's analysis in *PGA Tour, Inc. v. Martin*,[591] provides guidance. There, Casey Martin, a professional golfer, had a congenital circulatory condition called Klippel-Trenaunay-Weber Syndrome,[592] which withered Martin's right leg and often caused him significant pain when he walked.[593] Because Martin's condition substantially limited the major life activity of walking, Martin qualified as disabled under the ADA.[594] As a collegiate golfer, Martin was permitted to ride in a golf cart between his shots when he was experiencing pain.[595] PGA Tour rules, however, did not generally permit riding. Martin sought a permanent ruling permitting his cart use during PGA competitions.[596]

Martin based his argument on the "place of public accommodation" provision in Title III of the ADA. He asserted that because he paid to participate in the PGA's Qualifying School he was a customer of the PGA and that the PGA Tour discriminated against him in violation of the Act when it did not accommodate his disability by permitting cart use.[597] In addressing the matter, the district court accepted Martin's "place of public accommodation" premise and then considered whether cart use would fundamentally alter the game by advantaging Martin over competitors required to walk the course while playing.[598] The PGA argued that the universal walking rule was fundamental in that it "inject[ed] the element of fatigue into the skill of shot-making."[599] The court, however, disagreed and ordered that Martin be permitted to use a cart.[600] The Ninth Circuit affirmed, as did the United States Supreme Court.[601] The Supreme Court did not deem the walking rule as fundamental to PGA golf. Indeed, it found that the "rule is at best peripheral to the nature of [PGA golf] events, and thus it might be waived in individual cases without working a fundamental alteration."[602] The Court based its conclusion on the premise that guaranteeing identical playing conditions among competitors is impossible and that "pure chance may have a greater impact on the outcome of elite golf tournaments than the fatigue resulting from the enforcement of the walking rule."[603]

---

590. Maureen A. Weston, *The Intersection of Sports and Disability: Analyzing Reasonable Accommodations for Athletes with Disabilities*, 50 St. Louis U. L.J. 137, 159–62 (2005).
591. 532 U.S. 661 (2001).
592. *Id.* at 668.
593. *Id.*
594. *Id.*
595. *Id.*
596. *Id.*
597. *Id.*
598. *Id.* at 671–72.
599. *Id.* at 671.
600. *Id.* at 672.
601. *Id.* at 673, 691.
602. *Id.* at 689.
603. *Id.* at 687.

The Court's decision created an opportunity for Martin to pursue a career on the PGA Tour and was widely deemed a victory in the disabled community. Substantial uncertainty exists in the sports community, however, with respect to what qualifies as "fundamental" to a sport for purposes of the modification analysis.[604]

Even greater uncertainty reigns with respect to "modification" of a human being seeking to participate in sport. As discussed in Chapter 5, for instance, uneven rules prevail across the sports landscape with respect to requirements that intersex and transgender athletes endure hormone therapy in order to compete. Parameters around modification also exist in regard to disabled athletes, particularly around the issue of prosthetics.

[4] Prosthetics in Competition

While the Paralympic Games feature many athletes with visible physical disabilities, advances in prosthetic limb technology have opened a path for amputee athletes to credibly challenge able-bodied contemporaries in Olympic competition. Sport governing bodies, however, have in some cases objected to participation by prosthetics-aided athletes. In resolving such matters, arbitral panels have assessed the extent to which the prosthetics afford disabled athletes a net advantage over their competitors.[605]

The Oscar Pistorius case is illustrative. Pistorius was born with significant deficiencies in his lower legs, and both of his legs were amputated below the knee before he reached one year of age.[606] He walked with prosthetics, and as he grew older, he developed an interest in track and field.[607] With the help of "Cheetah" prosthetic legs, Pistorius ascended into a world class runner, setting multiple para-athlete world records in sprint events.[608] Pistorius then pursued the opportunity to compete against able-bodied runners, but the world governing body for track and field — the International Association of Athletics Federation ("IAAF"), now called World Athletics — attempted to bar him.[609] The IAAF argued that Pistorius' "Cheetah" legs violated an IAAF rule prohibiting the use of any "technical device that incorporates springs, wheels or any other element that provides the user with an advantage over another

---

604. *See* Weston, *supra* note 590, at 159–72. *Compare* Pottgen v. Mo. State High Sch. Activities Ass'n, 40 F.3d 926, 930 (8th Cir. 1994) (determining the maximum age rule for high school sports was fundamental), *and* Bowers v. Nat'l Collegiate Athletic Ass'n, 9 F. Supp. 2d 460, 466 (D.N.J. 1998) (holding academic eligibility requirements as fundamental for collegiate sports), *with* Cruz v. Pa. Interscholastic Athletic Ass'n, Inc., 157 F. Supp. 2d 485 (E.D. Pa. 2001) (finding that a waiver of the age rule for a learning disabled student would not fundamentally alter high school sports).

605. Christopher Bidlack, *The Prohibition of Prosthetic Limbs in American Sports: The Issues and the Role of the Americans with Disabilities Act*, 19 MARQ. SPORTS L. REV. 613 (2009).

606. Shawn M. Crincoli, *You Can Only Race if You Can't Win? The Curious Cases of Oscar Pistorius & Caster Semanya*, 12 TEX. REV. ENT. & SPORTS L. 133, 141 (2011).

607. *Id.*

608. *Id.* at 141–42.

609. *Id.* at 143.

athlete not using such a device."[610] Pistorius challenged the rule's application before the Court of Arbitration for Sport ("CAS").[611] Pistorius contended, among other things, that his baseline of having no legs below the knee put him at a profound disadvantage in running sprints and that the "Cheetah" legs, rather than provide him an "advantage" in violation of the rule, simply mitigated his obvious disadvantage.[612] CAS sided with Pistorius, finding that no scientific evidence indicated the "Cheetah" legs gave him a net advantage over his able-bodied competitors.[613] This cleared the path for Pistorius to vie for Olympic qualification. Although he failed to qualify for the 2008 Beijing Olympics, Pistorius qualified for and competed in the 2012 London Olympics.[614]

Pistorius' athletic success has inspired other amputee runners to utilize prosthetics in competing against able-bodied runners, and they too have faced regulatory obstacles. For instance, American 400-meter runner Blake Leeper attempted to qualify for the 2021 Tokyo games after dominating the 400 meter race at para-events and capturing fifth place in the event at the U.S. championships in 2019.[615] In 2020, World Athletics banned Leeper from competing with his prosthetics, which were similar to Pistorious' prosthetics, but longer.[616] World Athletics asserted Leeper's use of the prosthetics violated its Maximum Allowable Standing Height ("MASH") rule, which exists to prevent disabled athletes from "over-compensating for the absence of a missing limb."[617] Leeper challenged the ban before CAS in October of 2020, and the CAS tribunal ruled against him.[618] In an effort to continue competing in World Athletics events, Leeper began using legs that were two inches shorter than his previous pair, but in advance of the June 2021 United States Olympic trials, World Athletics banned the shorter legs as well.[619] The governing body determined that Leeper's torso length indicated he would have been 5 feet and 9 inches tall had he been born with legs, and that the disproportionately long prosthetic legs made him 6 feet tall, giving him

610. *Id.* at 142–43; Pistorius v. IAAF, CAS 2008/A/1480, 5 (May 16, 2008).

611. *Id.* at 143.

612. *Id.*

613. *Id.* at 148–49; *Pistorius*, CAS 2008/A/1480 at 14.

614. *Oscar Pistorius Makes Olympic History in 400m at London 2012*, BBC (Aug. 4, 2012), https://www.bbc.com/sport/olympics/18911479. It bears noting that Pistorius' career ended the following year when he was arrested for, and later convicted of, murdering his girlfriend in their home. Tim Hume, Faith Karimi & Nick Thompson, *Oscar Pistorius Sentenced to 6 Years in Prison for Girlfriend's Murder*, CNN (July 7, 2016), https://www.cnn.com/2016/07/06/africa/oscar-pistorius-sentence/index.html.

615. Adam Kilgore, *Paralympic Sprinter Blake Leeper's Application to Compete in Tokyo Olympics Denied*, WASHINGTON POST (Apr. 26, 2021), https://www.washingtonpost.com/sports/2021/04/26/blake-leeper-prostheses-tokyo-olympics-appeal/.

616. *Id.*

617. *Id.*

618. *Id.*; *The Court of Arbitration for Sport (CAS) Dismisses the 2nd Appeal of Blake Leeper*, COURT OF ARBITRATION FOR SPORT (June 11, 2021), https://www.tas-cas.org/fileadmin/user_upload/CAS_Media_Release_7930.pdf.

619. Kilgore, *supra* note 615.

an advantage.[620] Leeper challenged the more recent World Athletics decision before CAS as well, but he again lost and consequently did not have the opportunity to qualify for the 2021 Tokyo Olympics.[621]

As biomedical engineering continues to advance and technology provides additional means of supplementing disabled human bodies to compensate for deficiencies, questions as to whether the technology provides disabled athletes an advantage over their able-bodied competitors will persist and likely lead to additional CAS arbitrations.

[C] Disability and Employment

As employers, sports organizations are bound by Title I of the ADA, which mandates nondiscrimination and reasonable accommodation in the workplace.[622] As long as a "qualified" employee does not pose a direct threat to the health and safety of other employees, an employer may not discriminate against the employee because of the employee's disability.[623] A "qualified" employee under the statute is one who is "disabled" and can perform the essential functions of a job with or without a reasonable accommodation.[624] As noted above, to be recognized as "disabled" under the statute, an employee must have, or be regarded as having, a physical or mental impairment that substantially limits a major life activity.[625]

Importantly, inability to perform a specific specialized task — such as throwing a particular baseball pitch or dunking a basketball — does not constitute being substantially limited in a major life activity.[626] Major life activities recognized under the statute are everyday activities, such as walking, thinking, concentrating, and performing bodily functions.[627] Recall that golfer Casey Martin, discussed above in section 10.08[b][3] of this chapter suffers from Klippel-Trenaunay-Weber Syndrome, which renders him "disabled" in that he is substantially limited in the major life activity of walking. Martin brought his suit under the ADA's "place of public accommodation" prong, but had he been a golf team employee (professional golfers generally compete independently, as Martin did), and had the golf team taken an adverse employment

---

620. *Id.*

621. *Id.*

622. 42 U.S.C. § 12112(a)–(b).

623. 42 U.S.C. § 12113(b).

624. 42 U.S.C. § 12111(8).

625. 42 U.S.C. § 12102(3).

626. *See* Nuzum v. Ozark Auto. Distributors, Inc., 320 F. Supp. 2d 852, 863 (S.D. Iowa 2004), *aff'd*, 432 F.3d 839 (8th Cir. 2005) (Noting that "this Court concurs with the assessments of the courts cited above and finds that mowing the lawn, doing assorted outside chores, working on cars, coaching youth sports, throwing balls, driving a vehicle with a manual transmission, and tightly hugging one's spouse are not major life activities within the purview of the ADA's definition of such.").

627. 42 U.S.C. § 12102(2).

action against him because of his cart usage, he likely would have qualified as "disabled" under Title I of the ADA as well.

[1] Addiction

Although disability discrimination lawsuits in the sports employment context are rare, the Equal Employment Opportunity Commission — to which employment discrimination plaintiffs must submit their claims before filing suit in federal court — has recognized that sports organizations are not exempt from ADA employment discrimination suits. One case in which it did so was *Roy Tarpley v. Dallas Mavericks and NBA*.[628] Roy Tarpley was a standout college basketball player at the University of Michigan before the NBA's Dallas Mavericks selected him with the seventh overall pick in the 1986 NBA draft.[629] He played for the Mavericks until 1991, but during his career he abused illegal drugs and alcohol.[630] In 1991, the NBA banned him for cocaine use, and he played professionally in Greece through 1994 when the NBA reinstated him.[631] He then signed a six year, $20 million contract with the Mavericks.[632] The following year, the NBA permanently banned Tarpley for violating the terms of his reinstatement by using alcohol.[633] In 2003, Tarpley again applied for reinstatement, but his request was denied.[634]

In July 2006, Tarpley filed an EEOC charge of discrimination against the NBA and the Mavericks, asserting that he had passed all of the drug tests he had taken since being banned. He further alleged that the NBA and the Mavericks violated the ADA by discriminating against him because of his disability: drug and alcohol addiction.[635] The EEOC concluded reasonable cause existed to believe the NBA and the Mavericks violated Tarpley's rights under the ADA, and it issued Tarpley a right to sue letter, authorizing him to pursue federal litigation.[636] Tarpley filed federal suit in 2007 with a claim that tracked the ADA requirements, set out above. His complaint

---

628. Docket No. 4:07-cv-03132 (S.D. Tex. Filed Sept. 26, 2007). The EEOC has done so in other cases as well. *See, e.g.*, Stearns v. Bd. of Educ. for Warren Twp. High Sch. Dist. #121, 1999 WL 1044832, at *1 (N.D. Ill. Nov. 16, 1999) (holding that a high school's decision not to allow a student, who was a diagnosed alcoholic, to play basketball did not violate the ADA because he had previously violated the school's no alcohol policy); *see also* Len Pasquarelli, *Bengals' Thurman, Bucs' Cox File Discrimination Claims Against NFL*, ESPN (Aug. 17, 2007), https://www.espn.com/nfl/news/story?id=2978901 (reporting that two NFL players, viewed as alcoholics, filed a discrimination claim against the league for failing to reinstate them).
629. *Tarpley, Drug-Plagued Ex-Center, Dies*, USATODAY (Jan. 9, 2015), https://www.usatoday.com/story/sports/nba/2015/01/09/roy-tarpley-drug-plagued-former-mavericks-center-dies/21531289/.
630. *Id.*
631. *Id.*
632. *Id.*
633. *Id.*
634. *Ex-Mav Tarpley Alleges Discrimination by NBA, Team*, ESPN (Sept. 26, 2007), https://www.espn.com/nba/news/story?id=3038017.
635. *Id.*
636. *Id.*

read, in part, "Tarpley is a qualified individual with a disability within the meaning of the ADA, in that he has a disability in the form of past drug and alcohol abuse, which substantially limits at least one of his major life activities."[637] Under the ADA, an employer may enforce substance abuse policies against employees who use prohibited substances.[638] However, former substance abusers who have been successfully rehabilitated, as Tarpley claimed he had been, are protected under the statute.[639] Tarpley asserted that his major life activity substantially limited by alcoholism was working, and working is a well-established and accepted major life activity under ADA doctrine.[640] Although the parties exchanged motions and briefs for nearly a year, the ultimate strength of Tarpley's suit was untested, as the parties agreed to mediation and ultimately settled the matter.[641]

[2] Mental Health

Much more frequently than in the past, athletes are expressing vulnerability with respect to mental health. In 2021, for instance, two of the world's elite individual sport athletes — Naomi Osaka (tennis) and Simone Biles (gymnastics) — pulled out of major competitions, citing compromised mental health.[642] Elite team sport athletes, such as NBA player DeMar DeRozen, former NFL player Brandon Marshall, and MLB player Drew Robinson, have also famously shared their mental health struggles with the public.[643] None of these athletes have sought employment accommodation

637. ESPN, *supra* note 633; *see also* Tarpley v. National Basketball Association, Inc., Docket No. 4:07-cv-03132 (S.D. Tex. Sep 26, 2007) (Plaintiff's Complaint); *see also* Tarpley v. National Basketball Association, Inc., 4:07CV03132 (case was dismissed for settlement in 2009).

638. Americans with Disabilities Act Title III Technical Assistance Manual Covering Public Accommodations and Commercial Facilities, § 8.3, available at https://www.eeoc.gov/laws/guidance/technical-assistance-manual-employment-provisions-title-i-americans-disabilities-act; *see, e.g.*, Wood v. Indianapolis Power & Light Co., 210 F.3d 377 (7th Cir. 2000) (holding that a meter reader who tested positive for cocaine and marijuana use was not protected by the ADA).

639. 42 U.S.C. § 12114(b) (1994).

640. Robin L. Muir, *Drunk or Disabled? The Legal and Social Consequences of Roy Tarpley's Discrimination Claim Against the NBA*, 15 VILL. SPORTS & ENT. L.J. 333, 346 (2008).

641. Tarpley v. Nat'l Basketball Ass'n, Inc., Docket No. 4:07-cv-03132 (S.D. Tex. Sep 26, 2007) (Docket Sheet).

642. *Naomi Osaka Says Novak Djokovic, Others Reached Out to Offer Support After French Open Withdrawal*, ESPN (July 8, 2021), https://www.espn.com/tennis/story/_/id/31782152/naomi-osaka-says-novak-djokovic-others-reached-offer-support-french-open-withdrawal; Louise Radnofsky, *Simone Biles Will Make Dramatic Return to Tokyo Olympics on Balance Beam*, WALL STREET JOURNAL (Aug. 2, 2021), https://www.wsj.com/articles/simone-biles-balance-beam-final-tokyo-olympics-11627893493.

643. *See* Byron Jamar Terry, *Mental Health: The Human Side of DeMar DeRozan*, MEDIUM.COM (Apr. 14, 2020), https://medium.com/@terrybyron1/mental-health-the-human-side-of-demar-derozan-63a26eca1682 (speaking on DeMar DeRozan's mental health); *see also Brandon Marshall tries to break the stigma of mental illness*, USA TODAY (Nov. 27, 2020), https://www.usatoday.com/story/sports/nfl/2020/11/27/brandon-marshall-tries-to-break-the-stigma-of-mental-illness/43199299/ (noting Brandon Marshall's struggles with mental health); *see also* Jeff Passan, *San Francisco Giants outfielder Drew Robinson's remarkable second act*, ESPN (May 11, 2021), https://www.espn.com/mlb/story/_/id/30800732/san-francisco-giants-outfielder-drew-robinson-remarkable-second-act. Drew Robinson's story is particularly startling. He suffered severe depression for much of his life, and when the COVID-

under the ADA for a mental health disability. With the increasing prevalence of athletes publicly acknowledging mental health challenges, however, such an ADA lawsuit is a realistic possibility. Professor Michael McCann explores that possibility in analyzing the circumstances faced by Royce White as he attempted to launch an NBA career in 2012 while suffering from generalized anxiety disorder ("GAD") and obsessive-compulsive disorder ("OCD"). In his law review article, McCann examines the alleged discrimination White faced and how a court might have adjudicated the matter had White sued.[644]

White was a star basketball player at Iowa State University during the 2011–2012 season, leading his team in points, rebounds, assists, steals, and blocked shots.[645] He entered the NBA draft after the college season ended, and the Houston Rockets selected him in the first round, signing him to a multi-million dollar contract.[646] At Iowa State, White's GAD and OCD manifested in a fear of flying, though he was able to overcome that fear and flew to all but three of his club's away games (he was driven to those three).[647] His fear of flying, however, became more debilitating in the NBA.[648] White was initially able to fly to some pre-season activities, but he refused to participate in the club's training camp unless the Rockets assured him that they would let him travel by bus (at his own expense) to most of the club's away games.[649] The club agreed.[650] White was shortly thereafter assigned to the Rockets' NBA Development League[651] team, the Rio Grande Valley Vipers.[652]

White asserted that the Rockets demoted him in response to his insistence that the club agree to a mental health protocol that would govern aspects of his relationship with the club, including modes of travel.[653] Substantial discord followed, with White refusing to practice with the Vipers and the Rockets suspending him.[654] In January 2013, White and the Rockets agreed on mental health protocols that included a neutral mental health expert's involvement in future employment disputes regarding White's

---

19 pandemic hit, he spiraled downward. *Id.* Feeling inadequate and hopeless, he attempted to commit suicide, shooting himself in the head. *Id.* The attempt failed, and Robinson spent the following 20 hours in his apartment suffering from the gunshot wound to his head. *Id.* Though Robinson lost his right eye from the gunshot, he survived, has begun to more effectively treat his depression, and has returned to professional baseball. *Id.*

644. Michael A. McCann, *Do You Believe He Can Fly? Royce White and Reasonable Accommodations Under the Americans with Disabilities Act for NBA Players with Anxiety Disorder and Fear of Flying*, 41 PEPP. L. REV. 397 (2014).

645. *Id.* at 398–99.

646. *Id.* at 400.

647. *Id.* at 404.

648. *Id.* at 405–06.

649. *Id.*

650. *Id.* at 407.

651. In 2017, the NBA Development League executed a sponsorship deal with Gatorade and took the name the "G-League." Kareem Copeland, *D-League to be Renamed NBA Gatorade League*, NBA. COM (Feb. 14, 2017), https://www.nba.com/news/nba-d-league-renamed-nba-gatorade-league.

652. McCann, *supra* note 644, at 407.

653. *Id.* at 408.

654. *Id.*

mental health.[655] For the following several months, White played on and off with the Vipers, traveling by car when he played, and at other times not playing due to his mental health concerns.[656] The Rockets traded White to the Philadelphia 76ers after the season, but the 76ers released him within a few of months.[657] White thereafter played briefly for the NBA's Sacramento Kings and for a few teams overseas and has dabbled in mixed martial arts.[658]

No professional athlete had previously engaged with a club in such a public employment-related dispute over mental health accommodations. Mental health advocates commended White's courage and urged him to sue the Rockets for not appropriately accommodating his disability. As noted above, White did not sue. Had he done so, McCann argues White's suit most likely would have been unsuccessful.[659] To prevail, White would have to show that he was a "qualified" employee under the ADA, meaning he is "disabled" and can perform the essential functions of a job with or without a reasonable accommodation.[660] The first challenge would have been to establish that he is "disabled." While White would likely have been able to be establish that he legitimately suffered from GAD and OCD, he would have had to further establish that those conditions substantially limited a "major life activity."[661] In White's case, the "major life activity" in question was flying. Several cases have held that flying does not constitute a "major life activity" under the statute,[662] but those cases do not involve employment contexts in which flying is as frequent an occurrence as it is in the NBA.

Even assuming White was able to establish he is disabled under the statute, he would then have to establish that air travel is not an "essential function" of the job.[663] Because NBA teams play games all over the country with few days — and on some occasions no days — of rest in between, it would be difficult to argue air travel is not essential to the job. Even if White were to fund his own ground transportation, the distance between games would mean he would miss some games and likely show up poorly rested for others. Moreover, the NBA uniform player contract states that "a player assents to competitively and skillfully playing scheduled games,"[664] and relying strictly on ground transportation would not allow a player to fulfill that obligation. As such, air travel would likely be deemed an essential function of playing for an

---

655. *Id.*

656. *Id.* at 409.

657. *Id.* at 409–10.

658. Dan Martin, *NBA Bust Royce White Eyes Second Career as UFC Fighter*, NY Post (Feb. 27, 2019), https://nypost.com/2019/02/27/nba-bust-royce-white-eyes-second-career-as-ufc-fighter/ß.

659. McCann, *supra* note 644, at 438.

660. *Id.* at 414.

661. *Id.*

662. *Id.* at 415 (citing Bliss v. Nationwide Mut. Ins. Co., 2010 WL 11601326, at *11–12 (W.D. Tex. Feb. 25, 2010), and Cannizzaro v. Neiman Marcus, Inc., 979 F. Supp. 465, 476 (N.D. Tex. 1997) (holding that flying is not a major life activity for purposes of the ADA).

663. McCann, *supra* note 644, at 415.

664. *Id.* at 417.

NBA team, and an employer need not accommodate an employee's disability if the employee cannot perform an essential function of a job.

[D] Facility Access

The ADA requires that sports facilities, like other places of public accommodation, be accessible to people with disabilities.[665] Access extends beyond the entrance into the facility and must include access to restrooms, concessions, and other facility features and services.[666]

Notably, a facility's age bears on the facility owner's obligations to provide accommodations. Sports facilities built after 1993 are required to ensure that at least one percent of all seating is reserved and accessible for wheelchair bound spectators.[667] (Facilities built in 1993 or earlier are under no such regulation.) Moreover, the wheelchair seating required in newer stadiums must provide wheelchair users "lines of sight comparable to those for members of the general public."[668] This requirement has produced substantial litigation.

In *Miller v. Cal. Speedway Corp.*,[669] the California Speedway Corporation (the "Speedway") opened the California Speedway, a facility designed to host NASCAR events.[670] Robert Miller, a NASCAR fan, was a regular spectator at the Speedway.[671] Because he was paralyzed below the neck and restricted to a wheelchair, Miller always purchased tickets in the wheelchair section toward the top of the stadium.[672] Although his line of sight to the track was unobstructed when fans in front of him were sitting down, it was blocked when they stood up during exciting moments.[673] Miller sued the Speedway under the ADA for not providing him "lines of sight comparable to those for members of the general public."[674] The parties did not dispute whether wheelchair users had to be provided a clear line of sight while all spectators were sitting, but defendant did not believe that requirement extended to the intermittent moments when some spectators stood up. The district court found for the Speedway, but the Ninth Circuit reversed.[675] It relied on the Department of Justice's interpretation of the ADA's "line of sight" requirement as applying "in assembly areas where spectators can be expected to stand during the event or

---

665. *See Guide to the ADA Accessibility Standards, Chapter 10: Sports Facilities*, U.S. Access Board, https://www.access-board.gov/ada/guides/chapter-10-sports-facilities/ (last visited Feb. 18, 2022).

666. *See id.*

667. 42 U.S.C. § 12101 *et seq.* (1990) (Appendix 13 provides the accessibility guidelines for new stadiums).

668. *Id.*

669. 536 F.3d 1020 (9th Cir. 2008).

670. *Id.* at 1023.

671. *Id.*

672. *Id.*

673. *Id.*

674. *Id.* at 1024 (quoting 42 U.S.C. § 12101 *et seq.* (1990)).

675. *Id.*

show being viewed."[676] Deeming this interpretation "reasonable and therefore entitled to substantial deference," the court found for Miller.[677] Dispositions in "line of sight cases" are unpredictable, however, because: (1) these issues are factually dependent with regard to configuration of the seating and human bodies at sporting events; and (2) the Department of Justice periodically releases updated ADA Accessibility Guidelines,[678] which different courts have historically interpreted in different ways.[679]

While a disproportionate number of ADA accessibility cases at sports facilities involve the non-ambulatory, the statute extends generally to the disabled community. Indeed, a fair amount of litigation involves access to in-stadium aural programming for the hearing impaired. *Feldman v. Pro Football. Inc.*[680] is one such case. Pro Football, Inc. ("Pro Football") owns and operates the NFL's Washington Commanders. Plaintiffs, hearing-impaired fans, attended several games at the team's home stadium, FedEx Field. They alleged the team did not provide auxiliary aids or closed captioning such that hearing impaired spectators could benefit from the announcements broadcast via the stadium's public address system.[681] Plaintiffs sued Pro Football under the ADA, asserting the statute demands that "[n]o individual shall be discriminated against on the basis of disability in the full and equal enjoyment of the goods, services, facilities, privileges, advantages, or accommodations of any place of public accommodation...."[682] Pro Football noted that the team provided assisted listening devices and that "nothing in the law dictates that they provide captioning as opposed to other auxiliary services."[683] The plaintiffs, however, asserted — and Pro Football did not disagree — that the provided listening devices were not sufficient to provide them with "equal access to aural information broadcast at FedEx Field."[684] The plaintiffs further asserted that accommodation beyond the provided listening devices was necessary to provide equal access. Although Pro Football did not dispute the assertion, it responded that the ADA only obligates the team to provide the listening devices.[685]

---

676. *Id.* at 1032.
677. *Id.* at 1033.
678. The Department of Justice issued its most recent ADA Accessibility Guidelines in 2010 (with applicability to all stadiums built after March of 2012). These guidelines explicate that "wheelchair spaces shall be dispersed. Wheelchair spaces shall provide spectators with choices of seating locations and viewing angles...." 36 C.F.R. pt. 1191 app. B (2020).
679. *See, e.g.*, Caruso v. Blockbuster-Sony Music Entm't Centre at the Waterfront, 193 F.3d 730, 736–37 (3d Cir. 1999) (interpreting the ADA Accessibility Guidelines to not require lines of sight over standing spectators); Paralyzed Veterans of America v. D.C. Arena L.P., 117 F.3d 579, 587 (D.C. Cir. 1997) (interpreting the ADA Accessibility Guidelines to require lines of sight over standing spectators). While the ADA's 2010 Accessibility Guidelines were designed to reduce confusion about "line of sight" analysis, it is likely courts will reach conflicting decisions about this or other aspects of facility access under the ADA.
680. 579 F. Supp. 2d 697 (D. Md. 2008).
681. *Id.* at 699.
682. *Id.* at 708.
683. *Id.*
684. *Id.*
685. *Id.* at 709.

The court disagreed, admonishing Pro Football for claiming to have sufficiently accommodated plaintiffs while acknowledging the accommodation did not grant plaintiffs the equal access necessitated under the law.[686] In doing so, the court cited the Department of Justice regulations implementing Title III of the ADA, which read, "A public accommodation shall take those steps that may be necessary to ensure that no individual with a disability is excluded, denied services, segregated or otherwise treated differently than other individuals because of the absences of auxiliary aids and services."[687] The court's decision makes clear that sports teams and facility operators may not simply pick and choose which measures they will take to accommodate disabled spectators under the ADA. Rather, they must take whatever accommodative steps are necessary unless such steps would result in a "specific hardship or undue burden."[688]

---

686. *Id.*

687. *Id.* at 708–09.

688. *Id.* at 710. *See Innes v. Bd. of Regents of Univ. Sys. of Md.*, 29 F. Supp. 3d 566 (D. Md. 2014) (holding that two deaf spectators sufficiently stated a claim for ADA discrimination when University of Maryland failed to ensure effective communication at athletic events); *see also Sports Venues Facing More Legal Battles Over Captioning*, ATHLETIC BUSINESS (Dec. 13, 2013), https://www.athleticbusiness. com/operations/legal/article/15144984/sports-venues-facing-more-legal-battles-over-captioning (reporting on caption litigation with the Arizona Cardinals and The Ohio State University).

Chapter 11

Injury Compensation

§ 11.01 Introduction

This chapter discusses injuries to athletes and mechanisms available to compensate them for those injuries. It begins with a discussion of workers' compensation as a mechanism for compensating professional athletes for injuries occurring in the course of their employment. The chapter then discusses the viability of medical malpractice claims athletes assert against physicians and trainers. Next, it discusses the liability of defendants at all levels of sports to athletes who suffer concussion-related illnesses. The liability of manufacturers, sellers, and others for injuries to athletes involving allegedly defective equipment is also examined.

§ 11.02 Workers' Compensation

[A] Introduction

State-based workers' compensation statutes allow workers to receive compensation for injuries and medical expenses "arising out of and in the course of employment."[1] Workers' compensation statutes are premised on the idea that costs associated with compensating workers for work-related injuries are a production-related cost of doing business.[2] In exchange for a simplified no-fault mechanism for compensation, injured workers relinquish the right to pursue tort or other statutory remedies against their employers for covered injuries.[3] The relinquishment of employees' tort claims is accompanied by the loss of defenses (*e.g.*, assumption of the risk) that employers could assert against a tort claim. Under most workers' compensation statutes, however, employers are not exposed to the risk of liability for punitive damages and pain and suffering.[4] In exchange, workers' compensation statutes generally permit eligible

---

1. 5 ARTHUR LARSON, LEX K. LARSON & THOMAS A. ROBINSON, LARSON'S WORKERS' COMPENSATION LAW Chapter 1 Synopsis (2019).

2. 5 LARSON'S WORKERS' COMPENSATION LAW § 3.01.

3. *Id.*

4. MATTHEW J. MITTEN, ET AL., SPORTS LAW AND REGULATION: CASES, MATERIALS, AND PROBLEMS 961 (5th ed. 2020).

claimants to receive monetary benefits stemming from wage losses due to the claimant's "permanent symptoms and impairment" and "lifetime medical care."[5]

Under workers' compensation statutes, an employee's entitlement to compensation hinges primarily on whether: (1) the claimant falls within the relevant statute's definition of an employee, and (2) the injury for which the claimant seeks compensation arose "in the course of" the claimant's employment.[6] In contrast to college athletes,[7] professional athletes in team sports have encountered little difficultly in establishing the requisite employment relationship. In the seminal case of *Metropolitan Casualty Insurance Company of New York v. Huhn*,[8] the court found that a deceased baseball player fell within the definition of employee as set forth in the relevant workers' compensation statute.[9] Subsequent courts concur in finding that athletes in team sports are employees as defined by workers' compensation statutes.[10]

The foregoing analysis assumes, however, that a state workers' compensation statute does not exclude professional athletes from its definition of employee. Florida, Massachusetts, and Wyoming are among the states that explicitly exclude professional athletes from the definition of employee.[11] Other states indirectly exclude professional athletes from the reach of workers' compensation statutes by restricting employees who can assert claims to those whose incomes do not exceed a certain threshold, such as the percentage by which a player's salary exceeds the weekly average salaries of all workers within a state.[12] Yet, absent a statutory exclusion,[13] professional athletes in team sports meet the employment relationship requirement. It should also be noted that the statutory exclusion may be waived, where for example, a collective

---

5. Benjamin T. Boscolo & Gerald Herz, Ch. 17 — *Professional Athletes and the Law of Workers' Compensation: Rights and Remedies, in* GARY A. UBERSTINE, THE LAW OF PROFESSIONAL AND AMATEUR SPORT 17-3 (2021).

6. MITTEN, et al., *supra* note 4, at 961.

7. *See* discussion, Ch. 2, *supra*.

8. 142 S.E. 121 (Ga. 1928).

9. *Id.* at 125–27.

10. *See, e.g.*, Brinkman v. Buffalo Bills Football Club, 433 F. Supp. 699, 702 (W.D.N.Y. 1977) (player's tort claim was barred by workers' compensation statute); Pro-Football, Inc. v. Uhlenhake, 558 S.E.2d 571 (Va. Ct. App. 2002); Brocail v. Detroit Tigers, Inc., 268 S.W.3d 90 (Tex. Ct. App. 14th Dist. 2008) (workers' compensation was the exclusive remedy available to an injured player); Estate of Gross v. Three Rivers Inn, Inc., 706 N.E.2d 741 (N.Y. App. 1998); Farren v. Baltimore Ravens, Inc., 720 N.E.2d 590 (Ohio Ct. App. 8th Dist. 1998) (question of fact as to whether football player, who was not under contract and was injured while participating in off-season conditioning at team's training facility and was directed by the team, was an employee as defined by workers' compensation statute); Rudolph v. Miami Dolphins, 447 So. 2d 284 (Fla. Ct. App. 1st Dist. 1983) (statutory exclusion applies to players attempting to obtain roster spots on a team as well as those who have roster spots).

11. *See, e.g.*, Florida, FLA. STAT. §440.02(17)(c)(3); Massachusetts, MASS. GEN. LAWS ch. 152 §1(4); Wyoming, WYO. STAT. §27-14-102(a)(vii)(F).

12. *See, e.g.*, Michigan, MICH. COMP. LAW ANN. §418.360(1); Pennsylvania, 77 PA. STAT. ANN. §565(e); *see also* Lyons v. Workers' Compensation Appeals Bd., 803 A.2d 857 (Pa. Commw. Ct. 2002) (upholding the constitutionality of the limitation).

13. Florida law excludes professional athletes from the scope of workers' compensation. FLA. STAT. §440.02(17)(c)(3). Having said that, courts are often called upon to address related issues.

bargaining agreement requires a team to "obtain workers' compensation coverage or guarantee equivalent benefits."[14] Moreover, establishing employee status can be an impediment for professional athletes engaged in some individual sports and non-professional athletes injured while playing in an employer sponsored sporting event.[15] For a discussion of the tests employed by courts to determine employee status, see the discussion in Chapter 2.04, *supra*.

Assuming an injured player is able to meet the threshold requirement — the existence of an employment relationship — a host of other issues may arise including: (1) whether the aggravation of a prior injury is compensable;[16] (2) the effect of a player's failure to market the player's residual value;[17] (3) a team's entitlement to a set off against workers' compensation benefits for payments made to a player;[18] and (4) notice requirements.[19] The following discussion addresses other salient issues, including: (1) whether an injury arising in contact sports, such as football and hockey, is accidental and falls within the scope of workers' compensation statutes; (2) recovery for cumulative trauma and jurisdictional issues;[20] (3) residency requirements and the

---

14. Tampa Bay Area NFL Football, Inc. v. Jarvis, 668 So. 2d 217, 218 (Fla. Ct. App. 1st Dist. 1996), *reh'g denied* (Mar. 5, 1996); Sielicki v. New York Yankees, 388 So. 2d 25, 25 (Fla. Ct. App. 1980) (holding that Yankees purchase of workers' compensation insurance negated the professional athlete exclusion in the state's workers' compensation statute).

15. For cases involving whether jockeys are employees, see Clark v. Industrial Commission, 297 N.E.2d 154 (Ill. 1973) (because of defendant's lack of control, jockey was not an employee); Moore v. Clarke, 187 A. 887 (Md. 1936) (finding jockey was not an employee); Munday v. Churchill Downs, Inc., 600 S.W.2d 487 (Ky. Ct. App. 1980) (applying right to control test in concluding jockey was not an employee). *But see* Isenberg v. Calif. Employment Stabilization Comm'n, 180 P.2d 11, 15–16 (Cal. 1947) (applying right to control test and concluding jockey was an employee); Gross v. Pellicane, 167 A.2d 838 (N.J. Super. 1961) (applying right to control test in finding jockey was an employee). For discussions of cases in which courts found employee status for non-professional athletes injured in a company sponsored sporting activities see, *e.g.*, Bogert v. E.B. Design Air, Inc., 833 N.Y.S.2d 279 (N.Y.A.D. 2007); Bd. of Educ. of City of Chicago v. Industrial Comm'n, 405 N.E.2d 783 (Ill. 1980); Lybrand, Ross, Bros. and Montgomery v. Industrial Comm'n, 223 N.E.2d 150 (Ill. 1967). *But see* Lindsay v. Public Service Co. of Colo., 362 P.2d 407, 412 (Colo. 1961) (game in which employee was injured was not connected to the employer's business).

16. Brinkman v. Buffalo Bills Football Club, 433 F. Supp. 699 (W.D.N.Y. 1977).

17. Hamilton v. Pro-Football, Inc., 823 S.E.2d 13, 20 (Va. Ct. App. 2019) (denying benefits where claimant, a professional football player, failed to market his residual value (*i.e.*, actively look for work) after recovering from his injury).

18. Dubinsky v. St. Louis Blues Hockey Club, 229 S.W.3d 126 (Mo. App. 2007); Smith v. Richardson Sports Ltd., 616 S.E.2d 245 (N.C. Ct. App. 2005) (discussing the amount of credit employer is entitled as an offset against workers' compensation benefits to be paid to a player); Pittsburgh Steelers, Inc. v. W.C.A.B. (*Williams*), 814 A.2d 788, 792 (Pa. Commw. 2002); Ladd v. Cincinnati Bengals, Inc., 1998 WL 140093 (Ohio Ct. App. 1st Dist. 1998) (team entitled to dollar-for-dollar offset from workers' compensation to be paid to player for any amounts paid to the player).

19. *See, e.g.*, Pittsburgh Steelers, Inc. v. W.C.A.B., 814 A.2d 788, 792 (Pa. Commw. 2002) (discussing purposes of notice requirement and finding notice to the team's trainer was sufficient notice to the employer); *see generally* LARSON'S WORKERS' COMPENSATION LAW § 126 (2019) (discussing the notice requirement); *see also* Adams v. N.Y. Giants, 827 A.2d 299 (N.J. Super. Ct. 2003) (discussing statute of limitations).

20. *See* Dandenault v. Workers' Comp. Appeals Bd., 728 A.2d 1001 (Pa. Commw. 1999).

enforceability of forum selection clauses; (4) the applicability of the fraudulent mis-representation and intentional injury exceptions; and (5) the applicability of the co-employee exception, particularly as it relates to team doctors.

[B] Accidental Injury Arising in the Course of Employment?

Once the employee requirement is satisfied, a claimant's entitlement to workers' compensation benefits turns on whether the debilitating injury occurred in the course of an athlete's employment.[21] If the injury occurred on a team's premises and during a workout or a game, it will be deemed to have occurred in the course of an athlete's employment.[22] In *Dandenault v. Workers' Comp. Appeals Bd.*,[23] the court found that an injury suffered by a player during his participation in a summer hockey league that was not required by his employer, was not within the scope of the employee's employment.

In contact sports, such as football and hockey, in which violence appears to be in-herent to the sport, an additional issue arises — was the injury accidental. Despite some outlying authority to the contrary,[24] courts have generally found that such in-juries are compensable.[25] Courts reject employers' arguments that the nature of sports such as football and hockey, in which violent collisions occur, negates the requirement that the injury be the result of an accident.[26] The court in *Pro-Football, Inc. v. Uh-lenhake*[27] articulated the rationale for the rule that injuries incurred during a football game are accidental even though there may be an elevated risk of injury given the nature of the game:

> The commission properly rejected this misguided notion and ruled that "[t]he nature of the employment and the foreseeability of a potential injury does not determine whether an injury sustained in the ordinary course of

---

21. *See* Pro-Football, Inc. v. Tupa, 14 A.3d 678, 680, 686–92 (Md. Spec. App. 2011), *aff'd*, 51 A.3d 544 (Md. 2012); Renfro v. Richardson Sports Ltd., 616 S.E.2d 317, 322–23 (N.C. App. 2005).

22. *See* Boscolo & Herz, *supra* note 5, at 17-8.

23. 728 A.2d 1001 (Pa. Commw. Ct. 1999); *see also* Robinson v. Dept. of Labor & Indus., 326 P.3d 744, 753–54 (Wash. Ct. App. 2014) (finding that player, who was injured in off-season tryout, could not recover workers' compensation because of an absence of an employment relationship and the injury did not occur in the course of the claimant's employment even though the NFL's Seattle Seahawks paid certain of the claimant's expenses related to his attendance and participation in the camp).

24. *See, e.g.*, Rowe v. Baltimore Colts, 454 A.2d 872 (Md. Spec. App. 1983) (holding injury to pro-fessional football player was not accidental); Palmer v. Kansas City Chiefs Football Club, 621 S.W.2d 350 (Mo. Ct. App. 1981).

25. *See e.g.*, *Tupa*, 14 A.3d at 678; *Renfro*, 616 S.E.2d at 317.

26. *Tupa*, 14 A.3d at 690–91; Albrecht v. Industrial Comm'n, 648 N.E.2d 923 (Ill. Ct. App. 2006); *Renfro*, 616 S.E.2d at 317; Pro-Football v. Uhlenhake, 558 S.E.2d 571 (Va. Ct. App. 2002); Norfolk Ad-mirals v. Jones, 2005 WL 2847392, at *1 (Va. Ct. App. 2005); *see also* Pro-Football v. McCants, 51 A.3d 586 (Md. Ct. App. 2012); Estate of Gross v. Three Rivers Inn Inc., 706 N.E.2d 741 (N.Y.A.D. 1998).

27. 558 S.E.2d 571 (Va. Ct. App. 2002).

an employee's duties is an accident." The business of Pro-Football is to engage in the activity of professional football. It employs individuals to constantly perform in a strenuous activity that has risks and hazards. As with coal miners, steel workers, firefighters, and police officers, who are covered by the [Workers' Compensation] Act, other classes of employees are regularly exposed to known, actual risks of hazards because "the employment subject[s] the employee to the particular danger." The commission correctly ruled that professional football players are not exempt from the coverage of the Act when they suffer injuries in the game they are employed to perform.[28]

Similar reasoning was used in a case involving a hockey player's eligibility for workers' compensation. In that case, *Norfolk Admirals v. Jones*,[29] the court upheld the finding of the workers' compensation commission, which wrote that because "fighting is an integral part of the game of hockey and ... claimant's job on employer's hockey team was to be an 'enforcer,'" the claimant's injury was accidental and occurred in the course of his employment.

[C] Recovery for Cumulative Trauma and Jurisdiction Issues

Professional athletes often claim that they are disabled and therefore entitled to workers' compensation as a result of cumulative trauma: "repeated shocks to the human frame over a period of time ultimately causing recognizable injury."[30] California's workers' compensation statute has been interpreted as permitting athletes to recover for cumulative trauma. In other states, cumulative injury is not a compensable injury under state workers' compensation statutes. Thus, in *Pro-Football v. Uhlenhake,* the court interpreted Virginia's statute as not encompassing injury resulting from cumulative injuries.[31]

Players' perceptions of California's workers' compensation statute as more generous, resulted in players on teams located outside of California seeking benefits under California's statute. Players argued that they fell within the scope of California's statute because they played games against California-based teams and the injuries incurred in those games contributed to their disability. These claims led to litigation regarding the enforceability of forum selection clauses as teams sought to require that players assert workers' compensation claims in the state in which the team was located.

In one such case, *Matthews v. NFL Management Council*,[32] a former NFL player sought to file a workers' compensation claim in California notwithstanding a forum selection clause stipulating that he assert any such claim in Tennessee, the state in

28. *Id.* at 576 (citations omitted).
29. 2005 WL 2847392 at *5 (Va. Ct. App. Nov. 1, 2005).
30. Boscolo & Herz, *supra* note 5, at 17-11, 17-12.
31. *Uhlenhake*, 558 S.E.2d at 578.
32. 688 F.3d 1107 (9th Cir. 2012).

which the team that he spent most of his career playing for, the Tennessee Titans, is located. An arbitrator enforced the forum selection clause, and the player sought to vacate the award on public policy grounds. On appeal, the player argued: "Matthews contends that California has an explicit, well-defined and dominant public policy militating against agreements that purport to waive an employee's right to seek California workers' compensation benefits before a California tribunal, no matter how tenuous the connection between California and the employee or the employment."[33] In upholding the arbitrator's award, the Ninth Circuit ruled that the forum selection clause was not void against public policy. It further stated: "[Matthews] has not shown that he falls within the category of employees to whom the 'no waiver' rule applies. He has thus not shown that the arbitration award is contrary to a clear, well-defined and dominant public policy of the state of California."[34] To curb the litigation, California passed a statute in 2013 that limits cumulative trauma claims to professional athletes in sports, including football, basketball, and ice hockey, who played more than two seasons during their career for a California-based team and did not play more than seven seasons for a team headquartered in another state.[35]

[D] The Co-Employee Bar on Employee Tort Actions against Third Parties

Generally, workers' compensation statutes bar an injured employee from asserting tort claims against a co-employee. In sports, the co-employee rule has been extended to bar injured players' malpractice lawsuits against team doctors, trainers, and coaches.[36] In *Stringer v. Minn. Vikings Football Club, LLC.*,[37] the court initially articulated the rationale for the co-employee rule: "[The legislature] was concerned that allowing an employee to sue a co-employee for simple negligence 'tends to shift tort liability from employer to fellow employee in a manner never intended by the workers'

---

33. *Id.* at 1111.

34. *Id.* at 1114; *accord* Kansas City Chiefs v. Allen, 2013 WL 1339820 (W.D. Mo. Mar. 30, 2013) (refusing to vacate finding of arbitration that choice of law and/or forum selection clause did not violate public policy); Atlanta Falcons Football Club LLC v. Nat'l Football League Players Ass'n, 906 F.2d 1278, 1286–87 (N.D. Ga. 2012) (upholding arbitration award enforcing choice of forum provision requiring players on Georgia-based NFL team, who sought to file workers' compensation claims in California, to assert such claims in Georgia and rejecting players' assertion the provision violated public policy); Cincinnati Bengals, Inc. v. Abdullah, 2013 WL 154077, *8–9 (S.D. Ohio Jan. 15, 2013) (affirming arbitrator's award upholding forum selection provision). *But see Tupa*, 14 A.3d at 686 (finding forum selection clause violated public policy).

35. West Ann. Cal. Labor Code § 600.5.

36. Ellis v. Rocky Mtn. Empire Sports, Inc., 602 P.2d 895 (Colo. Ct. App. 1979) (barring player's tort claim against a coach due in part to the co-employee doctrine).

37. 705 N.W.2d 746 (Minn. 2005); *accord* Daniels v. Seattle Seahawks, 968 P.2d 883, 885 (Wash. Ct. App. 1998); Lotysz v. Montgomery, 766 N.Y.S.2d 28 (N.Y. App. Div. 2003); Jones v. Bouza, 160 N.W.2d 881, 882 (Mich. 1968); *see also* Matthew J. Mitten, *Medical malpractice liability of sports medicine care providers for injury to, or death of, athlete*, 33 A.L.R. 5th 619 § 8 (1995).

compensation system.'"[38] In *Stringer*, the relevant statutory language provided: "A co-employee working for the same employer is not liable for a personal injury incurred by another employee unless the injury resulted from the gross negligence of the co-employee or was intentionally inflicted by the co-employee."[39] The court interpreted the language as providing that an injured player's tort claim will be subject to the co-employee rule unless: (1) the co-employee owed a duty to the claimant, the breach of which resulted in the claimant's injury; and (2) the injury resulted from the co-employee's gross negligence or intentional conduct. With respect to the first factor, the court stated a personal duty arises to an injured employee only where the co-employee: (1) "take[s] direct action toward or ... direct[s] another to ... take[] direct action toward the injured employee..., [and (2)] acted outside the course and scope of employment...."[40] The court concluded that the defendants, the head trainer, assistant trainer, and medical services coordinator, did not owe a personal duty to the deceased athlete because the services they provided were within the course and scope of their employment.[41]

Similarly, in *Hendy v. Losse*,[42] the court examined the language of a workers' compensation statute in concluding that co-employee tort immunity extended to a team physician. As was true in *Stringer*, the facts demonstrated that a doctor acted within the course of his employment in treating a football player's injuries. Therefore, the player's malpractice claim against the physician was barred. Addressing the co-employee rule, the court in *Brocail v. Detroit Tigers*,[43] stated: "If the [medical] malpractice of a fellow employee, no less than any other negligence of a fellow employee, gives rise to a compensable injury, then workmen's compensation stands as the sole recourse."[44]

[E] Intentional Conduct and Fraudulent Concealment Exceptions

[1] The Intentional Conduct Exception

Workers' compensation statutes commonly allow injured employees the right to pursue tort claims against employers if the employee can establish that the employer's

---

38. *Stringer*, 705 N.W.2d at 755.

39. *Id.* at 754.

40. *Id.* at 757 (citations omitted).

41. *Id.* at. 762; *see also* McLeod v. Blasé, 659 S.E.2d 727, 730–31 (Ga. App. 2008).

42. 819 P.2d 1 (Cal 1991); *accord* Daniels v. Seattle Seahawks, 968 P.2d 883, 885 (Wash. Ct. App. 1998); Lotysz v. Montgomery, 766 N.Y.S.2d 28 (N.Y. App. Div. 2003); *see also* Mitten, *supra* note 37, § 8; McLeod v. Blasé, 659 S.E.2d 727, 730–31 (Ga. App. 2008) (co-employee rule precluded a professional basketball player's malpractice claim against a certified athletic trainer employed by the N.B.A.'s Atlanta Hawks); *see also* Evans v. Arizona Cardinals Football Club, LLC, 262 F. Supp. 3d 935, 940–41 (N.D. Cal. 2017) (rejecting player's intentional misconduct claim).

43. 268 S.W.3d 90, 108 (Tex. Ct. App. 2008) (quoting Jones v. Bouza, 160 N.W.2d 881, 882.)(Mich. 1968)).

44. *Id.*

conduct, which caused the injury, was willful, deliberate or intentional. Players have attempted to circumvent the exclusivity of workers' compensation statutes by asserting the intentional conduct exception to workers' compensation statutes' preclusion of tort claims.[45] Before discussing the intentional conduct exception, it is important to note that not all workers' compensation statutes allow for the exception.[46] In *Brocail*,[47] discussed *supra*, the court provided guidance for determining if conduct is intentional:

> An employer is deemed to have intended to injure if he had actual knowledge that an injury was certain to occur and willfully disregarded that knowledge. Knowledge must be actual; constructive, implied, or imputed knowledge is not sufficient. 'A plaintiff may establish a corporate employer's actual knowledge by showing that a supervisory or managerial employee had actual knowledge that an injury would follow from what the employer deliberately did or did not do.'[48]

The court in *DePiano v. Montreal Baseball Club, Ltd.*,[49] adopted a similar standard for determining the applicability of the intentional conduct exception. The plaintiff, a minor league baseball player, sued his minor league club and the parent club, the Montreal Expos, alleging "negligence in their failure to provide timely and adequate medical care for his injury, and for requiring him to continue playing despite his injury."[50] The alleged consequence of the defendants' alleged negligence was aggravation of the plaintiff's injury and the end of his baseball career.[51] The court found that the plaintiff had not alleged facts sufficient to establish an intentional tort as defined in New York's Workers' Compensation Act. "In order to constitute an intentional tort, the conduct must be engaged in with the desire to bring about the consequence of the act. A mere knowledge and appreciation of a risk is not the same as the intent to cause injury."[52]

---

45. *Id.* at 108; *accord* DePiano v. Montreal Baseball Club, 663 F. Supp. 116, 117 (W.D. Pa. 1987) (concluding that "there is nothing in the evidence to indicate that the defendants' intention was to injure plaintiff. Negligence alone, no matter the degree, does not satisfy the intentional injury exception to the compensation bar.").

46. *See, e.g.*, Evans v. Arizona Cardinals Football Club, LLC, 262 F. Supp. 3d 935, 941 (N.D. Cal. 2017) (interpreting California's workers' compensation statute as encompassing intentional conduct claims and Wisconsin statute as limiting the intentional conduct exception to assault); Ellis v. Rocky Mountain Empire Sports, Inc., 602 P.2d 895, 898 (Colo. App. 1979) (interpreting Colorado workers' compensation statute as encompassing intentional tort claims); *see also Brocail*, 268 S.W.3d at 90 (recognizing intentional tort exception but concluding it was time-barred by statute of limitations).

47. 268 S.W.3d 90 (Tex. Ct. App. 1988).

48. *Id.* at 108 (citations omitted).

49. 663 F. Supp. 116 (W.D. Pa. 1987).

50. *Id.* at 117.

51. *Id.*

52. *Id.* at 117 (quoting Finch v. Swingly, 348 N.Y.S.2d 266 (A.D. 1973)). *But see* Bass v. World Wrestling Federation Entertainment, Inc., 129 F. Supp. 2d 491, 509 (E.D.N.Y. 2001) (wrestler's claims of intentional tort sufficient to survive motion for summary judgment).

[2] The Fraud Exception

Players have also asserted that an employer's fraud eliminates the workers' compensation bar to tort claims. In *Gambrell v. Kansas City Chiefs Football Club, Inc.*,[53] the player alleged that team medical doctors conducted a physical examination and determined he was physically fit to play football. The player further alleged this determination was false because, at the time of the examination, he was disabled due to preexisting injuries that rendered him unfit. Finally, he alleged the doctors knew or should have known that their representations as to his fitness were false.

The court began its analysis by stating that, notwithstanding workers' compensation statutes, an employee may sue its employer in tort for "wrongs not comprehended within the Workmen's Compensation Act, such as false imprisonment and defamation."[54] The court noted that this exception also applies to claims of fraud but also stated that the application of the rule is more difficult to assess in the context of fraud.[55] Quoting Lex Larson, that court stated:

> The cases involving allegations of deceit, fraud, and false representation can
> best be sorted out by distinguishing those in which the deceit precedes and
> helps produce the injury, and those in which the deceit follows the injury
> and produces a second injury or loss.[56]

Relying on Larson's analysis, the court ruled that cases falling within the first of the two categories do not give rise to the fraud exception. In contrast, cases falling with the second group, "are not precluded by the Workmen's Compensation Act because 'the alleged deceit has acted, not upon plaintiff's physical condition, but upon his legal rights under the compensation act.'"[57] It concluded that the player's claim was barred because the alleged fraud "merge[d] into the injury for which a compensation remedy is provided."[58]

Although a different approach was adopted by the court in *Evans v. Arizona Cardinals Football Club, LLC*,[59] the result was the same. Like the court in *Gambrell*, the *Evans* court stated that the fraud exception is very narrow. It interpreted California's workers' compensation statute as requiring an employee to establish: "(1) the [team] knew of his work-related injury, (2) the [team] concealed that knowledge from him, and (3) the injury was aggravated as a result of such concealment."[60] The court added that the exception does not apply if the employee is aware of the injury at all times. It concluded that plaintiff failed to present evidence that the team concealed knowledge

---

53. 562 S.W.2d 163 (Mo. Ct. App. 1978).
54. *Id.* at 165.
55. *Id.* at 166.
56. *Id.* (quoting LARSON'S WORKMEN'S COMPENSATION LAW § 68.32, at 13–22).
57. *Id.* at 166.
58. *Id.*
59. 262 F. Supp. 3d 935 (N.D. Cal. 2017).
60. *Id.* at 939.

of the player's ankle injury of which he was aware at all times.[61] With respect to the player's assertion that the team failed to apprise him of the risk that certain medication would aggravate his injury, the court stated: "Plaintiffs cite no authority for the proposition that merely concealing generalized risks associated with work-related substances that can aggravate a work-related injury—as opposed to concealing knowledge of the specific work-related injury itself—satisfies the first element of the fraudulent-concealment exception."[62]

§ 11.03 Liability of Physicians and Trainers

A team physician has dual responsibilities.[63] On the one hand, the physician is employed by the club or institution and is thereby under pressure to avoid "unnecessary restriction of athletic activity" of athletes.[64] On the other, a team physician owes a responsibility to protect the athlete's health.[65] Ultimately, however, the team physician's primary responsibility is to "provide medical treatment and advice consistent with an individual athlete's best health interest because there is a physician-patient relationship between them."[66]

As is true in medical malpractice cases generally, the liability of medical care providers in sport (*i.e.*, physicians and athletic trainers) will be determined on a case-by-case basis.[67] Assuming the existence of a physician-patient relationship,[68] courts tend to adopt either a general standard of care or a standard focused on the sports-related medical specialization. With respect to the former, the standard is whether the physician's services conformed to that of a "reasonably competent medical practitioner under similar circumstances."[69] With respect to the latter, the standard is

---

61. *Id.*

62. *Id.* at 939–40; *see also Brocail*, 268 S.W.3d at 110–11 (finding that player's fraud and concealment claims were barred by statute of frauds); Rivers v. New York Jets, 460 F. Supp. 1233, 1238 (E.D. Mo. 1978) (athlete's concealment claim was barred by N.Y. workers' compensation statute).

63. Matthew J. Mitten, *Team Physicians and Competitive Athletes: Allocating Legal Responsibility for Athletic Injuries*, 55 U. PITT. L. REV. 129, 138 (1993).

64. *Id.* at 140.

65. *Id.*

66. *Id.*

67. Mitten, *supra* note 37.

68. *See, e.g.*, Powell v. Voy, 1994 WL 621970 (N.D. Cal. Nov. 1 1994) (finding physician-client relationship is a prerequisite to imposing negligence liability on a physician); Martin v. Niagara Frontier Hockey Corp., 578 N.Y.S.2d 25 (N.Y. App. 1991) (holding that a physician was not liable for alleged failure to diagnose the severity of a hockey player's knee injury because of the absence of physician-patient relationship); Murphy v. Blum, 554 N.Y.S.2d 640, 642 (N.Y. App. 1990) ("Since [physician] was retained by the NBA solely for the purpose of advising it whether Murphy would be physically capable of performing his duties as a referee . . . , no physician-patient relationship existed. . . . in this case").

69. WALTER T. CHAMPION, JR., FUNDAMENTALS OF SPORTS LAW § 4.1 (2020); *see also* Fleischmann v. Hanover Ins. Co., 470 So. 2d 216, 217 (La. Ct. App. 1985) (electing not to recognize sports medicine as a subspecialty); Weiss v. Pratt, 53 So. 3d 395, 401 (Fla. Ct. App. 2011) (articulating the general standard for assessing whether a physician committed malpractice).

whether the physician's provision of services departed from the accepted or reasonable standard of sports medicine care.[70] It is also notable that courts, depending on the jurisdiction, will apply one of these standards on a national, regional or local basis.[71]

Assuming that an athlete's tort claim is not displaced by a workers' compensation statute in professional sports, athletes have pursued diverse medical malpractice claims against physicians and trainers. One such claim is that a physician and/or trainer misdiagnosed the nature and/or severity of an athlete's injury. In these cases, athletes invariably assert that the medical provider's negligent misdiagnosis of the athlete's physical condition during an exam or the provider's negligent treatment exacerbated an existing injury and/or created a permanent disability, which jeopardized the athlete's ability to continue to play a sport.[72] For example, in *Searles v. Trustee of St. Joseph's Coll.*, a college athlete alleged that an athletic trainer "negligently conducted a course of treatment ... that contributed to a worsening of [the college athlete's] condition"[73] Similarly, in *Wani v. George Fox University*,[74] the plaintiff athlete

---

70. *See* Wani v. George Fox Univ., 2019 WL 1339586, at *3 (D. Ore. Mar. 25, 2019) (articulating the applicable standard as "the standard of care required of a reasonable athletic trainer in the community"); Gibson v. Digiglia, 980 So. 2d 739, 744 (La. Ct. App. 2008) (holding that plaintiffs failed to "present[] any evidence to support a claim that Dr. Digiglia's actions fell below the standard of care for that alleged sub-specialty of physicians"); Gill v. Tamalpais Union High Sch. Dist., 2008 WL 2043239, at *22 (Calf. Ct. App. 1st Dist. May 14, 2008) (stating lower court did not err in giving a jury instruction stating: "You must determine the level of skill, knowledge and care that other reasonably careful athletic trainers would use in similar circumstances, based only on the testimony of the expert witnesses...."); Searles v. Trustees of St. Joseph's Coll., 695 A.2d 1206, 1210 (Me. 1997) (in athlete's suit against an athletic trainer, court states the applicable standard is whether the trainer "has the duty to conform to the standard of care required of an ordinary careful trainer"); Mikkelsen v. Haslam, 764 P.2d 1384, 1386 (Utah Ct. App. 1988) (defining the applicable standard as whether the orthopedist "depart[ed] from orthopedic medical profession standards); Classen v. Izquierdo, 520 N.Y.S.2d 999 (N.Y. Sup. Ct. 1987) (holding physician's duty is measured by whether conduct was in "accordance with good and accepted standards of medical care"); *see also* CHAMPION, *supra* note 69, §4.1; MITTEN, *supra* note 4, at 950–51.

71. CHAMPION, *supra* note 69,

72. *See, e.g.*, Sorey v. Kellet, 849 F.2d 960 (5th Cir. 1988) (deceased athlete's mother filed lawsuit for negligent treatment by physician and trainer; court dismisses action because defendants were entitled to qualified immunity); Brocail v. Anderson, 132 S.W.3d 552, 554–55 (Tex. Ct. App. 14th Dist. 2004) (alleging a doctor negligently failed to discover or treat a torn ligament in his elbow but case dismissed for lack of jurisdiction); Dailey v. Winston, 1986 WL 12063 (Oct. 28, 1986) (alleging misdiagnosis and negligent treatment); Lowery v. Juvenal, 559 S.W.2d 119 (Tex. Ct. App. 1977) (former college player alleged negligent treatment by physician and trainer, but action barred by statute of limitations); Rosensweig v. State, 158 N.E.2d 229 (N.Y. App. Div. 1958) (alleging doctor's pre-fight examination of a boxer negligently failed to discover a pre-existing brain injury).

73. 695 A.2d 1206 (Mo. 1997). The athlete also alleged that the trainer failed to provide him with information sufficient to inform the coach that the athlete should not play basketball and that if he played before his injury completely healed, he would likely suffer permanent injury.

74. 2019 WL 1339586 (D. Ore. Mar. 25, 2019); Gillespie v. Southern Utah State College, 669 P.2d 861 (Utah 1983) (athlete alleged athletic trainer negligently treated the athlete's ankle injury); Speed v. State, 240 N.W.2d 901 (Iowa 1976) (finding doctors liable for malpractice in negligently treating athlete's injury); Toppel v. Redondo, 617 N.E.2d 403 (Ill. Ct. App. 1993) (athlete alleging negligent treatment of a knee injury).

alleged that the head football trainer's negligence in failing to diagnose and properly treat his thumb injury exacerbated the impact of the injury.[75]

Athletic trainers, in particular, have been sued for the negligent failure to refer athletes to physicians.[76] In such cases, athletes allege the trainer's negligence caused extended treatment and/or further injury. In *Jarreau v. Orleans Parish School Board*,[77] the athlete alleged, in part, that the trainer's delay in referring him to a physician to treat an arm fracture exacerbated the injury, extended his recovery period, and limited the results of treatment. The court noted that the trainer should have recognized his limitations and sought "expert medical advice for [his] players in the face of continuing complaints involving pain and swelling."[78]

Krueger v. San Francisco Forty Niners is representative of another type of claim athletes assert against physicians — failure to disclose accurate information regarding an athlete's medical condition.[79] There, a football player alleged that a physician, who treated Forty Niners players and had performed knee surgery on the plaintiff, fraudulently concealed the "true nature and extent of the damage to his left knee"[80] and of the adverse effects of the steroids he was required to take following the surgery.[81] The court characterized the dispositive issue as one involving informed consent, which it described as the duty imposed on physicians to "disclose to the patient all information necessary to make a knowledgeable decision about proposed treatment."[82] It stated that a critical element of a concealment claim is the intent, which it stated occurs when at "the time information was concealed defendant had the intent to induce plaintiff to adopt or abandon a course of action."[83] Reversing the lower court's judgment in favor of the team, the court concluded, "we think the record unequivocally demonstrates that, in its desire to keep appellant on the playing field, respondent consciously failed to make full, meaningful disclosure to him respecting the magnitude of the risk he took in continuing to play a violent contact sport with a profoundly damaged left knee."[84] The court also stated that "'[p]atients are generally persons un-

75. *Id.* at *3; *see also* Gardner v. Holified, 639 So. 2d 652 (Fla. Ct. App. 1994) (alleging physician negligently failed to discover the extent of an athlete's injury or to prescribe appropriate treatment); Martin v. Niagara Frontier Hockey Corp., 578 N.Y.S.2d 25 (N.Y. App. Div. 1991) (rejecting hockey player's claim that physician negligently failed to diagnosis nature of injury).

76. *See, e.g.*, Pinson v. State of Tennessee, 1995 WL 739820 (Tenn. Ct. Ap. Dec. 12, 1995) (trainer liable in negligence for failing to convey information regarding athlete to physician).

77. 600 So. 2d 1389, 1391 (La. Ct. App. 1992).

78. *Id.* at 1393.

79. 234 Cal. Rptr. 579 (Cal. Ct. App. 1987); *see also* Martin v. Casagrande, 559 N.Y.S.2d 68 (N.Y. App. Div. 1990) rejecting plaintiff's fraudulent concealment of medical information claim); *Anderson*, 132 S.W.3d at 554–55 (alleging team doctor intentionally failed to inform of the full extent of athlete's injury, but case dismissed for lack of jurisdiction).

80. *Krueger*, 234 Cal. Rptr. at 583.

81. *Id.* at 581.

82. *Id.* at 583.

83. *Id.*

84. *Id.* at 584.

learned in medical sciences, ...' and consequently are entitled to rely upon physicians for full disclosure of material medical information."[85]

§ 11.04 Compensation for Concussion-Related Injuries

[A] Introduction

A concussion is a form of traumatic brain injury that "may result from shaking the brain within the skull and, if severe, can cause shearing injuries to nerve fibers and neurons."[86] The adverse health consequences of a concussion may be temporary such as headaches, nausea, blurred vision, slurred speech, difficulty with coordination, and loss of concentration.[87] Longer term health diagnoses which have been linked to concussions include dementia and chronic traumatic encephalopathy ("CTE").[88] One court described CTE as "a neuropathological diagnosis that currently can only be made post mortem.... CTE involves the build-up of 'tau protein' in the brain, a result associated with repetitive head trauma."[89] One study estimated that 1.6 to 3.8 million sport and recreation-related concussions occur each year.[90] Unsurprisingly, athletes in both contact and non-contact sports and at all levels of sports — youth, high school, college, and professional — have sought recovery for the harmful health consequences of concussions. This chapter examines the types of claims athletes have asserted, against whom those claims have been asserted, and the defenses raised by defendants. It also discusses global settlement agreements that the NFL, NHL, and NCAA have entered into with athletes.

[B] High School and Youth Organizations

Under a primary assumption of the risk standard (see discussion in Chapter 10.02, *supra*), courts have ruled that an athlete sustaining a concussion from playing sports such as soccer and football is an inherent risk of participation. Therefore, in order to recover, a plaintiff must establish that the defendant's conduct enhanced the risk

---

85. *Id.*

86. Nitra Agarwal, Rut Thakkar & Khoi Tran, *Sports-related Head Injuries*, American Association of Neurological Surgeons, https://www.aans.org/Patients/Neurosurgical-Conditions-and-Treatments/Sports-related-Head-Injury (last visited Oct. 19, 2021).

87. *In re* Nat'l Football League Players Concussion Injury Litig., 821 F.3d 410, 421 (3d Cir. 2016) (hereinafter "*NFL Concussion Litigation*"); Richardson v. Southeastern Conference, 2020 WL 1515730, at *3 (N.D. Ill. Mar. 30, 2020).

88. *NFL Concussion Litigation*, 821 F.3d at 421; *Richardson*, 2020 WL 1515730, at *3.

89. Archie v. Pop Warner Little Scholars, Inc., 2019 WL 8230854 at *3 (C.D. Calif. Dec. 27, 2019); *Richardson*, 2020 WL 1515730, at *3–4.

90. Van Pelt et al., *A cohort study to identify and evaluate concussion risk factors across multiple injury settings; findings from the CARE Consortium*, 6 INJURY EPIDEMIOLOGY 1 (2019), https://injepi journal.biomedcentral.com/track/pdf/10.1186/s40621-018-0178-3.pdf.

of injuries related to concussions. In high school, athletes frequently assert that a coach's conduct, such as demanding or permitting an athlete to return to play after the athlete had sustained an initial concussion, enhanced the inherent risks. Absent such a showing, it is highly unlikely that an injured athlete will be able to recover. Accordingly, one court relied on primary assumption of the risk in finding that a plaintiff failed to present a prima facie case that the college and other defendants owed him a duty of care for injuries sustained as a result of a concussion.[91] In validating the defense, the court reasoned that neither the college nor the referee had reason to know that plaintiff had sustained an initial concussion.[92]

Liability may be imposed, however, where a coach's decision to require or permit an athlete to continue to play a sport after a concussion aggravated the effects of the concussion. In *Fiedler v. Stroudsburg Area School District*,[93] the court dismissed claims against a high school principal and district superintendent who were not directly involved in a coach's alleged insistence that a player who suffered a concussion return to practice thereby enhancing the risk of adverse effects of a concussion suffered during the practice. The court ruled, however, that the plaintiff's claim could proceed against a physical education teacher who allegedly required the player to practice even though she had suffered a concussion and thereby enhanced the risk associated with another concussion that she sustained.[94] In *Randall v. Michigan High School Athletic Association*,[95] the court ruled that a state statute intended to protect athletes who suffer concussions imposed a duty on a coach to immediately remove a concussed athlete from play.

Similarly, in *Mayall v. USA Water Polo, Inc.*,[96] a court permitted plaintiff's claim to move forward against a coach. There, the athlete was a member of a water polo team under the auspices of USA Water Polo.[97] Although the court adhered to California precedent established in *Kahn* (see Chapter 10.05[B][1], *supra*), which applied the primary assumption of the risk standard to claims by athletes against their coaches, the court reversed the trial court's dismissal of the athlete's claim against her coach.

---

91. Calderone v. Malloy College, 112 N.Y.S.3d 191 (N.Y. App. Div. 2019).
92. *Id*. at 193.
93. 427 F. Supp. 3d 539, 551 (M.D. Pa. 2019).
94. *Id*. at 551.The court stated the following elements of state created danger liability:
   1) the harm ultimately caused was foreseeable and fairly direct;
   2) a state actor acted with a degree of culpability that shocks the conscience;
   3) a relationship between the state and the plaintiff existed such that the plaintiff was a foreseeable victim of the defendant's acts, or a member of a discrete class of persons subjected to the potential harm brought about by the state's actions, as opposed to a member of the public in general; and
   4) a state actor affirmatively used his or her authority in a way that created a danger to the citizen or that rendered the citizen more vulnerable to danger than had the state not acted at all.
Id. at 550.
95. 2020 WL 6811661 (Mich. Ct. App. Nov. 19, 2020).
96. 909 F.3d 1055 (9th Cir. 2018).
97. *Id*. at 1058.

It found that the coach's decision to permit the athlete to return to play following a concussion contributed to the adverse health effects the athlete sustained. The court stated:

> Mayall concedes that H.C.'s first injury, incurred when she was hit in the face during the first game, was inherent in the game of water polo. However, the secondary injury, incurred when H.C. was hit in the head again after being returned to play, was not inherent in the game. "[D]azed" from the initial blow, H.C. swam to the side of the pool to speak with her coach…, but she received no guidance or instruction that would have removed her from play. As the Court of Appeal wrote in *Wattenberger*, "It requires no depth of analysis to recognize that when one injures himself, further use of the injured member will likely exacerbate the condition."[98]

According to the court, the coach's decision enhanced the concussion-related risk inherent in the athlete's participation in sport.[99] The court also agreed with the plaintiffs' allegations that "USA Water Polo voluntarily undertook the duty of ensuring that 'proper safety precautions have been taken to protect the personal welfare of … athletes,'" and committed itself to "creating a healthy and safe environment of all of [its] members."[100] The court concluded that USA Water Polo's awareness of the severe risk of repeat concussions and the need to implement a policy that addressed when the removal from play of a player who suffered a head injury, if true, would amount to gross negligence (*i.e.*, "an extreme departure from the ordinary standard of care") under California law.[101]

A plaintiff's claim will not survive dismissal if the injured athlete fails to present evidence establishing the requisite causation between their participation and alleged concussion-related injury.[102] Courts have articulated a two-pronged evidentiary standard relating to causation: "players would need to show both general causation (that repetitive head trauma is capable of causing ALS, Alzheimer's, and the like), and specific causation (that the brain trauma suffered by a particular player in fact caused his specific impairments)."[103] In *Adams v. BRG Sports, Inc.*,[104] a group of former high school football players alleged they sustained head injuries as a result of design defects in the helmets they wore when they played.[105] Plaintiffs alleged that defendant's design of both its newer and older lines of helmets failed to adequately protect them from concussive and sub-concussive blows to the head.[106] Plaintiffs also alleged that warn-

---

98. *Id.* at 1063–64 (quoting Wattenbarger v. Cincinnati Reds, Inc., 28 Cal. App. 4th 746, 33 Cal. Rptr. 2d. 732 (Cal. Ct. App. 1994)). *But see* Dugan v. Thayer Academy, 2015 WL 3500385 (Mass. Super. Ct. May 27, 2015) (electing to adopt a negligence rather than a recklessness standard).

99. *Id.*

100. *Id.* at 1066–68.

101. *Id.* at 1068.

102. *Archie*, 2019 WL 8230854.

103. *Id.* at 4.

104. 2021 WL 1517881 at *1 (N.D. Ill. Apr. 17, 2021).

105. *Id.* at *1.

106. *Id.*

ings placed on the helmets were deficient because the warnings failed to prompt plaintiffs "to avoid playing football altogether, choose a safer helmet, or play football differently."[107] The court ruled that the plaintiffs' failure to proffer evidence to establish general and specific causation warranted dismissal of their negligence- and strict liability-based design defect claims.[108]

Defendant school districts have also successfully applied qualified immunity to defeat tort claims premised on allegations that the conduct of coaches (*e.g.*, not requiring a plaintiff to wear a helmet or allowing a plaintiff to resume activities after having suffered a concussion) enhanced the risk of concussion-related injuries.[109] Courts have also rejected athletes' effort to fashion section 1983, Fourteenth Amendment substantive due process claims premised on a state-created danger theory of liability.[110]

[C] College Athletics

In 2011, Adrian Arrington, a former college football player, filed a putative class action against the NCAA alleging breach of contract, negligence, and unjust enrichment relating to the organization's alleged inadequate handling of college athlete concussions and the risk associated with concussions.[111] Several similar lawsuits filed after the *Arrington* suit were consolidated, and the plaintiffs were ultimately certified as a class.[112] The parties eventually reached a settlement agreement that was approved in 2019. The class action consisted of two subclasses, one for contact sport athletes and one for noncontact sport athletes who played at NCAA member colleges or universities prior to the Settlement's "Preliminary Approval Date."[113] The contact sports subclass included athletes who participated in football, lacrosse, wrestling, ice and field hockey, soccer, and basketball.[114] The noncontact sports subclass consisted of athletes who had participated in college golf, softball, baseball, volleyball, and track and field.[115]

The most salient terms of the settlement agreement include the following: (1) The NCAA will spend $70 million to fund a Medical Monitoring Fund to be used for ex-

---

107. *Id.* at *2. Without addressing the merits of plaintiffs' failure to warn claim, the court refused to grant defendants' motion for summary judgment because of their failure to address the causation element in their briefs. *Id.* at *7.

108. *Id.* at *6.

109. *See, e.g.*, Hickey v. Enterline, 304 F. Supp. 3d 456 (M.D. Pa. 2018); Aspinall v. Murrieta Valley Unified Sch. Dist., 2018 WL 1163182 (Cal. Ct. App. 4th Dist. Mar. 6, 2018); Maselli *ex rel.* Maselli v. Reg'l Sch. Dist. #10, 2018 WL 3337053 (Conn. Super. Ct. June 11, 2018); *see also* Stahr v. Lincoln Sudbury Regional High Sch. Dist., 102 N.E.3d 995, 1001 (Mass. Ct. App. 2018) (coach's alleged failure to implement proper concussion protocols fell within statutory provision immunizing public employees from liability for injuries to athletes).

110. *See e.g.*, *Hickey*, 304 F. Supp. 3d at 460–63.

111. *In re* Nat'l Collegiate Athletic Ass'n Student-Athlete Concussion Injury Litig., 332 F.R.D. 202, 208 (N.D. Ill. 2019); Complaint, Arrington v. NCAA, 2011 WL 4374451 (N.D. Ill. Sept. 12, 2011).

112. *In re Nat'l Collegiate Athletic Ass'n*, 332 F.R.D. at 208.

113. *Id.* at 210.

114. *Id.*

115. *Id.* at 210–11.

penses relating to, *inter alia*, screening questionnaire costs and medical evaluations;[116] (2) the monitoring program will last for 50 years;[117] and (3) during the first 10 years, the NCAA will provide an additional $7 million to fund concussion-related research.[118] The plaintiffs agreed to release certain claims but to retain others. According to the settlement, "class members agree[ed] ... to release" past, present, and future claims "'seeking damages for medical monitoring ... related to concussions or sub-concussive hits or contact ... sustained during participation in NCAA-sanctioned sports as an NCAA student-athlete.'"[119] Class members also agreed to release "all claims 'brought or pursued on a class-wide basis..., including but not limited to tort claims, claims for breach of contract, breach of statutory duties, actual or constructive fraud, negligence, conspiracy, misrepresentation, fraudulent inducement, fraudulent concealment, breach of fiduciary duty, compensatory and punitive damages, injunctive or declaratory relief.'"[120] Class members, however, retained the right to pursue "individual personal or bodily injury claims" or "personal or bodily injury class claims brought on behalf of a class of persons who allege injury resulting from their participation in a single NCAA-sanctioned sport at a single-NCAA member school" as well as "class claims that do not relate in any way to medical monitoring or medical treatment of concussions or sub-concussive hits or contact."[121]

Subsequent to the settlement, former college athletes have filed lawsuits against the NCAA and conferences seeking damages for alleged concussion-related illnesses. As could be expected, former athletes have asserted claims sounding in tort, specifically negligence[122] and fraudulent concealment. In *Richardson v. NCAA*,[123] a former University of Florida football player sought recovery against the Southeastern Conference ("SEC") and the NCAA for injuries allegedly arising from head trauma resulting from concussions and sub-concussive impact occurring during games and practice. He argued that the NCAA and SEC failed to adopt adequate concussion safety protocols and return-to-play guidelines during the period in which he played.[124] The plaintiff further alleged that the NCAA and SEC had knowledge of the causes and effects of concussions and concealed that information from plaintiffs. According to the plaintiffs, if they had that information they would have discontinued playing or

---

116. *Id.* at 211.

117. *Id.*

118. *Id.*

119. *Id.* at 213.

120. *Id.*

121. *Id.*

122. *See e.g.*, Greiber v. NCAA, 2017 WL 6940498 (N.Y. Sup. Ct. Sept. 8, 2017) (alleging NCAA was negligent in failing to "implement adequate regulations in order to address the detection, treatment, and prevention of head injuries"); *see also* Bradley v. NCAA, 464 F. Supp. 3d 273, 296 (D.D.C. 2020) (plaintiff asserted negligence claim against university but claim was barred by pre-injury waiver of liability athlete had signed; court also dismissed plaintiff's negligence claim against the NCAA because plaintiff offered no evidence that defendant assumed risk of alleged negligence healthcare that the plaintiff alleged resulted in her injury).

123. 2020 WL 1515730 (N.D. Ill. Mar. 30, 2020).

124. *Id.* at *1.

taken additional precautions following head trauma.[125] The court concluded plaintiff had raised a fraudulent concealment claim sufficient to survive the defendants' motion to dismiss.[126]

Plaintiffs have also turned to contract- and restitution-based claims in seeking recovery for concussion-related injuries.[127] In *Richardson*, the court concluded that plaintiff's allegations that the promise in his contract with the University of Florida that he would comply with NCAA rules created an express or implied promise by the NCAA to safeguard plaintiff's health.[128] The court also ruled that plaintiff had alleged facts sufficient to warrant rejection of the NCAA's defense that plaintiff was not the third party beneficiary of the contract between the NCAA and the University of Florida. The court concluded NCAA bylaws requiring colleges to abide by NCAA regulations "expressed specific commitments by the NCAA and UF in the regulation of UF's football program to safeguard the mental and physical well-being of its football players."[129] The court dismissed, however, the plaintiff's unjust enrichment claim against the NCAA because his pleading failed adequately to assert that "he directly conferred a benefit upon the NCAA."[130] The court was also unpersuaded by the plaintiff's argument that the NCAA indirectly benefited because the athlete's participation on the Florida football team generated revenues, which in turn provided revenue to the NCAA via its broadcasting and merchandising contracts and ticket sales.[131]

[D] Professional Sports — NFL and NHL Concussion Litigation

[1] NFL Concussion Litigation

In 2011, the first NFL concussion-related lawsuit in the United States was filed by 73 former professional football players in a California court against the NFL and

---

125. *Id.* at *7.

126. *Id.* at *10; *accord* Rose v. NCAA, 346 F. Supp. 3d 1212, 1227 (N.D. Ill. 2018); *see also* NCAA v. Finnerty, 170 N.E.3d 1111 (Ind. Ct. App. 2021) (in three consolidated cases, plaintiffs alleged fraudulent concealment claims against the NCAA).

127. In *Rose*, 346 F. Supp. 3d 1212, former football players sought to hold the NCAA liable for injuries resulting from repetitive brain trauma, including concussions. The players asserted negligence, fraudulent concealment, breach of express and implied contract, and restitution claims. The action was not adjudicated on the merits but was resolved pursuant to the comprehensive settlement. *In re NCAA Student-Athlete Concussion Injury Litigation*, 332 F.R.D. at 202.

128. *Richardson*, 2020 WL 1515730, at *11; *accord* Langston v. Mid-Atlantic Intercollegiate Athletics Ass'n, 448 F. Supp. 3d 938, 954–55 (N.D. Ill. 2020); Weston v. Big Sky Conference, 466 F. Supp. 3d 896, 909 (N.D. Ill. 2020); *see also Rose*, 346 F. Supp. 3d at 1227–28 (denying defendants' motion to dismiss the breach of express contract claim but granting dismissal of plaintiff's implied contract claim).

129. *Richardson*, 2020 WL 1515730, at *12; *accord Langston*, 448 F. Supp. 3d at 956; *Weston*, 466 F. Supp. 3d at 909.

130. *Richardson*, 2020 WL 1515730, at *13; *accord*, *Rose*, 346 F. Supp. 3d at 1229.

131. *Id. But see Weston*, 466 F. Supp. 3d at 911.

Riddell, Inc., a manufacturer of sports equipment.[132] Within a year, 96 similar lawsuits had been filed against the NFL and Riddell.[133] Plaintiffs in these and many subsequent lawsuits, including the first class action suit filed in 2012, alleged claims of fraudulent concealment, negligent misrepresentation, negligence, negligent hiring and retention, strict liability for design and manufacturing defects, failure to warn, wrongful death, and loss of consortium.[134] The gist of the retired players' lawsuits is that the "NFL failed to take reasonable actions to protect them from the chronic risks of head injuries in football."[135] The players also claimed that Riddell should be liable for the defective design of their helmets.[136] In addition, the former players "alleged that the NFL had a duty to provide players with rules and information to protect them from the health risks — both short and long-term — of brain injury, including Alzheimer's disease, dementia, depression, deficits in cognitive functioning, reduced processing speed, loss of memory, sleeplessness, mood swings, personality changes, and CTE."[137] Facing a multitude of lawsuits in 2011, the NFL and Riddell sought to consolidate the suits. In June 2012, the defendants' motions to consolidate were granted.[138]

The plaintiffs were certified as a class and reached a settlement agreement.[139] In 2016, the Third Circuit Courts of Appeals affirmed both the district court's certification of the class and approval of the settlement,[140] which the court described as having the following three components: (1) an uncapped Monetary Award Fund that provides compensation for retired players who submit proof of certain diagnoses (claims are likely to exceed $1 billion); (2) a $75 million Baseline Assessment Program that provides eligible retired players with free baseline assessment examinations of their objective neurological functioning; and (3) a $10 million Education Fund to instruct football players about injury prevention.[141] The class, which was approved by the district and appellate courts, consists of NFL players who retired prior to July 7, 2014.[142] Pursuant to the settlement, class members agreed to "release all claims and actions against the NFL 'arising out of, or relating to, head, brain and/or cognitive injury, as well as any injuries arising out of, or relating to, concussions and/or sub-concussive events,'" including claims relating to CTE.[143] The Settlement's release does not foreclose actions by players who opted out of the settlement, current NFL players, and players

---

132. *In re* Nat'l Football League Players Concussion Injury Litig., 821 F.3d 410, 421 (3d Cir. 2016) [hereinafter "*NFL Concussion Litigation*"].

133. Lawrence G. Cetrulo, *Sports player concussion litigation,* 4 Toxic Torts Litigation Guide § 38.10 (Dec. 2020).

134. *Id.*; Mitten et al., *supra* note 4, at 953–54.

135. *NFL Concussion Litigation*, 821 F.3d at 421.

136. *Id.*

137. *Id.*

138. *Id.*

139. *Id.* at 423.

140. *Id.* at 448.

141. *Id.* at 423.

142. *Id.* at 425.

143. *Id.*

who retired subsequent to July 7, 2014.[144] At the time of the Third Circuit's approval of the settlement, the class consisted of 5,000 former players. As of October 25, 2021, the number of registered class members stood at over 20,500.[145]

Subsequent to the approval of the settlement, the district court and the Settlement Fund's Special Master have resolved issues including: appeals of determinations finding that players failed to meet the eligibility standards for receiving compensation;[146] the sufficiency of a player's efforts to opt out;[147] whether the settlement forecloses loss of consortium claims (which it does);[148] and the entitlement of attorneys to fees.[149]

[2] NHL Concussion Litigation

Like their NFL counterparts, professional hockey players sued their league for concussion-related injuries. Hockey players have sought recovery for the "pathological and debilitating effects of brain injuries caused by concussive and sub-concussive impacts sustained by former NHL players during their professional careers."[150] Plaintiffs seek liability based on the NHL's alleged knowledge of the adverse health consequences of brain trauma and the league's failure to warn players.[151] Plaintiffs also allege that the league's promotion of violence during games contributed to brain trauma.

Following a federal court's denial of plaintiffs' request for class certification,[152] 146 former hockey players entered into a $18.9 million settlement with the NHL. Under the settlement, these former players were to receive at least $22,000 each. An administrative fund will pay up to $75,000 per player for costs relating to medical treatment for players demonstrating certain neurological conditions.

Players opting out of the settlement have filed lawsuits asserting state-law claims against the NHL sounding in negligence, failure to warn, concealment, and misrep-

---

144. *Id.*

145. NFL Concussion Settlement, *Program Statistics*, https://www.nflconcussionsettlement.com/ (last visited Oct. 30, 2021).

146. NFL Concussion Settlement, *Rules Governing Registration and Appeals*, https://www.nfl concussionsettlement.com/Docs/NFL_Rules_Governing_Registration_Appeals.pdf (last visited Oct. 29, 2021).

147. *In re* Nat'l Football League Players Concussion Injury Litig., 2019 WL 95917 (E.D. Pa. Jan. 3, 2019); *In re* Nat'l Football League Players Concussion Injury Litig., 2019 WL 188431 at *8–9 (E.D. Pa. Jan. 14, 2019).

148. *In re* Nat'l Football League Players Concussion Injury Litig., 2019 WL 188431 at *8–9.

149. *In re* Nat'l Football League Players Concussion Injury Litig., 2021 WL 3744100 (E.D. Pa. July 29, 2021).

150. *In re* Nat'l Hockey League Players Concussion Injury Litig., 327 F.R.D. 245, 249 (D. Minn. 2018).

151. *Id.*

152. *Id.* at 267.

resentation.[153] One the NHL's primary defenses is that plaintiffs' claims are preempted by Section 301 of the National Labor Relations Act subjecting the claims to dismissal.[154] In *Carcillo v. NHL*, the court stated that the preemption of a state claim pursuant to Section 301 depends on whether the claim is "inextricably intertwined with consideration of the terms of the labor contract."[155] The court held that the plaintiff's negligence action that was premised on the League's alleged glorification and promotion of violence, "which increased the risk of concussion injuries[,]" was rooted in the common law duty "to refrain from unreasonably harming others...."[156] Therefore, Section 301 did not preempt plaintiff's negligence claim.[157] The court also held, however, that to the extent the plaintiff's negligence claim was premised on the NHL's alleged "'*self-imposed and self-declared duties*' to keep Plaintiffs safe" and to advise them of concussion-related risk, the claim was subject to preemption.[158] The court concluded it would be impossible to define the scope of the NHL's duties without interpreting the NHL Collective Bargaining Agreement.[159] Because the NHL's alleged duty to disclose would arise from the League's fiduciary or contractual obligations, the court ruled it too was preempted.[160] It reached the same conclusion regarding plaintiff's failure to warn claim after finding that any duty to warn would necessarily be derived from the contractual agreement between the plaintiff and the NHL.[161]

§ 11.05 Defective Equipment and Products Liability

[A] Introduction

Athletes have sought compensation from sellers (*e.g.*, retailers), distributors, and manufacturers for injuries arising from defective equipment.[162] Their product liability

---

153. Carcillo v. NHL, 529 F. Supp. 3d 768 (N.D. Ill., 2021).

154. *Id.* Another defense that has been successfully asserted by the NHL and other defendants is lack of personal jurisdiction. *See e.g., In re* National Hockey League Players' Concussion Injury Litigation, 2019 WL 5088516 (D. Minn. Oct. 10, 2019); Peluso v. New Jersey Devils, LLC, 2018 WL 4054108 (D. Minn. Aug. 24, 2018).

155. *Carcillo,* 529 F. Supp. 3d at 778–79.

156. *Id.* at 779–80.

157. *Id.; accord* Montador v. NHL, 2020 WL 11647730 at *6 (N.D. Ill., Nov. 24, 2020).

158. *Carcillo,* 529 F. Supp. 3d at 780.

159. *Id.; accord Montador,* 2020 WL 11647730, at *4; Boogaard v. NHL, 211 F. Supp. 3d 1107, 1112 (N.D. Ill. 2016).

160. *Carcillo,* 529 F. Supp. 3d at 780.

161. *Id.* at 781–82. The court also found that plaintiff's duty to disclose misrepresentation claims were preempted because any such duty would have to be premised on the parties' contractual relationship and this would require consideration of the CBA. *Id.* at 782–83.

162. *See* RESTATEMENT (THIRD) OF TORTS: PRODUCTS LIABILITY § 1 [hereinafter RESTATEMENT OF TORTS].

actions have been brought pursuant to tort (*i.e.*, negligence and strict liability) and contract (*i.e.*, breach of express and implied warranties)[163] theories based on design defects, manufacturing defects, and inadequate warnings.[164] The alleged defective products for which athletes seek recovery encompass an array of sports equipment including helmets, protective eye wear, hockey sticks, baseball bats, and golf-related equipment.[165] Whether the action sounds in tort or contract, the ultimate question addressed in such cases is whether the product's condition causes it to "fail[] to perform the normal, anticipated, or specified use to which the manufacturer intends that it be put in a reasonable, adequate, and safe manner and is thus unreasonably dangerous to a plaintiff."[166]

Although the substantive claims vary, the core allegation is that an injury was caused by a defective product. As discussed below, in a negligence action, the plaintiff must show that the defendant "deviated from accepted standards of conduct in its actions or failure to act."[167] For strict liability actions, liability ensues when a plaintiff demonstrates that a manufacturer placed a product on the market, which was defective and thereby unreasonably dangerous.[168] Unlike negligence, the plaintiff need not prove the manner in which the product became defective only that it is defective.[169] Thus, the culpability of the defendant is not material. Even under a negligence theory, however, increasingly the plaintiff is not required to "prove any specific act of negligence on the part of a defendant, provided direct and circumstantial evidence permits the inference that the accident was caused by a defect."[170] One commentator states that the differences between a negligence and strict liability-based design defect claim is negligible.

> In design defect actions, negligence and strict liability theories overlap as both theories require the plaintiff to prove that the product was defectively designed, exposing the user to an unreasonable risk of harm. As proper design is an issue of reasonable fitness, strict liability adds little to negligence by the manufacturer.... In the past, courts made distinctions between strict liability claims and negligence claims within this category. As reflected in the Restatement Third, Torts: Products Liability, however, strict liability and

---

163. *Id.*

164. Theodore Z. Wyman, *Cause of Action for Injuries Caused by Defective Helmets*, 68 CAUSES OF ACTION 2d 373 (2021); RESTATEMENT OF TORTS § 1, cmt. 1 (recognizing the three ways in which products can be defective); Sollami v. Eaton, 772 N.E.2d 215, 219 (Ill. 2002) (identifying the three types of defects in a case involving an alleged defective trampoline).

165. *See generally* CHAMPION, *supra* note 69, § 5:2.

166. Wyman, *supra* note 164, § 4.

167. Charles J. Nagy, Jr., *Overview of Products Liability Law*, AM. L. PROD. LIAB. 3d § 1:10 (Aug. 2021).

168. Wyman, *supra* note 164, § 8.

169. *Id.* §§ 3:4 & 1:13 (noting that strict liability has been adopted in most states by common law or statute).

170. *Id.* § 14:1.

negligence theories are, in reality, quite similar and often indistinguishable in courts' analyses of particular facts....[171]

Unlike tort-based negligence and strict liability product defect actions, a breach of warranty action is premised on contract and arises as a consequence of representations (*i.e.*, an express warranty) made by a seller or by operation of law (*i.e.*, implied warranties) even under circumstances in which a seller, or in some instances a manufacturer, is unaware of the defective nature of the goods. It is important to note that the three above-described differing substantive grounds for recovery are not mutually exclusive and should be viewed as alternative grounds for recovery.[172]

[B] Negligence and Strict Liability

[1] Design Defects

A product liability action premised on a product's defective design requires a plaintiff to show: (1) the existence of a defect that existed when the product left the defendant's possession, (2) the injury was a type that the manufacturer reasonably could have anticipated, and (3) the design defect proximately caused the plaintiff's injury.[173] Notwithstanding a lack of unanimity by courts regarding the standard to employ in determining if a defective design exists, courts have gravitated toward two tests. The reasonable expectations test focuses on whether the "product perform[s] as safely as an ordinary consumer would expect when used in an intended and reasonably foreseeable manner."[174] Other courts have adopted a balancing test that asks

---

171. *Id.* § 5; *see, e.g.*, Jackson v. E-Z-GO Division of Textron, Inc., 326 F. Supp. 3d 375, 391 (W.D. Ky. 2018) (stating that "[u]nder Kentucky law, a plaintiff can bring a defective design claim under a theory of strict liability or negligence, the foundation of both theories being that the product is 'unreasonably dangerous.'"); Rogers *ex rel.* Rogers v. K2Sports LLC, 348 F. Supp. 3d 892, 905 (W.D. Wis. 2018) (identifying strict liability and negligence products liability claims as distinct and alternative forms of recovery but noting there is considerable overlap between the doctrines and that a plaintiff can rely on the same proof to establish a negligence claim that was relied to establish a strict liability claim); DuRocher v. Riddell, Inc., 97 F. Supp. 3d 1006, 1015 (S.D. Ind. 2015) (stating the state of Washington has, by statute, merged strict liability, negligence, and warranty claims into a single cause of action for product-related harm); Valente v. Textrone, Inc., 931 F. Supp. 2d 409, 437 (E.D.N.Y. 2013) (appearing to have merged strict products and negligence theories of liability).

172. *See* Nagy, *supra* note 167; Wyman, *supra* note 164; *see also* Monell v. Scooter Store, Ltd., 895 F. Supp. 2d 398, 410–11 (N.D.N.Y. 2012) (describing the substantive theories on which a plaintiff can base a products liability action).

173. *Id.* at 12; Nagy, *supra* note 167, § 1.26; CHAMPION, *supra* note 69; *see e.g.*, Sexton *ex rel.* Sexton v. Bell Helmets, Inc., 926 F.2d 331, 336 (4th Cir. 1991) (stating proof of defect is essential element of a design defect action); *Valente*, 931 F. Supp. 2d at 438 (plaintiff failed to establish causation element of design defect cause of action); Stringer v. NFL, 749 F. Supp. 2d 680 (S.D. Ohio) (discussing the causation requirement); Bennett v. Schuberth Werk GMBH & Co., 2002 WL 32153356, at *3–4 (D. Mont. 2002) (articulating the elements of a design defect cause of action and stating that causation is an element whether a claim sounds in product liability, negligence or warranty and plaintiff's failure to establish causation warrants dismissing the cause of action).

174. In *McCullough v. Nike, Inc.*, 2010 WL 2560407, at *5 (Cal. Ct. App. June 28, 2010), a case involving an alleged defectively designed baseball helmet, the court stated that the consumer expectation

whether the "benefits of the challenged design outweigh the risk of danger inherent in the design."[175] A few courts appear to have applied both tests.[176]

As it relates to causation, the Restatement (Third) of Torts provides that determining whether a product defect caused harm to a person involves applying the prevailing rules and principles governing causation in tort law, generally.[177] In short, a plaintiff must show that it is more likely than not that the conduct of the defendant was "a cause in fact of the injury; a mere possibility of causation is not enough."[178]

The elements of a defective design action were addressed in *A.K.W. ex rel. Steward v. Easton Bell Sports*,[179] in which a ninth-grade football player suffered a head injury after being tackled by an opposing player. The alleged design defect involved the padding used in the helmet worn by the boy at the time of his injury.[180] The court identified three elements of a design defect claim: (1) a defectively designed product; (2) that is unreasonably dangerous due to the defect; and (3) causation.[181] The court stated that a plaintiff successfully carries its burden of proving the existing defect by showing a "feasible design alternative," which it defined as "a design that would have to a reasonable probability prevented the harm without impairing the utility, usefulness, practicality or desirability of the product to users or consumers."[182] It added that the testimony of plaintiff's experts as to an alternative padding used by defendant's

---

test is used only in those cases in which the *everyday experience* of a user would lead to a conclusion that a product's design "violated minimum assumptions, and thus is defective regardless of expert opinion about the merits of the design." *See also* Horan v. Reebok Int'l Ltd., 2011 WL 4538038, at *2 (D. Conn. 2011) (acknowledging the two tests and discussing when the reasonable expectation test is applicable in the context of a strict liability action relating to a defectively designed product).

175. *Jackson*, 326 F. Supp. 3d at 391 (adopting risk-utility test); *McCullough*, 2010 WL 2560407; *Horan*, 2011 WL 4538038, at *2 (acknowledging the two test and discussing when the reasonable expectation test is applicable in the context of a strict liability action relating to a defectively designed product). This definition is consistent with that of the Restatement of Torts § 2(b), which provides that a design defect arises "when the foreseeable risks of harm posed by the product could have been reduced or avoided by the adoption of a reasonable alternative design by the seller or other distributor, or a predecessor in the distribution, and the omission of the alternative design renders the product not reasonably safe." *See also Valente*, 931 F. Supp. 2d at 437 (in case involving a golf cart, court discusses elements of a design defect cause of action); Mize v. HJC Corp., 2006 WL 2639477, at *5 (N.D. Ga. Sept. 13, 2006) (applying a balancing test that weighs "whether the design chosen [by the manufacturer] was a reasonable one from among the feasible choices of which the manufacturer was aware or should have been aware"; the court noted the significance of determining whether "the existence and feasibility of a safer and equally efficacious design diminishes the justification for using a challenged design").

176. *See e.g.*, *Valente*, 931 F.Supp.2d at 437; *DuRocher*, 97 F. Supp. 3d at 1006 (applying both).

177. RESTATEMENT OF TORTS § 15.

178. Wyman, *supra* note 164, § 7; *see also* A.K.W. v. Easton-Bell Sports, Inc., 454 F. App'x 244, 249 (5th Cir. 2011) (articulating the elements of a design defect cause of action, including causation); *Monell*, 895 F. Supp. 2d at 411 (applying a risk-benefit approach which includes a causation requirement).

179. 454 F. App'x 244 (5th Cir. 2011).

180. *Id.* at 246.

181. *Id.* at 247.

182. *Id.* at 248; *accord Jackson*, 326 F. Supp. 3d at 391 (requiring plaintiff provide "evidence of some practicable, feasible, safer, alternative design.").

competitors was instrumental in establishing the existence of an alternative feasible design.[183] On the issue of whether the design was unreasonably dangerous, the court found that evidence of an alternative feasible design used by the defendant's competitors was also proof that the defendant should have known about the dangerous condition of its helmet.[184] Turning to the issue of causation, the court stated, "[t]he plaintiff must introduce evidence … that it is more likely than not that the conduct of the defendant was a cause in fact of the result — [a] mere possibility of such causation is not enough."[185]

A different result was reached in *Stringer v. NFL*,[186] where a court rejected the plaintiff's design defect claim. The widow of a NFL player, who suffered a heat stroke during training camp and later died, alleged the football helmet and shoulder pads worn by the player acted as "an insulating blanket preventing evaporation and heat dissipation."[187] The court identified the following three elements of a cognizable design defect claim: "(1) that the defendant's product was in a defective condition unreasonably dangerous for its intended use; (2) that the defect existed when the product left the defendant's control; and (3) that the defect was the proximate cause of the injury sustained."[188] The court noted that Minnesota courts have adopted a reasonable-care balancing test, which it identified as an objective standard for determining if a product is designed defectively.[189] It stated that this test "'focuses on the conduct of the manufacturer in evaluating whether its choice of design struck an acceptable balance' between factors such as the likelihood and gravity of harm and the precautions necessary to prevent that harm."[190] The court concluded that the plaintiff failed to proffer evidence of "an alternative feasible design" that would have made the helmets and shoulder pads at issue safer to address heat-related illnesses.[191]

---

183. *Id.*; *see Valente*, 931 F. Supp. 2d at 437 (adopting a risk-benefit test for design defect determination and requiring plaintiff establish the "feasibility and efficacy of an alternative design, unless 'a reasonable alternative design is both obvious to and understandable by, a layperson.'"); *Sexton*, 926 F.2d at 337 (stating that in weighing the evidence of a design defect, "a product can only be defective if it is imperfect when measured against a standard existing at the time of sale or against reasonable consumer expectations held at the time of sale"); Lynn *ex rel.* Lynn v. Yamaha Golf-Car Co., 894 F. Supp. 2d 606, 628 (W.D. Pa. 2012) (in design defect case, "plaintiff must prove the availability of a technologically feasible and practical alternative design that would have reduced or prevented the harm sustained by the plaintiff"; finding plaintiff presented such evidence); *Mize*, 2006 WL 2639477, at *5 (applying a balancing test that weighs "whether the design chosen [by the manufacturer] was a reasonable one from among the feasible choices of which the manufacturer was aware or should have been aware"; the court notes the significance of determining whether "the existence and feasibility of a safer and equally efficacious design diminishes the justification for using a challenged design.").

184. *A.K.W.*, 454 F. App'x at 248.

185. *Id.* at 249.

186. 749 F. Supp. 2d 680 (S.D. Ohio 2009).

187. *Id.* at 684.

188. *Id.* at 695 (internal citations omitted).

189. *Id.*

190. *Id.* at 696.

191. *Id.* at 697; *see also Valente*, 931 F. Supp. 2d at 437 (holding plaintiff failed to present evidence of a feasible alternative design); *Mize*, 2006 WL 2639477 at *5–6 (rejecting plaintiff's claim because

In *Lynn ex rel. Lynn v. Yamaha Golf-Car Co.*,[192] recovery was sought pursuant to strict liability theory for injuries sustained by a minor child injured by an allegedly defective golf cart. On the issue of whether the design was defective, the court likewise adopted the risk-benefit balancing approach that focuses on whether there existed a "feasible and practical alternative design."[193] Adopting the Restatement (Third) of Torts elements of a strict liability products claim,[194] the court stated liability will be imposed on a defendant who is "[o]ne engaged in the business of selling or otherwise distributing products who sells or distributes a defective product ... for harm to persons or property *caused by the defect*."[195] On causation, the court stated that a plaintiff carries its burden by showing that the defect was a substantial factor in causing the plaintiff's injury.[196]

The elements of a design defect claim were also addressed in *Rogers ex rel. Rogers v. K2 Sports, LLC.*[197] In a case involving an alleged defective ski helmet, the court stated five elements of a strict products liability action: "(1) the product was defective; (2) the defect rendered the product unreasonably dangerous; (3) the defect existed when the product left the control of the manufacturer; (4) the product reached the consumer without substantial change; and (5) the defect caused the claimant's damages."[198] As for causation, the court stated that the relevant inquiry is whether the plaintiff can show that the "helmet had a design defect that caused [plaintiff's] injuries to be worse than they would have been without the defect."[199]

[2] Manufacturing Defects

The essence of a manufacturing defect is that the product is flawed and thus failed to perform as expected because of an error in its manufacture.[200] In *Derienzo v. Trek Bicycle Corp.*,[201] the court described a manufacturing defect as occurring from a "flaw

---

he failed to present evidence of an alternative feasible design); Wyman, *supra* note 164, §5 (stating plaintiff must establish a reasonable alternative design and that its omission makes the "product not reasonably safe"); *see* CHAMPION, *supra* note 69.

192. 894 F. Supp. 2d 606 (W.D. Pa 2012).

193. *Id.* at 628.

194. *Id.* at 628.

195. *Id.* (quoting the RESTATEMENT OF TORTS §1).

196. *Id.* at 637; *see also* Hauter v. Zogarts, 534 P.2d 377 (Cal. 1975). *But see* Patch v. Hillerich & Bradsby Co., 257 P.3d 383, 389 (Mont. 2011) (stating in a failure to warn case a more flexible approach to causation that "can be satisfied by evidence indicating that a warning would have altered the plaintiff's use of the product or prompted the plaintiff to take precautions to avoid the injury.").

197. 348 F. Supp. 3d 892 (W.D. Wis. 2018).

198. *Id.* at 901–03; *see also Patch*, 257 P.3d at 383 (stating similar elements in a case involving an alleged defective aluminum bat); *Sollami*, 772 N.E.2d at 219 (stating elements of a strict products liability action).

199. *Id.* at 902.

200. Wyman, *supra* note 164, §8; *see* Everett v. Bucky Warrant, Inc., 380 N.E.2d 653, 660 (Mass. 1978) (differentiating design and manufacturing defect claims).

201. 376 F. Supp. 2d 537 (S.D.N.Y. 2005).

that results from the manufacturer's plans not being carried out correctly, usually caused by an error during the product's manufacture or assembly."[202] In determining if a product is defective due to a manufacturing error, courts most frequently use one of two tests to assess whether the plaintiff has a cognizable action: did the product "deviate from its specifications or planned output" or did the product "fail to conform to the great majority of otherwise identical products manufactured in accordance with the same design by the same manufacturer."[203] In addition, the plaintiff must establish that the manufacturing defect was the cause of her injuries and the product was defective when it left the defendant's possession or control.[204]

In cases involving alleged manufacturing defects, there is considerable overlap between strict liability and negligence. In the latter, however, the salient issue is whether the manufacturer used reasonable care in the manufacture of the product.[205] Thus, the focus is on the manufacturer's fault. Under strict liability, however, the critical inquiry is whether the product is defective and thereby unreasonably dangerous.[206] In *DuRocher v. Riddell, Inc.*,[207] the court dismissed without prejudice the plaintiff's manufacturing defect claim.[208] The court stated that plaintiff failed to show that a manufacturer of helmets deviated materially from its "design specifications or performance standards…, or deviated in some material way from otherwise identical units of the same product line as required" by the relevant state statute.[209] In *Derienzo*, the court stated that the "crux of a strict liability manufacturing defect claim is the product's failure to perform as expected due to an error in the manufacturing process that resulted in a defect."[210]

[3] Failure to Warn and Inadequate Warning

A duty is imposed on manufacturers and sellers to warn potential users of the latent dangers associated with a product's use and to instruct them on how to properly use a product. Notes one commentator, "[t]he warning will be inadequate if it does not specify the risk presented by the product, it is inconsistent with how the products would be used, it does not provide the reason for the warnings, or if the warnings do not reach foreseeable users."[211] The Restatement (Third) of Torts further provides that a product: "is defective because of inadequate instructions or warnings when

---

202. *Id.* at 560; Lynch v. Trek Bicycle Corp., 2011 WL 1327032, at *3 (S.D. N.Y. Mar. 20, 2011) (similarly describing a manufacturing defect).

203. Wyman, *supra* note 164, §8 (adding that the "two tests are, at their core, deviation-from-the norm evaluations, based upon consumer expectancy that mass-produced products do not differ from their counterparts in ways that make them more dangerous than other").

204. *Id.*; *Derienzo*, 376 F. Supp. 2d at 560.

205. Wyman, *supra* note 164, §8.

206. *Id.*

207. 97 F. Supp. 3d 1006 (S.D. Ill. 2015).

208. *Id.*

209. *Id.* at 1023.

210. *Derienzo*, 376 F. Supp. 2d at 560.

211. CHAMPION, *supra* note 69.

the foreseeable risks of harm posed by the product could have been reduced or avoided by the provision of reasonable instructions or warnings by the seller or other distributor, or a predecessor in the commercial chain of distribution, and the omission of the instructions or warnings renders the product not reasonably safe."[212] The duty also requires the inclusion of "adequate instructions for the safe use of the product."[213] In addition, the duty to warn and whether the warning provided is adequate must be viewed within the context of the knowledge of those reasonably expected to use the product.[214]

In *Lynn*, the court provided the following guidance on determining if the plaintiff carries its burden of proof:

> [A] plaintiff must prove that adequate instructions or warnings were not provided and the omission of such warnings, which could have reduced or avoided the foreseeable risks of harm posed by the product, not only renders the product not reasonably safe but caused the plaintiff's harm. The test is one of reasonableness for judging the adequacy of product instructions and warnings. In making such an assessment, courts "[m]ust focus on various factors, such as content and comprehensibility, intensity of expression, and the characteristics of expected user groups."[215]

In *Stringer*,[216] the court stated that whether the defendant had a duty to warn hinges on:

> [W]hether the risk is reasonably foreseeable to the manufacturer. In determining whether the duty exists, the court goes to the event causing the damage and looks back to the alleged negligent act. If the connection is too remote to impose liability as a matter of public policy, the courts then hold there is no duty, and consequently no liability. On the other hand, if the consequence is direct and is the type of occurrence that was or should have been reasonably foreseeable, the courts then hold as a matter of law a duty exists.[217]

The court added there is no duty to warn of obvious risks.[218] The *Stringer* court found that a duty to warn existed because generalized knowledge that wearing a football helmet and shoulder pads would make the wearer hotter is different from the specific knowledge that such items worn under hot and humid conditions while a player is

---

212. RESTATEMENT OF TORTS § 2(c); *see also Patch*, 257 P.3d at 389 (in a strict liability action, stating elements of defect arising from a failure to warn or an inadequate warning).
213. Nagy, *supra* note 167, § 1.27.
214. *Id.*
215. *Lynn*, 894 F. Supp. 2d at 631–32, 639.
216. *Stringer*, 749 F. Supp. 2d at 680.
217. *Id.* at 687 (quoting German v. F.L. Smithe Mach. Co., 395 N.W.2d 922, 924 (Minn. 1986)).
218. *Id.; see also Sollami*, 772 N.E.2d at 219–23 (discussing open and obvious risk doctrine in case involving alleged defective trampoline).

engaged in strenuous activities could cause heat exhaustion and stroke.[219] The court concluded: "It was reasonably foreseeable to Defendants that a user of their helmets and shoulder pads during extremely hot and humid conditions might suffer from a heat stroke."[220]

The court also addressed the issue of causation. The court stated that in order to establish causation, the plaintiff was required to show that had a warning been given, the alleged injury would not have occurred.[221] This requires a showing that the warning would have resulted in a change in the injured party's behavior. In concluding that a warning would not have been relied on so as to cause a change in the player's behavior, the court relied on evidence demonstrating that the player would have continued to practice and participate in training camp.[222] The court ruled, however, that there were issues of material fact as to whether the warning would have changed the behavior of coaches and trainers.[223]

The court in *Mohney v. USA Hockey, Inc.*[224] addressed the plaintiff player's burden in establishing a cognizable strict liability failure to warn claim related to a helmet and mask. The court stated that the elements of a products liability action asserting an alleged inadequate warning are the same whether or not the action sounds in negligence or strict liability.[225] These are: (1) the manufacturer had a duty to warn; (2) the duty was breached; and (3) such breach was the cause of the plaintiff's injuries.[226] As it relates to the breach of the duty, the court stated: "The adequacy of such warnings is measured not only by what is stated, but also by the manner in which it is stated. A reasonable warning not only conveys a fair indication of the nature of the dangers involved, but also warns with the degree of intensity demanded by the nature of the risk. A warning may be found to be unreasonable in that it was unduly delayed, reluctant in tone or lacking in a sense of urgency."[227] The court added that proximate cause can be rebutted where the evidence established that the plaintiff did not read the warnings.[228]

---

219. *Stringer*, 749 F. Supp. 2d at 689.

220. *Id.* at 690; *see also Rogers*, 348 F. Supp.3d at 904 (stating that "the missing warning is a substantial factor in causing injury if a reasonable person would have heeded the warning and as a result avoided injury").

221. *Id.* at 691.

222. *Id.* at 691–92.

223. *Id.* at 692.

224. 300 F. Supp. 2d 556 (N.D. Ohio 2004).

225. *Id.* at 578.

226. *Id.* at 578; *see also* Arnold v. Riddell, Inc., 882 F. Supp. 979, 989 (D. Kan. 1995) (discussing evidence that establishes an inadequate warning); Westry v. Bell Helmets, Inc., 487 N.W.2d 781 (Mich. Ct. App. 1992) (finding factual circumstances supported finding of no duty to warn).

227. *Id.* at 578.

228. *Id.* For other cases involving an alleged failure to warn or inadequate warning involving sporting equipment, see *DuRocher*, 97 F. Supp. 3d at 1006 (alleged failure to warn of long-term risk associated with repeated head trauma); *Patch*, 257 P.3d at 389 (discussing elements of failure to warn claim); *Derienzo*, 376 F. Supp. 2d at 566 (discussing elements of failure to warn action); *Westry*, 457 N.W.2d at 783 (discussing elements of failure to warn claim).

[C] Warranty Claims

In addition to tort claims, athletes have asserted express and implied warranty claims to recover compensation for injuries for allegedly defective equipment. An express warranty arises when a seller makes an affirmation of fact or promise, rather than a statement of opinion,[229] which is a part of the basis of the bargain of the transaction.[230] A breach occurs when the product fails to conform to the affirmation of fact or promise and proximately causes the alleged injury.[231]

Injured players have also alleged breach of the implied warranty of merchantability and the implied warranty of fitness for particular purpose. A cognizable breach of implied warranty of merchantability arises when a plaintiff establishes that a merchant sold goods that were not merchantable at the time of sale, the defect or other condition of the goods proximately caused injury to the plaintiff or its property,[232] and the plaintiff timely notified the seller of the breach of warranty.[233] At a minimum, this warranty requires that goods be fit for their ordinary purpose. In *Valente v. Textron, Inc.*,[234] the court noted that a breach of implied warranty claim, unlike a strict products liability claim, "does not require a risk-utility balancing analysis, and, instead, only requires that the plaintiff prove that the product was not 'reasonably fit for the ordinary purpose for which it was intended.'"[235] The warranty of merchantability is also breached if the goods are not properly labeled, including providing appropriate warnings given the nature of the product.[236] The warranty of fitness for particular purpose arises when the seller knows or has reason to know of the buyer's particular purpose for goods and the buyer relies on the seller's skill or judgment.[237]

In *Hauter v. Zogarts*,[238] the plaintiff asserted breach of warranty claims in addition to a strict liability claim. A father purchased a device intended to assist his son in

---

229. *See e.g.*, Bell Sports, Inc. v. Yarusso, 759 A.2d 582 (Del. 2000) (finding that seller's statement that liners of helmets would reduce the risk of head injuries from blows gave rise to an express warranty). *But see* Wojcik v. Borough of Manville, 71 U.C.C. Rep. Serv. 2d 19 (N.J. Super. Ct. App. Div. 2010) (holding seller's statement could not provide basis for breach of express warranty claim because statements were opinions rather than affirmations of fact or promise); Masters *ex rel.* Masters v. Rishton, 863 S.W.2d 702 (Tenn. Ct. App. 1992) (concluding no cognizable breach of warranty claim arose where the plaintiff did not purchase a helmet from the defendant but borrowed it).

230. U.C.C. § 2-313. *See also* Salk v. Alpine Ski Shop. Inc., 342 A.2d 622, 625–26 (R.I. 1975) (finding that in the absence of affirmative of fact or promise no guarantee was given that could create an express warranty).

231. U.C.C. § 2-313.

232. *See* Trust Dept. of First Nat. Bank of Santa Fe, v. Burton Corp., 2013 WL 4884483, at *6 (D. Colo. Sept. 11, 2013) (discussing proximate causation); Jenish v. Monarch Velo LLC, 2007 WL 1364789 (E.D. Mich. May 9, 2007) (discussing the same).

233. Phillips v. Restaurant Management Corp., 552 S.E.2d 686 (N.C. App. 2001).

234. 931 F. Supp. 2d 409 (E.D.N.Y. 2013).

235. *Id.* at 439.

236. *See id.* at 439 (while dismissing plaintiff's failure to warn claim, recognizing such a claim can be premised on breach of an implied warranty of merchantability).

237. U.C.C. § 2-315; Filler v. Raytex Corp., 435 F.2d 336 (7th Cir. 1970).

238. 534 P.2d 377 (Cal. 1975).

improving the latter's golf play. The son was seriously injured while using the device. The court found that representations regarding the equipment's safety constituted an actionable express warranty rather than a mere statement of opinion.[239] Turning to plaintiff's claim that the product's defective design breached the implied warranty of merchantability, the court stated that design of the product rendered it unfit for its ordinary purpose and the product failed to conform to the representation of fact on the container or label, which constitute two of the ways in which the warranty of merchantability may be breached.[240] The plaintiff's breach of warranty claim was premised on the failure to warn of the dangers of using the device when the ball was not hit properly.[241]

When a plaintiff alleges breach of warranty claims arising from defective equipment, the defendant will likely assert a range of defenses. Sellers are likely to turn to language which effectively disclaims the implied warranties.[242] In addition, a seller is likely to assert other defenses available to sellers sued for breach of warranty, including that the transaction did not involve a contract for sale, a lack of privity, product misuse, the buyer's failure to comply with its obligations to notify a seller of breach, and the expiration of the statute of limitations.[243] The court in *Hemphill v. Sayers* addressed availability to defendants of two of these defenses.[244] The case involved a college football player who alleged he suffered a spinal injury as a result of a defective helmet. The court held that defendants, including the athletic director, head football coach and trainer could not be held liable under a breach of implied warranty theory because they were not sellers.[245] It also concluded that the helmet manufacturer was shielded from liability for breach of an implied warranty of merchantability because of an absence of privity. The court held that the plaintiff was not within the chain of distribution that the pertinent U.C.C. Article 2 privity provision was intended to protect.[246]

239. *Id.* at 383–84.
240. *Id.* at 385–86.
241. *Id.* at 385–86; *see also* Taub v. Cornell Univ., 1998 WL 187401, at *11 (N.D.N.Y. Apr. 15, 1998) (in case involving alleged defective rim of basketball hoop, court discussed differences between strict liability and breach of warranty claims); *Filler*, 435 F.2d at 336 (finding sunglasses designed for baseball player that shattered when batted ball hit plaintiff player in the eye breached an implied warranty of fitness for particular purpose). *But see* Lister v. Bill Kelley Athletic, Inc., 485 N.E.2d 483 (Ill. Ct. App. 1985) (rejecting athlete claims of a defective design and a failure to warn that helmet would not protect against injuries suffered by plaintiff).
242. U.C.C. §2-316.
243. Butler v. BRG Sports, LLC, 141 N.E.3d 1104 (Ill. App. 2019).
244. 552 F. Supp. 685 (S.D. Ill. 1982).
245. *Id.* at 689.
246. *Id.* at 692–93. *But see Filler*, 435 F.2d at 336 (stating privity not required for a breach of warranty claim in Indiana).

Part VI

Intellectual Property Issues in Sport

Chapter 12

Intellectual Property

§ 12.01 Introduction

In the early days of sport, the only way to experience a sporting event was to view it in person. Those days, however, are in the past. In the 21st century, radio, television, and digital platforms make sporting events widely available to the public. These sports programming delivery systems have transformed the economic realities of the sports industry. While peanuts, Cracker Jack, and other concession stand favorites still drive revenue, broadcasting rights have become the principal revenue drivers in the sports industry.[1] The NFL began the trend toward league-wide television broadcasting contracts in 1962 with its $4.65 million contract with CBS.[2] Club owners had no idea how profitable broadcasting rights would come to be. In 2021, the NFL finalized broadcasting agreements, valued at a total of $113 billion,[3] with NBC, CBS, ESPN/ABC, Fox, and Amazon all slated to begin in 2023 and run through 2033.[4] Other major professional sports leagues, which followed the NFL's lead into broadcasting partnerships, have found them similarly profitable. The NBA and MLB also receive over a billion dollars annually from their broadcasting deals.[5] The NCAA, too, has derived substantial revenue from broadcasting agreements.[6]

These extraordinarily lucrative broadcasts are the intellectual property of the sports organizations, and the agreements licensing them out are tightly structured and,

---

1. Gregory Bailey, *Streaming is the Name of the Game: Why Sports Leagues Should Adapt to Consumers and Follow Ad Dollars Towards Live Streaming*, 26 JEFFREY S. MOORAD SPORTS L.J. 323, 332 (2019).

2. JIM ROONEY, A DIFFERENT WAY TO WIN: DAN ROONEY'S STORY FROM THE SUPER BOWL TO THE ROONEY RULE 37 (2019).

3. H.J. Mai, *New $113 Billion NFL Media Rights Deal Gives Fans More Options to Watch Games*, NPR (Mar. 19, 2021), https://www.npr.org/2021/03/19/979178471/new-113-billion-nfl-media-rights-deal-gives-fans-more-options-to-watch-games.

4. *Id.*

5. *See* BROADCASTING RIGHTS REVENUE OF SELECTED SPORTS LEAGUES WORLDWIDE IN 2019, https://www.statista.com/statistics/1120170/broadcasting-rights-sports-by-league/ (last visited Aug. 27, 2021) (noting that NHL and MLS soccer broadcasting deals are modest by comparison, each totaling in the low hundreds of million); *see also* Mai, *supra* note 3.

6. REVENUE OF THE NCAA FROM TELEVISION BROADCAST PAYMENTS AND LICENSING RIGHTS FROM 2010 TO 2025, https://www.statista.com/statistics/219608/ncaa-revenue-from-television-rights-agreement/ (last visited Aug. 27, 2021).

obviously, implicate intellectual property law. However, the implications of intellectual property law borne of the dissemination of sports programming go beyond the broadcasts themselves. Wide exposure has increased the fan base and prompted a corresponding increased desire among fans to affiliate with their favorite teams by wearing supportive team paraphernalia and replica uniforms. These items feature league and team trademarks, which are also protected intellectual property.

This chapter examines three major categories of intellectual property rights and protections: those relating to publicity, trademarks, and sports broadcasting.

§ 12.02 Athlete Publicity Rights

[A] Introduction

Being a high-profile athlete brings with it the consequent ability to leverage celebrity into money eclipsing even the highest potential salary. That ability rests upon publicity rights, which protect the commercial value of a person's image. Even athletes who are essentially unrecognizable and have a minimal commercially viable "brand" on their own benefit from these rights when they are grouped together with those of star athletes and jointly marketed as a whole. Players unions (*e.g.*, the National Football League Players Association and Women's National Basketball Players Association) have taken this group-marketing path. Seizing opportunities to market a league's entire player population, players associations have created an additional dimension to athlete publicity rights, proving them useful for star players and marginal players alike.

Athlete publicity rights are a critical component of intellectual property in the sports industry, and it is important to understand the body of law that creates them.

[B] Foundations of the Right of Publicity

The foundation of an athlete's right of publicity lies in the common law. In particular, it lies in the common law right to privacy and the tort of defamation.

[1] Defamation

Professional and high-level amateur athletes' personal and professional lives are often scrutinized in the media. In some cases, that which is spoken and written about such athletes is potentially defamatory. Although judicial definitions of defamation vary, the following definition is representative:

> Defamation requires: "(a) a false ... statement concerning another; (b) an unprivileged communication to a third party; (c) fault amounting.... to negligence on the part of the publisher; and (d) either actionability of the statement irrespective of special harm or the existence of special harm caused by the publication."[7]

---

7. RESTATEMENT (SECOND) OF TORTS § 558 (1977).

An oral defamatory statement constitutes slander, while a written defamatory statement constitutes libel. Whether oral or written, however, athlete defamation cases are notoriously difficult to win. This is the case for many reasons, most notably the United States Supreme Court's 1964 decision in *New York Times v. Sullivan*.[8] Athletes are generally considered public figures, and *Sullivan* and its progeny create a heightened burden of proof in defamation cases brought by public figures.[9] A public figure must show by "clear and convincing evidence" (which is a higher standard than the "preponderance of the evidence" standard generally used in civil cases) that the statement in question was made with "actual malice."[10] This requires showing that the defendant knew the statement was false or acted with reckless disregard as to its potential falsity.[11] The actual malice requirement channels a First Amendment freedom of expression sensibility into defamation analysis, and the supporting policy rationale is clear. Meeting this more onerous burden of proof is particularly difficult for athletes, because much of the commentary regarding them is opinion-based, and the law does not want to chill such commentary.[12] Thus, a play-by-play announcer saying, "that quarterback just threw the worst pass I have ever seen," is unlikely to trigger any serious defamation concerns. If the announcer, however, said "that quarterback just threw the worst pass I have ever seen, and he has obviously taken a bribe to lose this game," liability would be a possibility if the quarterback could meet the above-described burden.

The "actual malice" burden is a heavy one, and defendants are often able to derail suits at the motion to dismiss stage when plaintiffs fall short of creating an inference that defendants acted with "actual malice." In *Zimmerman v. Al Jazeera America, LLC*,[13] however, MLB players Ryan Zimmerman and Ryan Howard were successful in securing denial of Al Jazeera's motion to dismiss in a case that involved the network's documentary titled, "The Dark Side: Secrets of the Sports Dopers."[14] The film displayed producers' "efforts to 'catch' on film individuals who purport to distribute [performance-enhancing drugs (PEDs)] to athletes" and, in plaintiffs' view, implicated them in PED use.[15] Zimmerman and Howard objected to representations made about them in the documentary and sued Al Jazeera for, among other things, defamation.[16] In denying defendant's motion to dismiss, the court acknowledged that "[b]ecause Zimmerman and Howard are public figures, their defamation ...

---

8. 376 U.S. 254 (1964).

9. *See id.* at 268. Although the *Sullivan* case dealt specifically with "public officials," a few years later in *Curtis Publishing Co. v. Butts*, the Court clarified that the *Sullivan* rule applies to all public figures. 388 U.S. 130, 162 (1967).

10. Cobb v. Time, Inc., 278 F.3d 629, 636 (6th Cir. 2002) (citing *Sullivan*, 376 U.S. at 285).

11. *Id.*

12. Time, Inc. v. Johnson, 448 F.2d 378, 380 (4th Cir. 1971).

13. 246 F. Supp. 3d 257 (D.D.C. 2017).

14. *Id.* at 288.

15. *Id.* at 263.

16. Initially, Zimmerman and Howard filed two separated cases, but the court consolidated them. *Id.* at 264.

action can only survive Defendant's motions to dismiss if it adequately alleges facts that support an inference that Defendants published the defamatory statements ... with actual malice."[17] It went on to conclude that plaintiffs did adequately assert such facts. Specifically, plaintiffs alleged that before the documentary was released, the documentary's producers learned that the person who accused them of using PEDs recanted, stating on camera:

> The statements on any recordings or communications that Al Jazeera intends to air are absolutely false and incorrect. To be clear, I am recanting any such statements and there is no truth to any statement of mine that Al Jazeera plans to air. Under no circumstances should any of those statements, communications, or recordings be aired.[18]

Nevertheless, Al Jazeera released the documentary.[19] These allegations were sufficient for plaintiffs to overcome defendant's motion to dismiss, but plaintiffs who are sports professionals generally have difficulty forwarding defamation claims.[20]

[2] Right of Privacy

Because most commentary about athletes is opinion-based, and because opinion-based commentary is generally protected under defamation principles, athletes have tended to rely on privacy torts, rather than the tort of defamation, when seeking to protect their reputation. The four basic categories of privacy torts are: "(1) intrusion upon seclusion or solitude; (2) public disclosure of embarrassing private facts; (3) publicity which places a person in a false light in the public eye; and (4) appropriation of name or likeness."[21] In regard to the first three categories, courts have found that sports industry professionals are, despite their celebrity, entitled to some measure of privacy.[22] The viability of common law claims asserting wrongful appropriation of

---

17. *Id.* at 280.

18. *Id.* at 269.

19. *Id.* at 270.

20. *See, e.g.,* Faigin v. Kelly, 978 F. Supp. 420 (D.N.H. 1997), *aff'd,* 184 F.3d 67 (1st Cir. 1999) (holding a sports agent was a public figure and denying the agent's defamation claim against a former NFL client and a sportswriter for failure to meet the actual malice standard); Bell v. Associated Press, 584 F. Supp. 128 (D.D.C. 1984) (holding that a former NFL player failed to meet his burden of proving actual malice in alleging defamation by a news service reporting on an arrest for lewdness by an individual posing as the player); Cottrell v. Nat'l Collegiate Athletic Ass'n, 975 So. 2d 306 (Ala. 2007) (denying a former college football coach's defamation claim because the coach was a limited-purpose public figure, and the NCAA did not act with actual malice in publishing statements regarding alleged recruitment violations).

21. PAUL WEILER, ET AL., SPORTS AND THE LAW: TEXT, CASES, AND PROBLEMS 575 (6th ed. 2019) (citing William Prosser, *Privacy,* 48 CAL. L. REV. 383, 389 (1960)).

22. *See, e.g.,* Jason Pierre-Paul v. ESPN, 2016 WL 4530884 (S.D. Fla. Aug 29, 2016) (finding that although medical reports related to football player Jason Pierre-Paul's fireworks related hand injury "were newsworthy," the extent of ESPN's "authority to make public facts private is not ... unlimited."); Bollea v. Gawker Media LLC, 2016 WL 4073660 (Fla. Cir. Ct. June 8, 2016) (enjoining Gawker from further publicly posting a sex tape involving Terry Bollea (also known as professional wrestler Hulk Hogan) and awarding Bollea millions of dollars in damages for Gawker's previous posting, notwithstanding Bollea's celebrity status); Andrews v. Marriott Int'l Inc., 61 N.E. 3d 1105 (Ill. App. Ct. 2016),

an athlete's name or likeness — the fourth category — has historically raised more questions, but courts now firmly recognize a right of publicity with respect to an athlete's name, image, and likeness. This right permits athletes to profit from their notoriety. The seminal case is *Haelen Laboratories v. Topps Chewing Gum*.[23] That case involved two companies, Haelen and Topps, which sold collectible cards featuring the images of baseball players.[24] Haelen had what it believed to be an exclusive contract to use the players' images, but Topps then entered into a contract with the athletes to use the same images.[25] Haelen sued Topps, and Topps defended by asserting that neither contract was binding as to the use of the images, because no property right in that use existed.[26] The Second Circuit, however, found for Haelen, determining that a property right in the use did exist.[27] Prior to *Haelen Laboratories*, courts had generally been unsympathetic to athletes' and celebrities' claims that their names or likenesses were misappropriated.[28] Since *Haelen Laboratories*, however, the overwhelming majority of states have established a publicity right that provides plaintiffs,[29] including athletes,[30] the opportunity to recover for misappropriation of their names, images, and likenesses.

[3] Federal Statutory Rights: The Lanham Act

Federal law, through the Lanham Act, provides potential support for athletes who believe their right of publicity has been misappropriated. The Lanham Act is a broad-based intellectual property statute designed to prevent customer confusion with

---

(awarding ESPN reporter $55 million in her invasion of privacy lawsuit after a "peeping tom" videoed her naked in her hotel room and posted the videos on the internet).

23. 202 F.2d 866 (2d Cir. 1953).

24. *Id.* at 867.

25. *Id.*

26. *Id.* at 868.

27. *Id.*

28. *See, e.g.*, O'Brien v. Pabst Sales, 124 F.2d 167 (5th Cir. 1941); *see also* Chaplin v. Nat'l Broad. Co., 15 F.R.D. 134, 140 (S.D.N.Y. 1953) (failing to grant privacy protection to the famous actor Charles Chaplin).

29. *See, e.g.*, Lugosi v. Universal Pictures, 603 P.2d 425, 428 (Cal. 1979) (explaining that an individual maintains the right to "create in his name and/or likeness ... a right of value"); *see also* Henley v. Dillard Dep't Stores, 46 F. Supp. 2d 587, 590 (N.D. Tex. 1999) (establishing the three elements necessary to recover under Texas law); Jim Henson Prods., Inc. v. John T. Brady & Assocs., Inc., 867 F. Supp. 175, 190 (S.D.N.Y. 1994) (holding that "Connecticut would interpret the right of publicity as descendible."); *but see* Dillinger, LLC v. Elec. Arts Inc., 795 F. Supp. 2d 829, 836 (S.D. Ind. 2011) (holding that "post-mortem right-of-publicity statute did not apply to a personality who died before its enactment" under Indiana law).

30. *See, e.g.*, Allison v. Vintage Sports Plaques, 136 F.3d 1443 (11th Cir. 1998) (holding under Alabama law that the first-sale doctrine barred the claim of a widow of a well-known race-car driver that a retailer violated the driver's right to publicity); Ventura v. Titan Sports, Inc., 65 F.3d 725 (8th Cir. 1995) (holding under Minnesota law that wrestler could recover for violation of his right to publicity by a wrestling organization); Newcombe v. Adolf Coors Co., 157 F.3d 686 (9th Cir. 1998) (reversing district court's grant of summary judgment for defendant in California right of publicity case). For further discussion, see 1 J. Thomas McCarthy, Rights of Publicity and Privacy (2d ed.), §§ 6:2–6:0 (Westlaw 2019).

respect to goods and services. Its provisions go well beyond right of publicity issues, but Section 43(a) of the statute provides a cause of action for misappropriation of name, image, or likeness.[31] It prohibits the use in commerce of "any word, term, name, symbol, or device, or any combination thereof…, which is likely to cause confusion, or to cause mistake, or to deceive as to … affiliation."[32] Importantly, the Lanham Act only covers items that operate as trademarks,[33] making it more limited in scope than many state laws. But with respect to trademarked items, courts assess Lanham Act right of publicity claims in much the same way they treat various state-created right of publicity claims.

[C] Effectuating the Right of Publicity

Different jurisdictions, of course, utilize different formulations and standards in adjudicating right of publicity and misappropriation claims, but certain themes are consistent. To effectuate a publicity right and recover for misappropriation of name, image or likeness, a plaintiff must establish that the defendant used the plaintiff's name, image, or likeness without permission and that the misappropriation caused plaintiff injury. While this may seem a straightforward analysis, it implicates many issues.

[1] Identifiability

To succeed on a right of publicity claim, a plaintiff must show that the name, image, or likeness being used is identifiably the plaintiff's.[34] When a defendant blatantly uses a plaintiff's name in a promotion without permission, it is generally actionable.[35] More difficult cases involve circumstances in which a defendant uses an obscured image of what appears to be the plaintiff. In such cases, identity is unclear, and courts engage in a factually intensive analysis, as illustrated in the seminal cases, *Ali v. Playgirl*[36] and *Newcombe v. Adolf Coors Co.*[37]

Ali involved a drawing published in the February 1978 issue of Playgirl Magazine. The drawing featured an unnamed Black male attired in boxing gear sitting in the corner of a boxing ring with his hands taped in manner customary for boxers, resting

---

31. 15 U.S.C. § 1125 (2012).

32. 15 U.S.C. § 1125(a) (2012).

33. ETW Corp. v. Jireh Publishing, Inc., 332 F.3d 915, 922 (6th Cir. 2003).

34. *See* Prima v. Darden Restaurants, Inc., 78 F. Supp. 2d 337, 352 (D.N.J. 2000) (noting that right of publicity elements are derived from copyright infringement and include 1) ownership in a valid copyright, and 2) copying of constituent elements of the work that are original); *see also* 31 CAUSES OF ACTION 2d 121 (originally published in 2006) (outlining four elements for the plaintiff to establish a prima facie case: 1) the defendant used plaintiff's identity or persona, 2) the appropriation of the persona was for the defendant's advantage, commercial or otherwise, 3) the plaintiff did not consent to the use of his or her identity, and 4) the appropriation is likely to cause an injury to the plaintiff).

35. Randall T.E. Coyne, *Toward a Modified Fair Use Defense in Right of Publicity Cases*, 29 WM. & MARY L. REV. 781, 799 (1988).

36. 447 F. Supp. 723 (S.D.N.Y 1978).

37. 157 F.3d 686 (9th Cir. 1998).

on the ropes of the ring.[38] The man was not identified by name — simply as "Mystery Man" — but an accompanying verse on the page described the man as "The Greatest."[39] Former heavyweight boxing champion Muhammad Ali, who was at the time internationally known as the "The Greatest," sued Playgirl Magazine for misappropriation of his likeness.[40] He sought an injunction requiring that Playgirl cease distributing the issue, recover all copies of the magazine that had been distributed but not yet sold, and deliver to him all printing plates and other devises used to print the drawing.[41] In reaching a decision, the court engaged in an optical analysis of the drawing to determine whether the unnamed boxer depicted was identifiably Ali. The court had little difficulty determining that: "[e]ven a cursory inspection of the picture which is the subject of this action strongly suggests that the facial characteristics of the black male portrayed are those of Muhammad Ali."[42] This, together with Playgirl's use of the appellation "The Greatest," led the court to conclude that the likeness in question was identifiable as Ali and that Playgirl had, therefore, misappropriated Ali's likeness.[43] Consequently, the court granted the requested injunctive relief.[44]

Ali's distinctive facial features made the court's task relatively easy, but as *Newcombe* illustrates, facial recognition is not necessary for a plaintiff to succeed in protecting against unauthorized use of their image or likeness.[45] In 1994, Sports Illustrated magazine published an advertisement for Killian's Red Beer that featured a "drawing of an old-time baseball game" next to a picture of a glass of beer.[46] Although the facial features of the pitcher in the drawing were not entirely visible, Don Newcombe, who had attained great fame as a professional baseball player decades earlier, believed the pitcher in the drawing matched his likeness.[47] Newcombe had not authorized Coors Brewing Co. (which owned Killian's Red Beer) to use his likeness and, as a former alcoholic who had dedicated his life to warning against alcohol consumption, he was distressed about his likeness being featured in the advertisement.[48] He therefore sued Coors for infringing on his right of publicity through its unauthorized use of his likeness.[49]

---

38. *Id.* at 726.
39. *Id.* at 727.
40. *Id.* at 725.
41. *Id.*
42. *Id.* at 726.
43. *Id.* at 727.
44. *Id.* at 732.
45. *See* Carson v. Here's Johnny Portable Toilets, Inc., 698 F.2d 831, 836 (6th Cir. 1983) (holding that an entertainer's right of publicity was invaded by intentional appropriation of his identity for commercial exploitation, notwithstanding that neither his name nor likeness were used); Abdul-Jabbar v. Gen. Motors Corp., 75 F.3d 1391, 1396 (9th Cir. 1996) (establishing that even an abandoned celebrity name may enjoy protection under the right of publicity).
46. *Id.* at 689.
47. *Id.*
48. *Id.*
49. *Id.*

In addition to the depicted pitcher's facial characteristics being unclear, the depiction featured neither Newcombe's team name nor jersey number.[50] The depicted pitcher's stance and body shape, however, perfectly mirrored Newcombe's real-life unorthodox pitching windup.[51] Coors argued that "stance alone cannot suffice to render a person readily identifiable" and that the depiction of the pitcher "was essentially generic and could have been any one of thousands of people who have taken to the pitcher's mound to throw a baseball."[52] Although the federal district court hearing the case granted summary judgment for Coors, the Ninth Circuit disagreed.[53] The Ninth Circuit emphasized that body shape and posture can be deemed as identifiable as facial features are for publicity right purposes.[54] The court wrote, "based on the record before us, Newcombe is the only [pitcher] who has such a stance. The record contains pictures of other pitchers in the windup position but none of these pitchers has a stance similar to Newcombe's."[55]

Ali and *Newcombe* reflect the law's general view on identifiability. Prohibition of unauthorized use extends beyond the use of an athlete's name or exact photographic representation to encompass less precise, but clearly identifiable, renderings.[56] A plaintiff will generally only be successful, however, if usage is commercial in nature.[57]

[2] Injury

An athlete's name, image, and likeness have value and are the fruits of the athlete's labor.[58] The enormity of an athlete's "public personality" value has become increasingly clear over the years as potential career endorsement income for athletes has climbed from the hundreds of thousands of dollars to the hundreds of millions of dollars. Diminution of that value, therefore, can be quite injurious, and injury can take multiple forms, including harm to reputation. Therefore, even if no pecuniary loss

---

50. *Id.* at 693.

51. *Id.* at 692.

52. *Id.*

53. *Id.* at 696.

54. *Id.* at 693.

55. *Id.* at 692.

56. *See* Upper Deck Co. v. Panini Am., Inc., 469 F. Supp. 3d 963 (S.D. Cal. 2020) (granting protection to a manufacturer's use of an athlete's name, image, and likeness on commercial trading cards); *see also* Hart v. Elec. Arts, Inc., 717 F.3d 141 (3d Cir. 2013) (finding that college football players have protection from video game developers using their name, image, and likeness).

57. *See, e.g., Hart,* 717 F.3d at 141 (reversing district court's grant of summary judgment for defendant video game developer in case in which defendant admits to "misappropriating [former college football player's] identity for commercial exploitation"); *see also In re NCAA Student-Athlete Name & Likeness Licensing Litig.*, 724 F.3d 1268, 1271 (9th Cir. 2013) (finding that a video game developer's use of a college athlete's likeness for commercial purposes is not protected under the First Amendment).

58. Uhlaender v. Henricksen, 316 F. Supp. 1277, 1282 (D. Minn. 1970).

results directly from the unauthorized use, an injury to reputation can support an actionable claim.[59]

[D] Limitations on the Right of Publicity

[1] First Amendment Limitations

The right of publicity is not absolute. Among the most notable limitations are the First Amendment and the "first-sale doctrine."

The right of publicity carries with it a public policy cost: potentially squelching free speech. A tension, therefore, exists between granting athletes and other celebrities control over their names, images, and likenesses and allowing third parties to explore and communicate ideas that involve those names, images, and likenesses. These tensions often arise in two very different expressive contexts: newscasts and works of art.

[a] Newscasts

Courts have struggled to determine when a defendant's First Amendment protections outweigh a plaintiff's right to publicity. Because a precise line cannot be drawn, courts have developed a sliding scale approach: an entirely commercial use of an athlete's identity, on the one hand, is entitled to little protection, while use in a purely informational newscast, on the other, is entitled to greater — though not absolute — protection.[60] The difficulty in separating permissible use from constitutionally impermissible use is illustrated by the Supreme Court's decision in *Zacchini v. Scripps-Howard Broadcasting*.[61] The plaintiff, Hugo Zacchini, was an acrobat and a daredevil whose show consisted of being shot out of a canon into a net 200 feet away.[62] In 1972, a county fair hired Zacchini to perform his stunt on a regular basis.[63] A television reporter recorded one of Zacchini's performances without his permission.[64] That night, Zacchini's entire 15-second "human cannonball"

---

59. *See* E.L.V.H. Inc. v. Bennett, 2020 WL 606755, at *7 (C.D. Cal. Feb. 6, 2020) (explaining that the harm to reputation outweighs the importance of receiving monetary recovery because it is "impossible to quantify" the monetary loss); *see also* Beachbody, LLC v. Kteam Enterprises, Ltd., 2017 WL 7806558, at *3 (C.D. Cal. June 19, 2017) (outlining elements for a plaintiff to obtain a permanent injunction: "(1) that it has suffered an irreparable injury; (2) that remedies available at law, such as monetary damages, are inadequate to compensate for that injury; (3) that, considering the balance of hardships between the plaintiff and defendant, a remedy in equity is warranted; and (4) that the public interest would not be disserved by a permanent injunction.") (citing eBay, Inc. v. MercExchange, LLL, 547 U.S. 388, 391 (2006)).

60. ETW Corp. v. Jireh Pub., Inc., 332 F.3d 915 (6th Cir. 2003); *see also* Dryer v. Nat'l Football League, 55 F. Supp.3d 1181, 1195–1200 (D. Minn. 2014) (holding that NFL's use of video footage of players in games was entitled to First Amendment protection, outweighing players' rights to publicity).

61. 433 U.S. 562 (1977).

62. *Id.* at 563.

63. *Id.*

64. *Id.* at 563–64.

performance appeared on the evening news.[65] Zacchini was displeased and sued the company that owned the television station for which the reporter worked.[66]

After years of litigation, the case reached the United States Supreme Court, which decided, by the narrowest of margins (five justices in the majority and four dissenting), in Zacchini's favor.[67] Recognizing the import of both Zacchini's right of publicity and First Amendment-protected newscasts, the Court concluded "the broadcast of a film of petitioner's entire act poses a substantial threat to the economic value of that performance" and thus the television station's free speech interest could not prevail.[68] The four dissenting justices disagreed, arguing the First Amendment comprehensively protects the content of legitimate news broadcasts.[69]

Although the Court viewed the issue before it as a close question, the key fact that influenced the majority's determination was that the television station aired Zacchini's entire performance. When only a short portion of a performance or sporting event is used, courts have little difficulty granting First Amendment protection.[70] This is why sporting event "highlight" segments are ubiquitous during sports newscasts.

[b] Artistic Expression

[i] Balancing Right of Publicity and the First Amendment with Respect to Works of Art

Courts struggle with First Amendment line drawing in the artistic context, just as they do when it comes to news broadcasts. Consequently, legal precedent provides imperfect guidance as to how a court will balance the right of publicity against the First Amendment. Two cases involving two very different athletes — former NHL brawler Tony Twist and golf legend Tiger Woods — and which produced very different outcomes are illustrative.

Doe, a/k/a Tony Twist v. TCI Cablevision[71] involved NHL enforcer Tony Twist who sued the creators of a comic book featuring a character who was a mob boss with the name Anthony "Tony Twist" Twistelli. Twist alleged the defendants violated his publicity rights.[72] The fictional Twistelli bore no physical resemblance to Twist, but the two shared the name as well as a "tough guy" reputation.[73] The Missouri

---

65. *Id.* at 564.
66. *Id.*
67. *Id.* at 578–79.
68. *Id.* at 562.
69. *Id.* at 580–81.
70. *See* ETW Corp. v. Jireh Pub., Inc., 332 F.3d 915 (6th Cir. 2003); *see also* Nat'l Football League v. Alley, Inc., 624 F. Supp. 6, 10 (S.D. Fla. 1983) (discussing that there must be an advertisement use for there to be a violation of a player's right to publicity); *see also* Gionfriddo v. Major League Baseball, 94 Cal. App. 4th 400, 114 Cal. Rptr. 2d 307, 313, 315 (2001) (explaining that there is public interest in making players' facts and data available and thus not awarding exclusive rights).
71. 110 S.W.3d 363 (Mo. 2003) (en banc).
72. *Id.* at 365.
73. *Id.* at 366.

Supreme Court concluded the usage was, at once, both artistic and commercial, but it determined that the use was more commercial than art.[74] It found that "the use and identity of Twist's name has become predominantly a ploy to sell comic books and related products rather than an artistic or literary expression, and under these circumstances, free speech must give way to the right of publicity."[75]

ETW Corp. v. Jireh Publishing, Inc.[76] involved golf great Tiger Woods, who sued Jireh Publishing, Inc., which created for sale prints of a painting called the "Masters of Augusta" that featured several prominent renderings of Woods during the 1997 Masters golf tournament.[77] Woods, who had not given Jireh permission,[78] sued but ultimately lost.[79] The court found Woods' right of publicity was "significantly outweighed by society's interest in freedom of artistic expression."[80]

In *ETW*, as in the *Twist* case, an athlete's right of publicity was invaded by an artist who created a work that was sold for profit, but in *ETW*, unlike in *Twist*, the court found against the athlete and for the artist. Those who have studied the two cases struggle to reconcile them. Consider the view of the late Harvard Law School Professor Emeritus Paul Weiler, and his co-authors:

> The Missouri Supreme Court in the *Tony Twist* case and the Sixth Circuit in the Tiger Woods case reached exactly opposite conclusions. The first determined that [the comic book's] use of Tony Twist's name was primarily commercial and thus not entitled to First Amendment protection, while the second concluded that [the] use of Tiger Woods' image in the painting was expressive, non-commercial, and thus protected. Is there something about the use of Woods' image that made it more worthy of constitutional immunity than the use of Twist's name in a comic book, or do the opinions simply reflect different judicial views about the balance between the right of publicity and the First Amendment?[81]

[ii] The Transformative Use Test

In 2001, the California Supreme Court developed the Transformative Use Test, which has become the leading test courts use to strike the balance between the right of publicity and the First Amendment in cases involving works of art. The court held in *Comedy III Productions, Inc. v. Gary Saderup, Inc.*,[82] that when a work of art is not just a "literal depiction," but instead contains "significant transformative elements," it is both worthy of First Amendment protection and "less likely to interfere with

---

74. *Id.* at 374.

75. *Id.*

76. 332 F.3d 915, 918 (6th Cir. 2003).

77. *Id.* at 918.

78. *Id.*

79. *Id.* at 919.

80. *Id.* at 938.

81. PAUL WEILER, ET AL., SPORTS AND THE LAW: TEXT, CASES, AND PROBLEMS 588 (6th ed. 2018).

82. 25 Cal. 4th 387 (2001).

the economic interest protected by the right of publicity."[83] Under the Transformative Use Test, protection is most appropriate when:

1) The likeness used is "one of the 'raw materials' from which an original work is synthesized" as opposed to "the very sum and substance of the work in question."

2) The work is "primarily the defendant's own expression" as long as that expression is "something other than the likeness of the celebrity."

3) The "creative elements" in the work "predominate" over the "literal and imitative" elements.

4) The "marketability and economic value" of the work do not "derive primarily from the fame of the celebrity depicted."

5) The "artist's skill and talent is [not] manifestly subordinated to the overall goal of creating a conventional portrait of a celebrity so as to commercially exploit his or her fame."[84]

The Ninth Circuit's decision in *In re NCAA Student-Athlete Name & Likeness Litigation*[85] illustrates the test's application. This case involved Electronic Arts ("EA"), a video game manufacturer, using college athletes' likenesses as a part of its video games.[86] The use was not tangential. Rather, EA sought to "replicate each school's entire team as accurately as possible."[87] This meant that each athlete on a university's team included in the game had "a corresponding avatar ... with the player's actual jersey number and virtually identical height, weight, build, skin tone, hair color, and home state."[88] In addition, avatars mimicked the real athletes' mannerisms, behaviors, and playing styles.[89] The only things differentiating the avatars from the real athletes were that the avatars had no names on the backs of their jerseys and were listed as being from a different home town than the real athletes.[90] Samuel Keller, a college quarterback, led a class action lawsuit claiming his right of publicity was violated.[91] In its analysis, the Ninth Circuit applied the five Transformative Use Test factors in concluding that "EA's use does not qualify for First Amendment protection as a matter of law because it literally recreates Keller in the very setting in which he has achieved renown."[92]

It is important to understand that a court that has not adopted the Transformative Use Test — of which there are many in the United States — might have found

83. *Id.* at 405.
84. *Id.* at 1274.
85. 724 F.3d 1268 (9th Cir. 2013).
86. *Id.* at 1271.
87. *Id.*
88. *Id.*
89. *Id.*
90. *Id.*
91. *Id.* at 1272.
92. *Id.* at 1271.

otherwise.[93] Paying close attention to jurisdiction is, therefore, critical when exploring an artistic expression right of publicity case.

[E] The First-Sale Doctrine

The first-sale doctrine creates an additional limitation on the right of publicity. Whereas the First Amendment can restrict the right of publicity in the first instance, the first-sale doctrine applies only after the right of publicity is originally effectuated. The doctrine has its roots in trademark and copyright law. In that context, it demands that once a party purchases a copyrighted or trademarked item, that party is free to sell or otherwise alienate the item. The concept has, over time, found traction in the right of publicity space. A key case in this regard is *Allison v. Vintage Sports Plaques*.[94] There, a sports memorabilia company, Vintage Sports Plaques, bought numerous sports trading cards featuring the names and photographs of professional sports figures.[95] It then repackaged the cards, framed them, and sold them for substantially more money.[96] The sports figures pictured on the cards sued Vintage Sports Plaques under state law for allegedly invading their right of publicity.[97] The Eleventh Circuit found for the defendant.[98] The court emphasized that its decision did not deprive athletes of their right to publicity and that they "would continue to enjoy the right to license the use of [their] image[s] in the first instance — and thus enjoy the power to determine when, or if, [their] image[s] will be distributed."[99] Abrogating the first-sale doctrine in the right of publicity context, the court warned, would produce all sorts of perverse outcomes. For instance, it would potentially "prevent a child from selling to a friend a baseball card that he had purchased, a consequence that undoubtedly would be contrary to the policies supporting [the] right [of publicity]."[100] The Eleventh Circuit's decision in *Allison* establishes the majority rule. After the first sale, an athlete's right of publicity with respect to an item generally dissolves.[101]

---

93. *See, e.g.*, Stayart v. Google Inc., 710 F.3d 719, 723 (7th Cir. 2013) (applying the "incidental use test," requiring that there be "substantial rather than an incidental connection between the use and the defendant's commercial purpose" for liability to be imposed); Rogers v. Grimaldi, 875 F.2d 994, 1004–05 (2d Cir. 1989) (creating the "Rogers test," which asks whether the use of an individual's name, image, and likeness are "disguised commercial advertisement"); Lohan v. Perez, 924 F. Supp. 2d 447, 454–55 (E.D.N.Y. 2013) (applying the "incidental use test"); Doe v. TCI Cablevision, 110 S.W.3d 363, 374 (Mo. 2003) (applying the "predominant use test" which determines that liability is appropriate "if a product is being sold that predominantly exploits the commercial value of an individual's identity ... even if there is some 'expressive' content in it that might qualify as 'speech' in other circumstances").

94. 136 F.3d 1443 (11th Cir. 1998).

95. *Id.* at 1444.

96. *Id.*

97. *Id.* at 1445.

98. *Id.* at 1450–51.

99. *Id.* at 1449.

100. *Id.*

101. *See* CENAPS Corp. v. Cmty. of Christ, 371 F. Supp. 3d 1024, 1028 (M.D. Fla. 2019) (citing Quality King Distributors, Inc. v. L'anza Research Intern., Inc., 523 U.S. 135, 152 (1998)) (explaining

§ 12.03 Trademark Protection and Infringement

[A] Introduction

A trademark identifies a product or service and distinguishes it from other similar products and services. A trademark can be a name, a slogan, a logo, or another distinctive mark. To illustrate, consider sports apparel. Imagine a blue sweatshirt with a placard obscuring its front. With the placard in place, the shirt appears generic and unremarkable. If, however, you remove the placard to reveal the famous Nike "swoosh," the shirt is instantly recognizable as a Nike product. If, instead, three stripes are revealed by moving the placard, you would know the shirt is an Adidas product. And if the placard's removal revealed, rather than a swoosh or three stripes, the silhouette of a large cat bounding forward, the first thing you would think is "Puma." The swoosh, the three stripes, and the silhouetted cat are all trademarks, indicating Nike, Adidas, and Puma, respectively. Those three names are also trademarks and work together with their respective logos to differentiate each company's products from others in the market.

Trademarks exists to prevent consumer confusion through establishing brand name recognition.[102] The idea is to try to ensure consumers receive the quality level they expect when they purchase a product or service. The trademark, which signals that quality, incentivizes companies to maintain high standards so that their brands are not tarnished. Unfortunately, it also incentivizes opportunists to cloak inferior products and services with trademarks that connote quality in an attempt to make a quick buck. This both reduces the trademark holder's profits (by losing confused consumers' sales to the opportunists) and damages the trademark holder's brand (by having inferior products and services associated with the trademark). As such, the law permits trademark holders to prevent such opportunists, known as trademark infringers, from deceptively using the holders' names and logos.[103]

Importantly, the United States operates a "first-to-use" rather than a "first-to-file" trademark regime, which means a trademark is yours once you begin to use it and do not abandon it.[104] Company A, for example, need not register a trademark to own it, and Company B may not take ownership of the trademark through registering it if Company A had previously established first use. However, the Lanham Act, the nation's most important statute regulating trademarks, encourages registration as early as possible, as registration constitutes "constructive use of the mark, conferring

---

that "the whole point of the first sale doctrine is that once the copyright owner places a copyrighted item in the stream of commerce by selling it, he has exhausted his exclusive statutory right to control its distribution"); *see also* Microsoft Corp. v. Big Boy Distribution LLC, 589 F. Supp. 2d 1308 (S.D. Fla. 2008) (declining to extend first sale protections to licensed software).

102. Star Indus., Inc. v. Bacardi & Co., 412 F.3d 373 (2d Cir. 2005).

103. 15 U.S.C. § 1114.

104. Leah Chan Grinvald, *A Tale of Two Theories of Well-Known Marks*, 13 VAND. J. ENT. & TECH. L. 1, 9–10 (2010).

a right of priority, nationwide in effect, on or in connection with the goods or services specified in the registration."[105]

When an entirely unaltered trademark is used without authorization, courts have little difficulty in concluding infringement has occurred. The close cases involve use of slightly altered trademarks, which trademark holders deem to be infringement but alleged infringers deem to be lawful use. The iconic Eddie Murphy film *Coming to America*, which features a small restaurant owner who secretly studies the McDonald's Operations Manuel in his attempts to compete with the fast-food behemoth, offers a fictional comedic illustration of the minor alterations that sometimes spur trademark enforcement litigation. After chasing McDonald's investigators off of his restaurant's grounds, the restaurant owner explains to one of his startled employees:

> Look ... me and the McDonald's people have this little misunderstanding. See, they're McDonald's.... I'm McDowell's. They have the Golden Arches, mine is the Golden Arcs. They have the Big Mac, I have the Big Mick. We both have two all-beef patties, special sauce, lettuce, cheese, pickles and onions, but their buns have sesame seeds. My buns have no seeds.[106]

The "misunderstanding" the fictional restauranteur references is impliedly a trademark infringement dispute; one the restauranteur will likely lose, as trademark law exists to prevent the very consumer confusion the restauranteur is clearly attempting to create.

Most trademark infringement cases, in sports and otherwise, that reach the courts are less cut and dried than the fictional McDonald's/McDowell's dispute, and they are also less humorous. Sports organizations, like organizations in other industries, invest tremendous resources in establishing a brand that attracts a loyal following, and they do not take lightly the prospect of consumers being confused or the brand being damaged.

[B] Trademark Infringement

[1] Team Names

What is in a name? For sports teams, the answer is clear: a great deal. Team names serve identification purposes, channel emotion for dedicated fans, and oftentimes reflect a team's desired personality. Trademark infringement with respect to a team name, therefore, is a serious matter. The applicable legal standard for trademark infringement has been articulated in different ways by different courts, but the "various formulations come down to whether it is likely that the challenged mark if permitted to be used by the defendant would cause the plaintiff to lose a substantial number of consumers."[107] In answering this question, pertinent considerations include:

---

105. 15 U.S.C. § 1057(c).

106. COMING TO AMERICA (Paramount Pictures 1988).

107. Indianapolis Colts, Inc. v. Metropolitan Baltimore Football Club Ltd. Partnership, 34 F.3d 410, 414 (7th Cir. 1994).

- the similarity of the marks;

- the similarity of the products;

- the knowledge of the average consumer of the product; and

- the overlap of the parties' geographical markets.[108]

The Seventh Circuit considered these factors when deciding *Indianapolis Colts v. Metropolitan Baltimore Football Club*,[109] a trademark infringement action borne of perhaps the most notorious club relocation episode in sports history. On March 28, 1984, in the middle of the night, Baltimore Colts owner Robert Irsay used a fleet of moving trucks to quietly pack up the team's belongings and transport them to the club's new home city.[110] He gave no prior notice to the community in Baltimore, where the club had played for years in front of a loyal fan base. Consequently, the move caused great distress to the community.[111] The City of Baltimore attempted to secure the team's return through litigation and other means, but to no avail.[112] In 1993, however, the Canadian Football League approved a franchise in Baltimore, promising a return of football to the city.[113] The owner of the new franchise desired to call the team the Baltimore Colts, but the NFL threatened to sue, at which point, the new owner adopted a slightly altered version: the Baltimore CFL Colts.[114] The NFL and the Indianapolis Colts viewed the alteration as insufficient and sued for trademark infringement under the Lanham Act.[115]

Considering the similarity of the marks, the similarity of the products, the average consumer's knowledge, and the overlap of the geographical markets, the Seventh Circuit affirmed the lower court's determination that the name "Baltimore CFL Colts ... was likely to confuse a substantial number of consumers" and found for the plaintiffs.[116]

Although not all courts apply the exact four factors that the Seventh Circuit applied in *Indianapolis Colts*, they generally follow the contours established in that case.[117] In *Board of Regents of the Univ. Sys. of Georgia v. Buzas Baseball, Inc.*,[118] for example, the court applied a seven-factor (rather than a four-factor) test to determine whether

---

108. *Id.* at 414.
109. *Id.* at 410.
110. *Id.* at 411.
111. *Id.*
112. *Id.*
113. *Id.*
114. *Id.*
115. *Id.*
116. *Id.* at 416.
117. *See, e.g.*, Johnny Blastoff, Inc. v. Los Angeles Rams Football Co., 188 F.3d 427, 435 (7th Cir. 1999) (referencing the similarity and geographical factors considered in *Indianapolis Colts*); Rust Env't & Infrastructure, Inc. v. Teunissen, 131 F.3d 1210, 1217 (7th Cir. 1997) (noting the consumer knowledge factor as referenced in *Indianapolis Colts*); Dallas Cowboys Football Club, Ltd. v. Am.'s Team Properties, Inc., 616 F. Supp. 2d 622, 632 (N.D. Tex. 2009) (noting the Northern District of Texas's application of the likelihood of confusion factors for the "America's Team" mark).
118. 176 F. Supp. 2d 1338 (N.D. Ga. 2001).

the challenged mark, if used, would cause the plaintiff to lose substantial market share. Importantly, the *Buzas Baseball* case also illustrates the challenge that the fact-intensive trademark infringement inquiry presents for parties seeking summary judgement. In the case, the Georgia Institute of Technology, known colloquially as "Georgia Tech," brought a trademark infringement suit against Buzas Baseball, owner of a Salt Lake City, Utah-based minor league baseball team called the Salt Lake Buzz. Georgia Tech's sports teams are called the Yellow Jackets, not the Buzz, but Georgia Tech had registered trademarks in the word "Buzz" and the graphic design of a yellow jacket.[119] Notwithstanding this, Buzas Baseball, used a mascot called "Buzzy" and sold "buzz" and "bee-like" merchandise to popularize the team.[120] Buzas Baseball denied infringement, claiming that "Buzz" was a reference to Utah being known as the "Beehive State" and that the monosyllabic, four letter team name ending in a double-z was designed to conjure thoughts of the state's most famous sports team, the Utah Jazz.[121] Both parties filed motions for summary judgment.[122]

The court considered the following seven factors adopted by the Eleventh Circuit: "(1) Type of mark; (2) similarity of mark; (3) similarity of the products the marks represent; (4) similarity of the parties' retail outlets (trade channels) and customers; (5) similarity of advertising media; (6) the defendant's intent; and (7) actual confusion."[123] Like the Seventh Circuit in *Indianapolis Colts*, the court focused primarily on consumer confusion and its consequences for the plaintiff in reaching its decision. Citing the numerous open questions of material fact, the court determined the case could not be resolved on summary judgment, as it could not "find as a matter of law that there is or is not a likelihood of confusion."[124] It was, therefore, "impossible to determine whether Buzas Baseball infringed on Georgia Tech's marks."[125] With neither party prevailing on summary judgment, the case went forward in litigation, but eventually settled.[126]

As is evident from the above discussion, courts apply different tests in trademark infringement suits involving team names and insignia. The ultimate outcome of these disputes, however, appears to turn on the possibility of confusion and the consequences of that confusion for a plaintiff.

[2] Merchandising

Sports is big business, and a considerable share of that business hinges on merchandising. Team names, accompanying insignia, and other trademarked words

---

119. *Id.* at 1344.
120. *Id.* at 1345.
121. *Id.*
122. *Id.*
123. *Id.* at 1351.
124. *Id.* at 1354.
125. *Id.*
126. *See* Bd. of Regents of the Univ. Sys. of Georgia v. Buzas Baseball, Inc., 176 F. Supp. 2d 1338 (N.D. Ga. 2001).

and images are critical to marketing team-themed merchandise and, therefore, driving revenue. Indeed, in bringing its lawsuit against Buzas Baseball, Georgia Tech was unlikely to have been concerned about fans confusedly cheering for the Salt Lake Buzz rather than the Georgia Tech baseball team in a particular instance. Its concern likely stemmed from the possibility that Georgia Tech fans or other interested consumers might buy "buzz"-related hats, shirts, and other merchandise from Buzas Baseball rather than from Georgia Tech, costing Georgia Tech money.

As discussed earlier in this chapter, however, trademark law traditionally has sought primarily to prevent the likelihood of consumer confusion. An expansion of trademark protection to merchandising goes beyond concerns about customer confusion. It broadens property rights in trademarks in a way that allows the trademark holder to maximize profits whether or not customer confusion exists, potentially thwarting competition and consequently driving up prices. For this reason, some legal scholars have opposed the expansion of trademark protection.[127] In 1975, however, the Fifth Circuit approved of a more expansive view of trademark protection, and other courts have tended to follow suit by granting "a 'right' to control merchandise that includes a team or university name."[128]

Boston Professional Hockey Association v. Dallas Cap and Emblem Mfg., Inc.[129] is illustrative. In that case, National Hockey League Services ("NHLS"), the NHL's licensing agent, had an agreement with the Lion Brothers Company that designated Lion Brothers as NHLS's exclusive licensee for producing embroidered patches with NHL teams' logos on them.[130] A Lion Brothers competitor, Dallas Cap & Emblem, tried to obtain such a license but failed.[131] Dallas Cap & Emblem then decided to manufacture patches for sale anyway.[132] NHL teams sued for trademark infringement.[133]

The case was relatively unique among trademark infringement cases, because the NHL teams' trademarks themselves were being sold as patches; they were not being attached to items such as shirts or towels. As such, there was no concern that a consumer would mistake a shirt or towel that was not an NHL team's product as being an NHL team's product. The district court acknowledged that NHL teams have an interest in their own individualized symbols that are "entitled to legal protection against ... unauthorized, intentional duplication."[134] It concluded, however, that the issue could be resolved through defendant informing purchasers that its patches were not "official" NHL patches. In reversing, the Fifth Circuit disagreed that a notice

127. Mark A. Lemley & Mark P. McKenna, *Owning Mark(et)s*, 109 Mich. L. Rev. 137, 168 (2010).

128. Paul Weiler, et al., *supra* note 81, at 620; Savannah Coll. of Art & Design, Inc. v. Sportswear, Inc., 983 F.3d 1273 (11th Cir. 2020); Bd. of Supervisors for Louisiana State Univ. Agric. & Mech. Coll. v. Smack Apparel Co., 550 F.3d 465 (5th Cir. 2008).

129. 510 F.2d 1004 (5th Cir. 1975).

130. *Id.* at 1009.

131. *Id.*

132. *Id.*

133. *Id.* at 1008.

134. *Id.*

informing purchasers would be enough, finding that the emblems only sold "because they bore the identifiable trademarks of plaintiffs."[135] The Fifth Circuit admitted that its decision "may slightly tilt the trademark laws from the purpose of protecting the public to the protection of the business interests of plaintiffs," but that the two are "so intermeshed ... that both the public and plaintiffs are better served by granting the relief sought."[136]

More than 45 years after *Boston Professional Hockey Association*, the court's expansion of trademark law remains controversial.[137] Nevertheless, it remains the majority view.[138]

[3] Trademark Dilution

In 1995, the United States Congress passed the Trademark Dilution Act, which amended the Lanham Act.[139] The amendment provides protection for the owner of a "famous mark" if another person or entity uses the mark without authorization in a way that dilutes the mark's distinctive quality.[140] In 2006, Congress passed the Trademark Dilution Revision Act, which further amended the Lanham Act.[141] This amendment requires that the party claiming dilution must show that the trademark in question is "widely recognized by the general consuming public of the United States as a designation of source of the goods or services of the mark's owner."[142] The names and logos of major professional sports leagues and teams are examples of famous marks, as are the NCAA and its logo. Names and logos of major sports events, such as the NFL's Super Bowl and The Preakness horse race also qualify.

Notably, a trademark dilution cause of action does not require the likelihood of confusion or economic harm (though such facts would certainly aid the trademark dilution claim). Blurring a famous mark's distinctiveness or tarnishing its reputation is sufficient to establish dilution. In the sports context, Trademark Dilution Act claims tend to revolve around the association of famous marks with inferior goods and services. The Trademark Dilution Revision Act does not provide courts substantial guidance in determining whether tarnishment has occurred, stating only that "dilution by tarnishment is association arising from the similarity between a mark or trade

---

135. *Id.* at 1013.

136. *Id.* at 1011.

137. Matthew J. Mitten, *From Dallas Cap to American Needle and Beyond: Antitrust Law's Limited Capacity to Stitch Consumer Harm from Professional Sports Club Trademark Monopolies*, 86 TUL. L REV. 901, 914 (2012).

138. *See* Savannah Coll. of Art & Design, Inc. v. Sportswear, Inc., 983 F.3d 1273 (11th Cir. 2020); *see also* Bd. of Supervisors for Louisiana State Univ. Agric. & Mech. Coll. v. Smack Apparel Co., 550 F.3d 465 (5th Cir. 2008) (establishing that a University's color scheme can acquire enough secondary meaning to warrant trademark protection); *but see* Univ. of Pittsburgh v. Champion Prod., Inc., 566 F. Supp. 711 (W.D. Pa. 1983), vacated (Feb. 2, 1984) (holding that there was no likelihood of confusion arising from a university's commercial use of an insignia because it was functional).

139. Federal Trademark Dilution Act, 15 U.S.C. § 1125(c).

140. *Id.*

141. *Id.*

142. *Id.* at § 1125(c)(2)(A)

name and a famous mark that harms the reputation of the famous mark."[143] The Act provides, however, six factors to guide courts in making their "blurring" assessment. The factors are non-exclusive and serve only to provide basic contours around a court's analysis. The factors are:

(i)   the degree of similarity between the mark or trade name and the famous mark;

(ii) the degree of inherent or acquired distinctiveness of the famous mark;

(iii) the extent to which the owner of the famous mark is engaging in substantially exclusive use of the mark;

(iv) the degree of recognition of the famous mark;

(v)   whether the user of the mark or trade name intended to create an association with the famous mark; and

(vi) any actual association between the mark or trade name and the famous mark.[144]

New York City Triathlon LLC v. NYC Triathlon Club Inc.[145] provides a paradigmatic example of a trademark dilution matter. The case involved New York City Triathlon, LLC, which organizes a well-known annual event called The New York City Triathlon. The New York City Triathlon, LLC, is sanctioned by USA Triathlon, the triathlon governing body in the United States.[146] The event first took place in 2001 and, over the years, has received national and international media coverage and has been viewed by over a billion people across the globe.[147] Since its inception, The New York City Triathlon, LLC used the marks "The New York City Triathlon," "The NYC Triathlon," and "The NYC Tri" in conjunction with the event.[148]

In 2010, a New York-based triathlon equipment retailer called SBR Triathlon Club changed its name to NYC Triathlon Club.[149] Within two months, The New York City Triathlon, LLC sought injunctive relief in federal court based on many grounds — including alleged Lanham Act trademark dilution grounds.[150] The court had little difficulty determining that The New York City Triathlon, LLC would likely be successful on the merits, and therefore granted the injunction.[151]

The court first found that the marks were, indeed, famous, noting that "the extent of publicity associated with Plaintiff's marks, and their widespread recognition supports a finding of fame."[152] The court then turned to the "blurring" and "tarnishing" assessments. It applied the aforementioned six factors to guide its "blurring"

---

143. *Id.* at § 1125(c)(2)(B).
144. *Id.*
145. 704 F. Supp. 2d 305 (S.D.N.Y. 2010).
146. *Id.* at 312.
147. *Id.*
148. *Id.* at 311.
149. *Id.* at 312–13.
150. *Id.* at 313.
151. *Id.* at 347.
152. *Id.* at 321.

assessment and found that they all factors cut clearly in favor a "blurring" finding.[153] With respect to tarnishment, because the record clearly revealed that the defendant had a history of "trading on others' goodwill and providing poor customer service," the court also found dilution by tarnishment was likely.[154] Having found likelihood of dilution by both blurring and tarnishment, the court granted the injunction against defendant.[155] The Trademark Dilution Revision Act's loose guidance on what constitutes dilution produces a free-flowing analysis that differs by jurisdiction,[156] but *New York City Triathlon*, offers a helpful illustration of a typical trademark dilution matter.

New York City Triathlon also addresses cybersquatting, a tactic that opportunists have long used to pry money away from trademark holders, including celebrity athletes and sports organizations. Under the scheme, the opportunist identifies an athlete or organization, purchases domain names that include various forms of the athlete's or organization's name, and then offers to sell the domain names to the athlete or organization for a massive profit or otherwise seeks enrichment through using the domain names. In 1999, Congress passed the Anti-Cybersquatting Consumer Protection Act, which provides a trademark owner a cause of action against anyone who, with "bad faith intent to profit," registers or uses a domain name that is "identical or confusingly similar" to a distinctive or famous trademark.[157]

In addition to its dilution claim, New York City Triathlon, LLC asserted a cybersquatting claim against NYC Triathlon Club. In granting the plaintiff's requested relief, the court found the defendant acquired in bad faith a domain name that was "nearly identical and certainly confusingly similar to" the plaintiff's.[158]

[4] Fair Use

As you'll note from the materials thus far, trademark law largely favors trademark holders, but unauthorized users do have defenses against infringement suits. Foremost among these is the "fair use" defense. Under this doctrine, parties may generally use others' trademarks when doing so serves to describe the user's product or service and does not create the impression of sponsorship or endorsement. Generally, the use of the trademark must be peripheral rather than the basis for generating profit.

In the sports context, fair use arguments have arisen in various contexts, often when a players' association — but not the league in which the players play — enters

---

153. *New York City Triathlon, LLC*, 704 F. Supp. 2d at 323.

154. *Id.*

155. *Id.* at 347.

156. *See, e.g.*, Savin Corp. v. Savin Grp., 391 F.3d 439, 455 (2d Cir. 2004) (establishing two elements for trademark dilution analysis under New York law: "(1) a distinctive mark capable of being diluted and (2) a likelihood of dilution. . . ."); *see also* Panavision Int'l, L.P. v. Toeppen, 141 F.3d 1316, 1324 (9th Cir. 1998) (noting that the California approach to trademark dilution additionally weighs the mark's "distinctive quality" and if the mark is "famous.").

157. 15 U.S.C. § 1125(d).

158. *New York City Triathlon, LLC*, 704 F. Supp. 2d at 324.

a sponsorship or licensing agreement with a third party. In *NFL v. Coors Brewing Co.*,[159] for instance, the NFL Players Association, through its licensing subsidiary Players Inc., entered a sponsorship agreement with Coors Brewing Co.[160] The agreement resulted in Coors being named the "Official Beer of the NFL Players."[161] The NFL, however, objected to the use of the "NFL" trademark and sued for an injunction.[162] The court rejected the NFLPA's argument that the use of the trademark was merely descriptive and therefore constituted fair use. Noting that the NFLPA was clearly seeking to "capitalize on the goodwill inherent in the NFL trademark,"[163] the court granted the injunction.

In a case involving a different league and a different players' association, Major League Baseball Properties, which is MLB's licensing arm, sued to enjoin Pacific Trading Cards from displaying MLB players' team uniforms on their cards without having first received a license from MLB to do so. Pacific Trading Cards had received a license from the MLB Players Association, but while the MLBPA has the right to license the players' images, team uniforms are MLB trademarks.[164] Nevertheless, the court refused to grant the injunction, finding that the depicted players, rather than the uniforms, drove any value associated with the cards.[165] In other words, Pacific Trading Cards was capitalizing on the goodwill of the players' images to which it had legitimate access, not the MLB uniforms to which it did not.

To avoid disputes such as the one litigated in *Major League Baseball Properties v. Pacific Trading Cards*, merchandisers now typically secure licenses from both the league and the players' association.[166] Still, trademark infringement cases often trigger fair use defenses, and the analysis generally revolves around whether the use is suggestive of endorsement or merely descriptive.

[5] Ambush Marketing

Ambush marketing involves an entity seeking to benefit commercially from an apparent connection to a sporting event when in fact there exists no sponsorship or endorsement arrangement.[167] The benefit may result from an increase in the ambushing entity's sales, a decrease in a competitor's sales, or both. Event organizers, understandably, loathe the ambush marketing concept, as it incentivizes free riding off of an event's popularity and disincentivizes paid sponsor relationships. Liability, however, flows only when the marketing campaign is deemed likely to cause confusion

---

159. 205 F.3d 1324 (2d Cir. 1999).

160. *Id.*

161. *Id.* at *1.

162. *Id.*

163. *Id.*

164. Major League Baseball Properties v. Pacific Trading Cards, 1998 WL 241904 (S.D. N.Y. May 14, 1998).

165. *Id.* at 3.

166. Sam Carp, *Marketing destiny: How the NBA and NFL stars are taking back control*, SPORTSPRO (Oct. 1, 2018), https://www.sportspromedia.com/from-the-magazine/nfl-nba-player-unions-interview.

167. Gerlinde Berger-Walliser, *Bavarian Blondes Don't Need a Visa: A Comparative Law Analysis of Ambush Marketing*, 21 TUL. J. INT'L & COMP. L. 1, 3 (2012).

as to the connection between the ambusher and the event in question. In 1961, Judge Henry Friendly articulated the governing standard in *Polaroid Corp. v. Polarad Elecs. Corp.*[168] and identified several non-exhaustive factors courts might consider in determining whether confusion will likely result from the campaign.[169] Factors include "the degree of similarity between the two marks," "defendant's good faith," and "the sophistication of the [consumers]."[170]

The analysis, however, is famously free-flowing, as evidenced in *Fed'n Internationale De Football Ass'n v. Nike, Inc.*,[171] a case involving FIFA's 2003 Women's World Cup soccer tournament. The tournament was held in the United States, and FIFA used the trademark "USA 2003" to advertise the event, while Nike, which sponsored the United States Women's National Soccer Team playing in the tournament, used the term "USA 03" as a part of its sponsorship efforts.[172] FIFA sued Nike, arguing that Nike's use of "USA 03" ambushed the World Cup and sought to promote a non-existent connection between the Nike brand and the tournament.[173] The court concluded that, on balance, Nike's use of "USA 03" did not create "a likelihood of customer confusion."[174] The court further observed that the demarcation line between a creative marketing campaign and unlawful ambush marketing is a thin one. Indeed, in finding for Nike, the court wrote that "Nike's careful use of a mark that might be affiliated with both [the Women's National Team and the World Cup] is not necessarily an indication of bad faith, but instead of savvy marketing."[175]

An incident at the 2010 FIFA World Cup in South Africa illustrates the difficulty courts encounter in distinguishing savvy marketing from unlawful marketing. Budweiser was the official beer sponsor of the World Cup, but a Netherlands-based brewer's novel marketing campaign made it the most talked about beer company at the event. The brewer, Bavaria, hired 36 women to attend a Netherlands match as a group clad in bright orange mini-dresses, similar in color to the Dutch players' uniforms and identical to dresses consumers received for free as a promotion when purchasing eight-packs of Bavaria beer back in the Netherlands.[176] The women, who attracted attention during the television broadcast, were discovered to be working for Bavaria and were expelled from the venue.[177] Bavaria, however, achieved its goal. The stunt, and Bavaria beer, became the talk of the World Cup for several days,

---

168. 287 F.2d 492, 495 (2d Cir. 1961).

169. *Id.*

170. *Id.*

171. 285 F. Supp. 2d 64 (D.D.C. 2003).

172. *Id.* at 66.

173. *Id.* at 67.

174. *Id.* at 74.

175. *Id.*

176. Rob Gray, Great Brand Blunders: The Worst Marketing and Social Media Meltdowns of All Time ... and How to Avoid Your Own 110 (2014); Marina Hyde, *Another triumph for FIFA's Chillingly Efficient Rights Protection Team*, TheGuardian.com, June 15, 2010, https://www.theguardian.com/football/2010/jun/16/fifa-world-cup-ambush-marketing.

177. Gray, *supra* note 176, at 110.

propelling the small beer merchandiser into an overnight international phenomenon.[178] Consider where you believe this campaign falls on the sliding scale between lawfully inventive and unlawfully infringing. FIFA, unsurprisingly, viewed it as the latter and brought legal action against Bavaria under the South African Merchandise Marks Act.[179] The parties settled the matter with undisclosed terms and Bavaria's agreement "to fully respect the integrity of FIFA's commercial programme until the end of the year 2022."[180]

Whether the Bavaria beer ambush marketing campaign would have violated the law in the United States is unclear. While liability would require customer confusion as to the connection between the ambusher and the event in question, such confusion can be hard to prove, particularly under a multi-factor analysis like that set forth in *Polaroid Corp*. Identically dressed spectators are commonplace at the World Cup, and this group of spectators, other than being at a World Cup match with tens of thousands of others, displayed no connection to the World Cup event. Their orange garb connected them to the Dutch team, but thousands of other fans appeared similarly connected to the various national teams in the tournament. Persuasive arguments could be offered in support of each party's position, and as with many trademark infringement disputes, different courts could reach different conclusions. This uncertainty is one reason American sports organizations rarely launch legal challenges against ambush marketing campaigns, and, consequently, why ambush marketing continues to proliferate.

Indeed, ambush marketing, particularly in the spectacular attention-grabbing Bavaria beer mode, has proven so successful that companies have begun to ambush events *of which they are official sponsors* to increase the impact of their sponsorship. The Coca-Cola Company, for instance, was a sponsor of the 2019 month-long NCAA college basketball tournament known as March Madness, during which it ran scores of advertisements touting its new Orange and Vanilla cola product.[181] As a seemingly unrelated matter, two men appearing to be twins — one dressed entirely in orange and one dressed entirely in white — showed up as spectators at numerous games throughout the tournament.[182] Their curious appearance attracted substantial attention at venues and during television broadcasts, and the attention increased as the tournament progressed. Well into the tournament, astute observers noted the men were usually holding cups of Coca-Cola, after which it became clear the men were planted at the games by the Coca-Cola Company as Orange and Vanilla personified.[183] The mystery surrounding the men created a story spectators

---

178. *Id.*

179. *Id.*

180. *Id.*

181. Matt Lombardi, *The Two Bearded Fans Who Have Been Going Viral During the NCAA Tournament Appear to Be Plants*, THE SPUN (Mar. 31, 2019), https://thespun.com/more/top-stories/orange-vanilla-coke-fans-ncaa-tournament.

182. *Id.*

183. *Id.*

followed for weeks. When the mystery was solved, the connection between Coca-Cola and the tournament intensified, presumably increasing the value of the sponsorship.[184]

The success of Orange and Vanilla personified as a marketing strategy is sure to spark ambush marketing attempts at future mass sporting events, potentially triggering trademark infringement. In such cases, trademark owners will have to determine the value of pursuing the ambushers when doing so will require establishing customer confusion as to the connection between the ambusher and the event. Other factors for owners to consider are the generally brief lifespan of ambush marketing campaigns, the possibility of litigation amplifying the ambusher's platform during that brief lifespan, and a potential freedom of expression defense similar to those addressed in the defamation and right of publicity contexts earlier in this chapter.

§ 12.04 Sports Broadcasting

[A] Introduction

As noted in the introduction to this chapter, broadcasting creates substantial revenue in the sports industry. In sport's early days, sports organizations derived revenue almost entirely from ticket sales and concessions. When they discovered that people unable to attend the games would enjoy the opportunity to follow the play-by-play game action, they began to work with media companies in broadcasting the games.[185] Famously, MLB's Pittsburgh Pirates in the early 1930s entered an exclusive contract with General Mills (which then subcontracted with NBC) to broadcast descriptions of Pirates' games on two Pittsburgh radio stations.[186] A different radio station, which had offices that provided a clear line of sight to the Pirates' home field, meanwhile broadcast games without authorization.[187] The Pirates sued for an injunction against the latter station and won, establishing a common law property right in game broadcasts.[188] While the law around exclusivity in sports broadcasting has evolved since then, the Pirates' assertion of dominion over accounts of its games and the court's recognition of that dominion offered a glimpse of sports broadcasting's promise as a major revenue generator.

That promise was realized when television came of age in the 1950s. Fewer than 10 million people owned a television set in 1950, but nearly 70 million people owned

184. *See 2020 Category Captain for Packaged Beverages: The Coca-Cola Co.*, CONVENIENCE STORE NEWS (Apr. 6, 2020), https://www.csnews.com/2020-category-captain-packaged-beverages-coca-cola-co (stating that "the rollout plan also successfully leveraged Coke's partnership with NCAA March Madness by launching Coke Orange Vanilla during the basketball tournament").

185. *See* Jack Moore, *Throwback Thursday: The TV Deal That Created Modern Sports*, VICE (Jun. 11, 2015).

186. Pittsburgh Athletic Co. v. KQV Broadcasting Co., 24 F. Supp. 490, 492 (W.D. Pa. 1938).

187. *Id.* at 491.

188. *Id.* at 493–94.

one by decade's end.[189] The National Football League observed the growth of television's popularity and seized upon it. By 1970, televisions were ubiquitous in the United States, and the NFL's television broadcast rights were worth $46.25 million (a tenfold increase over their worth just eight years earlier).[190] The value of the rights has continued to grow exponentially. The NFL's current national broadcasting deals with CBS, Fox, and NBC total over $3 billion annually.[191] While other sports organizations do not command dollar amounts that are quite as high, the NBA's national broadcasting deals exceed $2 billion annually,[192] MLB's national broadcasting deals exceed $1 billion annually,[193] and the NCAA's national broadcasting deal for its March Madness basketball tournament alone nears $1 billion annually.[194]

The economic value of these broadcasting deals underscores the importance of broadcasting rights and the body of law that protects them.

[B] Copyright Law as a Basis to Protect Broadcasts

The concept of copyright in the United States dates back to the nation's founding and is featured in Article I, Section 8 of the Constitution. It reads, "To promote the Progress of Science and useful Arts, by securing for limited Times to Authors and Inventors the exclusive Right to their respective Writings and Discoveries."[195] In the years since, Congress has passed and periodically amended copyright statutes, but the Copyright Act of 1976 was the first such statute to protect live sports broadcasts. Specifically, the Copyright Act gives the copyright owner the exclusive right to publicly perform or display "original works of authorship fixed in any tangible medium" and states that "[a] work consisting of sounds, images, or both, that are being transmitted, is 'fixed' ... if a fixation of the work is being made simultaneously with its transmission."[196] The Act provides copyright owners the exclusive right to duplicate and air — or authorize others to duplicate and air — a copyrighted broadcast of a

189. JIM ROONEY, A DIFFERENT WAY TO WIN: DAN ROONEY'S STORY FROM THE SUPER BOWL TO THE ROONEY RULE 26 (2020).

190. *Id.* at 37.

191. Jabari Young, *With football ratings on the rise, NFL officials look to raise TV broadcast fees on multiyear media deals*, CNBC (Dec. 30, 2019), https://www.cnbc.com/2019/12/30/nfl-ratings-recovering-new-media-deals-could-be-on-the-2020-agenda.html.

192. *NBA Announces 9-Year Extension With ESPN, Turner, Through 2025*, SPORTS MEDIA WATCH, https://www.sportsmediawatch.com/2014/10/nba-tv-deal-espn-abc-tnt-nine-year-deal-2025-24-billion-lockout.

193. Maury Brown, *MLB's $4 Billion ESPN Media Rights Extension Brings the League's Total Broadcast Value to $12 Billion Over 7 Years*, FORBES (May 14, 2021), https://www.forbes.com/sites/maurybrown/2021/05/14/espns-7-year-392-billion-renewal-with-mlb-starts-in-2022/?sh=6ccd35bf3b1c.

194. Joe Reedy, *CBS, Turner partnership on NCAA Tournament has huge benefits*, ABC NEWS (Mar. 17, 2021), https://abcnews.go.com/Entertainment/wireStory/cbs-turner-partnership-ncaa-tournament-huge-benefits-76504960.

195. U.S. CONST. art. I, § 8, cl. 8.

196. 17 U.S.C. §§ 101, 102(a)(6) (2002).

sports event.[197] Because sports broadcasts simultaneously transmit sounds and images, they are widely recognized to fall within the Act's protections. In addition, the Act provides copyright owners a copyright infringement cause of action against any person or entity violating these exclusive rights.[198]

[C] Limits of Copyright Protections

Copyright owners' rights are limited in three important ways. First, recording a sports broadcast for one's own in-home, personal consumption does not constitute copyright infringement. In 1984, the United States Supreme Court in *Sony Corp. of America v. Universal City Studios, Inc.*[199] characterized this activity not as infringement but as "time-shifting for private home use."[200] This decision allowed Videocassette Recorder ("VCR") and related recording technologies to flourish as a means of capturing live sports broadcasts for viewing at a later time.

Second, although the broadcast of a live sporting event is copyrightable, the "idea, procedure, process, system, method of operation, [and] concept ..." underlying a live sports event is not.[201] So, while the broadcast of a Major League Baseball game (with its distinctive designated hitter rule) between a team from New York and a team from Baltimore is copyrightable, the rules and mechanisms of the game itself are not.[202] Copyright law, therefore, can do nothing to prevent a rival league from staging or broadcasting a baseball game between other teams from those two cities, even if the playing rules are the exact rules used by Major League Baseball.[203]

Third, and relatedly, copyright law does not protect the events of a particular game, just the broadcast of those events, as the Second Circuit made clear in 1997 in *NBA v. Motorola, Inc.*[204] The dispute arose from Motorola's production of a paging device called SportsTrax. The device, which had a three-square inch screen and retailed for $200, displayed NBA games in progress, updating the score, which team had the ball, the time remaining, and other aspects of the game.[205] The information was fed into SportsTrax by individuals who were watching the game live on television or listening to it live on the radio.[206]

The NBA asserted copyright infringement claims against Motorola. The court had little trouble, however, concluding that the events of the NBA games (and other sporting events) were not copyrightable, as they did not constitute "original works

---

197. 17 U.S.C. § 106 (2002).
198. *Id.*
199. 464 U.S. 417 (1984).
200. *Id.* at 449.
201. 17 U.S.C. § 102 (2002).
202. M. NIMMER & D. NIMMER, NIMMER ON COPYRIGHT § 2.09[F] at 2-170.1 (1996).
203. Hoopla Sports and Entertainment, Inc. v. Nike, Inc., 947 F. Supp. 347 (N.D. Ill. 1996) (finding the format of an international all-star basketball game cannot be copyrighted).
204. 105 F.3d 841 (2d Cir. 1997).
205. *Id.* at 843–44.
206. *Id.* at 844.

of authorship" under the Copyright Act.[207] The court unsurprisingly concluded the broadcasts — the simultaneously-recorded transmission — of games were copyrightable, but it clearly distinguished those broadcasts from what Sportstrax was transmitting. The court wrote, "although the broadcasts are protected under copyright law, ... [Motorola] did not infringe NBA's copyright because they reproduced only facts from the broadcasts, not the expression or description of the game that constitutes the broadcasts."[208] As such, it found for Mortorola.[209] The precedent established in *Motorola* propelled the explosion of Internet-based real-time sports score updates, which are now available on any number of websites on any given day.[210]

Actual game broadcasts, of course, are broadly protected under copyright law, but technological advances make the contours of those protections difficult to define.

[D] Sports Broadcast Infringement: A Technological Cat and Mouse Game

The transmission of live sporting events has come a long way since NBC's Pittsburgh Pirates radio broadcasts in the 1930s and the NFL's pioneering television broadcast deals of the 1950s and 1960s. Technological progress has widened (with respect to both mode and breadth of transmission) opportunities to view live sports broadcasts, but it has also complicated the role of intellectual property in regulating them.

For instance, in the late 1990s, a satellite carrier called PrimeTime 24 Joint Venture transmitted copyrighted NFL television broadcasts to households with insufficient reception to view games on the NFL's primary television networks.[211] PrimeTime had a license to do this for United States customers, but without permission from the NFL, it did the same for customers in Canada.[212] In *NFL v. PrimeTime 24 Joint Venture*,[213] the NFL sued for copyright infringement with respect to the Canadian broadcasts and PrimeTime responded with a finely parsed defense.[214] It acknowledged that infringement occurs when copyrighted material has been publicly displayed, but

---

207. *Id.* at 846.

208. *Id.* at 847.

209. *Id.* at 855.

210. It bears noting that the Eleventh Circuit, in a case called *Morris Communications Corp. v. PGA Tour, Inc.*, 364 F.3d 1288 (11th Cir. 2002), seemed to take a different approach. In that case, the court found that the PGA Tour could prevent Morris Communications Corp. and other media entities from accessing its events and on-site media centers unless the entities agreed not to syndicate or otherwise distribute real-time golf updates. Morris Communications' suit, however, was based in antitrust law and, indeed, the court specifically stated "this case is not about copyright law." *Morris Communications Corp.*, 364 F.3d at 1292. This distinction may explain why *Morris Communications Corp.*, although decided five years after the *Motorola* case, did little to chill the proliferation of real-time sports score updates across the internet.

211. NFL v. PrimeTime 24 Joint Venture, 211 F.3d 10, 11 (2d Cir. 2000).

212. *Id.*

213. *Id.*

214. *Id.* at 12.

insisted that the public displays in question — the broadcasts in Canada — occurred outside of the United States and were therefore outside the reach of U.S. copyright law.[215] The Second Circuit disagreed, finding that the public displays did not occur only on television stations in Canada but rather at "each step in the process by which a protected work wends its way to the audience."[216] It therefore ruled for the NFL.[217]

In 2014, the Supreme Court in *American Broadcasting Companies, Inc. v. Aereo, Inc.*[218] grappled with the challenge of applying copyright law to broadcasts in the Internet Age. Although the case did not involve sports broadcasts, it involved broadcasts generally, and therefore bears on the sports context. Aereo, Inc. sold a service that provided subscribers the opportunity to watch live (or immaterially delayed) television programming on devices connected to the internet.[219] It did so in innovative technological fashion by providing each subscriber with a lease to their individual digital recorder and antenna, housed at a remote location, which each subscriber could use to access desired content.[220] The American Broadcasting Companies sued Aereo, alleging Aereo infringed on its copyright.[221] Aereo did not deny selling the subscriptions, but asserted it merely supplied the equipment and that the subscribers — by selecting their programming — were the parties who transmitted the copyrighted material.[222] As such, Aereo argued, it did not infringe.

The Court refused to accept Aereo's argument, finding that "[b]y means of its technology, Aereo's system 'receive[s] programs that have been released to the public and carr[ies] them by private channels to additional viewers.'"[223] The fact that the innovative and "technologically complex service"[224] gave individual users the power to select through their leased equipment the particular programming on a given day was, in the Court's view, immaterial.[225]

Dissenting justices, however, argued passionately that the subscriber's agency was the entire point, analogizing each subscriber's antenna to a library card.[226] "The key point," they asserted, "is that subscribers call all the shots: Aereo's automated system does not relay any program, copyrighted or not, until a subscriber selects the program and tells Aereo to relay it."[227] As such, the dissent concluded Aereo did not infringe, and in reaching this conclusion, the dissent conveyed a broader perspective making a bigger point. It noted that in *Sony Corp. of America*, decided three decades earlier

---

215. *Id.*
216. *Id.* at 13.
217. *Id.*
218. 573 U.S. 431 (2014).
219. *Id.* at 436.
220. *Id.*
221. *Id.* at 437.
222. *Id.*
223. *Id.* at 442–43.
224. *Id.* at 436.
225. *Id.* at 444.
226. *Id.* at 456.
227. *Id.*

and referenced above, the Supreme Court had almost declared the VCR to be "contraband" with a near majority predicting "that VCR technology would wreak all manner of havoc in the television and movie industries."[228] In the case *sub judice*, the dissent asserted, plaintiffs "make similarly dire predictions about Aereo."[229]

Aereo, Inc. reveals the challenge involved in applying copyright law with respect to broadcasts as technology develops. It also reveals that the Supreme Court's justices have long been polarized on the issue. As technology continues to develop and as innovators continue to create new means of offering sports broadcasts to customers, courts will be forced to continue grappling with what constitutes infringement.

---

228. *Id.* at 462.
229. *Id.*

Table of Cases

Index

Cumulative trauma, 389, 391, 392

Employer-employee relationship, 56, 58, 61

Fraudulent concealment exception, 393, 394

Intentional conduct exception, 393, 394

Statutory exclusion, 388

Tort action, impact on, 392–393

Workers' compensation act, 391, 394

Y

Youth Sports, 3–6

Amateur Athletic Union (AAU), 4

AAU Basketball, 4, 5

Club/travel sports, 4

Olympic Development Programs (ODP), 5